MyMaths for Key Stage 3

2C

Powered by MyMaths.co.uk

OXFORD
UNIVERSITY PRESS

OXFORD
UNIVERSITY PRESS

Great Clarendon Street, Oxford, OX2 6DP, United Kingdom

Oxford University Press is a department of the University of Oxford. It furthers the University's objective of excellence in research, scholarship, and education by publishing worldwide. Oxford is a registered trade mark of Oxford University Press in the UK and in certain other countries

First published in 2014

British Library Cataloguing in Publication Data
Data available

978-0-19-830458-6

11

Paper used in the production of this book is a natural, recyclable product made from wood grown in sustainable forests. The manufacturing process conforms to the environmental regulations of the country of origin.

Printed and bound by CPI Group (UK) Ltd Croydon CR0 4YY

Acknowledgements

Although we have made every effort to trace and contact copyright holders before publication this has not been possible in all cases. If notified, the publisher will rectify any errors or omissions at the earliest opportunity.

P2-3: John Lamb/Digital Vision/Getty Images; **P14:** Kosarev Alexander / Shutterstock.Com; **P15:** (B) Eti Swinford/Dreamstime; **P22-23:** Oliviero Olivieri/ Robert Harding World Imagery/Corbis; **P25:** Plasticrobot/ Dreamstime; **P40-41:** DAVID A. HARDY/SCIENCE PHOTO LIBRARY; **P66-67:** Martin Siepmann/Glow Images; **P73:** OUP; **P77:** Roel Smart/Istock; **P86-87:** Dennis Hallinan/Alamy; **P100-101:** Warren Faidley/Corbis/Glow Images; **P104:** Dwimages England/Alamy; **P106:** Mark Herreid/Shutterstock; **P111:** Silver-John/Shutterstock; **P122-123:** Sciencephotos/Alamy; **P126:** (T) Alexander Bushenkov/Dreamstime, (B) Manfred Konrad/Istockphoto; **P130:** (T) Marc Slingerland/Dreamstime; **P131:** Marc Slingerland/Dreamstime; **P136-137:** The Art Archive/ Alamy; **P154:** Vibrant Image Studio/Shutterstock; **P162-163:** Godong/Universal Images Group/Getty Images; **P180-181:** Grant Glendinning/Shutterstock; **P196-197:** Compuinfoto/Fotolia; **P203:** Egiss/Istockphoto; **P205:** Ziutograf/Istockphoto; **P216-217:** Eric Gevaert/ Shutterstock; **P229:** Dave Turner/Shutterstock; **P238-239:** Denys Rudyi/Fotolia; **P246:** Joshua Haviv/Dreamstime; **P252-253:** Jonathan Feinstein/Shutterstock; **P268-269:** Photodisc/OUP; **P271:** M.Brodie/Alamy; **P274:** Natalia Merzlyakova/Dreamstime; **P278:** (L) Anke Van Wyk/ Dreamstime, (R) Kitchner Bain/Dreamstime; **P279:** Sedmi/ Shutterstock; **P286-287:** Uppercut RF/Glow Images; **P289:** (B) Kamenetskiy Konstantin/Shutterstock; **P291:** (T) Nanisimova/Shutterstock, (B) Gors4730/Dreamstime

Artwork by; Phil Hackett , Erwin Haya, Paul Hostetler, Dusan Pavlic, Giulia Rivolta, Katri Valkamo & QBS.

Contents

Number

1 **Whole numbers and decimals**
Introduction 2
1a Factors, multiples and primes 4
1b Prime factor decomposition 6
1c LCM and HCF 8
1d Square roots and cube roots 10
1e Indices 12
1f Rounding and estimation 14
1g Trial-and-improvement 1 16
MySummary/MyReview 18
MyPractice 20

Geometry

2 **Measures, perimeter and area**
Introduction 22
2a Metric measure 24
2b Imperial measure 26
2c Area of a rectangle and a triangle 28
2d Area of a parallelogram and a trapezium 30
2e Circumference of a circle 32
2f Area of a circle 34
MySummary/MyReview 36
MyPractice 38

Algebra

3 **Expressions and formulae**
Introduction 40
3a Indices in algebra 42
3b Index laws 44
3c Collecting like terms including powers 46
3d Expanding brackets 48
3e Factorising expressions 50
3f Formulae 52
3g Rearranging formulae 54
3h Writing expressions 56
3i Algebraic fractions 58
MySummary/MyReview 60
MyPractice 62
Case study 1: Energy in the home 64

Number

4 **Fractions, decimals and percentages**
Introduction 66
4a Fractions and decimals 68
4b Adding and subtracting fractions 70
4c Multiplying and dividing fractions 72
4d Percentage change 74
4e Percentage problems 76
4f Fractions, decimals and percentages 78
MySummary/MyReview 80
MyPractice 82
MyAssesment 1 84

Geometry

5 Angles and 2D shapes
Introduction ... 86
5a Angles and parallel lines ... 88
5b Properties of a triangle and a quadrilateral ... 90
5c Properties of a polygon ... 92
5d Congruent shapes ... 94
MySummary/MyReview ... 96
MyPractice ... 98

Algebra

6 Graphs
Introduction ... 100
6a Graphs of linear functions ... 102
6b Equation of a straight line ... 104
6c Curved graphs ... 106
6d Midpoints of coordinate pairs ... 108
6e Graphs of implicit functions ... 110
6f Real-life graphs ... 112
6g Time series ... 114
MySummary/MyReview ... 116
MyPractice ... 118
Case study 2: Patchwork ... 120

Number

7 Mental calculations
Introduction ... 122
7a Arithmetic with negative integers ... 124
7b Powers of 10 ... 126
7c Mental addition and subtraction ... 128
7d Mental multiplication and division ... 130
MySummary/MyReview ... 132
MyPractice ... 134

Statistics

8 Statistics
Introduction ... 136
8a Planning a statistical investigation ... 138
8b Collecting data ... 140
8c Frequency tables ... 142
8d Constructing diagrams ... 144
8e Averages 1 ... 146
8f Averages 2 ... 148
8g Interpreting statistical diagrams ... 150
8h Scatter diagrams and correlation ... 152
8i Comparing distributions ... 154
MySummary/MyReview ... 156
MyPractice ... 158
MyAssessment 2 ... 160

Geometry

9 Transformations
Introduction ... 162
9a Transformations ... 164
9b Combinations of transformations ... 166
9c Symmetry ... 168

9d Enlargements 1 170
9e Enlargements 2 172
MySummary/MyReview 174
MyPractice 176
Case study 3: Food crops 178

Algebra

10 Equations
Introduction 180
10a Linear equations 1 182
10b Linear equations 2 184
10c Equations with fractions 186
10d Trial-and-improvement 2 188
10e Real-life equations 190
MySummary/MyReview 192
MyPractice 194

Number

11 Written and calculator methods
Introduction 196
11a Multiplication 198
11b Division 200
11c Calculator skills 202
11d Calculators in context 204
11e Order of operations 206
11f Written addition and subtraction 208
11g Multiplication and division problems 210
MySummary/MyReview 212
MyPractice 214

Geometry

12 Constructions
Introduction 216
12a Constructing triangles 1 218
12b Constructing triangles 2 220
12c Bisectors and perpendiculars 222
12d Scale drawings 224
12e Loci 226
12f Bearings 228
MySummary/MyReview 230
MyPractice 232
Case study 4: Paper folding 234
MyAssessment 3 236

Algebra

13 Sequences
Introduction 238
13a General term of a sequence 240
13b Sequences in context 242
13c Geometric sequences 244
13d Recursive sequences 246
MySummary/MyReview 248
MyPractice 250

Geometry

14 3D shapes

Introduction 252
14a 3D shapes 254
14b Plans and elevations 256
14c Surface area of a prism 258
14d Volume of a prism 260
MySummary/MyReview 262
MyPractice 264
Case study 5: Perspective 266

Ratio

15 Ratio and proportion

Introduction 268
15a Ratio 270
15b Division in a given ratio 272
15c Direct proportion 274
15d Ratio and proportion 276
15e Comparing proportions 278
15f Algebra and proportion 280
MySummary/MyReview 282
MyPractice 284

Statistics

16 Probability

Introduction 286
16a Two or more events 288
16b Tree diagrams 290
16c Mutually exclusive outcomes 292
16d Experimental probability 294
16e Comparing experimental and theoretical probability 296
16f Simulating experimental data 298
16g Venn diagrams and probability 300
MySummary/MyReview 302
MyPractice 304
Case study 6: Free-range 306
MyAssessment 4 308

Functional

17 Everyday maths

Introduction 310
17a Planning the trip to France 312
17b Camp Sarlat 314
17c The sports day 316
17d The expedition 318
17e Camp-life 320

Answers 322
Index 328

About this book

MyMaths for Key Stage 3 is an exciting new series designed for schools following the new National Curriculum for mathematics. This book has been written to help you to grow your mathematical knowledge and skills during Key Stage 3.

Each topic starts with an Introduction that shows why it is relevant to real life and includes a short *Check in* exercise to see if you are ready to start the topic.

Inside each chapter, you will find lots of worked examples and questions for you to try along with interesting facts. There's basic practice to build your confidence, as well as problem solving. You might also notice the **4-digit codes** at the bottom of the page, which you can type into the search bar on the *MyMaths* site to take you straight to the relevant *MyMaths* lesson for more help in understanding and extra practice.

At the end of each chapter you will find *My Summary*, which tests what you've learned and suggests what you could try next to improve your skills even further. The *What next?* box details further resources available in the supporting online products.

Maths is a vitally important subject, not just for you while you are at school but also for when you grow up. We hope that this book will lead to a greater enjoyment of the subject and that it will help you to realise how useful maths is to your everyday life.

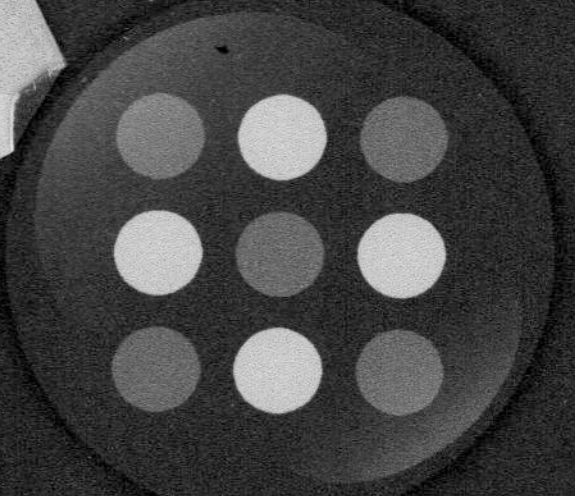

1 Whole numbers and decimals

Introduction

When your parents pay using a credit card on the internet they need to know that their financial details are safe. The financial transaction is turned into a secret code (encrypted) using the product of two very large prime numbers – the person receiving the message has to know both of these prime numbers so that they can decrypt the message.

The problems involved in writing very large numbers as the product of two prime numbers makes it very difficult for someone intercepting the message to crack the code.

What's the point?

Prime numbers allow people to rest assured that their bank accounts will not be hacked into.

Objectives

By the end of this chapter, you will have learned how to ...

- Use divisibility tests to find factors and identify primes.
- Find and use the lowest common multiple (LCM) and highest common factor (HCF) of two numbers using prime factors.
- Find square roots and cube roots.
- Use, multiply and divide numbers written in index form.
- Round numbers to a given power of 10 and use rounding to make estimates.
- Use trial-and-improvement to find square and cube roots.

Check in

1. Write all the factors of **a** 60 **b** 132 **c** 225
2. Find the HCF and LCM of **a** 8 and 12 **b** 15 and 20 **c** 18 and 27
3. Work out the value of **a** $2 \times 3 \times 5$ **b** $2^2 \times 3^2$ **c** $2 \times 5^2 \times 7$
4. Write out the first 20 prime numbers.
5. Work out these using a calculator where appropriate.

   a 9^2 **b** 5^3 **c** $\sqrt{36}$ **d** 1.7^3 **e** $\sqrt{45}$

Starter problem

A million dollar reward awaits the person who can find a rule (function) for generating all the prime numbers.

Here are some of the formulae that have been tried,

$6n + 1$

$6n - 1$

$n^2 - n + 41$

$2^n - 1$

Test out these formulae and see if they really work.

1a Factors multiples and primes

Any whole number can be writen as the product of two **factors**.

For example 12 = 3 × 4

The **multiples** of 3 are 3, 6, 9, **12**, 15, ...

Divisibility tests can be used to find larger **factors** of a number.

Example

Is 15 a factor of 255?

15 = 3 × 5

Use simple divisibility tests to check if 3 and 5 are factors of 255.

Number	Is it a factor of 255?
3	Yes: 2 + 5 + 5 = 12
5	Yes: 255 ends in a 5

3 and 5 are both factors of 255.

This means that 15 is also a factor of 255.

Check: 255 ÷ 15 = 17

Divisibility Tests

÷2	the number ends in a 0, 2, 4, 6 or 8
÷3	the sum of the digits is divisible by 3
÷4	the last two digits form a multiple of 4
÷5	the number ends in a 0 or a 5
÷6	the number is divisible by both 2 and 3
÷7	there is no simple check for divisibility by 7
÷8	half of the number is divisible by 4
÷9	the sum of the digits is a multiple of 9
÷10	the number ends in a 0
÷11	the alternating sum of the digits is a multiple of 11
÷12	the number is divisible by both 3 and 4

A **prime** number has exactly two factors: the number itself and 1.

Example

Is 139 a prime number?

Factor	Is it a factor of 139?
2	No: 139 ends in a 9
3	No: 1 + 3 + 9 = 13
5	No: 139 ends in a 9
7	No: 139 ÷ 7 = 19 r 6
11	No: 1 + 9 − 3 = 7

$13^2 = 169$ so you do not need to divide by any higher prime numbers.

139 is a prime number.

Exercise 1a

1 Complete the following factor pairs.

a $18 = \square \times 18 = \square \times 9 = \square \times 6$

b $20 = \square \times 20 = \square \times 10 = \square \times 5$

c $30 = \square \times 30 = \square \times 15 = \square \times 10$
$= \square \times 6$

d $35 = \square \times 35 = \square \times \square$

2 The first five multiples of 2 are 2, 4, 6, 8, 10. Write the first five multiples of

a 3 **b** 5 **c** 7
d 8 **e** 11 **f** 15

3 Use the divisibility tests, where possible, to answer each of these questions. In each case, explain your answer and then check your answer by division.

a Is 5 a factor of 385?
b Is 3 a factor of 746?
c Is 7 a factor of 164?
d Is 11 a factor of 3234?
e Is 12 a factor of 458?
f Is 15 a factor of 2010?
g Is 18 a factor of 1926?
h Is 24 a factor of 2712?

4 Write all the factors of

a 460 **b** 864 **c** 625
d 924 **e** 1024 **f** 1225

Remember factors always come in pairs: $16 = 1 \times 16$, 2×8 and 4×4

5 Use the divisibility tests to find which of these numbers are prime. In each case explain your answer.

a 199 **b** 161 **c** 221
d 239 **e** 301 **f** 379

6 Use your calculator to find all the prime numbers between 10000 and 10050.

Problem solving

7 Siobhan makes a sequence out of hexagons.

 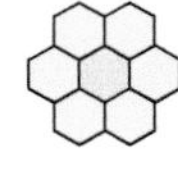 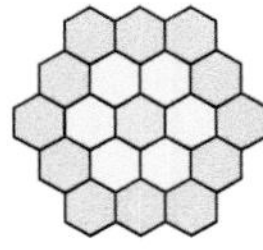 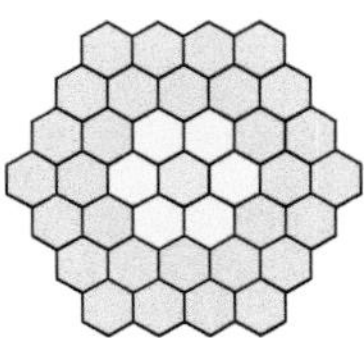

a How many hexagons are there in each diagram?

b How many hexagons will there be in each of the next two diagrams in this sequence?

c What do you notice about the types of numbers in your sequence?

d Investigate bigger numbers in this sequence.

8 Siobhan reads an article that says that all prime numbers can be described by mathematical formulae such as $6n + 1$.

For example

when $n = 1$, $6n + 1 = 7$ (a prime number)

when $n = 2$, $6n + 1 = 13$ (a prime number)

when $n = 3$, $6n + 1 = \ldots$

Investigate these formulae, to see which of them generate prime numbers.

a $6n + 1$
b $6n - 1$
c $n^2 - n + 41$
d $2^n - 1$

Write a report about what you have found out.

Did you know?

Searching for primes is very competitive. At the start of 2014 the largest known prime number is

That is one less than 2 multiplied by itself a lot of times! The number has 17425170 digits!

1b Prime factor decomposition

- Every whole number can be **decomposed** as the product of its **prime factors**.

Decompose means to write a number as the product of its prime factors.

Example

What number is represented by $2^3 \times 3 \times 5^2$?

$2^3 \times 3 \times 5^2 = 2 \times 2 \times 2 \times 3 \times 5 \times 5$
$= 600$

To write two numbers as the product of their prime factors you can use a **factor tree** or a method based on repeated division.

Example

Write each number as the product of its prime factors.

a 2100 **b** 1800

A factor tree can start with any pair of factors. It will always stop with the same prime factors.

a

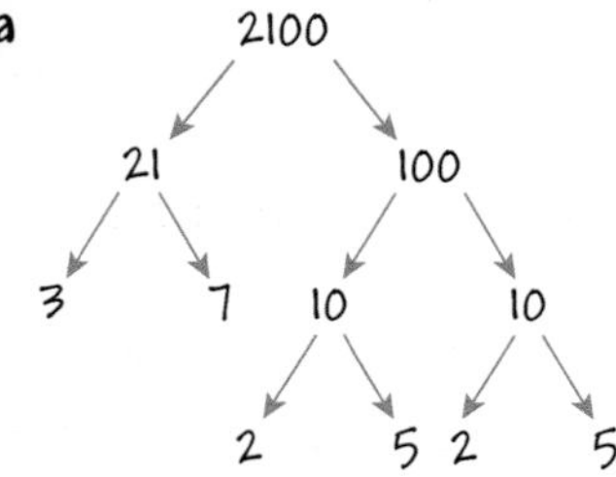

$2100 = 2 \times 2 \times 3 \times 5 \times 5 \times 7$
$= 2^2 \times 3 \times 5^2 \times 7$

b

2) 1800
2) 900
2) 450
3) 225
3) 75
5) 25
5 STOP

$1800 = 2 \times 2 \times 2 \times 3 \times 3 \times 5 \times 5$
$= 2^3 \times 3^2 \times 5^2$

In repeated division, it is easiest to divide by the smallest prime number you can. Stop when you reach a prime number.

The prime factors of a number can be used to list all of its factors.

Example

Write the factors of 140.

$140 = 2 \times 2 \times 5 \times 7$

In addition to 1, 2, 5 and 7 the factors of 140 are

$2 \times 2 = 4$	$2 \times 2 \times 5 = 20$	$2 \times 5 \times 7 = 70$
$2 \times 5 = 10$	$2 \times 2 \times 7 = 28$	$2 \times 2 \times 5 \times 7 = 140$
$2 \times 7 = 14$	$5 \times 7 = 35$	

The factors of 140 = {1, 2, 4, 5, 7, 10, 14, 20, 28, 35, 70 and 140}

Exercise 1b

1 Work out the value of

a $2^2 \times 3 \times 5$ **b** $2^2 \times 7$

c $2 \times 3^2 \times 5$ **d** $2^2 \times 5^2 \times 7$

e $2^2 \times 5 \times 11$ **f** $2^2 \times 3^2 \times 7$

g $2^3 \times 13$ **h** $2^2 \times 3^2 \times 7^2$

i $2^3 \times 3 \times 5^2 \times 7$ **j** $2^4 \times 5 \times 11$

2 Write each of these numbers as the product of its prime factors.

a 18 **b** 42 **c** 80

d 54 **e** 128 **f** 420

g 200 **h** 175 **i** 360

j 480 **k** 576 **l** 1080

m 2520 **n** 1296 **o** 2025

3 Gina has used the factor tree method to find all the prime factors of 12 600 and 26 460. Here is her working out.

i

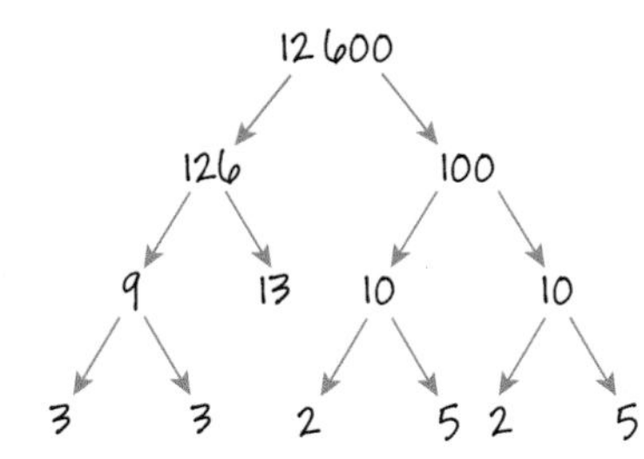

ii

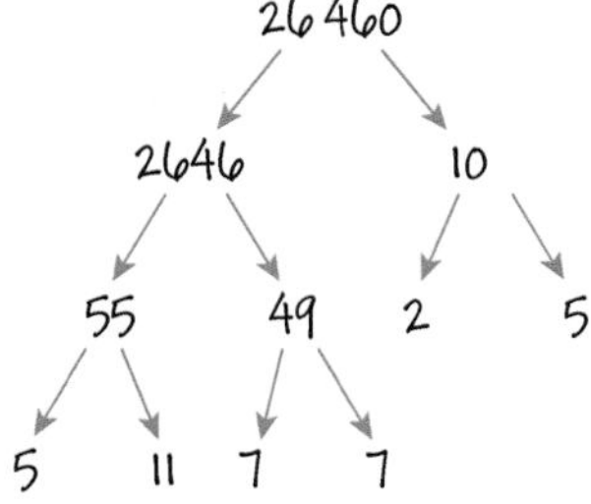

a Can you spot her mistakes?

b Copy and correct Gina's work.

c Write down any strategies you used to find Gina's mistakes.

4 List all the factors of these numbers.

a 80 **b** 180 **c** 450

d 330 **e** 1470 **f** 1000

5 How many factors do these numbers have?

a 2^2 **b** 2^3 **c** 2^4 **d** 3^2

e 3^3 **f** 3^4 **g** $2^2 \times 3^2$ **h** $2^3 \times 3^2$

Can you find a rule for the number of factors?

Look at the indices.

Problem solving

6 **a** A number has prime factors of 2, 3 and 5.
What are the smallest five values it could be?

b Find the smallest number greater than 200 with exactly four prime factors.

c Find the smallest number greater than 200 with four different prime factors.

7 Verity has to make 12 different numbers between 100 and 600. She is allowed to multiply any of the numbers 3, 5 and 7 together as many times as she likes.
Copy and complete Verity's table.

$3^2 \times 5^2 = 225$	$3 \times 5^2 \times 7 = 525$				
$3 \times 7^2 = 147$					

How many more examples can you find?

1c LCM and HCF

The **highest common factor** (**HCF**) and the **lowest common multiple** (**LCM**) of two numbers can be found using prime factors.

- The HCF is the largest number that will divide into the two numbers exactly.
- The LCM is the smallest number that both numbers will divide into exactly.

Example

Find the HCF and LCM of 240 and 540.

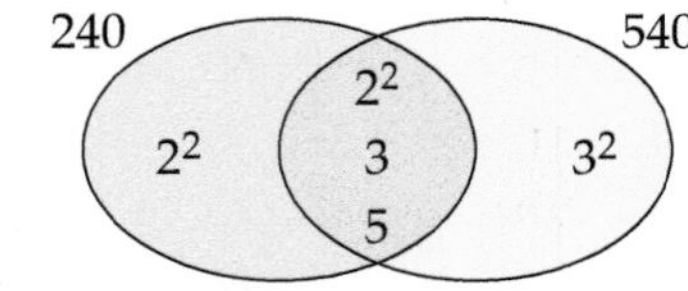

Write both numbers as the product of their prime factors

	240
2	120
2	60
2	30
2	15
3	5 STOP

	540
2	270
2	135
3	45
3	15
3	5 STOP

p.50 >

$240 = 2^4 \times 3 \times 5$ $\quad 540 = 2^2 \times 3^3 \times 5$

Multiply the prime factors they have in common

HCF of 240 and 540 $= 2^2 \times 3 \times 5 = 60$

Multiply the highest power of each of the prime factors

LCM of 240 and 540 $= 2^4 \times 3^3 \times 5 = 2160$

The LCM can be used to add or subtract fractions with different denominators, and the HCF used to simplify fractions.

Example

a Simplify $\frac{96}{168}$ **b** Calculate $\frac{23}{28} + \frac{17}{40}$

a The HCF of 96 and 168 is 24

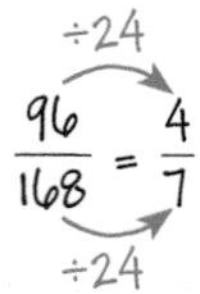

$\frac{96}{168} = \frac{4}{7}$ ($\div 24$)

b The LCM of 28 and 40 is 280

$\frac{23}{28} = \frac{230}{280}$ ($\times 10$) $\quad \frac{17}{40} = \frac{119}{280}$ ($\times 7$)

$\frac{23}{28} + \frac{17}{40} = \frac{230 + 119}{280} = \frac{349}{280} = 1\frac{69}{280}$

Exercise 1c

1 Find the HCF of

- **a** 10 and 15 **b** 35 and 50
- **c** 72 and 96 **d** 95 and 133
- **e** 6, 15 and 21 **f** 24, 40 and 64

2 Find the LCM of

- **a** 10 and 15 **b** 35 and 50
- **c** 68 and 85 **d** 140 and 196
- **e** 6, 15 and 21 **f** 10, 25 and 40

3 Find the HCF and LCM of

- **a** 108 and 144 **b** 280 and 360
- **c** 385 and 660 **d** 441 and 819
- **e** 480 and 1080 **f** 720 and 1260
- **g** 35, 56 and 63 **h** 45, 75 and 90

> Write each number as the product of its prime factors.

4 Cancel down each of these fractions into their simplest form.

a $\frac{24}{36}$ **b** $\frac{50}{90}$ **c** $\frac{72}{96}$ **d** $\frac{81}{135}$ **e** $\frac{120}{192}$

5 Work out these, leaving your answer as a fraction in its simplest form.

- **a** $\frac{7}{10} - \frac{7}{15}$ **b** $\frac{5}{12} + \frac{7}{15}$
- **c** $\frac{7}{20} + \frac{3}{25}$ **d** $\frac{12}{25} + \frac{13}{40}$

Did you know?

Venn diagrams were invented by John Venn. A stained glass window in the dining hall of Gonville and Caius College at Cambridge University celebrates Venn's work.

Problem solving

6 Find the missing numbers in these productogons. The number in a rectangle is the product of the numbers in the circles either side of it.

a

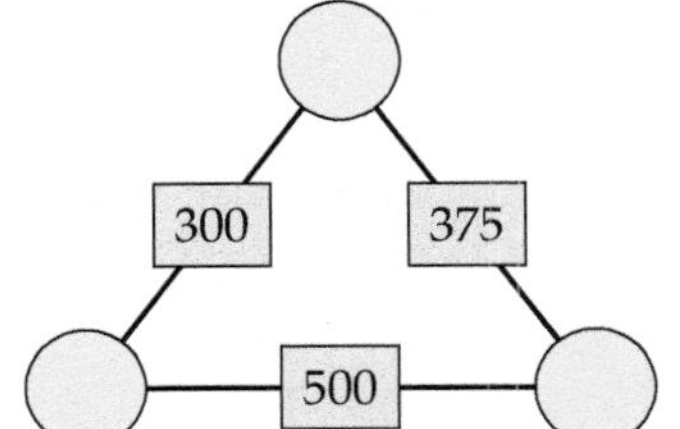

b

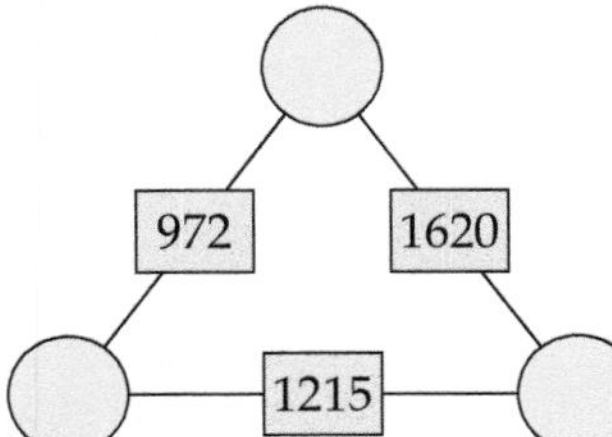

7 In a faraway galaxy, three planets are lined up around a giant sun. They have orbits of 28, 42 and 49 weeks.

- **a** After how many weeks will the three planets be next in line?
- **b** How many orbits will each planet have completed before they are back in alignment?

8 **a** The HCF of two numbers is 20. What could the two numbers be? Describe the answers you might expect as precisely as possible.

b The LCM of two numbers is 100. What could the two numbers be? Describe the answers you might expect as precisely as possible.

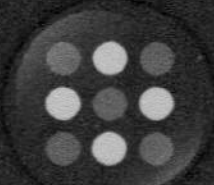

1d Square roots and cube roots

You can use the $\sqrt{\ }$ and $\sqrt[3]{\ }$ function keys on your calculator to find the **square root** of any positive number and the **cube root** of any number.

Not all calculators are the same, check the keys on yours.

Example

Work out the value of **a** $\sqrt{1849}$ **b** $\sqrt[3]{1849}$ **c** $\sqrt[3]{-2197}$

a To find $\sqrt{1849}$ type $\sqrt{\ }$ 1 8 4 9 =

$\sqrt{1849} = 43$

Check: $43^2 = 1849$, $(-43)^2$ is also equal to 1849.

The square roots of 1849 = ±43

b To find $\sqrt[3]{1849}$ type SHIFT $\sqrt[3]{\ }$ 1 8 4 9 =

$\sqrt[3]{1849} = 12.273\,797\,97\ldots$

$= 12.3$ (1 dp)

c $\sqrt[3]{-2197} = -13$

Check: $(-13)^3 = -13 \times -13 \times -13 = -2197$

±43 means +43 and −43. There are two square roots for a positive number, one positive and one negative. A negative number cannot have a square root.

When an answer is not a whole number, you need to round it to an appropriate degree of accuracy.

The cube root of a positive number is positive. The cube root of a negative number is negative.

It is sometimes possible to find the square root of a **square number** and the cube root of a **cube number** by using prime factors.

Example

Work out the value of **a** $\sqrt{784}$ **b** $\sqrt[3]{-64}$

a Find the prime factors of 784

$784 = 2 \times 2 \times 2 \times 2 \times 7 \times 7$

$\sqrt{784} = \sqrt{(2 \times 2 \times 2 \times 2 \times 7 \times 7)}$

$= \sqrt{(2 \times 2 \times 7) \times (2 \times 2 \times 7)}$

$= 2 \times 2 \times 7$

$= 28$

b Find the prime factors of 64

$64 = 2 \times 2 \times 2 \times 2 \times 2 \times 2$

$\sqrt[3]{-64} = \sqrt[3]{(-2 \times 2 \times -2 \times 2 \times -2 \times 2)}$

$= \sqrt[3]{(-2 \times 2) \times (-2 \times 2) \times (-2 \times 2)}$

$= -2 \times 2$

$= -4$

The prime factors of 784 make two identical groups of numbers. The prime factors of 64 make three identical groups of numbers.

Exercise 1d

1 Work out these using a calculator where appropriate.

a 12^2 **b** 19^2 **c** 25^2 **d** 7^3 **e** 13^3 **f** $(-8)^2$

g 10^3 **h** 3.5^2 **i** 20^3 **j** 4.2^3 **k** 12.1^3 **l** $(-5)^3$

2 Calculate these using a calculator where possible.
Give your answer to 1 dp.

1 dp means one decimal place.

a $\sqrt{70}$ **b** $\sqrt{120}$ **c** $\sqrt[3]{70}$ **d** $\sqrt[3]{400}$

e $\sqrt{200}$ **f** $\sqrt{-40}$ **g** $\sqrt[3]{-90}$ **h** $\sqrt[3]{-150}$

3 Calculate these **without** a calculator.

Hint: write each number as the product of its prime factors.

a $\sqrt{225}$ **b** $\sqrt{324}$ **c** $\sqrt{576}$ **d** $\sqrt[3]{216}$

e $\sqrt[3]{512}$ **f** $\sqrt{1296}$ **g** $\sqrt[3]{-125}$ **h** $\sqrt[3]{-343}$

Problem solving

4 **a** Two consecutive numbers are multiplied together.
The answer is 8930. What are the two numbers?

b Three consecutive numbers are multiplied together.
The answer is 185 136. What are the three numbers?

c A digital camera screen is in the shape of a square. It has an area of 70.56 cm². What length is the side of the screen?

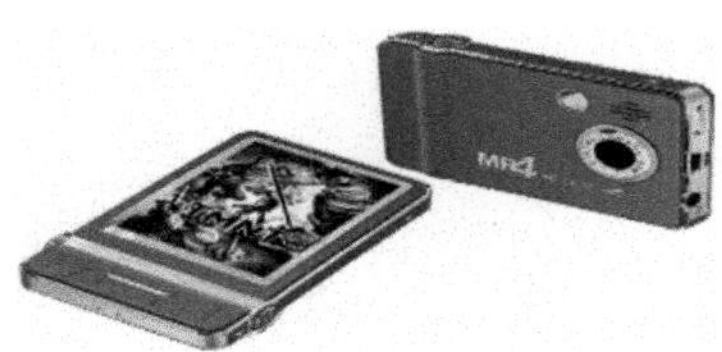

5 Hanif works out $\sqrt{10} = 3.16227766$
He then calculates 3.16227766^2 but the answer is not 10.
Explain why the answer is not 10.

6 Hatti has a trial and improvement method for finding $\sqrt{40}$ without using the $\sqrt{\ }$ key on her calculator. Here is her working.

Estimate	Check (square of estimate)	Answer	Result
6	6^2	36	Too small
7	7^2	49	Too big
6.5	6.5^2	42.25	Too big
6.3	6.3^2	39.69	Too small
6.4	6.4^2	40.96	Too big
6.35	6.35^2	40.3225	Too big

Make sure you have both upper and lower bounds for your answer.

$\sqrt{40} = 6.3$ (1 dp)

Use Hatti's method to estimate

a $\sqrt{20}$, $\sqrt{95}$, $\sqrt{300}$

b $\sqrt[3]{100}$, $\sqrt[3]{10}$, $\sqrt[3]{1600}$

Give your answers to 1 decimal place.

1e Indices

- When you have the same number multiplied by itself several times you can use index notation.

$2 \times 2 \times 2 = 2^3$ The small number is called the **index** or **power**. The big number is called the **base**.

You can use the y^x or ^ function on your calculator to evaluate indices.

Example

Work out the values of **a** 15^4 **b** 217^0 **c** 2^{-1}

a $15^4 = 15 \times 15 \times 15 \times 15 = 50\,625$

b $217^0 = 1$ Any number to the power of zero is 1

c $2^{-2} = \frac{1}{2^2} = \frac{1}{4}$ Negative powers mean one over the positive power.

- The decimal system is based upon powers of 10, and can be written using **index notation.**

1 thousand	$= 1000$	$= 10 \times 10 \times 10$	$= 10^3$
1 ten	$= 10$	$= 10$	$= 10^1$
1 unit	$= 1$		$= 10^0$
1 tenth	$= \frac{1}{10}$	$= \frac{1}{10^1}$	$= 10^{-1}$

Scientists use some very big and very small powers.
10^{-15} m = 1 femtometre
the size of an atomic nucleus.
10^{21} m = 1 zettametre
a typical distance between stars.

You can multiply numbers written in **index form**.

Example

Calculate **a** $5^3 \times 5^2$ **b** $5^2 \times 5^1$

a $5^3 \times 5^2 = (5 \times 5 \times 5) \times (5 \times 5) = 5^5$

$= 5^{3+2} = 5^5$

b $5^2 \times 5 = 5^{2+1} = 5^3$

Add the indices when multiplying. Remember the base number must be the same.

You can divide numbers written in index form.

Example

Calculate **a** $5^5 \div 5^2$ **b** $5^2 \div 5^4$

a $5^5 \div 5^2 = \frac{5 \times 5 \times 5 \times \cancel{5} \times \cancel{5}}{\cancel{5} \times \cancel{5}} = 5 \times 5 \times 5 = 5^3$

$= 5^{5-2} = 5^3$

b $5^2 \div 5^4 = 5^{2-4} = 5^{-2}$

Subtract the indices when dividing.

Exercise 1e

1 Calculate these.

a 5^3 b 2^6 c 3^3
d 1^7 e 5^0 f 10^5
g 2^1 h 7^0 i 10^{-2}
j 11^3 k 8^{-3} l 6^{-1}

2 Simplify each of these, leaving your answer as a single power of the number.

a $4^2 \times 4^3$ b $3^4 \times 3^2$ c $5^3 \times 5^4$
d $4^5 \times 4^2$ e $2^6 \times 2^2$ f $6^5 \times 6^4$
g $4^5 \div 4^2$ h $3^7 \div 3^3$ i $5^5 \div 5^3$
j $4^6 \div 4^4$ k $2^5 \div 2^4$ l $6^7 \div 6^5$

3 Calculate these, leaving your answer in index form where possible.

a $5^2 \times 2^3$ b $3^3 + 3^2$ c $4^3 - 2^4$
d $3^5 \div 4^2$ e $2^4 \div 2^5$ f $9^2 \div 3^3$

4 Simplify each of these, leaving your answer as a single power of the number.

a $3^2 \times 3^3 \times 3^2$ b $4^5 \times 4$
c $10^3 \times 10^4 \times 10^2$ d $\dfrac{2^4 \times 2^5}{2^3}$
e $\dfrac{4^2 \times 4^4 \times 4^3}{4^6}$ f $10^3 \div 10^5$
g $\dfrac{5^3 \times 5^6}{5^8 \div 5^4}$ h $3^{12} \div 3^9 \div 3^3$

Problem solving

5 Put these numbers in order from smallest to largest.

2^8 3^5 4^4 11^3

6 Jasmine knows that $2^8 = 256$.
Uri says that she can use this information to work out 2^{10}.
Explain how Jasmine can use 2^8 to work out 2^{10}.

7 Use the fact that $4^6 = 4096$ to work out

a 4^5 b 4^7

8 Use your calculator to find the power x in these questions.
The first one has been done for you.

a $3^x = 81$ b $2^x = 32$ c $10^x = 1\,000\,000$

a Guess $x = 5$, evaluate
$3^5 = 243$ too high,
try a lower value, $x = 4$
evaluate $3^4 = 81$
$3^x = 81$, $x = 4$

d $7^x = 49$ e $4^x = 1024$
f $6^x = 1296$ g $2^x = 256$
h $10^x = 0.1$ i $2.5^x = 6.25$

Did you know?

The Three Gorges Dam, in China, is the world's largest hydroelectric scheme. It will generate 22.5 gigawatts, or 2.25×10^{10} watts, of power!

9 Ali makes a cube using 125 smaller cubes.
He paints the outside of the cube with red paint.

a How many of the smaller cubes have 1 face painted red?

b How many of the smaller cubes have 0 faces painted red? 2 faces painted red? 3 faces painted red?

c Investigate other different-sized starting cubes.

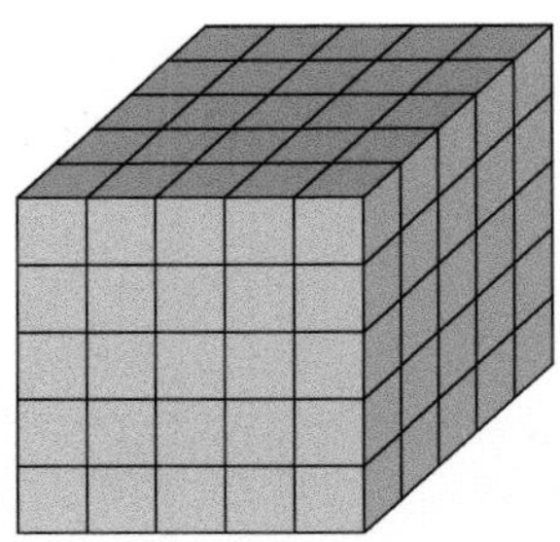

1f Rounding and estimation

- To round a number to the nearest **whole number** or a given number of **decimal places** you look at the next digit
  - if it is five or more, **round up**
  - if it is less than five, **round down**.

Example

Engineers must manufacture the components for formula 1 engines to very high accuracies in order to get the best performance.
The diameter of a piston is measured to be 9.75083 cm.
Write the diameter to 3 decimal places.

100	10	1	·	$\frac{1}{10}$	$\frac{1}{100}$	$\frac{1}{1000}$	$\frac{1}{10\,000}$	$\frac{1}{100\,000}$
		9	•	7	5	0	8	3

To round to 3 dp, look at the 4th dp.
The 4th dp is 8, so round up.

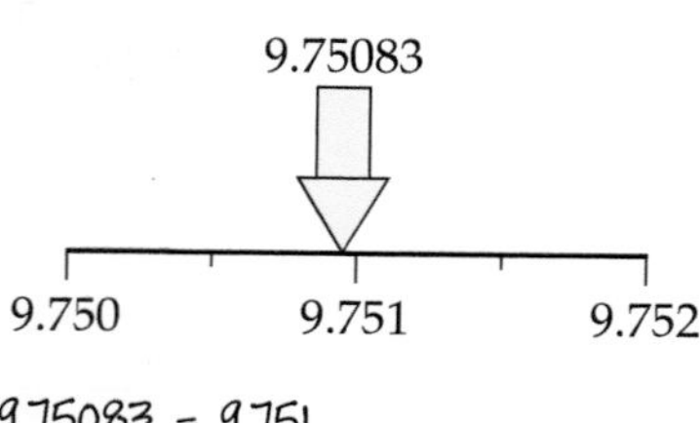

9.75083 = 9.751

- Rounding is used to make **estimates** in real-life situations.

Example

June works in the canteen of H.Elthy Eton School.
She needs to calculate how many dinners to make each day.
In a recent poll, 73% of pupils at the school ate school dinners.
The school is an 11–16 sports college with four form groups in each year.
June estimates that there are about 30 pupils in each form group.
How many dinners should June make?

Number of forms in school = 4 × 5 = 20

Fraction of pupils who eat school dinners = 73% ≈ $\frac{3}{4}$

Number of dinners ≈ $\frac{3}{4}$ of (30 × 20)

= $\frac{3}{4}$ of 600

= 450

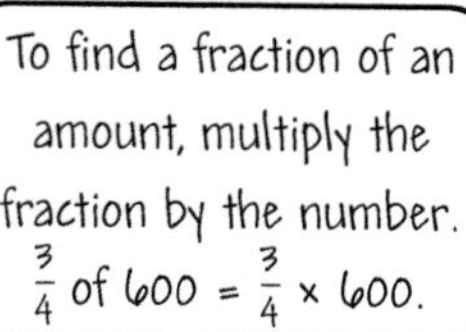

Exercise 1f

1 Round each number to the nearest

i 1000	ii 100	iii 10.
a 12 093	b 2397	c 894
d 8498	e 23 456	f 699
g 2987	h 1 436 384	i 9999
j 7474	k 4747	l 106 842
m 3 106 842	n 55 555	o 454 545

2 Round each number to the nearest

i whole number	ii 1 dp
iii 2 dp	iv 3 dp.
a 5.0472	b 3.4539
c 17.5166	d 3.04925
e 13.00854	f 130.2536
g 0.03047	h 7.90089

Problem solving

3 Here is some information about Brian the flea.
Each of the measurements has been rounded.
Length = 3.8 mm (1 dp)
Width = 1.26 mm (2 dp)
Write **i** the minimum value and
ii the maximum value that each of Brian's measurements could be.

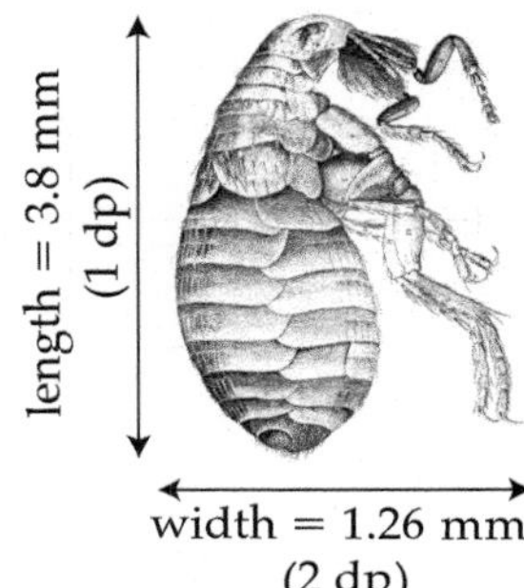

4 Work out an estimate for each of these problems.
Show all the steps of your working out.

a At R U Danzin Arts College the average height of a year 8 boy is 1.48 m and the average height of a year 8 girl is 1.35 m. There are 73 boys and 81 girls in year 8. Estimate, to the nearest metre, the total height of the pupils in year 8.

b A swimming club decided to raise money for charity by swimming the equivalent distance from Oxford to Carlisle. The distance from Oxford to Carlisle is 429.7 km. The length of the swimming pool was 24.6888 metres. The average time to swim one length was 51.3 secs.

i Estimate, to the nearest length, the number of lengths swum.

ii Estimate, to the nearest hour, the time taken for the swim.

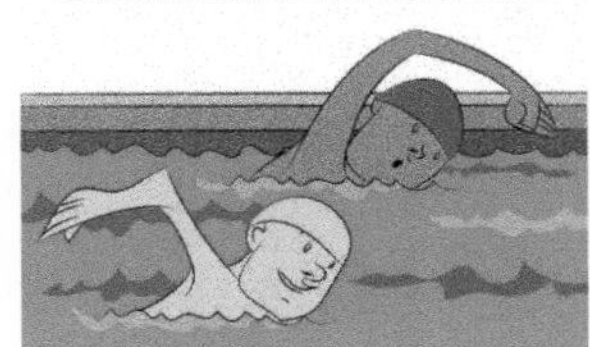

5 Kevin has measured the walls of his bedroom.
Length = 3.4 m (1 dp) Width = 2.3 m (1 dp)
He buys a rectangular piece of carpet with an area of 7.9 m^2, in the same shape as his bedroom. However the piece of carpet is not long or wide enough!
Explain what has happened.

1g Trial-and-improvement 1

‹ p.10
p.188 ›

You can find the **square root** of a number by trial-and-improvement.

Example

Estimate $\sqrt{60}$ to 2 dp.

First, you must find upper and lower bounds.

$7^2 = 49$ and $8^2 = 64$ so $7 < \sqrt{60} < 8$

Organise trials to sandwich the solution.

	A	B	C	D
1	Estimate	Estimate^2	Answer	Result
2	7	7^2	49	Low
3	8	8^2	64	High
4	7.5	7.5^2	56.25	Low
5	7.6	7.6^2	57.76	Low
6	7.7	7.7^2	59.29	Low
7	7.8	7.8^2	60.84	High
9	7.75	7.75^2	60.0625	High
10	7.74	7.74^2	59.9076	Low
11	7.745	7.745^2	59.98503	Low

7.7 too small and 7.8 too big $7.7 < \sqrt{60} < 7.8$

7.74 too small and 7.75 too big $7.74 < \sqrt{60} < 7.75$

7.745 too small and 7.750 too big $7.745 < \sqrt{60} < 7.750$

$\sqrt{60}$ is between 7.745 and 7.750

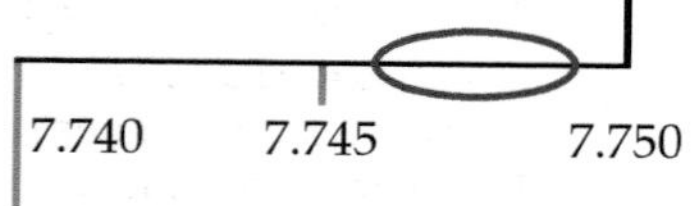

Stop because both 7.745 and 7.750 round to 7.75 (2 dp).

$\sqrt{60} = 7.75$ (2 dp)

You can find the **cube root** of a number by trial-and-improvement.

Example

Estimate $\sqrt[3]{100}$ to 2 dp.

$4^3 = 64$ and $5^3 = 125$ so $4 < \sqrt[3]{100} < 5$

	A	B	C	D
1	Estimate	Estimate^3	Answer	Result
2	4	4^3	64	Low
3	5	5^3	125	High
4	4.5	4.5^3	91.125	Low
5	4.6	4.6^3	97.336	Low
6	4.7	4.7^3	103.823	High
7	4.65	4.65^3	100.5446	High
9	4.64	4.64^3	99.89734	Low
10	4.645	4.645^3	100.2206	High

4.6 too small and 4.7 too big
$4.6 < \sqrt[3]{100} < 4.7$

4.64 too small and 4.65 too big
$4.64 < \sqrt[3]{100} < 4.65$

4.640 too small and 4.645 too big
$4.640 < \sqrt[3]{100} < 4.645$

$\sqrt[3]{100}$ lies between 4.640 and 4.645

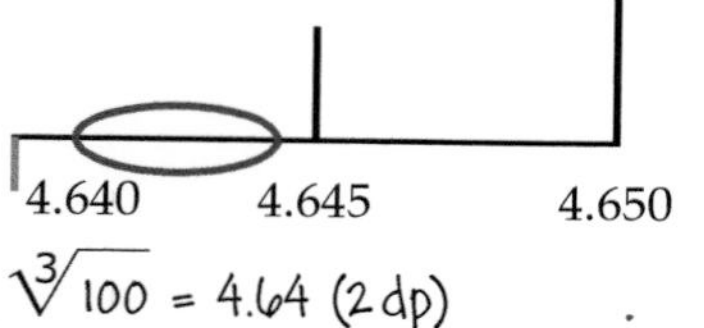

The answer is **less** than 4.645 so it rounds to 4.64 (2 dp).

$\sqrt[3]{100} = 4.64$ (2 dp)

Exercise 1g

1 Laura is working out $\sqrt{75}$ to 2 dp.
Here is her working out.

	Estimate	Estimate²	Answer	Result
	8.6	8.6^2	73.96	Low
	8.7	8.7^2	75.69	High
	8.66	8.66^2	74.996	Low
	8.67	8.67^2	75.169	High

a Does she need to do any more working to find the answer? Explain your thinking.

b Continue Laura method to find $\sqrt{75}$ to 3 dp.

2 Use a trial-and-improvement method to find the square root of each of these numbers to 2 dp.

a $\sqrt{30}$ **b** $\sqrt{70}$ **c** $\sqrt{145}$
d $\sqrt{180}$ **e** $\sqrt{250}$ **f** $\sqrt{600}$

Use the square root key on your calculator to check your answers.

3 Use a trial-and-improvement method to find the cube root of each of these numbers to 1 dp.

a $\sqrt[3]{40}$ **b** $\sqrt[3]{200}$ **c** $\sqrt[3]{70}$
d $\sqrt[3]{13}$ **e** $\sqrt[3]{2000}$ **f** $\sqrt[3]{5000}$

Use the cube root key on your calculator to check your answers.

Did you know?

This Babylonian tablet says

$$\sqrt{2} = 1 + \frac{24}{60} + \frac{51}{60^2} + \frac{10}{60^3}$$
$$= 1.414\,213 \text{ (6 dp)}$$

The calculation was done 3700 years ago without calculators.

Problem solving

4 Yvette is trying to find $\sqrt{60}$ using a method called iteration.
It takes an 'old' estimate and calculates an improved 'new' estimate.
This is the formula she is using.

$$\text{new} = \frac{1}{2} \times \left(\text{old} + \frac{60}{\text{old}}\right)$$

She tries 10 as her 'old' estimate.

$$\text{new} = \frac{1}{2} \times \left(10 + \frac{60}{10}\right) = 8$$

She then uses her 'new' estimate, 8, as the 'old' estimate.

$$\text{new} = \frac{1}{2} \times \left(8 + \frac{60}{8}\right) = 7.75$$

She uses her 'new' estimate, 7.75, as the 'old' estimate, and repeats …

a Continue using Yvette's method for finding $\sqrt{60}$.

b After a few goes, use your calculator to check the value of $\sqrt{60}$.
Write what you notice.

c Try finding $\sqrt{300}$ using the same method.

d If you have access to a computer, use this formula in a spreadsheet.

e The iteration will stop if new = old.
Call this value x, write an equation for x and solve it.

1 MySummary

Check out

You should now be able to ...

Test it ➡ Questions

You should now be able to ...	Level	Questions
✓ Use divisibility tests to find factors and identify primes.	5	1, 2
✓ Find and use the HCF and LCM of two numbers using prime factors.	6	3 – 5
✓ Find square roots and cube roots.	6	6, 7
✓ Use, multiply and divide numbers written in index form.	6	8
✓ Round numbers to a given power of 10 and use rounding to make estimates.	6	9, 10
✓ Use trial-and-improvement to find square and cube roots.	6	11

Language	Meaning	Example
Prime number	A number divisible by itself and 1	2, 3, 5, 7, 11, 13 ...
Factor	A quantity that divides another given quantity without a remainder	2 and 3 are factors of 6, because $2 \times 3 = 6$
Multiple	The product of any quantity and an integer	3, 6, 9, 12 are multiples of 3
Prime factor decomposition	Writing a number as a product of prime factors	$2000 = 2^4 \times 5^3$
Factor tree	A method for finding the prime factors of a number	See p 6
Highest Common Factor (HCF)	The largest number that divides each of a given set of numbers exactly	For 12 and 18 the HCF is 6 and the LCM is 36
Lowest Common Multiple (LCM)	The smallest number that each of a given set of numbers divides into exactly	
Square root	A square root is a number that when multiplied by itself is equal to a given number.	$\sqrt{25} = 5$ because $5 \times 5 = 5^2 = 25$
Cube root	A cube root is a number that when multiplied by itself three times is equal to a given number.	$\sqrt[3]{27} = 3$ because $3 \times 3 \times 3 = 3^3 = 27$
Indices	A compact way of writing a repeated product	$5^3 = 5 \times 5 \times 5$

1 MyReview

1 Use divisibility tests to answer these questions. Explain your answer.

a Is 8 a factor of 508?

b Is 6822 divisible by 6?

c Is 617 a multiple of 3?

d Is 127 a prime number?

2 Write each of these numbers as a product of its prime factors. Use index notation in your answers.

a 297 **b** 2450

3 Find the highest common factor of each pair of numbers.

a 27 and 117

b 385 and 144

4 Find the lowest common multiple of each pair of numbers.

a 35 and 77

b 126 and 588

5 Work these out. Leave each answer as a fraction in its simplest form.

a $\frac{5}{6} + \frac{8}{9}$ **b** $\frac{11}{12} - \frac{7}{15}$

6 Find these using a calculator. Give your answer to 2 dp where possible.

a $\sqrt{250}$ **b** $\sqrt{-225}$

c $\sqrt[3]{500}$ **d** $\sqrt[3]{-160}$

7 Find these without using a calculator.

a 11^2 **b** $\sqrt{169}$

c 8^3 **d** $\sqrt[3]{-64}$

8 Evaluate these expressions. Leave each answer in index form where possible.

a $4^6 \times 4$ **b** $5^0 \times 5^7$

c $12^6 \div 12^4$ **d** $6^2 \div 3^2$

e $3^4 - 3^2$ **f** $2^7 \times 2^5 \div 2^{10}$

9 Round 160.0952 to the nearest

a whole number **b** 1 dp

c 2 dp **d** 3 dp.

10 A table is measured to be 95 cm long to the nearest cm. What is the

a shortest

b longest length the table could actually be?

11 Use trial and improvement to find $\sqrt[3]{20}$ to 1 dp. Show your working clearly.

What next?

Score		
0 – 4		Your knowledge of this topic is still developing. To improve look at Formative test: 2C-1; MyMaths: 1001, 1032, 1033, 1034, 1035, 1044, 1053, 1057 and 1968
5 – 9		You are gaining a secure knowledge of this topic. To improve look at InvisiPen: 112, 135, 172, 173, 174, 181, 184 and 221
10 – 11		You have mastered this topic. Well done, you are ready to progress!

1 MyPractice

1a

1 Write all the factors of these numbers.

a 200 **b** 288 **c** 289 **d** 300 **e** 440 **f** 256
g 500 **h** 639 **i** 777 **j** 999 **k** 1000 **l** 2304

2 Use the divisibility tests to say which of these numbers are prime.
In each case explain your answer.

a 401 **b** 413 **c** 419 **d** 437 **e** 451 **f** 479

1b

3 Write each of these numbers as the product of its prime factors.

a 22 **b** 46 **c** 84 **d** 58 **e** 132 **f** 104
g 185 **h** 425 **i** 205 **j** 181 **k** 366 **l** 309
m 489 **n** 585 **o** 1089 **p** 2529 **q** 1305 **r** 3025

4 Use prime factors to list all the factors of these numbers.

a 60 **b** 96 **c** 110 **d** 165 **e** 430 **f** 600
g 950 **h** 1225 **i** 2116 **j** 1764 **k** 3136 **l** 3969

1c

5 Find the HCF and LCM of

a 100 and 120 **b** 144 and 192 **c** 210 and 240 **d** 336 and 378
e 315 and 495 **f** 616 and 728 **g** 40, 56 and 72 **h** 48, 80 and 176

6 Cancel down each of these fractions into its simplest form.

You can use the HCF.

a $\frac{35}{49}$ **b** $\frac{100}{120}$ **c** $\frac{144}{192}$ **d** $\frac{210}{240}$ **e** $\frac{105}{175}$
f $\frac{234}{273}$ **g** $\frac{210}{378}$ **h** $\frac{96}{528}$ **i** $\frac{477}{583}$ **j** $\frac{198}{858}$

1d

7 Find these using a calculator. Give your answers to 1 dp.

a $\sqrt{11}$ **b** $\sqrt{111}$ **c** $\sqrt[3]{111}$ **d** $\sqrt[3]{-111}$ **e** $\sqrt{-9}$ **f** $\sqrt[3]{91}$

8 **a** Three consecutive numbers are multiplied together to give -1716.
What are the three numbers?

b Two consecutive numbers are multiplied together to give 1806.
Find the two possible pairs of consecutive numbers.

9 Find these without a calculator.

a $\sqrt{256}$ **b** $\sqrt{441}$ **c** $\sqrt{729}$
d $\sqrt[3]{1728}$ **e** $\sqrt[3]{3375}$ **f** $\sqrt{2025}$

1e

10 Use your calculator to find the power x in these questions.

a $3^x = 2187$ **b** $2^x = 512$ **c** $4^x = 65536$ **d** $5^x = 15625$
e $10^x = 1$ **f** $7^x = 16807$ **g** $4^x = 1$ **h** $6^x = 7776$
i $2^x = 16$ **j** $2^x = 0.5$

11 Simplify each of these, leaving your answer as a single power of the number.

a $2^3 \times 2^4$ **b** $7^4 \times 7^8$ **c** $4^3 \times 4^9$ **d** $3^5 \times 3^0$ **e** $6^5 \times 6^5$
f $2^5 \div 2^3$ **g** $2^7 \div 2^7$ **h** $4^5 \div 4^4$ **i** $3^6 \div 3$ **j** $10^5 \div 10^6$

12 Calculate these, leaving your answer in index form where possible.

a $3^4 \times 4^3$ **b** $2^3 + 4^2$ **c** $5^3 - 2^4$ **d** $4^5 \div 2^2$ **e** $3^2 \times 3^2$

13 Simplify each of these, leaving your answer as a single power of the number.

a $5^3 \times 5^3 \times 5^3$ **b** $3^5 \times 3^5 \times 3^5$ **c** $10^4 \times 10^4 \times 10^4$
d $(2^4)^3$ **e** $(5^3)^3$ **f** $8^9 \div 8^9$
g $\frac{3^4 \times 3^3}{3^2}$ **h** $\frac{2^2 \times 2^4 \times 2^6}{2^8}$ **i** $10^3 \div 10^3$

1f

14 Round each of these numbers to the nearest

i whole number **ii** 1 dp **iii** 2 dp **iv** 3 dp.

a 6.1583 **b** 4.5648 **c** 18.6262 **d** 4.15494 **e** 16.00468
f 3.90909 **g** 9.99999 **h** 87.65432 **i** 0.000707 **j** 0.282828...

15 Work out an estimate for each of these problems.
Show all the steps of your working out.

a The average height of a man in Scotland is 1.78 m. There are 662954 people living in Glasgow, of whom 49% are men. Estimate the combined height of all the men in Glasgow.
Give your answer to the nearest kilometre.

b Giuseppe runs the marathon which is 42.195 km in length.
He covers each kilometre in 3 mins 48 secs.
Estimate the time it will take Giuseppe to complete the race.
Give your answer to the nearest minute.

1g

16 Use a trial and improvement method to find the square root of each of these numbers to 2 dp.

a $\sqrt{45}$ **b** $\sqrt{13}$ **c** $\sqrt{361}$ **d** $\sqrt{876}$ **e** $\sqrt{2640}$

Use the square root key on your calculator to check your answers.

17 Use a trial and improvement method to find the cube root of each of these numbers to 1 decimal place.

a $\sqrt[3]{95}$ **b** $\sqrt[3]{300}$ **c** $\sqrt[3]{10}$ **d** $\sqrt[3]{999}$ **e** $\sqrt[3]{87654}$

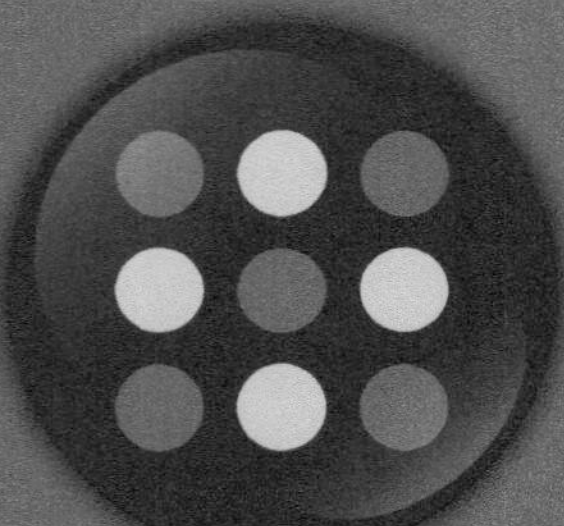

2 Measures, perimeter and area

Introduction

Geometry evolved because of the need to measure shapes. The ancient Egyptians are often credited as being the first people who used geometry as a major feature of their society. Besides building pyramids for pharaohs, geometry was used to solve practical problems such as measuring the area of a farmer's land so that he could be taxed appropriately. This often proved difficult due to the annual flooding of the river Nile.

What's the point?

Being able to measure things is as important as being able to count – it means you can share things out fairly!

Objectives

By the end of this chapter, you will have learned how to ...

- Use appropriate metric units to measure length, mass, capacity and area.
- Convert between metric units and between metric and Imperial units.
- Read and interpret scales on a range of measuring instruments.
- Calculate the area of a rectangle, a triangle, a parallelogram and a trapezium.
- Know the names of parts of a circle.
- Calculate the circumference and area of a circle.

Check in

1 List all the units of measurement that you know for

a Length   b Mass   c Capacity

2 Calculate

	i	ii	iii	iv
a	7.4×10	$3.9 \div 10$	0.6×100	$250 \div 1000$
b	25×0.6	12×4.5	5.5×30	5.5×2.2
c	$126 \div 4.5$	$2 \div 2.5$	$480 \div 1.6$	$5.4 \div 0.6$

3 Calculate the perimeter and the area of these rectangles.

a 8 m by 5 m   **b** 4.5 cm by 6 cm   **c** 25 mm by 12.5 mm

Starter problem

A band is fastened around three identical circles with a radius of 10 cm.

Find the perimeter of the band and the area enclosed by the band.

Investigate.

10 cm

2a Metric measure

- The **length** of an object is its linear extent.
  - The metric units for length are millimetres (mm), centimetres (cm), metres (m) and kilometres (km).
    1 cm = 10 mm
    1 m = 1000 mm = 100 cm
    1 km = 1000 m

▲ You can walk about 1 km in 15 minutes.

- **Area** is the amount of surface a shape covers.
  - The metric units for area are square millimetres (mm^2), square centimetres (cm^2), square metres (m^2) and square kilometres (km^2).
    1 hectare (ha) = 10000 m^2

▲ A bag of sugar weighs 1 kg.

- The **mass** of an object is how much matter it contains.
  - The metric units for mass are grams (g), kilograms (kg) and tonnes (t).
    1 kg = 1000 g
    1 tonne (t) = 1000 kg

▲ A carton of fruit juice holds 1 ℓ.

- **Capacity** is the amount of liquid a container holds.
  - The metric units for capacity are millilitres (mℓ), centilitres (cℓ) and litres (ℓ).
    1 litre (ℓ) = 1000 mℓ = 100 cℓ

Example

A rectangular football pitch measures 120 metres by 90 metres. Calculate the area of the pitch in hectares.

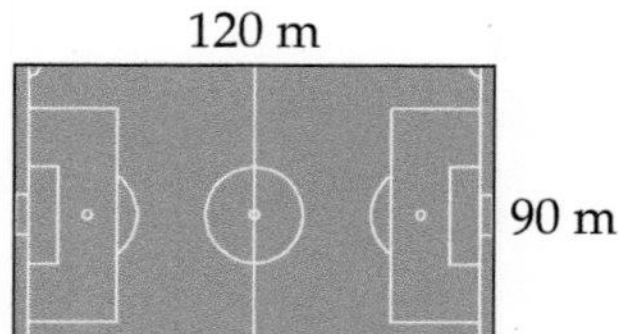

Area = 120 × 90
= 10 800 m^2
= 10 800 ÷ 10 000 ha
= 1.08 hectares

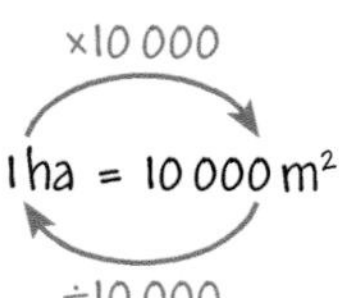

Example

Convert these measurements into the units indicated in brackets.

a 4.7 km (into m) **b** 75 cℓ (into ℓ)

a 4.7 km = 4.7 × 1000 m
= 4700 m

×1000
1 km = 1000 m
÷1000

b 75 cℓ = 75 ÷ 100 ℓ
= 0.75 ℓ

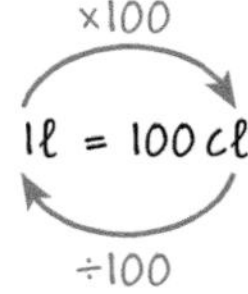

Exercise 2a

1 Choose the most appropriate metric unit to measure each of these quantities and give a possible value in each case.
   - **a** The amount of water in a swimming pool
   - **b** The diagonal distance across a flat-screen television
   - **c** The surface of the cover of this textbook
   - **d** The amount of petrol in a car
   - **e** The weight of a Year 8 pupil
   - **f** The distance across an ocean
   - **g** The height of a skyscraper
   - **h** The weight of a box of drawing pins
   - **i** The surface area of a DVD
   - **j** The capacity of a cup.

2 A sunflower grows to 1.76 metres tall. Calculate the height in
   a centimetres **b** millimetres.

3 Calculate the number of metres in a 50 km race.

4 Convert these measurements to the units in the brackets.
   - **a** 40 cm (mm) **b** 0.2 kg (g)
   - **c** 2.5 ha (m^2) **d** 8.5 km (m)
   - **e** 6.5 ℓ (cℓ) **f** 500 ml (ℓ)
   - **g** 6300 kg (t) **h** 800 mm (cm)
   - **i** 14.1 t (kg) **j** 138 000 m^2 (ha)
   - **k** 100 mℓ (cℓ) **l** 5 km (cm)
   - **m** 1 000 000 mg (kg)

Problem solving

5 What is the total of these weights in
   a grams **b** kilograms?

4.5 kg 825 g 3.05 kg

Did you know?

One litre of water weighs one kilogram.

One millilitre of water weighs one gram.

6 Shahid is running a 10 km road race. He has already run 5230 metres. How much further has he to run?

7 A 250 ml bottle of hair shampoo costs 99 p. A one-litre bottle of the same shampoo costs £3.99. Which bottle is better value for money? Show your working to explain your answer.

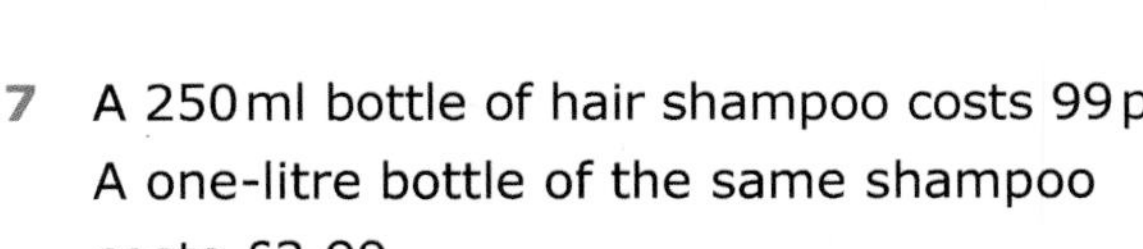

8 One teaspoon holds 5 millilitres. How many teaspoons of medicine can be poured from a 15 cl medicine bottle?

9 A square field has an area of exactly 1 hectare. Calculate the length and width of the field in metres.

10 10 sheets of A4 paper stack to a height of 1 millimetre. How many sheets of A4 paper would you need to stack to your height?

2b Imperial measure

Measurements can use **metric** or **imperial** units.
Imperial units include for ...

length and distance
inch, foot, yard and mile

1 foot	= 12 inches
1 yard	= 3 feet
1 mile	= 1760 yards

mass
ounce (oz), pound (lb) and stone

1 pound	= 16 ounces
1 stone	= 14 pounds
1 ton	= 160 stones

capacity
pint and gallon.

1 gallon = 8 pints

Imperial to metric conversions

1 inch ≈ 2.5 cm	1 oz ≈ 30 g	1 pint ≈ 600 ml
1 yard ≈ 1 metre	1 kg ≈ 2.2 lb	1 pint ≈ 0.6 l
1 mile ≈ 1.6 km		1 gallon ≈ 4.5 l
5 miles ≈ 8 km		

You can convert between metric and imperial measures using these conversions...

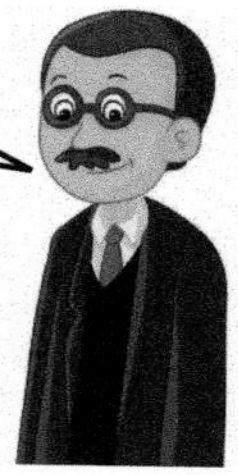

Example

a Convert 4.5 pints to litres.

b Convert 480 g to ounces.

a 4.5 pints ≈ 4.5 × 0.6 litres
= 2.7 litres

1 pint ≈ 0.6 l (×0.6, ÷0.6)

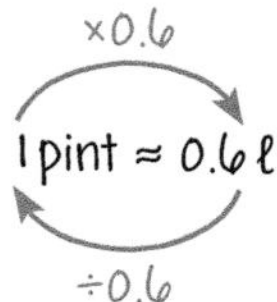

b 480 g ≈ 480 ÷ 30 ounces
= 16 oz

1 oz ≈ 30 g (×30, ÷30)

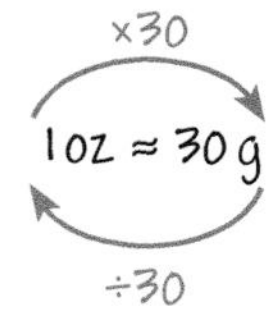

To use a measuring **instrument** to measure both metric and imperial quantities you will need to understand the **scale**.

Example

Write the reading on each of the scales.

a

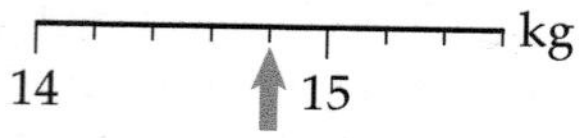

b

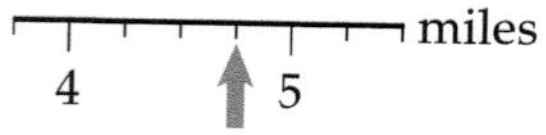

a This scale goes up in 1 kg intervals.
The 5 spaces between represent 1000 g.
Each individual space represents 200 g.
The scale reads 14 kg 800 g or 14.8 kg

b This scale goes up in 1 mile intervals.
The 4 spaces between represent 1 mile.
Each individual space represents 0.25 mile.
The scale reads 4.75 miles.

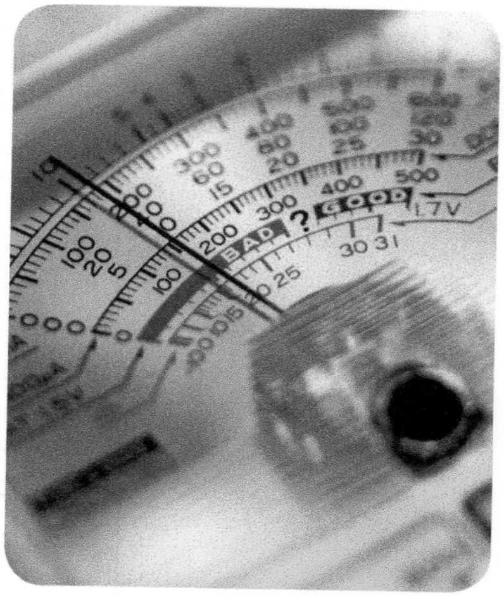

▲ A multimeter can have several scales.

Exercise 2b

1 State the larger unit of measurement.
- **a** inch or centimetre
- **b** pound (lb) or kilogram
- **c** pint or litre
- **d** mile or kilometre
- **e** yard or metre

2 Convert these measurements to the units in brackets.

a	6 pints (ℓ)	**b**	4.5 kg (lb)
c	10 gallons (ℓ)	**d**	70 miles (km)
e	36 inches (cm)	**f**	45 kg (lb)
g	2.5 pints (mℓ)	**h**	5 feet (cm)
i	4.5 oz (g)	**j**	100 km (miles)

3 Convert these measurements to the units in brackets.

a	30 cm (inches)	**b**	4.2 litres (pints)
c	12 km (miles)	**d**	300 ml (pints)
e	40.5 litres (gallons)	**f**	103.4 lb (kg)
g	450 g (oz)	**h**	240 mm (inches)
i	6.6 m (feet)	**j**	125 cm (inches)

4 Write down the readings on each scale. Give two answers for each arrow.

a 10 12 t

b 8 9 cm

c 2 3 inch

d

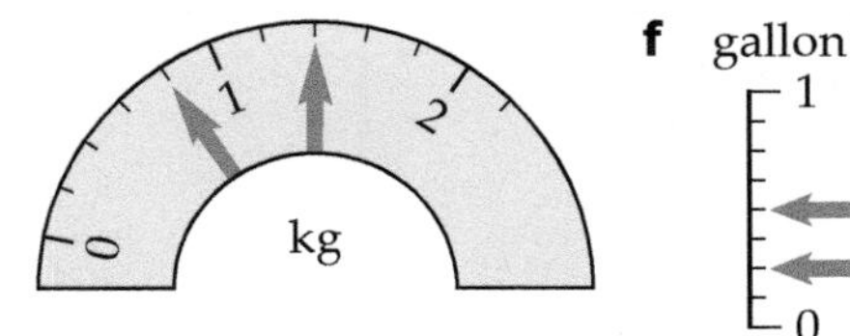

Problem solving

5 Charles Blondin was a French tightrope walker. He crossed the gorge below Niagara Falls on a tightrope, 1100 feet long and 160 feet above the water. Convert the distances to
a inches **b** centimetres **c** metres.

6 A litre of petrol costs £1.24. What will a gallon cost?

7 The speed limit on a canal is 8 km per hour. Convert this speed to miles per hour.

8 You should drink 2 litres of water every day. How many pints is this in one year?

9 **a** Look at the parallelogram. Is AB longer than BC?
b Measure AB and BC in centimetres.
c Convert each measurement into inches.

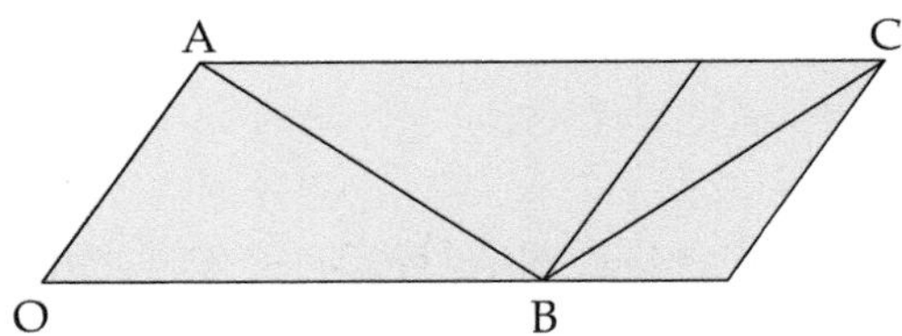

Sander's parallelogram illusion

10 An Imperial pint is 20 fluid ounces. An American pint is 16 fluid ounces. A gallon is 8 pints for both Imperial and American units. How many litres are there in an American gallon?

2c Area of a rectangle and a triangle

The **area** of a shape is the amount of surface it covers. Units for area include mm^2, cm^2, m^2 or km^2.

▲ You can find the area of a shape by counting how many squares fit inside it.

The area of a rectangle = length × width

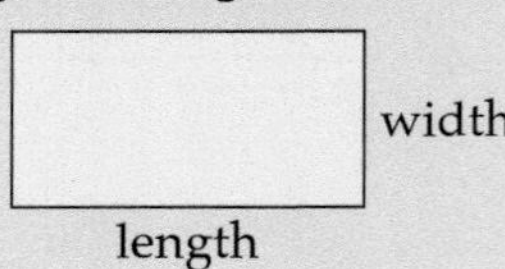

Example

Calculate the perimeter and area of this shape made from rectangles.

10 cm, 4 cm, 3 cm, 9 cm, 5 cm, 7 cm

First calculate the missing lengths.

10 − 7 = 3 cm   9 − 4 = 5 cm

Perimeter = 10 cm + 9 cm + 7 cm + 5 cm + 3 cm + 4 cm = 38 cm

Area = 10 × 4 + 7 × 5
= 40 + 35
= 75 cm^2

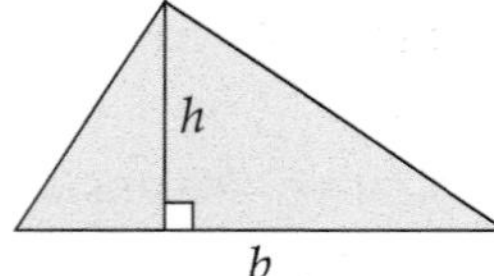

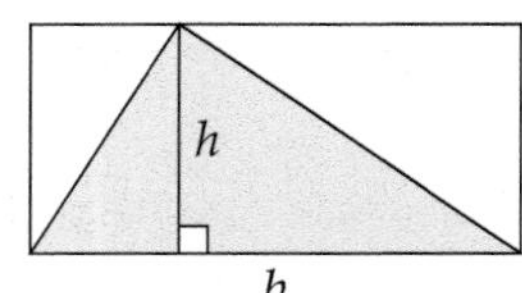

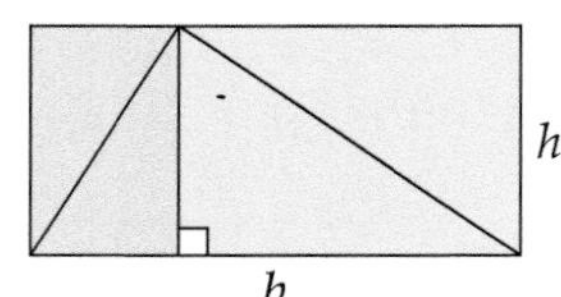

The area of a **triangle** is half the area of the surrounding rectangle.
The area of the rectangle = $b \times h$

The area of a triangle $= \frac{1}{2} \times b \times h$
$= \frac{1}{2} \times$ **base** × **perpendicular** height

Example

A square is drawn inside another square.
Calculate the area of the shaded square.

Area of the large square = 15 × 15 = 225 cm^2
Area of one triangle = $\frac{1}{2} \times 10 \times 5$
= 25 cm^2
Area of all four triangles = 4 × 25 = 100 cm^2
Area of the shaded square = 225 − 100
= 125 cm^2

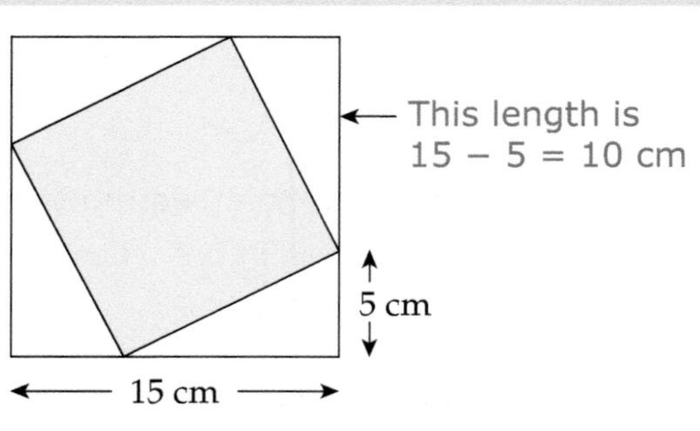

Exercise 2c

1 Calculate the perimeter and area of these shapes made from rectangles.

a

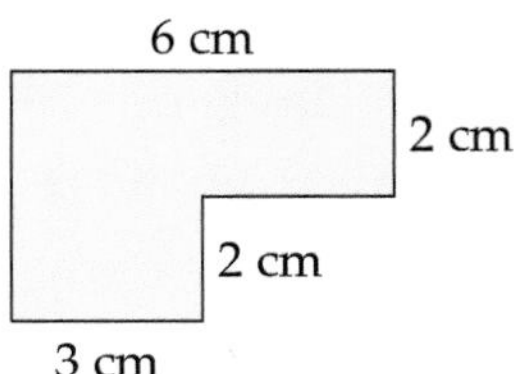

b

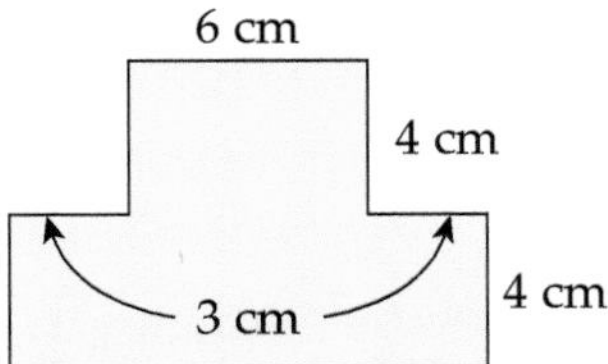

c

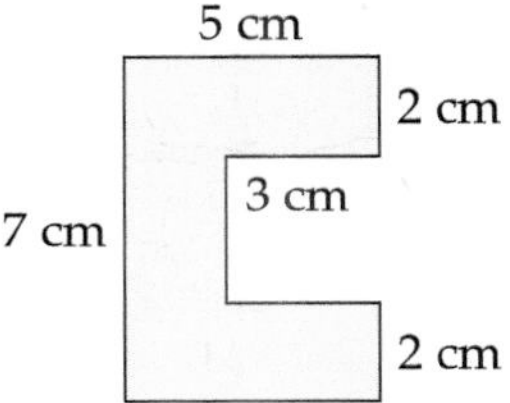

2 Calculate the area of these triangles.

a

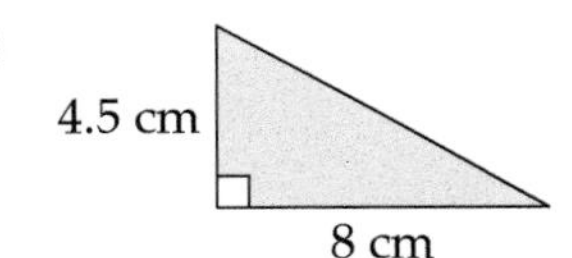

b

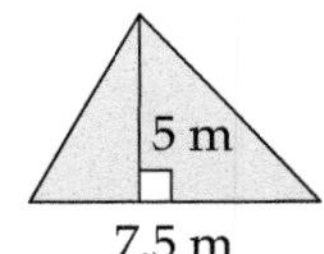

c

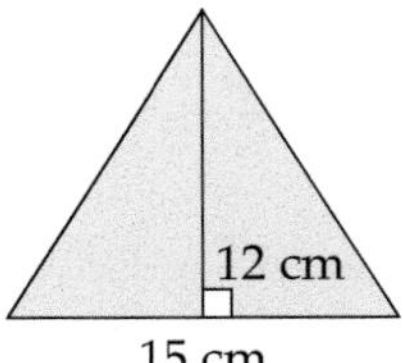

d

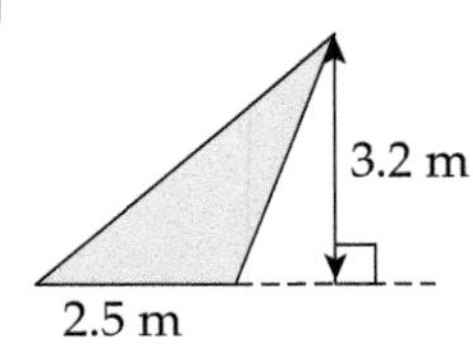

3 Calculate the unknown length in each of these shapes.

a

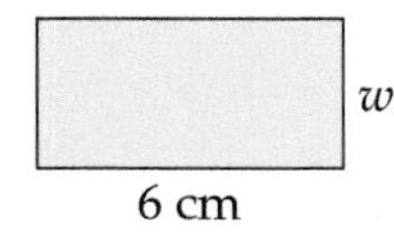

Area = $18\,cm^2$

b

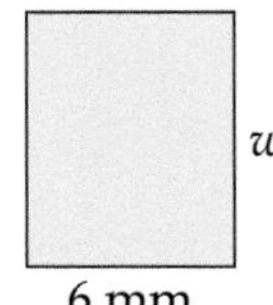

Area = $45\,mm^2$

c

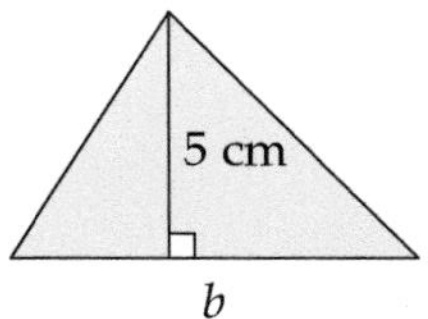

Area = $20\,cm^2$

d

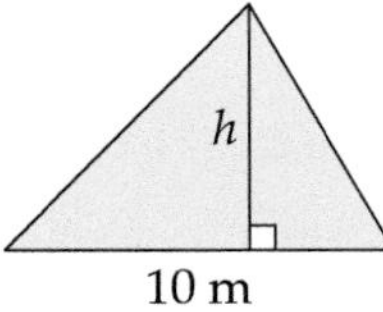

Area = $36\,m^2$

e

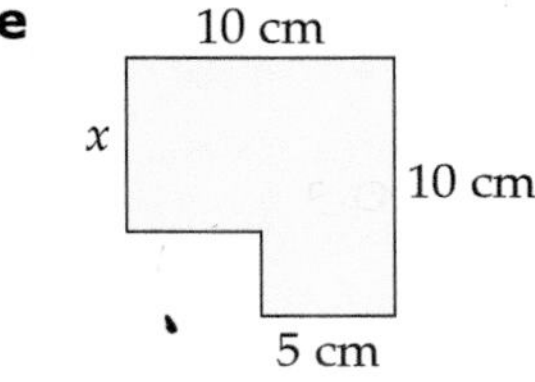

Area = $80\,cm^2$

f

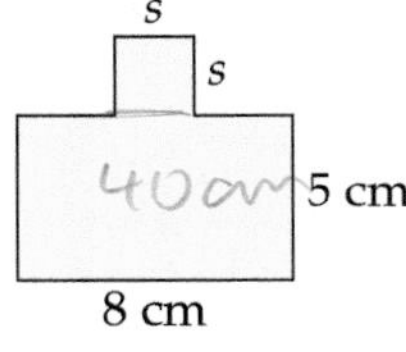

Area = $44\,cm^2$

4 Calculate the area of the shaded shapes.

a

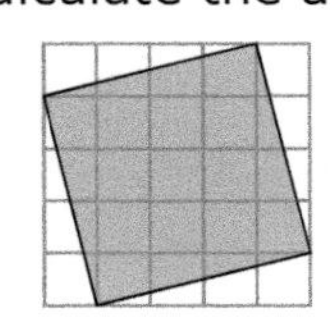

b

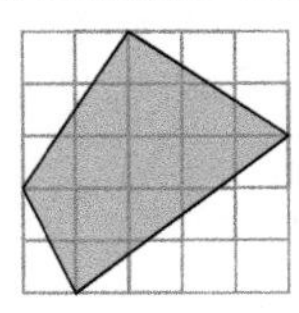

c

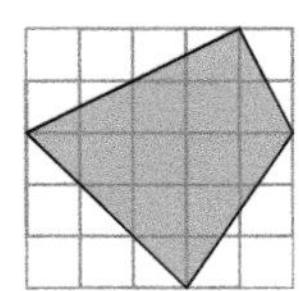

d

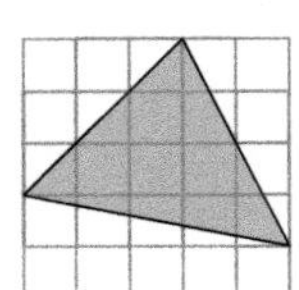

Problem solving

5 The area of the rectangle and the triangle are the same.
Calculate the value of h.

7.5 cm
12 cm
h
20 cm

6 A rope is knotted to form a loop of length 30 metres.
The rope forms a rectangle.
Calculate the largest area that can be enclosed by the rope.

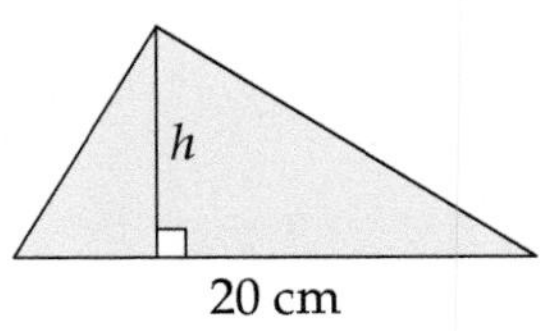

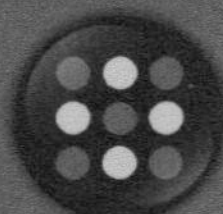

2d Area of a parallelogram and a trapezium

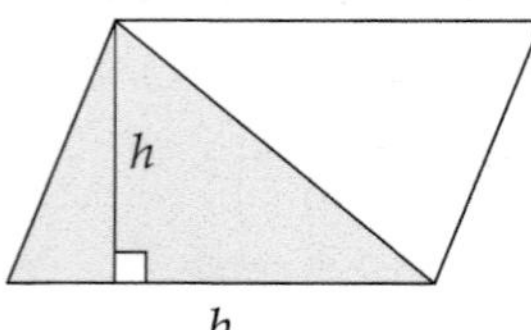

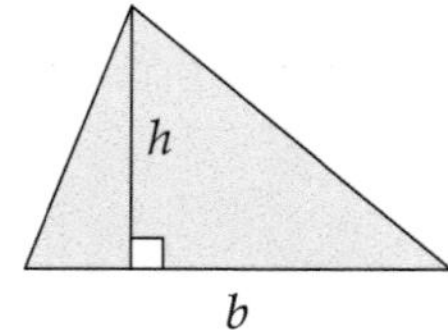

b is the base. h is the perpendicular height. Perpendicular means 'at right angles to'.

The **area** of the **parallelogram** is double the area of the triangle.

Area of the triangle $= \frac{1}{2} \times b \times h$

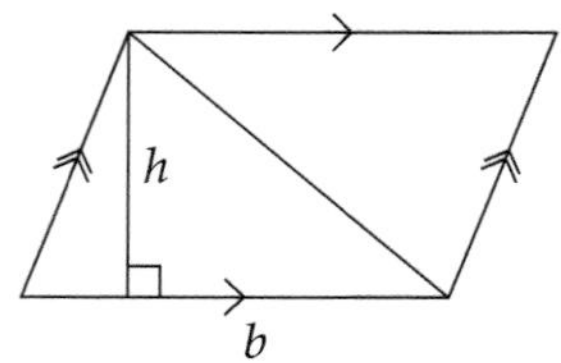

The area of a parallelogram $= b \times h$

Example

The area of the parallelogram is 45 cm². Calculate the length of the base.

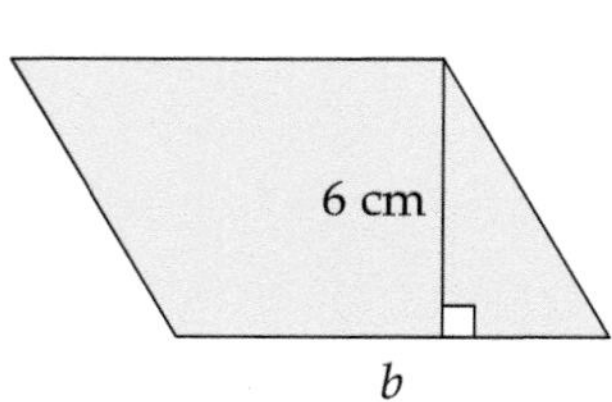

Area $= b \times h$

$45 = b \times 6$

$b = 7.5$ cm

$45 \div 6 = 7.5$

A parallelogram has two pairs of parallel sides. b is the base. h is the perpedicular height.

You can fit two identical **trapeziums** together to make a parallelogram.

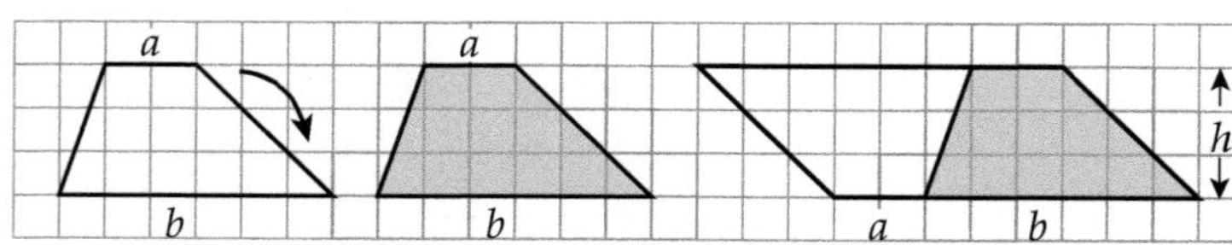

The area of the green trapezium is half the area of the parallelogram.

Area of the parallelogram $= (a + b) \times h$

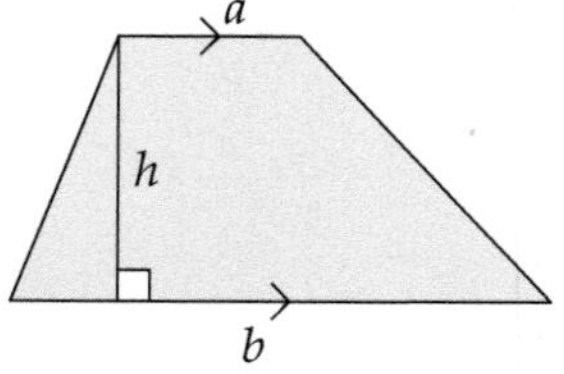

The area of a trapezium $= \frac{1}{2} \times (a + b) \times h$

Example

Calculate the area of this trapezium.

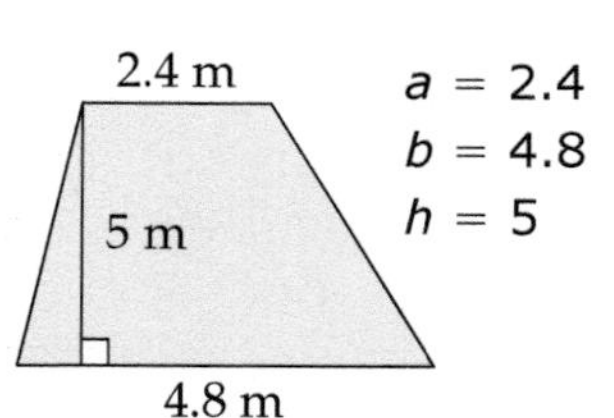

$a = 2.4$
$b = 4.8$
$h = 5$

Area $= \frac{1}{2} \times (a + b) \times h$

Area $= \frac{1}{2} \times (2.4 + 4.8) \times 5$

$= \frac{1}{2} \times 7.2 \times 5 = 18\text{m}^2$

Exercise 2d

1 Calculate the area of these shapes. Include units in your answer.

a

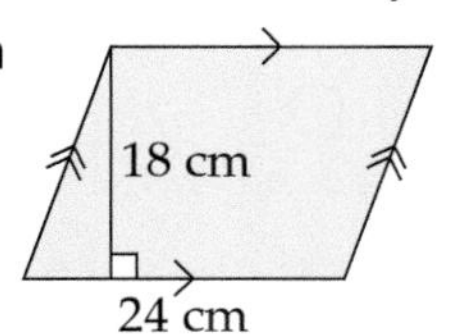

b

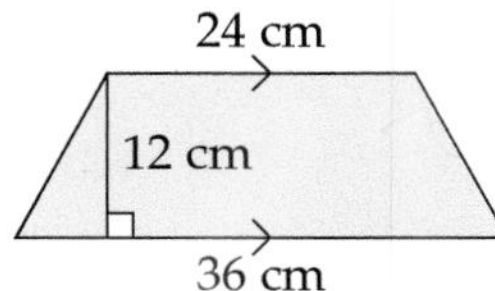

c

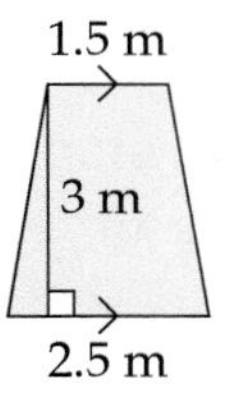

d

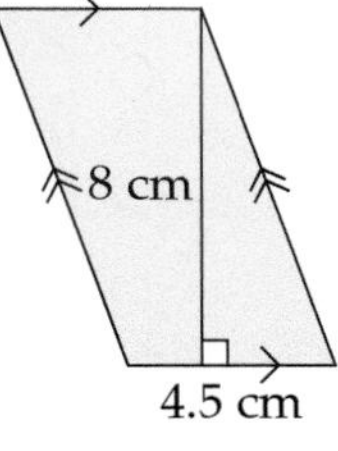

e

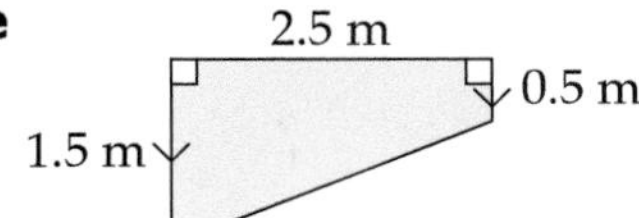

f 4 mm, 2 mm, 4 mm

2 Use the formula Area $= b \times h$ to find the area of each parallelogram when

a $b = 10\,\text{cm}, h = 5\,\text{cm}$

b $b = 1.25\,\text{mm}, h = 16\,\text{mm}$

c $b = 8.4\,\text{m}, h = 6.6\,\text{m}$

d $b = 95\,\text{cm}, h = 1.2\,\text{m}$

Give your answer to part **d** in both cm² and m².

3 Use the formula Area $= \frac{1}{2} \times (a + b) \times h$ to find the area of each trapezium when

a $a = 8\,\text{cm}, b = 12\,\text{cm}, h = 14\,\text{cm}$

b $a = 7\,\text{cm}, b = 14\,\text{cm}, h = 19\,\text{cm}$

c $a = 8.1\,\text{m}, b = 5.7\,\text{m}, h = 6.4\,\text{m}$

4 Find the unknown lengths in these shapes for each of the given areas.

a

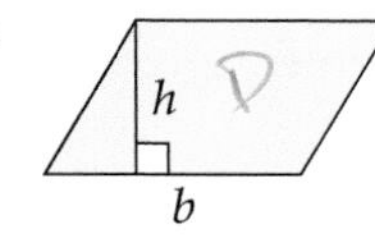

i $b = 4\,\text{cm}$, area $= 10\,\text{cm}^2$

ii $b = 4.5\,\text{m}$, area $= 27\,\text{m}^2$

b

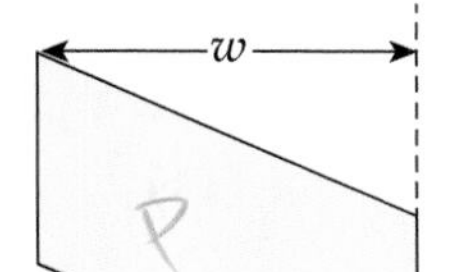

i $l = 3\,\text{cm}$, area $= 14.25\,\text{cm}^2$

ii $w = 2.5\,\text{mm}$, area $= 12.5\,\text{mm}^2$

c

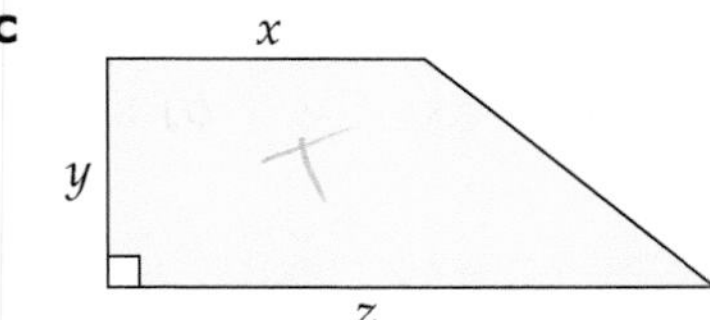

i $x = 13\,\text{mm}, z = 19\,\text{mm}$, area $= 352\,\text{mm}^2$

ii $y = 7\,\text{cm}, z = 21\,\text{cm}$, area $= 122.5\,\text{cm}^2$

Problem solving

5 Mike wants to paint the end wall of his terrace house with a protective weather-resistant paint.

a Calculate the area of the wall.

b One litre of paint covers approximately $5\,\text{m}^2$. How many litres of paint does Mike need?

20 m, 14 m, 20 m

6 The area of this trapezium is $25\,\text{cm}^2$. The length a is less than the length b. Write down five different pairs of possible values for a and b.

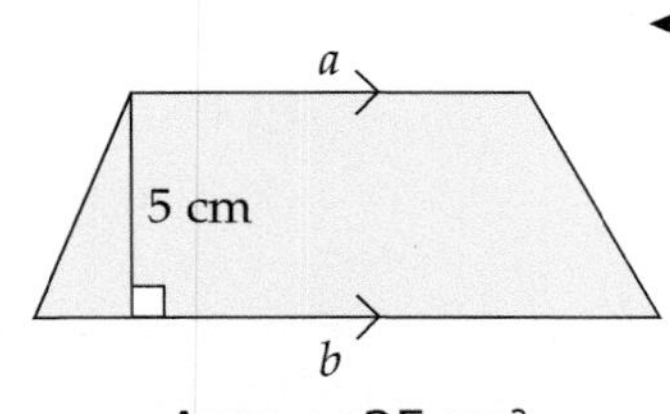

Area $= 25\,\text{cm}^2$

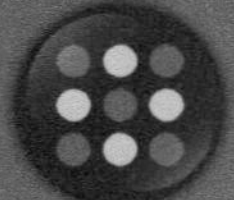

2e Circumference of a circle

- A circle is a set of points equidistant from its **centre**.
  Equidistant means 'the same distance'.

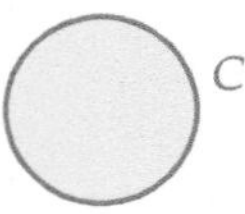

The **circumference** (C) is the distance around the circle.

The perimeter of the circle is called the circumference.

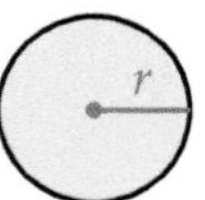

The **radius** (r) is the distance from the centre to the circumference.

Radii is the plural of radius.

Part of the circumference is called an **arc**.

Arcs can be different lengths.

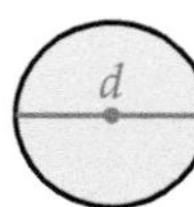

The **diameter** (d) is the distance across the centre of the circle.

The diameter is twice the length of the radius. $d = 2 \times r$

The circumference of the circle is '3 and a bit' × the diameter. You can use the Greek letter **π (pi)** for the exact value of '3 and a bit'.

d 2d 3d 4d
3.14d

- Circumference = π × diameter $C = \pi d$

- Circumference = π × 2 × radius $C = 2\pi r$

Example

Calculate the circumference of each circle.
Take π to be 3.14

a

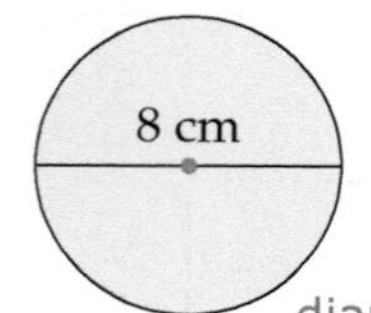

diameter = 8 cm

b

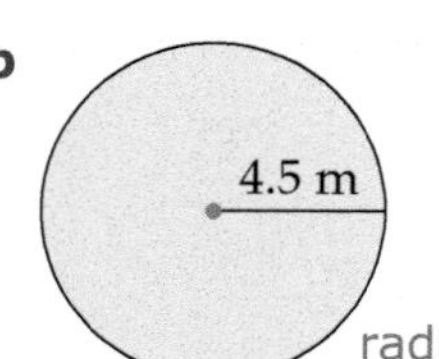

radius = 4.5 m

a $C = \pi d$
$= 3.14 \times 8$
$= 25.12$ cm

b $C = 2\pi r$
$= 2 \times 3.14 \times 4.5$
$= 28.26$ m

Exercise 2e

1 $\pi = 3.141\ 592\ 653\ 589\ 793\ 238\ 46\ldots$

Which of these approximations is the nearest to π?

a 3.1 **b** $\frac{22}{7}$ **c** 3 **d** 3.142

2 Measure and write down the radius and diameter of each circle.

State the units of your answers.

a

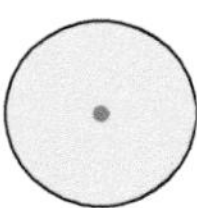

b

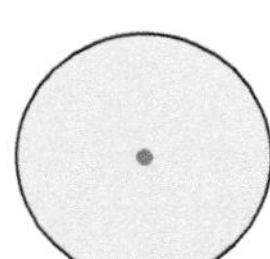

c

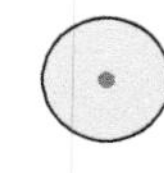

Calculate the circumference of each circle. (Take $\pi = 3.14$)

3 Calculate the circumference of each circle. (Take $\pi = 3.14$)

a

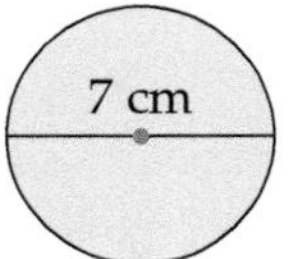

b

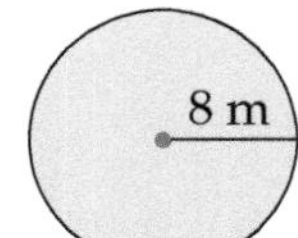

c

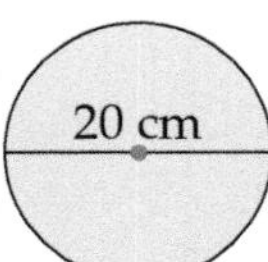

d

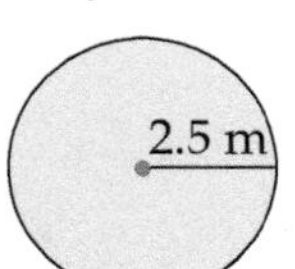

4 Calculate the circumference of each circle for the given diameter, d, or radius, r. (Take $\pi = 3.14$)

a $d = 12$ cm **b** $r = 2.1$ mm **c** $d = 1.25$ m **d** $r = 35$ mm

Did you know?

3, 1, 4, 1, 5, 9, 2, 6, 5, 3, 5, 8, 9, 7, 9, 3, 2, 3, 8, 4, 6, 2, 6, 4, 3, 3, 8, 3, 2, 7, 9, 5, 0, 2, 8, 8...

In 2006, Akira Haraguchi from Japan claimed to have broken the World record for memorising the number π. He needed more than 16 hours to recite the number to 100 000 decimal places.

Problem solving

5 A circle fits exactly inside a square.

The square has sides of length 10 cm.

a Calculate the perimeter of the square.

b Using $\pi = 3.14$, calculate the circumference of the circle.

c Explain why you know the answer to part **a** should be larger than the answer to part **b**.

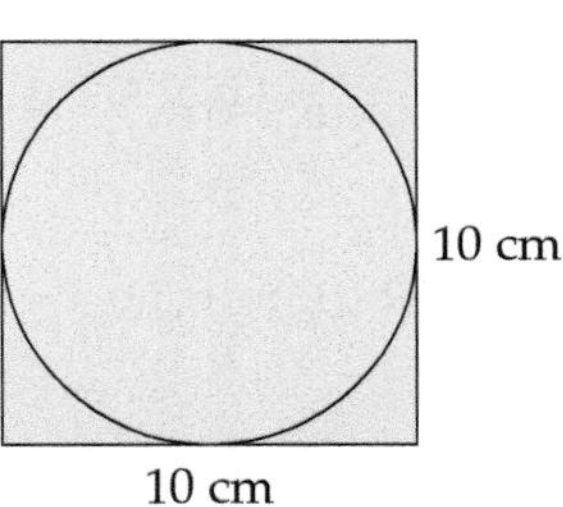

6 Make a collection of circular objects, such as coins, plates and so on.

Use a ruler and string to measure the diameter and the circumference of your objects.

Copy and complete the table to show your results.

Object	Circumference (C)	Diameter (d)	$C \div d$
Coin			
Plate			
...			

Circumference ÷ diameter should be about the same number for each circle.

What is this number?

Give your answers to 1 dp where appropriate.

7 Find the **i** diameter and **ii** radius of a circle with circumference

a 18.85 cm **b** 49 mm **c** 54 m **d** 84.5 m

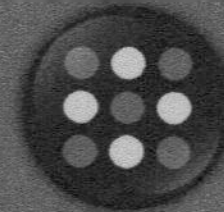

2f Area of a circle

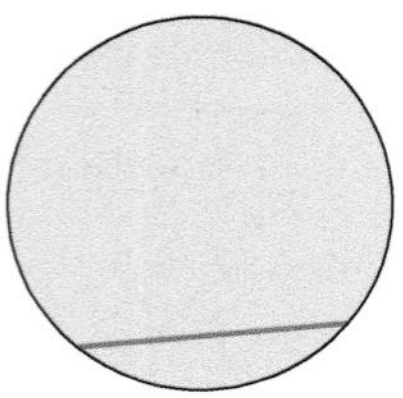

A **chord** is a line joining two points on the circumference.

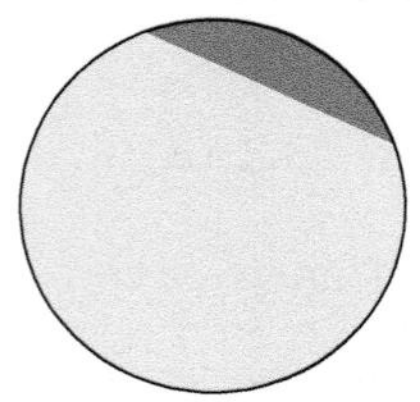

A **segment** is the region enclosed between a chord and an arc.

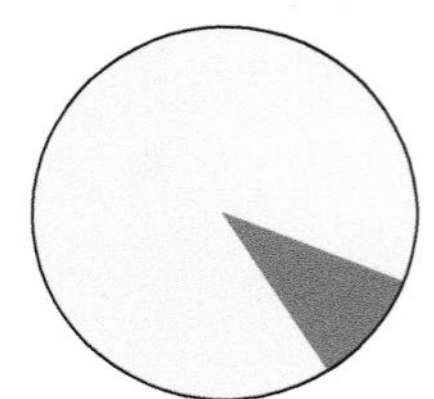

A **sector** is the region enclosed by an arc and two radii.

Area of a circle = π × radius × radius

Area = πr^2

Example

Calculate the area of each circle. Take π to be 3.14

a

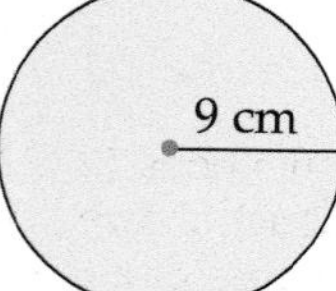

radius = 9 cm

b

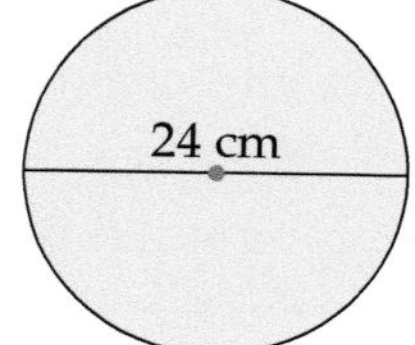

diameter = 24 cm

a Area $= \pi r^2$

$= 3.14 \times 9 \times 9$

$= 254.34\ \text{cm}^2$

b Radius $= 24 \div 2 = 12\ \text{cm}$

Area $= \pi r^2$

$= 3.14 \times 12 \times 12$

$= 452.16\ \text{cm}^2$

Example

The radius of the large circle is 8 cm and the radius of the small circle is 3 cm. Calculate the blue area. Take π to be 3.14

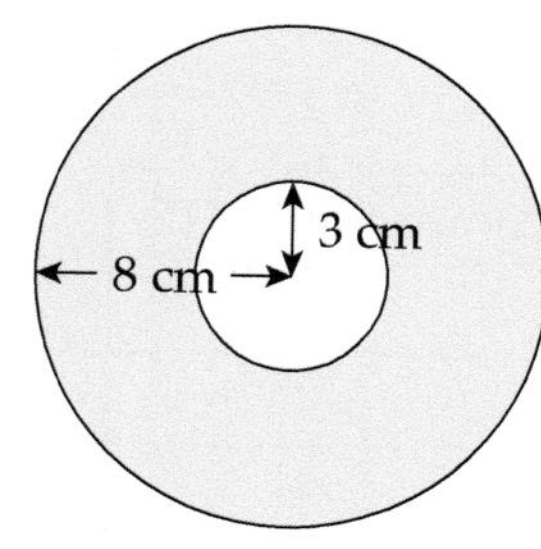

Area of the large circle $= \pi r^2$

$= 3.14 \times 8 \times 8$

$= 200.96\ \text{cm}^2$

$= 201\ \text{cm}^2$

Area of the small circle $= \pi r^2$

$= 3.14 \times 3 \times 3$

$= 28.26\ \text{cm}^2$

$= 28.3\ \text{cm}^2$

Area of the blue annulus $= 200.96 - 28.26$

$= 172.7\ \text{cm}^2$

$= 173\ \text{cm}^2$

Exercise 2f

1 Calculate the area of these circles. State the units of your answers.

> Take $\pi = 3.14$ for all the questions on this page.

a

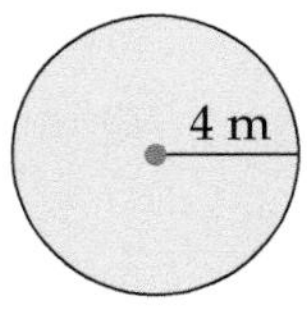

radius = 4 m

b

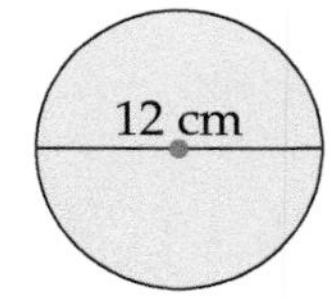

diameter = 12 cm

c

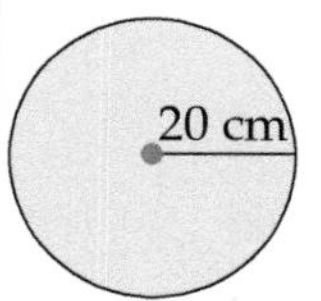

radius = 20 cm

d	radius = 7 cm	**e**	diameter = 16 cm	**f**	diameter = 30 m
g	diameter = 23 mm	**h**	radius = 18 m	**i**	diameter = 22 cm
j	diameter = 160 cm	**k**	radius = 75 mm	**l**	radius = 45 m
m	diameter = 13.6 cm	**n**	radius = 12.1 mm	**o**	diameter = 3.15 m

2 Calculate the area of these shapes.

a

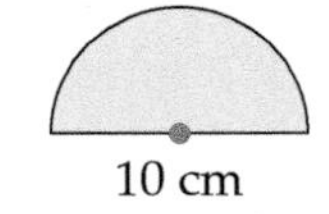

> Half a circle is called a semicircle.

b

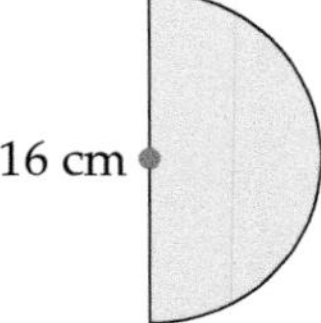

c

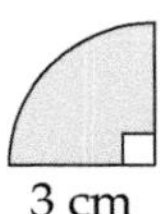

Did you know?

Archimedes (2872–212 BC) showed that the area of a circle equals the area of a right-angled triangle of base the circle's circumference and height its radius.

3 Calculate the area of the shaded regions.

a

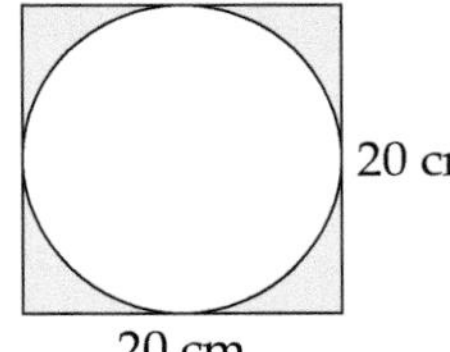

b

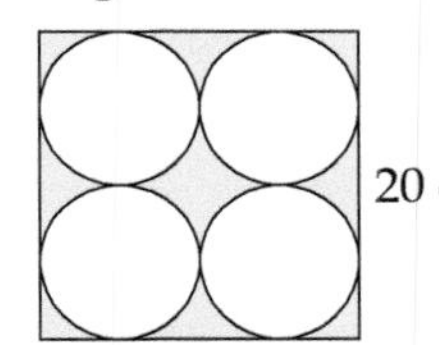

Problem solving

4 A church window is made using a semicircle and a rectangle.
Calculate the area of glass in the window.

90 cm

50 cm

5 The radius of the large circle is 10 cm and the radius of the small circle is 5 cm.
Calculate pink area in each diagram.

a

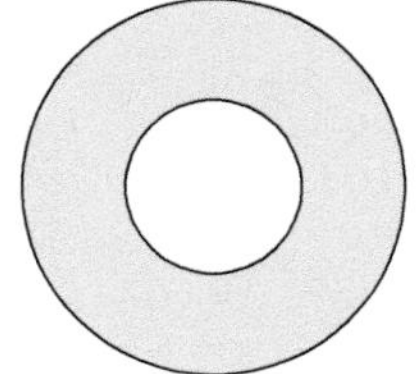

b

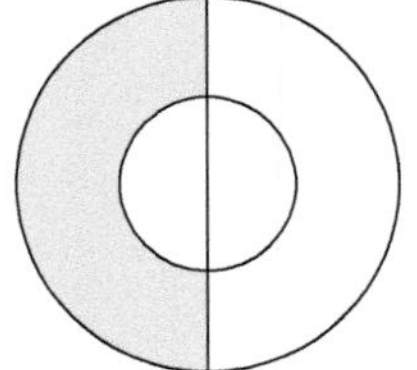

c

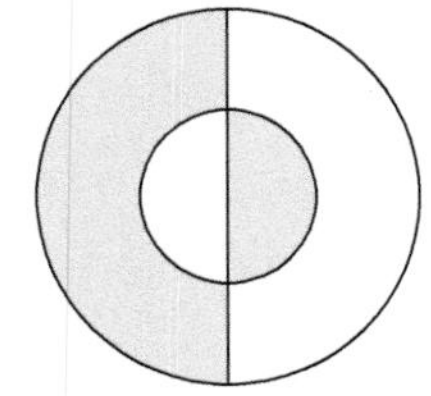

6 The radius of a circle is doubled.
Does the area of the circle double? Explain your answer.

2 MySummary

Check out

You should now be able to ...

Test it ➡ Questions

You should now be able to ...	Level	Questions
✓ Use appropriate metric units to measure length, mass, capacity and area.	5	1
✓ Convert between metric units and metric and Imperial units.	5	2, 3
✓ Read and interpret scales on a range of measuring instruments	5	4
✓ Calculate the area of a rectangle and a triangle.	5	5 – 8
✓ Calculate the area of a parallelogram and trapezium.	6	9, 10
✓ Know the names of parts of a circle.	6	11
✓ Calculate the circumference and area of a circle.	6	11

Language	Meaning	Example
Metric measurement	An international system of measurement based on the decimal system	m = metre, kg = kilogram ℓ = litre
Imperial measurement	System of measurement used in the US, Liberia and Myanmar as well as occasionally in the UK	yd = yard, lb = pound pt = pint
Perimeter	The sum of all the sides of a two-dimensional shape	The perimeter of a square = 4 × length of its side
Circumference	The perimeter of a circle	$\pi \times$ diameter
Arc	Part of the circumference	arc
Radius	The distance from the centre of the circle to the circumference	$r = \frac{\text{diameter}}{2}$
Diameter	The diameter is the distance across the circle through the centre	$D = 2r$

1 Write an appropriate metric unit for each measurement.

a The amount of water in a bucket.

b The length of a pair of sunglasses.

c The distance from London to Newcastle.

2 **a** Convert 2.5 km into cm.

b Convert 3000 g into tonnes.

3 **a** Convert 4.5 kg into pounds.

b Convert 3 pints into millilitres

4 Write down the readings on this scale.

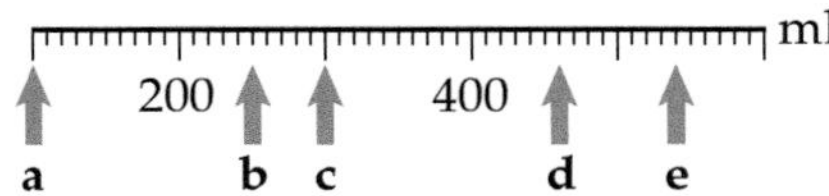

5 Calculate the area of this rectangle.

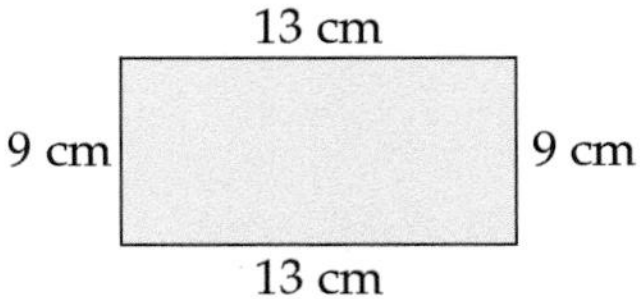

6 The area of this rectangle is 35 m². What is its perimeter?

7 Calculate the area of this triangle.

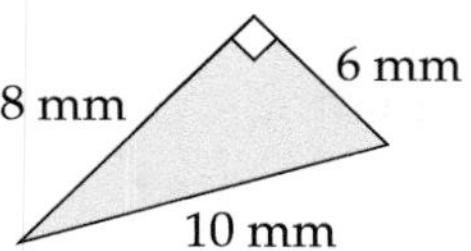

8 Calculate the area of this shape which has been made using two rectangles.

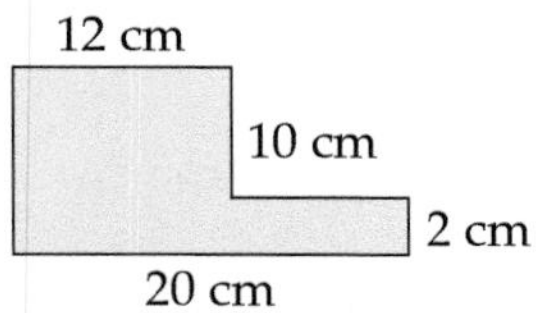

9 A parallelogram has a base of length 13 cm and an area of 104 cm². What is the height of the parallelogram?

10

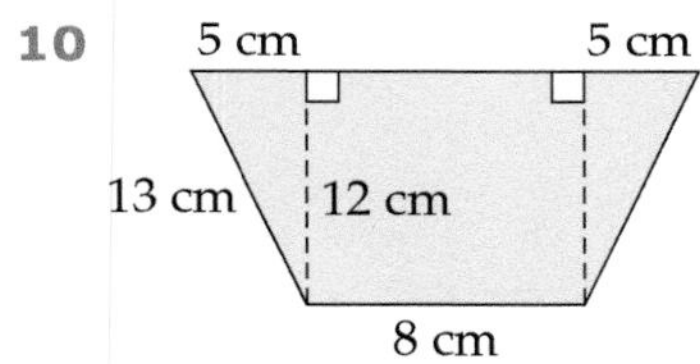

a What is this shape called?

b Calculate the area of the shape.

11

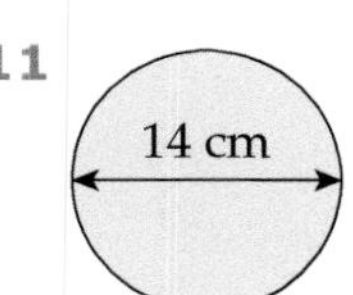

For this circle, calculate

a its area

b its circumference.

What next?

Score		
0 – 4		Your knowledge of this topic is still developing. To improve look at Formative test: 2C-2; MyMaths: 1061, 1083, 1084, 1088, 1108, 1110, 1128, 1129 and 1191
5 – 9		You are gaining a secure knowledge of this topic. To improve look at InvisiPen: 314, 315, 332, 333, 351 and 352
10 – 11		You have mastered this topic. Well done, you are ready to progress!

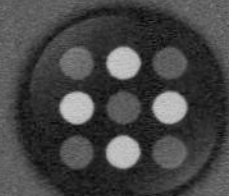

2 MyPractice

2a

1 Calculate the number of 10 cm lengths of string that can be cut from a 5 m ball of string.

2 Convert these measurements to the units indicated in brackets.

a 8.5 ℓ (mℓ) **b** 456 mm (cm) **c** 8.5 ha (m^2) **d** 25 cl (mℓ) **e** 4.2 t (kg)

2b

3 Convert these measurements to the units indicated in brackets.

a 27.5 kg (lbs) **b** 120 cm (inches) **c** 135 g (oz)

d 750 ml (pints) **e** 850 miles (km)

4 Write down each reading on the scales.
Give an answer for each arrow.

a

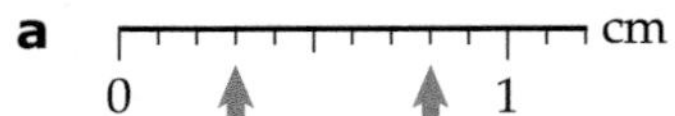

b

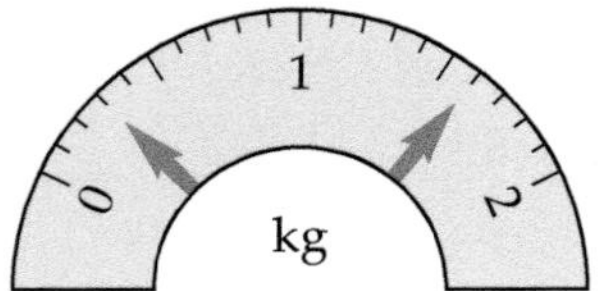

c

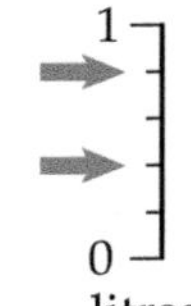

2c

5 Six identical rectangles are arranged in the shape of a large rectangle.
Calculate the area of one of the rectangles.

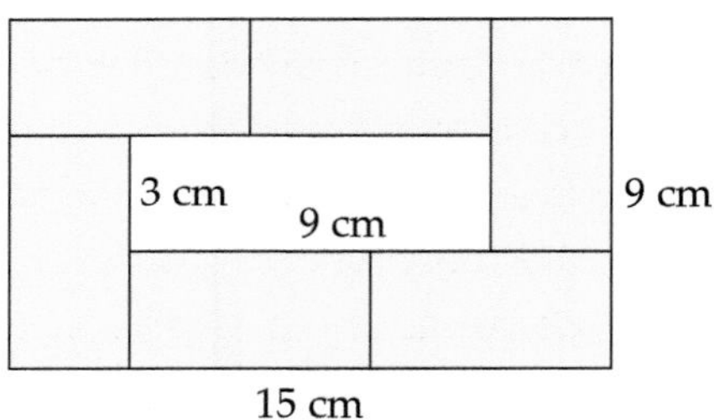

6 The area of each of these triangles is 40 cm^2.
Calculate the unknown values.

a

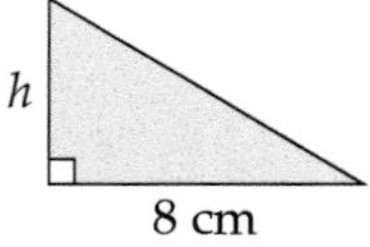

b

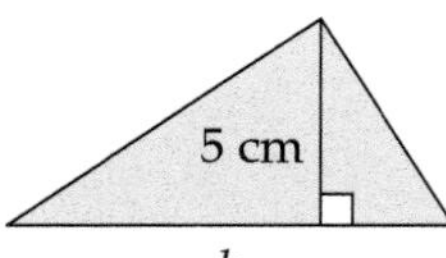

c

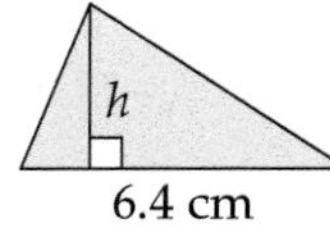

d

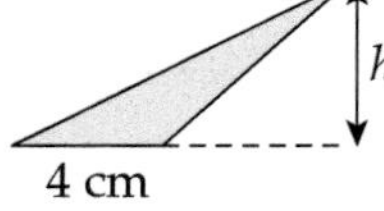

2d

7 Calculate the areas of the parallelogram and trapezia.

a

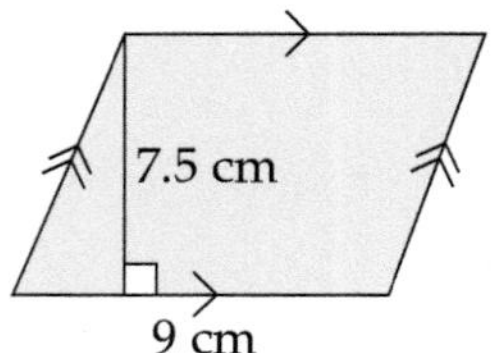

b

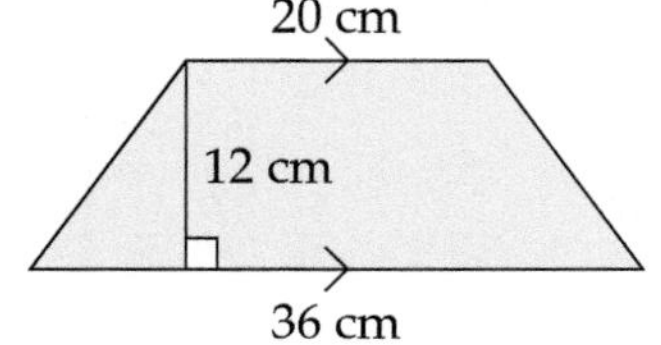

c

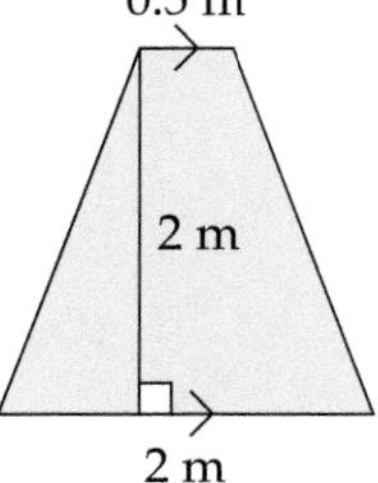

2d

8 The area of the parallelogram and the trapezium are the same.
Calculate the value of h.

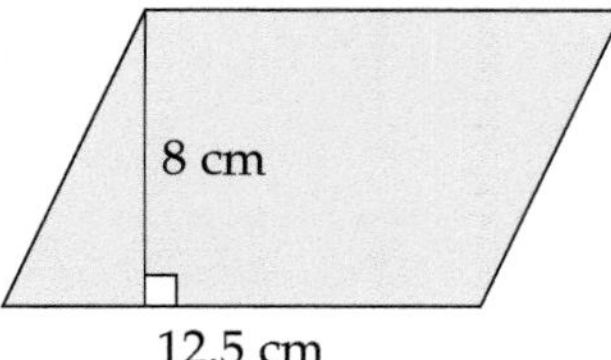

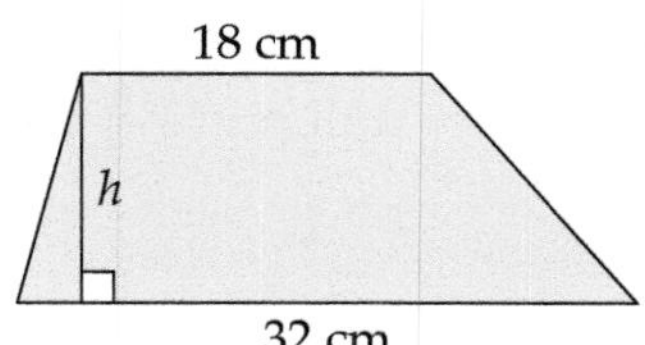

2e

Use $\pi = 3.14$ for the remaining questions on this page.

9 A penny-farthing was a type of bike used in the 19th century.
The diameter of the large wheel is 120 cm and is 3 times larger than the diameter of the small wheel.
Calculate

- **a** the diameter of the small wheel
- **b** the circumference of the small wheel
- **c** the circumference of the large wheel.

The large wheel turns one complete revolution.

- **d** How many times will the small wheel turn?

10 Six equilateral triangles of side 6 cm are arranged to form a hexagon.
A circle is drawn passing through the vertices of the hexagon.
Calculate the circumference of the circle.

2f

11 A circular pond has a radius of 5 metres.
Calculate the surface area of the water.

12 The 'No entry' sign consists of a white rectangle on a red circle of radius 30 cm.
The rectangle has dimensions of 50 cm by 11.5 cm.
Calculate the red area of the sign.

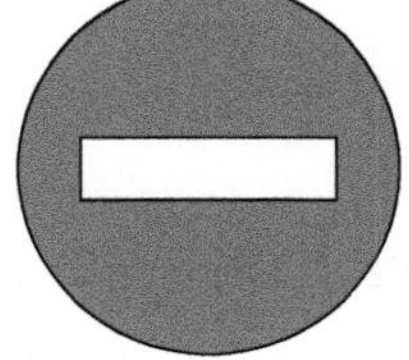

13 Calculate the shaded areas.

a

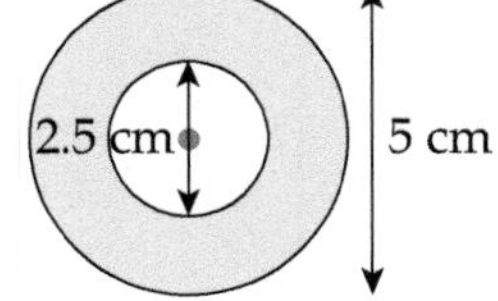

b

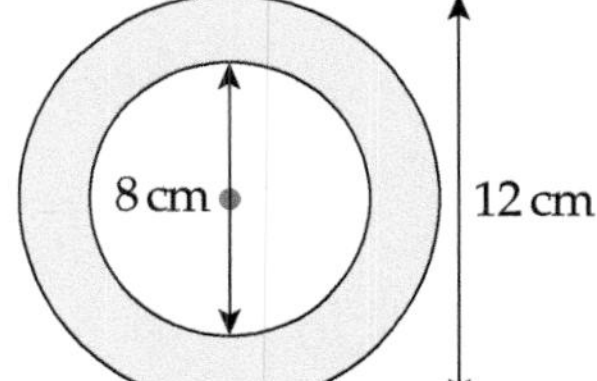

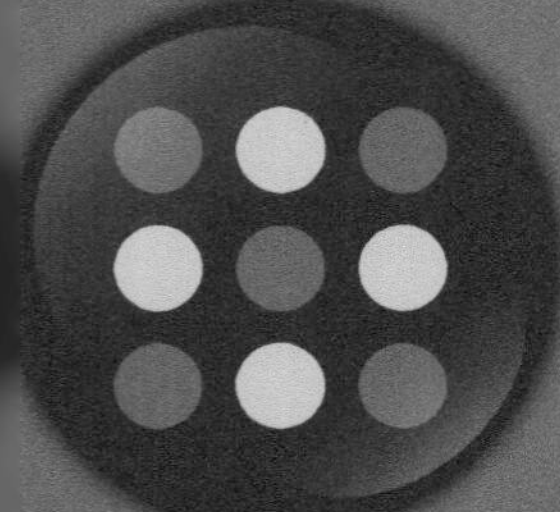

3 Expressions and formulae

Introduction

Engineers use algebraic formulae to represent the flight of a spacecraft, such as the NASA's Voyager 1 space probe which was launched in 1977 and has now recently left our solar system, the first man-made object ever to have done so. These formulae are often very complex, and they have allowed people on the ground to predict and control the spacecraft's progress with great accuracy.

What's the point?

Without the use of formulae to model and predict what happens in the real world, we would have no idea what might happen next in complex situations. An expensive space rocket would probably not even leave the launchpad!

Objectives

By the end of this chapter, you will have learned how to ...

- Use index notation, including negative indices, and basic index laws.
- Simplify algebraic expression by collecting like terms.
- Expand single brackets.
- Factorise an expression by taking out a common factor.
- Derive and substitute into a formula.
- Change the subject of a formula.
- Add and subtract simple algebraic fractions.

Check in

1 Given that $a = 2$ and $b = 5$, evaluate each of these.

a $5a$	**b** $b + 3$	**c** $4b - 3$	**d** $3a + 2b$
e ab	**f** $2(a + 4)$	**g** b^2	**h** $\frac{b + 7}{3}$

2 Simplify these algebraic expressions, where possible.

a $x + x$	**b** $y + y + y$	**c** $2a + a$	**d** $5b - 3b$
e $5p + q$	**f** $8k - 3$	**g** $7x + y - 2x$	**h** $10m - 4n - 6m + n$

3 Evaluate each of these calculations.

a $\frac{1}{5} + \frac{2}{5}$	**b** $\frac{8}{9} - \frac{1}{9}$	**c** $\frac{3}{4} - \frac{3}{8}$	**d** $\frac{4}{5} - \frac{1}{15}$
e $\frac{2}{3} + \frac{2}{9}$	**f** $\frac{5}{6} - \frac{1}{4}$	**g** $\frac{3}{4} + \frac{2}{5}$	**h** $\frac{7}{12} + \frac{3}{8}$

Starter problem

Here is a polygon drawn on square dotty paper.

Investigate different polygons and find the connection between the area, the number of dots on the inside and the number of dots on the perimeter.

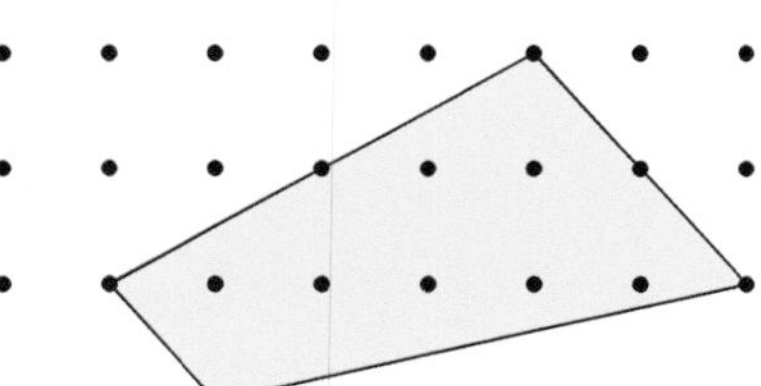

3a Indices in algebra

p.12

- Long products of the same number can be written using **index** notation.

2 is the base and 8 is the index or power. 2^8 is not the same as $2 \times 8 = 16$.

$$2 \times 2 \times 2 \times 2 \times 2 \times 2 \times 2 \times 2 = 2^8 = 256$$

Example

Evaluate these numbers without a calculator.

a 4^3 **b** 22^0

a $4^3 = 4 \times 4 \times 4 = 64$

b $22^0 = 1$ A number raised to the power 0 is always 1.

- To work out a number raised to a negative index, write the **reciprocal** with a positive index.

$$3^{-2} = \frac{1}{3^2} = \frac{1}{9}$$

Example

Evaluate these numbers without a calculator.

a 2^{-5} **b** $\left(\frac{2}{5}\right)^{-2}$

a $2^{-5} = \frac{1}{2^5} = \frac{1}{32}$

b $\left(\frac{2}{5}\right)^{-2} = \left(\frac{5}{2}\right)^{2} = \frac{5}{2} \times \frac{5}{2} = \frac{25}{4} = 6\frac{1}{4}$

- **Indices** in algebra follow the same rules as in arithmetic.

$a^5 = a \times a \times a \times a \times a \qquad n^0 = 1$

- Operations in algebra, like those in arithmetic, follow the rules of BIDMAS.

Brackets, Indices, Division and Multiplication, Addition and Subtraction.

Example

Given that $a = 3$, $b = -2$ and $c = \frac{1}{2}$, evaluate these expressions.

a $5a^2$ **b** $10 - b^2$ **c** $bc + a^3$

a $5a^2 = 5 \times 3^2$
$= 5 \times 9$
$= 45$

b $10 - b^2 = 10 - (-2)^2$
$= 10 - 4$
$= 6$

c $bc + a^3 = -2 \times \frac{1}{2} + 3^3$
$= -1 + 27$
$= 26$

To evaluate an algebraic expression you **substitute** a given number for a **variable**.

Exercise 3a

1 Evaluate these indices without a calculator.

a 3^2 b 2^6 c 10^5 d 1^{10}
e 0^4 f 4^0 g $(-1)^3$ h $(-3)^4$

2 Evaluate these negative indices without a calculator.

a 2^{-4} b 6^{-2} c 5^{-3} d 1^{-8}
e $\left(\frac{1}{2}\right)^{-5}$ f $\left(\frac{1}{3}\right)^{-3}$ g $\left(\frac{2}{3}\right)^{-4}$ h $\left(\frac{4}{9}\right)^{-2}$

3 State whether each of these algebraic statements is true or false. If false, give a reason.

Are these statements true if you substitute numbers for the variables?

a $a + a + a = 3a$ b $x^3 = x \times 3$
c $p \times 9 = 9p$ d $xy = yx$
e $t \div 7 = \frac{t}{7}$ f $y - 4 = 4 - y$
g $n \times n = n^2$ h $3b^2 = (3b)^2$
i $-n \times -n = -n^2$ j $(-a)^5 = -a^5$

4 Given that $a = -3$, evaluate these algebraic expressions and arrange the cards in ascending order.

$4a$ a^3 $2a^2$
a^0 $(2a)^2$ a^{-2}

5 Given that $x = 2$ and $y = -5$, find the value of these algebraic expressions.

a x^7 b y^3
c $5x^3$ d $(2x)^3$
e $3x + y^2$ f $2x^3 - y$
g $x^2 y$ h $(x^4 - y^2)^2$
i $\frac{x^4}{y^2}$ j $(x^2y)^2$

Problem solving

6 A mouhefanggai is a solid shape made from the space where two cylinders meet at right angles. If the cylinders have radius r, the volume of the mouhefanggai is $\frac{16}{3}r^3$.

Find the volume of a mouhefanggai made from cylinders with these radii.

a $r = 3$ b $r = 6$ c $r = 2$ d $r = 4$

Did you know?

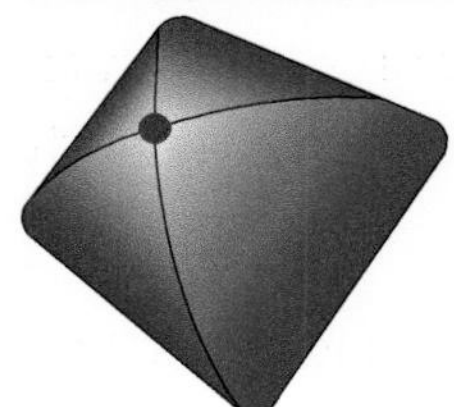

Mouhefanggai is Chinese for 'two square umbrellas'.

7 Write these expressions as a single power of the base.

a $2^3 \times 2^3$ b $3^2 \times 3^3 \times 3^4$ c $x^7 \times x^5$ d $y^5 \times y^{-3}$

8 $(2^2)^2 = 2^2 \times 2^2 = 2^{2+2} = 2^4$

Giving your answers in index form, work out

a $(2^2)^3$ b $(3^2)^4$ c $(4^5)^3$

Can you write a rule to work out a power of a power: $(2^m)^n = 2^{\square}$?

You may find it helpful to write the expression out in full and then simplify.

3b Index laws

Example

Evaluate

a $2^3 \times 3^2$ **b** $3^5 \div 9^2$

a $2^3 \times 3^2 = (2 \times 2 \times 2) \times (3 \times 3)$
$= 8 \times 9$
$= 72$

b $3^5 \div 9^2 = \frac{3 \times 3 \times 3 \times 3 \times 3}{9 \times 9}$
$= \frac{243}{81}$
$= 3$

- When multiplying indices involving the same base number, add the indices.
- When dividing indices involving the same base number, subtract the indices.

Indices in algebra follow the same rules as in arithmetic.

Example

Evaluate

a $3^5 \times 3^2$ **b** $7^5 \div 7^3$ **c** $a^5 \times a^2$ **d** $y^5 \div y^2$

a $3^5 \times 3^2 = (3 \times 3 \times 3 \times 3 \times 3) \times (3 \times 3)$
$= 3^{5+2}$
$= 3^7$

b $7^5 \div 7^3 = \frac{7 \times 7 \times 7 \times 7 \times 7}{7 \times 7 \times 7}$
$= 7^{5-3}$
$= 7^2$

c $a^5 \times a^2 = (a \times a \times a \times a \times a) \times (a \times a)$
$= a^{5+2}$
$= a^7$

d $y^5 \div y^2 = \frac{y \times y \times y \times y \times y}{y \times y}$
$= y^{5-2}$
$= y^3$

- When raising an index to an index, multiply the indices.

Example

Simplify

a $(4^3)^2$ **b** $(a^2)^4$ **c** $(3b^5)^2$

a $(4^3)^2 = 4^3 \times 4^3$
$= 4^{3 \times 2}$
$= 4^6$

b $(a^2)^4 = a^2 \times a^2 \times a^2 \times a^2$
$= a^{2 \times 4}$
$= a^8$

c $(3b^5)^2 = 3b^5 \times 3b^5$
$= 3^2 \times (b^5)^2$
$= 9b^{10}$

When possible leave your answer as an index number.

Exercise 3b

1 Write these in index form.

a $2 \times 2 \times 2$

b $5 \times 5 \times 5 \times 5 \times 5$

c $8 \times 8 \times 8 \times 8 \times 8 \times 8$

d $x \times x \times x \times x$

e $k \times k$

f $(-3) \times (-3) \times (-3) \times (-3)$

g $4 \times 4 \times 4 \times 7 \times 7$

h $a \times a \times a \times a \times a \times b \times b \times b$

2 Evaluate these without a calculator.

a 4^2 b 2^5

c 3^4 d 10^6

e 5^3 f 1^{20}

g $(-2)^3$ h $(-1)^8$

3 Simplify these multiplications, leaving your answer in index form.

a $3^2 \times 3^4$ b $6^5 \times 6^3$

c $2^8 \times 2^3$ d 9×9^7

e $x^4 \times x^5$ f $y^4 \times y^6$

g $p^2 \times p^3 \times p^4$ h $q \times q^3 \times q^5 \times q^7$

4 Simplify these divisions, leaving your answer in index form.

a $5^8 \div 5^3$ b $\frac{10^6}{10^4}$

c $7^{10} \div 7$ d $4^5 \div 4^5$

e $\frac{x^{12}}{x^5}$ f $\frac{y^6}{y^5}$

5 Simplify these, leaving your answer in index form.

a $(4^3)^5$ b $(10^2)^9$

c $(a^4)^6$ d $(2k^3)^6$

e $(3t^5)^4$ f $(-2b^3)^3$

g $(-b)^{10}$ h $((5a^2)^3)^2$

Problem solving

6 The number of diagonals in a polygon with n sides is given by the formula

$\frac{1}{2}(n^2 - 3n)$

Work out the number of diagonals in

a a pentagon b a square

c a heptagon d a decagon.

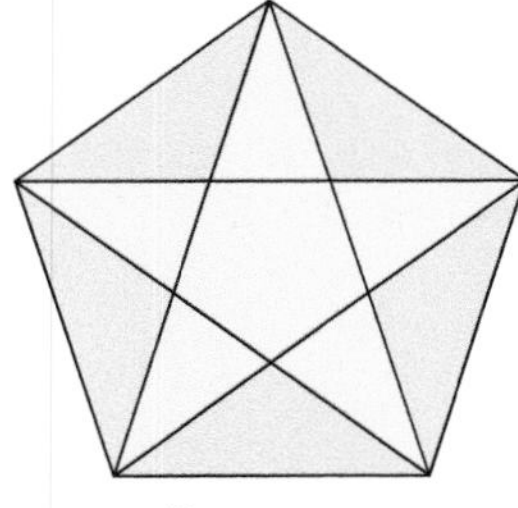

Pentagon

The diagonals of a shape are found by joining each vertex to another non-adjacent vertex.

7 Copy and complete.

a $8^6 \times \square = 8^{10}$ b $\square \div 3^2 = 3^5$ c $(6^3)^{\square} = 6^{15}$ d $x^4 \div \square = x^6$

e $y^6 \times \square = y^8$ f $k^5 \div \square = k$ g $3p^{\square} \times \square p^3 = 6p^5$ h $(5q^3)^{\square} = 25q^{\square}$

8 a Using the laws of indices simplify $4^{\frac{1}{2}} \times 4^{\frac{1}{2}}$?

b What is the value of $4^{\frac{1}{2}}$?

c Evaluate

i $9^{\frac{1}{2}}$ ii $16^{\frac{1}{2}}$ iii $81^{\frac{1}{2}}$ iv $144^{\frac{1}{2}}$

d What is the value of $27^{\frac{1}{3}}$?

3c Collecting like terms including powers

- Terms that involve the same unknown are **like terms**.
- You can **collect** together terms that involve exactly the same combination of letters to **simplify** an algebraic **expression**.

3a, 12a and 5a are like terms. 8xy and −3yx are like terms. 2x and −2x² are not like terms because they have different powers.

Example

Simplify these algebraic expressions by collecting like terms.

a $3a + 8b + 7a + 2$

b $8xy + 4y - 3yx - 3y$

c $4x^2 - 2x + x^2 - 3$

a $3a + 8b + 7a + 2 = 3a + 7a + 8b + 2 = 10a + 8b + 2$

b $8xy + 4y - 3yx - 3y = 8xy - 3xy + 4y - 3y = 5xy + y$

c $4x^2 - 2x + x^2 - 3 = 4x^2 + x^2 - 2x - 3 = 5x^2 - 2x - 3$

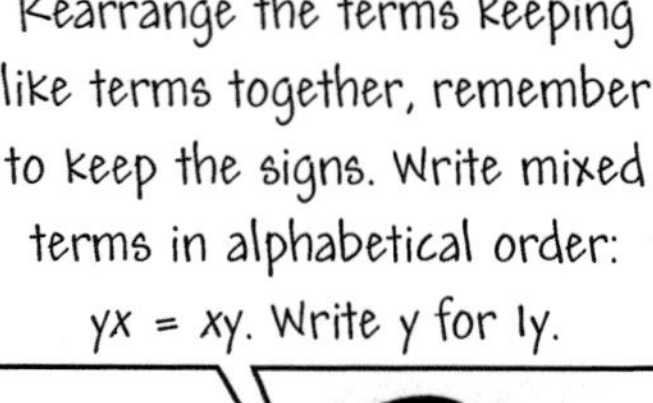

- To simplify expressions involving multiplications, rearrange the multiplication so that all the numbers are together and all the letters are together.

Example

Simplify

a $2t \times 3t^2$

b $4ab \times 5b^2$

a $2t \times 3t^2 = 2 \times t \times 3 \times t \times t$

$= 2 \times 3 \times t \times t + t$

$= 6t^3$

b $4ab \times 5b^2 = 4 \times a \times b \times 5 \times b \times b$

$= 4 \times 5 \times a \times b \times b \times b$

$= 20ab^3$

Separate the numbers from the letters. Multiply the numbers and write the letters in index form.

- To simplify expressions involving divisions, cancel common factors. Deal with the numbers and letters separately.

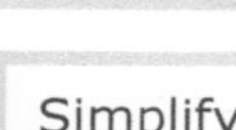

Example

Simplify

a $x^2y \div x$

b $\frac{10a^2}{5a}$

a $x^2y \div x = \frac{x^2y}{x}$

$= \frac{x \times \cancel{x} \times y}{\cancel{x}}$

$= xy$

b $\frac{10a^2}{5a} = \frac{10 \times a \times \cancel{a}}{5 \times \cancel{a}}$

$= 2a$

Rewrite the division as a fraction and cancel common factors. Make sure that you remember to divide any numbers.

Exercise 3c

1 Copy the table. Place each of these algebraic expressions under the correct heading in the table and simplify where possible.

$4x + 1$ $\quad 5a^2 - 2a$ $\quad p^2 + p^2$ $\quad 3g \times 8h$

$6m - 3m + n$ $\quad \frac{14b}{7}$ $\quad ab + 3ba$ $\quad \frac{2k + k^2}{2}$

Can be simplified	Cannot be simplified

2 Simplify these expressions, where possible, by collecting like terms,

- **a** $x + x + x$
- **b** $4m + 8m$
- **c** $10t - 3t$
- **d** $3a^2 + 5a^2 - 7a^2$
- **e** $4p^2 + 7p - p^2 + 2p$
- **f** $7k + 3 - 5k^2$
- **g** $9ab + 6bc - 4ba - 1$
- **h** $8g^3 + 5p^2 - 7g^3 - 2p$
- **i** $2 + 2x + x^0 + x^2$

3 Sort these cards into pairs of equivalent algebraic expressions. Show all your working.

$4 \times a \times a$	$4a^2b^2$
$4a \times 2$	$8ab$
$2a \times 4b$	$4a^2$
$2ab \times 2ba$	$8a$

4 Simplify these expressions as fully as possible.

- **a** $x \div 3$
- **b** $8a \div 2$
- **c** $\frac{3q}{3}$
- **d** $\frac{12t}{3t}$
- **e** $\frac{25gh}{5h}$
- **f** $\frac{20b^2}{4b}$
- **g** $\frac{30p^2q}{6q}$
- **h** $\frac{24mn^2}{8mn}$
- **i** $\frac{4a + 8}{4}$
- **j** $\frac{3k - k^2}{k}$

Problem solving

5 Write an algebraic expression for the volume of these solids.

The volume of a cube or cuboid is given by its length × width × height.

a

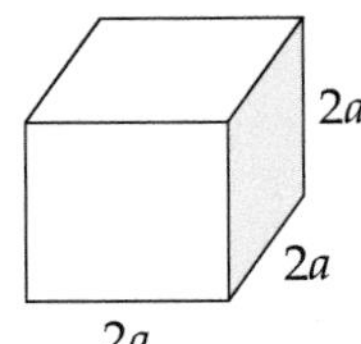

b

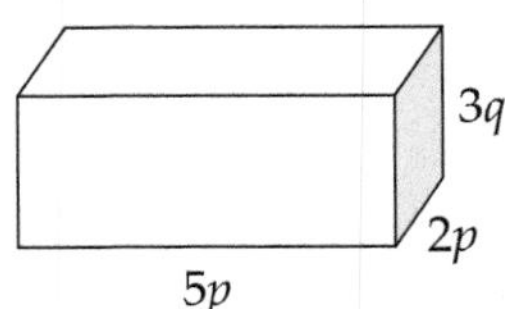

6 In this algebra pyramid, each brick is the sum of the two bricks below it.

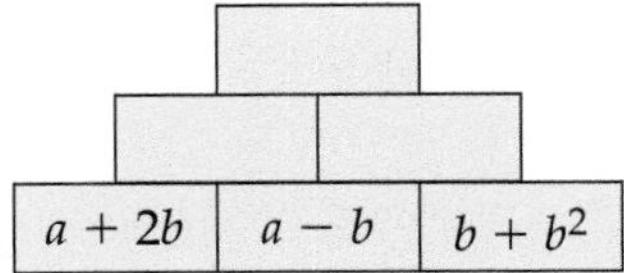

In this algebra pyramid, each brick is the product of the two bricks below it.

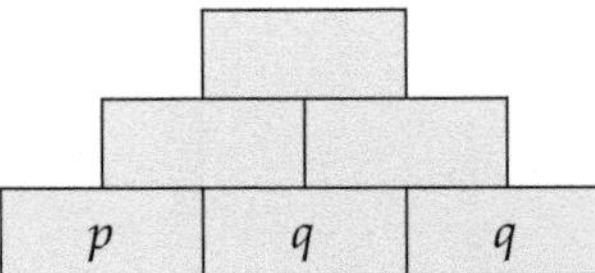

a Copy and complete the pyramids.

b Design some pyramids of your own.

3d Expanding brackets

- To **expand** a **bracket** you multiply each term inside the bracket by the term outside the bracket.

Example

Expand these brackets.

a $k(k + 2)$ **b** $-2(3p + 1)$

a $k(k + 2) = k \times k + 2 \times k$
$= k^2 + 2k$

b $-2(3p + 1) = -2 \times 3p + -2 \times 1$
$= -6p + -2$
$= -6p - 2$

Use the rules for multiplying with negative numbers.

- An **expression** may have several pairs of brackets. Expand each pair of brackets and then **simplify** by collecting like terms.

Example

Find the difference in area between these rectangles.
Fully simplify your answer.

A: 5 by $2x + 1$ B: 3 by $x - 1$

area of A $= 5(2x + 1)$
area of B $= 3(x - 1)$
area A − area B $= 5(2x - 1) - 3(x - 1)$
$= 10x + 5 - 3x + 3$
$= 7x + 8$

Remember that $-3 \times -1 = 3$.

- An expression may involve indices. Terms which have different powers of a variable are not like terms and must be treated separately.

Example

Expand and simplify $x(2x - 5) - 6(x - 2)$.

$x(2x - 5) - 6(x - 2) = 2x^2 - 5x - 6x + 12$
$= 2x^2 - 11x + 12$

Exercise 3d

1 Expand these brackets.

- **a** $3(x + 4)$ **b** $4(2f - 1)$
- **c** $t(t + 9)$ **d** $m(n - 7)$
- **e** $p(10 - q)$ **f** $3a(a + b)$
- **g** $-8(4 - 2y)$ **h** $-x(x - 10)$

2 Expand and simplify these expressions.

- **a** $4(x + 2) + 3(x + 5)$ **b** $2(3p + 2) + 5(p + 3)$
- **c** $3(3a - 4) + 6(2a + 1)$ **d** $7(t - 3) + 3(9 - 2t)$
- **e** $5(k + 4) - 3(k + 1)$ **f** $2(2y - 1) - 3(y + 2)$
- **g** $4(3m + 1) - 5(2m - 3)$ **h** $8(2n - 5) - 4(3n - 10)$

Problem solving

3 Write an algebraic expression for the area of each rectangle.
Expand the brackets.

a $k - 1$ by 6

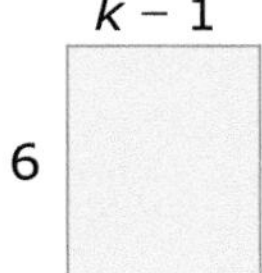

b k by $k + 5$

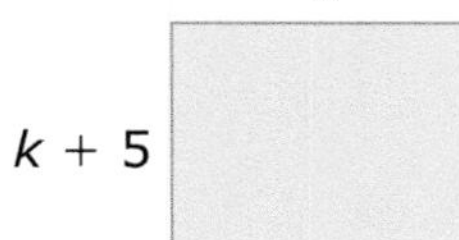

c $3x - 4$ by 5

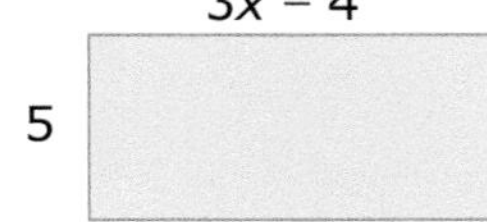

d p by $2p + q$

4 Find the surface area of this cuboid.

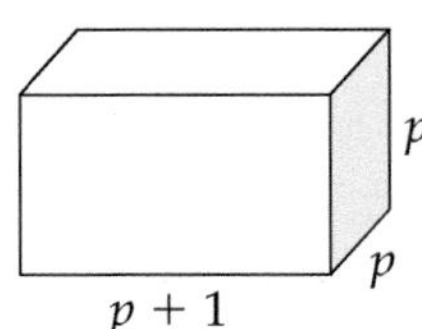

To find the surface area of a cuboid, calculate the area of each individual face and then sum your answers.

Did you know?

	Quarter 1
Revenues	
Membership Sales	175,000.00
Supplement Sales	25,000.00
Misc.	50,000.00
Total Revenues	250,000.00
Expenses	
Rent	50,000.00
Salaries	100,000.00
Supplies	50,000.00
Misc.	53,000.00
Total Expenses	253,000.00
Net Income	(3,000.00)

Accountants sometimes write negative amounts in brackets or use red ink.

5 Sort these algebraic expressions into pairs by expanding the brackets and simplifying.
Write the odd one out.

$x(x + 1) + 2(x - 5)$ $2x(x - 2) + 3(2 - x)$ $x(x + 5) - 2(x + 5)$

$3(x + 2) - 2x(2 - x)$ $5x(x + 1) - 3x(x + 4) + 6$

6 These brackets have been expanded.
Can you work out each original expression?

- **a** $3(\square + 2) = 3x + 6$ **b** $2(p + \square) = 2p + 8$ **c** $5(y - \square) = 5y - 10$
- **d** $4(\square + \square) = 4k + 12$ **e** $\square(2t + \square) = 6t + 15$ **f** $\square(\square - 2) = 15a - 10$

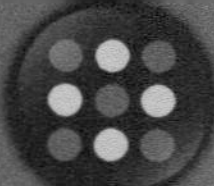

3e Factorising expressions

- Factorising is the reverse of expanding. When factorising an expression you put brackets back into the expression.

A factor of a number is any number that divides into it without leaving a remainder.

$$3(x + 2) \xrightarrow{\text{Expand}} 3x + 6$$

$$3(x + 2) \xleftarrow[\text{Factorise}]{} 3x + 6$$

‹ p.8

- To **factorise**, look for **factors** that are common to all terms and choose the **highest common factor (HCF)**.

Example

Factorise

a $5x + 15$ **b** $8a + 12$

a $5x + 15 = 5 \times x + 5 \times 3$
$= 5(x + 3)$

b $8a + 12 = 4 \times 2a + 4 \times 3$
$= 4(2a + 3)$

The HCF of 5x and 15 is 5. The HCF of 8a and 12 is 4.

Expressions to be factorised can involve powers.

Example

Factorise

a $y^2 + 3y$ **b** $2p^2 - 10pq$

a $y^2 + 3y = y \times y + y \times 3$
$= y(y + 3)$

b $2p^2 - 10pq = 2p \times p - 2p \times 5q$
$= 2p(p - 5q)$

To fully factorise an expression: Write the HCF outside the bracket. Divide each term in the expression by the HCF and write the answer inside the bracket.

Factorising is useful when trying to solve equations.

Example

Solve $30x - 18 = 42$

$30x - 18 = 42$	Factorise the left-hand side of the equation.
$6(5x - 3) = 42$	Divide each side by 6.
$5x - 3 = 7$	Add 3 to each side.
$5x = 10$	Divide each side by 5.
$x = 2$	

Exercise 3e

1 Write the HCF of these.

a 4 and 6 **b** 9 and 15 **c** 12 and 18 **d** 15 and 20

e $3x$ and $9x$ **f** $8x$ and $20y$ **g** $6p$ and $18p^2$ **h** $4t$, $10t$ and $14t^2$

2 Factorise these expressions fully.

a $3x + 6$ **b** $4a - 12$ **c** $12b - 15$ **d** $10k + 15$ **e** $16 - 6p$

f $7 - 7t$ **g** $mn + 2m$ **h** $8a - 2b$ **i** $5pq + 2$ **j** $6xy - 18x$

Problem solving

3 Ada and Ava are twins. Using a to stand for Ada and Ava's age, you can write an equation using Ada's description

Mum's age = $4a - 12$

a Write an equation using Ava's description.

b Use factorisation to convince Ada and Ava that they are both right.

c Ada and Ava are 14 years old.
Work out their Mum's age.

Ada says ... Ava says ...

Ada: To find my Mum's age, I multiply my age by 4 and then subtract 12 from my answer.

Ava: To find my Mum's age, I subtract 3 from my age and then multiply my answer by 4.

4 Maggie has got all of her factorisation homework wrong. Explain each mistake.

a	b	c
$3x^2 + 6x$	$8a + 10a^2$	$8k^2 - 16k$
$= 3(x^2 + 2x)$	$= a(8 + 10a)$	$= 4k(2k - 4)$
d	**e**	**f**
$9t^2 - 15t$	$2p + 6p^2$	$15xy - 10x^2$
$= 3t(3t - 15)$	$= 2p(3p)$	$= 5x(3y - 10^2)$

5 Solve this equation using two different methods.

$4x + 20 = 32$

Check that your answer is the same for each method.

Think up other equations that can be solved using two methods and swap with a partner.

Factorise the left-hand side.

6 Alexander thinks of a number, adds 2 and multiplies by 5.
William takes the same number, subtracts 2 and multiplies by 3.

a Write Alexander's thought process as an algebraic expression.

b Write William's thought process as an algebraic expression.

c Prove that the difference between these two expressions is always an even number.

3f Formulae

- A **formula** is a relationship or rule expressed in symbols.

The formula for the area of a triangle is $A = \frac{1}{2}bh$.

The **subject** of this formula is A, it is the variable that equals an expression.

You can **substitute** into a formula to find an unknown variable.

The formula connects the **variables** A = area, b = base and h = height.

Example

Isla bakes fairy cakes in her gas oven at Gas Mark 4.
What temperature should Flora use in her electric oven?

$T = 14g + 121$, In this formula T is the temperature in °C and g is the Gas Mark.

Substitute 4 (Gas Mark) for g.

$T = 14g + 121$
$= 14 \times 4 + 121$
$= 177°C$

- You can derive a formula to suit a real-life situation.
- Derive means find or deduce from the information given.

Example

A plumber's call-out charge is £50. His hourly rate is £25.
Derive a formula for the cost of hiring this plumber.

Number of hours worked, *h*	Cost of hours worked in £	Call-out charge in £	Total cost, *C*
1	$1 \times 25 = 25$	50	75
2	$2 \times 25 = 50$	50	100
3	$3 \times 25 = 75$	50	125
h	$h \times 25 = 25h$	50	$25h + 50$

$c = 25h + 50$, where
c = cost and h = hours worked.

Make a table containing examples. Generalise to derive a formula. Remember to say what each variable means.

You may be able to use diagrams to derive a formula and explain how it works.

Example

Write a formula for the perimeter, P, of any rectangle whose length is twice its width, w.

$P = 2w + w + 2w + w$ Collect like terms.
$P = 6w$

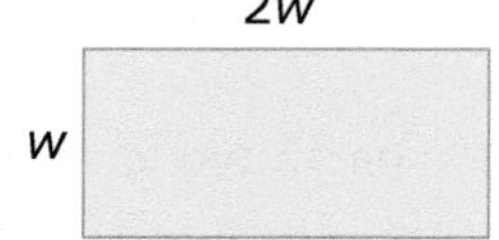

Exercise 3f

1 Find the value of the required variable in each of these formulae.

a $P = 4L$

Find P when $L = 7$.

b $s = \dfrac{d}{t}$

Find s when $d = 120$ and $t = 2.5$.

c $F = \dfrac{9}{5}C + 32$

Find F when $C = 30$.

d $s = ut + \dfrac{1}{2}at^2$

Find s when $u = 0$, $a = 2$ and $t = 5$.

Problem solving

2 Jason uses two routes to cycle from his house to Clare's house.

Route A: 10 miles

Route B: 14 kilometres

To convert a distance in miles, m, to a distance in kilometres, k, use the formula $k = \dfrac{8}{5}m$

Advise Jason of the shortest route.

3 The sum of all the integers from 1 to n is given by the formula

$$\text{Sum} = \frac{n(n+1)}{2}$$

a Use this formula to find the sum of the numbers from 1 to 5. Check your answer mentally.

b Calculate the sum of the first 100 numbers.

Did you know?

▲ Carl Friedrich Gauss (b 1777) was one of the most influential mathematicians ever. When he was a boy it is said that his maths teacher asked the class to add up the first 100 numbers. Gauss produced the only correct answer within minutes.

4 Lynda sees these two adverts for plumbers in her area.

a Derive a formula to find the cost of hiring out

i Mike the Plumber **ii** Phil's Plumbing.

b Use your formulae to advise Lynda of the cheapest plumber if the work takes

i 2 hours **ii** 5 hours.

c Find the number of hours work for which these plumbers charge the same amount.

PHIL'S PLUMBING

£50 call-out charge
£15 per hour thereafter

MIKE THE PLUMBER

Call-out fee £35
Hourly rate £20

5 The number of red squares, r, is connected to the length of a side of the inner white square, l, by the formula

$$r = 4l + 4$$

a Explain why this formula works.

b Use your formula to find the number of red squares surrounding a white square of length 10.

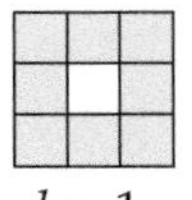
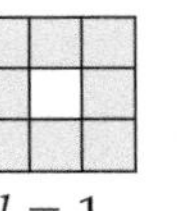
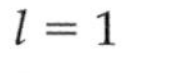

$l = 1$

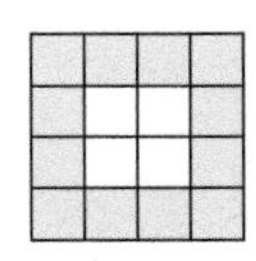

$l = 2$

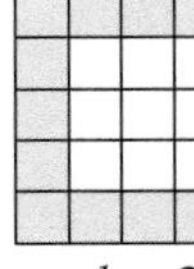

$l = 3$

6 Research the formulae in question **1**. What are they used for? What do the variables stand for? Investigate other real life formulae.

3g Rearranging formulae

The **subject** of a formula is the **variable** that stands alone on one side of the formula. You can **rearrange** a formula to make a different variable the subject.

$s = \frac{d}{t}$ — s is the subject.

$t = \frac{d}{s}$ — t is the subject.

$d = st$ — d is the subject.

- To change the subject of a formula you need to 'undo' each operation in turn. Use **inverse** operations.
  - Addition is the inverse of subtraction.
  - Division is the inverse of multiplication.

Read the formula starting with the variable that you want to make the subject. This formula reads: 'Start with x, multiply by m and add c to get y'.

Example

Rearrange $y = mx + c$ to make x the subject.

$y = mx + c$

$y - c = mx$ — Subtract c from both sides.

$\frac{y - c}{m} = x$ — Divide both sides by m.

Sometimes you need to change the subject of a formula to **evaluate** a variable.

Example

A travel brochure gives the average temperatures during July. The formula that connects temperature in °F to temperature in °C is $F = \frac{9}{5}C + 32$.

Rearrange this formula and find the temperature in °C.

$F = \frac{9}{5}C + 32$

$F - 32 = \frac{9}{5}C$ — Subtract 32 from both sides.

$5(F - 32) = 9C$ — Multiply both sides by 5.

$\frac{5(F - 32)}{9} = C$ — Divide both sides by 9.

$C = \frac{5(77 - 32)}{9} = \frac{5 \times 45}{9} = \frac{225}{9} = 25$ Substituting 77 for F.

The average July temperature in Positano, Italy is 25°C.

Exercise 3g

1 Make x the subject of these formulae.

a $x + b = a$ **b** $y = x - t$ **c** $p + x = q + r$ **d** $p = x + y + z$

e $x - y = 2y$ **f** $m^2 = x - n$ **g** $ab + x = c$ **h** $pq + r = r + x$

2 Make y the subject of these formulae.

a $xy = z$ **b** $py = q + r$ **c** $a = by - c$ **d** $a = r + xy$

e $m + ny = p - m$ **f** $dy - e = f - e$ **g** $xyz = p$ **h** $kly = m + n$

3 For each of these formulae, change the subject to the variable shown in red.

a $P = x + y + z$ **b** $P = 4l$ **c** $A = lw$ **d** $P = 2a + 2b$

e $C = 2\pi r$ **f** $y = mx + c$ **g** $v = u + at$ **h** $m = \frac{1}{2}(a + b)$

Problem solving

4 The formula for the perimeter of this isosceles triangle is $P = 2a + b$.

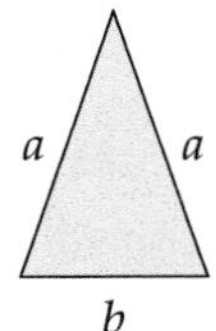

a Explain why this formula works.

b Rearrange this formula to make b the subject.

c Find b when $P = 33$ and $a = 12$.

5 The formula for the perimeter of this rectangle is $P = 2l + 2w$.

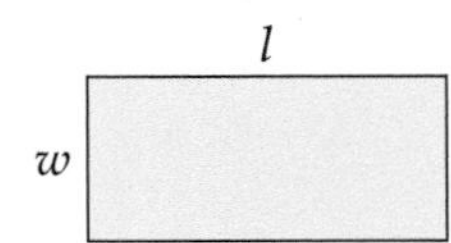

a Explain why this formula works.

b Rearrange this formula to make w the subject.

c Find w when $P = 28$ and $l = 9$.

d Derive a formula to find the perimeter of a rectangle whose length is three times its width.

6 The surface area, S, of a cuboid is given by the formula $S = 2lw + 2hw + 2hl$ where l is the length, w is the width and h is the height.

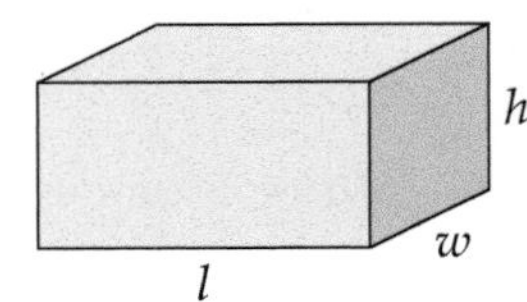

a By forming and solving an equation, find w when $S = 76$, $l = 4$ and $h = 5$.

b Find the length of a cuboid with a surface area of 94, a width of 3 and a height of 4.

c Explain why this formula works.

7 **a** Make x the subject of these formulae.

i $a - x = b$ **ii** $p - qx = r$

b Create some more formulae involving a negative x term and challenge your partner to rearrange your formulae to make x the subject. Discuss your methods.

c Make x the subject of these formulae.

i $\frac{a}{x} = b$ **ii** $p + q = \frac{r}{x}$

d Create some more formulae involving x as the denominator of a fraction and challenge your partner to rearrange your formulae to make x the subject. Discuss your methods.

3h Writing expressions

- An algebraic expression can be **simplified** by collecting **like terms**.

Example

Write a simplified expression for the missing length in this rectangle.

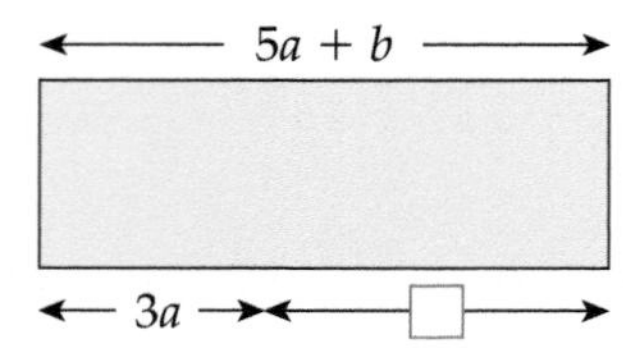

$\square = 5a + b - 3a$

$= 5a - 3a + b$ Keep the sign in front with the term.

$= 2a + b$ Collect like terms.

- To simplify an expression involving **brackets, expand** each pair of brackets and then collect like terms.

Substitute length = $4x - y$ and width = $2y$ into the formula for the perimeter.

Example

Find the perimeter of this rectangle.
Fully simplify your answer.

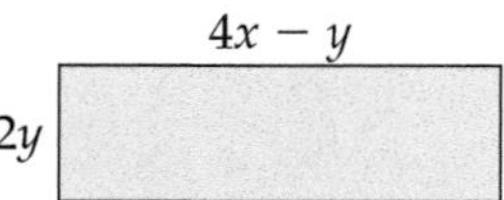

Perimeter = 2(length + width)

$= 2(4x - y + 2y)$ Collect like terms.

$= 2(4x + y)$ Multiply each term inside the bracket by 2.

$= 8x + 2y$

Example

a Write an algebraic expression using brackets for the shaded area of this rectangle.

b Expand the brackets.

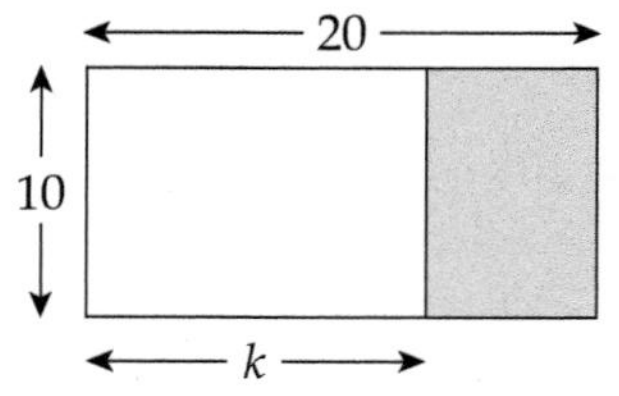

The shaded area has length = 10 and width = $20 - k$.

a Shaded area = $10(20 - k)$

b $10(20 - k) = 200 - 10k$ Multiply each term inside the bracket by 10.

Exercise 3h

1 Guide Xavier along the grid of Milton Keynes streets to his office building.

One block right = $+a$
One block left = $-a$
One block up = $+b$
One block down = $-b$

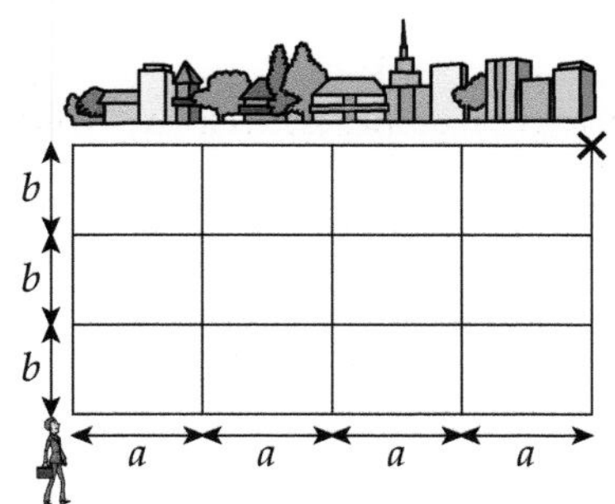

Going three blocks right and two block up becomes:
$+a+a+a+b+b$
$=3a+2b$

a Devise three different routes that Xavier can take to work and write these as algebraic expressions.

b For each expression, simplify by collecting like terms. Write what you notice.

2 In a magic square, the sum of each row, column and diagonal is the same.
Show that this is a magic square.

$b-a$	$3a+2b$	a
$3a$	$a+b$	$2b-a$
$a+2b$	$-a$	$3a+b$

3 Write a simplified expression for the missing lengths on each of these rectangles.

a
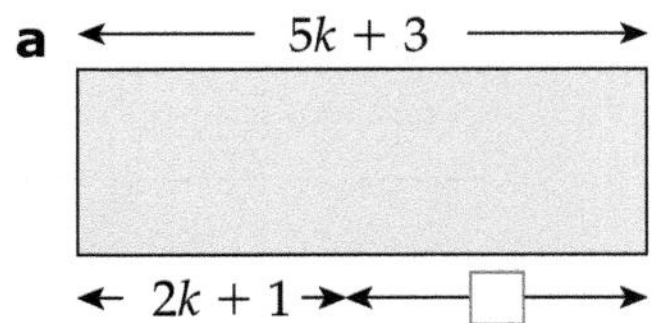

b
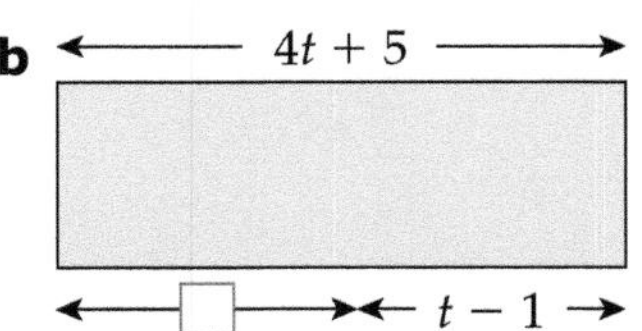

4 i Write an algebraic expression using brackets for each of these shaded areas.
ii Expand the brackets.

a
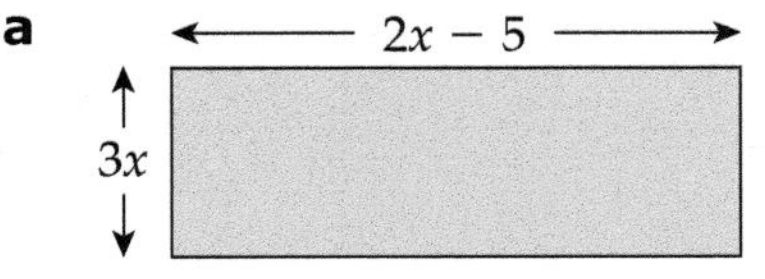

b
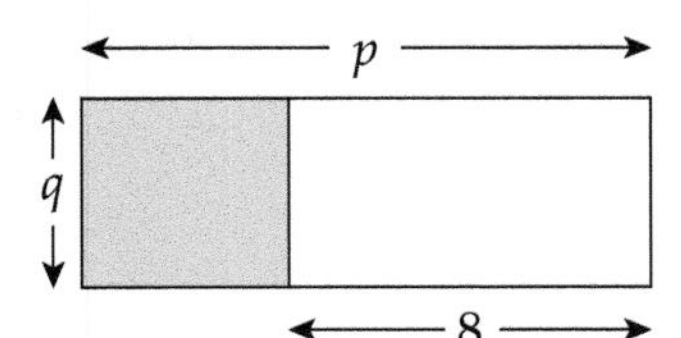

c
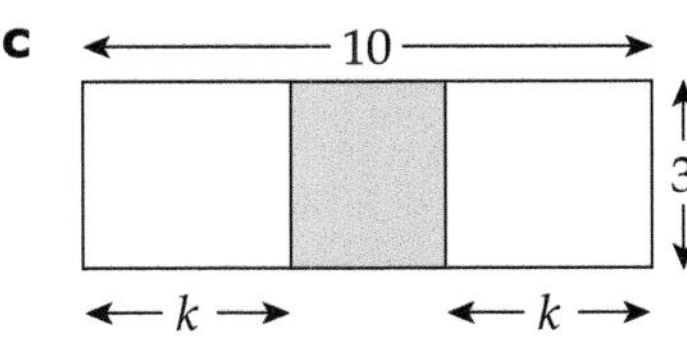

5 a In this rectangle, length = $y+3$ and width = $y+2$.
The area of this rectangle = $(y+3)(y+2)$.
By writing an expression for the area of each of the four small rectangles, summing and collecting like terms, find an expression equivalent to $(y+3)(y+2)$.

b Can you use this method to expand $(x+1)(x+4)$?

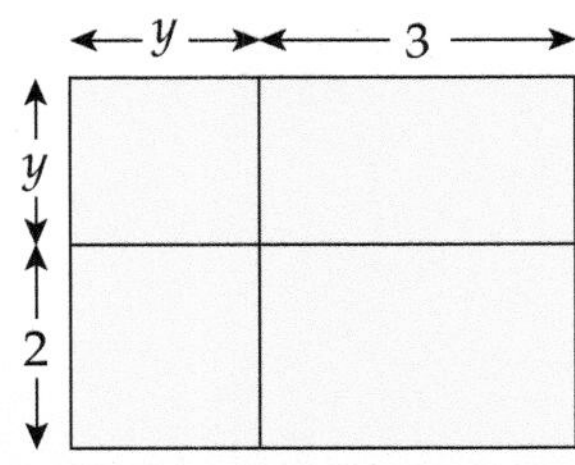

3i Algebraic fractions

- Fractions can be added and subtracted if they have a **common denominator**.
- When the fractions have different denominators, find a common denominator and use **equivalent fractions**.

Example

Calculate

a $\frac{2}{7}+\frac{3}{7}$ **b** $\frac{3}{5}-\frac{1}{2}$

a $\frac{2}{7}+\frac{3}{7}=\frac{5}{7}$

b $\frac{3}{5}-\frac{1}{2}=\frac{6}{10}-\frac{5}{10}$

$=\frac{1}{10}$

p.70 ›

Use the LCM to make equivalent fractions. The LCM of 5 and 2 is 10.

$\frac{3}{5}=\frac{6}{10}$ (×2) and $\frac{1}{2}=\frac{5}{10}$ (×5)

- **Algebraic fractions** have algebraic expressions in the numerator or denominator or in both.
Algebraic fractions follow the same rules as numerical fractions.

Example

Calculate

a $\frac{x}{2}+\frac{x}{3}$ **b** $\frac{2}{x}+\frac{5}{y}$ **c** $\frac{4}{x^2}-\frac{3}{x}$

a $\frac{x}{2}+\frac{x}{3}=\frac{3x}{6}+\frac{2x}{6}$ The LCM of 2 and 3 is 6.

$=\frac{5x}{6}$

b $\frac{2}{x}+\frac{5}{y}=\frac{2y}{xy}+\frac{5x}{xy}$ The LCM of x and y is xy.

$=\frac{5x+2y}{xy}$ $5x$ and $2y$ are not like terms so cannot be added.

c $\frac{4}{x^2}-\frac{3}{x}=\frac{4}{x^2}-\frac{3x}{x^2}$ The LCM of x and x^2 is x^2.

$=\frac{4-3x}{x^2}$ 4 and $-3x$ are not like terms so cannot be added.

Take extra care when the algebraic terms are in the denominator.

Exercise 3i

1 Work these out, simplifying your answer as necessary.

a $\frac{1}{7}+\frac{3}{7}$ b $\frac{5}{9}-\frac{1}{9}$

c $\frac{3}{5}+\frac{1}{5}$ d $\frac{8}{11}-\frac{4}{11}$

e $\frac{3}{4}-\frac{1}{4}$ f $\frac{5}{6}+\frac{1}{6}$

g $\frac{7}{8}-\frac{5}{8}$ h $\frac{7}{12}+\frac{11}{12}$

2 Simplify these expressions.

a $\frac{x}{3}+\frac{x}{3}$ b $\frac{x}{4}+\frac{y}{4}$

c $\frac{2a}{5}+\frac{a}{5}$ d $\frac{4}{7}t-\frac{3}{7}t$

e $\frac{1}{6}p+\frac{5}{6}q$ f $\frac{1}{x}+\frac{2}{x}$

g $\frac{8}{k}-\frac{3}{k}$ h $\frac{5}{x^2}-\frac{2}{x^2}$

3 Sort these cards into pairs of equivalent fractions.

$\frac{x}{5}$ $\frac{xy}{2y}$ $\frac{2}{x}$ $\frac{x^2}{10x}$

$\frac{10}{5x}$ $\frac{2x}{10}$ $\frac{x}{2}$ $\frac{x}{10}$

4 Work these out using equivalent fractions.

a $\frac{1}{3}+\frac{1}{9}$ b $\frac{2}{3}+\frac{1}{6}$

c $\frac{7}{10}-\frac{2}{5}$ d $\frac{5}{8}-\frac{1}{4}$

e $\frac{1}{2}+\frac{1}{3}$ f $\frac{4}{5}-\frac{2}{3}$

g $\frac{3}{4}-\frac{1}{5}$ h $\frac{5}{6}+\frac{3}{4}$

5 Simplify these expressions.

a $\frac{x}{2}+\frac{x}{4}$ b $\frac{p}{3}-\frac{p}{6}$

c $\frac{2a}{3}+\frac{a}{4}$ d $\frac{4}{5}b-\frac{1}{2}b$

e $\frac{z}{3}-\frac{2z}{15}$ f $\frac{x^2}{8}+\frac{x^2}{2}$

g $\frac{y^2}{3}-\frac{4y^2}{27}$ h $\frac{5xy}{12}+\frac{xy}{3}$

6 Simplify these expressions.

a $\frac{6}{x}-\frac{3}{x^2}$ b $\frac{2}{3x^2}+\frac{1}{x}$

c $\frac{2}{y}-\frac{3}{z}$ d $\frac{3}{5xy}+\frac{2}{3x}$

Problem solving

7 A box of chocolate chunks contains c chocolates. Ashim and Aesha share a box of chocolate chunks. This is how much they eat.

a Write and simplify an algebraic expression to show the fraction of the box of chocolate chunks that Ashim and Aesha have eaten.

b Ashim and Aesha have eaten 26 chocolate chunks. Work out the number of chocolate chunks, c, in a box.

3 MySummary

Check out

You should now be able to ...

Test it ➡ Questions

You should now be able to ...	Level	Questions
✓ Use index notation and basic index laws.	7	1 – 3
✓ Simplify algebraic expressions by collecting like terms.	6	4
✓ Expand single brackets.	6	5, 6
✓ Factorise an expression by taking out a common factor.	6	7
✓ Derive and substitute into a formula.	6	8 – 10
✓ Change the subject of a formula.	6	11
✓ Add and subtract simple algebraic fractions.	7	12

Language	Meaning	Example
Index notation	A way to show repeated multiplication	$10^3 = 10 \times 10 \times 10 = 1000$ $x \times x \times x = x^3$
Reciprocal	The reciprocal of a number is $\frac{1}{\text{number}}$	The reciprocal of $\frac{5}{4}$ is $\frac{4}{5}$
Expanding brackets	Multiplying each term inside the bracket by the term outside the bracket	$3(5 + 2) = 3 \times 5 + 3 \times 2$
Simplify expressions	Rearrange or cancel common factors to arrive at an equation which is easier to solve!	$3b + 2b - 2 + b = 6b - 2$
Like terms	Terms that have the same variables and powers	$2x^2$ and $4x^2$ are like terms $2x^2$ and $2x$ are not like terms
Factorising expressions	This is the reverse of expanding brackets – divide each term in the expression by the HCF and write the answer inside the bracket	$4c^2 + 8c = 4c(c + 2)$
Algebraic fractions	Fractions whose numerator and/or denominator are algebraic expressions	$\frac{5x + 2y}{xy}$

1 Evaluate these indices without a calculator.

a 5^0 b 3^{-2} c $(-5)^3$ d $(2^3)^2$

2 Given that $x = 2$ and $y = -3$, evaluate these expressions.

a x^4 b $2y^3$
c $(2xy)^{-1}$ d $(x^2 - y^2)^2$

3 Simplify each of these.
Use indices in your answers.

a $2 \times 2 \times 2$ b $1 \div (3^2 \times 3)$
c $x^6 \times x^4 \times x$ d $y^6 \div y^8$
e $\frac{x^3}{x^{-2}}$ f $(2a^4)^3$

4 Simplify these expressions.

a $16a - 12b + 9 - 15b - 18a$
b $3y + 4y^2 + 5y + y^2$
c $3cd + 5d + 8dc - 2c$
d $\frac{15pq^2}{30p^3q}$

5 Expand these brackets.

a $7(8 - 2a)$ b $-2(2b - 7)$
c $c(c + 1)$ d $-d(2d - 7)$

6 Expand these brackets and collect like terms.

a $3(r + 4) + 2(2r - 1)$
b $7(4s - 3) - 6(5s - 4)$

7 Factorise fully these expressions.

a $12x - 4$ b $7a + 14b$
c $15pq + 45p$ d $6st^2 - 9t$

8 $v = u + at$
Use this formula to find the value of v when $u = 5$, $a = 2$ and $t = 7$

9 A soft play area charges £50 to host a child's Birthday party, plus an additional cost of £3.50 per guest for food.
Derive a formula to find the cost, £C, of a party for n people.

10 Write a simplified expression for the shaded area.

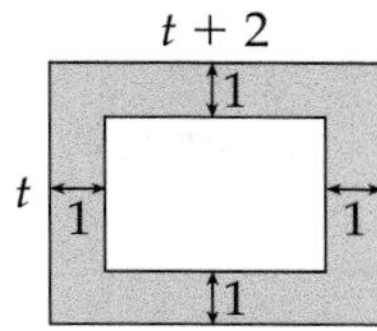

11 Make x the subject of the formulae

a $x - 2b = c$ b $7 + x = y - 12$
c $ax = b$ d $3x - y = 2y + 9$

12 Simplify

a $\frac{x}{5} + \frac{2x}{15}$ b $\frac{3a}{5} - \frac{a}{4}$
c $\frac{2}{x} + \frac{3}{xy}$ d $\frac{5}{p} - \frac{q}{p^2}$

What next?

Score		
	0 – 5	Your knowledge of this topic is still developing. To improve look at Formative test: 2C-3; MyMaths: 1033, 1155, 1158, 1178, 1179, 1186, 1187, 1247 and 1951
	6 – 10	You are gaining a secure knowledge of this topic. To improve look at InvisiPen: 145, 174, 184, 185, 212, 213, 214, 221, 222, 223, 251 and 256
	11 – 12	You have mastered this topic. Well done, you are ready to progress!

3 MyPractice

3a

1 Evaluate these numbers without a calculator.

a 5^2 b 3^4 c 2^8 d 6^0 e 4^{-3} f 8^{-2} g $\left(\frac{1}{2}\right)^{-7}$ h $\left(\frac{3}{4}\right)^{-2}$

2 Given that $m = 3$ and $n = -2$, find the value of these algebraic expressions.

a $2m^3$ b $6n^2$ c $(2n)^2$ d $3m + n^4$ e mn^2 f $(m^2 - n^2)^2$

3b

3 Simplify these, giving your answer in index form.

a $2^3 \times 2^5$ b $4^8 \times 4^2$ c 7×7^4 d $5^7 \times 5^2$

e $a^4 \times a^6$ f $b^3 \times b^2 \times b$ g $2x^7 \times 5x^2$ h $3y^3 \times 4y^8$

4 Simplify these, giving your answer in index form.

a $6^7 \div 6^4$ b $10^6 \div 10$ c $\frac{8^4}{8^3}$ d $\frac{p^{10}}{p^3}$ e $16k^8 \div k^6$ f $12t^8 \div 6t^8$

5 Simplify these, giving your answer in index form.

a $(3^5)^2$ b $(12^3)^5$ c $(m^4)^9$ d $(n^2)^7$ e $(4d^5)^3$ f $(-2x^2)^5$

3c

6 Simplify these expressions, where possible, by collecting like terms.

a $3x + 8x - 2x$ b $4a^2 - 6a^2 + 10a^2$ c $10m + 7n - 3n - 5m$

d $4p^2 + 8 - 3p$ e $12ab - 6ba + ab$ f $3g^3 - 4g^3 + 2g^2$

7 Simplify these expressions as fully as possible.

a $\frac{20x}{5}$ b $\frac{12y}{4y}$ c $\frac{21pq}{7q}$ d $\frac{30k^2}{18k}$ e $\frac{24gh^2}{16h}$ f $\frac{3b + 12}{3}$

3d

8 Use brackets to write an expression for the area of this rectangle. Then expand the brackets.

9 Expand and simplify these expressions.

a $5(a + 2) + 3(a + 4)$ b $3(4x + 1) + 6(2x - 1)$

c $3(4p + 3) + 7(1 - p)$ d $5(3b - 2) - 2(4b + 1)$

e $8(m + 2) - 3(2m - 3)$ f $6(4n - 3) - 4(5n - 4)$

3e

10 Factorise these expressions fully.

a $2x + 4$ b $5y + 20$ c $6g - 2$ d $8t - 12$

e $18 - 15k$ f $10p + 15q$ g $7a + ab$ h $15mn - 9n$

11 a Three consecutive numbers are summed. Using n to represent the first of these numbers, write and simplify an algebraic expression.

b Prove that the sum of three consecutive numbers is always equal to three times the middle number.

3f

12 Entry to the Cheeky Monkeys play barn costs £3.50 per child, adults are free.

a Work out the cost of one child paying 4 visits to Cheeky Monkeys.

b Derive a formula for the cost, C, of one child paying n visits to Cheeky Monkeys.

A parent or carer can spend £10 for membership of Cheeky Monkeys for one year. Members pay only £2.50 entry fee per child.

c Derive a formula to work out the cost, C, of one child paying n visits to Cheeky Monkeys if their parent or carer is a member.

d Sam takes her only daughter, Aysha, to Cheeky Monkeys once a month. Work out whether or not it is worth Sam becoming a member of Cheeky Monkeys.

13 The diagrams show a pattern of red and white tiles.

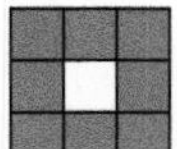

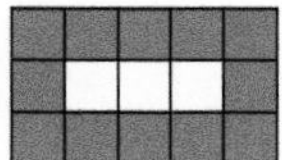

a Write a formula to connect the numbers of white tiles, w, and red tiles, r.

b Explain why this formula works.

c Use your formula to find the number of red tiles surrounding 100 white tiles.

3g

14 Make x the subject of each of these formulae.

a $p = x + r$ **b** $a + b = x - c$ **c** $x + 3y = z$

d $3p + x = 5p$ **e** $a = x - a^2$ **f** $x - mn = p + mn$

15 Make y the subject of each of these formulae.

a $m = ny$ **b** $b^2y = a$ **c** $p - 3 = qy$

d $g = fy + h$ **e** $aby = x$ **f** $y(\pi + 2) = r$

3h

16 Write an algebraic expression for each missing length on this rectangle.

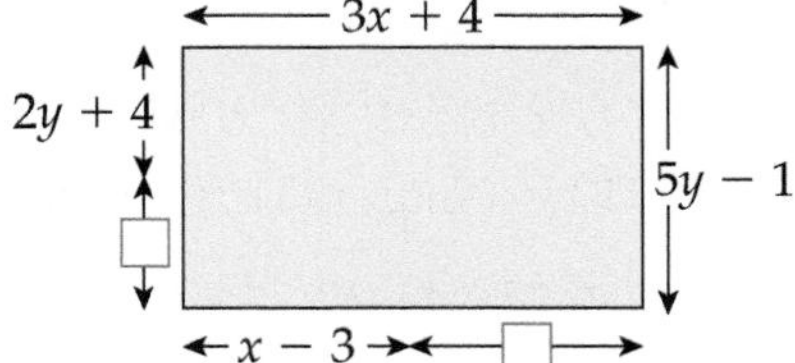

17 **i** Write an algebraic expression using brackets for the shaded areas in these rectangles.

ii Expand the brackets.

a

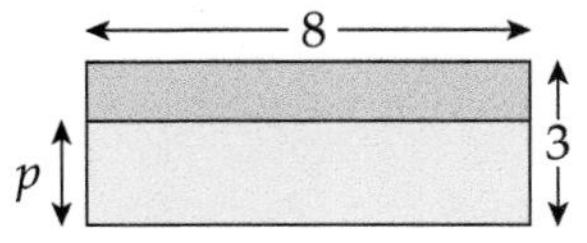

b

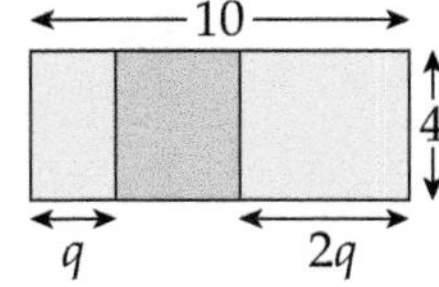

3i

18 Simplify these expressions.

a $\frac{x}{5} + \frac{2x}{5}$ **b** $\frac{p}{8} - \frac{q}{8}$ **c** $\frac{5}{9}a - \frac{1}{9}a$ **d** $\frac{10}{t} - \frac{3}{t}$

19 Simplify these using equivalent fractions.

a $\frac{k}{4} + \frac{k}{8}$ **b** $\frac{2y}{5} - \frac{y}{100}$ **c** $\frac{3}{8}m + \frac{1}{2}m$ **d** $\frac{3}{10}n - \frac{1}{8}n$

e $\frac{3}{a} + \frac{2}{b}$ **f** $\frac{6}{p} - \frac{1}{q}$ **g** $\frac{10}{t} - \frac{7}{t^2}$ **h** $\frac{5}{xy} - \frac{3}{x}$

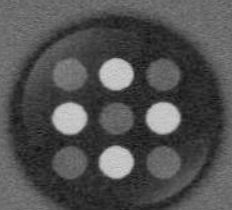

Case study 1: Energy in the home

With headlines like these, many people are looking at alternative forms of energy and other ways of saving energy in their homes.

ELECTRICITY PRICE SHOCK!

Oil cost hits new high

Gas price explodes

Solar power

Save up to 70% on your yearly hot water bill.
Save money on your electricity bill forever.
Cut your CO_2 emissions.
Use an everlasting FREE source of energy!

Task 1

a Look at all the green labels. Work out how long it would take for the savings to repay the cost of installing the item.

b i Which things do you think are most cost effective?

ii Which are not so cost effective?

c Would the length of time you are going to live in the same house alter your decisions?

Loft insulation
Cost £350
Save £200 per year

Lagging hot water tank
Cost £20
Save £50 per year

Efficient A rated boiler
Cost £2000
Save £150 per year

New heating controls
Cost £150
Save £50 per year

Ground based heat pump
Cost £12000
Save £800 per year

Double glazing
Cost £3500
Save £100 per year

Solar water heating
Cost £5000
Save £100 per year

Small wind generator
Cost £5000
Save £250 per year

Task 2

An average house in the UK uses around 3300 kWh of electricity in a year.

A typical solar panel will generate 825 kWh per year. The costs and saving are shown below

a How many solar panels would a house need to meet all of its electricity demands?

b What would be the total cost of fitting these solar panels?

c How long would it take to make a saving on having solar panels fitted?

Solar panels
Cost £6000 per panel
Save £120 per panel per year

Cavity wall insulation
Cost £350
Save £200 per year

Energy efficient light bulbs

Task 3

A **standard** light bulb can last up to 1000 hours switched on.

A typical **energy efficient** bulb can last up to 15000 hours.

a Think about a light bulb in your house.

i How many hours would it be switched on per day on average?

ii Estimate how many hours it would be switched on per year.

b How long would this bulb last **i** if it is energy-efficient **ii** if it is standard?

c In reality, an energy-efficient bulb might typically last for only 40% of this time.

Using your answer to **b**, estimate how long in years a typical energy-efficient bulb might last.

Draught proofing
Cost £120
Save £50 per year

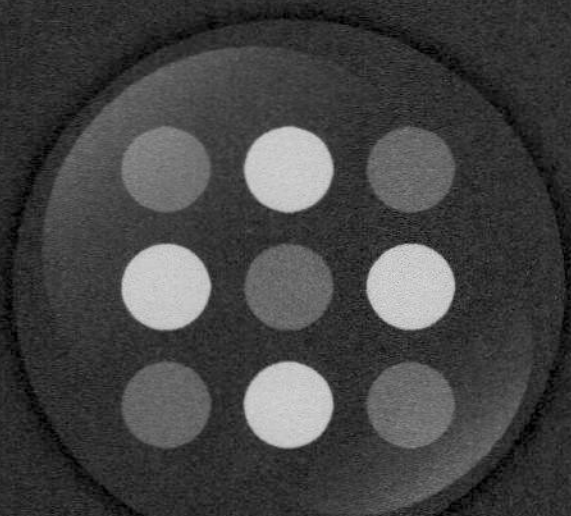

4 Fractions, decimals and percentages

Introduction

You use fractions in your everyday life. Although you might not actually use the word fraction in your sentences, the coins you use to buy things are all fractions of a pound, the measurements you use for distance are fractions of a metre, and when you are telling the time you do actually say the fractions out loud!

What's the point?

Using fractions allows you to describe amounts that are not a whole number.

Objectives

By the end of this chapter, you will have learned how to …

- Convert between decimals and fractions and order them.
- Add and subtract fractions with different denominators.
- Multiply and divide fractions.
- Calculate percentages of an amount and percentage changes.
- Calculate an original amount from the result of a percentage change.
- Convert between percentages, fractions and decimals.

Check in

1 Write these decimals as fractions.

a 1.5 **b** 0.78 **c** 0.125

Write any fractions in their simplest form.

2 Write these fractions as decimals without using a calculator.

a $\frac{7}{10}$ **b** $\frac{27}{20}$ **c** $\frac{13}{25}$ **d** $\frac{35}{40}$

3 Calculate each of these additions and subtractions, giving your answer as a fraction.

a $\frac{2}{5} + \frac{1}{4}$ **b** $\frac{6}{7} - \frac{2}{3}$

4 Use a mental method to calculate

a $1\frac{2}{3}$ of £39 **b** $\frac{7}{8}$ of 400 kg

5 Calculate each of these.

a $10 \times \frac{4}{7}$ **b** $8 \div \frac{2}{3}$

6 Copy and complete the table.

Fraction	Decimal	Percentage
$\frac{13}{20}$		
	0.125	

Starter problem

A pair of trainers cost £80. They are increased in price by 10%.

By what percentage do they need to be reduced to get back to the original cost of £80?

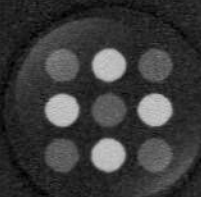

4a Fractions and decimals

- A decimal is another way of writing a fraction.
- A **terminating decimal** is one whose last digits are all zero.

To write a terminating decimal as a fraction you can use your knowledge of place values.

Example

Convert these decimals into fractions in their simplest form.

a 0.6 **b** 0.15 **c** 0.315

$0.6 = \frac{6}{10} = \frac{3}{5}$ (÷2)

$0.15 = \frac{15}{100} = \frac{3}{20}$ (÷5)

$0.315 = \frac{315}{1000} = \frac{63}{200}$ (÷5)

- A **recurring decimal** is one whose last digits keep repeating.

You can use division to convert a fraction into a decimal by dividing the numerator by the denominator.

Example

Convert $\frac{4}{33}$ into a decimal using short division.

$\frac{4}{33} = 4 \div 33$

$= 0.1212...$

$= 0.\dot{1}\dot{2}$

$33\overline{)4.^{4}0^{7}0^{4}0^{7}0}$ = 0.1212...

40 − 33 = 7
70 − 66 = 4

- You can compare and order fractions and decimals by converting them into decimals.

Example

Put these fractions and decimals in order from lowest to highest.

$\frac{2}{9}$ $\frac{3}{11}$ 0.22

Convert any fractions into decimals using division.

$\frac{2}{9} = 2 \div 9 = 0.222...$ $\frac{3}{11} = 3 \div 11 = 0.2727...$ 0.22

Order the decimals. 0.22 0.222... 0.2727...

So the order is 0.22 $\frac{2}{9}$ $\frac{3}{11}$

Exercise 4a

1 Write these decimals as fractions in their simplest form.

a 0.4 b 1.12 c 0.36
d 0.98 e 0.166 f 2.625

2 Write these fractions as decimals without using a calculator.

a $\frac{3}{10}$ b $\frac{23}{20}$ c $\frac{19}{25}$ d $\frac{63}{50}$
e $\frac{55}{25}$ f $\frac{8}{5}$ g $\frac{3}{20}$ h $\frac{33}{40}$
i $\frac{14}{40}$ j $\frac{85}{80}$ k $\frac{305}{125}$ l $\frac{37}{8}$

3 Change these fractions into decimals using division. Use an appropriate method. Give your answers to 5 decimal places where appropriate.

a $\frac{5}{16}$ b $\frac{3}{32}$ c $\frac{4}{11}$
d $\frac{3}{7}$ e $\frac{17}{6}$ f $\frac{22}{7}$

4 Place $<$ or $>$ between these pairs of numbers to show which number is the largest.

a $0.5 \square \frac{4}{7}$ b $\frac{7}{12} \square \frac{5}{8}$
c $\frac{3}{7} \square 0.42$ d $0.69 \square \frac{11}{16}$
e $\frac{4}{9} \square 0.45$ f $0.462 \square \frac{6}{13}$
g $\frac{7}{9} \square 0.8$ h $0.1765 \square \frac{3}{17}$

5 Put these fractions and decimals in order from lowest to highest.

a $\frac{3}{7}$ 0.43 $\frac{7}{16}$ 0.425
b $\frac{1}{9}$ $\frac{1}{8}$ 0.11 0.12
c $\frac{4}{7}$ $\frac{19}{33}$ 0.6 $\frac{571}{999}$
d $0.\dot{3}$ $\frac{2}{7}$ 0.333 $\frac{22}{63}$
e $\frac{1}{11}$ $0.0\dot{8}$ 0.09 $\frac{3}{29}$

Problem solving

6 The variable p represents a decimal number with one decimal place. Write a list of the possible values of p if

a $\frac{3}{7} < p < \frac{5}{7}$ b $\frac{1}{4} < p < \frac{3}{4}$ and $\frac{3}{8} < p < \frac{7}{8}$

7 Given that $\frac{1}{11} = 0.0909...$, work out the decimal equivalents of these fractions without a calculator.

a $\frac{2}{11}$ b $\frac{3}{11}$ c $\frac{4}{11}$
d $\frac{5}{11}$ e $\frac{6}{11}$ f $\frac{10}{11}$

Write down what you notice.

8 Petra changes a fraction into a decimal using her calculator. The answer on her calculator says 0.6842105263. Both the numbers in her fraction are less than 20. What fraction did Petra type into her calculator?

9 a Let $x = 0.4444....$

i Write a similar expression for $10x$.

ii Use your two expressions to solve for x as a fraction.

b Use a similar method to find

i 0.5555.... ii 0.15151515....

10 a Calculate $\frac{1}{7}$ by a written method of division.

b Your answer should have six repeating digits. This is the most repeating digits that 7 can have, why?

c i Calculate $\frac{1}{19}$ by a written method of division.

ii How many repeating digits does your answer have? Is this a worst case?

4b Adding and subtracting fractions

p.8

You can add or subtract fractions with different denominators by first writing them as **equivalent fractions** with the same **common denominator**.

Example

Calculate

a $\frac{7}{12} + \frac{1}{5}$ **b** $\frac{7}{18} - \frac{5}{24}$

60 is the LCM of 12 and 5.

a $\frac{7}{12} = \frac{35}{60}$ (×5) $\frac{1}{5} = \frac{12}{60}$ (×12)

$\frac{35}{60} + \frac{12}{60} = \frac{35 + 12}{60}$

$= \frac{47}{60}$

72 is the LCM of 18 and 24.

b $\frac{7}{18} = \frac{28}{72}$ (×4) $\frac{5}{24} = \frac{15}{72}$ (×3)

$\frac{28}{72} - \frac{15}{72} = \frac{28 - 15}{72}$

$= \frac{13}{72}$

You need to be careful when you calculate with mixed numbers and improper ('top heavy') fractions.

Example

Calculate

a $2\frac{3}{8} - 1\frac{7}{12}$ **b** $3\frac{3}{5} + 2\frac{5}{7}$

a $2\frac{3}{8} = \frac{19}{8}$ $1\frac{7}{12} = \frac{19}{12}$

24 is the LCM of 8 and 12.

$\frac{19}{8} = \frac{57}{24}$ (×3) $\frac{19}{12} = \frac{38}{24}$ (×2)

$\frac{57}{24} - \frac{38}{24} = \frac{57 - 38}{24}$

$= \frac{19}{24}$

$2\frac{3}{8} - 1\frac{7}{12} = \frac{19}{24}$

b $3\frac{3}{5} + 2\frac{5}{7} = 5 + \frac{3}{5} + \frac{5}{7}$

35 is the LCM of 5 and 7.

$\frac{3}{5} = \frac{21}{35}$ (×7) $\frac{5}{7} = \frac{25}{35}$ (×5)

$\frac{21}{35} + \frac{25}{35} = \frac{46}{35}$

$= 1\frac{11}{35}$

$3\frac{3}{5} + 2\frac{5}{7} = 5 + 1\frac{11}{35}$

$= 6\frac{11}{35}$

6

Exercise 4b

Give each answer as a fraction in its simplest form.

1 Calculate each of these.

a $\frac{3}{7}+\frac{1}{7}$ **b** $\frac{17}{20}-\frac{7}{20}$

c $1\frac{7}{12}+2\frac{6}{12}$ **d** $3\frac{4}{9}-1\frac{7}{9}$

2 Calculate each of these additions and subtractions.

a $\frac{3}{8}+\frac{5}{9}$ **b** $\frac{4}{7}+\frac{6}{11}$ **c** $\frac{3}{15}+\frac{4}{7}$

d $\frac{12}{13}-\frac{13}{15}$ **e** $\frac{14}{17}-\frac{11}{15}$ **f** $\frac{14}{27}+\frac{3}{16}$

g $\frac{5}{16}-\frac{2}{13}$ **h** $\frac{7}{12}+\frac{5}{16}$

3 Work these out.

a $\frac{13}{15}-\frac{7}{30}$ **b** $\frac{14}{15}+\frac{9}{20}$ **c** $\frac{17}{28}-\frac{14}{35}$

d $\frac{17}{20}+\frac{7}{24}$ **e** $\frac{11}{16}+\frac{7}{24}$ **f** $\frac{21}{32}-\frac{7}{16}$

g $\frac{29}{36}+\frac{17}{45}$ **h** $\frac{17}{60}+\frac{11}{36}$

4 Work these out.

a $1\frac{3}{8}+\frac{1}{2}$ **b** $2\frac{1}{4}-\frac{3}{8}$ **c** $2\frac{2}{3}+2\frac{5}{6}$

d $3\frac{3}{10}-2\frac{3}{5}$ **e** $2\frac{3}{7}+1\frac{4}{9}$ **f** $2\frac{3}{5}+1\frac{2}{3}$

g $3\frac{4}{5}-2\frac{7}{8}$ **h** $1\frac{4}{7}+2\frac{1}{3}$

Problem solving

5 **a** Paige wants to download a very big file from a website. In the first hour she downloads $\frac{2}{7}$ of the file. In the second hour she downloads the next $\frac{3}{8}$ of the file.

i What fraction of the file has she downloaded after 2 hours?

ii What fraction of the file has she not yet downloaded?

b Dylan is making a cake. He uses $\frac{3}{4}$kg of flour, $\frac{3}{8}$kg of butter and $\frac{7}{16}$kg of sugar. He puts all the ingredients into a bowl. What is the total weight of the ingredients?

6 **a** A photograph has a length of $4\frac{3}{4}$ inches and a width of $3\frac{1}{3}$ inches. Calculate the perimeter of the photograph.

b Naomi takes a bus journey from Keswick to Seatoller. The total distance is 12 km. Find the distance between Rosthwaite and Seatoller.

Keswick

$6\frac{2}{5}$ km

Grange

$3\frac{1}{8}$ km

Rosthwaite

Seatoller

7 Here are five weights, each with a different mass. You can use the weights to measure the mass of different amounts.

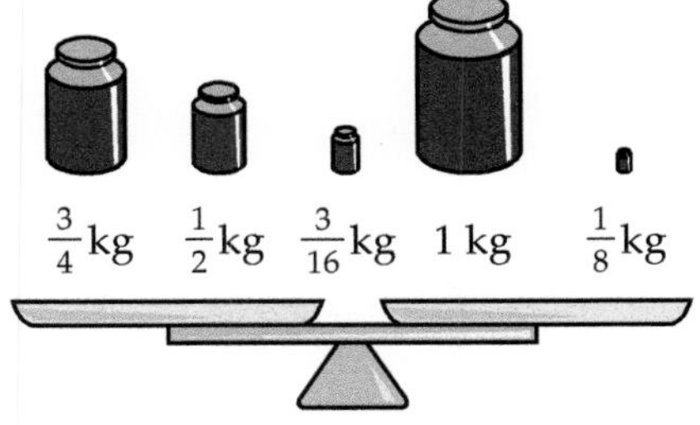

a What is the total mass of all five weights?

b Which two weights have a combined mass of $\frac{15}{16}$ kg?

c Investigate what different masses you could weigh using these weights.

Did you know?

Musicians use notes of fractional duration.

breve	2	notes
semibreve	1	note
minim	$\frac{1}{2}$	note
crotchet	$\frac{1}{4}$	note
quaver	$\frac{1}{8}$	note
semiquaver	$\frac{1}{16}$	note

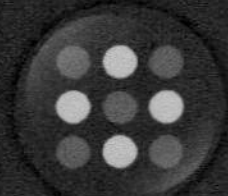

4c Multiplying and dividing fractions

- You can find a **fraction of a number** or quantity using multiplication.

Example

Calculate $\frac{5}{18}$ of 30 kg.

$\frac{5}{18}$ of 30

$= \frac{5}{18} \times 30 = \frac{5}{\cancel{18}_3} \times \cancel{30}^5$ Use cancellation to simplify the product.

$= \frac{25}{3}$

$= 8\frac{1}{3}$ kg Convert your answer to a **mixed number** using division.

- When you multiply a pair of fractions, the numerators are multiplied together and the denominators are multiplied together.

Example

Calculate

a $\frac{3}{5} \times \frac{4}{7}$

b $\frac{7}{12} \times \frac{6}{11}$

a $\frac{3}{5} \times \frac{4}{7} = \frac{3 \times 4}{5 \times 7}$

$= \frac{12}{35}$

b $\frac{7}{12} \times \frac{6}{11} = \frac{7}{\cancel{12}_2} \times \frac{\cancel{6}^1}{11}$

$= \frac{7 \times 1}{2 \times 11}$

$= \frac{7}{22}$

- Dividing by fraction is the same as multiplying by its reciprocal. This is sometimes called the inverse rule.

Example

Calculate $\frac{2}{5} \div \frac{3}{7}$

$\frac{2}{5} \div \frac{3}{7} = \frac{2}{5} \times \frac{7}{3}$ Change the division into a multiplication and invert the fraction.

$= \frac{2 \times 7}{5 \times 3}$

$= \frac{14}{15}$

Exercise 4c

1 Calculate

a $3 \times \frac{2}{7}$ **b** $4 \times \frac{1}{9}$ **c** $2 \times \frac{5}{16}$

d $3 \times \frac{3}{11}$ **e** $2 \times \frac{5}{14}$ **f** $3 \times \frac{5}{8}$

g $4 \times \frac{3}{5}$ **h** $5 \times \frac{7}{8}$

2 Calculate

a $6 \times \frac{2}{3}$ **b** $15 \times \frac{3}{10}$ **c** $18 \times \frac{5}{12}$

d $15 \times \frac{11}{12}$ **e** $18 \times \frac{7}{24}$ **f** $15 \times \frac{13}{25}$

g $35 \times \frac{9}{14}$ **h** $16 \times \frac{5}{28}$

3 Calculate

a $\frac{5}{8}$ of 6 feet **b** $\frac{6}{13}$ of 52

c $\frac{4}{9}$ of 12 inches **d** $\frac{17}{12}$ of 66 mins

e $1\frac{3}{16}$ of 30 GB **f** $2\frac{7}{10}$ of 110 m

4 Calculate

a $\frac{3}{5} \times \frac{2}{7}$ **b** $\frac{3}{8} \times \frac{5}{6}$ **c** $\frac{3}{4} \times \frac{5}{9}$

d $\frac{5}{6} \times \frac{3}{10}$ **e** $\frac{4}{9} \times \frac{3}{8}$ **f** $\frac{5}{6} \times \frac{9}{20}$

g $\frac{6}{7} \times \frac{14}{15}$ **h** $\frac{12}{25} \times \frac{10}{21}$

5 Calculate

a $5 \div \frac{5}{6}$ **b** $8 \div \frac{4}{5}$ **c** $6 \div \frac{2}{5}$

d $9 \div \frac{3}{7}$ **e** $5 \div \frac{4}{9}$ **f** $10 \div \frac{4}{7}$

g $12 \div \frac{8}{11}$ **h** $15 \div \frac{12}{13}$

6 Calculate

a $\frac{3}{5} \div \frac{4}{7}$ **b** $\frac{5}{8} \div \frac{5}{6}$

c $\frac{7}{9} \div \frac{2}{3}$ **d** $\frac{7}{10} \div \frac{5}{7}$

e $\frac{45}{27} \div \frac{20}{3}$ **f** $\frac{9}{11} \div \frac{1}{33}$

Always simplify any fractions and write improper fractions as mixed numbers.

Remember to cancel if you can.

Problem solving

7 a A postcard is $4\frac{1}{2}$ inches wide and $7\frac{3}{4}$ inches long.
What is the area of the postcard?

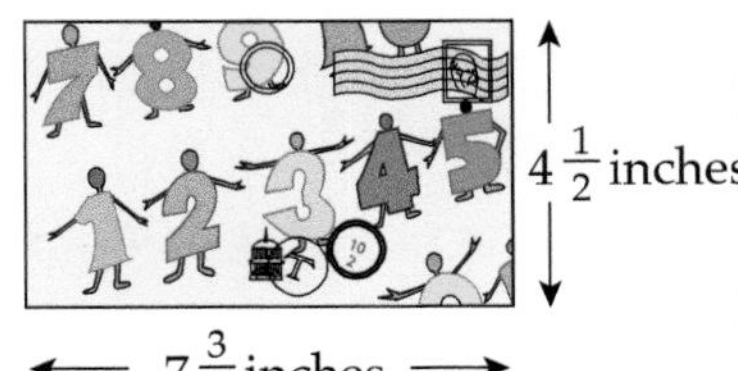

b A bag of cherries weighs $\frac{7}{10}$ kg. In a week Hanif eats $2\frac{1}{4}$ bags of cherries. How many kilograms of cherries does he eat?

8 A bag of sugar weighs 1 kg. Nial uses $\frac{1}{4}$ of the bag to make some biscuits. Colleen uses $\frac{2}{3}$ of the remaining sugar to make a cake.

i How many grams of sugar are left?

ii What fraction of the bag of sugar is left?

9 Calculate

a $18 \div 2\frac{1}{4}$ **b** $2\frac{5}{8} \div 1\frac{1}{3}$

10 a The product of two fractions is $\frac{5}{6}$.
What could the two fractions be?

b The product of two fractions is $\frac{6}{35}$.
What could the two fractions be?

11 a Choose a starting fraction, such as $\frac{3}{7}$.

b Work out $\frac{1 - \text{your fraction}}{1 + \text{your fraction}}$ then $\frac{1 - \text{your new fraction}}{1 + \text{your new fraction}}$

c Repeat for several different starting fractions.

d Write what you notice and try to explain what has happened.

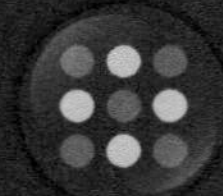

4d Percentage change

- A percentage is a fraction written as the number of parts per 100.

$$23\% = \frac{23}{100} \qquad 5\% = \frac{5}{100} = \frac{1}{20}$$

(÷5 applied to numerator and denominator)

- You can calculate a percentage of an amount using mental, written and calculator methods.

Example

Calculate 11% of £45.

Mental method

10% of £45 = £4.50
+ 1% of £45 = £0.45
11% of £45 = £4.95

Written method

11% of £45 = $\frac{11}{100}$ of 45
= $\frac{495}{100}$ = £4.95

Calculator method

11% of £45 = 0.11 of 45
= £4.95

- You can calculate a **percentage increase** or **decrease** in a single calculation using an equivalent decimal.

Example

a

In a sale all prices are reduced by 22%.
A pair of trainers normally cost £80.
What is the sale price of the pair of trainers?

b

Jasmine earns £24 a week from her newspaper round.
This week her wage is increased by 7%.
What is her new weekly wage?

a

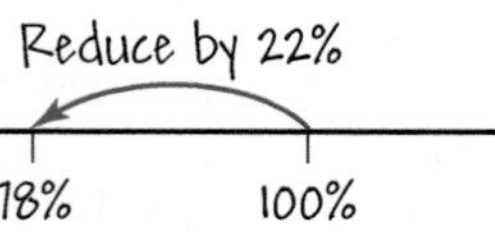

In the sale the prices decrease by 22%

Sale price = (100 − 22)% of old price
= 78% of £80
= 0.78 × 80
= £62.40

b

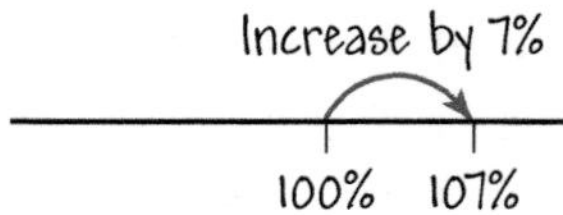

Jasmine's wage increases by 7%

New wage = (100 + 7)% of old wage
= 107% of £24
= 1.07 × £24
= £25.68

Exercise 4d

1 Calculate these using an appropriate method.

a	15% of £70	b	25% of 180 m
c	78% of 58 kg	d	35% of 240 ml
e	62% of £99	f	35% of 85 GB
g	45% of $58	h	99% of 99 m
i	3% of 120 mm	j	17.5% of 250 MB
k	3.5% of 3 m	l	4.75% of £27 000
m	60% of 245 km	n	105% of 665 g
o	11% of 6 tonnes	p	2% of £2 500 000

2 Calculate these percentage changes.

- **a** Increase £40 by 12%
- **b** Decrease £360 by 21%
- **c** Increase 48 km by 5%
- **d** Decrease 36 mm by 15%
- **e** Increase 125 kg by 18%
- **f** Decrease £3700 by 35%
- **g** Increase £19 by 17.5%
- **h** Decrease 68 kJ by 4.5%

Problem solving

3 Thomas can buy a QII Games Console for one cash payment of £299, or pay a deposit of 30% and then twelve equal monthly payments of £19.

Which is the better option? Explain and justify your answer.

Give all answers to 2 dp as necessary

4 **a** Heather weighs 45 kg. Two weeks later her weight has increased by 8%. What is Heather's new weight?

b In a sale all prices are reduced by 30%. A DVD costs £13 before the sale. What is the sale price of the DVD?

c Last month Chris scored 40 marks on a history test. This month he improves his score by 15%. How many marks did he score in his history test this month?

d Shahida is given £240 by her uncle. She spends 23% of the money. How much money does she have left?

5 Barry plays a computer game every week. Each week he improves his highest score by 13%. This week his highest score is 282 500.

- **a** What will his highest score be next week?
- **b** What was his highest score last week?

6 Imran is 6 years old and is 90 cm tall. His father notices that Imran has increased in height by 9% each year for the last two years. If Imran grows at 9% a year:

- **a** How tall will Imran be when he is 7 years old?
- **b** How tall will Imran be when he is 10 years old?
- **c** How tall will Imran be when he is 16 years old?
- **d** Do you think Imran will grow at 9% a year?

Explain your answer.

Did you know?

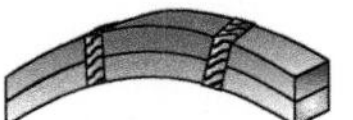

Metals expand when heated, for example, the length of a copper bar will increase by 0.17% if heated by 100°C. Differences in expansion rates are used to make bimetallic strips that bend when heated or cooled.

4e Percentage problems

- You can use **percentage change** to solve problems.

Example

In a sale all the prices are reduced by 20%.
A football shirt costs £36 in the sale.
What was the original price of the football shirt?

A 20% reduction means that the shirt cost 80% of the original amount.

You can use the **unitary method** to find 1% of the original price.

You can use the **inverse operation** method to find the original amount by division.

	80% of the original price	= £36	
÷80	1% of the original price	= £0.45	÷80
×100	100% of the original price	= £45	×100

To work out 80% of the price you multiply by 0.8

Original price £? → ×0.8 → Sale price £36
Sale price £36 → ÷0.8 → Original price £?

The inverse of multiplying by 0.8 is dividing by 0.8

Original price = Sale price ÷ 0.8
= £36 ÷ 0.8 = £45

Example

Next year the number of students at Notterhall Sports College is expected to increase by 15% to 966 students. How many students are there in the current year?

A 15% increase means that the number of students will increase to 115% of what it is in the current year.

Using the **unitary method**

115% of students in current year = 966 students
1% of students in current year = 966 ÷ 115
= 8.4 students
100% of students in current year = 8.4 × 100
= 840 students

Using the **inverse operation** method

To work out an increase of 15% you multiply by 1.15
The inverse of multiplying by 1.15 is dividing by 1.15
Students in current year = 966 ÷ 1.15
= 840 students

Exercise 4e

Problem solving

1 Jackson decides to increase the wages of everybody in his factory by 4%. Copy and complete his new payroll list.

Name	Old wage	New wage
James	£300	
Bernie	£275	
Vikki		£520
Rufus		£364

2 **a** A pair of trainers are on sale for £84 which is 70% of the original price. What was the original price of the trainers?

b A computer has been reduced in price by 25% to £345. What was the original price of the computer?

c A packet of McDitty's chocolate fingers is increased in mass. The label says that the packet is now 35% bigger. The weight of the packet is now 324 g. What was the original weight of a packet of McDitty's chocolate fingers?

3 **a** Gareth bought a computer game in a sale and saved £5. The label said that it was a 25% reduction. What was the original price of the computer game?

b Mandy bought a box of cereal on Monday. On Friday she bought a box of the same cereal but with 30% extra free. Mandy worked out that she got an extra 150 g of cereal in the new packet. How much cereal was there in the original packet?

4 Violet and Nita each bought an identical coat from the same shop. Violet bought hers on Saturday when there was 20% off the original price. Nita bought hers on Monday when there was 30% off the original price. Violet paid £15 more than Nita.

a What was the original price of the coat?

b How much did Violet pay for the coat?

c How much did Nita pay for the coat?

5 The population of the Earth in the year 2012 was 7078 million.

a If the population of the Earth has increased by 2% a year, what was the population of the Earth in 2011?

b What was the population of the Earth in the year 2000?

c Investigate the population of the Earth at different times in history.

4f Fractions, decimals and percentages

You can **convert** between **fractions**, **decimals** and **percentages** using a range of methods.

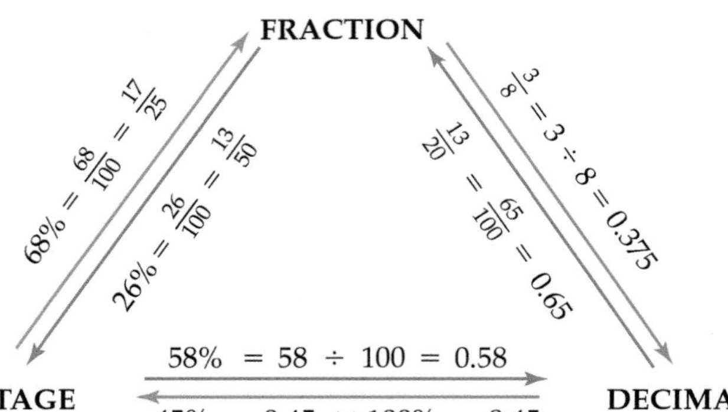

Example

Copy and complete this table.

Fraction	Decimal	Percentage
	0.325	
$\frac{3}{7}$		

$0.325 = \frac{325}{1000} = \frac{13}{40}$ (÷25)

$\frac{3}{7} = 3 \div 7$

$= 0.429$ (3 dp)

$0.325 = 0.325 \times 100\%$

$= 32.5\%$

$\frac{3}{7} = (3 \div 7) \times 100\%$

$= 42.9\%$ (1 dp)

Fraction	Decimal	Percentage
$\frac{13}{40}$	0.325	32.5%
$\frac{3}{7}$	0.429	42.9%

- You can express the **change** in an amount as a percentage of the original amount.

Example

A computer is reduced in price from £420 to £357.
What is the percentage reduction?

Price reduction $= £420 - £357$
$= £63$ — Calculate the reduction in price.

Reduction $= \frac{63}{420}$ of the original price — Express the reduction as a fraction.

Percentage reduction $= (63 \div 420) \times 100\%$
$= 15\%$ — Change the fraction into a percentage using division.

Check your answer by working out 15% reduction of £420 = 0.85 × 420 = £357

Exercise 4f

1 Copy and complete this table.
Clearly show your working out.

Fraction	$\frac{7}{40}$			$\frac{7}{12}$	
Decimal		0.07			0.0475
Percentage			135%		

Give your answers as
- decimals to 4 decimal places
- percentages to 2 decimal places
- fractions in their simplest form.

Problem solving

2 These are the marks scored by Seung in his recent exams.
He needs to score 35% or more to pass.

a In which subjects did he pass the exam?
Explain your answer.

b In which subject did he do the worst? Explain your answer.

c By changing each of his marks to a percentage, put the subjects in order from Seung's worst subject to his best.

EXAM REPORT	
Engineering	9/24
Maths	14/40
Media	45/56
German	11/30
Art	12/35
Geography	17/49
Sports Studies	34%

3 **a** An HD TV is reduced in price from £480 to £408.
What is the percentage reduction?

b Last month Vikram earned £2300. This month his pay is £2369. What is the percentage increase in Vikram's pay?

c Last year, the average number of people watching Manchester Rovers home games was 68 000. This year there are an average of 71 400 people watching the games.
What is the percentage increase in the crowd at Manchester Rovers?

4 A water tank contains 800 litres of water. At night the water freezes and expands in volume to 872 litres of ice.
Use this information to work out the percentage increase in volume of water when it turns into ice.

5 Over time the prices of things you buy usually increase.
These are the prices of eight items in 1987 and 2012.

a For each item, work out the percentage increase (or decrease) over the 25-year period.

b Investigate price increases over longer periods of time.

c Find out why prices usually increase.

Object	1987 price	2012 price	% increase or decrease
House	£23 000	£195 000	
Salary	£7000	£23 000	
TV	£300	£150	
Petrol (litre)	£0.34	£1.04	
Marz bar	£0.16	£0.45	
Milk (pint)	£0.20	£0.36	
Man Utd season ticket	£64	£437	
Portable music player	£80	£20	

4 MySummary

Check out

You should now be able to ...

Test it ➡

Questions

		Level	Questions
✓	Convert between decimals and fractions and order them.	6	1 – 3
✓	Add and subtract fractions with different denominators.	6	4, 5
✓	Multiply and divide fractions.	7	6 – 8
✓	Calculate percentages of an amount and percentage changes.	7	9, 10
✓	Calculate an original amount from the result of a percentage change.	7	11, 12
✓	Convert between percentages, fractions and decimals.	7	13, 14

Language	Meaning	Example
Terminating decimal	A decimal whose last digits are all zero	0.125
Recurring decimal	A decimal whose last digits have a repeating (non-zero) pattern	$0.\dot{3} = 0.3333...$
Percentage	A fraction where the denominator is 100	50% of 10 is 5
Numerator	The number on the top of a fraction	In $\frac{2}{3}$ 2 is the numerator 3 is the denominator
Denominator	The number on the bottom of a fraction	
Common denominator	If two fractions have the same denominator they are said to both have a common denominator	$\frac{3}{4}$ and $\frac{1}{4}$ have a common denominator of 4.
Mixed number	A mixed number is written in terms of both integers and fractions	$2\frac{1}{2}$ is an example of a mixed number
Improper fraction	A fraction in which the numerator is larger than the denominator	$\frac{7}{5}$ is an improper since $7 > 5$
Equivalent fractions	Fractions that have the same value	$\frac{3}{5}$ and $\frac{15}{25}$

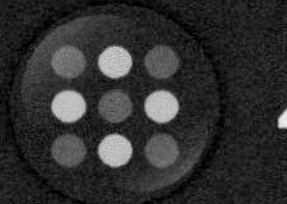

4 MyReview

1 Write these fractions as decimals
Do not use a calculator.

a $\frac{19}{25}$ **b** $\frac{36}{60}$ **c** $\frac{2}{9}$ **d** $\frac{13}{11}$

2 Write these decimals as fractions.
Do not use a calculator.

a 0.625 **b** 0.16 **c** $0.\dot{6}$ **d** 3.2

3 Put these numbers in order from lowest to highest.

a $\frac{1}{9}$ $\frac{1}{7}$ 0.1 $\frac{2}{15}$

b $\frac{3}{7}$ $0.\dot{4}$ $\frac{5}{12}$ 0.4

4 Calculate these and give your answer as a fraction in its simplest form

a $\frac{2}{7} + \frac{4}{21}$ **b** $\frac{9}{10} - \frac{2}{15}$

c $\frac{4}{5} + \frac{5}{6}$ **d** $\frac{11}{18} - \frac{2}{27}$

5 Calculate these; write your answers as improper fractions.

a $1\frac{2}{3} + 3\frac{1}{7}$ **b** $4\frac{1}{10} - 2\frac{5}{6}$

6 Use a mental method to calculate these.

a $\frac{2}{7}$ of £56 **b** $1\frac{2}{3}$ of 2 m

7 Calculate these using a mental or written method; simplify your answers.

a $14 \times \frac{5}{21}$ **b** $\frac{2}{11} \times \frac{33}{40}$

8 Calculate and simplify your answers.

a $12 \div \frac{3}{4}$ **b** $\frac{3}{10} \div \frac{4}{15}$

9 Calculate these percentages using a suitable method.

a 35% of 880 **b** 98% of 1230

c 110% of 752 **d** 5.7% of 24

10 Calculate these percentage changes.

a Increase 70 by 5%

b Decrease 17 by 32%

11 A car is reduced in price by 30%.
The new price is £5250.
What was the original price?

12 This year a school has 240 students in year 7, an increase of approximately 12% from the year before. How many students were there the year before?

13 An oil painting increases in value from £1200 to £1560.
What is the percentage increase?

14 A colour printer is reduced in price from £250 to £180.
What is the percentage reduction?

What next?

Score		
0 – 5		Your knowledge of this topic is still developing. To improve look at Formative test: 2C-4; MyMaths: 1015, 1016, 1017, 1040, 1046, 1047, 1060, 1074, 1075, 1302 and 1934
6 – 11		You are gaining a secure knowledge of this topic. To improve look at InvisiPen: 143, 144, 145, 152, 153, 154, 161 and 162
12 – 14		You have mastered this topic. Well done, you are ready to progress!

4 MyPractice

4a

1 Change these fractions into decimals using division. Use an appropriate method.

Give your answers to 5 dp where appropriate.

a $\frac{9}{16}$ b $\frac{5}{17}$ c $\frac{3}{13}$ d $\frac{6}{7}$ e $\frac{11}{19}$

2 Place $<$ or $>$ between these pairs of numbers to show which number is the largest.

a $0.4 \square \frac{3}{7}$ b $\frac{6}{13} \square \frac{7}{15}$ c $\frac{5}{8} \square 0.6$ d $0.39 \square \frac{7}{19}$

3 Put these fractions and decimals in order from lowest to highest.

a $\frac{8}{13}$ 0.623 $\frac{5}{8}$ 0.63 b $\frac{3}{13}$ $\frac{4}{17}$ 0.229 0.23

4b

4 Work out

a $\frac{12}{15} - \frac{7}{18}$ b $\frac{13}{15} + \frac{11}{25}$ c $\frac{14}{27} + \frac{13}{18}$ d $\frac{7}{14} + \frac{7}{21}$

e $\frac{13}{16} + \frac{7}{20}$ f $\frac{24}{35} - \frac{5}{28}$ g $\frac{23}{36} + \frac{7}{54}$ h $\frac{13}{60} + \frac{8}{15}$

5 Hector has $2\frac{1}{2}$ litres of water. Jenny has $\frac{3}{5}$ of a litre of blackcurrant cordial. They mix the two drinks together. What is the total amount of liquid?

6 Work out

a $2\frac{1}{5} + \frac{1}{3}$ b $1\frac{1}{4} - \frac{5}{8}$ c $3\frac{2}{5} + 1\frac{2}{3}$ d $2\frac{5}{8} - 1\frac{11}{12}$

4c

7 Calculate

a $\frac{3}{4}$ of 5 yards b $\frac{5}{12}$ of 60 kg c $\frac{3}{8}$ of 20 mm d $\frac{4}{13}$ of 39 km

e $1\frac{5}{16}$ of 40 miles f $3\frac{7}{8}$ of 200 m^2 g $1\frac{5}{12}$ of 340 $m\ell$ h $3\frac{8}{25}$ of 1 century

8 Calculate

a $\frac{4}{7} \times \frac{5}{3}$ b $\frac{2}{5} \times \frac{3}{8}$ c $\frac{5}{6} \times \frac{4}{5}$ d $\frac{7}{8} \times \frac{3}{4}$

e $\frac{14}{15} \times \frac{12}{35}$ f $\frac{12}{35} \times \frac{15}{21}$ g $\frac{22}{16} \times \frac{32}{18}$ h $\frac{5}{8} \times \frac{24}{15}$

9 Calculate

a $4 \div \frac{4}{7}$ b $12 \div \frac{4}{3}$ c $16 \div \frac{8}{9}$ d $10 \div \frac{5}{7}$

e $3 \div \frac{5}{11}$ f $14 \div \frac{7}{4}$ g $15 \div \frac{10}{11}$ h $18 \div \frac{9}{13}$

4c

10 Calculate

a $\frac{4}{7} \div \frac{5}{8}$ **b** $\frac{6}{9} \div \frac{6}{7}$ **c** $\frac{8}{11} \div \frac{3}{4}$ **d** $\frac{8}{13} \div \frac{4}{7}$

e $\frac{5}{6} \div \frac{4}{9}$ **f** $\frac{9}{10} \div \frac{3}{5}$ **g** $\frac{3}{14} \div \frac{12}{35}$ **h** $\frac{8}{9} \div \frac{32}{45}$

4d

11 Calculate these percentage changes.

a Increase £50 by 28%

b Decrease £640 by 45%

c Increase 180 km by 6%

d Decrease 270 mm by 3.5%

e Increase 85 kg by 8%

f Decrease £9 000 000 by 1.2%

12 a Monica earns £35 each weekend, working in her mum's shop. Next weekend her pay will be increased by 4%. How much will Monica earn next weekend?

b In a sale all prices are reduced by 15%. A DVD costs £12.49 before the sale. What is the sale price of the DVD?

4e

13 a A laptop is on sale for £330 which is 60% of the original price.
What was the original price of the laptop?

b A Porsche 911 increased in price from 1982 to 2007 by 263%.
The price for a Porsche 911 in 2007 was £60 621.
What was the price of the Porsche in 1982?

14 a Kerry bought a mobile phone in a sale and saved £12.
The label said that it was a 15% reduction.
What was the original price of the mobile phone?

b In a special offer, a packet of biscuits says that it contains 20% extra.
The weight of the packet is 64 g heavier than it was before the special offer.
How much did the packet of biscuits used to weigh?

4f

15 Copy and complete this table. Show clearly your working out.

Fraction	Decimal	Percentage
$\frac{7}{15}$		
	0.995	
		12.5%
$\frac{4}{13}$		
	1.0377	

Give your answers as
- decimals to 4 decimal places
- percentages to 2 decimal places
- fractions in their simplest form.

16 a An DVD costs £13. In a sale the price is reduced to £11.44.
What is the percentage reduction?

b A laptop is reduced in price from £880 to £836.
What is the percentage reduction?

MyAssessment 1

These questions will test your knowledge of the topics in Chapters 1 to 4.
They give you practice in the questions that you may see in your GCSE exams.
There are 70 marks in total.

1 Here is a set of statements. Say whether each statement is true (T) or false (F).

- **a** One of the prime factors of 375 is 3. (1 mark)
- **b** The HCF of 20 and 30 is 2. (1 mark)
- **c** 121 is divisible by 3. (1 mark)
- **d** 51 is a prime number. (1 mark)
- **e** The LCM of 20 and 30 is 60. (1 mark)

2 Find the value of these roots where possible.

- **a** $\sqrt{25}$ (1 mark) **b** $\sqrt[3]{27}$ (1 mark)
- **c** $\sqrt[3]{-125}$ (1 mark) **d** $\sqrt{-49}$ (1 mark)

3 Simplify each of these. Leave your answer as a single power of the number.

- **a** $3^4 \times 3^2$ (1 mark) **b** $5^4 \div 5^3$ (1 mark)
- **c** $5^4 \div 4^5$ (1 mark) **d** $2^6 \times 2^3$ (1 mark)

4 Round these numbers to the accuracy stated.

- **a** 3698 to the nearest 100 (1 mark)
- **b** 14.978 to 2 dp (1 mark)
- **c** 32.95 km to the nearest 100 metres (1 mark)

5 Use a trial-and-improvement method to find the roots of these numbers to 2 dp.

- **a** 40 (2 marks) **b** $\sqrt[3]{60}$ (2 marks)

6 Arrange these quantities in order of size from smallest to largest.

2 cℓ 2 pints 2 mℓ 2 litres 2 gallons (3 marks)

7 The area of this triangle is 35 cm².
Calculate the vertical height of the triangle. (2 marks)

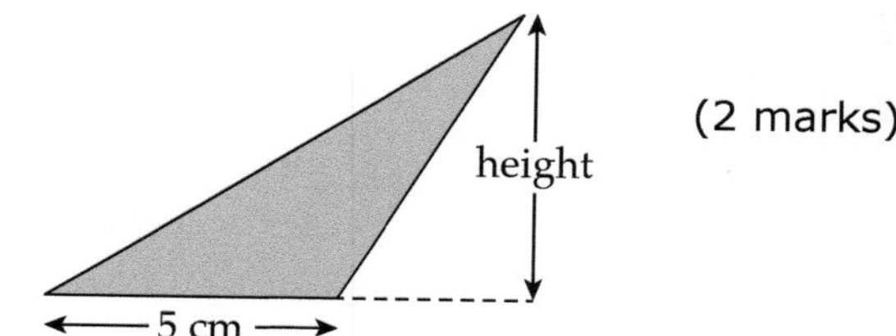

8 Each of these two shapes has the same area of 120 cm² and the same vertical height of 6 cm. Calculate

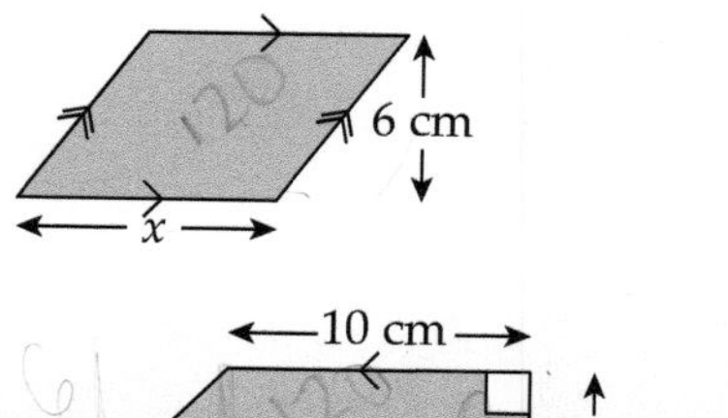

- **a** the base length, x of the parallelogram (2 marks)
- **b** the base length, y of the trapezium. (3 marks)

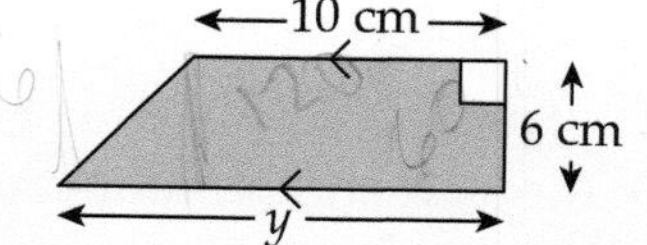

9 A circular hole, 5.4 cm in diameter, is being cut into a piece of wood 8 cm by 8 cm.

a What is the circumference of the hole? (2 marks)

b What is the area of wood that remains after the hole is drilled? Use $\pi = 3.14$. (3 marks)

10 Given that $x = 2$, find the value of these algebraic expressions.

a $3x^2$ (1 mark) **b** $(3x)^2$ (1 mark)

c $3x^{-2}$ (1 mark) **b** $(3x)^{-2}$ (1 mark)

11 Simplify these expressions, leaving your answer in index form.

a $p^2 \times p^7$ (1 mark) **b** $3g^8 \div g^5$ (1 mark)

c $(k^7)^2$ (1 mark) **d** $(5m^4)^3$ (1 mark)

12 Simplify these expressions by collecting like terms.

a $3x^2 + 4x - x^2 + 9x - 3$ (1 mark) **b** $11p^3 - 4p + 3p^3 - p^2 + 9p$ (1 mark)

c $-8t + 4t^2 - 5t + 8t^3 - t$ (1 mark) **d** $3n^2 - 4n - 7n^2 - 6n + 4n^2$ (1 mark)

13 A cuboid has side lengths x, $x + 3$ and $x - 1$.
Calculate the total surface area of the cuboid and give the answer in the simplest form. (4 marks)

14 Factorise these expressions.

a $3x^2 + 4x$ (1 mark) **b** $10p^2 - 5pq$ (1 mark)

15 Rearrange these formulae to make the letter in bold the subject.

a $v = u + a\boldsymbol{t}$ (1 mark) **b** $V = \pi r^2\boldsymbol{h}$ (1 mark)

16 A photographic image $8\frac{1}{2}$ inches long by $5\frac{1}{4}$ inches wide is being cropped by $\frac{1}{3}$ inch along its length and width.

a What is area of the original image? (2 marks)

b What is the new length and width of the new image? (2 marks)

c What is the difference in area between the original and new images? (3 marks)

17 A new car was bought at a cost of £12 000. Each year the value depreciates by 15%.

a What is the car worth after one year? (2 marks)

b What is the car worth after three years? (3 marks)

18 A vase was bought at a car boot sale for £4.75 and was sold a year later at an auction for £67. What was the percentage profit? (3 marks)

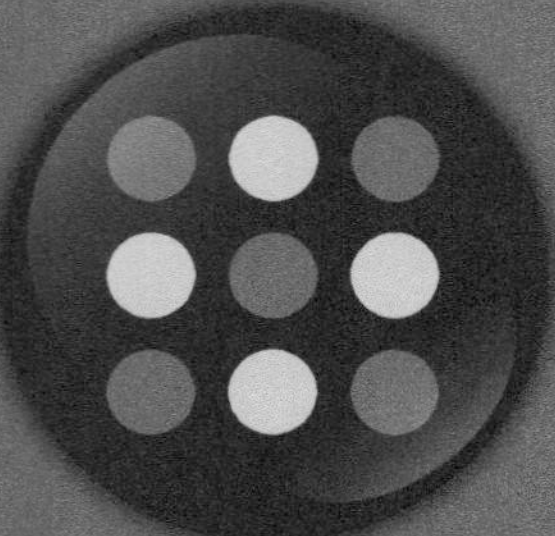

5 Angles and 2D shapes

Introduction

In computer games, 3D characters and objects are made from thousands of triangles. Computer programmers write a piece of computer code to represent a triangle and then repeat this over and over again to represent much more complex shapes. The triangles are then given different colours to create the illusion of three dimensions.

What's the point?

The triangle is the most basic polygon. By understanding triangles, people can create highly sophisticated shapes in computer technology and in architecture.

Objectives

By the end of this chapter, you will have learned how to ...

- Reason geometrically using the properties of angles at a point and on a line and intersecting and parallel lines.
- Recognise the different types of triangles and quadrilaterals and use their properties.
- Recognise the different types of polygons and calculate interior and exterior angles for regular polygons.
- Identify congruent shapes.

Check in

1 Use a protractor to measure these angles.
State whether the angles are acute, obtuse or reflex.

a AOB **b** AOC **c** AOD

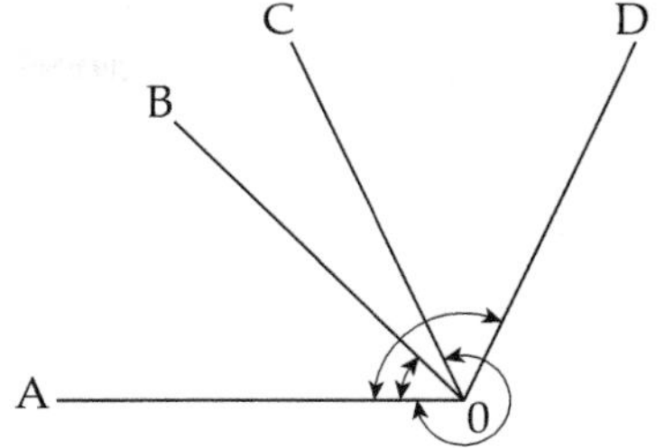

2 Solve these equations.

a $5a = 180$ **b** $8b + 36 = 180$ **c** $15c = 360$

3 What are the interior angles of a square?
If we tilt one of the sides by 10°,
what are the interior angles now?
If we add them all up, are they the
same as for the square?

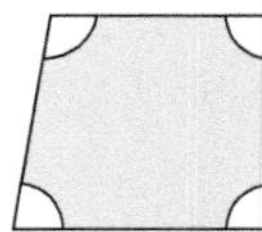

Starter problem

A tessellation is a tiling pattern with no gaps or overlaps.
Which regular polygons tessellate?
Which combinations of different regular polygons will tessellate?

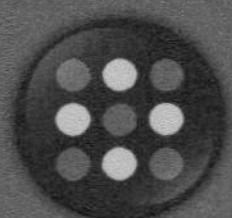

5a Angles and parallel lines

Here are some useful geometrical facts.

These facts can help you to find missing angles.

360° 180° 90°

▲ There are 360° at a point.

▲ There are 180° on a straight line.

▲ **Perpendicular** lines meet at right angles.

Parallel lines are always the same distance apart.

Vertically opposite angles are equal.

When two lines **intersect**, 4 angles are formed.

The 2 pink, acute angles are equal. The 2 blue, obtuse angles are equal.

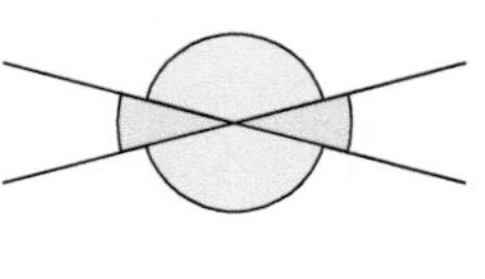

When a line intersects two parallel lines, 8 angles are formed.

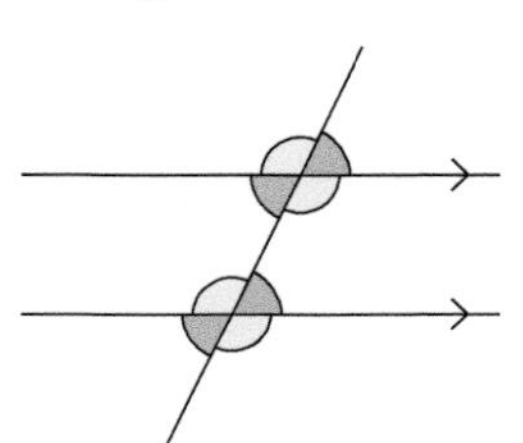

The 4 pink, acute angles are equal. The 4 blue, obtuse angles are equal.

Alternate angles are equal.

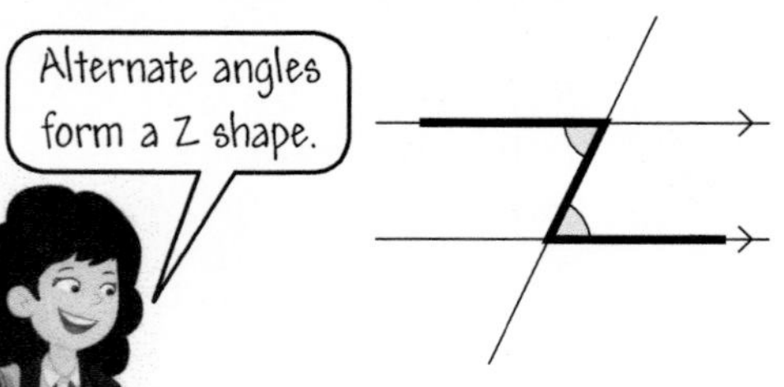

Corresponding angles are equal.

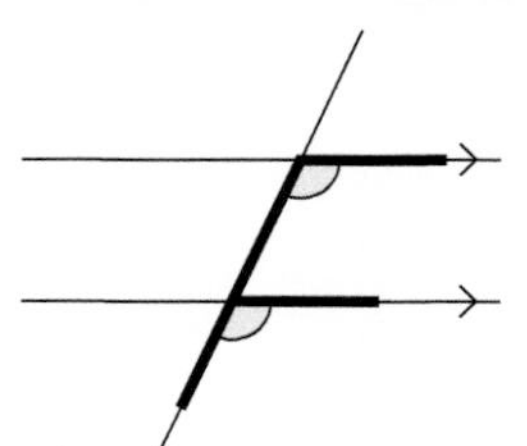

Corresponding angles form an F shape.

Example

Calculate the values of the angles a, b and c.

$a = 135°$ Alternate angles are equal.

$b = 45°$ Angles on a straight line add to 180°.

$c = 135°$ Corresponding angles are equal.
or Vertically opposite angles are equal.
or Angles on a straight line add to 180°.

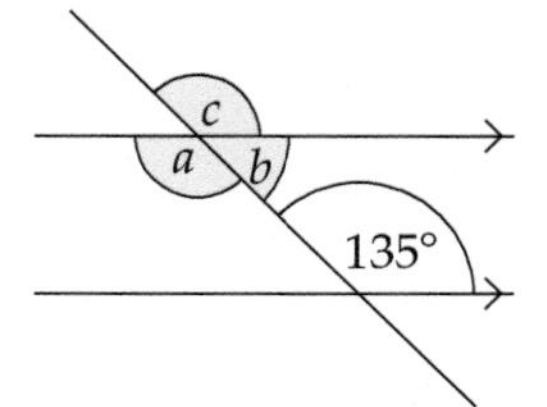

Exercise 5a

1 Calculate the unknown angles.

a

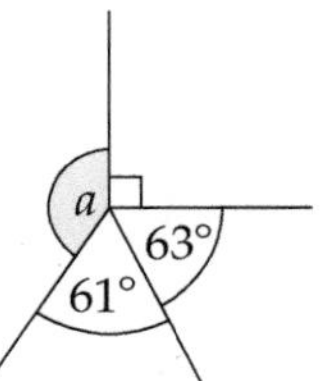

b

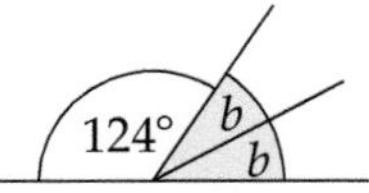

c

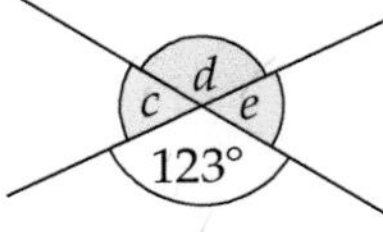

2 Calculate the angles marked with a letter, giving a reason in each case.

a

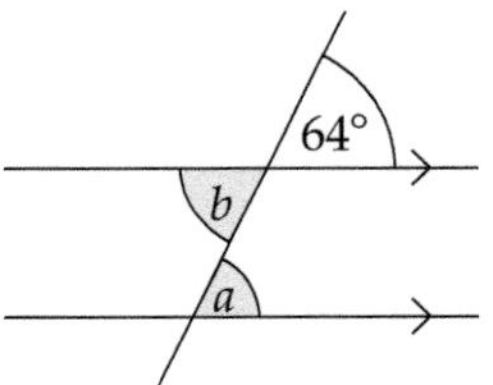

b

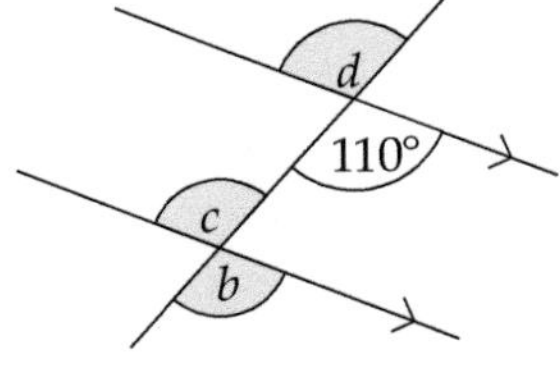

c

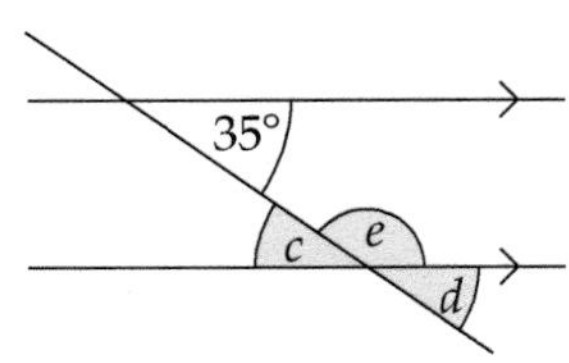

2 **d**

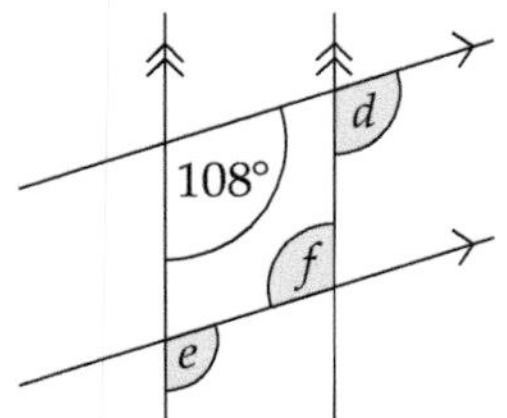

e

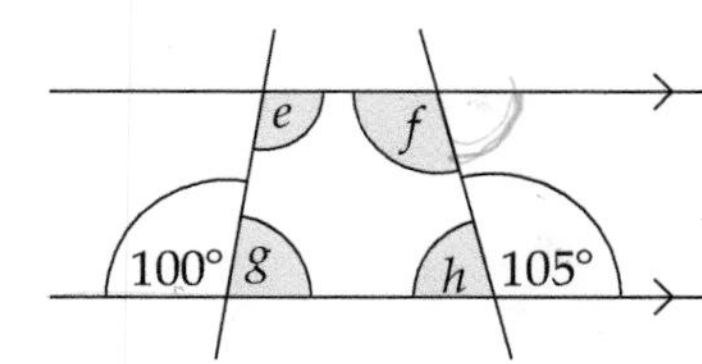

f

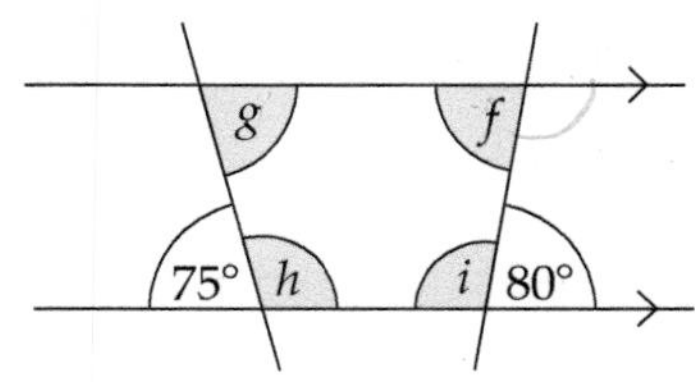

3 Calculate the value of the letters.

a

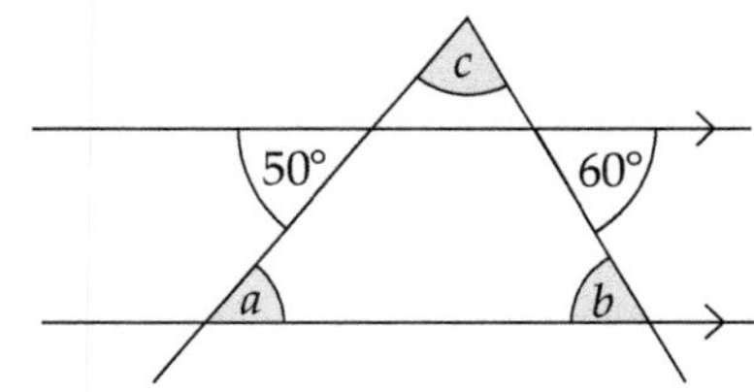

b

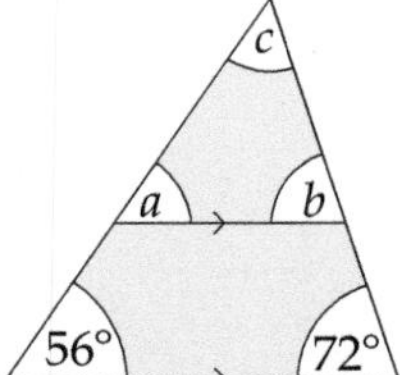

Problem solving

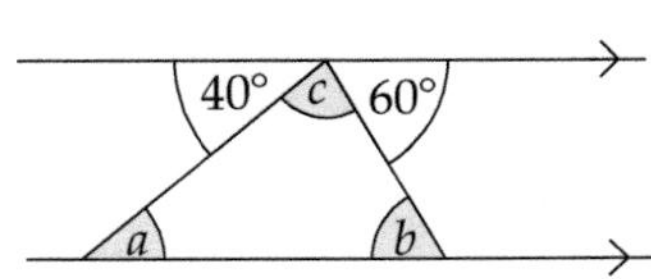

4 **a** Find the values of a and b.

b Using angles on a straight line, find the value of c.

c Find the total of a, b and c.

d Choose your own values for the angles marked 40° and 60° and find the new total of a, b and c.

e What does this prove?

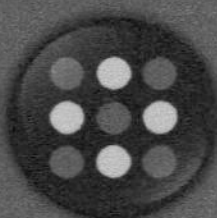

5b Properties of a triangle and a quadrilateral

- The **interior** angles of a **triangle** add to 180°
- The **exterior** angle of a triangle is equal to the sum of the two opposite interior angles.

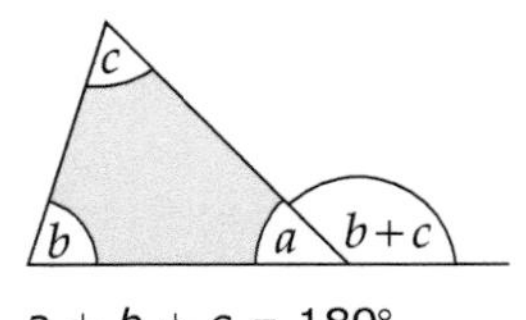

$a + b + c = 180°$

Equilateral

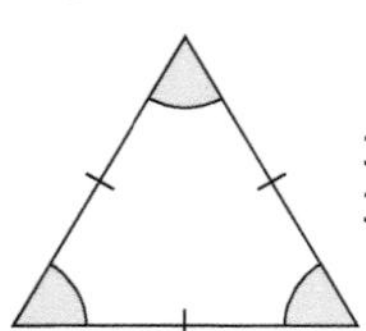

3 equal sides
3 equal angles

Isosceles

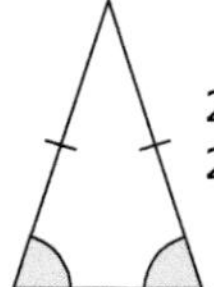

2 equal sides
2 equal angles

Scalene

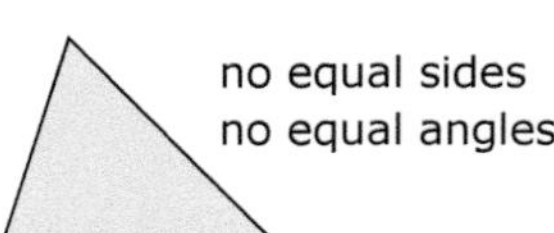

no equal sides
no equal angles

Right-angled

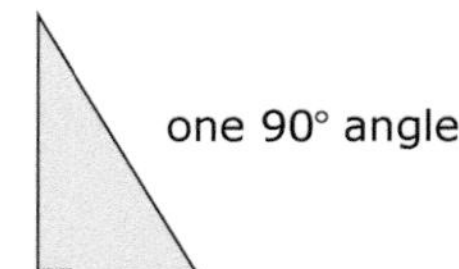

one 90° angle

- The interior angles of a **quadrilateral** add to 360°.

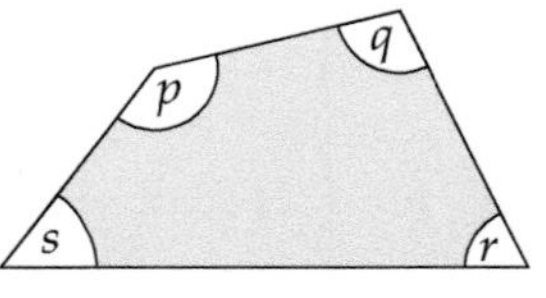

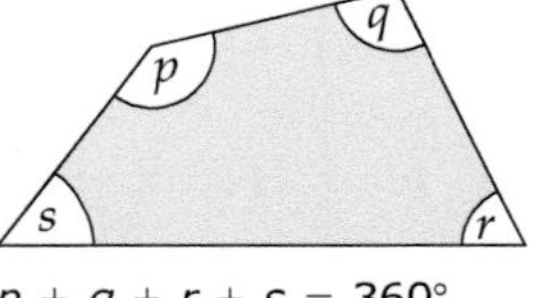

$p + q + r + s = 360°$

You should know the mathematical name of these quadrilaterals.

Square

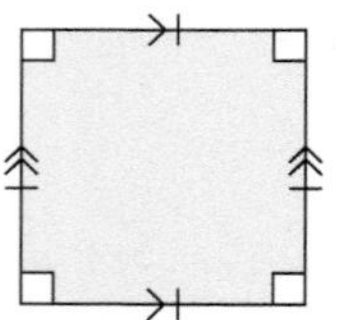

4 equal sides
4 90° angles
2 sets of parallel sides

Rectangle

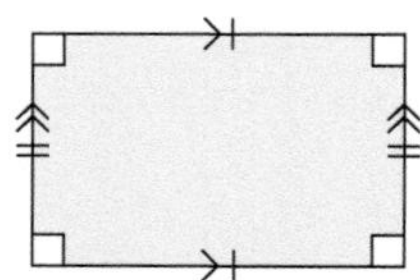

2 sets of equal sides
4 90° angles
2 sets of parallel sides

Rhombus

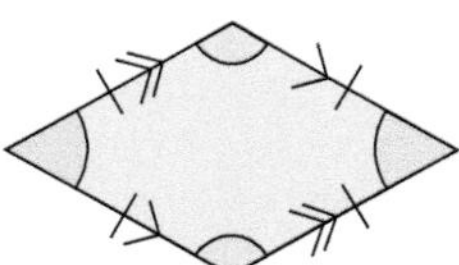

4 equal sides
2 pairs of equal angles
2 sets of parallel sides

Parallelogram

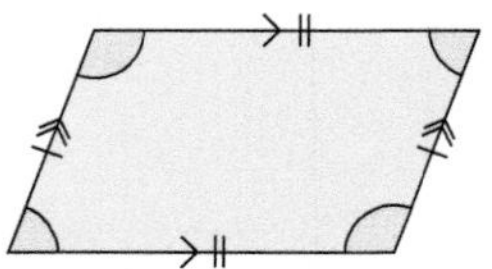

2 sets of equal sides
2 pairs of equal angles
2 sets of parallel sides

Trapezium

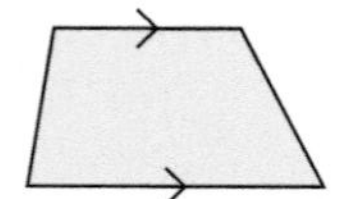

1 set of parallel sides

Isosceles trapezium

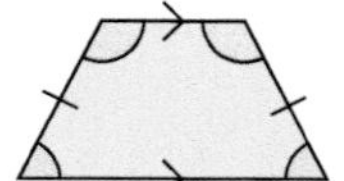

1 set of equal sides
2 pairs of equal angles
1 set of parallel sides

Kite

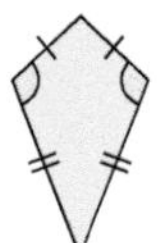

2 sets of equal sides
1 pair of equal angles
no parallel sides

Arrowhead

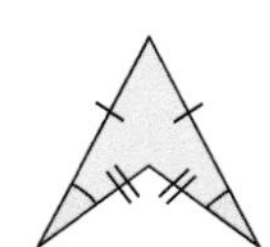

2 sets of equal sides
1 pair of equal angles
no parallel sides

Exercise 5b

1 Calculate the third angle in each of these triangles and state the type of triangle.

   a 60°, 60° b 33°, 114°

   c 36°, 54° d 71°, 29°

2 Name the different types of quadrilaterals you can see in this regular hexagon.

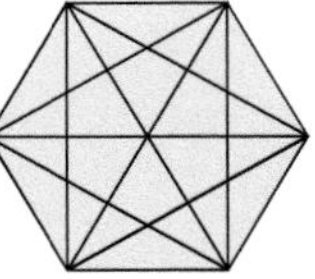

3 Calculate the fourth angle in each of these quadrilaterals. State the type of quadrilateral – there could be several answers for each question.

   a 45°, 45°, 135° b 47°, 63°, 125°

   c 20°, 20°, 65° d 20°, 20°, 270°

4 Calculate the value of the unknown angles.

   a b

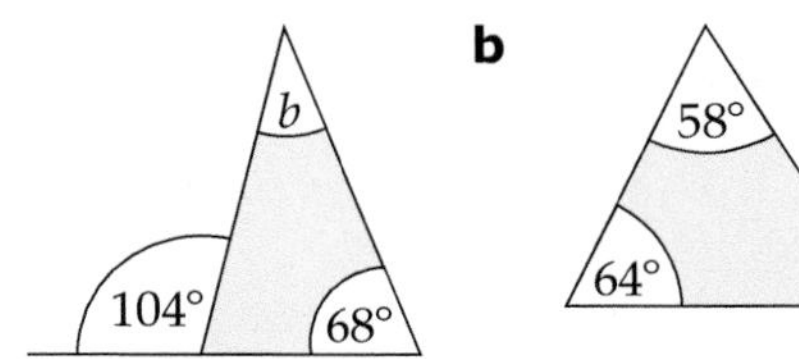

   c

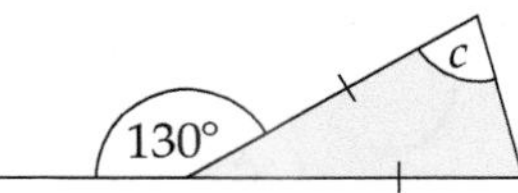

   d

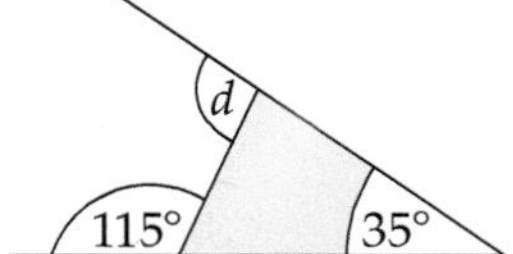

Problem solving

5 Name the quadrilaterals with diagonals that

   a bisect each other

   b are perpendicular

   c are equal in length

   d are equal in length and are perpendicular

   e are equal in length but are not perpendicular.

6 Two identical equilateral triangles are placed together edge to edge.

   a What is the name of the shape that is formed?

   b Explain the properties of this shape to justify your answer.

7 A rectangle is drawn inside a circle of radius 6 cm.
The rectangle fits along two perpendicular radii of the circle.

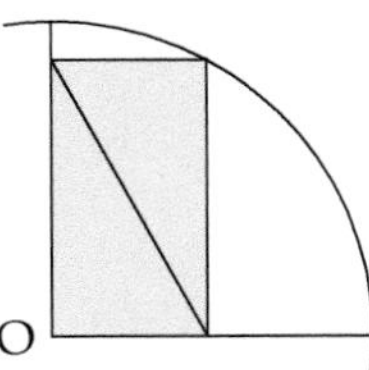

   a Find the length of the diagonal of the rectangle.

   b Can you draw any other rectangles within the circle that have the same length diagonal?

Did you know?

▲ A red kite is a bird of prey. A hovering toy kite is named after the bird and the mathematical shape after the toy!

5c Properties of a polygon

- A **polygon** is a 2D shape with straight sides.

You should know the names of these polygons.

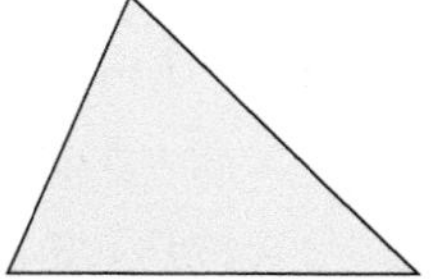

Triangle: 3 sides

Quadrilateral: 4 sides

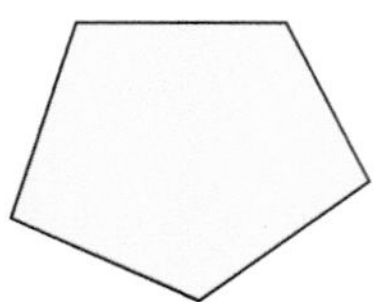

Pentagon: 5 sides

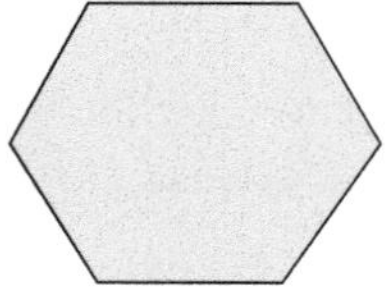

Hexagon: 6 sides

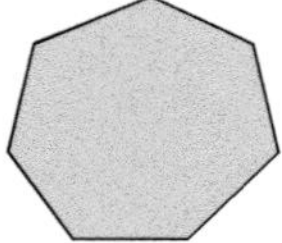

Heptagon: 7 sides

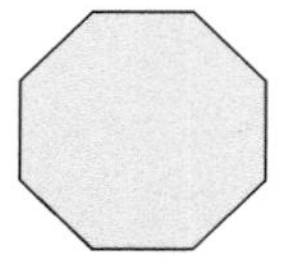

Octagon: 8 sides

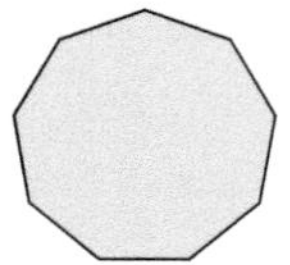

Nonagon: 9 sides

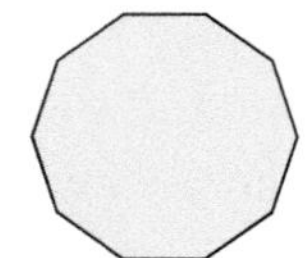

Decagon: 10 sides

You call the angles inside a shape **interior** angles.

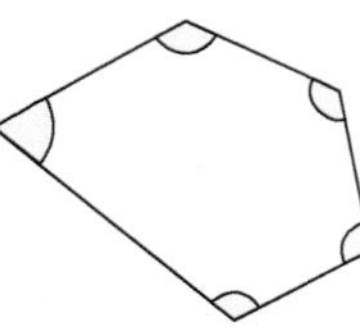

You can find the **exterior** angles of a 2D shape by extending one side at each corner.

- Interior angle + exterior angle = 180°

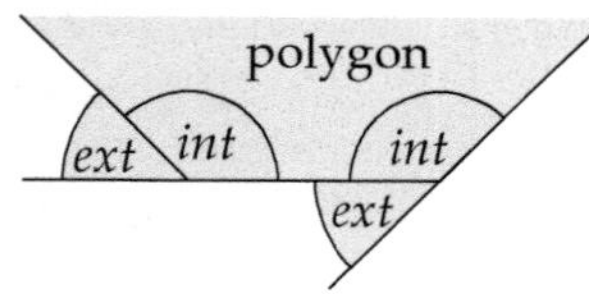

Angles on a straight line add to 180°.

- The exterior angles of any polygon add to 360°.

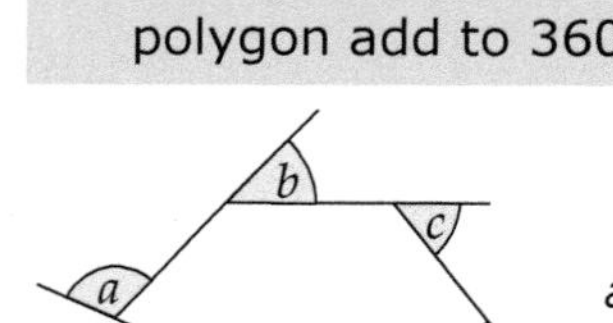

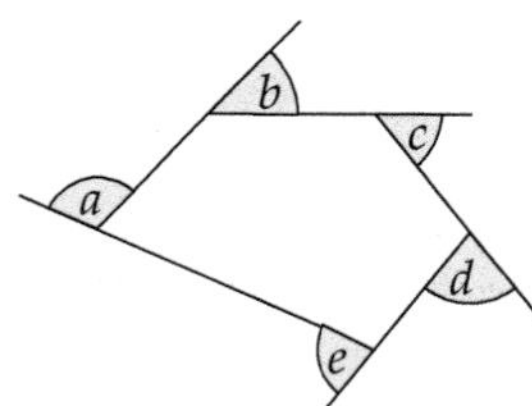

$a + b + c + d + e = 360°$

- A **regular** shape has equal sides *and* equal angles.

A regular pentagon has 5 equal sides and 5 equal angles.

Example

Calculate the exterior and interior angle of a regular octagon.

The exterior angles of any polygon add to 360° and there are 8 equal exterior angles in a regular octagon.

$360° \div 8 = 45°$ Each exterior angle is 45°

$180° - 45° = 135°$ Each interior angle is 135°

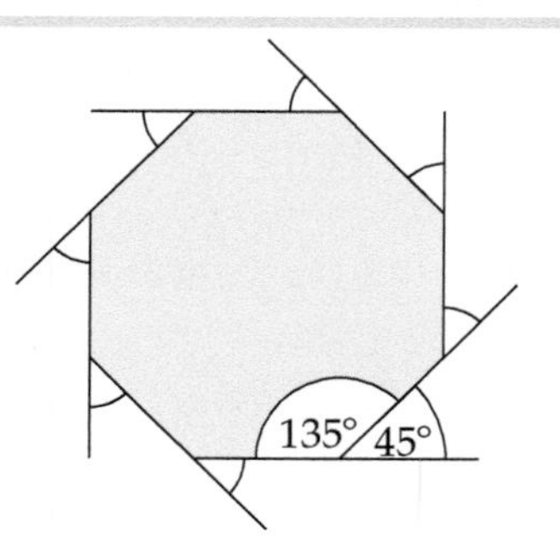

Exercise 5c

1 A **tessellation** is a tiling pattern with no gaps. Tessellate each polygon on square grid paper.

a 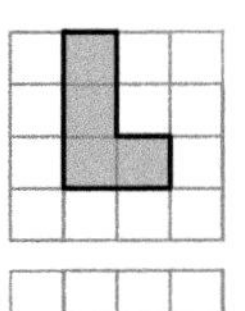

b 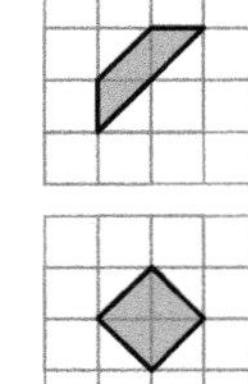

c

d

2 When you draw the diagonal of a quadrilateral, two triangles are formed.
The sum of the interior angles of a quadrilateral is $2 \times 180° = 360°$

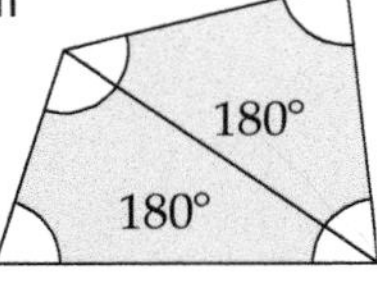

a Draw a pentagon and draw the diagonals from one vertex to form three triangles.

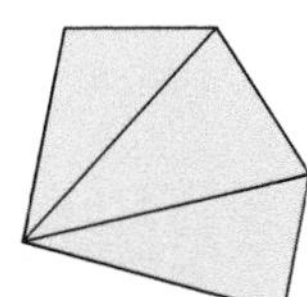

2 b Copy and complete the table for all polygons up to a decagon.

Name	Number of triangles	Sum of the interior angles
triangle	1	$1 \times 180° = 180°$
quadrilateral	2	$2 \times 180° = 360°$
pentagon	3	

3 Calculate the exterior and interior angles of

a an equilateral triangle

b a regular hexagon

c a regular nonagon

d a regular decagon

e a regular 18-sided polygon

f a regular 24-sided polygon.

Problem solving

4 Regular pentagons do not tessellate, rhombuses are needed to fill in the gaps.

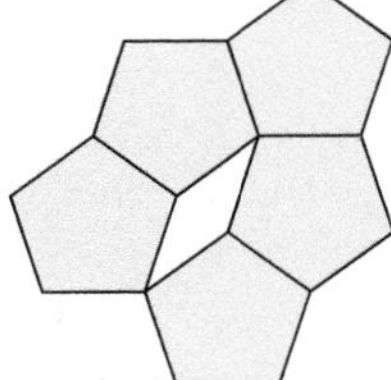

a Calculate the size of the exterior angle of a regular pentagon.

b Calculate the size of the interior angle of a regular pentagon.

c Calculate each of the four angles in the rhombus.

5 Draw a circle.
Use a protractor to mark off points on the circumference at 60° intervals at 0°, 60°, 120° etc.
Draw the regular hexagon and six of the diagonals.
Cut out the 12 triangles and colour the obtuse angles.

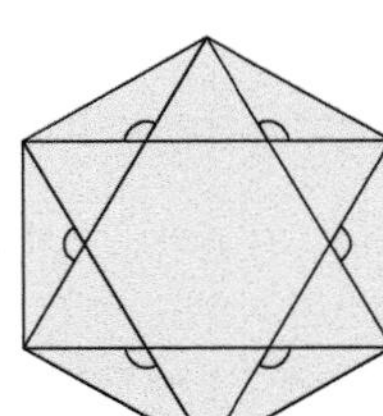

a Rearrange the six isosceles triangles to make a regular hexagon.

b Use angles at a point to calculate this obtuse angle.

c Hence state the value of the interior angle of a regular hexagon.

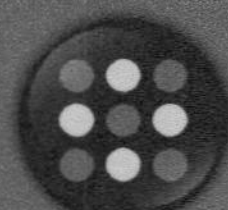

5d Congruent shapes

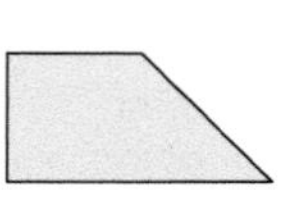
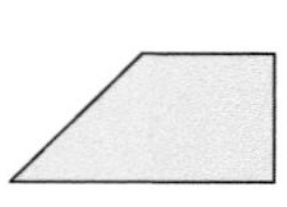
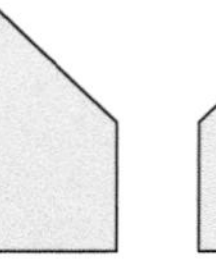
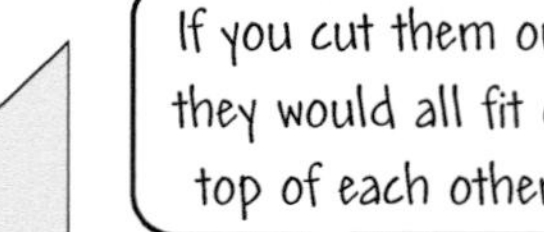

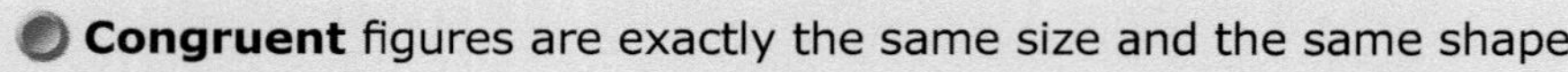

Congruent figures are exactly the same size and the same shape.

Example

Write the letters of the congruent shapes.

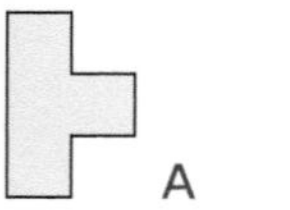
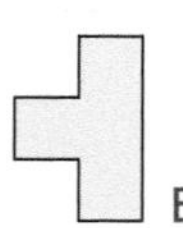
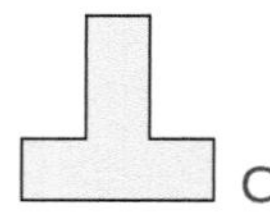
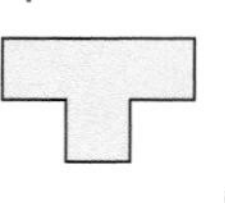
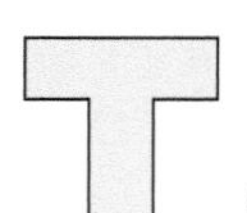

A B C D E

A, B and D are congruent
C and E are congruent.

The figures are the same size and the same shape.

If shapes are congruent, then
- **corresponding angles** are equal
- **corresponding sides** are equal.

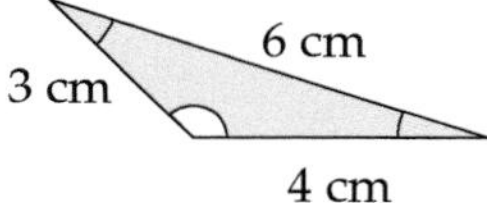

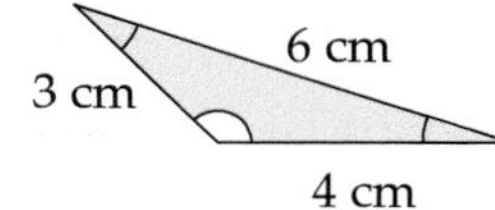

Example

The green triangle and the yellow triangle are congruent. State the lengths of

a AB
b AC
c BC

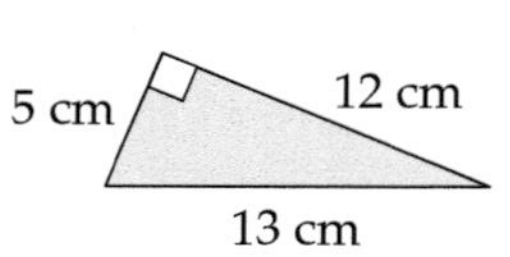

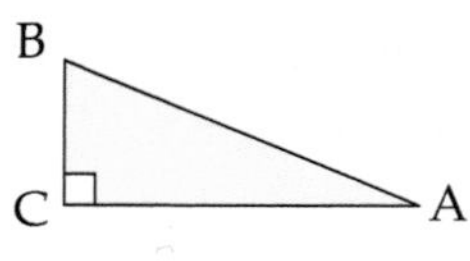

Rotate and flip over the yellow triangle so that the triangle could fit on top of the green triangle.

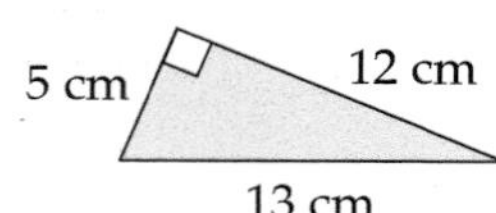

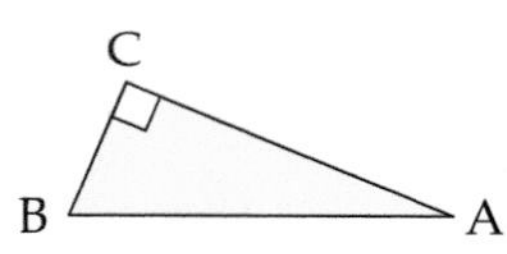

Compare the triangles.

a AB = 13 cm
b AC = 12 cm
c BC = 5 cm

Exercise 5d

1 Draw the shape that is not congruent to the others.

a

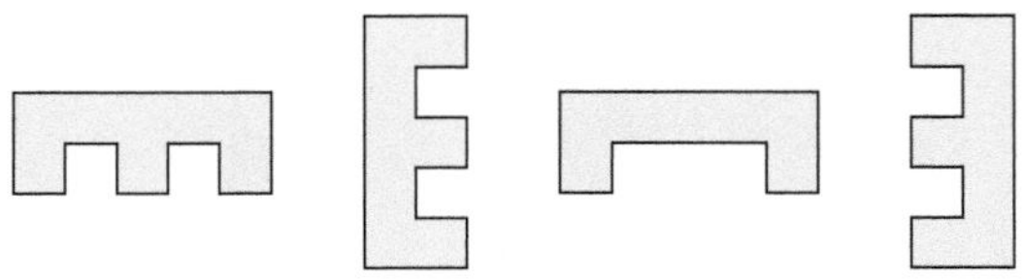

b

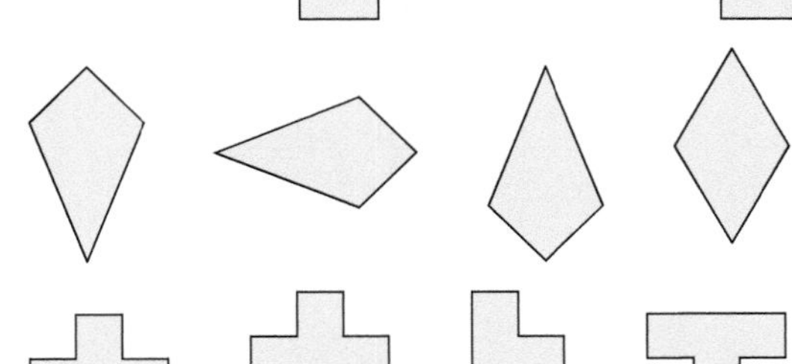

c

d

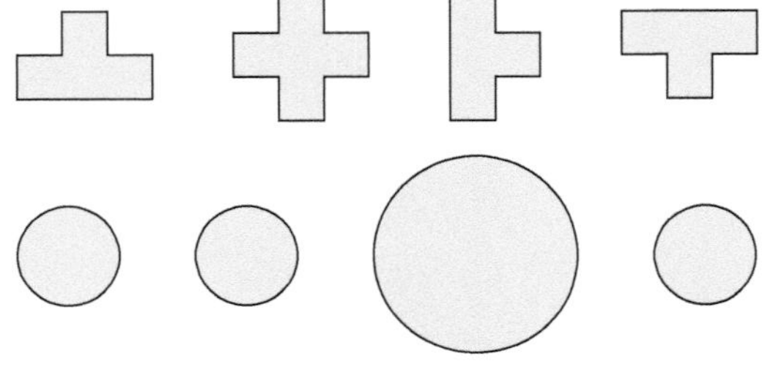

2 **a** Which triangles are congruent to the green triangle?

b Which triangles are congruent to the orange triangle?

c Which triangle is not congruent to the others?

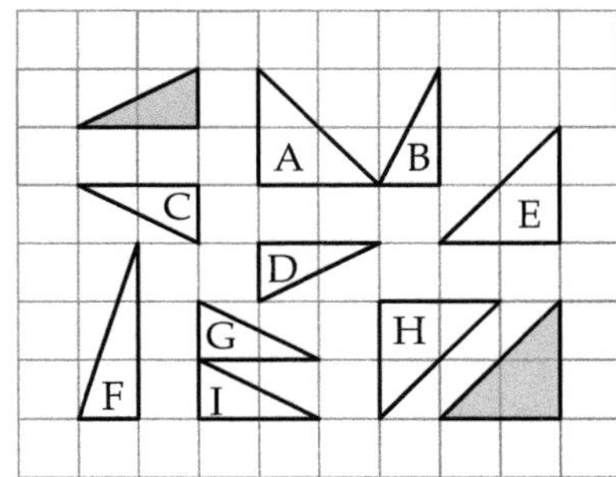

Problem solving

3 The blue parallelogram and the green parallelogram are congruent. State the values of angles A, B, C and D.

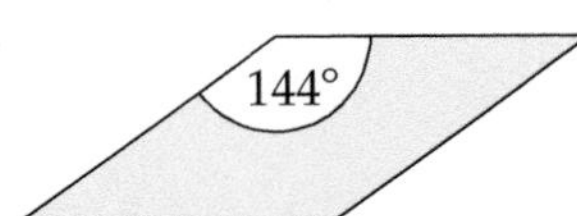

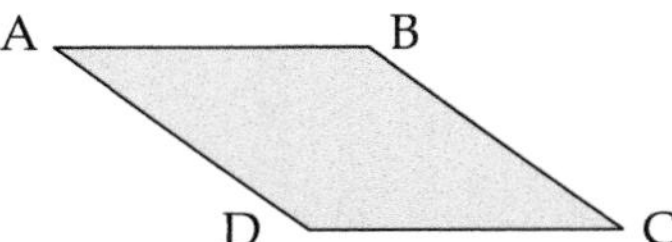

4 The yellow triangle and the orange triangle are congruent.

State the lengths of **a** AB

b AC

c BC

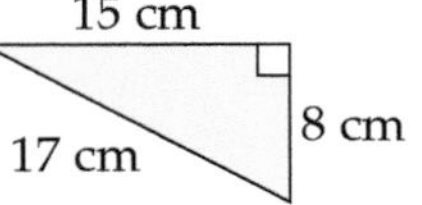

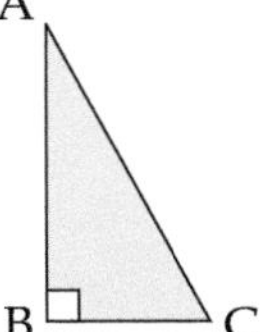

5 A 4 by 4 grid can be divided into two congruent shapes in many different ways.

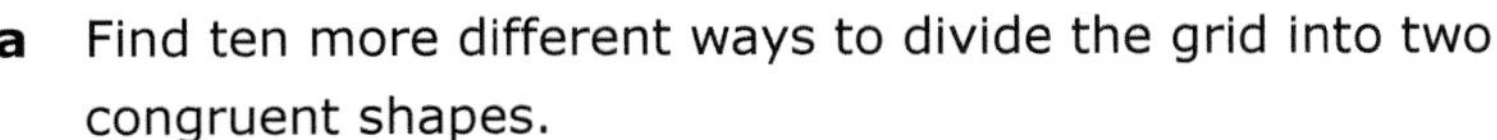

a Find ten more different ways to divide the grid into two congruent shapes.

b What do you notice about all of the congruent shapes you have drawn?

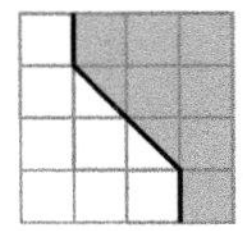

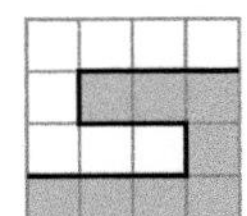

5 MySummary

Check out

You should now be able to ...

		Test it ➡ Questions
✓ Reason geometrically using the properties of the angles at a point and on a line and intersecting and parallel lines.	6	1
✓ Recognise the different types of triangles and quadrilateral and use their properties.	6	2, 3
✓ Recognise the different types of polygons and calculate interior and exterior angles for regular polygons.	6	4, 5
✓ Identify and use congruence.	6	6

Language	Meaning	Example
Parallel lines	Lines that are always the same distance apart from each other	Railway tracks
Perpendicular lines	Two lines that are at right angles to each other	A crossroads
Quadrilateral	A shape with four straight sides	A parallelogram
Polygon	A two-dimensional shape with three or more straight sides	Triangles, rectangles and hexagons are all polygons
Regular shape	A shape that has equal sides and equal angles	A square
Interior angle	The angle between adjacent sides in a polygon	int ext
Exterior angle	The angle between one side and the next side extended in a polygon	
Congruent	Two shapes are congruent if they have both the same size and the same shape	Two triangles that are identical, but one is rotated or reflected relative to the other.

1 Calculate the values of the labelled angles. State which geometric fact you used in each case.

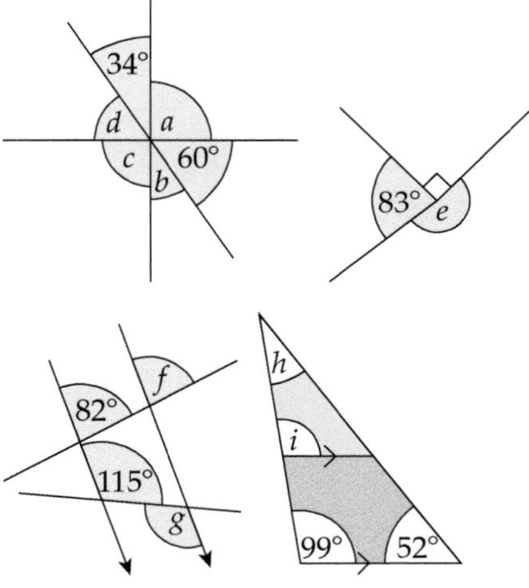

2 Calculate the value of the letters.

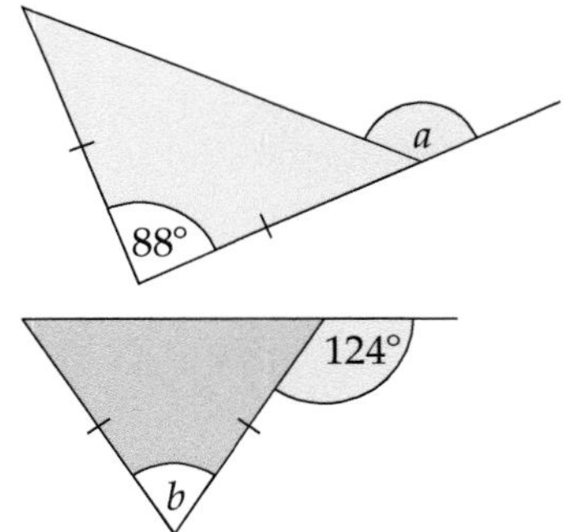

3 Which quadrilateral has

a 2 sets of equal sides, 2 pairs of equal angles and 2 sets of parallel sides?

b 1 set of equal sides, 2 pairs of equal angles and 1 set of parallel sides?

4 Calculate the size of

a the exterior angles of a regular nonagon

b the interior angles of a regular pentagon.

5 Accurately draw a regular hexagon.

6 The two parallelograms are congruent, state

a the length of AB

b the size of angle B

c the size of angle C

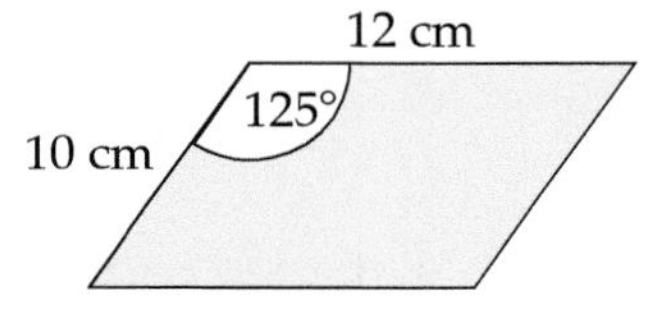

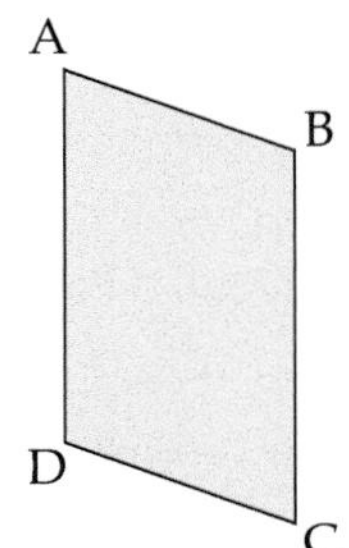

What next?

Score			
	0 – 2		Your knowledge of this topic is still developing. To improve look at Formative test: 2C-5; MyMaths: 1082, 1100, 1102, 1109 and 1141
	3 – 5		You are gaining a secure knowledge of this topic. To improve look at InvisiPen: 317, 342, 343, 344, 345, 346 and 374
	6		You have mastered this topic. Well done, you are ready to progress!

5a

1 Calculate the angles marked with a letter, giving a reason in each case.

a

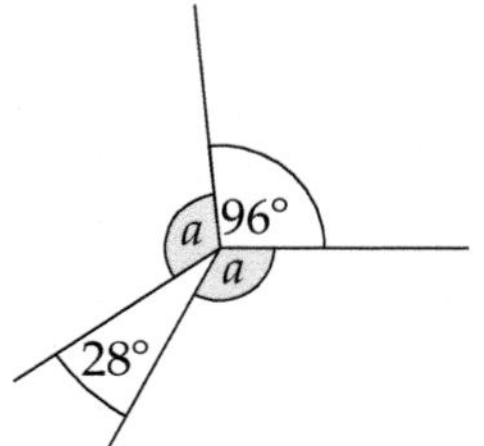

b

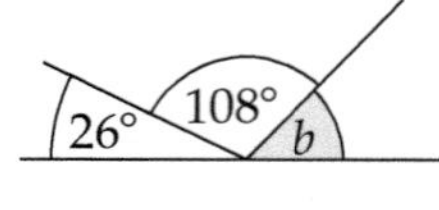

c

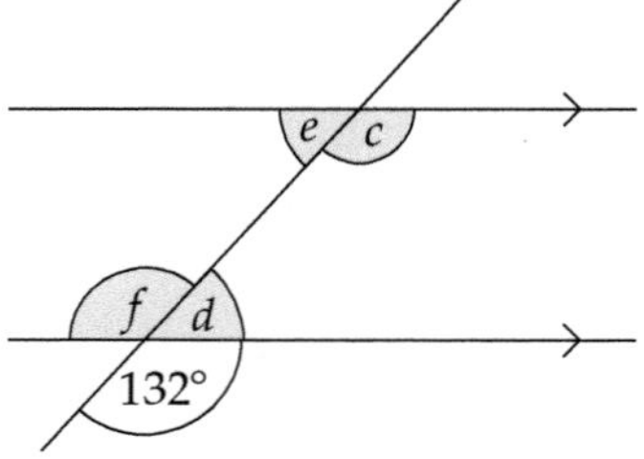

2 Find the value of

a a

b b

c $a + b$

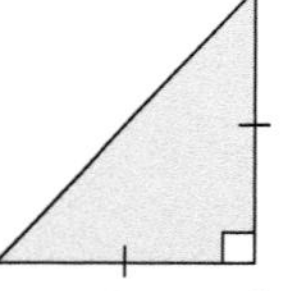

5b

3 Calculate the value of the unknown angles.
Give a reason in each case.

a

b

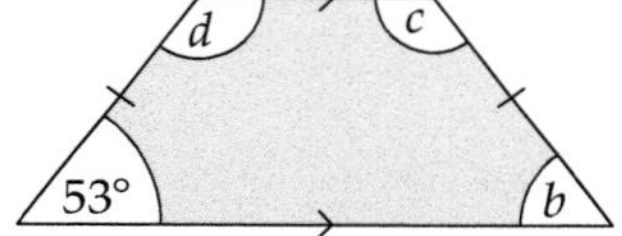

c

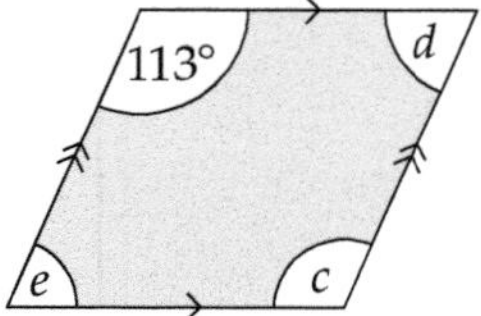

4 Two identical right-angled isosceles triangles are placed edge to edge.
Draw diagrams to show

a a square

b a right-angled isosceles triangle

c a parallelogram.

Use the properties of the right-angled triangles to show that each shape is the required quadrilateral.

5 Calculate the value of the unknown angles.

a

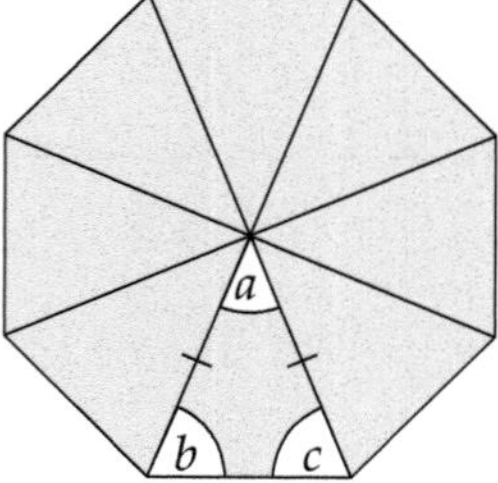

▲ A regular octagon.

b

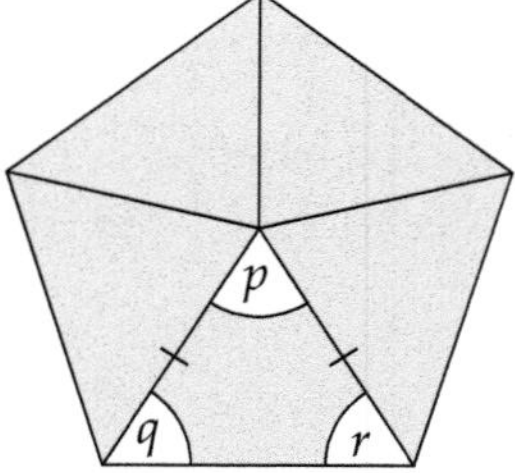

▲ A regular pentagon.

5c

6 **a** Copy these shapes and draw all the diagonals from each vertex.

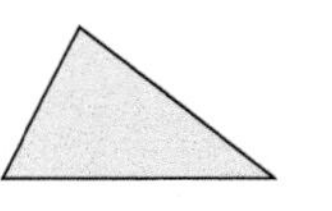
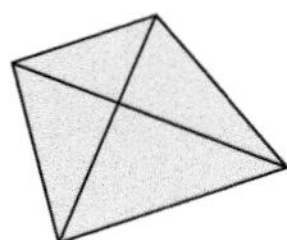
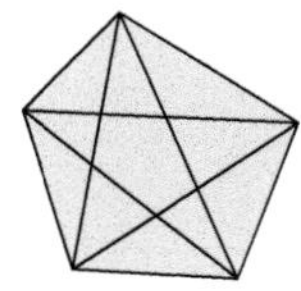
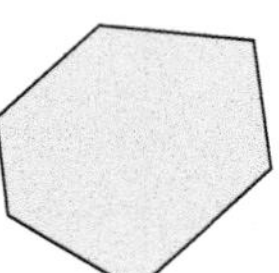
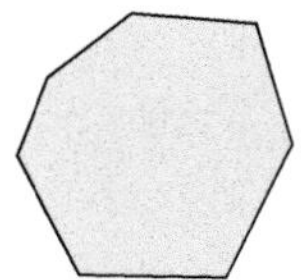
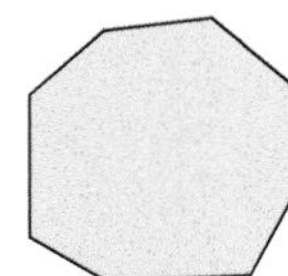

b Copy and complete the table.

Polygon	Number of sides	Number of diagonals
triangle	3	0
quadrilateral	4	2
pentagon	5	

5d

7 **a** Tessellate four congruent 'L' shapes on a 4 by 4 square grid.

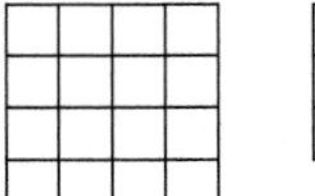

b Draw a different arrangement using the same shapes on the grid.

8 List the shapes which are congruent to one another.

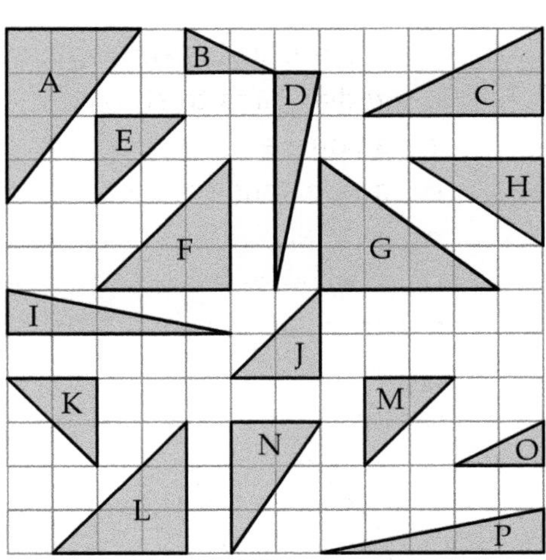

9 These two quadrilaterals are congruent.

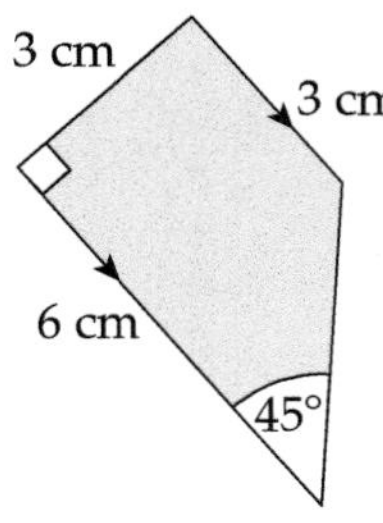

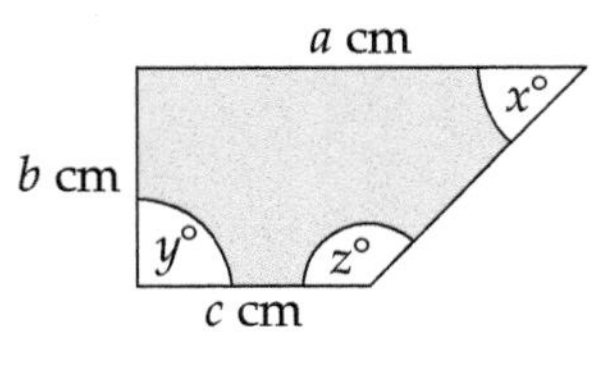

a State the size of angles x, y and z

b State the lengths of sides a, b and c

6 Graphs

Introduction

The world is increasingly feeling the adverse effects of climate change on the environment, such as melting polar ice caps and severe hurricanes.

Meteorologists use complex mathematical models of the Earth's climate, from which they can create functions and draw graphs to predict likely future weather patterns as the Earth warms up.

What's the point?

Graphs provide a clear picture of real-life data, allowing us to see patterns and predict what might happen next. This is vital as the world gets hotter, so we can know what precautions to take.

Objectives

By the end of this chapter, you will have learned how to ...

- Plot the graph of a linear function and use the equation of a straight line.
- Plot the graph of a non-linear function.
- Find the midpoint of a pair of coordinates.
- Plot the graph of an implicit function.
- Plot and interpret graphs of real life situations.
- Plot and interpret time series graphs.

Check in

1 Find the value of y in these equations if **i** $x = 2$ **ii** $x = -1$ **iii** $x = \frac{3}{2}$

a $y = 3 + 4x$ **b** $y = 7 - 5x$ **c** $2x + 3y = 16$ **d** $y = 2x^2 - x$

2 **a** Copy and complete the table for some points on the line.

x	0		3
y		3	

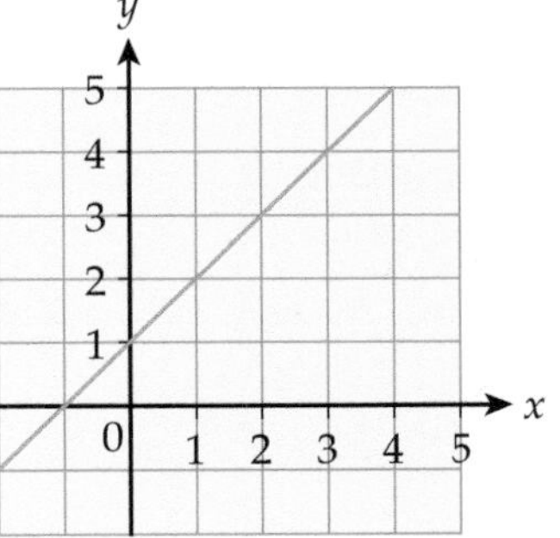

b Copy and complete this sentence:

'The y-coordinate is equal to the x-coordinate ☐ ☐'

c Use part **b** to write the equation of the line.

Starter problem

A man wants to enclose part of his garden in the shape of a rectangle.

He uses an outside wall of his house as one side of the rectangle, and uses 40 m of fencing to enclose the other three sides.

What is the maximum area of rectangle he can enclose?

Wall

Fencing

6a Graphs of linear functions

- A **graph** shows the relationship between two **variables**.
- To plot the graph of a **function**, find three or more points that satisfy the given equation.

A linear function will not contain variables with powers. $x + y = 5$ is a linear function. $y = x^2 + 3x + 2$ is not a linear function.

This is a table of values for the equation $y = x + 4$. The y-values are always 4 more than the x-values. You can read off three coordinate pairs. (1,5), (2,6) and (3,7).

x	1	2	3
y	5	6	7

- The graph of a **linear** function will always be a straight line.

Plot the points (1,5), (2,6) and (3,7) on a set of coordinate axes and join with a ruler.

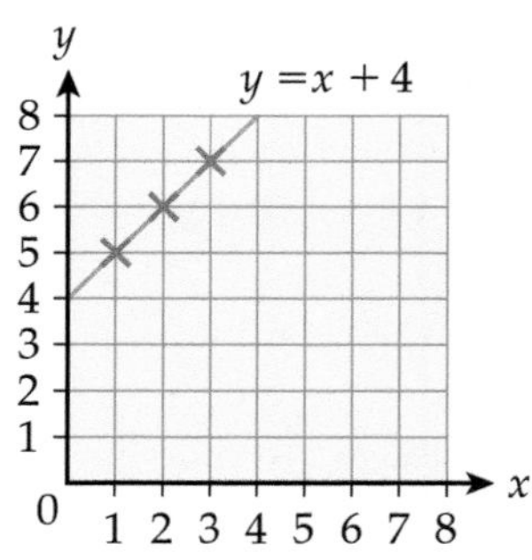

If you plot three points and do not have a straight line then you have made a mistake!

Example

a Plot the graphs $y = 3$ and $y = 2x - 1$ on the same set of coordinate axes.

b Write the coordinates of the point of intersection.

a

x	1	2	3
y	3	3	3

If $y = 3$ then the y-values are always 3.

x	1	2	3
y	1	3	5

If $y = 2x - 1$ then you double each x-value and subtract 1 to get each y-value.

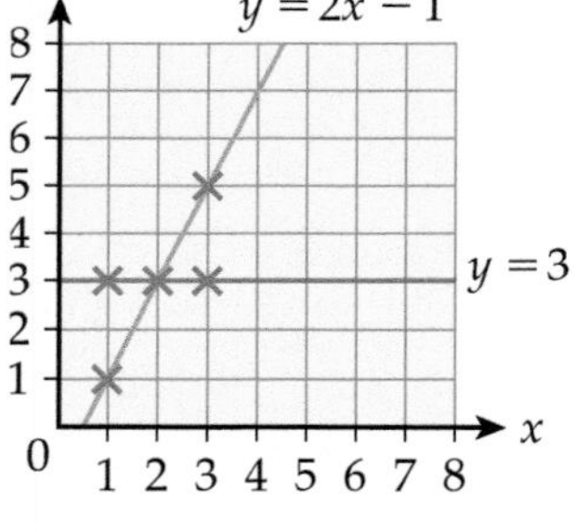

b The point of intersection is (2, 3).

- Equations of the form $y = c$, where c is a number, produce horizontal line graphs.
- Equations of the form $x = c$, where c is a number, produce vertical line graphs.

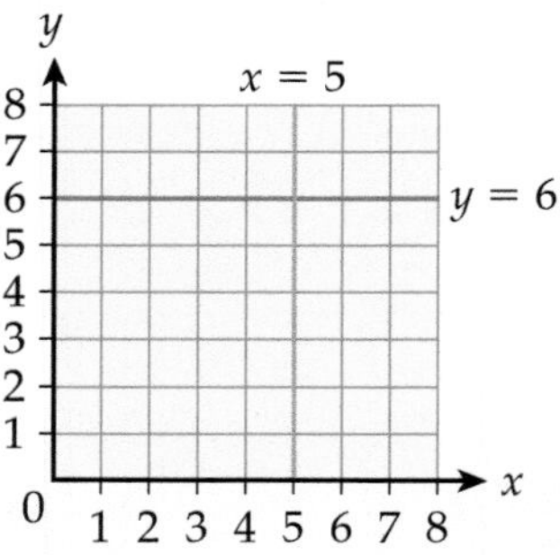

Exercise 6a

1 Match each equation with one of these cards.

Horizontal line	Vertical line
Sloping line	Not a straight line

a $x = 5$ **b** $y = 3x + 2$

c $x + y = 10$ **d** $y = 0$

e $y = x^2$ **f** $y = \frac{1}{3}x$

g $x = -1$ **h** $y = 2(x - 1)$

2 **a** Copy and complete the table of values for the equation $y = 3 - 2x$.

x	0	1	2
y		1	

b Plot these points on a set of coordinate axes with values from -2 to 4 in both the x and y directions.

c Write the coordinates of the point where the line $y = 3 - 2x$ cuts the x-axis.

Problem solving

3 **a** On a set of coordinate axes with values from 0 to 5 in both the x and y directions, plot the graphs of $x = 1$ and $y = 3$. Write the coordinates of the point where these lines intersect.

b Without drawing the graphs, write the coordinates of the point where these lines intersect.

i $x = 2$ and $y = 4$ **ii** $x = 3$ and $y = -1$ **iii** $x = \frac{1}{2}$ and $y = 1$

4 Which of these lines passes through the point (2,5)?

Line	$y = x + 3$	$x + y = 7$	$y = 3x$	$y = 2x - 1$	$y = \frac{3}{2}x + 2$
✓ **or** ✗					

5 **a** For each equation, copy and complete this table of values.

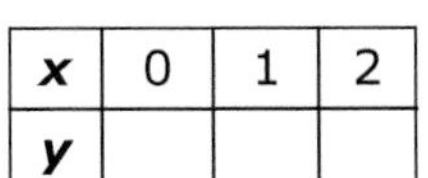

x	0	1	2
y			

i $y = 2x - 1$ **ii** $y = 2x$ **iii** $y = 2x + 1$ **iv** $y = 2x + 2$

b Plot the graph of each equation on the same set of coordinate axes.

c What do you notice about these graphs?
Compare each graph with its equation, mentioning both its slope and the coordinates of the point where the graph cuts the y-axis.

6 Repeat question **5** for each of these equations.

i $y = \frac{1}{2}x + 1$ **ii** $y = x + 1$ **iii** $y = 2x + 1$ **iv** $y = 3x + 1$

7 Here are the equations of five straight lines.

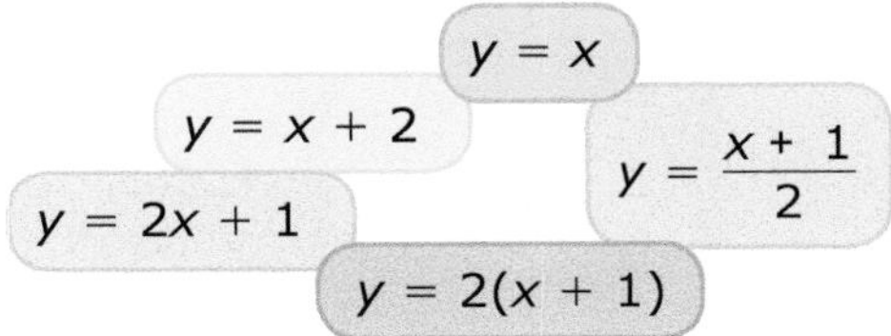

Can you find two pairs of parallel lines?
Which is the odd one out?
Suggest the equation of a line that is parallel to this line.

Did you know?

▲ The ABC, or Atanasoff-Berry computer, was the first electronic computer. It was built to find where systems of linear equations crossed.

6b Equation of a straight line

- The equation of a straight-line graph can be written $y = mx + c$
  - The **gradient**, m, describes the steepness or **slope** of the line.

$y = 2x + 1$

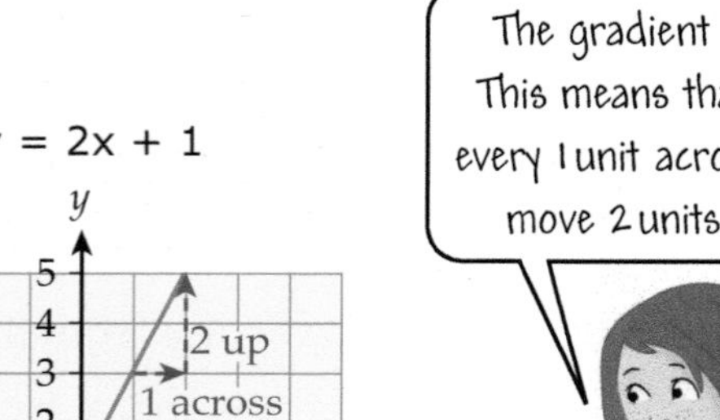

The gradient is 2. This means that for every 1 unit across you move 2 units up.

$y = \frac{1}{2}x + 3$

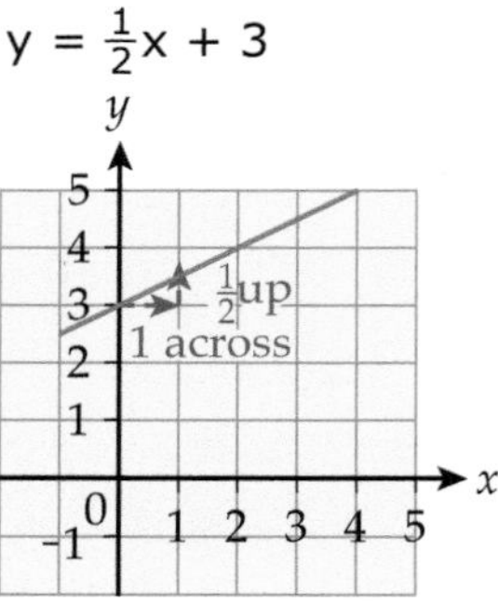

The gradient is $\frac{1}{2}$. This means for every 1 unit across you move $\frac{1}{2}$ a unit up.

- The y-**intercept**, c, is the point at which the line cuts the y-axis. The coordinates of this point are $(0, c)$.

$y = 3x - 1$

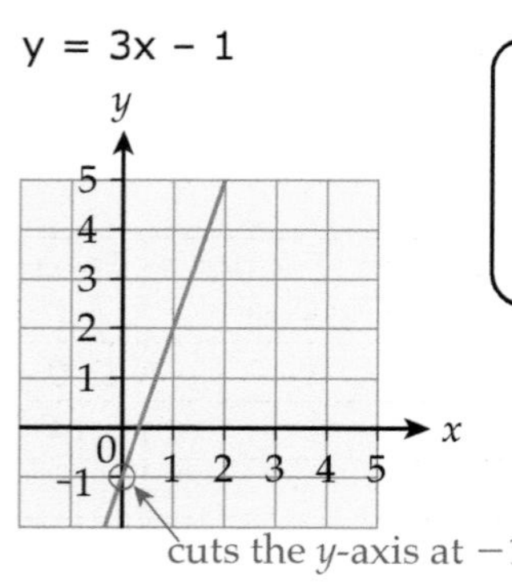

$c = -1$. The coordinates of the y-intercept are $(0, -1)$.

$y = -x + 3$ or $y = 3 - x$

cuts the y-axis at 3

$c = 3$. The coordinates of the y-intercept are $(0, 3)$. This line has a negative gradient of −1. The line slopes down in a negative direction.

Example

Find the equation of each of these straight lines.

a The line is vertical. The coordinates of some points on the line are (3, 0), (3, 1) and (3, 2). The x-value is always 3.
The equation of the line is $x = 3$.

b $m = +\frac{1}{2}$ because for every 1 unit across you move $\frac{1}{2}$ a unit *up*. The y-intercept is (0, 0) so $c = 0$.
The equation of the line is $y = \frac{1}{2}x$.

c $m = -2$ because for every 1 unit across you move 2 units *down*. The y-intercept is (0, 5) so $c = 5$.
The equation of the line is $y = -2x + 5$ or $y = 5 - 2x$.

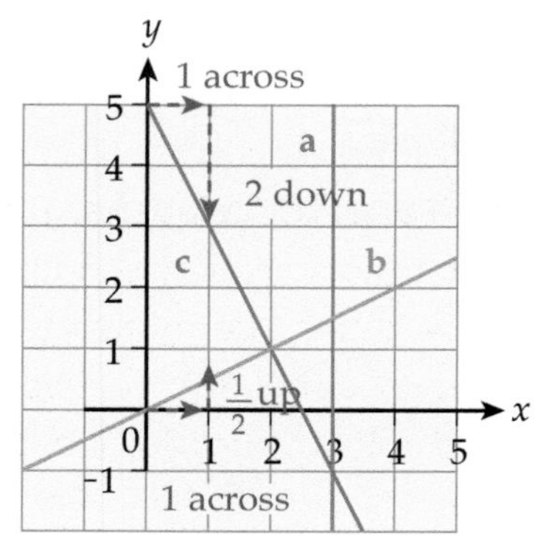

Exercise 6b

1 Copy and complete the table for each of these equations.

a $y = 3x + 2$ **b** $y = 4x - 1$

c $y = 2x$ **d** $y = \frac{1}{2}x + 3$

e $y = \frac{x}{2} - 5$ **f** $y = 3(x + 2)$

g $y = 4 - \frac{3}{2}x$ **h** $y = 10 - x$

Equation	Gradient	Coordinates of y-intercept

2 Write the equations of these three straight lines.

a Line A has a gradient of 2 and y-intercept at (0, 1).

b Line B cuts the y-axis at -4 and has a gradient of 1.

c Line C has m = -3 and $c = \frac{1}{2}$.

3 For each of these tables of coordinates, write the equation of the line on which these points lie.

a

x	0	1	2	3	4
y	5	5	5	5	5

b

x	0	1	2	3	4
y	0	2	4	6	8

c

x	0	1	2	3	4
y	5	4	3	2	1

d

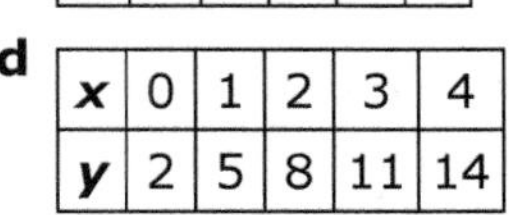

x	0	1	2	3	4
y	2	5	8	11	14

4 Find the equation of each of these straight lines.

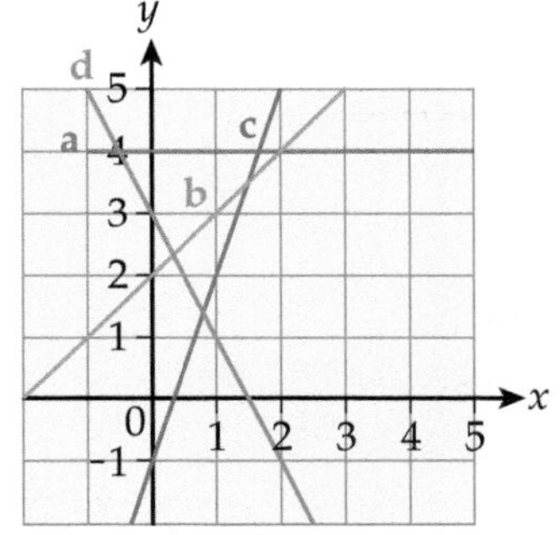

Problem solving

5 'Fab Cabs' taxis took these fares from three customers.

Name	Journey length (miles)	Fare
Mrs Mackay	4	£10
Mike	6	£14
Alicia Williams	2.5	£7

a Plot this information on a graph. Use axes with x-values from 0 to 8 (representing the journey length in miles) and y-values from 0 to 20 (representing the fare). Do you think plotting the graph makes the information easier to understand?

b Write the equation that the taxi company uses to calculate each fare.
Explain how this works, mentioning the cost per mile of hiring a taxi.

c 'Fair Fares' taxis charges £1 per mile and puts £5 on the meter at the start of each journey.
Add this information to your graph and determine which of these two companies you would choose to travel with.
Explain your decision.

6 Rearrange these equations so that y is the subject, and then write the gradient and y-intercept of each equation.

$x + y = 10$ $2y = x + 4$ $3y = 4x - 3$ $2y + x = 6$ $4y + 2x - 3 = 0$

- A function which has x^2 as its highest power of x is called a **quadratic** function.
  - A quadratic function produces a curved graph called a **parabola**.

$y = x^2$, $y = x^2 + 2x - 3$ and $y = 4x^2 - 1$ are all quadratic functions. $y = x + 5$, $y = 3x$ and $y = 4 - 3x$ are all linear functions.

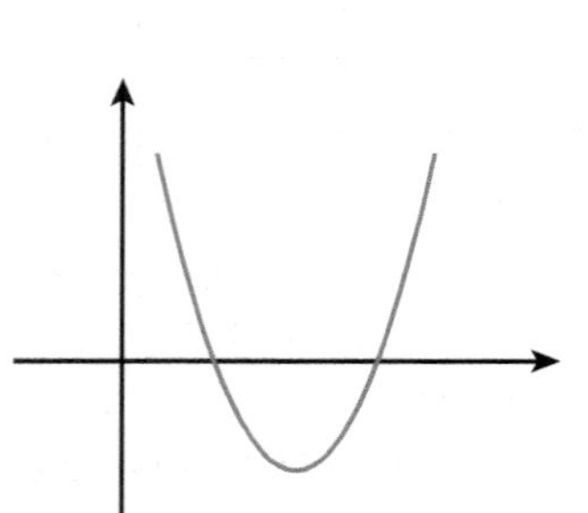

This graph is a symmetrical ∪ shape.

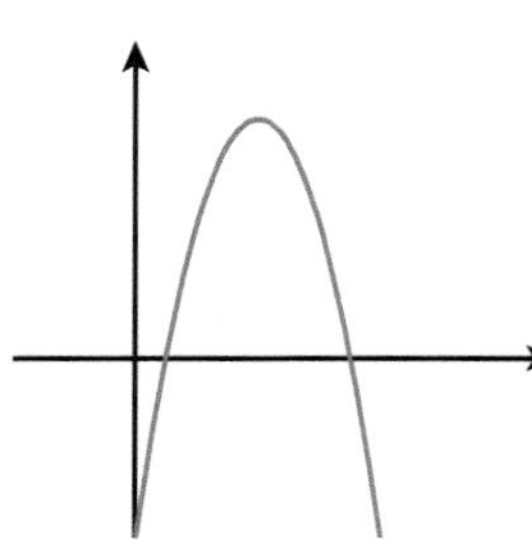

This graph is a symmetrical ∩ shape.

Example

Plot the graph of the function $y = x^2$.

Construct a table of values.

x	-3	-2	-1	0	1	2	3
y	9	4	1	0	1	4	9

$(-3)^2 = -3 \times -3 = 9$ $\quad 2^2 = 2 \times 2 = 4$

Plot the coordinate pairs (-3, 9), (-2, 4), (-1, 1), (0, 0), (1, 1), (2, 4) and (3, 9).

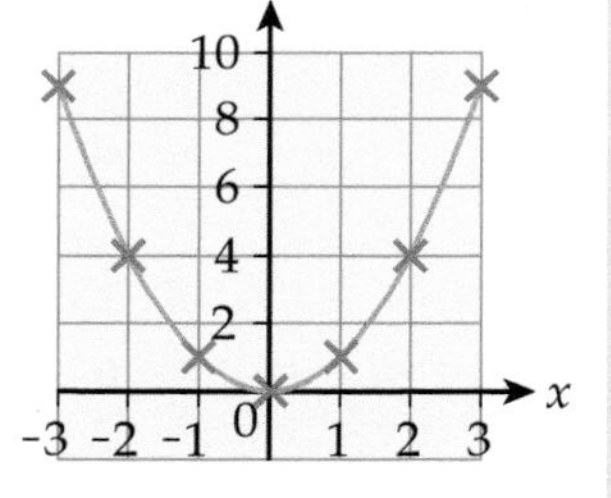

Example

Plot the graph of the function $y = -x^2 - x + 1$.

Construct a table of values.

x	-2	-1	0	1	2
$-x^2$	-4	-1	0	-1	-4
$-x$	+2	+1	0	-1	-2
+1	+1	+1	+1	+1	+1
y	-1	+1	+1	-1	-5

Plot the coordinate pairs (-2, 1), (-1, 1), (0, 1), (1, -1) and (2, -5).

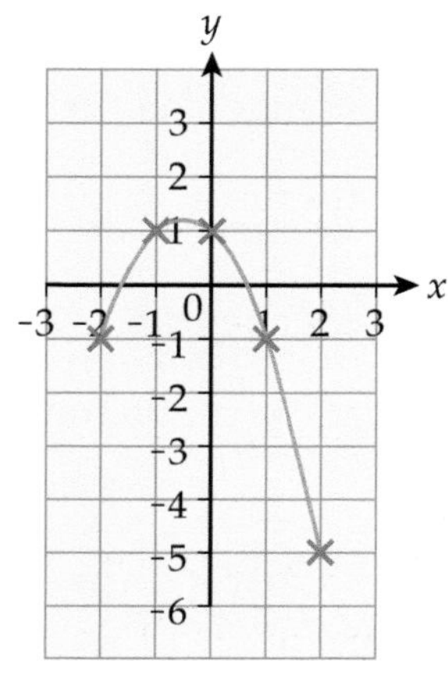

▲ The basketball follows a parabolic path.

Exercise 6c

1 Match each equation with one of these cards.

Linear graph	Quadratic graph

a $y = 10 - 3x$ b $y = 2$
c $x + y = 8$ d $y = x^2 - 7x + 10$
e $y = 2x^2$ f $x = -3$
g $y = 3(x + 1)$ h $y = x(x - 1)$

2 a Copy and complete the table of values for the equation $y = x^2 + 2$.

x	-3	-2	-1	0	1	2	3
x^2		4					
+2		2					
y		6					

b Plot these points on a set of coordinate axes with x-values from -4 to 4 and y-values from 0 to 12. Join the points with a smooth curve.

c Write the coordinates of the point where $y = x^2 + 2$ cuts the y-axis.

d Write the coordinates of the minimum point of $y = x^2 + 2$.

3 a Copy and complete the table of values for the equation $y = x^2 - 2x$.

x	-2	-1	0	1	2	3	4
x^2		1					
$-2x$		2					
y		3					

b Plot these points on a set of coordinate axes with x-values from -3 to 5 and y-values from -2 to 10. Join the points with a smooth curve.

c Write the coordinates of the points where $y = x^2 - 2x$ cuts the x-axis.

d Write the equation of the vertical line about which $y = x^2 - 2x$ is symmetrical.

Problem solving

4 The most general form for a quadratic equation is $y = ax^2 + bx + c$ where a, b and c are numbers.

a Choose values for a, b and c and use a computer graphing tool to plot your quadratic equation.

b What is the effect of increasing or decreasing c?
How many times does the curve intercept the x-axis?
How does your answer change as c changes?

c What is the effect of increasing or decreasing b?

d Your graph should have a vertical line of symmetry. What is its equation?
How does the equation of this line change as b changes?

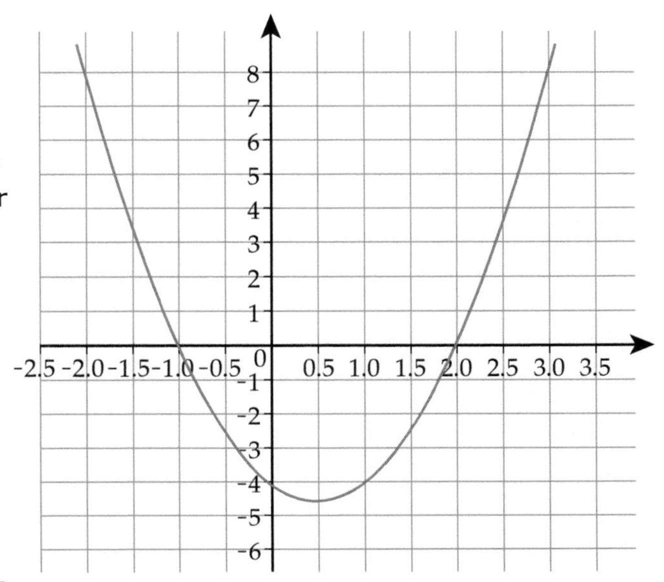

6d Midpoints of coordinate pairs

A line segment AB can be defined by giving the **coordinates** of its end points for example: A (3, 2) and B (7,4).

The **midpoint** M is the point that lies an equal distance from A and B on the line joining them.

The x-coordinate

$3 + \frac{1}{2}(7 - 3) = \frac{1}{2}(3 + 7) = 5$

The y-coordinate

$2 + \frac{1}{2}(4 - 2) = \frac{1}{2}(2 + 4) = 3$

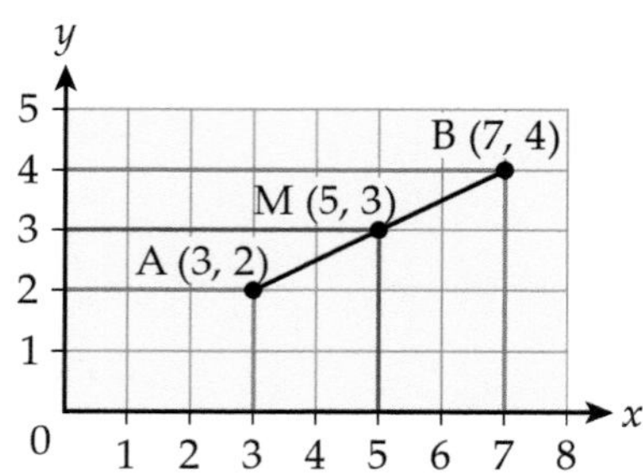

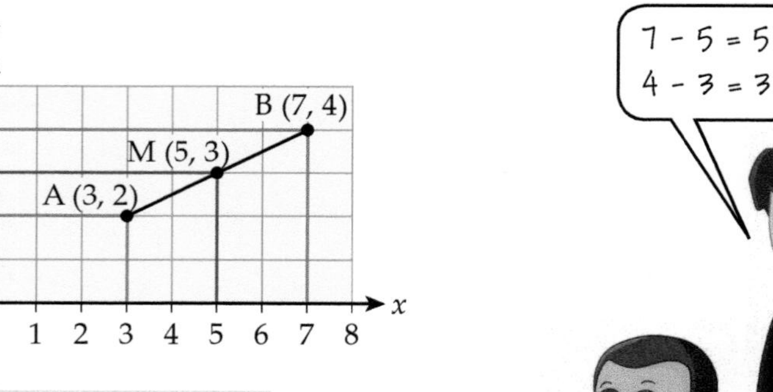

The midpoint M of the line segment joining A (x_A, y_A) and B (x_B, y_B) is given by

$$\left(\frac{x_A + x_B}{2}, \frac{y_A + y_B}{2}\right)$$

Example

Let A and B be the end points of a line segment and M be its midpoint.

a Given A (4, -1) and B (-2, -2) find M.

b Given A (3, -1) and M (5, -2) find B.

a $M = \left(\frac{4 - 2}{2}, \frac{-1 - 2}{2}\right)$

$= \left(\frac{2}{2}, \frac{-3}{2}\right) = (1, -1.5)$

b Let B = (x, y)

$(5, -2) = \left(\frac{3 + x}{2}, \frac{-1 + y}{2}\right)$

This gives 2 equations.

$\frac{3 + x}{2} = 5$ $\qquad$ $\frac{-1 + y}{2} = -2$

$3 + x = 10$ $\qquad$ $-1 + y = -4$

$x = 7$ $\qquad$ $y = -3$

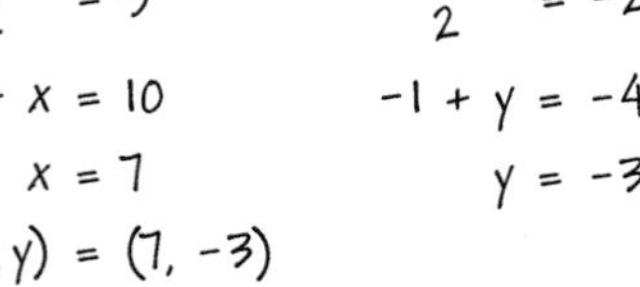

B (x, y) = (7, -3)

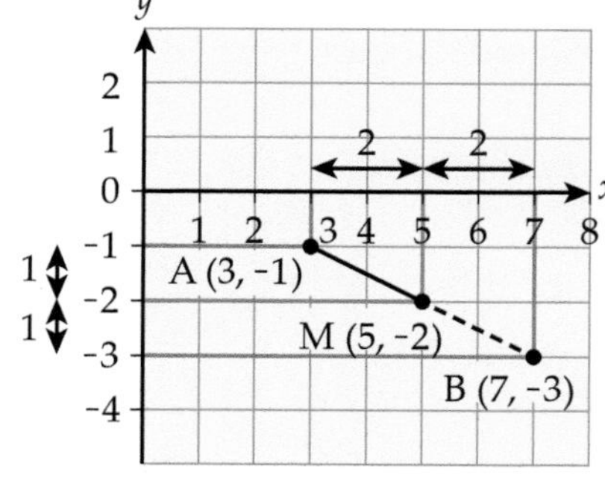

Exercise 6d

1 Find the midpoints of these pairs of points.

a (2, 3) and (4, 7)
b (4, -2) and (4, -4)
c (6, 6) and (-6, -6)
d (-5, -2) and (-3, -8)
e (-2, 4) and (-1, 5)
f (1.2, 5.3) and (7.2, -3.2)

2 A line segment AB has midpoint M. Given A and M find the coordinates of B.

a A (2, 2) and M (3, 4)
b A (-1, 3) and M (3, 4)
c A (2, 2) and M (-1, 3)
d A(-1, -3) and M (-2, -3)
e A (2.3, -1.3) and M (-3.4, -2.5)

Problem solving

3 The following sets of coordinates give the vertices of a quadrilateral ABCD. For each set

i give the name of the quadrilateral
ii calculate the coordinates of the midpoints of the lines joining opposite vertices M_{AC} and M_{BD}
iii comment on what you find.

a A (0, -1) B (1, 2) C (5, 5) and D (4, 2)
b A (-5, -2) B (-5, 3) C (-1, 0) and D (-1, -5)
c A (2, -3) B (2, -1) C (5, 2) and D (5, -6)

You can plot these shapes on a graph with x and y coordinates from -6 to 6.

4 Show that the points A, B and their midpoint lie on the given line.

a A (-1, -4) B (3, 4) line $y = -2 + 2x$
b A (1, 3) B (2, 5) line $y = 1 + 2x$
c A (0, 1) B (6, -1) line $x + 3y = 3$
d A (-2, 5) B $(3, 2\frac{1}{2})$ line $y = 4 - \frac{1}{2}x$

5 A and B lie on the line $y = 2x + 3$.
A has x-coordinate 1. B has y-coordinate 13.
Find the midpoint of AB.

6 Find the point P on the line segment AB which is one third of the way from A.

a A (0, 0) B (3, 0)
b A (0, 2) B (0, 8)
c A (1, 3) B (7, 6)
d A (-2, -3) B (-5, 3)
e A (4, -6) B (-2, 2)
f A (1.2, 2.1) B (0.6, 0.6)

7 a On 1 cm graph paper draw a set of axes from 0 to 8. Choose three sets of coordinate pairs and plot these as points A, B and C. Join A, B and C to form a triangle.

b Find the point M with coordinates $\left(\frac{x_A + x_B + x_C}{3}, \frac{y_A + y_B + y_C}{3}\right)$ and plot it.

c Carefully cut out the triangle. Can you balance it on the point M?

d Repeat for other triangles and other polygons where the coordinates of M are the mean average of the coordinates of the vertices.

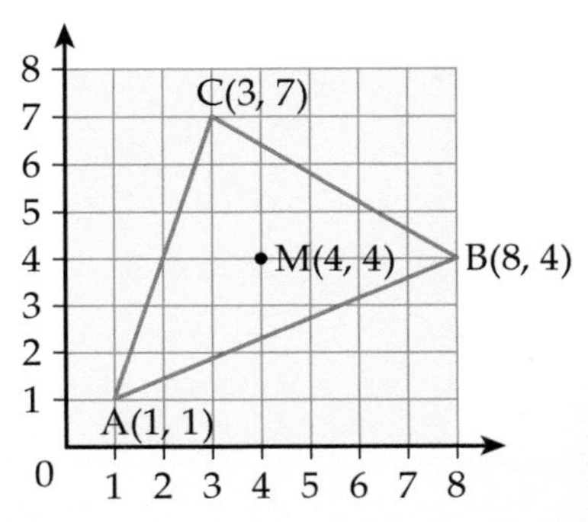

6e Graphs of implicit functions

- When y is the **subject**, the equation is an **explicit** equation.

$y = 3x + 2$, $y = 4x$ and $y = \frac{1}{2}x - 1$ are explicit equations.

- When y is not the subject, the equation is an **implicit** equation.

$y - 3x = 2$, $\frac{y}{4} - x = 0$ and $2y - x + 2 = 0$ are implicit equations.

You can **rearrange** implicit equations to make y the subject.

Equations of the form $y = mx + c$ produce straight-line graphs.

Example

For each of these implicit equations, rearrange for 'y' to find an equivalent explicit equation.

a $2x + y - 3 = 0$ **b** $4y - 2x = 3$

a $2x + y - 3 = 0$

$2x + y = 3$ $\quad +3$

$y = 3 - 2x$ $\quad -2x$

b $4y - 2x = 3$

$4y = 2x + 3$ $\quad +2x$

$y = \frac{2}{4}x + \frac{3}{4}$ $\quad \div 4$

$y = \frac{1}{2}x + \frac{3}{4}$

You must do the same to both sides of the equation.

- To plot the graph of an implicit function, either
  - rearrange to make the equation explicit, or
  - find the coordinates of the two points where the graph cuts the axes.

To find the coordinates of the points where the graph cuts the axes, first substitute $x = 0$ and then $y = 0$ into each implicit equation.

Example

a Plot $x + y = 5$ and $x - 2y = 2$ on the same axes and find their point of intersection.

b Show that the coordinates of the point of intersection satisfy both equations.

a $x + y = 5$ $\quad y = 0,\ x = 5 \Rightarrow (5, 0)$

$x = 0,\ y = 5 \Rightarrow (0, 5)$

$x - 2y = 2$ $\quad y = 0 \quad x = 2 \Rightarrow (2, 0)$

$x = 0 \quad -2y = 2 \quad \div -2$

$y = \frac{2}{-2} = -1 \Rightarrow (0, -1)$

The coordinates of the point of intersection are (4, 1).

b Substitute $x = 4$ and $y = 1$ into each equation.

$x + y = 4 + 1 = 5$ ✓ $\quad x - 2y = 4 - 2 \times 1 = 2$ ✓

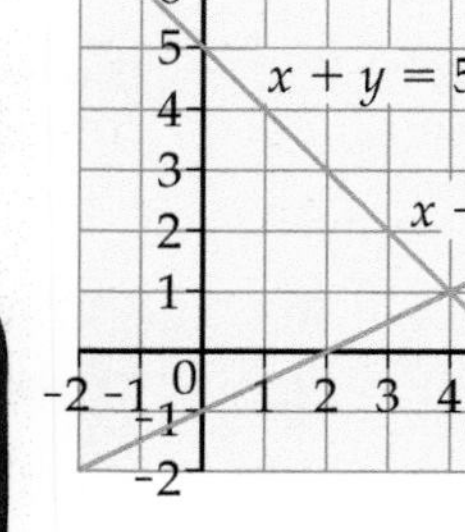

Exercise 6e

1 Rearrange these implicit equations to make y the subject.

a $x + y = 8$ **b** $2x + y = 1$

c $y - 3 = 4x$ **d** $3x + y - 2 = 0$

e $2y - x = 6$ **f** $3y + 2x = 3$

g $\frac{y}{3} - x = 0$ **h** $12 - 4y + x = 0$

2 Find the value of y in these equations when

i $x = 0$ **ii** $x = 3$ **iii** $x = -2$

a $4y + 3x = 3$

b $8 - 2y + 5x = 0$

c $x = 3(y - 2)$

d $\frac{2x + y}{3} = 5$

3 For each implicit equation, copy and complete the table of values and hence plot the graph of the function. You don't need to rearrange the equation.

a $x + y = 4$

x	0	2	
y			0

b $2x + y = 8$

x	0	2	
y			0

c $x + 3y = 6$

x	0	3	
y			0

Problem solving

4 **a** Using these graphs, write the coordinates of the points of intersection of these pairs of equations.

i $x + y = 6$ and $2y - 3x = 2$

ii $x + y = 6$ and $3y - 2x = 3$

iii $2y - 3x = 2$ and $3y - 2x = 3$

b Show that the coordinates of each point of intersection satisfy both equations in each pair.

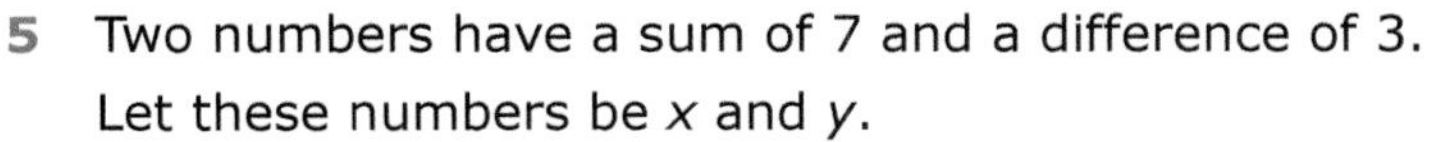

5 Two numbers have a sum of 7 and a difference of 3. Let these numbers be x and y.

a Write a pair of implicit equations to represent this information.

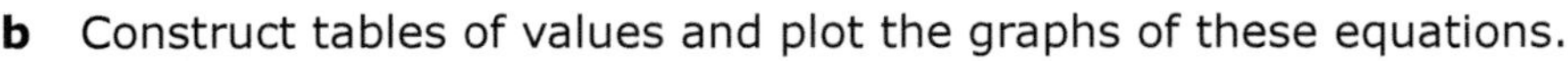

b Construct tables of values and plot the graphs of these equations.

c Write the point of intersection of your graphs and prove that these coordinates satisfy the equations in part **a**.

6 Two adults and two children visit the zoo at a cost of £50. One adult and three children visit the zoo at a cost of £45.

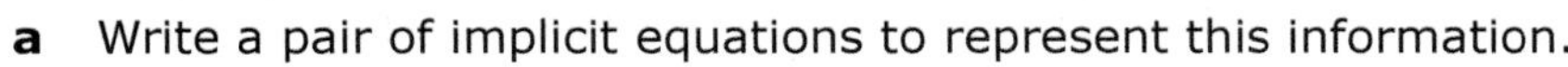

a Write a pair of implicit equations to represent this information.

b Using graphical software or a graphical calculator, plot the graphs of these equations on the same axes.

c Work out the cost of an adult's ticket and a child's ticket.

6f Real life graphs

- A real life situation can be represented by a **sketch graph**.

You do not need data to sketch a graph, but you should make sure that the general shape of the graph models the situation.

Example

Clare washes up a milk pan after breakfast.
Sketch a graph to show the depth of water in the washing-up bowl over a period of time.

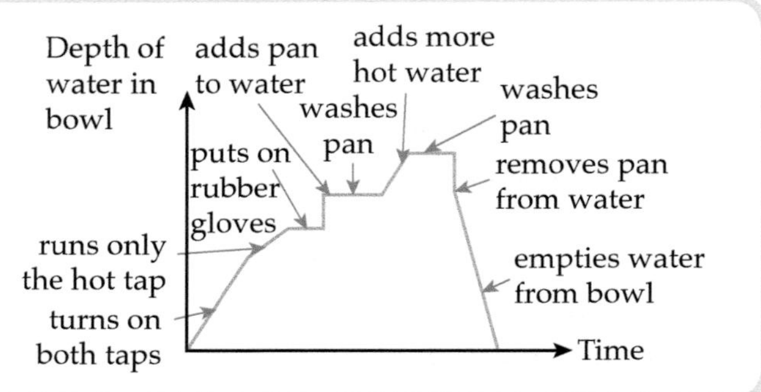

- A **distance–time graph** represents a real life journey.
- The **gradient** of a line on a distance-time graph represents the **speed**.

Example

Jason leaves his home at 07:00 and cycles to work. He cycles a distance of 10 km in half an hour and then stops for 10 mins to repair a puncture. He cycles the remaining 10 km to work in 20 mins. Jason spends only 2 hours at work before feeling unwell and being driven home in a colleague's car. He arrives home 25 mins later.

a Draw a distance–time graph to represent this information.

b Calculate the speed at which Jason's colleague drove him home.

a

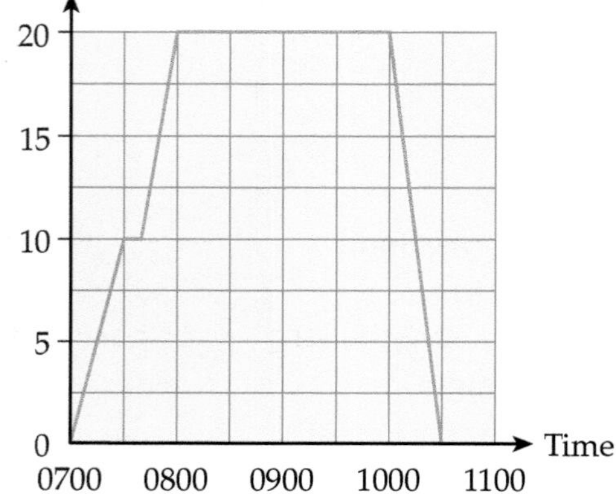

b Jason's colleague drives him 20 km in 25 mins.

$$\text{speed} = \frac{\text{Distance}}{\text{Time}}$$

$$\text{speed} = \frac{20\text{ km}}{\left(\frac{25}{60}\right)\text{ hours}}$$

$$= 20 \times \frac{60}{25}$$

$$= 48\text{ km/h}$$

$25\text{ min} = \frac{25}{60}\text{hrs}$

Exercise 6f

1 The graph represents the depth of tea in Sandeep's cup.

Depth of tea in cup

A B C D E F

Time

- **a** Match each section of the graph marked by a letter with one of the statements below.
  - **i** Sandeep drains her cup.
  - **ii** Sandeep adds a splash of cold water from the tap.
  - **iii** Sandeep drinks some tea.
  - **iv** Sandeep solves a sudoku puzzle.
  - **v** Sandeep uses the teapot to top up the tea in her cup.
  - **vi** Sandeep pours a cup of tea from her teapot.
- **b** Draw a sketch graph of the temperature of Sandeep's tea over the same period of time.

2 Samantha leaves her house at 11 a.m. and walks 3 km in half an hour to 'Atlas' delicatessen. She spends 15 mins buying some groceries and then walks for 15 mins towards home at a speed of 4 km per hour. A passing friend then picks her up on his tandem and together they cycle the rest of the journey in 5 mins.

- **a** Draw a distance–time graph to represent this information.
- **b** At what time does Samantha arrive home?
- **c** What is the average speed of the tandem?

Problem solving

3 Water is poured at a constant rate into each container A, B, C and D. Match each of these containers with one of the graphs.

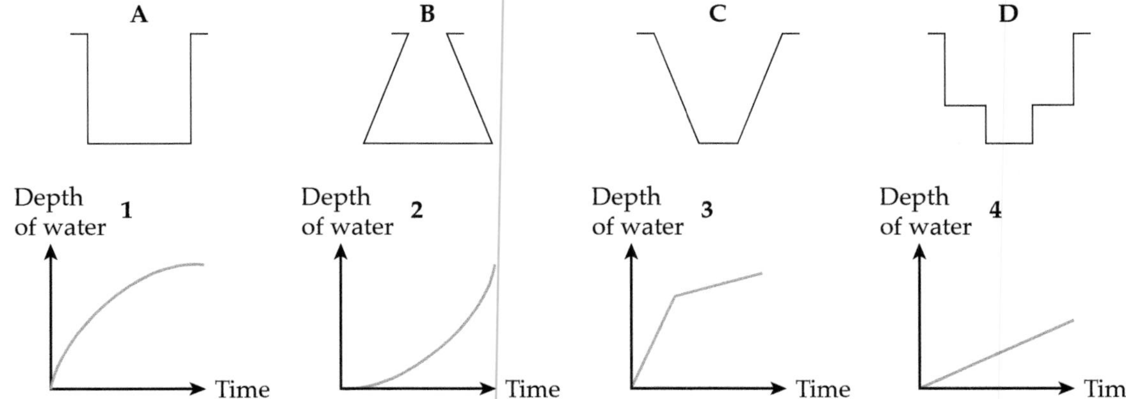

4 Using ideas from question **2**, draw a variety of containers and challenge your partner to sketch a related graph of the depth of the water against time.
Make sure you can check their answers!

6g Time series

Data is often collected over a period of time. For example, your weight on your birthday or the height of the water in an estuary at different times of day.
The pairs of variables can be plotted as coordinates (value, time) on a graph.

A time series is a type of line graph.

- A variable plotted against time on the x-axis is called a **time series graph**.

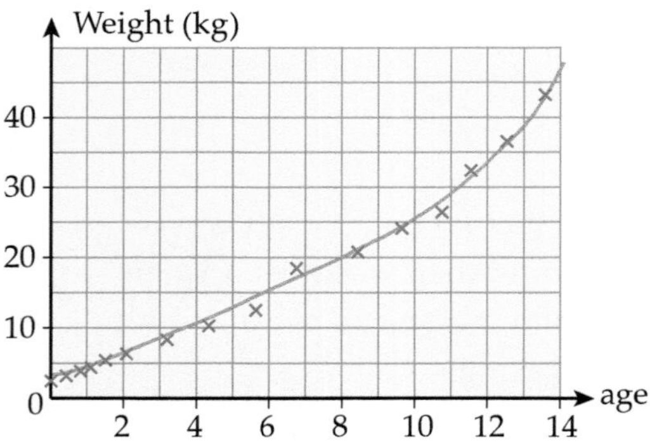

The long-term **trend** is for weight to increase.

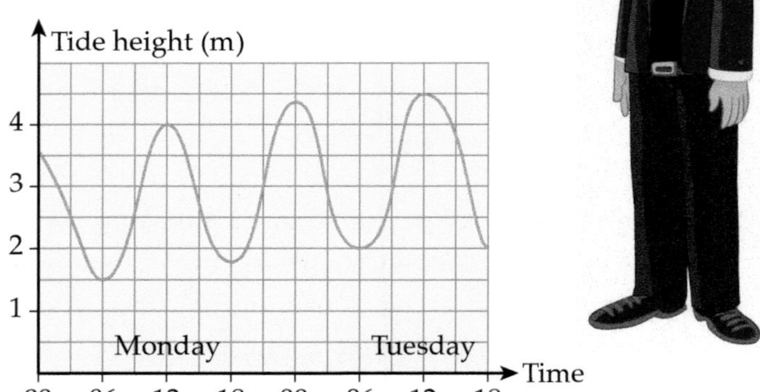

The short-term behaviour shows a fairly regular, repeating pattern with a **period** of 12 hours.

Example

Describe any patterns in this data for a household's electricity bill.

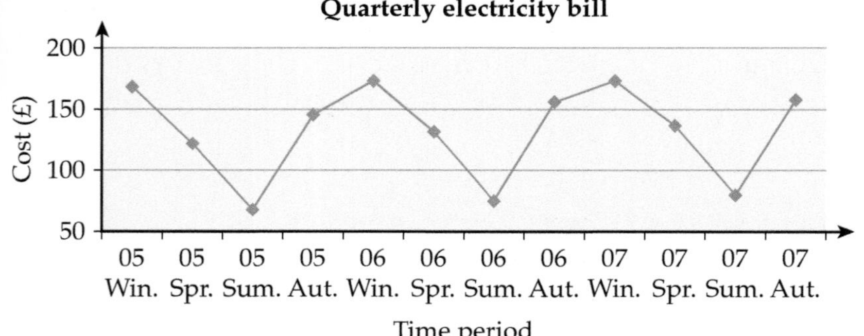

Comment on

a the short-term (yearly) **variation**

b the long-term variation.

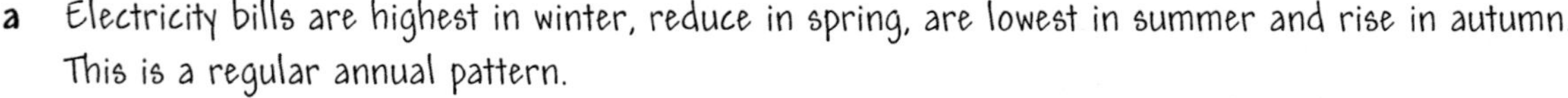

a Electricity bills are highest in winter, reduce in spring, are lowest in summer and rise in autumn. This is a regular annual pattern.

b Comparing equivalent quarterly electricity bills, the year-on-year trend is upward indicating rising electricity costs.

Exercise 6g

1 Describe the behaviour seen in these time series graphs.

a

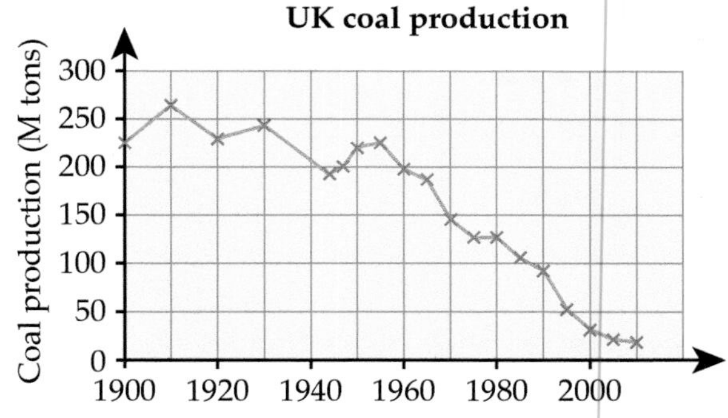

b

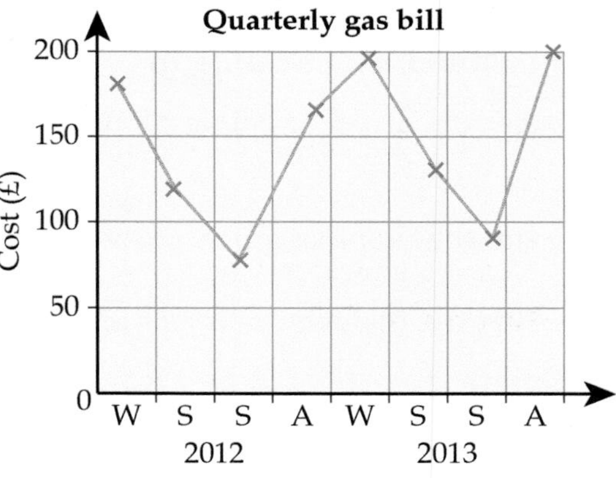

Problem solving

2 The graph below shows the number of minutes Sasha has used her mobile phone for in one billing period, which started on a Tuesday.

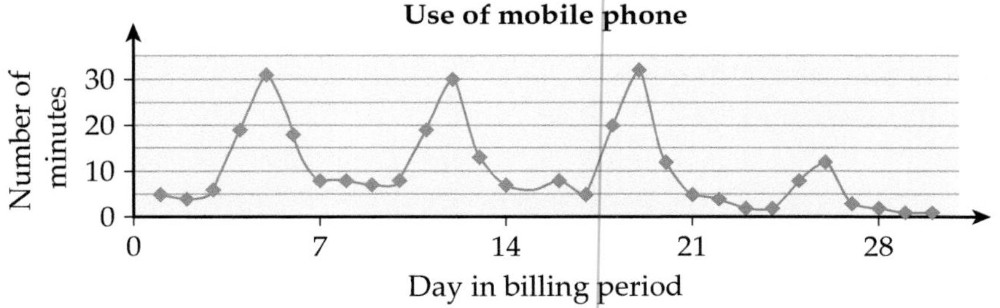

a Describe any patterns you see in the use of her phone.

b Her contract includes 300 free minutes in each billing period. She checks her account online after 20 days and sees that she has used 266 minutes already. Comment on what the graph tells you about her use of the phone for the rest of the month.

Did you know?

▲ Predicting the future behaviour of a variable using time series is very important in business.

3 For each set of data **i** draw a time series graph to show the data
ii describe the behaviour seen in the graph.

a The table shows the monthly ice cream sales in Cinzia's deli for one year.

Jan	Feb	Mar	Apr	May	Jun	Jul	Aug	Sep	Oct	Nov	Dec
£16	£10	£8	£16	£22	£36	£48	£50	£12	£15	£16	£39

b The table shows how much money Thomas earned from odd jobs during three years.

	Spr.	Sum.	Aut.	Win.
2010	£15	£35	£20	£10
2011	£18	£42	£24	£13
2012	£25	£50	£31	£19

6 MySummary

Check out

You should now be able to ...

Test it ➡ Questions

You should now be able to ...	Level	Questions
✓ Plot the graph of a linear function and use the equation of a straight line.	6	1 – 4
✓ Plot the graph of a non-linear function.	6	5
✓ Find the midpoint of a pair of coordinates.	6	6, 7
✓ Plot the graph of an implicit function.	7	8, 9
✓ Plot and interpret graphs of real life situations.	7	10
✓ Plot and interpret time series graphs.	6	11

Language	Meaning	Example
Linear function	A function whose graph is always a straight line	$y = mx + c$
Gradient	The slope of a line	If $y = mx + c$, m is the gradient
Intercept	Where a line touches the x-axis or y-axis	If $y = mx + c$, c is the intercept with the y-axis
Midpoint	The point that lies halfway between its two endpoints	The midpoint of the line joining (1, 4) and (7, 8) is (4, 6)
Parabola	The shape you get if you plot a quadratic function	$y = x^2$
Explicit equation	An equation where y is the subject	$y = 2x + 1$, $y = mx + c$, $y = 3x^2$
Implicit equation	An equation where y is not the subject	$2y + 3x = 5$, $y - c = mx$, $y = x + y^3$
Distance-time graph	A graph where time is plotted on the x-axis and distance is plotted on the y-axis	See p. 112

1 For the equation $y = 4x - 5$

a copy and complete the table

x	0	1	2	3
y				

b plot the graph of the equation.

2 Does the line $y = 5x - 2$ pass through the point (3, 12)?

3 For each equation write down its slope and where it crosses the y-axis.

a $y = 7x + 3$ **b** $y = x - 4$

c $y = 8 - 2x$ **d** $y = \frac{1}{2}x$

e $y = 5$ **f** $y = 5x + 4$

4 Find the equations of each of these straight lines.

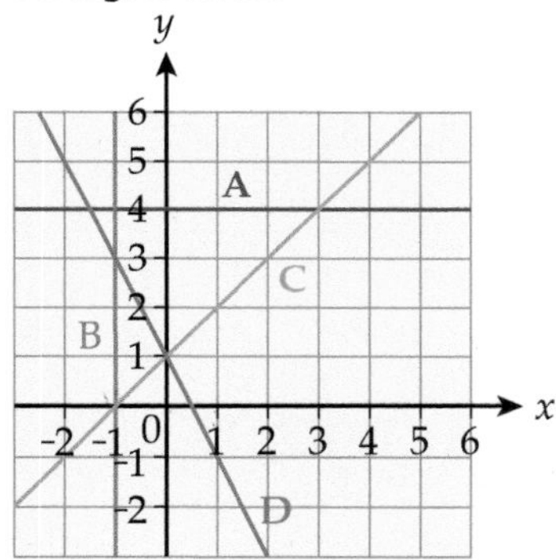

5 **a** Copy and complete the table of values for the equation $y = x^2 - 1$

x	-3	-2	-1	0	1	2	3
x^2							
-1							
y							

5 **b** Use the table to draw the graph of the equation

6 Find the midpoints of these pairs of points.

a (5, 8) and (13, 11)

b (3, -6) and (-8, -2)

7 M (8, 3) is the centre of the square ABCD. The coordinates of A are (5, 7).

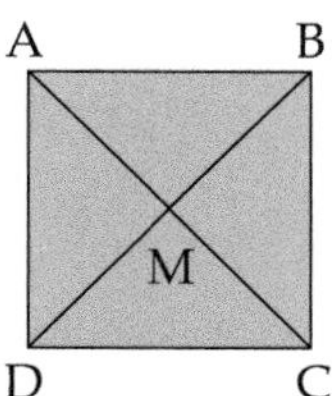

What are the coordinates of C?

8 Rearrange these to make y the subject.

a $x + y = 11$ **b** $2x + 3y = 18$

c $15 - 5y = 10x$ **d** $\frac{y}{2} - 7x = 13$

9 Plot the graph of $3x + y = 9$

10 Kat leaves her school which is 3 km from her home at 15:15. She takes 25 minutes to walk 2 km towards her home with a friend. She then stops at the friend's house for 15 minutes. Kat walks the rest of the way home at a speed of 6 km per hour.
Draw this journey on a distance-time graph.

What next?

Score		
0 – 4		Your knowledge of this topic is still developing. To improve look at Formative test: 2C-6; MyMaths: 1153, 1168, 1184, 1394, 1395, 1396 and 1939
5 – 8		You are gaining a secure knowledge of this topic. To improve look at InvisiPen: 256, 265, 266, 273, 275 and 278
9 – 10		You have mastered this topic. Well done, you are ready to progress!

6 MyPractice

6a

1 **a** Copy and complete the table of values for the equation $y = 2x + 1$.

x	0	1	2
$2x$			
$+1$			
y	1		

b Plot these points on a set of coordinate axes with x and y values from 0 to 8. Join your points with a straight line.

c On the same set of axes, plot the graph of $y = 7 - x$.

d Write the coordinates of the point of intersection of these graphs.

2 True or false?

The graphs of the functions $x = 2$ and $y = -3$ intersect at the point (-3, 2).

6b

3 Write the gradient and y-intercept of these straight lines.

a $y = 2x + 1$

b $y = 3x - 2$

c $y = \frac{1}{2}x + 5$

d $y = 8x$

e $y = x - 2$

f $y = 4 - 3x$

g $y = 1 - \frac{1}{3}x$

h $y = 3(2 - x)$

4 Find the equation of each of these straight lines.

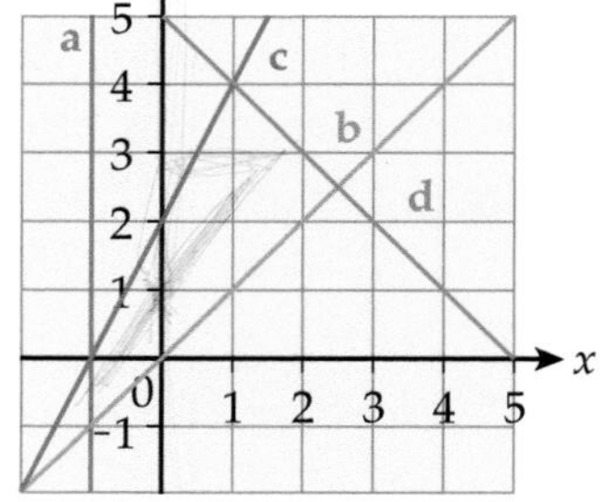

5 True or false?

The graph of the function $y = x^2 + 5x + 6$ passes through the point (1, 12).

Explain your answer.

6 **a** Copy and complete the table of values for the equation $y = x^2 - x$.

b Plot these points on a set of coordinate axes with x-values from -3 to 4 and y-values from -1 to 8.

Join the points with a smooth curve.

x	-2	-1	0	1	2	3
x^2	4					
$-x$	2					
y	6					

c Write the coordinates of the points where the line $y = x^2 - x$ cuts the x-axis.

d Write the equation of the vertical line about which $y = x^2 - x$ is symmetrical.

6d

7 M is the midpoint of the line segment AB.

Find M or B given the following information.

a $A(4, 2)$ $B\ (6, 4)$

b $A(-1, 7)$ $B\ (3, 3)$

c $A(5, 6)$ $B\ (1, -2)$

d $A(-2, -3)$ $B\ (-4, 2)$

e $A(-2, -1)$ $M\ (0, 1)$

f $A(6, 4)$ $M\ (2, 2)$

6e

8 **a** Copy and complete the tables and plot the graphs of these implicit functions on the same set of axes.

$x + y = 5$

x	0	1	2
y			

$5x - y = 1$

x	0	1	2
y			

b Write the coordinates of the point of intersection of these graphs.

c Show that the coordinates of the point of intersection satisfy each equation.

6f

9 Patrick leaves his home at 08:00. He jogs 3 km in 20 mins and then stops for 30 mins to have breakfast at a local café. Patrick sprints home in 10 mins. Patrick's wife, Giselle, leaves home at 08:15. She runs to the same café as Patrick in 15 mins and joins her husband for breakfast. Giselle leaves at the same time as Patrick and quickly walks back home, arriving at 09:15.

a Draw each of these journeys on the same distance-time graph.

b How long did Patrick and Giselle spend together over breakfast?

c Calculate the average speed at which

i Patrick ran home **ii** Giselle walked home.

6g

10 Karim runs a newsagent which sells CDs. The time series graph shows the number sold recently in each quarter. Describe two features of the graph.

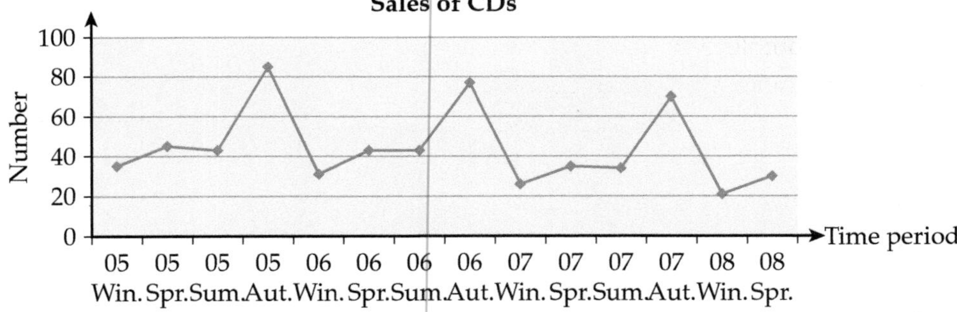

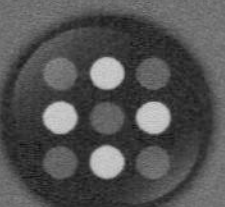

Case study 2: Patchwork

Patchworks are made by sewing together several small pieces of fabric, often polygons that are chosen because they fit together to make the desired design. You can describe these designs as tessellations, because they fit together without leaving gaps.

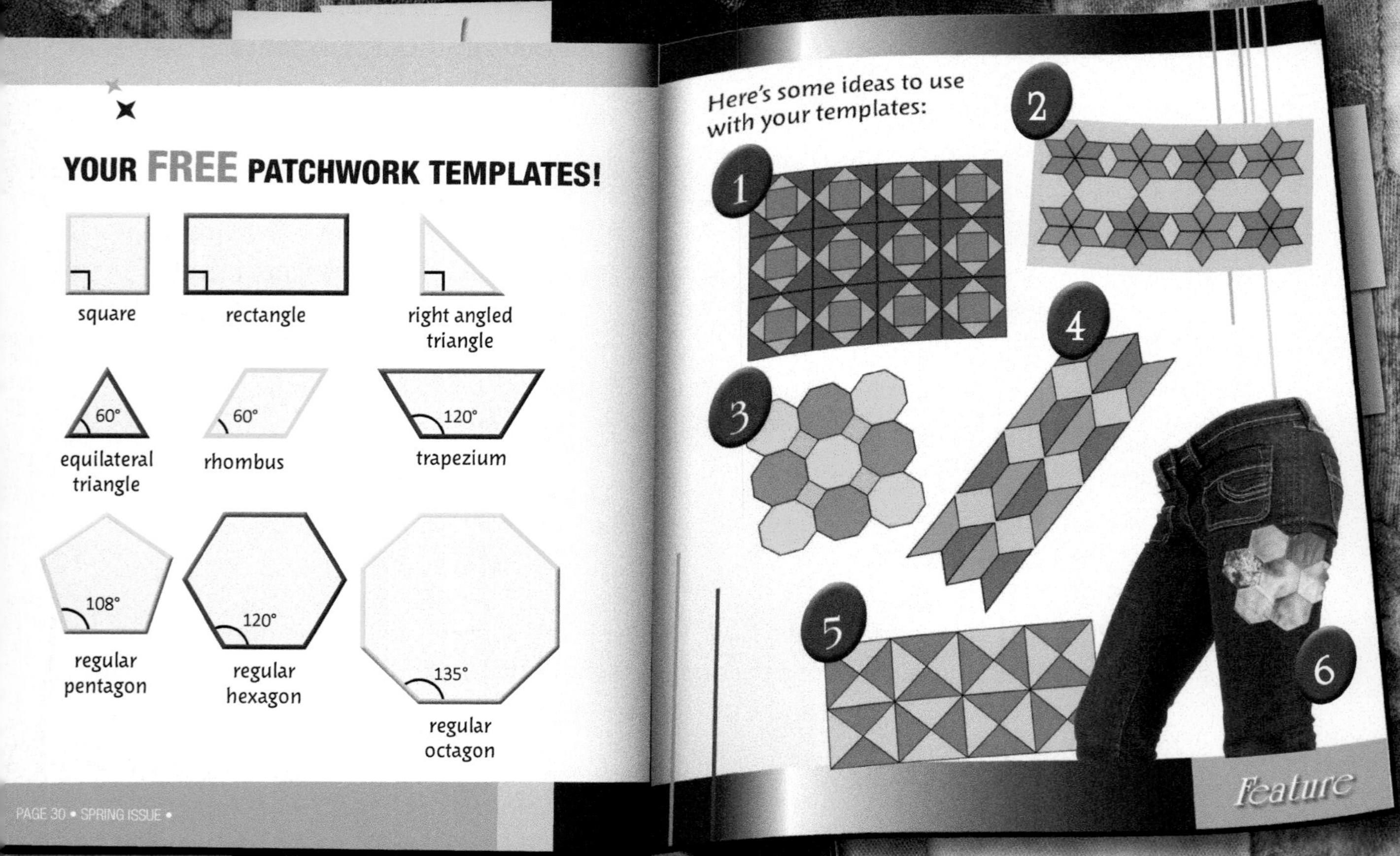

YOUR FREE PATCHWORK TEMPLATES!

square

rectangle

right angled triangle

60°
equilateral triangle

60°
rhombus

120°
trapezium

108°
regular pentagon

120°
regular hexagon

135°
regular octagon

PAGE 30 • SPRING ISSUE •

Here's some ideas to use with your templates:

1

2

3

4

5

6

Feature

Mix tunes

Task 1

Look at the patchwork templates, and the ideas 1 to 6 in the magazine above.

a For each of the ideas 1 to 6, describe which templates have been used.

b **i** Which patchworks use only one template?

ii Which patchworks use more than one?

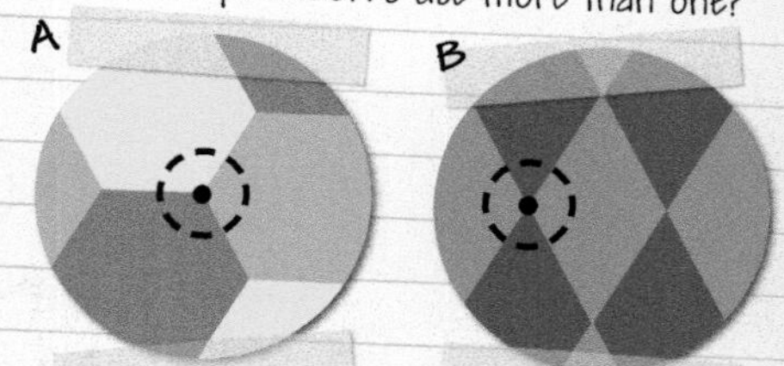

Task 2

Look at the patterns A and B. They are made up of the patchwork templates shown in the magazine.

a For each pattern A and B, describe which template has been used.

b (Harder) The angles at a point add up to 360°. Can you explain why regular hexagons tessellate but regular pentagons do not?

c What other combinations of the templates might tessellate? You can combine two or more templates.

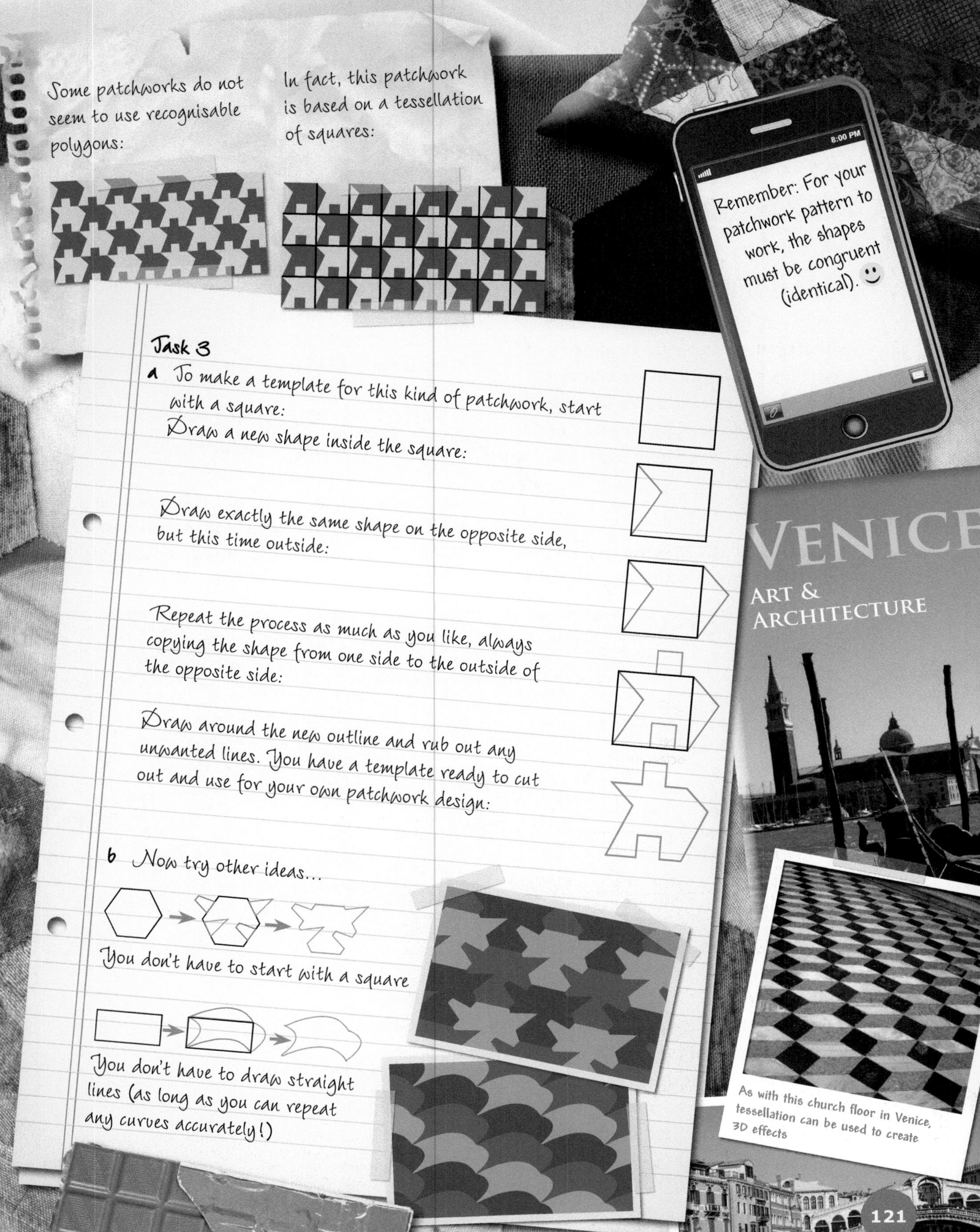

Some patchworks do not seem to use recognisable polygons:

In fact, this patchwork is based on a tessellation of squares:

Task 3

a To make a template for this kind of patchwork, start with a square:

Draw a new shape inside the square:

Draw exactly the same shape on the opposite side, but this time outside:

Repeat the process as much as you like, always copying the shape from one side to the outside of the opposite side:

Draw around the new outline and rub out any unwanted lines. You have a template ready to cut out and use for your own patchwork design:

b Now try other ideas…

You don't have to start with a square

You don't have to draw straight lines (as long as you can repeat any curves accurately!)

As with this church floor in Venice, tessellation can be used to create 3D effects

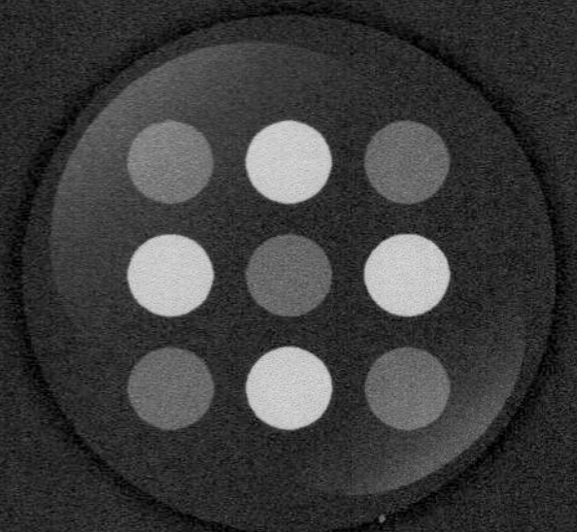

7 Mental calculations

Introduction

Human beings have always tried to use technology to make all aspects of their lives easier and more efficient. Mathematical calculation is no exception and the first devices invented to perform this task were called abacuses. They were mainly used to help them with the buying and selling of goods.

It wasn't until 1642 (some two thousand years later) that Pascal invented the first mechanical calculator called the Pascaline. It then took until the 1960s before Sharp produced the first battery powered calculator called the QT-8D.

What's the point?

Calculators help you perform calculations with large and awkward numbers. However you still need to understand what you're asking the calculator to work out, and check whether the answer is sensible.

Objectives

By the end of this chapter, you will have learned how to ...

- Use the rules of arithmetic with negative numbers.
- Calculate with positive and negative powers of ten.
- Perform mental addition, subtraction, multiplication and division.
- Use standard written methods for addition and subtraction with decimals.

Check in

1 Calculate these using an appropriate method.

a $5.42 + 324.9 + 8$ b $44.7 + 198.5 - 38.6$

c $528.38 - 129.7 - 32 - 0.78$ d $456.97 + 99.99 - 1.99$

2 Calculate these using a written method.
Remember to do a mental approximation first.

a 13×4.68 b 47×4.95 c 5.3×49.6 d 57.3×0.85

3 Calculate these using an appropriate method.
Give your answer as a decimal to 1 dp where appropriate.

a $563 \div 3.8$ b $922 \div 4.8$ c $722 \div 1.9$ d $697 \div 4.1$

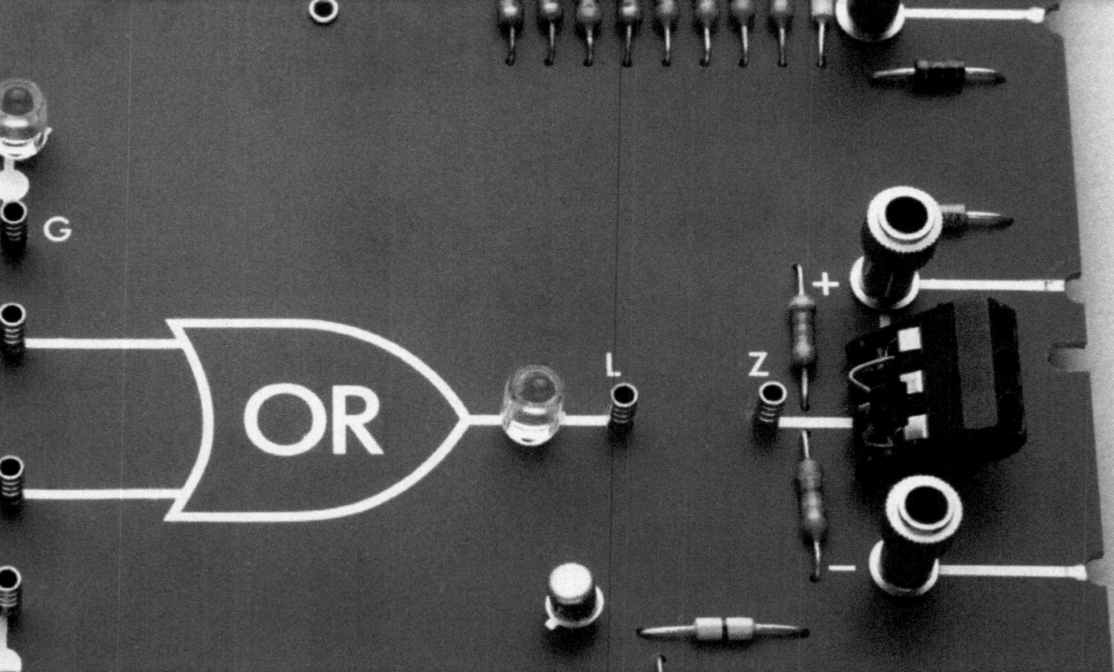

Starter problem

Here is a route of the streets a postman must walk along for his daily route.
He starts at the sorting office which is labelled A.
What is the shortest distance he can cover so that travels along every street at least once and returns to his sorting office at A?

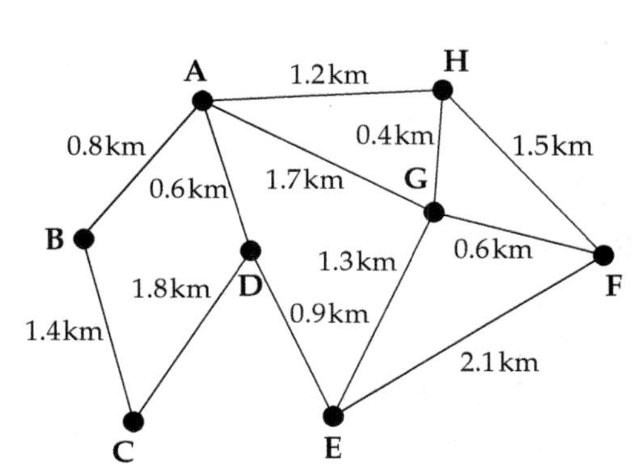

7a Arithmetic with negative integers

Negative numbers appear to the left of zero on the number line.

On a number line smaller numbers are always to the left of larger numbers.

Example

Put these numbers in order from smallest to largest.

-4.7   -3.9   − 5

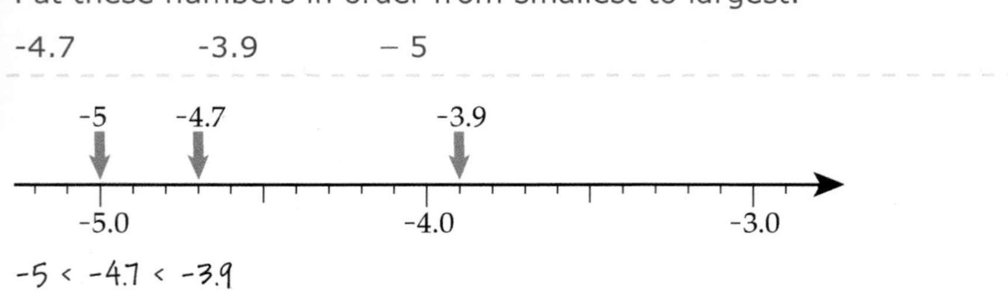

$-5 < -4.7 < -3.9$

To calculate with **negative integers** make sure that both the size and the sign of the answer are correct.

Example

Calculate

a $-27 + -31$ **b** $-18 - -14$

−31

−58   −27   0

+14

−18   −4   0

a $-27 + -31 = -27 - 31$
$= -58$

Add -31 is the same as subtract 31

b $-18 - -14 = -18 + 14$
$= -4$

Subtract -14 is the same as add 14

Adding a negative is the same as subtracting a positive. Subtracting a negative is the same as adding a positive.

When you are multiplying or dividing a pair of numbers a good rule to remember for the sign of the answer is:

		First number	
	Multiply or divide	Positive	Negative
Second number	Positive	+ Answer	− Answer
	Negative	− Answer	+ Answer

If the signs are the same, the answer will be positive. If the signs are different the answer will be negative.

Example

Calculate

a -8×6 **b** $-48 \div -8$ **c** $-48 \div 6$ **d** -8×-6 **e** $48 \div -6$

a -8×6
$= -48$
negative answer

b $-48 \div -8$
$= 6$
positive answer

c $-48 \div 6$
$= -8$
negative answer

d -8×-6
$= 48$
positive answer

e $48 \div -6$
$= -8$
negative answer

Exercise 7a

1 Place $<$ 'less than' or $>$ 'greater than' between these pairs of numbers to show which number is the larger.

a -8 and -6 **b** -3.5 and -5
c -5.8 and -6 **d** -3.2 and -3.19
e -0.05 and -0.489
f -1.271 and -1.268

2 Put these numbers in order from smallest to largest.

a	-1.8	-2	5	1.5	-3
b	-2.7	-3.4	-3.8	-3.2	-3
c	-5.2	-5.28	-5.3	5.4	-5.25

3 Calculate

a 7 + -11 **b** -12 + -9
c -8 − -15 **d** -6 − -15
e -19 + -15 **f** -5 + 7 − -4
g -6 − -8 + -7 **h** -12 + 32 + -27
i 33 + -16 − 24

4 Calculate

a 9 × -4 **b** -12 × 15
c -14 × -6 **d** -15 × -7
e -250 ÷ -5 **f** -306 ÷ 6
g -184 ÷ -8 **h** 288 ÷ -9

5 Copy and complete these calculations.

a □ + −8 = 0 **b** 5 × □ = -10
c 8 − □ = -7 **d** □ ÷ 7 = -13
e 7 + □ = -9 **f** □ × -6 = 84
g □ − -23 = -7 **h** -72 ÷ □ = 12
i □ ÷ -3 = -8

6 Here are six calculations

a □ ÷ □ = -4 **b** □ − □ = -10
c □ + □ = 12 **d** □ × □ = 36
e □ × □ = 0 **f** □ + □ = 0

Suggest, with reasons, what the missing numbers could be in each question.

Problem solving

7 a Copy and complete this multiplication grid.
Try to find two different ways to complete it.

b Design your own multiplication grid problem. What is the least amount of information that you need to include to obtain a unique solution?

×		**2**	**-7**	
		-12	42	
-5		-10		
	32			-12
				27

Did you know?

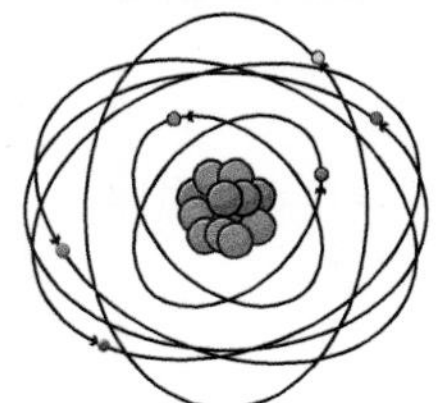

In Coulomb's law, the force between two electric charges is attractive or repulsive depending on the sign of their product.

8 Calculate

a -2 × -3 × -5 **b** -4 × -4 × -4 × -4
c $(-1)^3$ **d** $(-1)^{101}$
e (-3 × 4) − (-2 × -5) **f** -(7 × -6) + (-3 × -4)

7b Powers of 10

- The decimal system is based upon powers of 10, and can be written using **index notation**.

1 thousand (kilo) $= 1000 \quad = 10 \times 10 \times 10 = 10^3$

1 tenth (deci) $= \frac{1}{10} = 0.1 = \frac{1}{10^1} = 10^{-1}$

1 hundredth (centi) $= \frac{1}{100} = 0.01 = \frac{1}{10^2} = 10^{-2}$

Science and engineering use very large and very small numbers, for example 3 400 000 000 000 = 3.4×10^{12}

- The decimal system makes it easy to multiply and divide by powers of ten.
  - Multiplying by 0.1 is the same as dividing by 10.
  - Multiplying by 0.01 is the same as dividing by 100.
  - Dividing by 0.1 is the same as multiplying by 10.
  - Dividing by 0.01 is the same as multiplying by 100.

Example

Calculate

a 45×0.1 **b** 13×10^{-2}

c $4.5 \div 10^{-1}$ **d** $0.13 \div 0.01$

a 45×0.1
$= 45 \times \frac{1}{10}$
$= 45 \div 10$
$= 4.5$

b 13×10^{-2}
$= 13 \times \frac{1}{100}$
$= 13 \div 100$
$= 0.13$

c $4.5 \div 10^{-1}$
$= 4.5 \div \frac{1}{10}$

$= 4.5 \times 10$
$= 45$

d $0.13 \div 0.01$
$= 0.13 \div \frac{1}{100}$
$= 0.13 \times 100$
$= 13$

Multiplying by $\frac{1}{100}$ is the same as dividing by 100.

Dividing by $\frac{1}{100}$ is the same as multiplying by 100.

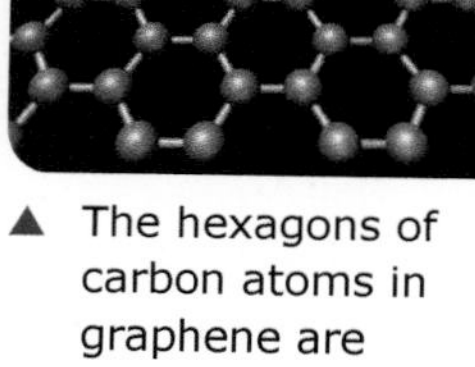

▲ The hexagons of carbon atoms in graphene are 3×10^{-10} m across

▲ The Andromeda galaxy contains about 10^{12} stars

Exercise 7b

1 Calculate

a 26×0.1 b $338 \div 0.1$
c 4.7×0.1 d $5.3 \div 0.1$
e $28.5 \div 0.01$ f $0.82 \div 0.01$
g 25.4×0.1 h 3.8×0.01

2 Calculate

a 28×10^2 b 3×10^3
c $275 \div 10^2$ d $4170 \div 10^3$
e 8.3×10^3 f 4.2×10^2
g $377 \div 10^2$ h $251 \div 10^2$
i 0.32×10^3 j 1.07×10^3
k $4.1 \div 10^2$ l 0.038×10^2

3 Calculate

a 29×10^{-1} b 3.8×10^{-1}
c 51×10^{-2} d 3.2×10^{-2}
e $36 \div 10^{-1}$ f $9.2 \div 10^{-1}$
g $65 \div 10^{-2}$ h $0.51 \div 10^{-2}$
i 317×10^{-1} j 299×10^{-1}
k 8.15×10^{-2} l 0.602×10^{-2}

4 Write each number as a decimal.

a 3.3×10^3 b 2.4×10^4
c 4.7×10^4 d 6.3×10^5
e 2.7×10^7 f 4.7×10^{-3}
g 2.9×10^{-5} h 1.01×10^9

Problem solving

5 Use one of the six number cards to complete each statement.

a $4 \times \square = 400$ b $0.23 \div \square = 23$ c $24 \div \square = 0.24$
d $5 \times \square = 0.05$ e $0.08 \div \square = 80$ f $830 \times \square = 83$

10^2 10^1 10^3
10^{-2} 10^{-1} 10^{-3}

6 Jack works out $15.8 \times 14.7 = 232.26$
Use this information to work out these calculations.
In each case, explain clearly the method you have used.

a 158×14.7 b 1.58×1.47
c 1580×0.147
d What other multiplications can you work out?
Represent your answers on a spider diagram.
e Can you use Jack's calculation to work out any divisions?

$15.8 \times 14.7 = 232.26$
$1.58 \times 1.47 =$
$158 \times 14.7 =$
$1580 \times 0.147 =$

7 Brogan is explaining to Shane how she can multiply numbers by powers of 10. Brogan says 'just look at the power and move the digits that number of places to the left of the decimal point'.

a Investigate Brogan's method by trying out some examples of your own.
b Does Brogan's method work for negative powers of 10?
Explain your answer.

8 Write each number as a decimal.

a $(12 \times 10^2) \times (4 \times 10^3)$ b $(4 \times 10^{-2}) \times (5 \times 10^4)$
c $(6 \times 10^3) \div (3 \times 10)$ d $(72 \times 10^{-3}) \div (8 \times 10^{-2})$

7c Mental addition and subtraction

When you are adding or subtracting decimals, first see if you can work it out in your head.

Example

Calculate

a 9.6 + 8.8 **b** 8.49 − 1.97

a Using partitioning

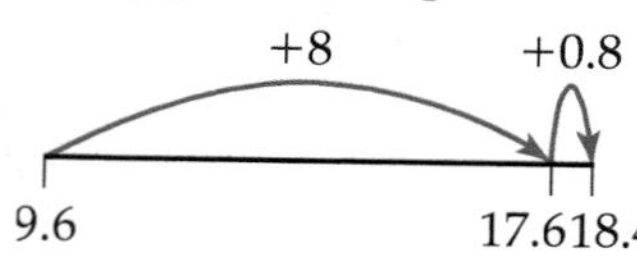

9.6 + 8.8 = 9.6 + 8 + 0.8
= 17.6 + 0.8
= 18.4

b Using compensation

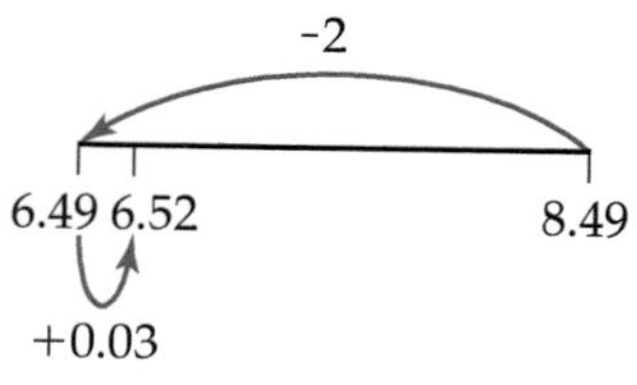

8.49 − 1.97 = 8.49 − 2 + 0.03
= 6.49 + 0.03
= 6.52

Always make an **approximation** before you try to solve a problem involving addition and subtraction.

Example

Barry wins £5000 on the lottery.
He decides to buy these three items.
How much money does he have left?

Approximate

Total cost = £3842 + £95 + £8 ≈ £3900 + £100 + £10
= £4010

Money left ≈ £5000 − £4010 = £990

Calculate, using mental methods

Total cost = £3842 + £95 + £8 = £3945

Money left = £5000 − £3945 = £1055

Exercise 7c

1 Choose a suitable method to calculate each of these.

a 12.7 + 8.6 b 4.78 + 8.9
c 7.8 + 8.95 d 3.29 + 7.99
e 18.3 − 6.49 f 8.76 − 4.93

2 Find the missing numbers in each of these number sentences.

a 3.73 + □ = 5 b 6.85 + □ = 20
c □ + 9.03 = 15 d 2.99 + □ = 50
e □ − 17.35 = 5 f 21.24 − □ = 15

Problem solving

3 This is a diagram of a road network.

a What is the shortest route from Pi to Epsilon? Explain your answer.

b Miss Wilton is a teacher. She travels from her home in Alpha to her school in Phi every day. How many kilometres does she travel in a week?

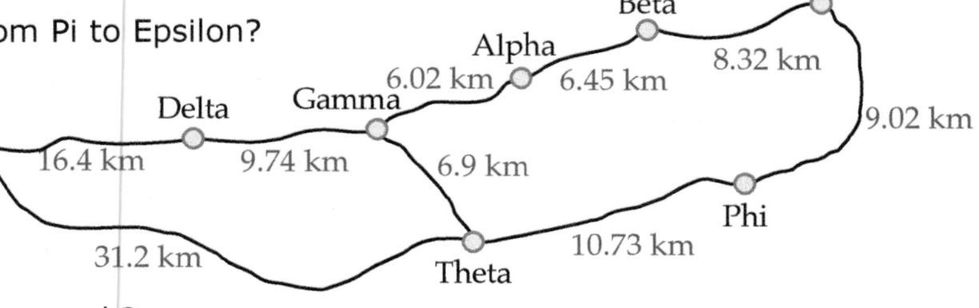

4 Read this information carefully and then answer the questions.

Ian is 1.63 m tall.
Kiefer is 0.23 m taller than Ian.
Hanif is 0.25 m shorter than Jason but 0.08 m taller than Guiseppe.
Liam is 0.51 m taller than Guiseppe.
Kiefer is 7 cm shorter than Liam.

a Who is the tallest pupil and what is their height?

b How much taller than Hanif is Kiefer?

c Put the boys in order of height from shortest to tallest.

5 Here are some items for sale in a shop. The shop is trying out two special offers.

£9.99

£16.39

£5.85

£7.99

Which is the better offer? Explain and justify your answer.

7d Mental multiplication and division

Some problems can be solved by breaking down the working out into smaller steps which each involve just one mathematical operation.

Example

Karim pays £36 800 for printing 20 000 holiday guidebooks.
The printing costs are

1.5 p per page 16 p for the cover

How many pages are there in Karim's guidebook?

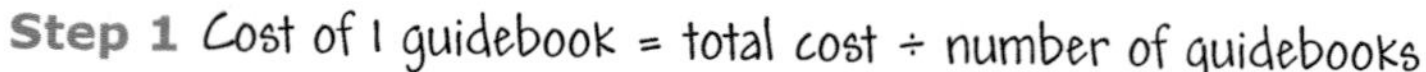

Step 1 Cost of 1 guidebook = total cost ÷ number of guidebooks
= £36 800 ÷ 20 000
= £1.84 (Use factors ÷ 10 000 and then ÷ 2)

Step 2 Cost of all pages = 184p − 16p (Convert all quantities to pence.)
= 168p

Step 3 Number of pages = cost of all pages ÷ cost of one page (Use equivalent calculation 168 ÷ 1.5 = 336 ÷ 3)
= 168 ÷ 1.5
= 112 pages

You should always check your working by performing an **approximation** whenever you solve a problem involving multiplication or division.

Example

Heath is looking at the cost of tickets for Liverton United football matches.

Adult £27.99 Child £18.99

He wants to buy 4 adult tickets and 6 child tickets. He has £230.
Will he have enough money to pay for the tickets?

Estimated calculation

4 adult tickets = 4 × £27.99 ≈ 4 × £30 = £120
6 child tickets = 6 × £18.99 ≈ 6 × £20 = £120
Total cost ≈ £240

Exact calculation

Total cost = 4 × £27.99 + 6 × £18.99
= (4 × £28) − 4p + (6 × £19) − 6p
= £112 + £114 − 10p
= £225.90

Change = £230 − £225.90 = £4.10

Heath will have enough money to pay for the tickets.

The estimation is an over-estimate because all the prices were rounded up.

Exercise 7d

Try to use a mental method, plus jottings, for all of these questions.

1 **a** 12 × 15 **b** 14 × 8
c 187 × 300 **d** 921 × 15
e 19 × 37 **f** 31 × 68
g 0.8 × 2.3 **h** 0.07 × 0.73

2 **a** 840 ÷ 15 **b** 2133 ÷ 9
c 16 860 ÷ 30 **d** 25 200 ÷ 700
e 357 ÷ 17 **f** 1344 ÷ 42
g 13.6 ÷ 0.8 **h** 0.143 ÷ 2.6

3 Joachim is trying to improve his fitness levels. Here is how fast his heart beats per minute for three activities.

cycling 83 running 91 swimming 75

Each day Joachim cycles for 15 mins, runs for 13 mins and swims for 17 mins.
In which activity does Joachim's heart beat the greatest number of times in total?
Explain and justify your answer.

4 Derek pays £9750 for printing 15 000 holiday guidebooks.
The printing costs are

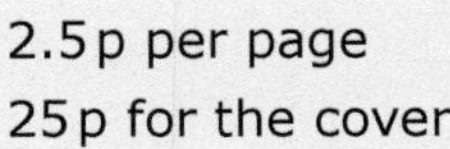

2.5 p per page
25 p for the cover

How many pages are there in Derek's guidebook?

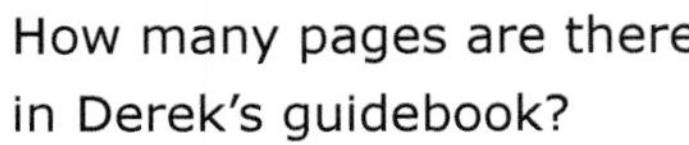

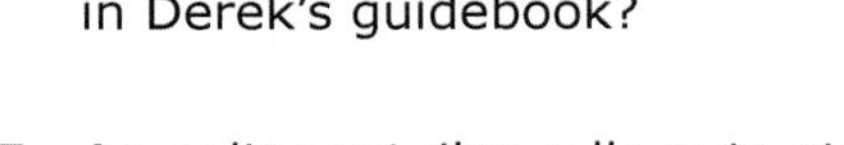

5 An online retailer sells nuts at these prices.

Almonds	£7.95 per kg
Peanuts	£4.85 per kg
Pecans	£14.95 per kg
Walnuts	£9.99 per kg

Work out, using an approximation, if each of these people has enough money for the cost of their orders.

Explain and justify your answers.

a Alesha orders 3 kg of almonds, 2 kg of peanuts and 4 kg of walnuts. She has £75.

b Jameela orders 8 kg of walnuts and 15 kg of pecans. She has £300.

c Bert orders 17 kg of almonds, 15 kg of peanuts and 12 kg of pecans. He has £350.

6 Every person is recommended to consume 5 portions of fruit and vegetables every day. A 150 ml glass of fruit juice counts as one daily portion. A carton of fruit juice normally contains 1000 ml (= 1 litre). This week the fruit juice is in special Xtra packs with 15% extra free.

a How many recommended daily portions of fruit juice are there in one Xtra carton?

b A family of 4 decide to each drink 150 ml of fruit juice every day.

i How much fruit juice will they drink in 1 week?

ii How many Xtra cartons of fruit juice will they need to buy?

c A carton of Xtra fruit juice costs £1.80
What is the approximate cost in a year for the family of 4 to each drink 150 ml of fruit juice a day?

7 MySummary

Check out

You should now be able to ...

Test it ➡ Questions

		Questions
✓ Use the rules of arithmetic with negative numbers.	5	1, 2
✓ Calculate with positive and negative powers of 10.	6	3
✓ Perform mental addition, subtraction, multiplication and division.	5	4 – 7

Language	Meaning	Example
Negative integer	Whole numbers less than 0	-2
Index notation	A way of writing numbers as 'powers'	360 can be written as either $2 \times 2 \times 2 \times 3 \times 3 \times 5$ or as $2^3 \times 3^2 \times 5$
Compensation	Using number bonds to find the sum or difference	$8.49 - 1.97$ $= 8.49 - 2 + 0.03$ $= 6.49 + 0.03$ $= 6.52$
Partition	A way of working out maths problems that involve large numbers by splitting them into smaller units so they're easier to work with.	$9.6 + 8.8 = 9.6 + 8 + 0.8$ $= 17.6 + 0.8$ $= 18.4$
Approximation	The use of rounding to simplify a calculation. An approximate answer can be used to check an exact calculation.	2.19×32.6 $\approx 2 \times 33 \approx 66$ Exact $= 71.394$ ≈ 66 ✓

7 MyReview

1 Place < or > between these pairs of numbers to show which number is the larger.

  a -8.9 and -8.7

  b -0.031 and -0.1

2 Copy and complete these calculations.

  a $12 + \square = 5$

  b $\square \times 8 = -32$

  c $-9 - \square = -14$

  d $-23 - \square = 5$

  e $-45 \div \square = 9$

3 Calculate

  a 6.51×10^3 **b** $0.34 \div 10^2$

  c 240×10^{-3} **d** 0.62×10^{-1}

  e $35.7 \div 10^{-2}$ **f** $10.4 \div 10^{-3}$

4 Use a mental method to do these calculations.

  a $5.76 + 3.4$ **b** $11.9 + 13.7$

  c $17.6 - 6.45$ **d** $6.78 - 0.79$

5 Four babies are weighed at a clinic.
Jack weighs 8.6 kg.
Emily weighs 1.2 kg more than Jack but 500 g less than Sophie.
Alex weighs 1.5 kg less than Sophie.

  a Who is the heaviest baby and what is their weight?

  b How much heavier is Emily than Alex?

  c Put the babies in order of weight from lightest to heaviest.

6 Use a mental method to do these calculations.

  a 5×24.1 **b** 6.99×8

  c $96.3 \div 1.5$ **d** £169 ÷ 7

7 Harry is taking his three children ten-pin bowling.
The cost per game is £7.99 per adult and £4.99 per child. If you pay two games the second is half price.
Harry has £35, is this enough to pay for two games?
Explain how you know.

8 Use a written method to do these calculations.

  a $0.435 + 11.03$

  b $12.6 + 7.89 + 172$

  c $23.67 - 5.478$

  d $56.89 - 7.98 + 32.7$

9 A box and its contents weighs 4.562 kg in total.
Inside the box are four books that weigh an average of 670 g, a torch that weighs 1.3 kg and some socks that weigh 105.2 g.
What is the weight of the empty box?

What next?

Score		
0 – 3		Your knowledge of this topic is still developing. To improve look at Formative test: 2C-7; MyMaths: 1002, 1013, 1026, 1068 and 1380
4 – 7		You are gaining a secure knowledge of this topic. To improve look at InvisiPen: 113, 121, 122 and 182
8 – 9		You have mastered this topic. Well done, you are ready to progress!

7a

1 Put these numbers in order from smallest to largest.

a -0.5 -3 2 0.5 -2

b -2.5 -3.5 -4.5 -1.5 -0.5

c -4.5 -4.6 -5 -5.2 3

2 Calculate

a $5 + -10$ **b** $-11 + -13$ **c** $-6 - -18$ **d** $-5 - -12$

e $-17 + -13$ **f** $13 + -19$ **g** $-24 + -23$ **h** $-35 - -38$

i $48 - -52$ **j** $-37 + -35.5$ **k** $-7 - 8 - 9$ **l** $-7 - -8 - -9$

3 Calculate

a 7×-9 **b** -8×9 **c** -11×-7 **d** -13×-9

e -12×15 **f** 17×-15 **g** -18×13 **h** -19×-9

i -15×-23 **j** -21×19 **k** $-150 \div -6$ **l** $-231 \div 7$

m $-216 \div -8$ **n** $-306 \div -9$ **o** $372 \div -12$ **p** $-345 \div -15$

7b

4 Calculate

a 39×10^3 **b** 7×10^2 **c** $416 \div 10^1$ **d** $3703 \div 10^2$

e 5.3×10^{-1} **f** 7.7×10^1 **g** $562 \div 10^3$ **h** $327 \div 10^3$

i 0.49×10^{-2} **j** 2.7×10^{-1} **k** $6.4 \div 10^{-2}$ **l** 0.057×10^{-2}

5 Write each number as a decimal

a 4.7×10^3 **b** 3.9×10^{-2} **c** 8.2×10^4 **d** 2.9×10^5

e 7.3×10^6 **f** 8.07×10^{-4} **g** 6.3×10^5 **h** 2.05×10^7

7c

6 Here are the distances in kilometres between six towns.
Helen walks from Aley to Bright to Deeton to Fite.
Jenny walks from Aley to Ceough to Esville to Fite.
Who walks the furthest distance and by how much?

Aley					
3.17 km	Bright				
5.86 km	6.45 km	Ceough			
3.7 km	4.08 km	1.74 km	Deeton		
6.32 km	5.04 km	2.64 km	1.84 km	Esville	
6.10 km	6.03 km	4.93 km	4.56 km	3.75 km	Fite

7c

7 Calculate these mentally.

a 11.8 + 7.4	**b** 2.68 + 8.9	**c** 4.8 + 5.92	**d** 3.07 + 2.98
e 13.7 − 8.88	**f** 6.99 − 3.49	**g** 8.71 − 4.8	**h** 9.67 − 3.85
i 0.867 − 0.577	**j** 1.006 − 0.756	**k** 8.349 − 2.022	**l** 19.73 − 7.605

8 Calculate these mentally.

a 109.9 + 12.2	**b** 99.9 − 45.5	**c** 28.3 − 7.49	**d** 15.78 + 7.9
e 899.5 − 98.6	**f** 41.8 − 38.9	**g** 1.37 + 5.69	**h** 12.85 + 19.55

9 Sayed has a 4 m length of cable. If he uses 197 cm how much does he have left?

10 Alexis sells used cars. She has four cars ready to sell at £3999; £5449; £7950 and £1750.

- **a** What is the difference between the highest and lowest priced cars?
- **b** What is the total price of all four cars?

7d

11 Calculate these mentally.

a 7.3 × 11	**b** 6.4 × 9	**c** 14 × 5.2	**d** 13 × 31
e 4.7 × 21	**f** 406 ÷ 7	**g** 3.4 × 13	**h** 300 ÷ 9
i 235 ÷ 4	**j** 16 × 1.9	**k** 576 ÷ 8	**l** 3.7 × 15

12 Calculate these mentally

a 5.02 × 6	**b** 9.9 × 12	**c** 3.4 × 5	**d** 1.49 × 4
e 98 × 7	**f** 2.6 × 3	**g** 0.22 × 5	**h** 0.06 × 0.5
i 376 ÷ 8	**j** 585 ÷ 15	**k** 7.2 ÷ 0.12	**l** 13.8 ÷ 0.6
m 2272 ÷ 4	**n** 0.0063 ÷ 0.9	**o** 0.64 ÷ 128	**p** 1365 ÷ 21

13 Calculate the cost of a day out for the Adams family: two adults and three children

Adult £29.50
Child £4.90

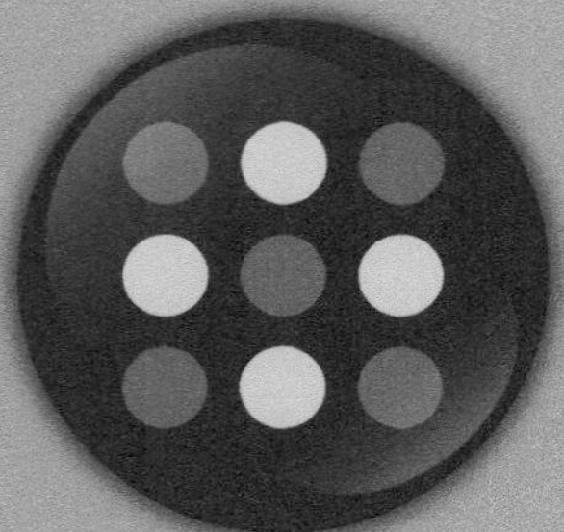

8 Statistics

Introduction

A census has taken place every ten years in the United Kingdom since 1801. A census is a huge survey carried out by the government. It gathers information about every member of the population.

The first census was undertaken by the Babylonians in about 3800 BC. In this census the government counted the number of people, their livestock and quantities of food and useful materials. Another very famous historical census was the Domesday Book, commissioned by William the Conqueror in December 1085, which was a full audit of the land and resources held in England at the time, so that he could work out how much tax to charge.

What's the point?

Statistical information is used to help governments and businesses make important decisions based on understanding the attitudes, behaviours and needs of real people. Without this information, they would more often make the wrong decisions.

Objectives

By the end of this chapter, you will have learned how to ...

- Plan a statistical investigation using the data handling cycle.
- Understand different types of data and how they may be analysed.
- Create questionnaires and record sheets and use them to collect data.
- Analyse data in terms of frequency and averages.
- Draw statistical charts such as stem-and-leaf diagrams and pie charts.
- Analyse scatter diagrams and time-series data.
- Compare different types of statistical distributions.

Check in

1 A survey asked how often people went to the cinema and gave options of

a a lot **b** regularly **c** not very often **d** never

Suggest better response options.

2 Andrea was going to ask people coming out of the cinema to fill out the survey in question **1**. Explain why this will give biased results.

3 For the this data, find the 5, 7, 6, 5, 9, 4

a mean **b** median **c** mode **d** range

Starter problem

How do pupils travel to your school?

What is the average time taken to travel to school?

Do boys take less time than the girls?

Do the pupils who live nearer the school take less time than the pupils who live further away?

Investigate and write a short report on your results.

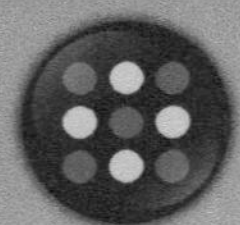

8a Planning a statistical investigation

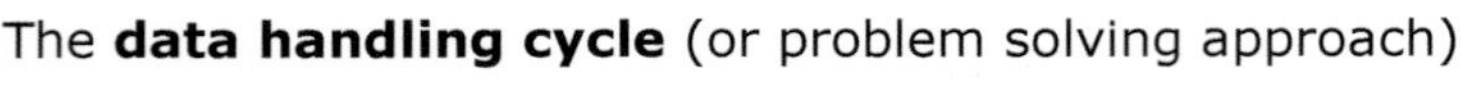

The **data handling cycle** (or problem solving approach) breaks a statistical investigation down into stages.

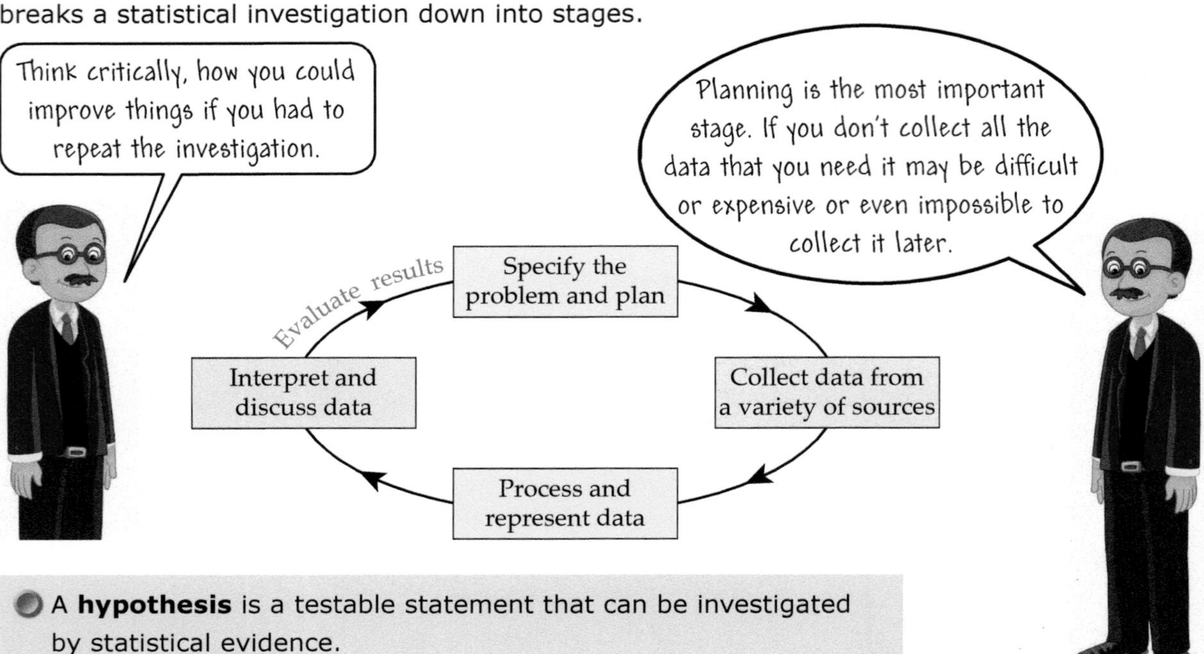

A **hypothesis** is a testable statement that can be investigated by statistical evidence.

Example

Charlie is spinning coins on a table.
She wonders how long it would be possible to keep a coin spinning.
Write three hypotheses that Charlie could investigate.

1. A 10p coin will spin for longer than a 5p coin.
2. An older coin will spin for longer than a new coin.
3. If you spin a coin five times, the longest spin will be the fifth one.

Example

Traffic lights and roundabouts allow traffic coming from different directions to have priority at different times.
What data would you want to collect if you were planning a junction coming out of a new housing estate?

The critical factor is the traffic flow at different times of the day.
So important data will include

- The number of houses.
- The profile of the community; does every household own a car?
- What direction cars are likely to turn at the junction?
- How busy is the road the traffic wants to get out onto?

Exercise 8a

1 A psychologist wants to look at factors that may affect memory. She thinks gender is likely to be a factor, that is, males and females might be different.

  a How could the psychologist test her theory?

  b Write down any other factors which you think might make a difference to memory.

2 A road safety organisation is concerned about the speeds of cars on the road. They want to plan an advertising campaign to target groups of drivers. They plan to do some research to find out what types of drivers, or types of cars, are particularly bad about speed on the roads.
Suggest categories of people or types of cars which you think they should look at.

3 A medical student is doing some research into the effects of alcohol on people's reaction times. He plans to measure their reaction times without taking any alcohol, and also after taking 1, 2 and 3 units of alcohol. A friend tells him that alcohol affects women more.
Suggest other factors which might make a difference to the effect of the alcohol.

4 For each of the following situations, write a formal hypothesis.

  a Do males have better memories than females?

  b Does memory get worse as you get older?

  c Do people under 22 drive faster than older people?

  d Do drivers of performance cars drive faster than drivers of family cars?

  e Does the same amount of alcohol have a bigger effect on people who do not normally drink alcohol?

  f Does the time of day affect how long it will take to make a delivery to a client?

5 Look back at the different factors you have suggested in each of questions **1**–**3**.

  a How would you collect data on each of them easily?

  b You are only given sufficient resources to collect a sample that is big enough to investigate two factors. In each case say which two factors you think will be most important.

8b Collecting data

In a statistical investigation a **variable** is a quantity that you can attach a value to.

- It is important to consider how simple it is to collect the data you want.

Some data is easy to collect. Some is very difficult or expensive to collect. Some requires special powers, such as only the police have.

Example

A university wants to carry out a survey to investigate the mental health of its students. It plans to collect the following information.

a name
b gender
c place of residence
d general health.

How easy will it be to collect the data?

a This will be hard, many students will wish to remain anonymous.
b Straightforward.
c This will be made easier if 'tick boxes' are provided:
☐ hall of residence ☐ family home
☐ shared, private house ☐ other
d This is too vague; it needs to specify a quantity you can measure such as blood pressure or BMI.

A **record sheet** is used to collect together data from different sources.

Name	Gender	Living at home?	Stage of course	health score	Age
Helen K.	F	Y	last year	36	22
Amir F.	M	Y	last year	32	21
Javier G.	M	N	last year	35	22
...					

A record sheet should include the information that is relevant to the hypothesis.

A **sample** is used when it is too expensive, time consuming or difficult to use the whole **population**.

- The larger a sample size, the more accurate the results.

Sometimes you can automate data collection and obtain much larger data samples. This is known as **data logging**.
Putting data on a computer often makes it easier to investigate.

Exercise 8b

1 A large teaching hospital is planning to conduct a study on the factors leading to increased risk of heart disease. The variables being considered are

i age **ii** gender
iii weight **iv** blood pressure
v amount smoked **vi** alcohol consumption.

Say whether you think data could be collected on each of the variables, and if so how.

2 A botanist wants to investigate the best conditions for growing a particular species. Make a list of variables which you think are factors she should consider and say how each might be measured.

3 Katie wants to investigate how long pupils sleep on nights before schooldays. She thinks that there may be differences between boys and girls, that it may change with age and that it may be different for single children and those with brothers or sisters.

a Design a short questionnaire she could use to collect the information she is interested in from each person.

b Design a record sheet to show all the data together.

Questionnaire reminders

- Ask relevant, unbiased questions.
- Make it easy to complete: use 'tick boxes', make options unambiguous and include an 'other' option.
- Avoid personal questions.

4 Christiano is investigating how long pupils spend on homework. He thinks that there may be differences between boys and girls, that it may change with age and that it may be different for single children and those with brothers or sisters.

He draws up a list of his friends to ask how long they spend on homework. The table shows how many friends he can ask in each category.

a Make one criticism of how Christiano plans to collect the data other than small sample sizes.

b The small numbers in some of the groups means that Christiano will not be able to answer all of the questions he was interested in. What would he have enough information to investigate?

c How could Christiano improve his survey?

	Age 12	Age 13	Age 14	Age 15
Boys, only child	7	8	2	1
Girls, only child	5	5	0	1
Boys with siblings	12	16	5	2
Girls with siblings	10	13	3	3

8c Frequency tables

- Using **frequency tables** and graphs often makes data easier to interpret.

If data takes a small number of discrete values you can individually list each value.

Example

Data has been collected on the general health, as measured by a 'health score', for university students who live at home or away from home.

Health score	30	31	32	33	34	35	36	37	38	Total
Home	0	1	0	2	4	16	14	8	2	47
Away	3	5	6	15	11	7	5	4	0	56

Compare the two groups of students.

Median = 36 home 24th student's score
= 33 away middle of 28th and 29th students' scores

Range = 7 home 38–31
= 7 away 37–30

On average, the students who live at home have a higher health score than those who don't. Whilst the range of health scores is the same for the two groups, the health scores of those who live at home generally lie closer to their median than do those of students who live away from home.

If the data takes many values or is continuous it should be grouped into suitable **class intervals** in a **grouped frequency table**.

- Use 6 to 10 intervals.
- Take care that intervals do not overlap or leave gaps.
- Class intervals can be of unequal widths, care must be taken when interpreting some aspects of tables and graphs when intervals are unequal.

$1 < x \le 2,\ 2 < x \le 3$ ✓
$1 \le x \le 2,\ 2 \le x \le 3$ ✗
$1 < x < 2,\ 2 < x < 3$ ✗

Example

The whole of Year 8 sat a test.
The lowest score was 42 and the highest was 94; most of the scores lie between 65 and 85.
Suggest suitable class intervals for a grouped frequency table.

40–49, 50–59, 60–64, 65–69, 70–74, 75–79, 80–84, 85–94

Using smaller interval widths allows you to collect more detailed information. Remember that you should not have more than 10 intervals.

Exercise 8c

1 The speeds of 60 cars on a single carriageway are recorded by a police mobile speed camera. The speeds are shown below in miles per hour.

61, 63, 58, 55, 73, 84, 61, 53, 67, 59, 63, 78, 57, 43, 58,
62, 62, 69, 55, 46, 79, 58, 51, 59, 62, 67, 58, 49, 64, 111,
63, 48, 57, 59, 60, 57, 59, 63, 61, 89, 61, 64, 58, 59, 56,
52, 59, 61, 63, 74, 81, 56, 56, 70, 58, 61, 60, 57, 75, 62

a Summarise this information in a grouped frequency table. Use the intervals ≤ 54, 55–59, 60–64, 65–69, 70–74, 75–84 and ≥ 85.

b In which interval does the median lie?

Did you know?

▲ The speed limit on a single carriageway is 60 mph.

2 After a permanent speed camera and warning signs were installed on the single carriageway in question **1**, the speeds of another 100 cars are recorded.

Speed, *v* (mph)	≤ 54	55–59	60–64	65–69	70–74	75–84	≥ 85
Frequency	15	49	26	8	1	1	0

a In which interval does the median lie?

b Compare the speeds recorded before and after the permanent speed camera and warning signs were installed.

3 **a** There are very few observations in the last three intervals in the set of data in question **2**. Explain why it would not be a good idea to combine them into a single interval ≥ 70.

b Police do not usually prosecute motorists if they are less than 5 mph over the speed limit. What proportions of the drivers are likely to be prosecuted for speeding both before and after the traffic calming measures were introduced?

4 Speed cameras cause a lot of anger and frustration in some motorists who often see them as a way of the government raising money from fines imposed on those caught speeding.
They often see parking fines in the same way.
Do you think there are any differences between the two?

8d Constructing diagrams

A **stem-and-leaf diagram** displays numerical data.
The stem-and-leaf diagram is ordered if the data is in numerical order.

Turned on its side, a stem-and-leaf diagram is effectively a bar chart.

Example

Draw a stem-and-leaf diagram for the following data on the heights of plants, in cm, and use it to find their median height.
61, 74, 59, 61, 82, 59, 64, 57, 63, 77, 71, 67, 78

```
5 | 9 9 7                      5 | 7 9 9
6 | 1 1 4 3 7     order →      6 | 1 1 3 (4) 7
7 | 4 7 1 8                    7 | 1 4 7 8
8 | 2                          8 | 2
```

median height = 64 cm   Key 5 | 7 means 57 cm

There are 13 plants, so the median height is the 7th value.

Draw the diagram and then order the data.

Statistical graphs show the same data in different ways.

	Advantage	Disadvantage
Pie chart 20 – 29, 30 – 39, 0 – 9, 10 – 19	• Quite easy to compare relative sizes of groups as group sizes are proportional to the angles. • Easy to compare proportions of the whole sample.	• Cannot tell the actual sizes of the groups. • Lose individual data values.
Bar chart 0, 2, 4, 6 0–9 10–19 20–29 30–39	• Shows the shape of a distribution. • Easy to compare relative sizes of groups. • Comparative bar charts make it easy to compare several data sets.	• Not so easy to compare a group's proportion of the whole sample. • Lose individual data values.
Stem-and-leaf diagram 0 | 3 4 4 7 9 9 1 | 5 5 7 2 | 0 1 3 | 6 Key 1 | 5 means 15	• Shows the shape of a distribution. • Keeps all the individual data values.	• Difficult to read for large data sets.

Exercise 8d

1 Car speeds recorded on a motorway are shown below.

61, 63, 72, 78, 73, 84, 68, 53, 74, 83, 79, 58, 77, 82, 91,
67, 58, 77, 89, 68, 61, 64, 68, 59, 73, 71, 81, 61, 63, 74

Show this information in a stem-and-leaf diagram.

2 The gender and age of the 36 members of a golf club who expressed interest in taking part in a charity golf event are shown below.

M35, F37, M41, M39, F55, M44, F47, M31, M41, F61, M29, M46,
F42, F49, M36, M32, F39, M46, M61, M35, M51, F38, F57, M43
M45, F41, M60, M34, F63, F49, M37, M57, M49, F52, F34, F47

a Draw a stem-and-leaf diagram to show the ages of the males.

b Draw a stem-and-leaf diagram to show the ages of the females.

c Find the median age of each group.

d Make any comparisons you can between the males and females who express interest.

Problem solving

3 The table below gives data on the number of pupils in four schools who achieve different levels in Intermediate Maths Challenge.

School	No award	Bronze	Silver	Gold	Total
A	53	22	12	4	91
B	37	28	18	9	92
C	44	21	16	7	88
D	41	25	17	5	88

For the following draw a pie chart, a bar chart or a comparative bar chart, choosing whichever is most appropriate.

a To compare the numbers at different levels in schools A and D.

b To see the proportions at different levels in school B.

c To see the numbers at different levels in school C.

4 If you drew a comparative bar chart to show the data on all four schools, you would have 16 bars. If there was data on 10 schools you would have 40 bars. How many schools do you think you can draw on a comparative bar chart and still make sense of the graph?

8e Averages 1

For large data samples, summary statistics such as averages or measures of spread are used to investigate the overall picture.

- The **mode** is the data value that occurs most often.
- The **median** is the middle data value when arranged in order.
- The **range** is the difference between the highest and lowest data values.

Example

Find the mode, median and range of this data on the price of chocolate bars.
50p, 56p, 30p, £1.20, 60p, 45p, £1.10, 60p, 30p, 60p

Convert all prices to pence and order the list.
30, 30, 45, 50, 56, 60, 60, 60, 110, 120
Mode = 60p

$$\text{Median} = \frac{(56 + 60)}{2} = 58\text{p}$$

Range = 120 − 30 = 90p

- For large data sets, a **grouped frequency table** is used to organise the data into more manageable intervals.
  - The **modal class** is the interval with the highest frequency.
  - The **median class** is the interval that contains the middle value.

Example

The table shows the resting pulse rates of a number of Year 8 students.

Pulse rate, p	$60 \le p < 65$	$65 \le p < 70$	$70 \le p < 75$	$75 \le p < 80$	$80 \le p < 85$
Frequency	6	14	35	22	8

For this data, what can you say about the **a** median **b** mode **c** range?

a Number of students = 6 + 14 + 35 + 22 + 8 = 85. The median is the $\frac{85+1}{2}$ = 43rd value in an ordered list. It is only possible to say which class this value occurs in.
median class is $70 \le p < 75$.

b It is not possible to say which pulse rate occurs most often.
modal class is $70 \le p < 75$.

c It is not possible to say what are the actual highest and lowest pulse rates.
Estimated range = 85 − 60 = 25
This is its largest possible value.

7

Exercise 8e

1 Find the mode, median and range of these lengths.
45 cm, 26 cm, 1.11 m, 70 cm, 0.45 m, 0.9 m,
650 mm, 80 cm, 1.2 m, 60 cm, 1.45 m, 145 mm

2 The table shows the times taken, in minutes, for a group of Year 8 students to complete a Sudoku puzzle.

Time, t	$0 \le t < 5$	$5 \le t < 10$	$10 \le t < 15$	$15 \le t < 20$
Frequency	2	18	12	3

a Find the modal class for the time taken to solve the puzzle.
b Find the class containing the median time taken to solve the puzzle.
c Find the range of the times taken to solve the puzzle.

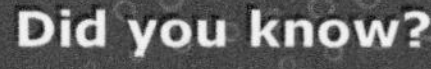

There are 6.67×10^{21} possible ways of filling in a blank suduko grid. However only 5.47×10^9 solutions are distinct after allowing for symmetries and relabellings.

3 Louise is going to Africa to do some volunteer work. A number of her friends decide to do a sponsored walk to raise money for her. The amounts they raised are listed below (in £).

45, 58, 62, 46, 35, 72, 65, 46, 40, 82, 39, 46, 52
58, 43, 45, 49, 56, 47, 48, 49, 76, 62, 67, 54, 48

a Construct a frequency table with intervals 30–39, 40–49, 50–59, 60–69, 70–79 and 80–89.
b Find the modal class for the amount raised.
c Find the class containing the median amount raised.
d Find the actual median from the list of values.

4 The table shows the times taken, in minutes, for people doing a 5 km fun run.

Time, t	$10 \le t < 15$	$15 \le t < 20$	$20 \le t < 25$	$25 \le t < 30$	$30 \le t < 35$
Frequency	345	598	2007	865	84

a Find the modal class for the time taken.
b Find the class containing the median time.
c Find the range of the times taken.

5 A teacher set a maths exam at the end of the year. The marks went from 22 to 80 with a median of 57. She decided that the exam was harder than in previous years so she would add 10 to each mark. Discuss whether the following statements must be true, must be false, or could be either.

a The median does not change but the range increases by 10.
b The range does not change but the median increases by 10.
c The highest mark will be 88.

8f Averages 2

The **mean** is the total of the data values divided by the number of values.

Example

Calculate the mean of these lengths.
1.05 m, 102 cm, 99 cm, 1050 mm, 0.98 m, 103 cm

Number of measurements = 6

Sum of lengths = 105 + 102 + 99 + 105 + 98 + 103 = 612 cm

$$\text{Mean} = \frac{612}{6} = 102\text{ cm}$$

$$\text{Mean} = 100 + \frac{(5 + 2 - 1 + 5 - 2 + 3)}{6} = 100 + \frac{12}{6} = 102\text{ cm}$$

When you have a lot of data it is helpful to organise it using a **frequency table**.

Example

The list shows the number of radios that are in the homes of Mrs Bowler's Year 8 form class.

2, 3, 1, 2, 0, 1, 5, 2, 3, 1, 2, 3, 2, 1, 0,
0, 2, 3, 1, 1, 1, 1, 2, 5, 2, 3, 2, 0, 2, 3

Calculate the mean number of radios per household.

Number of radios, n	Tally	Frequency, f	$n \times f$
0	||||	4	0
1	~~||||~~ |||	8	8
2	~~||||~~ ||||	10	20
3	~~||||~~ |	6	18
4		0	0
5	||	2	10
	Total	30	56

$$\text{Mean} = \frac{56}{30} \quad \frac{\text{total number of radios}}{\text{total number of households}}$$

$$= 1.86 = 1.9 \text{ (1 dp)}$$

Exercise 8f

1 Calculate the mean of these weights.
813 g, 807 g, 0.81 kg, 796 g, 0.817 kg, 800 g

Problem solving

2 A tailor will throw away material if there is less than 20 cm left on the roll.
The table shows the lengths, to the nearest 5 cm, of the bits thrown away at the end of 30 rolls.

Length, *l*	Frequency, *n*
0	7
5	10
10	6
15	5
20	2

a Find the mean length thrown away at the end of a roll.

b Is your calculation of the mean exact or is it an estimate? Explain your answer.

3 The list shows the number of televisions that are in the homes of Mrs Bowler's Year 8 form class.
2, 3, 2, 4, 1, 3, 6, 0, 4, 3, 3, 4, 1, 3, 2,
1, 2, 0, 1, 5, 3, 4, 3, 2, 4, 3, 3, 1, 2, 4

a Construct a frequency table and hence calculate the mean number of televisions per household.

b Comment on the distributions of radios from the example opposite, and televisions in the households.

4 The table shows the times taken, to the nearest 5 minutes, for the people taking part in a 5 km fun run.

Time, *t*	15	20	25	30	35
Frequency	345	598	2007	865	84

Calculate the mean time taken for the fun run.

You may use a calculator.

5 Look back at question **5** in the previous lesson. There is no information at all about the mean mark on the actual examination.
Can you say anything at all about the revised mean after the teacher has changed the marks?

6 John spilt ink on his table. Can you find the missing frequency?

x	0	1	2	3	4	5
F	6	4	2	8	[illegible]	8

Mean = 3

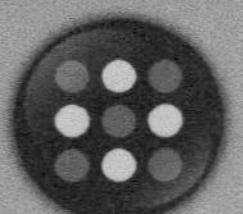

8g Interpreting statistical diagrams

- Two sets of data can be compared using a back-to-back **stem-and-leaf diagram**.

Example

The pulse rates of a group of Year 8 students are taken before exercise when they are resting, and again after 5 minutes of brisk exercise.

	Before exercise		After exercise	
(2)	9 7	6		(0)
(6)	8 6 6 3 2 1	7	8	(1)
(6)	7 7 5 4 1 0	8	0 3 5 6 6 9	(6)
(2)	0 0	9	0 1 1 8 8 9	(6)
(0)		10	0 1 3	(3)

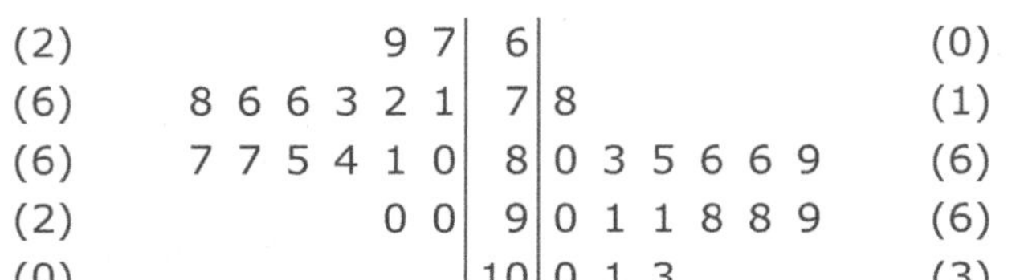

Key 1 | 8 |5 means 81 before exercise, and 85 after exercise

a For each data set, find **i** the range **ii** the median.

b Comment on what you find.

a i Before exercise range $= 90 - 67 = 23$ After exercise range $= 103 - 78 = 25$

ii median $= \frac{(78 + 80)}{2} = 79$ median $= \frac{(90 + 91)}{2} = 90.5$

b The pulse rates before exercise are lower on average than the rates after the exercise, and there is a similar spread for the two sets of data.

- **Pie charts** are a good way to compare proportions.

Maths results

School A

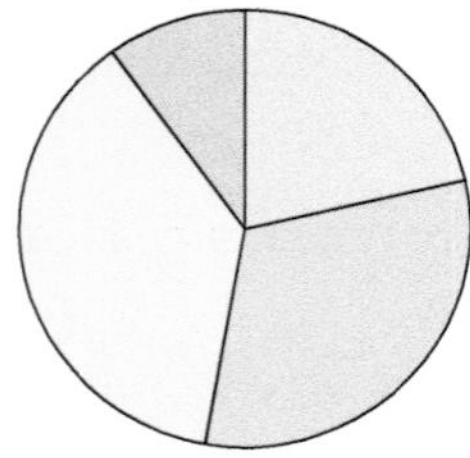

School B

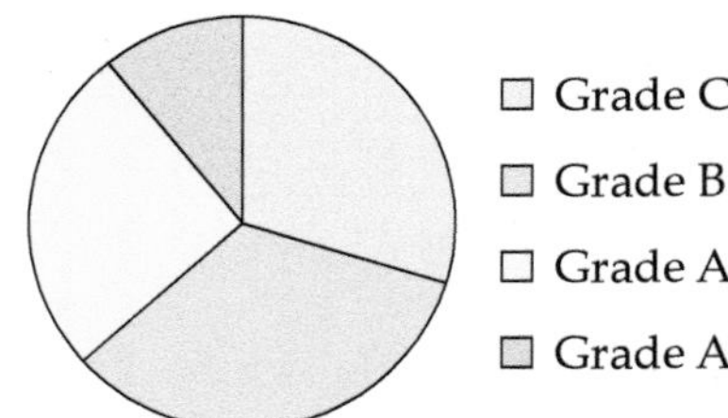

Pie charts do not tell you the actual numbers in a category. School B could have twice as many students as school A.

It is important to know what you are able to conclude.

True

School A has larger proportions achieving higher results.

Not necessarily true

School A has more grade A's than School B.

Exercise 8g

1 The lists show the times taken, in seconds, to run 100 metres for a men's squad and a ladies' squad at a football club.

Men

13.3, 12.7, 11.7, 14.2, 13.7, 12.7, 13.6, 13.0, 13.6, 13.0, 12.8, 14.1, 12.1, 12.4, 12.2, 11.9

Ladies

14.3, 14.6, 16.0, 13.2, 13.7, 13.7, 14.8, 15.6, 12.8, 15.5, 13.5, 14.5, 14.2, 13.9, 14.0, 13.6

a Draw a back-to-back stem-and-leaf diagram for the two data sets.

b Find the median time for the two squads.

c Compare the times taken by the two squads.

Did you know?

In 2013 the 100m world record for men was 9.58s set by Usain Bolt and for women was 10.49s set by Florence Griffith–Joyner.

2 The pie charts show the ages of guests at two camp sites.

Camp A

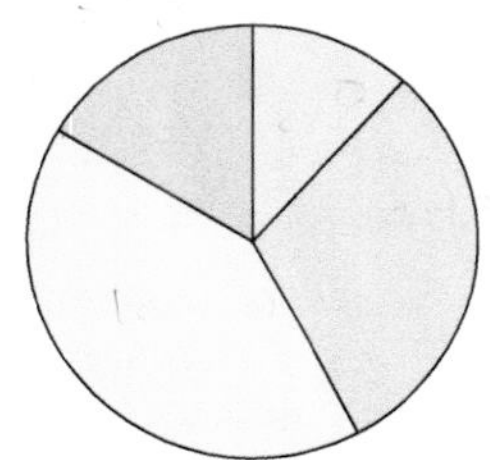

Camp B

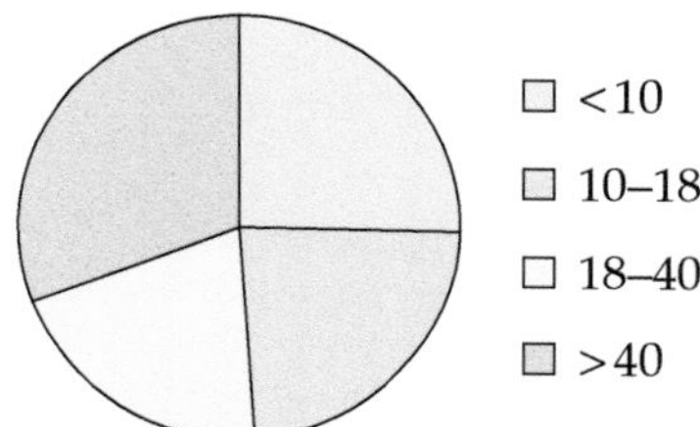

a Compare the proportions of different ages at the two sites.

b Katie has 2 children aged 5 and 7. She decides to send them to camp B because she thinks there will be more young children there. Explain why she cannot be sure of this.

Problem solving

3 Data on the Key Stage 3 Maths results for a school and for the county that it is in are summarised in the table.

	Level 4	Level 5	Level 6	Level 7
School	15	45	25	35
County	254	481	180	134

Hint: for each level, write the number of entries as a fraction of the total and take this proportion of 360°.

a Draw pie charts to show the school's results and the county's results.

b Compare the performance of the school in maths with the general performance in the county.

4 The actual numbers for the pie charts in the example on the page opposite are given in the table.

	Level 4	Level 5	Level 6	Level 7	Total
School A	26	38	45	12	121
School B	22	25	19	8	74

Can you think of how you might draw pie charts which would allow you to compare not only the proportions but also the actual numbers at the different levels?

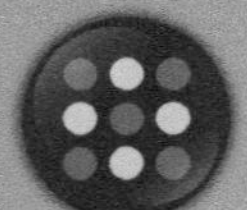

8h Scatter diagrams and correlation

- Pairs of variables can be plotted as coordinates in a **scatter graph**.

This scatter graph shows the times taken to complete the 100 m and 200 m by members of an athletics club and a soccer team.

This soccer player ran the 100 m in 16.5 s and the 200 m in 38.0 s. It is plotted at (16.5, 38.0).

For both groups, the 200 m time is just over twice the 100 m time. The athletes' performance is better and more consistent than the soccer players' performance.

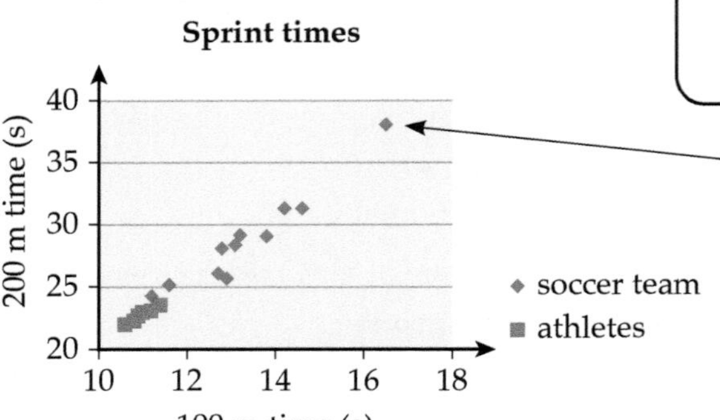

The closer the data is to lying on a straight line, the stronger is the correlation.

- **Correlation** is a way of describing any linear association there is between the two variables in a **scatter graph**.

The 100 m and 200 m sprint times for the soccer team show a **strong positive correlation**.

High values of the two variables occur together, as do low values.

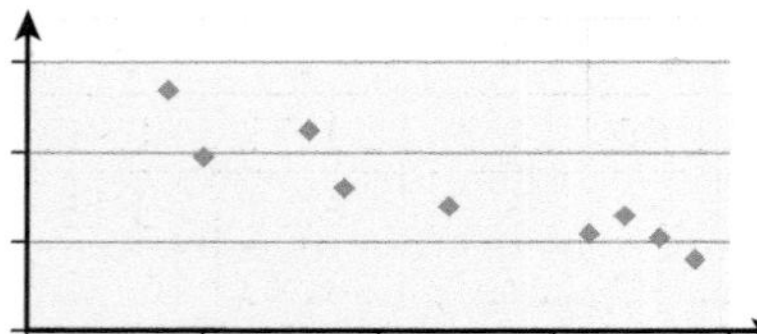

When a trend is decreasing, there is **negative correlation** between the variables.

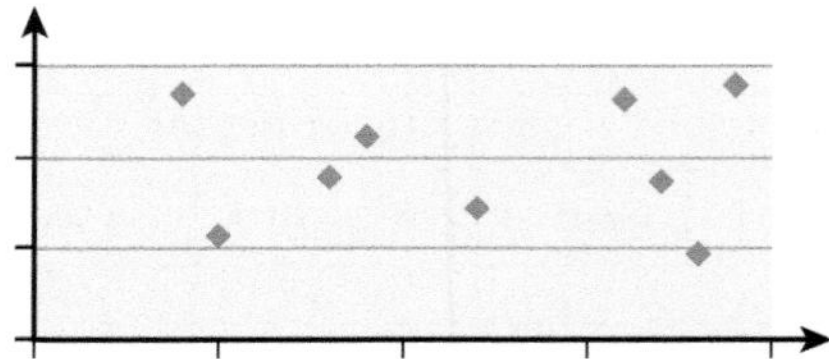

When no trend is obvious, there is **no correlation** between the variables.

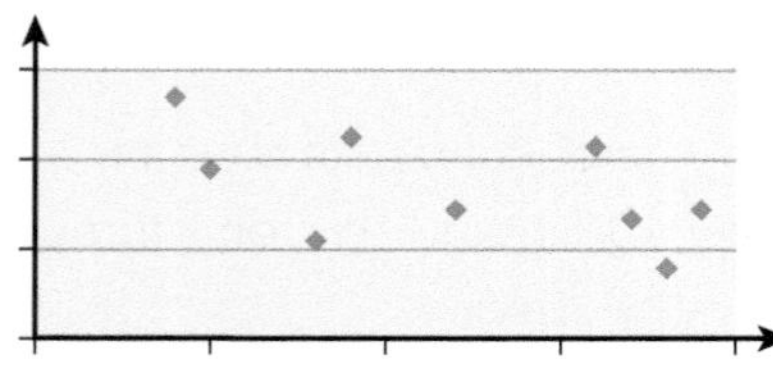

If there is an obvious trend, but the values are not so close to a straight line, there is a **moderate** (in this case negative) correlation.

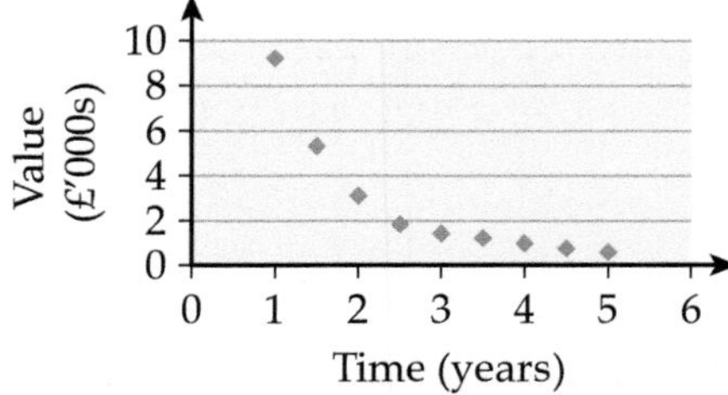

Sometimes there is a strong relationship between two variables, but it is not a straight-line relationship.

Exercise 8h

1 A medical student finds some data on the blood pressures, given in mmHg, of a number of men and women, taken in 1993.

Men	**Age (years)**	18	22	27	31	33	35	39	41	46	46	48	52	57	64	69
	Blood pressure	64	68	67	71	74	73	77	79	85	81	83	81	86	84	87
Women	**Age (years)**	17	19	23	35	37	39	41	44	47	51	55	61	63	67	70
	Blood pressure	66	67	67	74	75	76	76	79	78	78	80	79	81	82	32

a Plot a scatter graph to show the men's and women's data.

b Describe any trend you see in blood pressures as men get older.

c The medical student thinks that a data pair was misrecorded. Which point do you think it is and what may have happened?

d Do you think there was any difference between the blood pressures of men and women in 1993?

Use different symbols or colours for the men's and women's data points.

2 For these diagrams, describe any correlation you see.

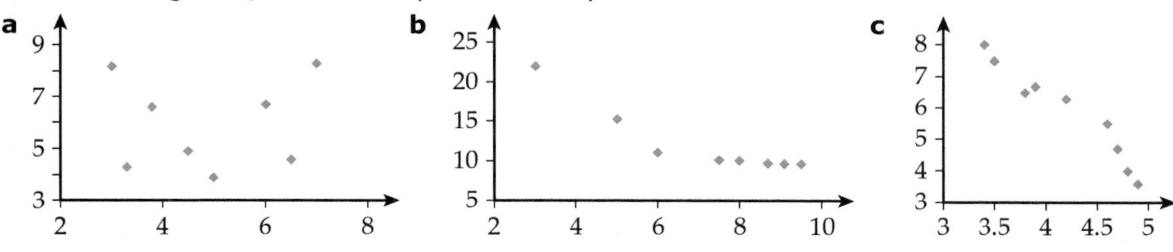

Problem solving

3 The table shows the performances of 10 athletes in three of the events in a decathlon competition.

	A	B	C	D	E	F	G	H	I	J
100 m (s)	11.25	11.30	11.4	11.45	11.50	11.50	11.60	11.7	11.73	11.90
Long jump (m)	6.78	6.67	6.56	6.68	6.40	6.37	6.25	6.38	6.11	6.15
Shot-put (m)	11.20	11.45	11.65	11.80	12.10	11.28	11.90	12.06	11.78	11.93

a Draw a scatter graph showing the times for the 100 m on the horizontal axis, and the distances for the shot-put on the vertical axis.

b On the same scatter graph, using a different colour or symbol, plot the long jump distances against the times for the 100 m.

c Describe the correlation between the times for the 100 m and the distances thrown in the shot-put, and the correlation between performances in the 100 m and the long jump.

4 Use your scatter graphs for question **3** for these questions.

a Taking the 100 m and the long jump together, which athletes do you think were the best and worst over the two events. Give reasons for your answers.

b Taking the three events together who were the best and worst athletes?

8i Comparing distributions

You can calculate statistics to summarise data and make comparisons.

Example

The depth of water (in m) at a number of high tides is measured in early February and in late March.

Early February	3.5	3.7	3.6	3.7	3.8	3.5	3.8	3.7	3.7	3.6
Late March	3.8	3.9	4.1	3.8	3.9	4.7	4.0	3.9	3.9	4.0

a For each month, calculate

i the mean

ii the median

iii the range.

b Use this information to compare the two distributions.

c Comment on the effect of the very high tide (4.7 m) on the results for late March.

If the data contains unusual values or is not symmetrical then the median is likely to give a more typical value than the mean.

a

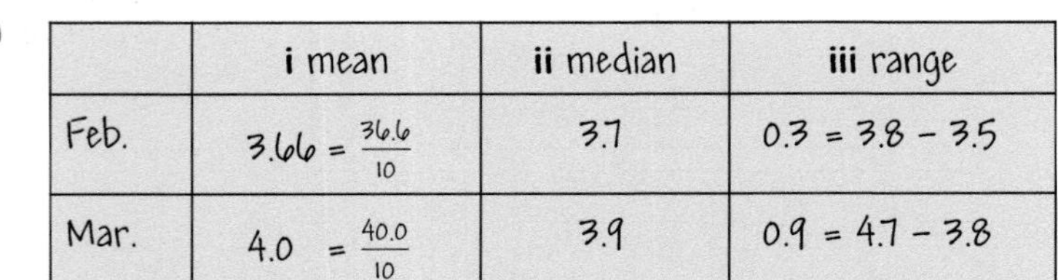

	i mean	ii median	iii range
Feb.	$3.66 = \frac{36.6}{10}$	3.7	0.3 = 3.8 − 3.5
Mar.	$4.0 = \frac{40.0}{10}$	3.9	0.9 = 4.7 − 3.8

b The averages show that the tides in late March were generally higher than in early February. The range in late March is much larger than in early February.

c The very high tide has a large effect on the range, which is sensitive to exceptional values. It also makes a significant contribution to the mean but less so to the median. This causes a noticeable difference between the two averages.

Quoting the range, mean and median does not tell us that every early February tide is lower than every late March tide.

Using summary statistics means that:

- large data sets become more manageable, <u>but</u> ...
- ... important detail within the data can be lost.

Exercise 8i

1 A training programme is designed to improve memory. To assess its effectiveness, tests were carried out before and after the training for 14 participants.

	Mean	Range
Before	35.4	15.2
After	48.1	12.3

a Compare the performance on the two tests.

b Do you think this provides strong evidence that the training is effective in improving memory?

Did you know?

▲ Tides are caused by the gravitational pull of the Sun and Moon acting on the Earth's oceans. Tidal ranges vary as the relative positions in the solar system vary.

2 A nurse records the LDL cholesterol levels and the gender of all the patients he sees during a morning surgery.

F3.7 means a female patient with a cholesterol level of 3.7.

F3.7, M3.2, M2.8, M3.1, F3.6, F3.4, F3.7, M3.1, F3.6, M3.2, M3.7, M3.1, M3.5, M3.1, F3.5, F3.1, F3.7, F3.1, M3.6, M3.1, M3.1, F3.4

a Find the median cholesterol levels for male and female patients seen that morning.

b Compare the cholesterol levels for these male and female patients.

3 The road safety officer in a large town collects information on the speeds of cars when they are 50 m from two sets of traffic lights.

Speed, v (mph)	$20 \le v < 25$	$25 \le v < 30$	$30 \le v < 35$	$35 \le v < 40$	$40 \le v < 45$
Frequency at set A	7	28	6	1	0
Frequency at set B	0	12	15	8	4

Set A is on a stretch of road with warnings about the presence of speed cameras.
Set B is on a similar road that does not have speed cameras.

a Find the intervals which contain the median speed approaching each set of traffic lights.

b Find the largest possible range of the speeds approaching each set of traffic lights.

c Compare the speeds of the cars approaching the two sets of traffic lights.

4 If a local politician visited the surgery and saw the data described in question **2**, why should she not take these medians as estimates of the median LDL cholesterol levels for males and females in her constituency?

8 MySummary

Check out

You should now be able to ...

Test it ➡ **Questions**

You should now be able to ...	Level	Questions
✓ Collect suitable data using questionnaires, data sheets and samples.	6	1
✓ Create and interpret a grouped frequency table.	6	2
✓ Create and interpret a stem-and-leaf diagram.	6	3
✓ Calculate averages, including from a frequency table.	6	4
✓ Create and interpret scatter diagrams and time series commenting on correlations and trends.	6	5
✓ Compare distributions.	7	6

Language	Meaning	Example
The data handling cycle	A way to organise a statistical investigation	Specify the problem; collect the data; process the data; interpret the data
Hypothesis	A testable statement that is either true or false	In Year 8 boys are taller than girls
Population	The complete set of 'objects' being studied	Population: the students in your school
Sample	A sub-set of a population	Sample: the students in Year 8
Scatter diagram	A graph showing paired data plotted as (x, y) points	See p. 152
Correlation	A measure of how close points are to lying on a straight line	Can be positive or negative, strong or weak, or no correlation
Time series	A scatter diagram with time as x-coordinate	The weekly rainfall over a year

1 Pippa plans to stand at the entrance to a supermarket and record how customers travelled to the shop, their gender and if they have come alone or not.
Design a record sheet for her to use.

2 The list gives the ages of people at a gym.

21 32 24 55 18 33 42 49
59 50 63 28 26 30 38 44
47 53 68 27 30 32 41 45

Construct a grouped frequency table for this data. Use the groups: ≤15, 16–19, 20–29, 30–39, 40–49, 50–59, ≥60.

3 Use the data from question **2**.

a Draw an ordered stem and leaf diagram to represent the ages of people in a gym.

b Find the mean age.

4 Jason records how many cakes are in lots of different packets.

Cakes, c	Frequency
1	5
2	8
3	0
4	25
5	1
6	43

Find the

a mean **b** median **c** mode.

5 The table shows the number of scarves sold at a shop and the outside temperature.

Temperature (°C)	-2	9	3	0	5	8
Scarves	15	2	11	14	5	3

a Draw a scatter diagram for this data.

b Describe the correlation.

6 The back-to-back stem-and-leaf diagram gives reaction times for girls and boys.

Boys		Girls
9	3	
1 8	4	9
2 4 6 8 8 9	5	2 4 4 7 8
3 4 4 7 8	6	0 4 5 5 8 9
0 3 5	7	1 3 3 7 8 8
2	8	0 1 4
8	9	0 1

Key 2 | 9 | 8 means 0.92 for a boy and 0.98 for a girl

a Find the median for girls and for boys.

b Find the range for girls and for boys.

c Compare the reaction times of girls and boys.

What next?

Score		
0 – 2		Your knowledge of this topic is still developing. To improve look at Formative test: 2C–8; MyMaths: 1192, 1196, 1201, 1202, 1206, 1213, 1215 and 1249
3 – 5		You are gaining a secure knowledge of this topic. To improve look at InvisiPen: 412, 413, 414, 427, 431, 444, 445, 446, 454 and 455
6		You have mastered this topic. Well done, you are ready to progress!

8 MyPractice

8a

1 A drug company wants to test the effectiveness of different doses of a new drug and whether the drug will affect some groups of people differently.

A patient's general health is important when taking medication.
You may wish to consider factors affecting general health.

a Suggest six ways to group people you think might react differently to the drug, for example, by gender if you think males and females might react differently.

b For each of your groups, write down a hypothesis which could be investigated.

8b

2 **a** Make a list of the variables the company will need to collect data on in order to investigate the hypotheses you wrote for question **1**.

b If the initial trials are to be done with groups of volunteers, say how easy you think it will be to get the information for each variable.

c Are there any of the variables you think will be harder to get information on when the people involved are not volunteers?

d The drugs company says you can only investigate three variables, which three variables do you think will be most important and why?

8c

3 The ages of a group of patients in a nursing home who were given the new drug are given below.

67, 63, 52, 49, 71, 82, 71, 59, 61, 57
81, 80, 56, 53, 59, 63, 67, 64, 47, 51
73, 71, 59, 62, 57, 46, 62, 70, 49, 57

64, 72, 56, 48, 59,64, 70, 53, 49, 67,
60, 76, 70, 61, 53, 52, 59, 72, 86, 49,
62, 70, 49, 80, 66, 47, 55, 90, 53, 61

a Summarise this information in a grouped frequency table using the intervals ≤ 54, 55–59, 60–64, 65–69, 70–74, 75–84, ≥ 85.

b In which interval does the median lie?

8d

4 A sample consisting of the first half of the population used in question **3** is taken.

a Draw a stem and leaf diagram to show the ages of these patients.

b Hence find the median of this sample.

8e

5 The table shows the times taken, in minutes, for a group of Year 8 students to complete a cross-country run.

Time, t	$10 \le t < 12$	$12 \le t < 14$	$14 \le t < 16$	$16 \le t < 18$	$18 \le t < 20$
Frequency	7	24	15	6	2

a Find the modal class for the time taken for the run.

b Find the class containing the median time taken for the run.

c Estimate the range of the times taken for the run.

8f

6 Sally sells some raffle tickets. Using the table calculate the mean number bought per person.

Number of tickets	1	2	3	4	5
Frequency	8	5	2	1	9

8g

7 100 people in London and in Belfast were asked to choose which food they preferred. The results are shown in the pie charts.

London

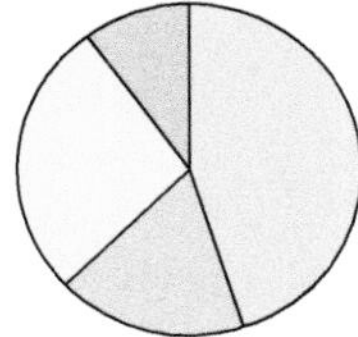

Belfast

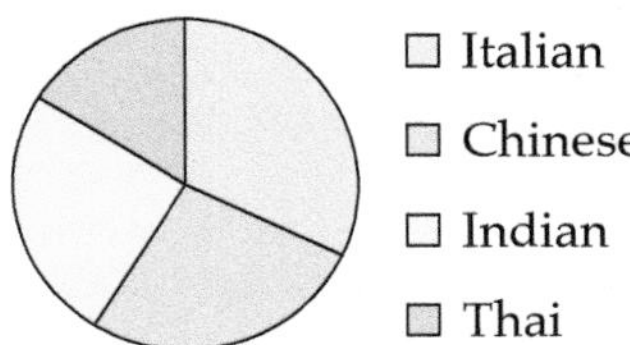

a Compare the food preferences of people in London and Belfast.

b In which city do you think most Chinese food was eaten? Explain your answer.

8h

8 Choose three pairs of variables and sketch the corresponding three scatter graphs to show each type of correlation (positive, negative and no correlation).

8i

9 A careers teacher has collected data from some sixth form pupils who left school to start a job on whether they did A-level maths and their starting salary (in £'000s).

Y15.7, N13.7, Y13.5, Y14.2,
N14.0, Y14.8, Y13.9, N13.7,
Y13.9, N14.2, Y14.6, Y13.9,
N13.8, N14.3, Y14.8, Y13.9,
Y15.1, N13.6, Y14.3, Y14.1

a Find the range and median starting salaries for the two groups.

b Is it reasonable to say that on average people with an A-level in maths earn more than those without one?

Y15.7 means yes did A-level maths, starting salary £15.7k

MyAssessment 2

These questions test your knowledge of the topics in chapters 5 to 8.
They give you practice in the questions that you may see in your GCSE exams.
There are 55 marks in total.

1 Calculate the value of the four angles marked with a letter. (4 marks)

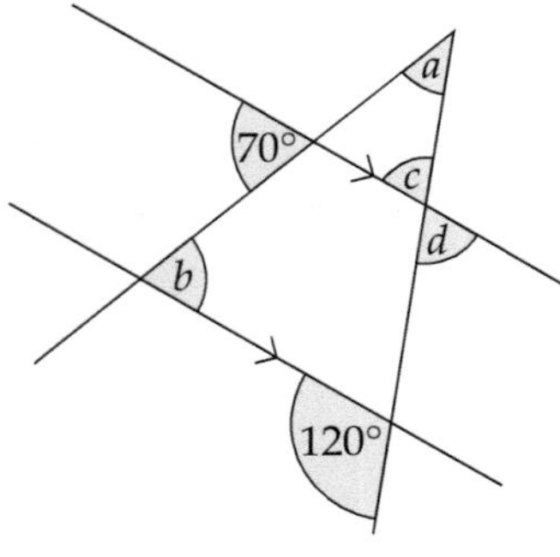

2 Name the quadrilateral that has these three properties. (2 marks)

- Only one pair of parallel sides.
- Only one line of symmetry.
- No rotational symmetry.

3 Look at this shape which shows four regular pentagons joined together.

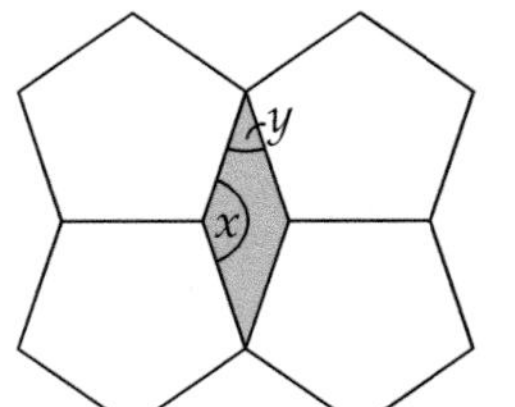

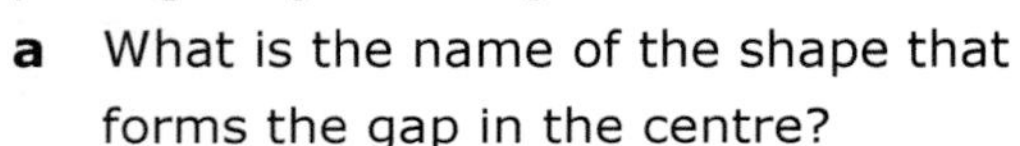

a What is the name of the shape that forms the gap in the centre? (1 mark)

b Calculate the two angles marked with a letter. (3 marks)

4 **a** State the gradient and y-intercept of the following straight lines. (4 marks)

i $y = 2x + 5$ **ii** $y = -1 - 2x$ **iii** $2y + 3x = 3$ **iv** $12 = 3x + 4y$

b On a graph with x-axis from -3 to 3 and y-axis from -4 to 12 draw the lines given by the equations in parts **a i** and **iii**. (5 marks)

c What are the coordinates of the point where the two lines intersect? (1 mark)

5 **a** Copy and complete the table of values for the equation $y = x^2 + 3x$ (2 marks)

x	-4	-3	-2	-1	0	1
y						

b Plot these points on a set of coordinate axes with x-values from -5 to 2 and y-values form -3 to 5. Join the points with a smooth curve. (4 marks)

c What name do we give to this shaped curve? (1 mark)

d What is the equation for the line of symmetry for this curve? (1 mark)

e Write the coordinates of the points where the curve cuts the x-axis? (2 marks)

6 Calculate

a $264 \div 0.01$ (1 mark) **b** 0.61×10^2 (1 mark)

c 8.7×10^{-1} (1 mark) **d** $1.71 \div 10^{-2}$ (1 mark)

7 On my birthday I received £65 in cash and decided to spend it on a book for £7.99, a memory pen for £6.99 and a DVD for £9.99.

a How much did I spend altogether? (2 marks)

b How much change did I have left? (2 marks)

c With the remaining money I bought some artists materials including six pencils costing 65p each and 8 sheets of drawing paper at £1.20 each. How much did I spend on art materials? (2 marks)

8 A survey was carried out to record the time taken to travel to school (to the nearest minute).

7	35	21	44	31	46	25	20	21	11
15	19	27	8	40	57	23	14	15	31
38	41	16	29	33	9	35	43	17	11

a Draw a stem-and-leaf diagram to show this information. (3 marks)

b Summarise this information in a grouped frequency table using the intervals 1 – 9, 10 – 19, 20 – 29, 30 – 39, 40 – 49 and 50 – 59 (3 marks)

c Answer these questions using the information in the frequency table.

i In which interval does the median lie? (1 mark)

ii In which interval does the mode lie? (1 mark)

iii What is the range of the data? (1 mark)

9 The table shows the number of competitors taking part in the Winter Olympic Games between 1952 and 2002.

1952	1956	1960	1964	1968	1972	1976
694	820	665	1091	1158	1006	1123
1980	1984	1988	1992	1994	1998	2002
1072	1274	1423	1801	1737	2302	2400

a Plot a scatter graph to show this data. (3 marks)

b Describe any trend you see in your graph. (1 mark)

c Draw the best straight line through the points. (1 mark)

d What type of correlation does this scatter represent? (1 mark)

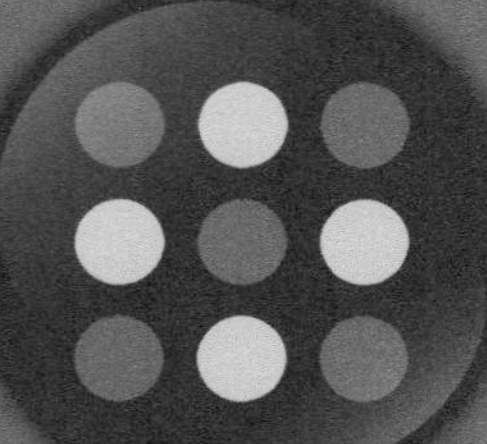

9 Transformations and symmetry

Introduction

Buddhist sand mandalas are made of coloured sand, often taking months to produce by skilled monks. A mandala symbolises the universe and is typically destroyed ritually after it is finished, as a symbol of impermanence. There are many other examples of complex geometric patterns in art, from designs in Islamic architecture, to Hindu Rangoli designs, and the work of more contemporary artists such as M C Escher.

What's the point?

Symmetry is a key feature of the natural world, often associated with beauty and simplicity. Understanding different types of symmetry allows you to create beautiful artistic compositions.

Objectives

By the end of this chapter, you will have learned how to ...

- Carry out and specify rotations, reflections and translations.
- Carry out combinations of transformations.
- Identify all the symmetries of shapes.
- Carry out and specify an enlargement.
- Use and interpret scale drawings.

Check in

1 Convert these measurements to the units in the brackets.

a 80 cm (mm) **b** 0.2 km (m) **c** 3.5 m (cm) **d** 450 m (km)

2 **a** Draw a coordinate grid with x- and y-axes from -4 to 4.

Plot and join the points (-4, 2), (0, 2) and (-2, -2) to form a triangle.

The triangle is moved 4 units to the right.

b Draw the new position of the triangle and give the coordinates of the vertices.

This triangle can be reflected back to the starting position.

c Describe where you would put the mirror line.

Starter problem

A shape (object) is reflected in the line $y = x$.
To find the new coordinates of each vertex of the shape (image), simply swap the x- and y-coordinates around.
Investigate rules for finding the image coordinates for this and other transformations.

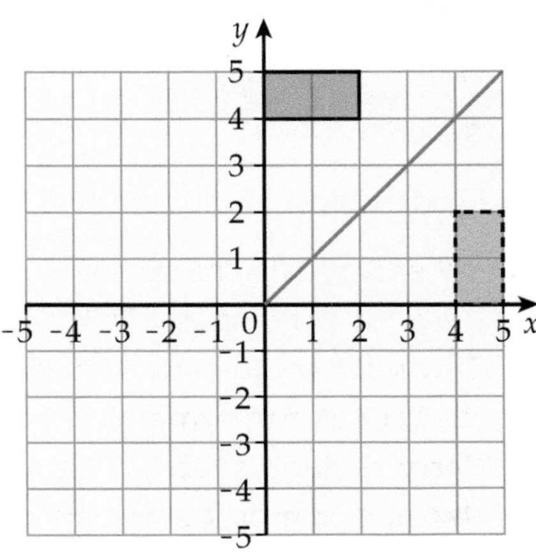

9a Transformations

- A **transformation** moves a shape to a new position.

The starting shape is called the **object**.
The **image** is the shape after the transformation.

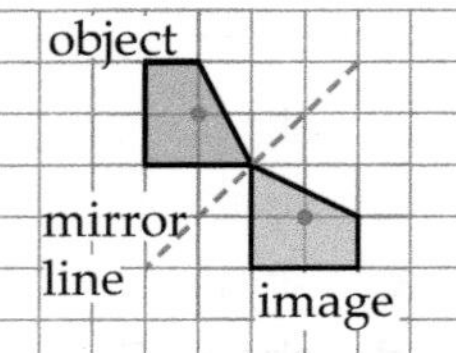

- A **reflection** flips an object over a mirror line.

You describe a reflection by giving the mirror line.

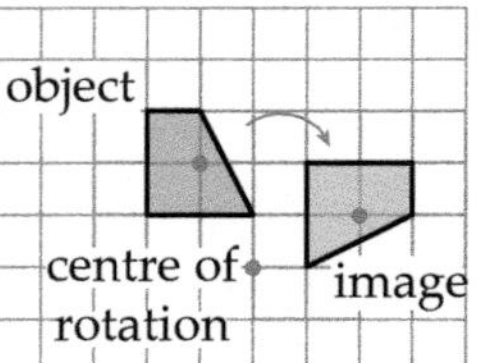

- A **rotation** turns an object about a point, called the **centre of rotation**.

You describe a rotation by giving
- the centre of rotation
- the angle of rotation
- the direction of turn (clockwise or anticlockwise).

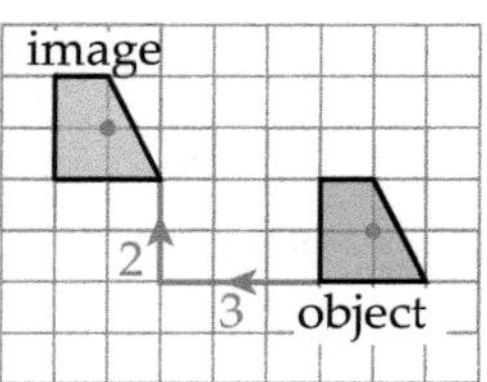

- A **translation** slides an object.

You describe a translation by giving the distance moved left or right, then the distance moved up or down.

The object and the image are **congruent** for reflections, rotations and translations.

Example

The orange octagon is rotated to the green octagon.
Use a trial and improvement approach to find the centre of rotation and the angle of rotation.

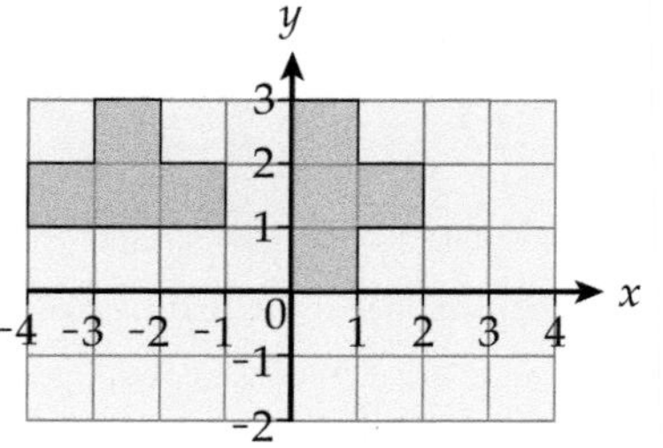

The transformation is an anticlockwise rotation of 90° about the point (−1, 0).

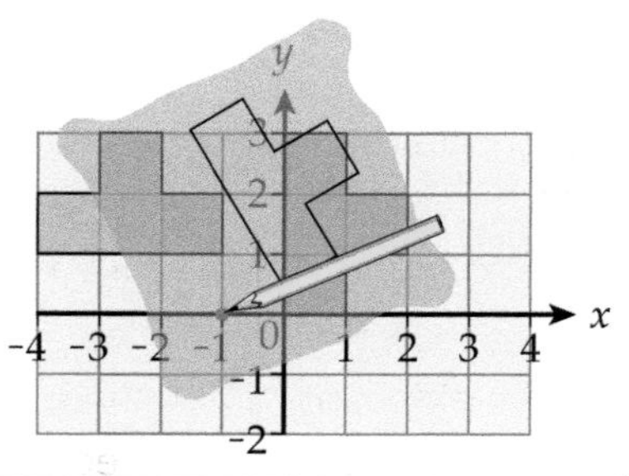

Exercise 9a

1 reflection rotation translation

Use these description cards to describe the transformations that move the pink shape to

- **a** shape A
- **b** shape B
- **c** shape C
- **d** shape D
- **e** shape E.

2 Copy the diagram.

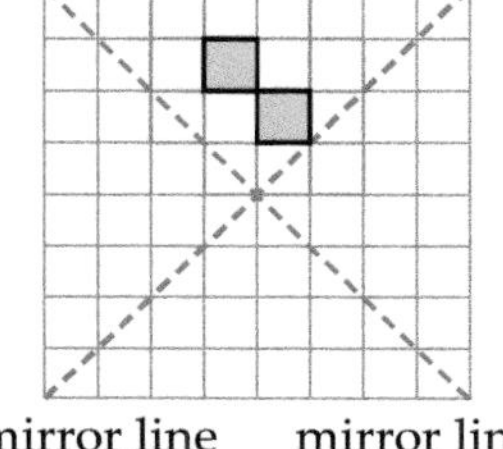

- **a** Reflect the two squares in one of the mirror lines.
- **b** Reflect the four squares in the other mirror line.

3 **a** The blue triangle is rotated to the green triangle. Find the centre of rotation and the angle of rotation.

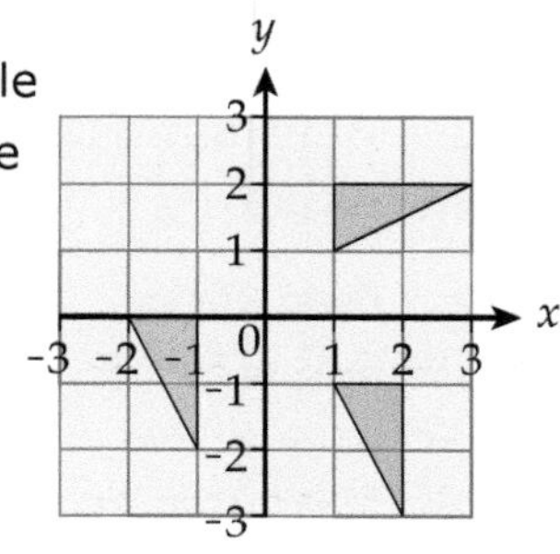

b The green triangle is rotated to the orange triangle. Find the centre of rotation and the angle of rotation.

c Describe fully the transformation that moves

- **i** the orange triangle to the blue triangle
- **ii** the blue triangle to the orange triangle.

Problem solving

4 **a** Rotate a scalene triangle through 180° about the midpoint of a side.

b Mark the equal angles and the equal sides on the completed quadrilateral.

c Show that the completed quadrilateral is a parallelogram.

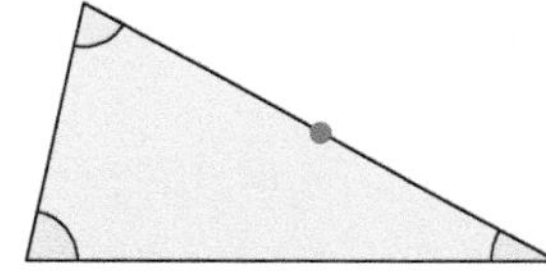

5 **a** Draw the 4 by 4 grid and copy this outline.

b Draw the reflection of the outline in the mirror line.

c Can you see a vase or two faces in your completed drawing?

d Colour either the vase or the faces.

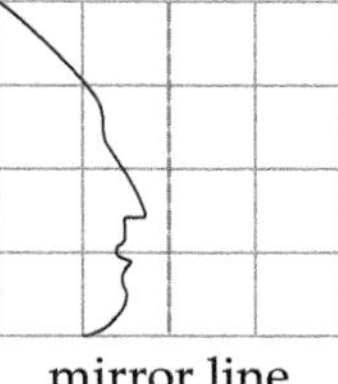

6 **a** Copy the diagram.
Reflect the blue shape in mirror line M1 and then reflect the image in mirror line M2.

b Describe the single transformation that takes the blue shape to the final image.

c Repeat this procedure for different initial shapes and different pairs of mirror lines. Can you find the connection between the two mirror lines and the single transformation?

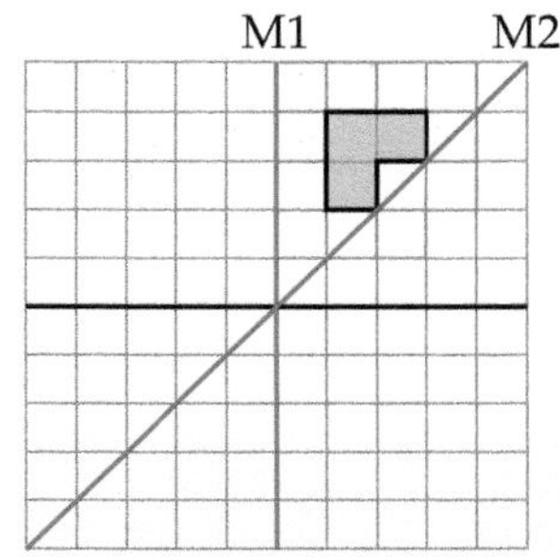

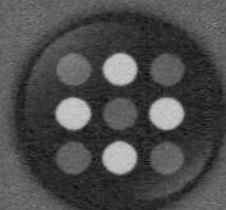

9b Combinations of transformations

You can transform 2D shapes using repeated **reflections**, **rotations** and **translations**.

Example

a Reflect the blue triangle in the line $x = 2$. Call the image I_1.

b Reflect the image in the line $y = 0$. Call the image I_2.

c Describe a single transformation that moves the blue triangle to I_2.

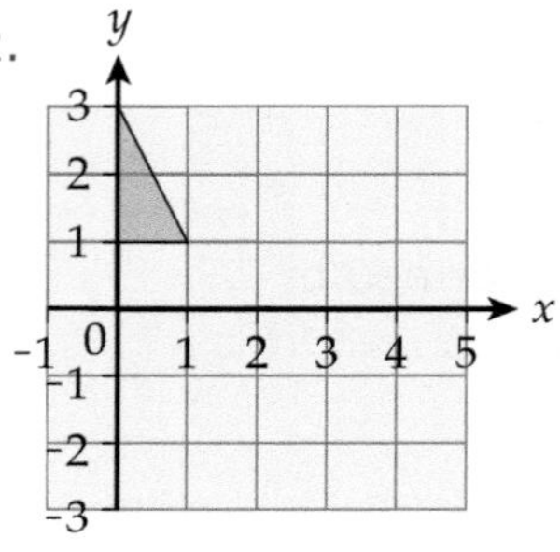

a, b

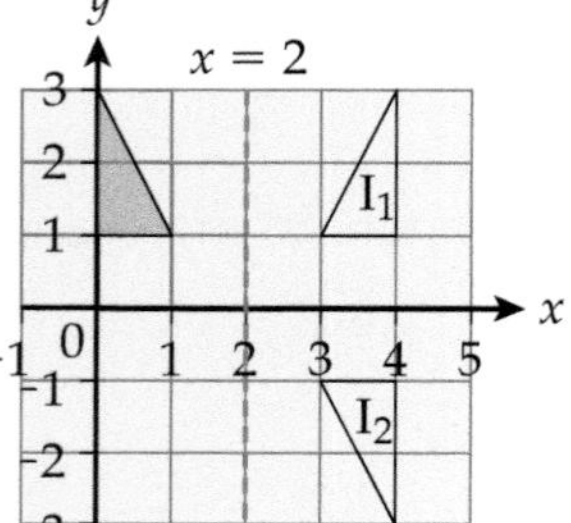

c A rotation of 180° about (2, 0).

This means these two reflections are **equivalent** to one half-turn rotation.

p.94

A **tessellation** is a tiling pattern with no gaps or overlaps.

You can tessellate shapes by repeating the same transformation.

Example

a Tessellate a scalene triangle using repeated rotations of 180° about the midpoints of the sides.

b Colour the equal angles in your tessellation.

c Which angle properties are shown in the tessellation?

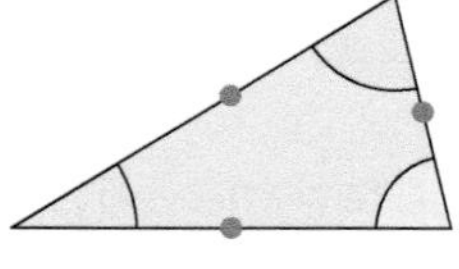

a, b

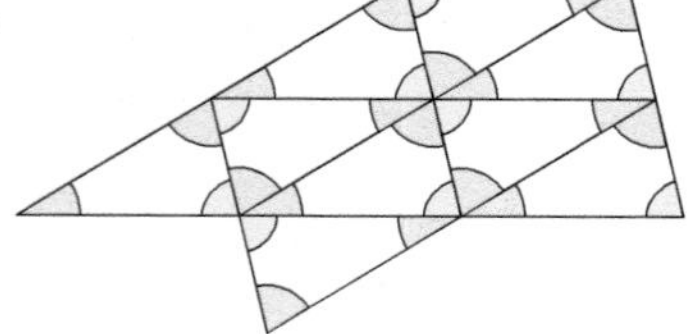

c
- Vertically opposite angles are equal.
- The exterior angle of a triangle is equal to the sum of the two opposite interior angles.
- Alternate angles are equal for parallel lines.
- Corresponding angles are equal for parallel lines.
- Sum of internal angles in a triangle equals the angle on a straight line, 180°.

Exercise 9b

1 Draw this isosceles trapezium on isometric paper.
The shape is rotated clockwise through 120° about the black dot.
The image is again rotated clockwise through 120° about the dot.
Name the shape that is formed by the object and the images.

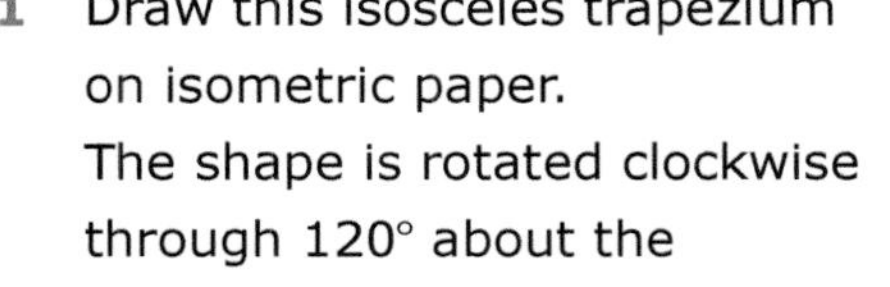

2 **a** Tessellate a quadrilateral using repeated rotations of 180° about the midpoint of the sides.

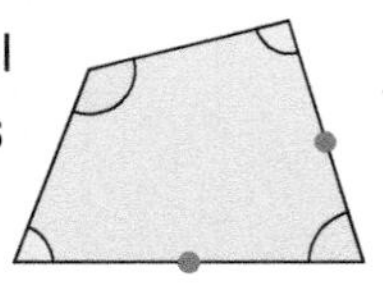

b Colour the equal angles in your tessellation.

c What angle properties are shown in the tessellation?

Problem solving

3 Two mirrors M_1 and M_2 are 4 units apart.
A pink flag is placed halfway between the mirrors.

a Draw the flag after a reflection in the mirror M_1. Label this image I_1.

b Draw the reflection of I_1 using the mirror M_2. Label this new image I_2.

c Describe the single transformation that moves the pink flag to I_2.

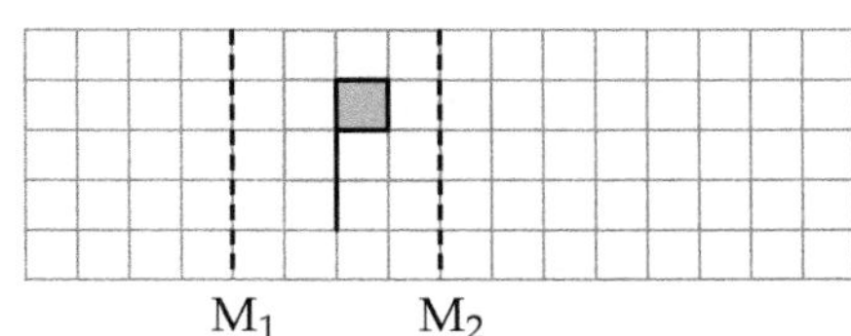

4 The green triangle is rotated clockwise through 180° about (0,0).

a Draw the image and label it I_1.

b The triangle I_1 is reflected in the x-axis. Draw the new image and call it I_2.

c Describe the single transformation that moves the green triangle to I_2.

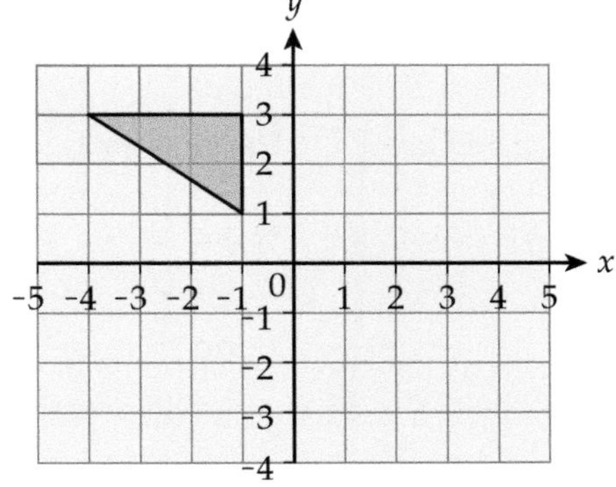

5 Use three squares to draw a hexagon.

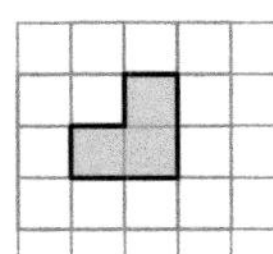

Colour your tessellation.

Remove a triangle and rotate the shape through 180°.

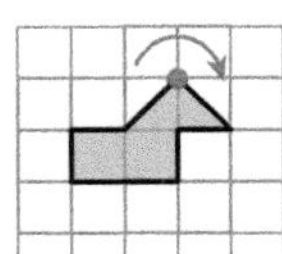

Show that this shape tessellates using repeated rotations.

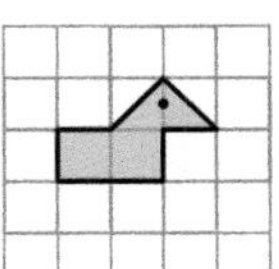

9c Symmetry

- A **line of symmetry** divides a shape into two identical mirror images.

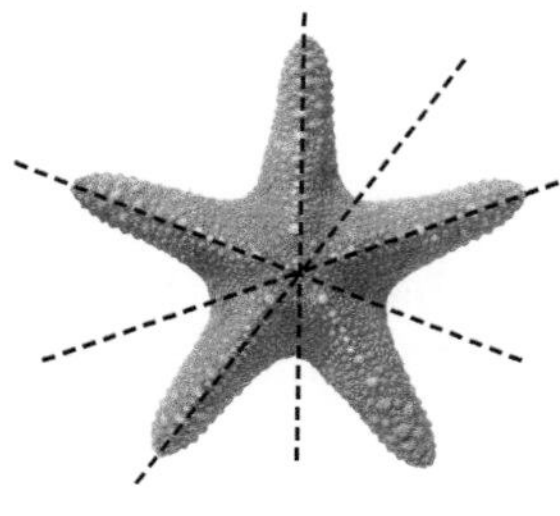

- A shape has **reflection symmetry** if it has at least one line of symmetry.

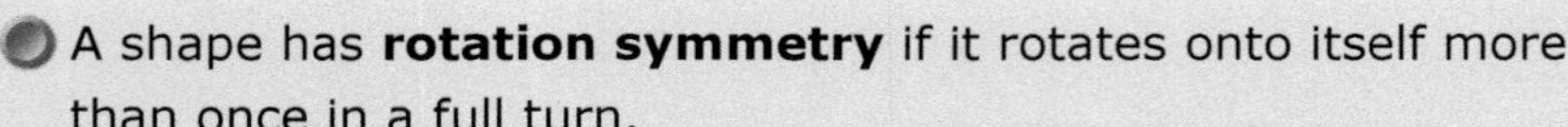

- A shape has **rotation symmetry** if it rotates onto itself more than once in a full turn.
  - The **order of rotation symmetry** is the number of times a shape looks exactly like itself in a complete turn.

The starfish has 5 lines of symmetry and rotation symmetry of order 5.

You should know the symmetry properties of these quadrilaterals.

Square	**Rectangle**	**Rhombus**	**Parallelogram**
4 lines of symmetry Rotation symmetry of order 4	2 lines of symmetry Rotation symmetry of order 2	2 lines of symmetry Rotation symmetry of order 2	0 lines of symmetry Rotation symmetry of order 2

Trapezium	**Isosceles trapezium**	**Kite**	**Arrowhead**
0 lines of symmetry No rotation symmetry	1 line of symmetry No rotation symmetry	1 line of symmetry No rotation symmetry	1 line of symmetry No rotation symmetry

Example

a Draw a shape using five squares that has 4 lines of reflection symmetry and rotation symmetry of order 4.

b Draw the 4 lines of symmetry.

a

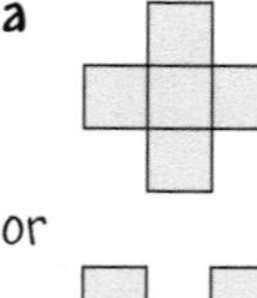

or

b

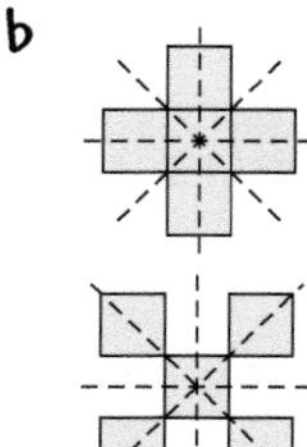

Exercise 9c

1 These symbols are on Abdi's mobile phone. Draw each symbol and draw any lines of symmetry. State the order of rotation symmetry in each case.

a #   b ▭

c ✳   d ☎

e ⇧   f

2 i Draw each of these shapes and draw any lines of symmetry.

ii State the order of rotation symmetry in each case.

a an equilateral triangle

b a square

c a regular pentagon

d a regular hexagon

e a regular octagon

A **regular** shape has equal sides and equal angles.

Problem solving

3 Make three copies of this diagram.

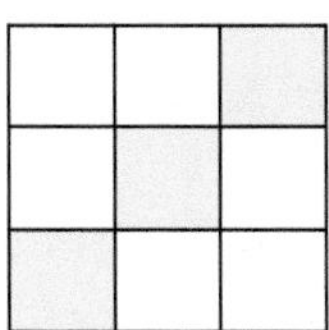

a On the first diagram add the lines of symmetry and state the order of rotation symmetry.

b On the second diagram colour in one square so that the shape has one line of symmetry, but no rotation symmetry. Draw the line of symmetry.

c On the third diagram colour in two squares so that the shape has no lines of symmetry, and rotation symmetry of order 2.

Did you know?

A kaleidoscope uses mirrors and repeated reflections to create symmetrical patterns.

4 This diagram has a vertical and a horizontal line of symmetry.

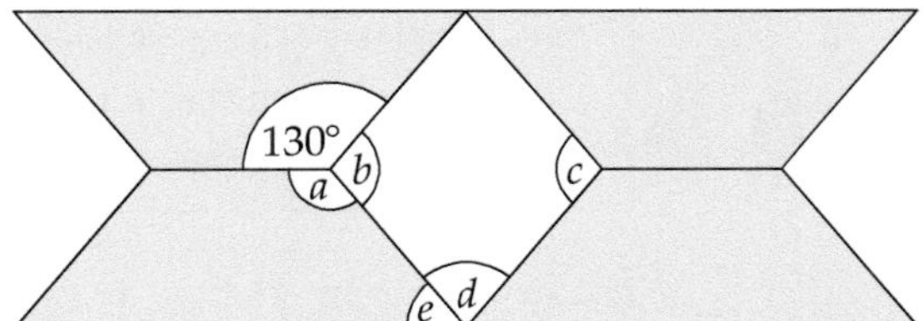

The angle shown is 130°.
Calculate the angles a, b, c, d and e.

5 The number 1001 has 2 lines of reflection symmetry and rotation symmetry of order 2.

1001

Are there any other numbers between 1000 and 2000 that have both reflection and rotation symmetry?

6 This Latin inscription has been found in Pompeii and other Roman cities. It translates as 'the farmer Arepo has ploughing as work'.
Describe all its symmetries.

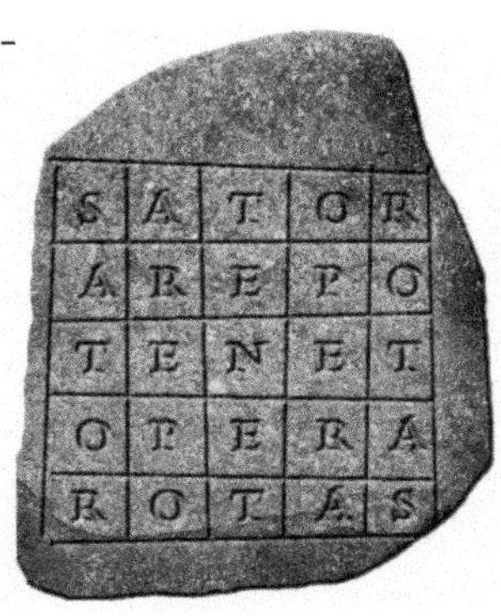

9d Enlargements 1

You enlarge a shape by multiplying the lengths by the **scale factor**.

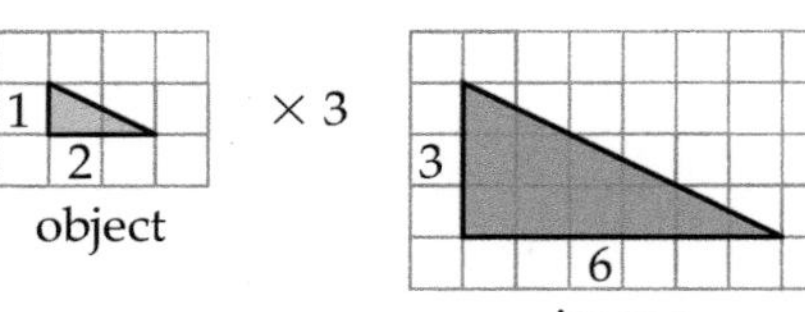

The scale factor is 3.

- An **enlargement** is a type of **transformation** that changes the size of a shape.
  - ▶ The **object** and the **image** are **similar shapes**.

The position of the image is fixed if you use a **centre of enlargement**.

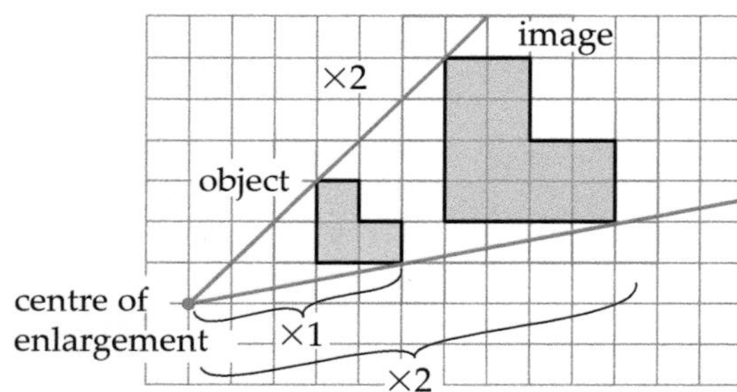

This enlargement is scale factor 2.

- You describe an enlargement by giving
  - the scale factor
  - the centre of enlargement.

Example

Draw the enlargement of the shape using a scale factor of 3 and the marked centre of enlargement.

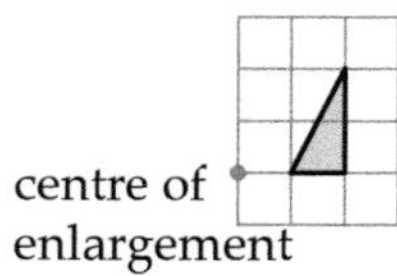

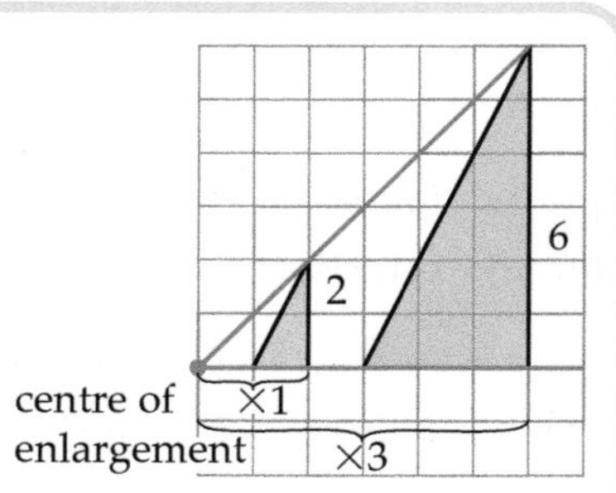

Exercise 9d

1 A photograph measuring 10 cm by 15 cm is enlarged to make mathematically similar photographs.
Calculate the scale factor of each enlargement.

a 20 cm by 30 cm **b** 30 cm by 45 cm
c 25 cm by 37.5 cm

2 Copy these diagrams on graph paper and draw on coordinate axes.
The blue shapes are enlarged to give the green shapes.
Calculate the scale factor between the small and large shape in each diagram and find the coordinates of the centre of enlargement.

a

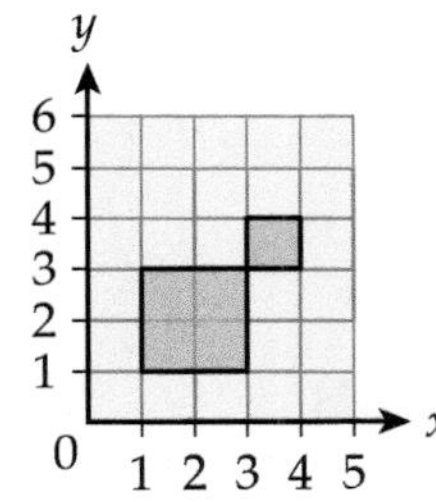

b

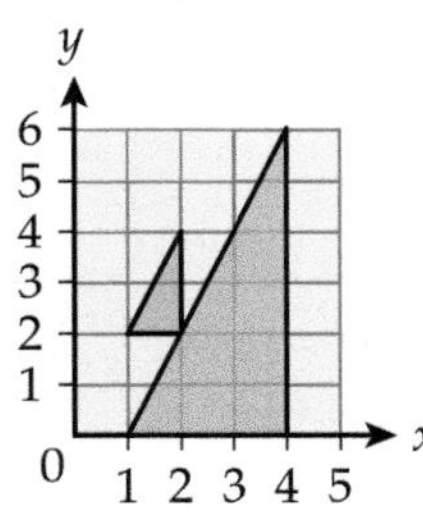

2 c

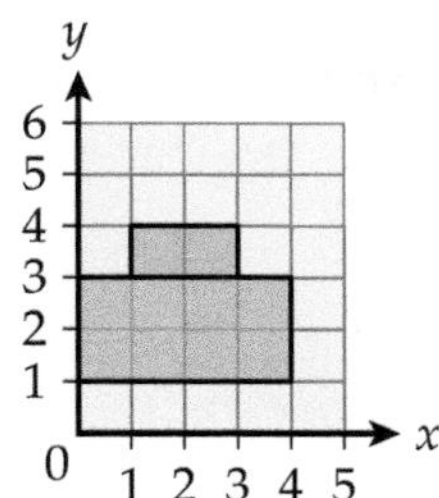

d

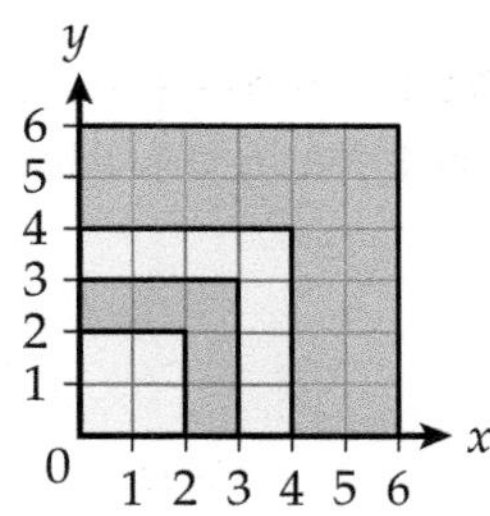

3 Copy these shapes on square grid paper.
Draw the enlargement of each shape using the dot as the centre of enlargement and the given scale factor.

a

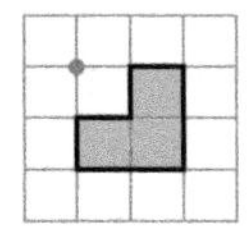

scale factor 2

b

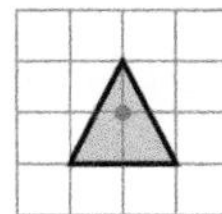

scale factor 3

c

scale factor 4

d

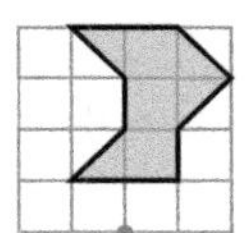

scale factor 2

Problem solving

4 The pink rectangle is enlarged to give a green rectangle using (0, 5) as the centre of enlargement.
Part of the green rectangle is shown.
The point (1, 5) moves to (4, 5).

Find **a** the scale factor of the enlargement
b the four coordinates of the green rectangle.

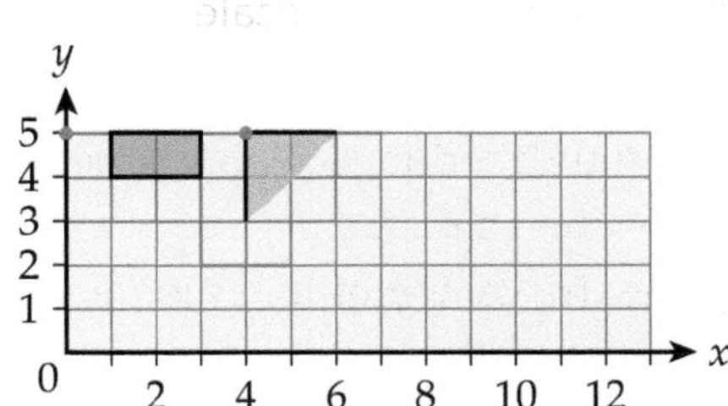

5 An equilateral triangle is enlarged by scale factor 2.
Four small triangles will fit inside the image.
The small triangle is enlarged by scale factor 10.

a How many small triangles will fit inside the image?
b Draw the enlarged shape on isometric paper.

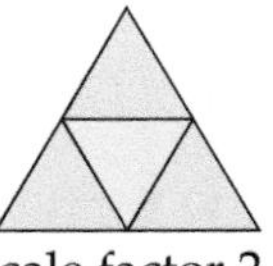

scale factor 2

9e Enlargements 2

An **enlargement** with a **scale factor** of $\frac{1}{2}$ results in an **image** that is smaller than the **object**.

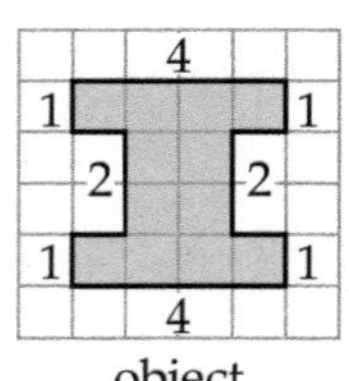

$\times \frac{1}{2}$

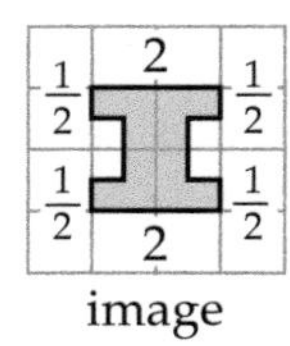

- The object and the image are **similar** – the lengths change in proportion – the angles stay the same.
  - If the scale factor is greater than 1, the image is larger than the object.
  - If the scale factor is less than 1, the image is smaller than the object.

The position of the image is fixed, if you use a **centre of enlargement**. This enlargement has scale factor $\frac{1}{3}$.

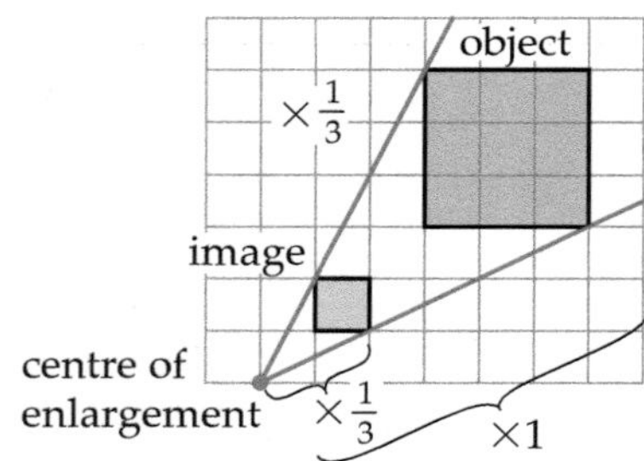

Example

Draw the enlargement of the orange triangle using a scale factor of $\frac{1}{2}$ using the origin as centre of enlargement.

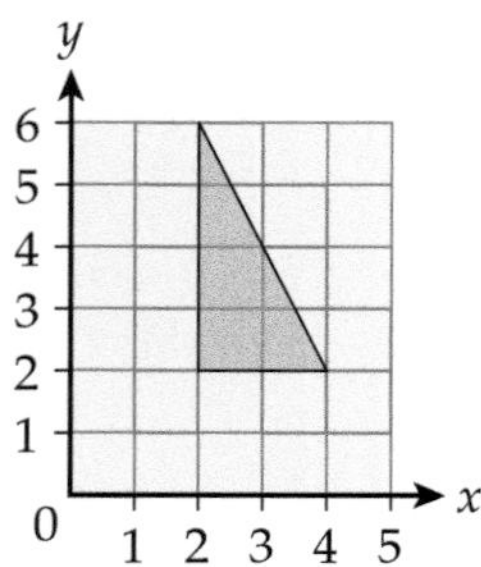

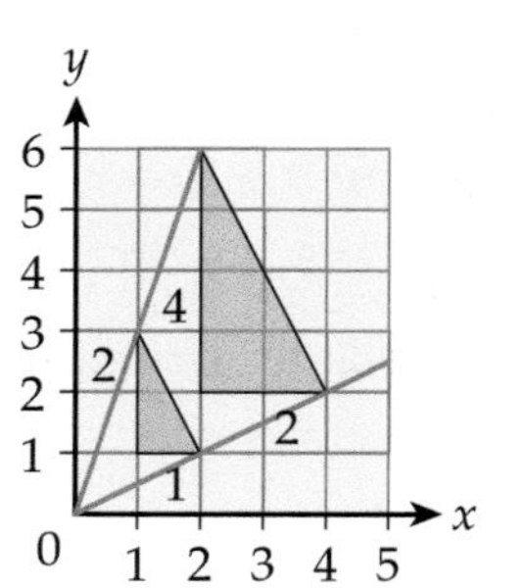

Check that each side of the large triangle has been multiplied by $\frac{1}{2}$.
$4 \times \frac{1}{2} = 2 \quad 2 \times \frac{1}{2} = 1$

Exercise 9e

1 Copy the shapes on square grid paper.
Enlarge each shape by the given scale factor.
There is no centre of enlargement.

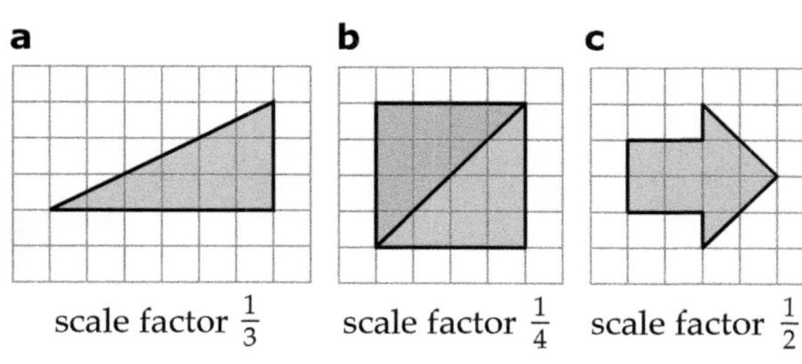

2 Copy these shapes on square grid paper.
Enlarge each shape using the dot as the centre of enlargement and the given scale factor.

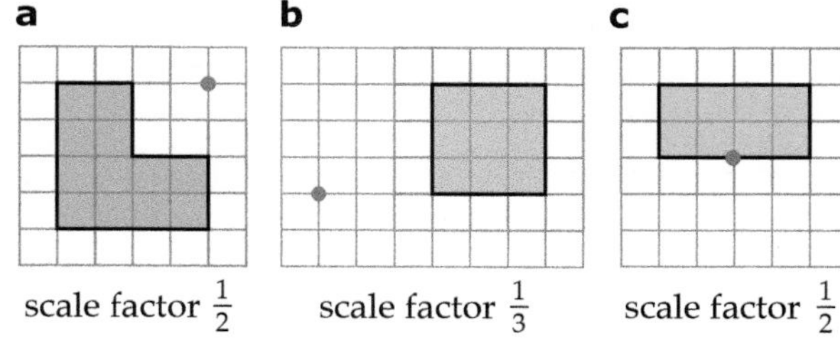

Problem solving

3 **a** Copy this coordinate grid onto graph paper and plot the points A(2,2), B(8,0), C(12,8) and D(4,6).

b State the mathematical name of quadrilateral ABCD.

c Using (2,4) as the centre of enlargement, enlarge ABCD by scale factor $\frac{1}{2}$.

d Write the coordinates of the vertices of the image.

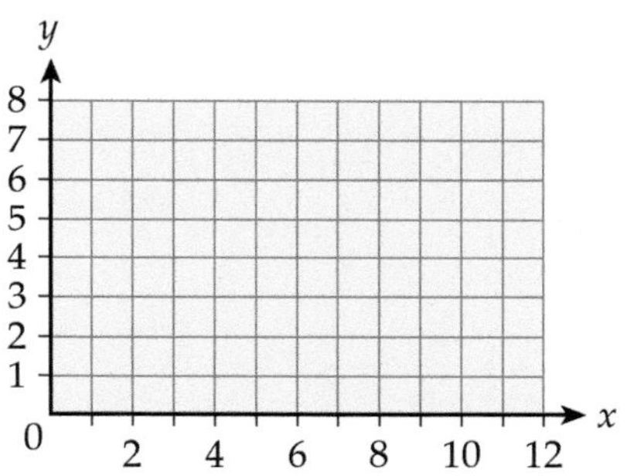

4 A triangle is enlarged by scale factor 4.
What is the scale factor of the enlargement that takes the image back to the object?

5 The smaller triangle is an enlargement of the larger triangle.
Calculate

a the scale factor of the enlargement

b the value of x

c the perimeter of each triangle.

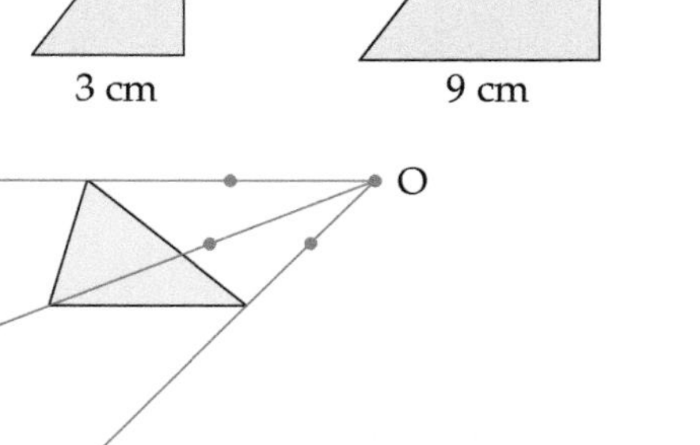

6 Draw a large triangle.
Mark a point O outside the triangle.
Draw lines from O to the vertices of the triangle.
Find the midpoint of each line and join the three midpoints to form a triangle.

O

Is this triangle similar to the first triangle?
What is the scale factor of the enlargement?

9 MySummary

Check out

You should now be able to ...

You should now be able to ...	Level	Test it ➡ Questions
✓ Carry out and specify reflections, rotations and translations.	5	1, 2
✓ Carry out combinations of transformations.	6	3
✓ Recognise rotation and reflection symmetry.	5	4, 5
✓ Carry out and specify an enlargement.	6	6, 7

Language	Meaning	Example
Object	The starting shape	p. 164
Image	The resulting shape after the transformations have been applied	
Reflection	The object is flipped over a given mirror line	Looking at this book in a mirror is a reflection.
Rotation	Rotates an object around a central point (like a car wheel turning)	Turning this book through 90° clockwise about its bottom right corner is a rotation.
Translation	A transformation which slides an object	Sliding this book across your desk is a translation.
Enlargement	A transformation that changes the size of the object.	If you enlarged this book by scale factor 2 about its centre, it would grow to twice its size
Scale factor	In an enlargement, the number that you multiply lengths on the object by to get corresponding lengths on the image	

1

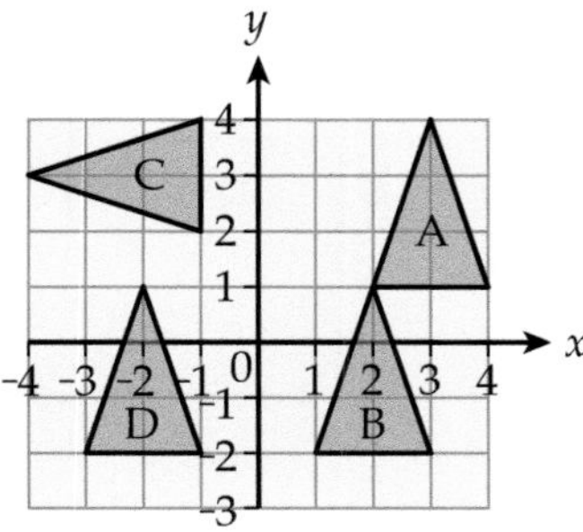

Describe the transformation that moves

a A to B **b** A to C **c** B to D

2 Copy this shape on squared paper. Reflect the shape in the mirror line.

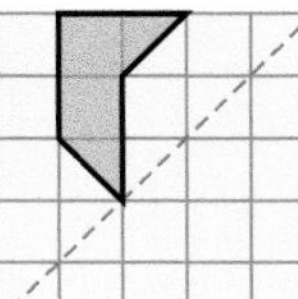

3

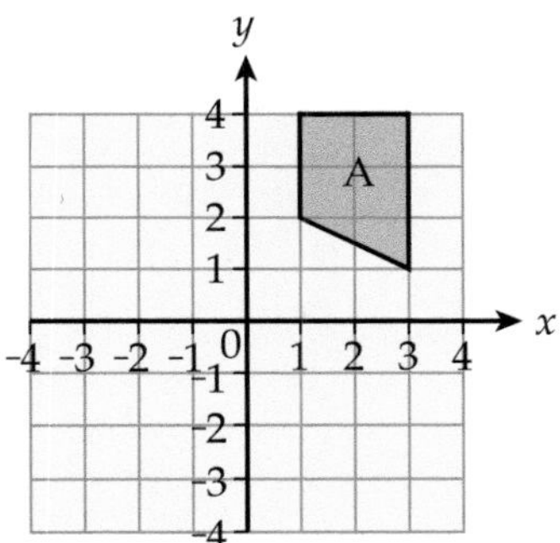

Copy the diagram.

a Rotate the trapezium 180° about (0, 0) and label the image B.

b Reflect B in the line $x = 0$ and label the image C.

c Describe fully the single transformation that moves A to C.

4 How many lines of symmetry do the following have?

a Regular decagon **b** Rectangle

5 State the order of rotation symmetry of

a an isosceles triangle

b a regular nonagon.

6 B is enlarged to give B′, calculate the scale factor and find the coordinates of the centre of enlargement.

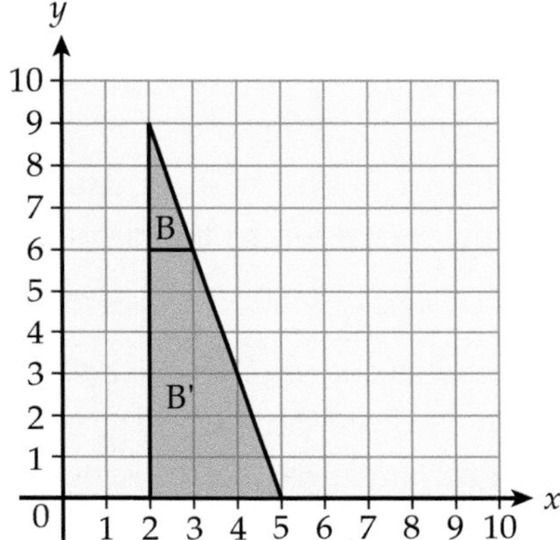

7 Copy the shape onto squared grid paper and enlarge it by scale factor $\frac{1}{2}$ using the dot as the centre of enlargement

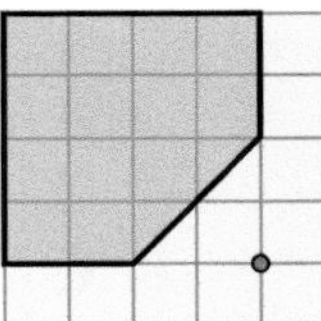

What next?

Score		
0 – 3		Your knowledge of this topic is still developing. To improve look at Formative test: 2C-9; MyMaths: 1099, 1113, 1114, 1115 1116, 1125, 1127 and 1230
4 – 6		You are gaining a secure knowledge of this topic. To improve look at InvisiPen: 361, 362, 363, 364, 366 and 368
7		You have mastered this topic. Well done, you are ready to progress!

9 MyPractice

9a

1 Copy the diagram on square grid paper.
Describe fully the transformation that moves the pink shape to
- **a** shape A
- **b** shape B
- **c** shape C.

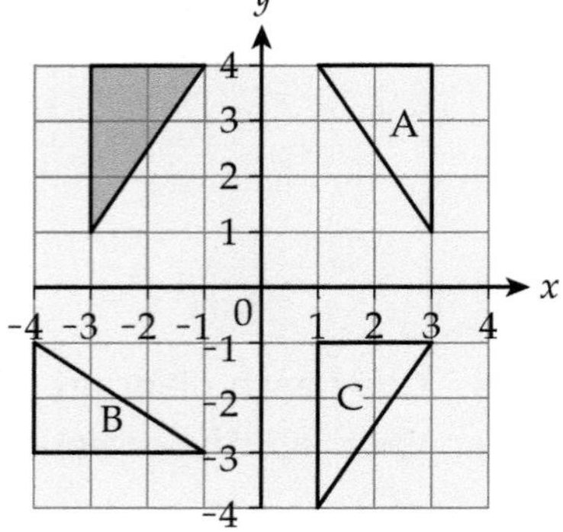

2 Copy the diagram on square grid paper.
- **a** Reflect the green hexagon in the line $y = x$.
Colour the image orange.
- **b** Describe a different transformation that moves the green hexagon to the orange hexagon.

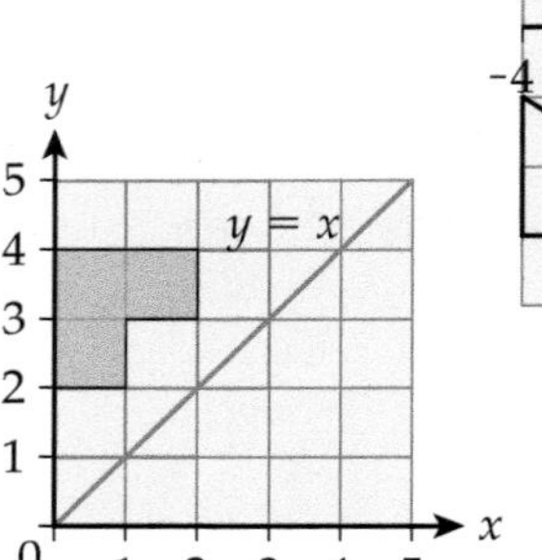

9b

3 **a** Tessellate a regular hexagon using repeated translations.
b Which other repeated transformations can you use to tessellate a regular hexagon?

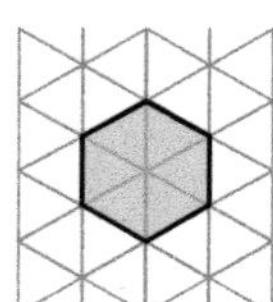

4 The pink triangle is rotated clockwise through 90° about (0, 0).
- **a** Draw the image and label it I_1.
- **b** The triangle I_1 is reflected in the y-axis.
Draw the new image and call it I_2.
- **c** The triangle I_2 is reflected in the x-axis.
Draw the new image and call it I_3.
- **d** Describe the single transformation that moves the pink triangle to I_3.

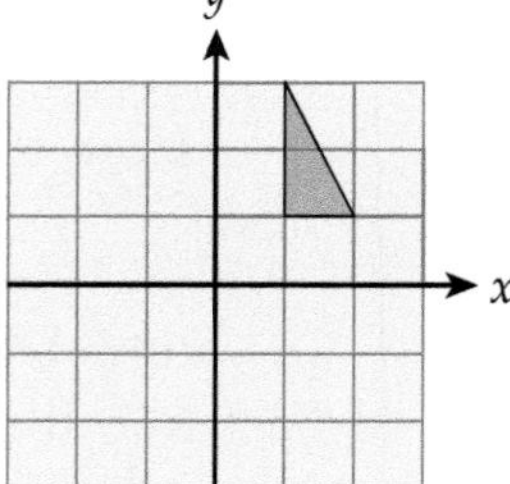

9c

5 Draw these currency symbols.
Draw any lines of reflection symmetry and state the order of rotation symmetry for each symbol.

a € **b** $ **c** S **d** ¥ **e** ₦

6 This triangle has one vertical line of symmetry.
- **a** State the values of a and b.
- **b** Explain your reasoning.

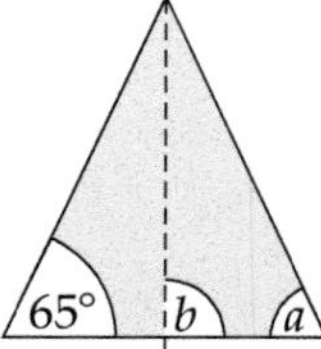

9d

7 Copy the shapes on square grid paper.
Draw the enlargement of each shape using the dot as the centre of enlargement and the given scale factor.

a 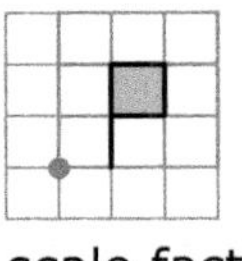
scale factor 3

b 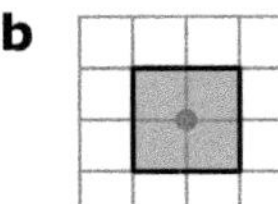 
scale fator 2

c 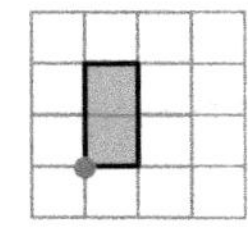
scale factor 4

8 Copy each diagram. The green shape has been enlarged to give the orange shape. Calculate the scale factors and give the coordinates of the centre of enlargement.

a 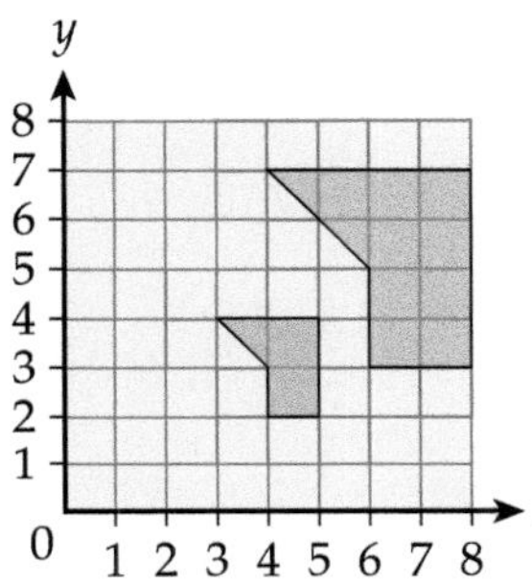

b 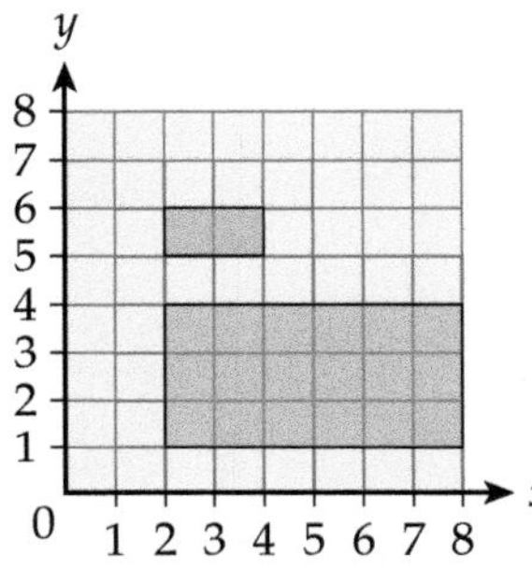

c 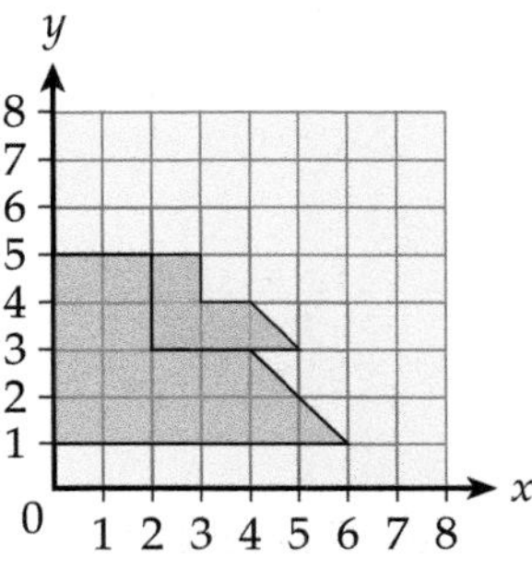

9e

9 **a** Plot the points A (4,0), B (7,0) and C (4,6) on the coordinate axes.

b What is the mathematical name of the shape ABC?

c Using (1,3) as the centre of enlargement, enlarge the shape ABC by scale factor $\frac{1}{3}$.

d Write down the coordinates of the image A′B′C′.

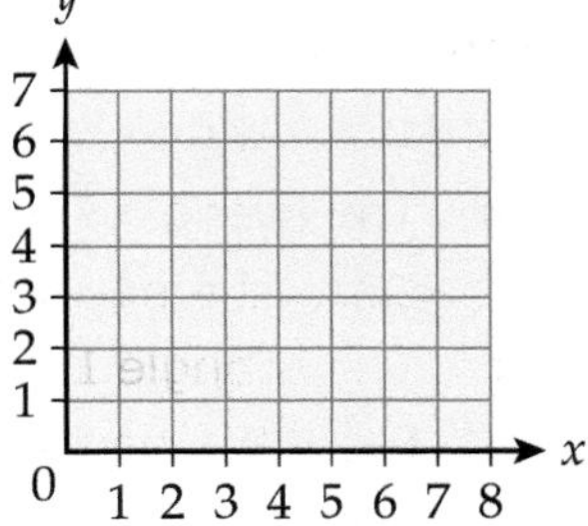

10 **a** The smaller triangle is an enlargement of the larger triangle, what is the scale factor?

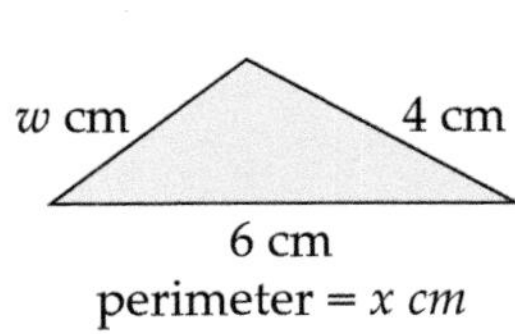

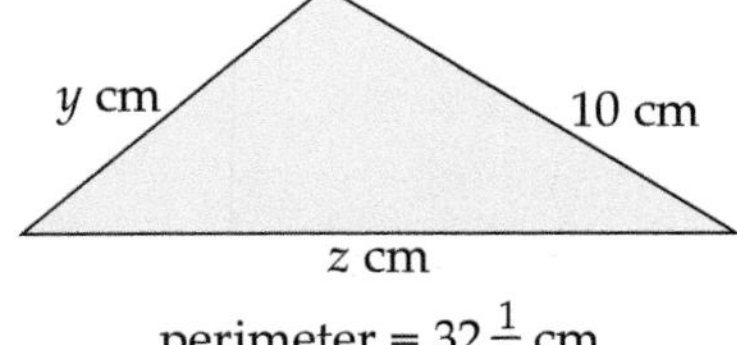

b Find the values of w, x, y and z.

Case study 3: Food crops

Wheat has been cultivated for around 10 000 years, originating from an area that is now part of Iran. It is still vitally important to us today, and keeping the world fed is a delicate balance between production and consumption.

Task 1

The table shows world wheat production between the years 2002 and 2008. The row labelled 'stocks' shows how much wheat is left in reserve.

1	World wheat production, consumption and stocks (million tonnes)						
2		02/03	03/04	04/05	05/06	06/07	07/08
3	produced	566	556	628	620		608
4	consumed	601	596	616		611	612
5	stocks	169	129		137	123	

a Find the figure '129' in the spreadsheet. Can you work out how it was calculated? Show your workings.

b Complete the missing entries in the spreadsheet.

c In how many years does consumption of wheat exceed production?

d What is happening to the stocks of wheat that are held in reserve?

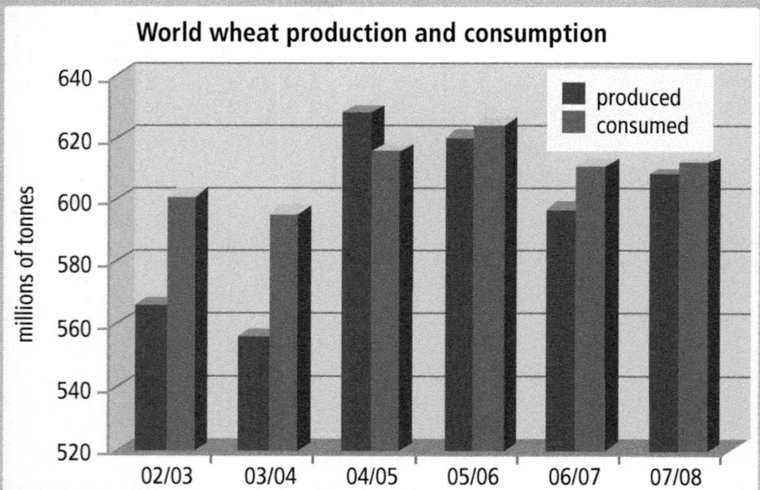

Task 2

Here is a bar chart generated from the spreadsheet.

For the first two years, the 'produced' bar is roughly half the height of the 'consumed' bar.

a How does that compare with the figures in the spreadsheet for those years?

b Do you think that the chart is a good representation of the actual figures? Explain your reasoning. Suggest improvements if appropriate.

The graph shows the price of wheat between 2003 and 2008.
A 'bushel' is an agricultural unit, usually of weight.

Wheat prices continue to rise

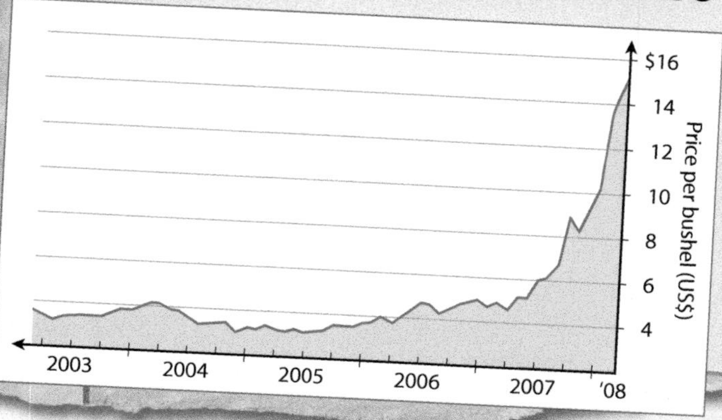

Task 3

a Roughly what is the lowest price a bushel of wheat has cost since 2003?

b When was the price at its lowest?

c How long did the price take to double from its lowest value?

d How long did it take to double again?

Crops are not only used for food.
Some crops, such as rapeseed, are used to make biodiesel, which is an alternative source of fuel.
The bar chart shows the trend in production of biodiesel in the EU between 2002 and 2007.

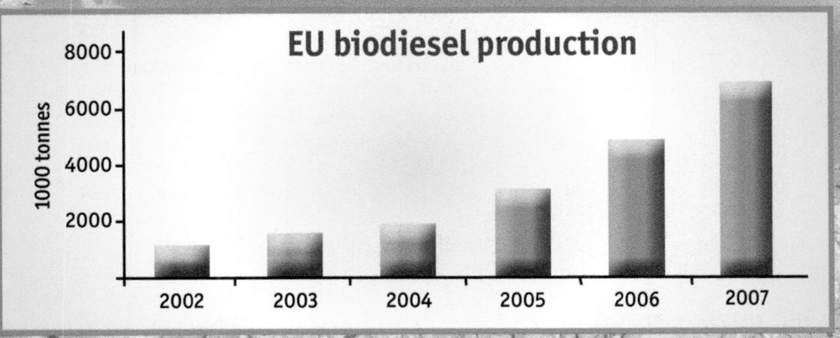

Task 4

a Write down estimated values for the biodiesel production for each year from 2002 to 2007.

b Roughly how many times bigger is the production of biodiesel in 2007 than it was in 2002?

c (Harder) Looking at the trend, what do you think the EU biodiesel production would have been in 2012? See if you can find the real value on the Internet and compare with your estimate. How close are you?

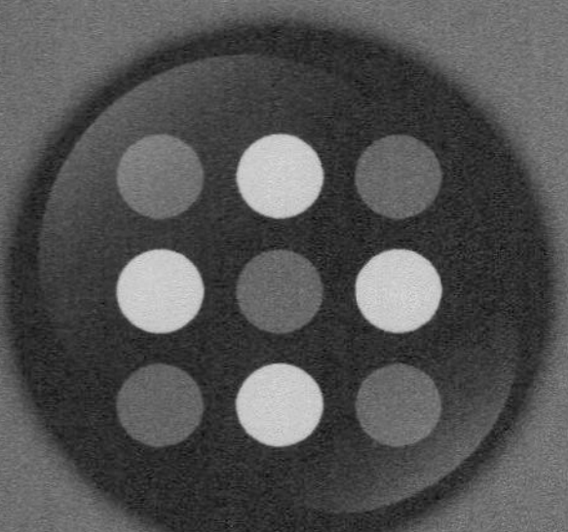

10 Equations

Introduction

Biologists use equations to predict the likely growth or decline of populations of endangered animals, such as the red kite which was saved from virtual extinction in the UK. Re-introduced into England in the Chilterns, the red kite is now thriving again with around 2000 breeding pairs.

What's the point?

Population growth is complex and involves a multitude of factors. By solving equations that include as many of these factors as possible, people can predict how populations can change.

Objectives

By the end of this chapter, you will have learned how to …

- Solve linear equations that involve
  - brackets
  - the unknown appearing more than once
  - negative numbers
  - fractions.
- Use trial and improvement methods to solve equations.

Check in

1 Solve these equations.

a $x + 3 = 8$ **b** $2y + 7 = 15$ **c** $4p - 3 = 21$ **d** $8k - 4 = 20$

e $7 - 2w = 3$ **f** $21 - 3z = 6$ **g** $\frac{x}{3} + 4 = 7$ **h** $5 - \frac{y}{2} = 3$

2 Expand these, simplifying where possible.

a $2(a + 5)$ **b** $3(b - 10)$ **c** $x(x + 2)$

d $a(b - 3)$ **e** $3t(t - 1)$ **f** $2p(3q + 4)$

g $4(k + 3) + 5(k - 2)$ **h** $5(3n + 2) - 2(4n - 1)$

Starter problem

In this diagram the equation $3x + 2 = 17$ has been changed in different ways, but all of these ways still give the same solution of $x = 5$.

Describe each change to the equation.

Continue each change for at least one more step.

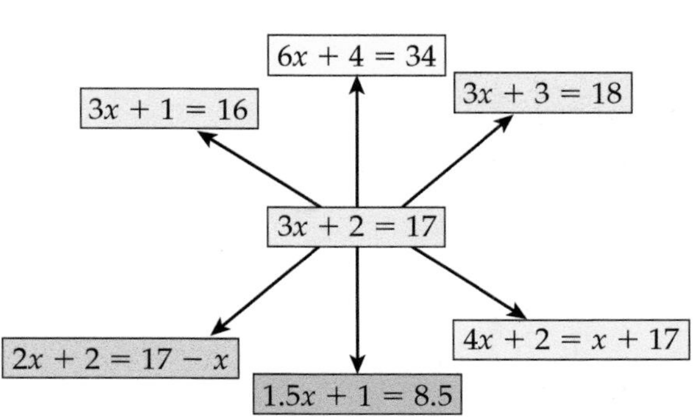

10a Linear equations 1

- An **equation** is a mathematical statement that two expressions are equal.

7x + 5 = 3x + 9 is an equation. The two sides are equal. 7x + 5 and 3x + 9 are **expressions**.

To **solve** an equation, you find the value of the unknown. Think of the equation $7x + 5 = 3x + 9$ as a set of scales, balanced at the equals sign.

$7x + 5 = 3x + 9$  Subtract $3x$ from both sides.

$4x + 5 = 9$ 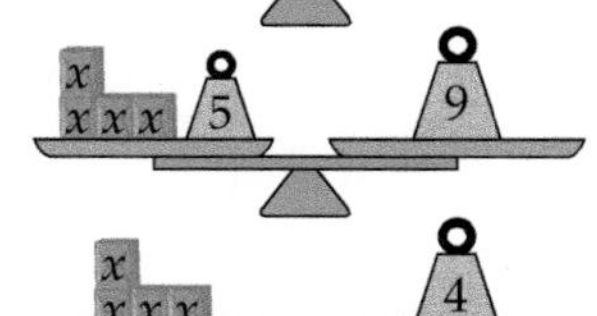 Subtract 5 from both sides.

$4x = 4$ 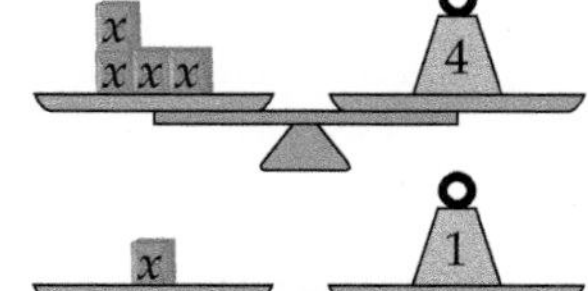 Divide both sides by 4.

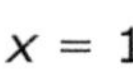

$x = 1$

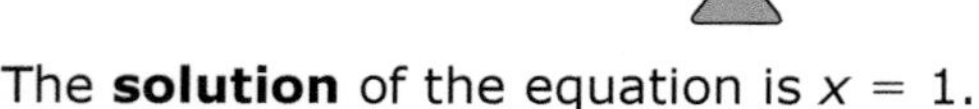

The **solution** of the equation is $x = 1$.

- To ensure that the scales balance, you must perform the same operation on each side of the equation.

Example

Solve these equations.

a $2(5x - 4) = 12$ **b** $\frac{3a + 4}{2} = 11$

a

$2(5x - 4) = 12$	Expand the brackets.
$10x - 8 = 12$	+ 8 to both sides.
$10x = 20$	÷ 10 on both sides.
$x = 2$	

b

$\frac{3a + 4}{2} = 11$	× 2 on both sides.
$3a + 4 = 22$	− 4 from both sides.
$3a = 18$	÷ 3 on both sides.
$a = 6$	

- To solve an equation with the unknown on both sides, remove the smallest algebraic term from both sides.

Example

Solve these equations.

a $4x + 6 = 9x - 4$ **b** $2(5n + 3) = 4(2n - 1)$

a

$4x + 6 = 9x - 4$	− 4x from both sides.
$6 = 5x - 4$	+ 4 to both sides.
$10 = 5x$	÷ 5 on both sides.
$2 = x$	
$x = 2$	

b

$2(5n + 3) = 4(2n - 1)$	expand the brackets.
$10n + 6 = 8n - 4$	− 8*n* from both sides.
$2n + 6 = -4$	− 6 from both sides.
$2n = -10$	÷ 2 on both sides.
$n = -5$	

Exercise 10a

1 Solve these equations.

- **a** $x + 4 = 7$
- **b** $5z = 20$
- **c** $2n - 6 = 4$
- **d** $11 = 3p + 2$
- **e** $9 + 6t = 9$
- **f** $20 = 7h - 1$
- **g** $4k - 1 = 1$
- **h** $9 + 8y = 1$

2 Arrange these equations into pairs that have the same solution. Which is the odd equation out?

- **A** $3(x + 5) = 21$
- **B** $12 = 4(x - 3)$
- **C** $\frac{x}{2} + 9 = 8$
- **D** $\frac{5x + 4}{7} = 2$
- **E** $\frac{2x + 7}{3} = 1$
- **F** $2(10 + x) = 8$
- **G** $\frac{x}{3} + 5 = 7$

3 Solve these equations by expanding the brackets and collecting like terms.

- **a** $2(x + 3) + 4(x + 1) = 22$
- **b** $7(a - 3) + 5(a + 2) = 37$
- **c** $3(p - 2) + 2(p - 5) = 14$
- **d** $2(2k - 1) + 4(3k + 1) = 18$
- **e** $5(2y + 3) - 6(y + 1) = 29$
- **f** $4(5n - 2) - 6(3n - 1) = 12$

4 Solve these equations with unknowns on both sides.

- **a** $3x + 5 = 2x + 10$
- **b** $6q - 10 = 2q + 10$
- **c** $4a - 11 = 7a - 17$
- **d** $9b - 2 = 2(3b + 5)$
- **e** $3m - 7 = 5m - 8$
- **f** $3(4 + 3n) = 4(n - 2)$

Problem solving

5 For each of these questions, form an equation and solve it to find the answer to the problem.

- **a** I think of a number, add 6 and multiply the result by 3. I get 33. What is my number?
- **b** This rectangle has an area of 35 units². Calculate x.

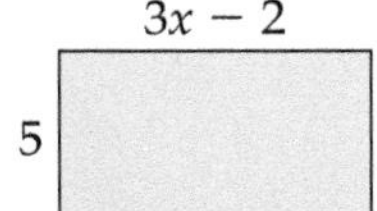

- **c** Find x and hence the angles of this triangle.

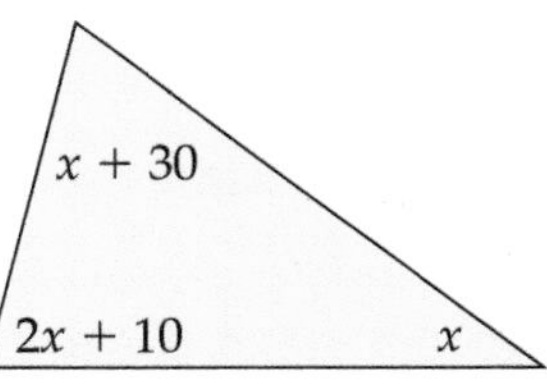

6 For each of these questions, form an equation and solve it to find the answer to the problem.

- **a** I think of a number, multiply by 5 and add 4. I get the same answer when I multiply by 3 and add 14. What is my number?
- **b** This triangle is isosceles. Find the value of x.

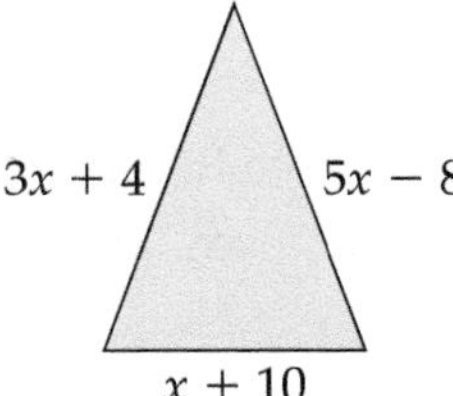

7 The sum of three consecutive even numbers is 48.
If x is the first number, form and solve an equation in x to find these numbers.
Can you make up some similar puzzles of your own?

10b Linear equations 2

- To **solve** an **equation** with a negative algebraic term, add this term to both sides of the equation.

Example

Solve these equations.

a $12 - 5k = 2$ **b** $4 - 3a = 7$

a

$12 - 5k = 2$	$+ 5k$ to both sides.
$12 = 2 + 5k$	$- 2$ from both sides.
$10 = 5k$	$\div 5$ on both sides.
$2 = k$	
$k = 2$	

b

$4 - 3a = 7$	$+ 3a$ to both sides.
$4 = 7 + 3a$	$- 7$ from both sides.
$-3 = 3a$	$\div 3$ on both sides.
$-1 = a$	
$a = -1$	

- To solve an equation with algebraic terms on both sides, subtract the smallest algebraic term from both sides.

Example

Solve these equations.

a $3x + 1 = 11 - 2x$ **b** $5 - 2n = 8 - 4n$

a

$3x + 1 = 11 - 2x$	$+ 2x$ to both sides.
$5x + 1 = 11$	$- 1$ from both sides.
$5x = 10$	$\div 5$ on both sides.
$x = 2$	

b

$5 - 2n = 8 - 4n$	$+ 4n$ to both sides.
$5 + 2n = 8$	$- 5$ from both sides.
$2n = 3$	$\div 2$ on both sides.
$n = \frac{3}{2}$	
$n = 1\frac{1}{2}$	

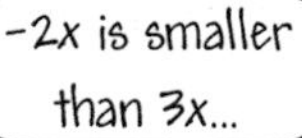

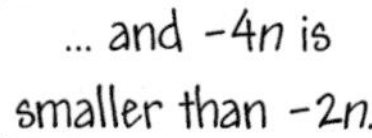

Exercise 10b

1 Solve these equations.

a $12 - x = 5$ **b** $-7a = 14$

c $6 - 4n = 2$ **d** $21 - 4m = 5$

e $15 - 3t = 0$ **f** $8 = 18 - 5p$

g $5 = 6 - 2k$ **h** $8 - y = 9$

i $5 - 4b = 13$ **j** $3 = 8 - 2d$

2 Prove that all of these equations have the same solution.

$2(5 - x) = 4$

$3x - 4(x - 2) = 5$

$\frac{14 - 3x}{5} = 1$

$12 - 4x = 0$

$4(9 - 2x) = 12$

3 Solve these equations with unknowns on both sides.

a $2x + 1 = 7 - x$

b $3t - 2 = 3 - 2t$

c $19 - 3p = 4p + 5$

d $14 - 5k = 3k - 10$

e $9n + 5 = 5 - n$

f $4 - a = 16 - 3a$

g $3 - 2b = 13 - 4b$

h $11 - 8m = 1 - 3m$

i $2(5 - y) = 22 - 5y$

j $3(5 - 2d) = 3 - 2d$

k $5(3 - 2q) = 2(7 - q)$

l $2(4 - x) = 5(1 - x)$

Problem solving

4 For each of these questions, form an equation and solve it to find the number that I am thinking of.

a I think of a number, multiply it by 2 and add 4.
I get the same answer as when I subtract my number *from* 19.

b I think of a number, double it and subtract it *from* 10.
I get the same answer as when I multiply my number by 4 and subtract 8.

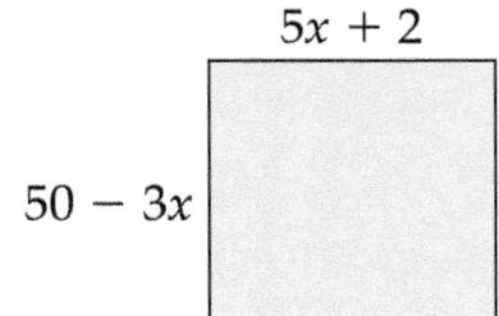

5 Find the length of a side of the blue square to the right.

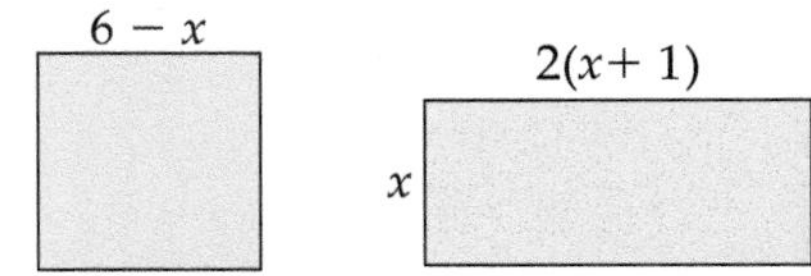

6 The pink square and the green rectangle have the same perimeter. Find the length of the rectangle.

7 A right-angled triangle has a perimeter of 15 m and a circle of radius r also has a perimeter of 15 m. What is the radius of the circle? Write your answer to 2 decimal places.

8 The equation $x^2 = 16$ has two solutions.
Work out these two solutions.
Using this knowledge, can you now write the two solutions for each of these equations?

One solution is positive and one is negative.

a $x^2 = 4$ **b** $x^2 = 25$ **c** $x^2 = 100$

d $x^2 + 1 = 10$ **e** $2x^2 = 128$ **f** $37 - 3x^2 = 10$

Research the name of this type of equation.

10c Equations with fractions

‹ p.54

- When solving equations, a fraction can be thought of as a division.
  - ▶ You undo a division by multiplying.

Start with x, add 5 and then divide by 3 to get 2.

$$\frac{x+5}{3} = 2$$

Multiplication and division are inverse operations.

Multiplying by 3 on both sides of $\frac{x+5}{3} = 2$ gives $x + 5 = 6$ and so $x = 1$.

Example

Solve these equations.

a $\frac{3x+4}{5} = 2$ **b** $\frac{x}{3} - 6 = 1$

a

$\frac{3x+4}{5} = 2$ × 5 on both sides

$3x + 4 = 10$ − 4

$3x = 6$ ÷ 3

$x = 2$

b

$\frac{x}{3} - 6 = 1$ + 6 to both sides.

$\frac{x}{3} = 7$ × 3

$x = 21$

The operation that was performed last is −6 so deal with this first.

- To solve an equation with fractions on both sides, you will need to perform two multiplications. This is known as **cross-multiplying**.

Example

Solve this equation.

$$\frac{3x-4}{5} = \frac{x+4}{3}$$

$\frac{3x-4}{5} = \frac{x+4}{3}$ × 5 on both sides.

$3x - 4 = \frac{5(x+4)}{3}$ × 3 on both sides.

$3(3x - 4) = 5(x + 4)$ expand the brackets.

$9x - 12 = 5x + 20$ − 5x

$4x - 12 = 20$ + 12

$4x = 32$ ÷ 4

$x = 8$

$\frac{3(3x-4)}{5} = \frac{5(x+4)}{3}$

Cross-multiplying is performing these two multiplications at the same time.

Exercise 10c

1 Solve these equations involving a fraction on one side.

a $\frac{x}{9} = 7$ **b** $5 = \frac{a}{8}$

c $\frac{3y}{4} = 1$ **d** $\frac{5k}{3} = 3$

e $\frac{n}{5} + 2 = 4$ **f** $3 + \frac{p}{4} = 5$

g $\frac{1}{3}t - 5 = 2$ **h** $5 = \frac{2}{3}b - 1$

i $\frac{m + 4}{5} = 3$ **j** $\frac{q - 8}{3} = 2$

k $9 = \frac{2d + 5}{3}$ **l** $\frac{4(g - 1)}{10} = 2$

2 Solve these equations where the unknown is in the denominator of the fraction.

a $\frac{6}{a} = 3$ **b** $4 = \frac{20}{y}$

c $\frac{2}{k} = 3$ **d** $4 = \frac{7}{t}$

2 **e** $\frac{10}{b} + 3 = 8$ **f** $7 + \frac{15}{x} = 10$

g $\frac{6}{p} - 3 = 1$ **h** $10 - \frac{4}{m} = 7$

i $\frac{6}{n + 1} = 3$ **j** $\frac{9}{2d - 1} = 3$

k $\frac{20}{6 - g} = 4$ **l** $4 = \frac{8}{3(1 - q)}$

3 Solve these equations by cross-multiplying.

a $\frac{x}{2} = \frac{x + 6}{4}$ **b** $\frac{y + 3}{2} = \frac{4y}{5}$

c $\frac{t + 7}{5} = \frac{t + 1}{2}$ **d** $\frac{p + 4}{7} = \frac{p - 4}{3}$

e $\frac{3a - 1}{4} = \frac{a + 7}{5}$ **f** $\frac{2k + 4}{7} = \frac{3k - 5}{5}$

g $\frac{4m - 1}{3} = \frac{3m - 2}{2}$

h $\frac{2(b + 3)}{5} = \frac{3b - 2}{2}$

Problem solving

4

I add 7 to my Mum's age and then divide by 5. I get the same answer as if I subtract 2 from my Mum's age and then divide by 4. Work out my Mum's age.

5 The rectangle and the triangle have the same area. Write and solve an equation for x and hence find the area of these shapes.

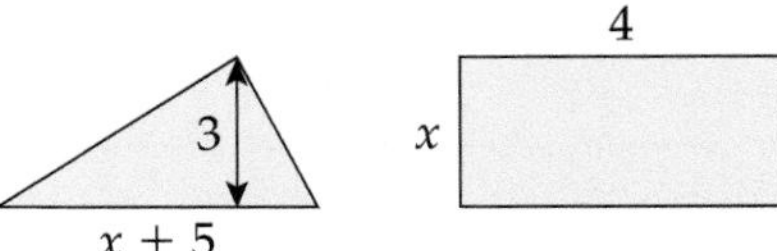

6 The sum of the external angles of a polygon is 360°.

a Write an algebraic expression for the size of an external angle of a regular n-sided polygon.

p.92

b By forming and solving an equation, find the number of sides of a regular polygon with an external angle of

i 72° **ii** 36° **iii** 45°

c Is a regular polygon with external angle 48° possible? Explain your answer.

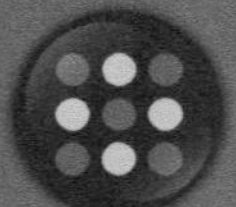

10d Trial and improvement 2

- Equations can be solved using a **trial and improvement** method.

Example

Solve $x^3 - x = 120$ using a trial and improvement method.

Try 4 $\quad 4^3 - 4 = 60$ too small
Try 6 $\quad 6^3 - 6 = 210$ too large
Try 5 $\quad 5^3 - 5 = 120$ correct
The solution is $x = 5$.

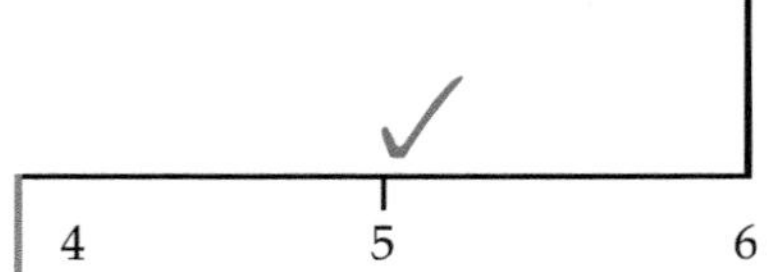

- Trial and improvement is often used to find **approximate** solutions to complex equations.

Example

Find a positive solution of $x^2 + \frac{1}{x} = 10$ by trial and improvement. Give your answer to 1 decimal place.

x	x^2	$\frac{1}{x}$	$x^2 + \frac{1}{x}$	Result
3	9	$\frac{1}{3}$	$9\frac{1}{3}$	low
4	16	$\frac{1}{4}$	$16\frac{1}{4}$	high
3.2	10.24	0.3125	10.5525	high
3.1	9.61	0.3225...	9.9325...	low
3.15	9.9225	0.3174...	10.2399...	high

The solution lies between 3.10 and 3.15
Any number between 3.10 and 3.15 rounds to 3.1 to 1 dp.
The solution is 3.1 (1 dp).

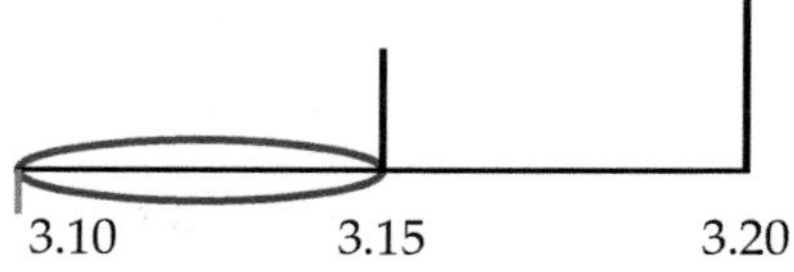

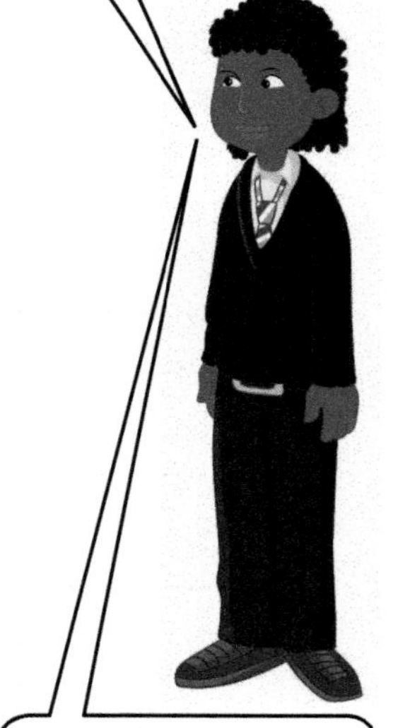

Exercise 10d

Give all approximate solutions to one decimal place

1 Copy and complete this table to find a positive solution of $x^2 + x = 240$.

x	x^2	$x^2 + x$	Result
10	100	110	low

2 Find a positive solution for each of these equations using a trial and improvement method.

a $x^2 - x = 90$ **b** $x^2 - 2x = 63$

c $x^3 + 3x = 536$ **d** $2^x = 1024$

e $x + \sqrt{x} = 56$ **f** $2x - \frac{30}{x} = 4$

3 Copy and complete this table to find a positive solution of $x^3 - 2x = 100$.

x	x^3	2x	$x^3 - 2x$	Result
4	64	8	56	low
5	125	10	115	high

4 Find a positive solution for each of these equations using a trial and improvement method.

a $x^4 = 60$ **b** $x(x - 3) = 25$

c $3^x = 50$ **d** $x + \frac{10}{x} = 9$

Problem solving

5 A rectangle has width w cm and length $w + 1$ cm. The area of the rectangle is 100 cm^2. Use trial and improvement to find w.

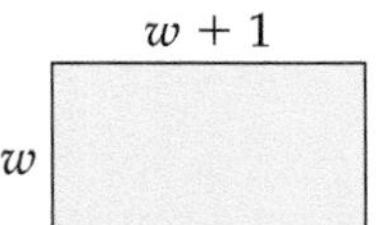

6 A cuboid has a square cross-section. The length of the cuboid is 1 more than a side of this square.

a Write an algebraic expression for the volume of the cuboid.

b Given that the volume of the cuboid is 90 cm^3, find k.

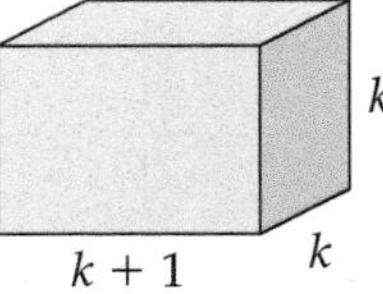

7 Here is a **quadratic** equation.

$x^2 + 2x = 20$

Use a spreadsheet to solve this equation by trial and improvement.

Start by inputting these formulae.

	A	B	C	D
1	x	x^2	$2x$	$x^2 + 2x$
2	1	= A2^2	= 2*A2	= B2+C2
3	= A2+1	= A3^2	= 2*A3	= B3+C3
4	= A3+1	= A4^2	= 2*A4	= B4+C4
5	= A4+1	= A5^2	= 2*A5	= B5+C5

Choose new values for x based on your results from the spreadsheet above. Continue until you find x.

10e Real-life equations

You meet equations in real life all the time.

An equation connecting real life quantities is often called a **formula**.

The equation for converting between temperatures given in Celsius, C, and Fahrenheit, F, is
$F = 1.8C + 32$

If £1 buys you \$1.50 then the equation for the exchange rate between x pounds and y dollars is
$y = 1.5x$

Example

The equation for converting Celsius, C, to Fahrenheit, F, is
$F = 1.8C + 32$

a 10 °C to °F **b** 25 °C to °F
c 86 °F to °C **d** 302 °F to °C

a $F = 1.8 \times 10 + 32$
$= 18 + 32$
$= 50$

b $F = 1.8 \times 25 + 32$
$= 45 + 32$
$= 77$

c $86 = 1.8C + 32$
$54 = 1.8C$
$C = 54 \div 1.8$
$= 30$

d $302 = 1.8C + 32$
$1.8C = 270$
$C = 270 \div 1.8$
$= 150$

Example

A taxi company charges £2.00 per journey plus 30 pence per mile.

a Write down an equation for £T, the total cost of a journey of m miles.
b How much would it cost to travel 5 miles?
c If I am charged £4.70 for my journey, how far did I travel?

a Total cost is £2 + £0.30 per mile
$T = 2 + 0.3m$

b $T = 2 + 0.3 \times 5 = 2 + 1.5 = 3.5$
My journey cost £3.50

c $4.7 = 2 + 0.3m$ Subtract 2
$2.7 = 0.3m$ Divide by 0.3
$9 = m$
The journey was 9 miles.

If the cost is written in pence the equation is $T = 200 + 30m$

Exercise 10e

1 Use the equation $F = 1.8C + 32$ to convert
  - **a** 100 °C to °F
  - **b** -40 °C to °F
  - **c** 140 °F to °C
  - **d** 0 °F to °C

2 Write down equations connecting the number of miles, m, and the total cost of the journey, £T, for these taxi companies.
  - **a** A fixed charge of £3.00 plus 25 pence per mile
  - **b** A fixed charge of £2.50 plus 35 pence per mile
  - **c** A fixed charge of £2.00 plus 40 pence per mile
  - **d** No fixed charge plus 48 pence per mile

3 For each of the taxi companies, **a** – **d**, in question **2**
  - **i** What is the cost of a 12 mile journey?
  - **ii** If the cost of a journey was £6 how far did you travel?

4 An equation connecting the number of dollars, y, you get per pound, x, at the bank is given as $y = 1.532x$. Use this equation to convert
  - **a** £100 into dollars
  - **b** £250 into dollars
  - **c** £820 into dollars
  - **d** $750 into pounds
  - **e** $1532 into pounds
  - **f** $10 500 into pounds

Problem solving

5 Two mobile phone companies, CheapTalk and BargainPhone, are advertising their newest tariffs to customers.

  - **a** Write down an equation for the total cost per month, £y, in terms of the number of minutes used, x, of a phone purchased from **i** CheapTalk.
    ii BargainPhone.
  - **b** Which of the phone companies will be cheaper if you want to talk for
    - **i** 20 minutes per month
    - **ii** 50 minutes per month
    - **iii** 150 minutes per month?
  - **c** **i** Write an equation for the number of minutes used if the cost using a CheapTalk phone equals the cost of using a BargainPhone phone.
    ii Solve the equation for the number of minutes.
  - **d** Explain how you should choose the best phone company based on how many minutes you expect to use your phone a month.

10 MySummary

Check out

You should now be able to ...

Test it ➡ Questions

You should now be able to ...	Level	Questions
Solve linear equations that involve ✓ Brackets	6	1
✓ The unknown appearing more than once	6	2, 3
✓ Negative numbers	6	2
✓ Fractions	7	3, 4
✓ Solve nonlinear equations using a trial and improvement method	6	5 – 7

Language	Meaning	Example
Expression	A mathematical statement	$3y + 6x$
Equation	A mathematical statement that two expressions are equal	$3y = 6$
Linear equation	An equation where the highest power is 1	$2x = 4$
Expand	To multiply out all brackets and then collect like terms	Expanding $2(3x + 5) - 7 + 4x$ gives $10x + 3$
Trial and improvement	A method for solving complex equations by making a guess, then improving on that guess until you are very close to the correct answer.	The equation $x^3 + x = 245$ can be solved by trial and improvement

10 MyReview

1 Solve these equations.

a $6 + 5a = 6$

b $4(2b - 5) = 12$

c $3(2c - 7) + 4(3c - 2) = 61$

d $8(2d + 5) - 3(8d - 9) = -21$

e $4e - 9 = 3e - 2$

f $6(2f - 13) = 5(10f - 8)$

2 Solve these equations.

a $22 - 9g = 4$

b $3h + 7 = 23 - h$

c $21 - 6i = 69 + 2i$

d $4(6j - 15) = 6(38 - 2j)$

e $12 - 5k = -66 - 11k$

f $3(12 - 4m) = 21 - 13m$

3 Solve these equations.

a $\frac{n + 2}{5} = 11$

b $\frac{3p - 2}{4} = 7$

c $3 + \frac{q}{4} = 0$

d $11 = \frac{3}{4}r - 19$

e $\frac{15}{s} = 3$

f $20 - \frac{8}{t} = 18$

g $\frac{45}{1 - 2u} = 5$

h $\frac{40 + v}{3(5 + v)} = 2$

4 Solve these equations.

a $\frac{w}{3} = \frac{w + 2}{4}$

b $\frac{x}{5} = \frac{x - 3}{4}$

c $\frac{y + 3}{3} = \frac{5y - 1}{7}$

d $\frac{5(z - 4)}{11} = \frac{3z + 1}{4}$

5 Copy and complete this table to find a solution of $x^3 - 2x = 329$.

x	x^3	$x^3 - 2x$	result
10	1000	980	high

6 Use a trial and improvement method to find a positive solution of the following equations. Give your answers correct to 1 decimal place.

a $x^5 = 19$

b $4^x = 37$

c $2x - \frac{5}{x} = 13$

d $x^3 + x^2 = 3$

7 A cuboid has side lengths p, p and $p-1$. The volume of the cuboid is 40 cm³. Find p correct to 1 decimal place.

What next?

Score		
0 – 3		Your knowledge of this topic is still developing. To improve look at Formative test: 2C-10; MyMaths: 1057, 1154, 1158, 1182, 1928 and 1929
4 – 6		You are gaining a secure knowledge of this topic. To improve look at InvisiPen: 234, 235, 236, 237, 241, 242, 243, 362, 363 and 364
7		You have mastered this topic. Well done, you are ready to progress!

10 MyPractice

10a

1 Solve these equations.

a $7x + 3 = 6x + 8$ **b** $6y + 9 = 4y + 17$

c $2a + 5 = 5a - 7$ **d** $5b - 3 = 9b - 7$

e $p + 24 = 7p$ **f** $4(q - 1) = 6q - 5$

g $3(k - 4) = 2(4k - 1)$ **h** $\frac{2}{3}t - 2 = \frac{1}{3}t + 2$

2 For each of these questions, form an equation and solve it to find the answer to the problem.

a Find the length of this rectangle.

$3x + 2$

$8(x - 1)$

b The areas of these shapes are equal.

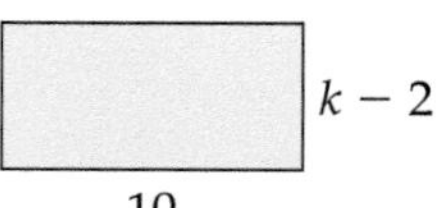

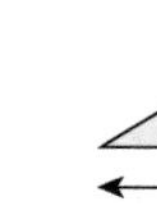

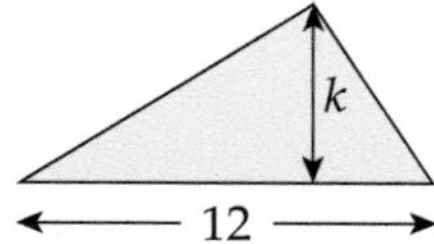

Find k and hence the dimensions of each shape.

3 **a** Think of a number, multiply it by 5 and then subtract 3. If you double the same number and add 15, you get the same answer. Find the number.

b This mobile is made from different shapes. It can hang from the ceiling. If the square shape has a mass of 60 grams, find the masses of all the other shapes.

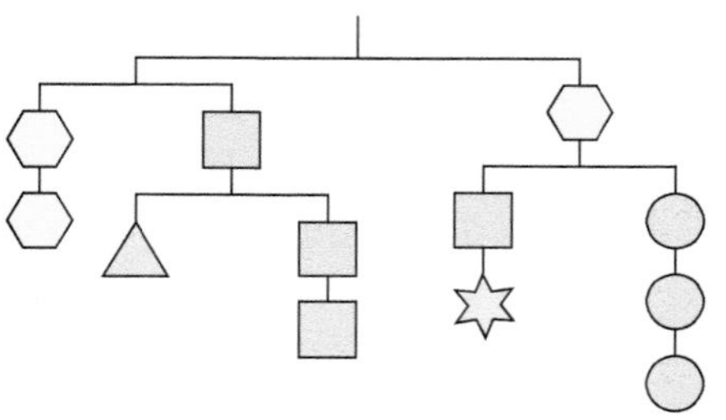

10b

4 Solve these equations.

a $10 - x = 7$ **b** $15 - 2y = 5$

c $11 = 21 - 5m$ **d** $0 = 18 - 6n$

e $9 - 3d = 8$ **f** $4 - 7f = 11$

g $8 - 2k = 5$ **h** $12 - 3t = 7$

5 Solve these equations.

a $4x + 3 = 8 - x$ **b** $2k + 5 = 17 - 4k$

c $3p - 5 = 5 - 2p$ **d** $10 - 3t = t - 2$

e $7 - a = 15 - 2a$ **f** $11 - 5b = 5 - 2b$

g $8(3 - y) = 2 + 3y$ **h** $2(7 - 2g) = 3(4 - g)$

10c

6 Solve these equations.

a $\frac{a}{3} = \frac{a+4}{5}$

b $\frac{b-1}{3} = \frac{2b}{7}$

c $\frac{x+5}{3} = \frac{x+11}{5}$

d $\frac{y+6}{9} = \frac{y-2}{5}$

e $\frac{2p-1}{9} = \frac{p-3}{2}$

f $\frac{5q-1}{4} = \frac{7q-5}{5}$

g $\frac{3m+1}{7} = \frac{5m-6}{4}$

h $\frac{3n-2}{5} = \frac{5n-8}{6}$

7 Tim and Tom are identical twins.

Tim says "My age is three years less than one quarter my mum's age".

Tom says "If you take 6 from my mum's age then my age is one-fifth of the result".

a Write two equations for Tim's and Tom's ages in terms of their mother's age.

b Hence find the ages of Tim and Tom and their mother.

10d

8 Copy and complete this table to find a positive solution of $x^3 - x = 50$, correct to 1 dp.

x	x^3	$x^3 - x$	Result
4	64	60	high
3	27	24	low

9 A number plus ten times its square root is equal to one thousand.

a Write down an equation whose solution gives this number.

b Solve your equation using trial and improvement.
Give your answer to 2 decimal places.

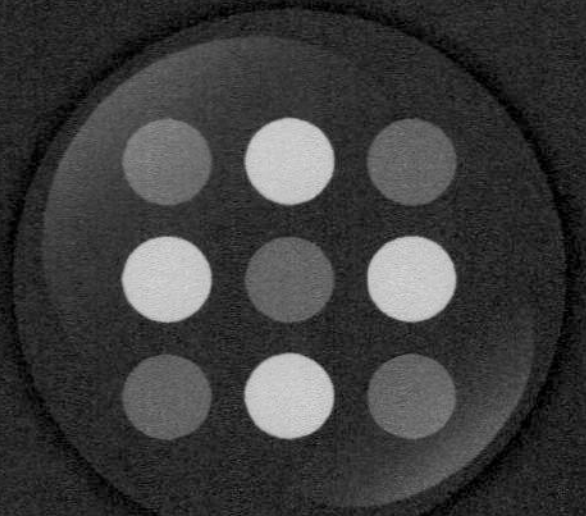

11 Written and calculator methods

Introduction

When you write down a mathematical calculation it might seem obvious to work through it from left to right across the page, in the same way that you read a book. But languages don't all work in the same way. Arabic and Hebrew read from right to left across the page, whereas traditional Chinese and Japanese are read from top to bottom in vertical columns! Mathematics is an international language, so mathematicians around the world agreed a convention for clarifying which operations should be performed first in a written calculation.

What's the point?

Scientists and mathematicians across the world write down all their calculations using the same order of operations – this allows them to understand each other's work and to exchange their ideas without confusion.

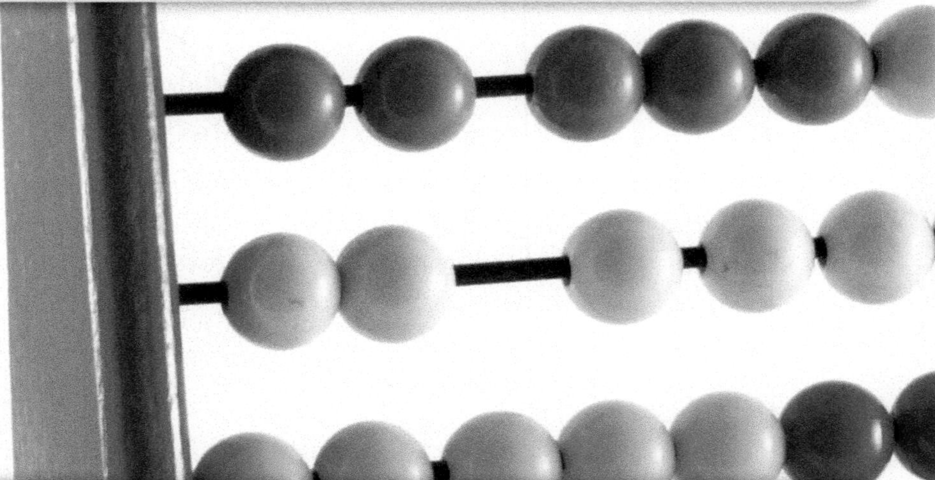

Objectives

By the end of this chapter, you will have learned how to ...

- Perform mental multiplication and division.
- Use standard written methods for addition, subtraction, multiplication and division.
- Use a calculator to calculate with powers, roots, brackets and fractions.
- Interpret the results of a calculation in context.
- Apply the BIDMAS rules to do a calculation in the correct order.

Check in

1 Round each of these numbers to the nearest **i** integer **ii** 1 dp.

a 6.0972 **b** 15.533 **c** 217.386 **d** 0.057

2 Calculate these using an appropriate method.

a $8.7 + 3.4$ **b** $15.7 - 7.29$ **c** $29.46 + 8.7$ **d** $12.3 - 8.49$

3 Calculate

a 12×10 **b** 38×0.1 **c** 3.7×0.01 **d** $48 \div 0.1$

4 Work out these calculations using the order of operations.

a $(3 + 2^2) \times 4$ **b** $28 - 2^2 - 7$ **c** $2 \times 7^2 + 6$

Starter problem

MAN EATS ELEPHANT!

Make up an amazing story using this information

Weight of a Blue Whale:	120 tonnes
Weight of elephant:	7500 kg
Weight of a mouse:	22 g
Average weight of 1 mouthful of a man:	9 g
Average time for eating 1 mouthful:	19.3 seconds
Average number of mouthfuls in a meal:	62

11a Multiplication

- Always try to work out multiplications in your head first.

Example

Calculate

a 26×0.05 **b** 6.4×21

a Using factors

$26 \times 0.05 = 26 \times 5 \times 0.01$

$= 130 \times 0.01$

$= 1.3$

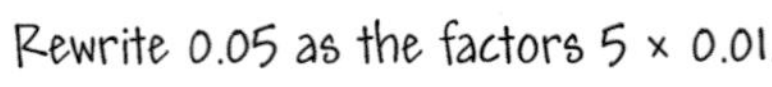

b Using partitioning

$6.4 \times 21 = (6.4 \times 20) + (6.4 \times 1)$

$= 128 + 6.4$

$= 134.4$

Split 21 into two parts, 20 and 1.

- For more difficult multiplications convert to an **equivalent whole-number calculation**.

Example

Hugh is a baker. He orders 66.5 kg of raspberry jam to make 200 Bakewell tarts.
He is charged £0.93 for each kilogram of jam.
How much does Hugh have to pay for the jam?

Estimate the answer first.

$66.5 \times 0.93 \approx 70 \times 1 = £70$

Convert to an equivalent whole number calculation.

$66.5 \times 10 = 665$ and $0.93 \times 100 = 93$

$66.5 \times 0.93 = 665 \times 93 \div 10 \div 100$

Using the standard method:

```
   665
 ×  93
 59850   = 90 × 665
    54
 + 1995  =  3 × 665
    11
 61845
  111
```

$66.5 \times 93 = 61845 \div 10 \div 100$

$= 61.845$

The total cost of the jam = £61.845

= £61.85 (2 dp)

Make sure you give your final answer in the context of the question.

Exercise 11a

1 Calculate these using an appropriate method.

a	28 × 43	b	52 × 93
c	4238 × 7	d	2654 × 9
e	284 × 45	f	19 × 716
g	8888 × 8	h	88 × 888

2 Calculate these using an appropriate method.

a	21 × 5.8	b	24 × 0.02
c	31 × 0.33	d	49 × 7.1
e	31 × 4.6	f	29 × 2.3
g	75 × 0.05	h	13 × 0.07

3 Calculate these using a written method.

a	9 × 5.18	b	7 × 3.92
c	23 × 5.4	d	36 × 4.4
e	28 × 0.26	f	56 × 0.45
g	78 × 29.1	h	43 × 6.18
i	37 × 2.95	j	71 × 6.21
k	2.8 × 46.1	l	3.8 × 29.8
m	8.3 × 2.04	n	16.3 × 0.35
o	27.5 × 0.57	p	46.5 × 0.78

4 Calculate these using a written method.

a	1234 × 56	b	789 × 789
c	36.05 × 47	d	2.45 × 6.17
e	4.198 × 0.43	f	0.318 × 7.25

Problem solving

5 **a** Jacob buys 37 kg of marmalade.
The marmalade is sold in 1 kg jars at a cost of £1.45 a jar.
How much does the 37 kg of marmalade cost?

b Kayleigh needs to make 385 small cakes.
Each cake requires 100 g of flour.
The flour costs £0.96 for 1 kg.
How much does the flour cost to make all 385 cakes?

c Every Monday morning Liam fills his car with petrol. He uses 45.6 litres of fuel each week. Petrol costs £1.25 per litre. His car travels 16.3 km for each litre of fuel.

i How much does Liam pay for fuel each week?

ii How far can he travel in his car each week?

d Horse feed costs £0.49 per kg. Monika works out that on average her horse Neddy eats 19.6 kg of feed each week.

i What is the weekly cost of feed for her horse?

ii What is the annual cost of feeding her horse?

e The exchange rate for pounds to dollars is £1 = $1.62178
How many dollars could you buy with

i £4000 **ii** £5275?

6 The sum of two numbers is 19.

a What is the greatest product you could make with the two numbers?

The sum of three numbers is 19.

b What is the greatest product you could make with the three numbers?

c Investigate splitting different numbers. Can you generalise your results?

11b Division

- Always try to work out divisions in your head first.

Example

Calculate

a 435 ÷ 15 **b** 450 ÷ 13

a Using factors

435 ÷ 15 = 435 ÷ 5 ÷ 3

= 87 ÷ 3

= 29

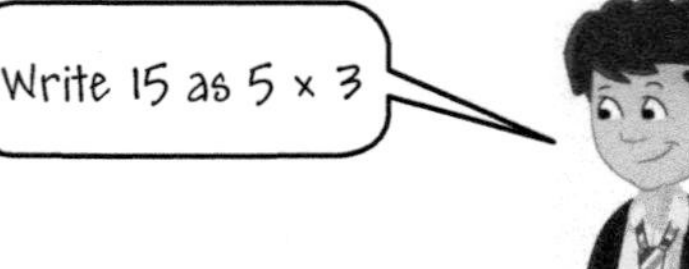

b Using partitioning

450 ÷ 13 = (390 ÷ 13) + (60 ÷ 13)

= 30 + 4 r 8

= 34 r 8

Split 450 into 390 and 60.

- When you are dividing a number by a decimal you need to change to an **equivalent calculation** with an integer divisor.

Example

Calculate 532 ÷ 3.9 giving your answer to 1 decimal place.

Re-write the calculation as an integer divisor.

532 ÷ 3.9 = 5320 ÷ 39

Multiply the dividend and divisor by 10.

Work out 5320 ÷ 39 using an appropriate written method.

Using **long division**

```
     136.41
39 ) 5320.000
    -39          39 × 1 = 39
     142
    -117         39 × 3 = 117
      250
     -234        39 × 6 = 234
       160
      -156       39 × 4 = 156
         40
        -39      39 × 1 = 39
          1
```

5320 ÷ 39 = 136.4 (1dp)

Using **short division**

```
     1 3 6 . 4 1
39 ) 5 3¹⁴2²⁵0¹⁶.0⁴0¹0
```

Think 53 ÷ 39 = 1 remainder 14

142 ÷ 39 = 3 remainder 25

250 ÷ 39 = 6 remainder 16

160 ÷ 39 = 4 remainder 4

40 ÷ 39 = 1 remainder 1

5320 ÷ 39 = 136.4 (1dp)

Check against an **estimate**
532 ÷ 3.9 ≈ 560 ÷ 4 = 140

Exercise 11b

1 Calculate these using an appropriate mental method.

a	84 ÷ 6	**b**	135 ÷ 9
c	156 ÷ 12	**d**	315 ÷ 15
e	440 ÷ 20	**f**	540 ÷ 12
g	936 ÷ 18	**h**	495 ÷ 15
i	784 ÷ 14	**j**	3115 ÷ 35
k	672 ÷ 21	**l**	1488 ÷ 16

2 Calculate these using an appropriate mental method. Give your answer with a remainder where appropriate.

a	240 ÷ 14	**b**	330 ÷ 17
c	341 ÷ 31	**d**	368 ÷ 16
e	279 ÷ 15	**f**	440 ÷ 19
g	610 ÷ 21	**h**	680 ÷ 12
i	412 ÷ 39	**j**	704 ÷ 23
k	1328 ÷ 26	**l**	5987 ÷ 27

3 Calculate these using an appropriate method. Give your answer as a decimal to 1 dp where appropriate.

a	45.6 ÷ 6	**b**	60.8 ÷ 8
c	68.8 ÷ 7	**d**	78.2 ÷ 17
e	70.2 ÷ 18	**f**	81.6 ÷ 16
g	13 ÷ 8	**h**	92 ÷ 7
i	115 ÷ 6	**j**	265 ÷ 14
k	38.7 ÷ 15	**l**	44.5 ÷ 16

4 Calculate these by changing to an equivalent calculation with an integer divisor. Give your answer as a decimal to 1 dp where appropriate.

a	475 ÷ 3.6	**b**	458 ÷ 2.8
c	716 ÷ 1.9	**d**	671 ÷ 4.1
e	538 ÷ 3.7	**f**	625 ÷ 2.5
g	196 ÷ 1.4	**h**	782 ÷ 2.2

Problem solving

5 Give your answers to these as either a remainder or as a decimal to 2 dp, depending upon the problem.

a Vincent is an Olympic sprinter. In the semi-final he runs the 100 m in 9.8 seconds.
What is his speed in metres per second?

b Irene works on a coffee plantation in Africa. Each day she has to pack 350 kg of Fair Trade coffee. She packs the coffee into 1.5 kg packs.
How many packs can she fill with coffee?

c Eric has been collecting 2 p coins for years and now has a pile that weighs 14.5 kg. A 2 p coin weighs 7.12 g. How much money does Eric have?

6 Georgia works out 42.8 × 0.57
= 24.396

Use this information to work out these calculations.
In each case, explain clearly the method you have used.

a **i** 24.396 ÷ 42.8
ii 243.96 ÷ 42.8
iii 2439.6 ÷ 4.28

b What other divisions can you work out? Represent your answers on a spider diagram.

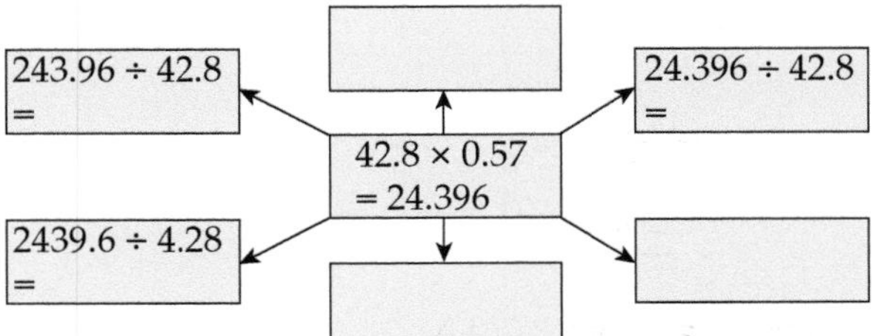

11c Calculator skills

- When solving more complex problems involving numbers with lots of decimal places, square roots, fractions and powers, use a calculator.

Beware, not all calculators are the same!

Fraction key

Example

Calculate $\frac{3}{4} + \frac{2}{7}$

Using the calculator, type

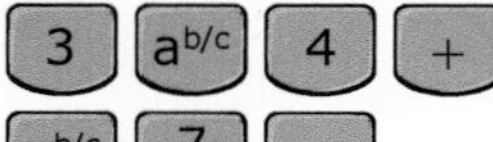

The answer is $\frac{29}{28} = 1\frac{1}{28}$

Power key

Example

Calculate $(6.34)^5$

Using the calculator, type

The answer is 10 243.450 88

Sign change

Example

Calculate $5.67 \times (-3.45)^2$

Using the calculator, type

The brackets ensure you calculate -3.45×-3.45 not -3.45×3.45

The answer is 67.487 175

Square root key

Example

Calculate $\sqrt{12.65 \times 3.98}$ to 3 dp.

Using the calculator, type

The brackets ensure you calculate $\sqrt{12.65 \times 3.98}$ not $\sqrt{12.65} \times 3.98$

The answer is 7.096 to 3 dp

- **Check** the answer by using mental estimates to see if the answer is the correct **order of magnitude**.

$5.67 \times (-3.45)^2 \approx$
$6 \times (-3)^2 = 6 \times 9 = 54 \approx$
67.487175 ✓

Exercise 11c

1 Without using a calculator, choose the most likely answer for each of these questions.
In each case explain the reasoning behind your choices.

a $(297)^2 = 88\,209$ or $91\,204$ or 5940

b $155 \div 0.62 = 96.1$ or 250 or 961

2 Use your calculator to calculate these questions.

a $\frac{6}{11} + \frac{2}{3}$ **b** $\frac{2}{9} + \frac{5}{13}$

c $(2.14)^6$ **d** $(6.75)^4$

e $3.43 \times (-2.71)^3$ **f** $0.5 \times (-6.4)^2$

g $\sqrt{0.22 \times 7.05}$ **h** $\sqrt{3.97 \times 1.98}$

Problem solving

3 **a** The rectangle and the square have exactly the same area.
How long is each side of the square?
Give your answer to 2 dp.

b The area of the new school sports building is $593\,\text{m}^2$.
The width of the changing room is $\frac{2}{5}$ of the length of the changing room.
What is the length of the side of the sports hall?
Give your answer to 2 dp.

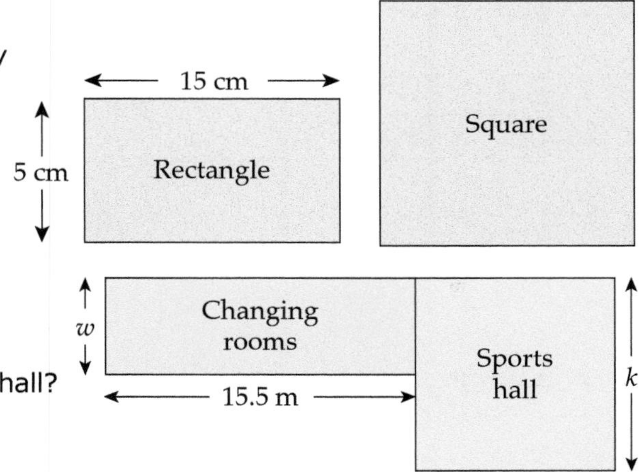

4 **a** Kevin says that when you square a number the answer always gets bigger.
Give two examples to show that this is not always true.

b Griselda says that when you find the square root of a number the answer always gets smaller.
Give two examples to show that this is not always true.

c Write a sentence which explains what happens to the size of a number when you find the square and the square root of it.

d **i** Plot your results on a graph. Add enough points so that you can draw a smooth curve to join them.

ii Comment on the shapes of the square and square root graphs.

5 Olaf is trying to solve a puzzle.

$$\frac{\sqrt{\square\square^2 + \square\square}}{\square} = 2$$

He must use each of the numbers 1, 3, 5, 7 and 9 only once to make this mathematical calculation correct.
Copy and complete the calculation so that it is correct.

Did you know?

Originally a calculator was the person who operated a hand cranked mechanical calculating machine.

11d Calculators in context

- When doing division using a calculator, you should interpret any **remainder** in the context of the problem.
  - ► It could be written as a whole number, a fraction or a decimal.

Example

Tyrone pays £10 000 for 60 video game consoles for his shop.
How much did he pay for each video game console?

Using a calculator

10000÷60
166.6666667

Answer Each console cost £166.67

- It is very important to interpret the remainder when you are **converting between units**.

Example

a Convert 10 000 seconds into hours, minutes and seconds.
b Convert 10 000 ounces into kilograms.
c Convert 1001 days into years, weeks and days.

a Convert the secs into mins. $10\,000 \div 60 = 166.6666...$

Change the remainder to an integer by multiplying it by the **divisor**.

$0.6666...\text{ mins} = 0.6666... \times 60\text{ secs}$
$= 40\text{ seconds}$

1 min = 60 secs
1 hour = 60 mins

Convert the mins into hrs. $166 \div 60 = 2.7666...$

Change the remainder to an integer by multiplying it by the **divisor**.

$0.7666...\text{ hours} = 0.7666... \times 60\text{ mins}$
$= 46\text{ minutes}$

10 000 seconds = 2 hours, 46 minutes and 40 seconds

1 oz ≈ 30 g
1000 g = 1 kg

p.26

b Convert the ounces into grams. $10\,000 \times 30 = 300\,000\text{ g}$

Convert the g into kg. $300\,000 \div 1000 = 300\text{ kg}$

$10\,000\text{ ounces} \approx 300\text{ kg}$

c $1001\text{ days} = 1001 \div 365 = 2.742465...\text{ years}$
$0.742465...\text{ years} = 0.742465... \times 365 = 271\text{ days}$
$271\text{ days} = 271 \div 7 = 38.714285...\text{ weeks}$
$0.714285... = 0.714285... \times 7$
$= 5\text{ days}$
1001 days = 2 years, 38 weeks and 5 days

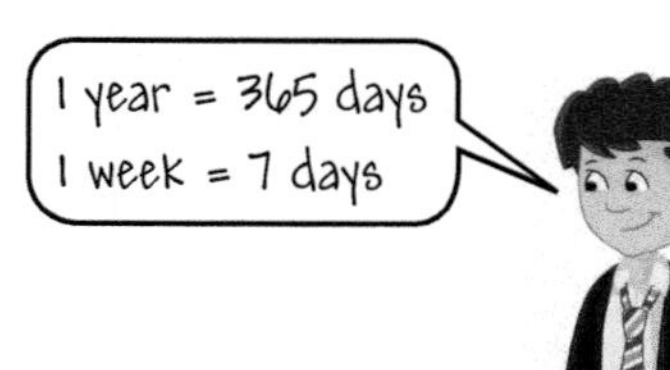

Exercise 11d

1 Convert these metric measurements to the units indicated in brackets.
- a 3865 cm (m and cm)
- b 373 068 cm (km, m and cm)
- c 7427 mℓ (ℓ and mℓ)
- d 15 863 320 g (tonnes, kg and g)
- e 12.25 m (feet and inches)
- f 58 000 cm^2 (m^2)
- g 25 kg (pounds)
- h 400 mm^2 (cm^2)

1 inch ≈ 2.5 cm
10 000 cm^2 = 1 m^2
100 mm^2 = 1 cm^2
1 kg ≈ 2.2 pounds

2 Convert these measurements of time into the units indicated in brackets.
- a 1000 secs (mins and secs)
- b 5420 secs (hours, mins and secs)
- c 400 000 secs (days, hours, mins and secs)
- d 100 000 days (years, weeks and days)
- e 9 999 999 secs (years, weeks, days, hours, mins and secs)

Problem solving

3 Solve these problems.
Give each of your answers in a form appropriate to the question.
- a Hanif sells small cars at his garage. He finds the total cost of his 5 small cars is £59 647. What price should he quote in his newspaper advert for a 'typical small car'?
- b The Year 8 pupils at Heswick High School are going on a trip to Alton Towers theme park. There are 233 pupils and 20 staff going on the trip. Each coach can hold 43 people. How many coaches should be ordered?
- c Ben takes an exam. There are 60 marks in total available on the exam paper and Ben gets 38 marks correct. How well did Ben do on the test?

Did you know?

Sexagesimal (base 60) numbers originated with the ancient Sumerians. We still use them to tell the time and measure angles.

4 Jimmi McFast is an athlete. He completes the 100 m at the Olympics in 9.92 seconds.
- a How fast did he run the 100 m race?
  Give your answer in metres per second (to 1 dp).
- b Convert Jimmi's speed into kilometres per hour.
- c Investigate some other speeds using these examples.
  - An aeroplane's cruising speed is 400 miles per hour.
  - A cheetah can run at 110 km per hour.
  - A TGV train can travel at 105 metres per second.
  - A space shuttle needs to travel at about 17 000 miles per hour to escape from the Earth.

1 mile ≈ 1.6 km

11e Order of operations

- When a calculation contains more than one **operation**, you must do the operations in the correct **order**.
  - ▶ The correct order for working out operations follows **BIDMAS**.

Brackets

Indices

Multiply | Divide

Add | Subtract

- A fraction often works as a pair of **brackets**. It is very useful to put brackets around the numerator and denominator when using a calculator.

Example

Calculate

a $(5 - 3^2)^2 - 2^3$ **b** $(3^2 + 5)^2 - 2^3$

a $(5 - 3^2)^2 - 2^3$ **b** $(3^2 + 5)^2 - 2^3$ — Work out the brackets. Inside the brackets are a power and also a subtraction/addition.

$= (5 - 9)^2 - 2^3$ $= (9 + 5)^2 - 2^3$

$= (-4)^2 - 2^3$ $= (14)^2 - 2^3$ — Work out the powers.

$= 16 - 8$ $= 196 - 8$ — Work out the subtraction.

$= 8$ $= 188$

Example

Calculate $\dfrac{\sqrt{(8+3)} \times (5-2)^3}{2 \times 8}$. Give your answer to 2 dp.

Rewrite using brackets. $[\sqrt{(8+3)} \times (5-2)^3] \div [2 \times 8]$

Key in

Estimate $\dfrac{\sqrt{11} \times 3^3}{16}$

$\simeq \dfrac{3 \times 30}{15} = 6$

The calculator displays 5.596 804…

= 5.60 (2 dp)

Exercise 11e

Give answers to 2 decimal places where appropriate.

1 Calculate these

a $(7 - 2^3)^2 - 5^2$

b $(3^2 - 2^3)^5 \times 2 - 3$

c $2 - 3 - 7 + 8 \div 4 - 2^2$

d $\dfrac{(8-3)^2}{(5-2)^2}$

e $\dfrac{(3^2-1)(5-2)^2}{(9-4)^2}$

f $\dfrac{(7-3)^2\sqrt{(28-3)}}{(10-8)^3}$

2 Use a calculator to work out these calculations.

a $[2.5^2 + (5 - 2.8)]^2$

b $3.4 + [6.8 - (11.7 \times 3.2)]$

c $8 \times (2.5 - 4.6)^2$

d $\dfrac{4.37 \times 31.6}{1.09 \times (6.4 \times 2.8)^2}$

e $\dfrac{3 \times \sqrt{(4.3^2 + 6^2)}}{5}$

f $\dfrac{(5^2+2)^2}{6 \times \sqrt{(7.8^2 - 9)}}$

Problem solving

3 Fern and Caroline both sat a test but did not agree on the answers.

	Question	Fern	Caroline
a	$(3 + 4^2) \times 2$	38	98
b	$5 - 3^2 - 3$	1	-7
c	$6 - 5^2$	31	-19
d	$(-5)^2 + 6$	31	-19
e	$60 \div (4 + 8) - 7 + (5 - 2)^3$	25	39
f	$(3 \times 5^2) \div (3 \times 5)$	15	5
g	$(3 \times 8)^2 \div (3 \times 2)$	96	16

For each question, calculate the correct answer to see who is right. Show your workings. Explain how every mistake was made.

4 a Jackie and Vlad are working out this calculation:

$$\left(\frac{5}{3}\right)^2$$

Jackie types $\frac{5}{3}$ into her calculator and squares it.
Vlad works out 5^2 and divides by 3^2.
They both get the same answer.
Explain how and why both methods work.

b Investigate

i $3^2 \times 5^2$ **ii** $(3 \times 5)^2$ **iii** $\sqrt{12} \times \sqrt{3}$ **iv** $\sqrt{12} \div \sqrt{3}$

Did you know?

Brackets can be used to denote an interval. (1, 5) means all the numbers between 1 and 5 but not 1 and 5 themselves. [1, 5] means all the numbers between 1 and 5 including 1 and 5.

11f Written addition and subtraction

- When mental addition or subtraction is too hard, use a written method.

Example

Calculate

a 4587 + 345.002 + 0.0067

b 4783.29 − 36.87 − 21.83

a Estimate = 4600 + 350 + 0 = 4950

Use standard addition method.

```
  4587.0000
   345.0020
 +   0.0067
  4932.0087
```

Answer = 4932.0087

b Estimate = 4800 − 40 − 20 = 4740

Break the calculation into two steps.

```
   36.87
 + 21.83
   58.70

 4783.29
 - 58.70
 4724.59
```

Answer = 4724.59

- Some problems can be solved by breaking down the working out into smaller steps.

Example

Tobias records the weights of all the parts of the space shuttle.

2 booster rockets = 1.186M kg.	crew + other = 0.00157M kg
separate fuel tank = 0.7538M kg	shuttle body = ?
payload = 0.02M kg	total weight = 2.000M kg

Use this information to calculate the weight of the shuttle body.

Step 1 Find the weight of all the parts of the space shuttle.

```
   1.18600
   0.75380
   0.02000
 + 0.00157
   1.96137
```

Step 2 Subtract the weight of all the parts from the total weight.

```
   2.00000
 - 1.96137
   0.03863
```

Weight of shuttle body = 0.03863 M kg

Exercise 11f

1 Calculate these using a written method.

a 645.9 − 77.3
b 548.62 + 73.8
c 45.75 + 730.4
d 963.2 − 271.6
e 358.23 − 71.7
f 213.8 + 7.26

2 Calculate these using a written method.

a 6.72 + 524.3 + 7
b 73.2 + 105.7 + 41.27
c 513.4 + 29.27 + 0.078
d 1349.2 + 31.05 − 8.8
e 187.8 − 51 − 26.7
f 48.7 + 193.5 − 89.37

Problem solving

3 Tron2 is a robot chef.
He measures all his ingredients very precisely.
Work out the total weight of each of his recipes.

Risotto Twist	
25.38 g	butter
154.4 g	onions
0.22 g	rice
59 g	water
0.065 g	salt

Spiced Rice Cakes	
13.475 g	ghee
215.07 g	rice
0.4 g	water
0.075 g	salt
6.63 g	tumeric

4 Verity has measured the perimeter of the main school building.
Here is a plan showing the measurements she has made.
The perimeter of the whole school building is 158.11 m.
What is the length of the side

a marked y **b** marked x?

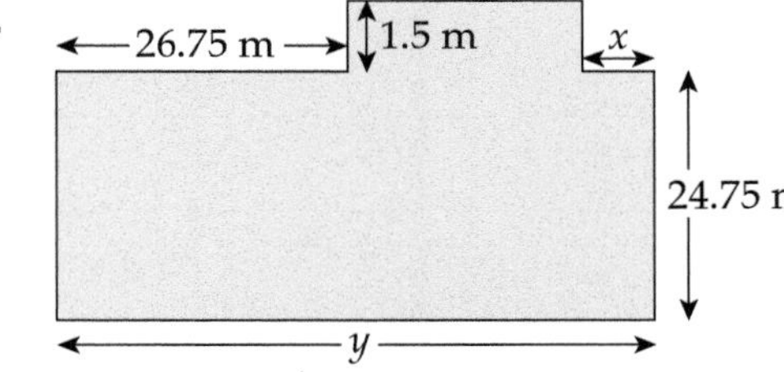

5 Find the missing amount in each of these number sentences.

a □ + 4065 g = 13 kg
b 1570 m + 0.08 km + □ = 5 km
c 908 ml + □ + 1.02 litres = 2 litres
d 1.8 tonnes + 1570 kg + 2.6 kg + 25 g = □ tonnes
e 2.3 km + 800 m + 27 cm + 76 mm = □ km

1 tonne = 1000 kg

6 Kirsty is delivering packages to a factory.
At the factory, all the packages are weighed on a giant weighing scale.
Use the information in these three diagrams to work out Kirsty's weight.

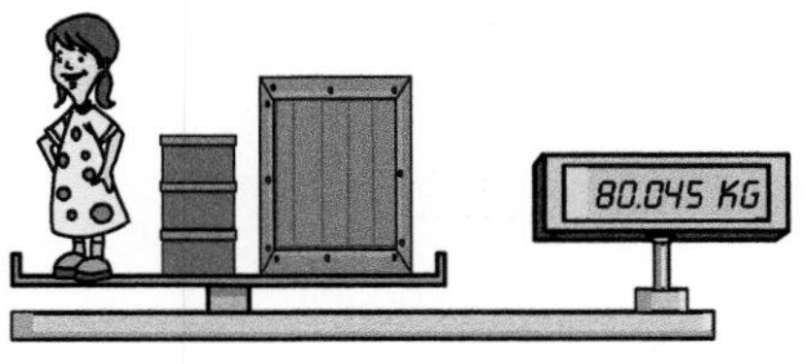

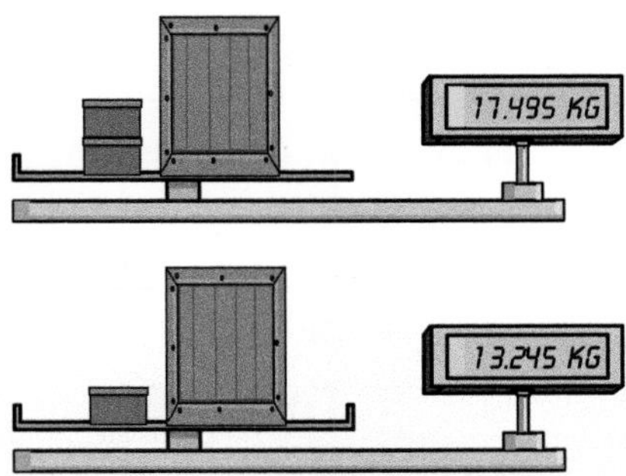

11g Multiplication and division problems

- Write the information you know and the information you are trying to find out when solving a problem.

Example

Here are the prices for buying calculators in bulk.
Gary buys 65 DAZIO CX 283P calculators.
Norbet buys 45 CHIP TQ 83SE calculators.
Who spends the most money on calculators?

Number ordered	DAZIO CX 283	DAZIO CX 283P	CHIP TQ 83S	CHIP TQ 83SE
1–10	£3.45	£3.85	£4.85	£5.15
11–30	£3.30	£3.70	£4.49	£4.99
31–50	£3.19	£3.55	£4.30	£4.89
Over 50	£3.09	£3.40	£4.19	£4.79

	Price each	Number
Gary	£3.40	65
Norbet	£4.89	45

Gary's total

$$\begin{array}{r} 65 \\ \times\ 34 \\ \hline 1950 \\ +\ 260 \\ \hline 2210 \end{array}$$

Gary spends £221.00

Norbet's total

$$\begin{array}{r} 489 \\ \times\ 45 \\ \hline 19560 \\ +\ 2445 \\ \hline 22005 \end{array}$$

Norbet spends £220.05

Difference = £221.00 − £220.05 = £0.95

Gary spends 95p more than Norbet.

- Check answers to a division (or multiplication) problem by taking the answer and performing the **inverse operation**.

Example

Mr Barnes wants to take 867 pupils and teachers from High Class Comprehensive to the theatre.
He has ordered 18 coaches, which can each carry 48 people, for the trip.
Has he ordered the correct number?

His answer × 48 = total number of pupils and teachers?

$18 \times 48 = 864 < 867$

This is smaller than the actual number of pupils and teachers, so Mr Barnes has not ordered enough coaches.

$$\begin{array}{r} 48 \\ \times\ 18 \\ \hline 480 \\ +\ 384 \\ \hline 864 \end{array}$$

Exercise 11g

Problem solving

1 Here are the offers from four phone companies for text messages.

Number ordered	CO2	Yello	Four	Skyte
1 – 9	4.25p	4.5p	4.25p	4.8p
10 – 49	4.2p	4.3p	4.15p	4.35p
50 – 99	4.15p	4.1p	4.05p	3.9p
Over 100	4.1p	3.9p	3.95p	3.45p

a Karl buys 35 text messages from CO2. How much money would he save if he switched to Four to buy his text messages?

b Zak buys 160 text messages a week from Yello.

i How much money would he save each week if he switched to Skyte?

ii How much money would he save in a year if he switched?

c Which phone company would you recommend to these people?

i Pete spends about £1.50 a week on text messages

ii Josh spends about £3 a week on text messages

iii Kath spends about £5 a week on text messages

In each case, explain your choice.

2 Maude is working out the costs of her motoring each week.
Petrol costs £1.18 a litre.
Maude's car travels 9.8 km for each litre of petrol.
Each week Maude travels 343 km in her car.

a How much money does Maude spend on petrol each week?

b How much money would you expect Maude to spend on petrol in a year? Explain your answer.

3 **a** Roger drives on the motorway at an average speed of 64 mph for 1.2 hours. Sarah completes the same journey in 1.6 hours. At what speed does Sarah drive?

b Isobel travels at 60 mph for 6 hours. Investigate other speeds and the time it would take to complete the same journey.

4 **a** Miss McCloud wants to take 650 pupils and teachers to a football match. She orders 11 coaches, which can each carry 58 people. Has she ordered the correct number? Explain your answer.

b Mr Kinsella wants to organise the 250 pupils in Year 8 into nine maths groups. There are supposed to be no more than 28 pupils in any class. Can Mr Kinsella fit the pupils into the 9 groups? Explain your thinking.

Check out

You should now be able to ...

Test it ➡ Questions

You should now be able to ...	Level	Questions
✓ Use mental methods for division and multiplication.	5	1
✓ Use standard written methods for addition, subtraction, multiplication and division.	6	2 – 6
✓ Use a calculator to calculate with powers, roots, brackets and fractions.	6	7
✓ Interpret the results of a calculation in context.	7	8, 9
✓ Use the BIDMAS rules to do a calculation in the correct order.	6	10

Language	Meaning	Example
Equivalent calculation	A way to write a decimal calculation as a whole number calculation	0.13×2.3 $= (13 \times 23) \div 1000$
Order of magnitude	Two numbers are the same order of magnitude if the difference between them is much smaller than either number	106 and 95 because $106 - 95 = 11$ and 11 is much less than 106 or 95
Inverse operation	The operation, $+ - \times \div$, that undoes the effect of another operation	The inverse of -7 is $+7$ $\div 3$ is $\times 3$
BIDMAS	The correct order for working out operations – Brackets, Indices, Divide, Multiply, Add, Subtract	$(3 + 2^2) + 2 \times 4$ $= 9 + 8 = 17$
Long division	A way of setting out workings when dividing by a multi-digit number	110 r 4 12)1324 12 12 12 04
Long multiplication	A way of setting out workings when multiplying	317 × 51 15850 + 3̊17 (carry 3) 16167 1

11 MyReview

1 Calculate these using a mental method.

a 28×0.04 b 19×2.2
c $555 \div 15$ d $50.4 \div 0.24$

2 Calculate these using a written method.

a 12×4.31 b 8.3×90.4
c 54.8×0.78 d 0.57×0.894

3 Calculate these, give your answer to 1 dp.

a $35.2 \div 6$ b $823 \div 12$
c $19 \div 8$ d $718 \div 1.8$
e $839 \div 0.62$ f $10.5 \div 4.5$

4 Rob is going to bake 178 cakes. Each cake requires 65 g of butter. The butter costs £1.45 for a 250 g pack.
How much does the butter for all the cakes cost in total?

5 Joe runs the 110 m hurdles in 16.2 s, what is his speed in metres per second? Give your answer to 2 dp.

6 Vijay's energy bill shows that he used 1224.89 kWh (kilowatt hours) of gas and 1133 kWh of electricity in one quarter of the year.
The price of gas was 4.217p per kWh and the price of electricity was 12.139p per kWh
In addition, he must pay a standing charge of 23.276p per day for gas and 15.219p per day for electricity.
There were 91 days in the quarter.
VAT at 5% of the total must also be added on.
Calculate the total cost of his energy bill (including VAT).

7 Use your calculator to work out

a $\sqrt{132.5 - 4.2^3}$

b $\dfrac{-5 - \sqrt{5^2 - 18 - 2 \times 3}}{-2}$

c $\dfrac{\sqrt{25 - 3^2}}{4^2 - 8}$

d $\dfrac{10.9 - 2.3 \times 1.4}{0.3(7.3 - 2.4)^2}$

8 Convert

a 7520 minutes to days, hours and minutes.
b 1 000 000 seconds to weeks, days, hours, minutes and seconds.

9 Convert these imperial measurements to the metric measurements indicated.

a 14 pounds to kg
b 5 feet, 9 inches to m

10 The following calculations are incorrect. Give the correct answer and explain the mistake.

a $(2 \times 3 + 5)^2 - 7 = 249$
b $(-4)^2 + 18 = 2$
c $72 \div (3 \times 2^2) - 5 + (7 - 8)^3 = 12$
d $(5 \times 8)^2 \div (5 \times 2) = 16$

What next?

Score		
	0 – 4	Your knowledge of this topic is still developing. To improve look at Formative test: 2C-11; MyMaths: 1007, 1008, 1010, 1011, 1026, 1041, 1167, 1905, 1914, 1916, 1917 and 1932
	5 – 8	You are gaining a secure knowledge of this topic. To improve look at InvisiPen: 122, 123, 124, 126, 127, 128, 131, 133 and 134
	9 – 10	You have mastered this topic. Well done, you are ready to progress!

11 MyPractice

11a

1 Calculate these using a written method.
Remember to do a mental approximation first.

a	82×0.65	**b**	64×0.57	**c**	82×91.3	**d**	93×26.5
e	36×1.86	**f**	72×9.51	**g**	16×2.19	**h**	8.3×86.7
i	63.7×0.91	**j**	38.4×0.69	**k**	57.2×0.61	**l**	93.9×0.93

11b

2 Calculate these using an appropriate method.
Give your answer as a decimal to 1 dp where appropriate.

a	$48.6 \div 6$	**b**	$67.4 \div 8$	**c**	$82.8 \div 7$	**d**	$38.5 \div 14$
e	$62.5 \div 15$	**f**	$31.2 \div 16$	**g**	$327 \div 4.6$	**h**	$912 \div 5.6$
i	$304 \div 2.4$	**j**	$441 \div 2.1$	**k**	$327 \div 8.2$	**l**	$955 \div 3.7$

11c

3 Use your calculator to work out the answers to these sets of instructions.

- **a** Input the number 12. Square your answer. Add 23.
  Find the square root. Add -8. Cube your answer.
- **b** Input the fraction $\frac{7}{8}$. Square your answer. Divide by 2.
  Add 14. Square root your answer.
- **c** Write the sets of instructions in parts **a** and **b** as calculations using the correct order of operations.

11d

4 Solve these problems.
Give each of your answers in a form appropriate to the question.

- **a** Jasmine's syndicate wins £3 454 123.23 on the Euro millions. There are 17 people in the syndicate. How much does each person receive?
- **b** The population of Smalltown is 48. Each year the population is predicted to increase by 6%. What will the population be in one year's time?

11e

5 Calculate these, giving your answer to 2 dp where appropriate.

a $\dfrac{(7-2)^3}{(8-3)^2}$ **b** $\dfrac{(4^2-1.2)(7-2.5)^2}{(9-4.1)^3}$ **c** $\dfrac{(3^2-2)^2\sqrt{(31-2^3)}}{(17-5)^2}$

6 Use a calculator to work out these calculations.
Give your answers to 2 dp where appropriate.

- **a** $[1.8^3 + (17 - 2.3^2)]^2$
- **b** $8.2 + [3.7^2 - (12.7 \div 2.6)]$
- **c** $9.2 \times (1.05 - 2.1)^3$
- **d** $\dfrac{5.03 \times 1.9^3}{4.23 \times (8.7 - 3.3)^2}$

11f

7 Calculate these using an appropriate method.

a 7.6 + 4.3 + 11 **b** 79 + 115.6 + 41 **c** 9.27 + 0.9 + 9 + 0.95

d 999.9 + 99.99 + 0.099 **e** 33.3 + 333.3 − 3.33 **f** 2473.5 + 40.79 − 4.6

8 An airline baggage handler has 1.35 tonnes of capacity left on a plane. Can she load all of the following packages?

car parts, 560 kg   cut flowers, 34.6 kg   a sack of letters 76 kg
two sacks of parcels 98 kg each   a crate of mangoes 425 kg

9 Darren is having trouble with his arithmetic. For each problem

i work out the correct answer **ii** explain Darren's probable mistake.

a 346.95 + 564.32   Darren's answer, 811.27

b 1.0046 − 0.045   Darren's answer, 1.0001

c 627.43 − 451.62   Darren's answer, 275.81

d 126.6 + 59.3 + 384.13   Darren's answer, 4027.2

11g

10 Calculate these using the standard method.

a 19 × 3.68 **b** 27 × 4.18 **c** 46 × 5.53 **d** 62 × 7.26

e 49 × 5.69 **f** 74 × 8.57 **g** 79 × 8.37 **h** 99 × 9.99

11 Calculate these using an appropriate method. Give your answer as a decimal rounded to 1 decimal place where appropriate.

a 36.7 ÷ 8 **b** 43.6 ÷ 7 **c** 25.6 ÷ 6 **d** 35.7 ÷ 9

e 50.4 ÷ 24 **f** 52.7 ÷ 39 **g** 91.6 ÷ 24 **h** 41.8 ÷ 17

12 Depak is driving the 249 miles home from holiday.

a His average speed is 45 miles per hour. How long will it take him?

b His fuel consumption is 33 miles per gallon. How much fuel will he need?

c When full his petrol tank holds 14 gallons but at the start of this journey it is only five-eighths full. Can he make it home without having to fill up?

d Depak doesn't know it but his car has a leak, and it is losing 0.15 gallons of petrol every hour. Will he still make it home?

13 a Elliot is cooking an 8.5 kg turkey for his family. The instructions say cook at a high heat for 5 min per kg, then turn the heat down and cook for 25 min per kg and finally cook for 30 min at the high heat again.
How long will it take to cook the turkey?

b After cooking the turkey must rest for 45 min. It will take Elliot a further 20 min to carve and serve. If Elliot wants to serve dinner at 4 o'clock in the afternoon, when should he put the turkey in the oven?

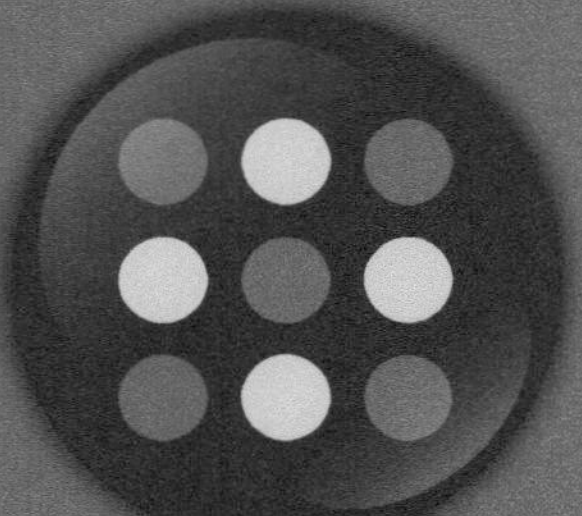

12 Constructions

Introduction

As supermarket companies get bigger they open new branches in different towns. The warehouses which supply to each branch need to be positioned carefully. In order to save costs the supermarket companies try to choose a site which has good transport links and which is close to an equal distance from each branch that it services.

This problem can be solved using mathematical constructions by finding the regions on a map that are approximately an equal distance from each branch.

What's the point?

Accurate geometrical constructions allow you to solve real-life problems involving scale drawings and maps.

Objectives

By the end of this chapter, you will have learned how to ...

- Construct a unique triangle given sufficient information on the size of its angles and lengths of its sides.
- Construct bisectors and perpendiculars.
- Construct simple loci.
- Use three figure bearings.

Check in

1 Use angle properties of parallel lines to calculate the unknown angles.

a

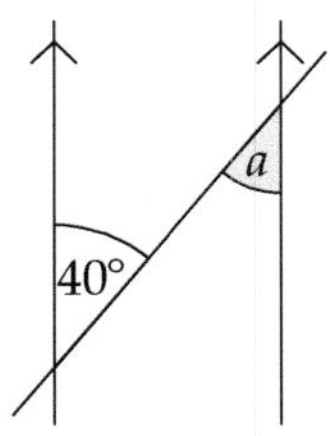

b

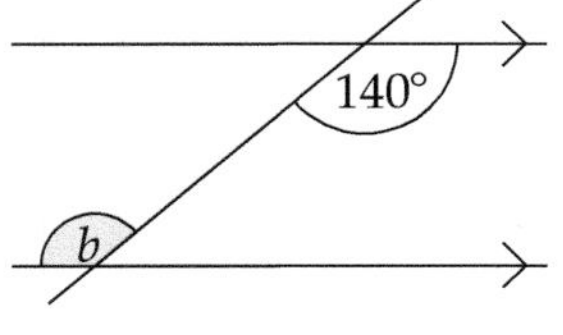

c

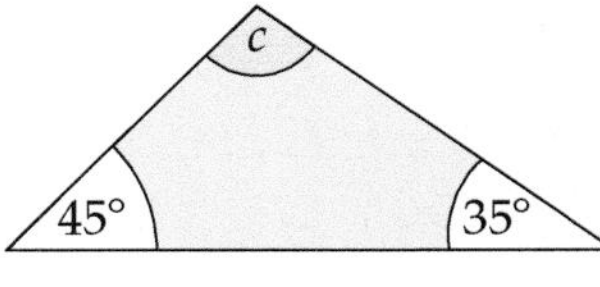

2 **a** Draw two lines AB and AC, with AB = 5 cm, AC = 6.5 cm and angle BAC = 60°.

b Measure the distance BC.

Starter problem

When you construct the perpendicular bisectors of an equilateral triangle, the lines meet at a point. This point is the centre of a circle which passes through each of the three corners of the equilateral triangle.

Does this work for all types of triangles?

Does it work for quadrilaterals?

Does it work for any polygons?

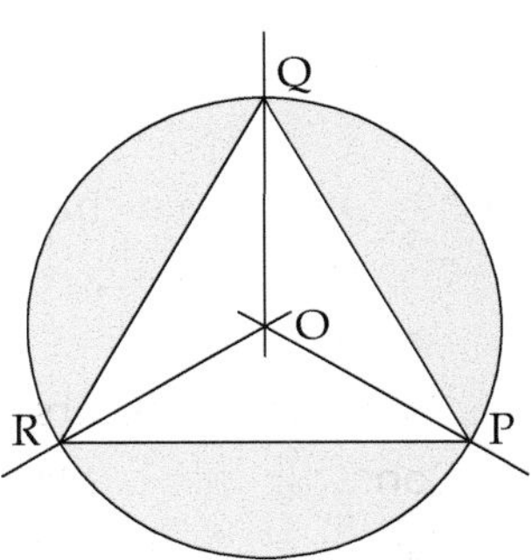

12a Constructing triangles 1

You can **construct** a **triangle** using a **ruler** and a **protractor**.

- You always construct **congruent** triangles, when you are given
  - either

    two angles and the included side (ASA)

    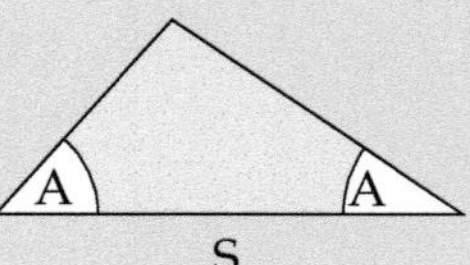

  - or

    two sides and the included angle (SAS)

    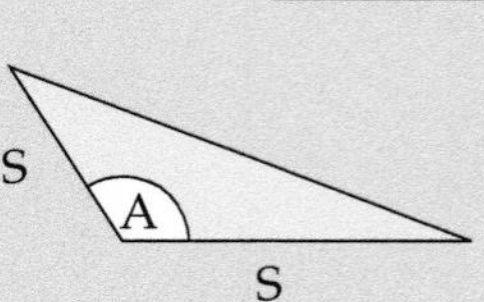

Example

Construct the triangle ABC so that

AC = 5 cm angle A = 53° angle C = 74°.

First draw a sketch of the triangle.

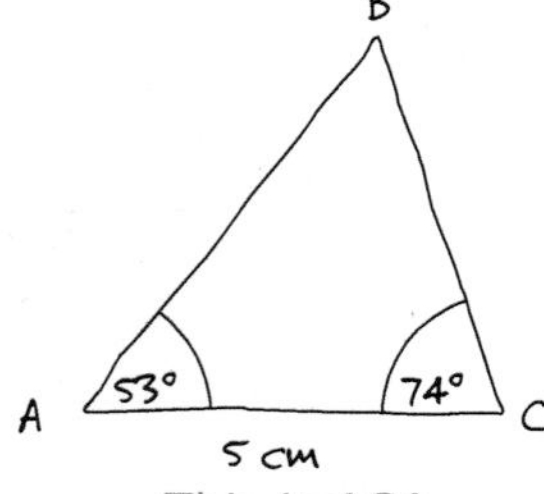

This is ASA.

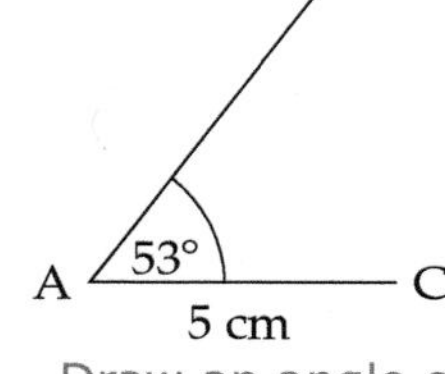

Draw the base line of 5 cm using a ruler.

Draw an angle of 53° at A using a protractor.

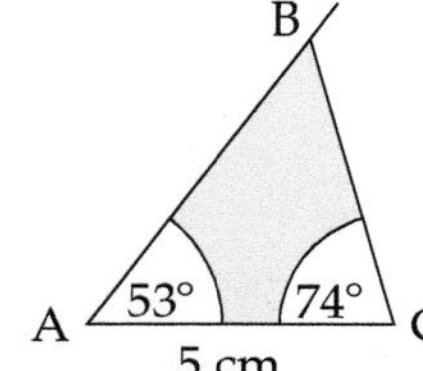

Draw an angle of 74° at C using a protractor to complete the triangle.

Example

a Construct the triangle DEF so that

DF = 4 cm EF = 3 cm angle F = 40°.

b Measure DE and calculate the perimeter of the triangle.

a

First draw a sketch of the triangle.

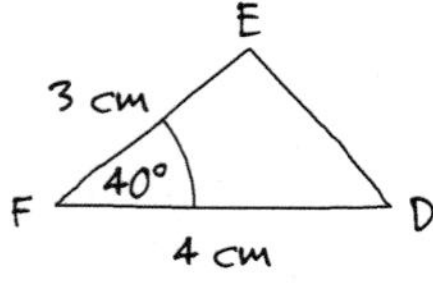

This is SAS.

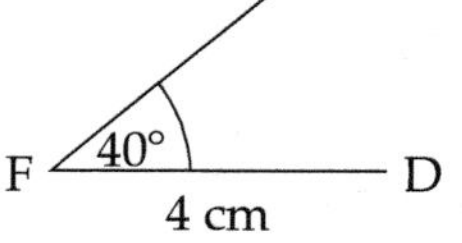

Draw the base line of 4 cm using a ruler.

Draw an angle of 40° at F using a protractor.

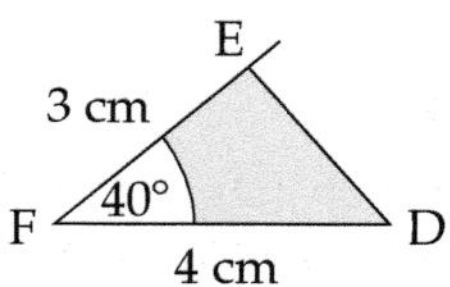

Mark E at 3 cm from F and draw DE to complete the triangle.

b DE is 2.6 cm

Perimeter = 4 + 3 + 2.6 = 9.6 cm

Exercise 12a

1 Construct these triangles.
Measure and calculate the perimeter of each triangle.

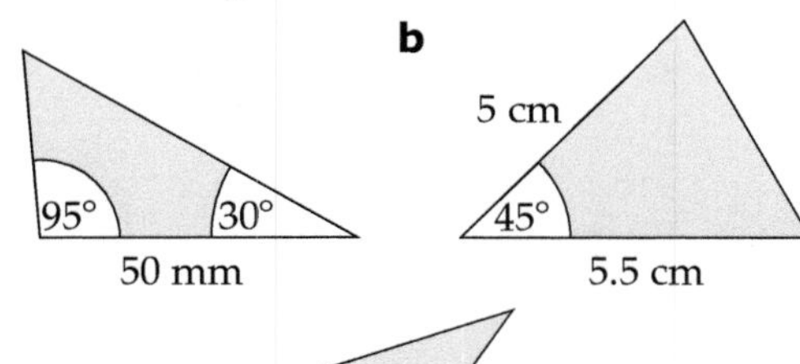

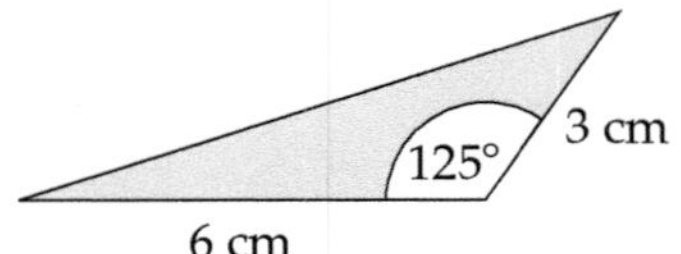

2 Construct these triangles and give the mathematical name of each triangle.
Draw a sketch first.

- **a** AC = 6.5 cm angle A = 30°
  angle C = 75°
- **b** angle Q = 40° angle R = 50°
  QR = 55 mm
- **c** EF = 7 cm angle F = 120°
  FD = 4 cm
- **d** XY = 5 cm angle Y = 45°
  ZY = 7.1 cm

3 Calculate the unknown angles and then construct each triangle.

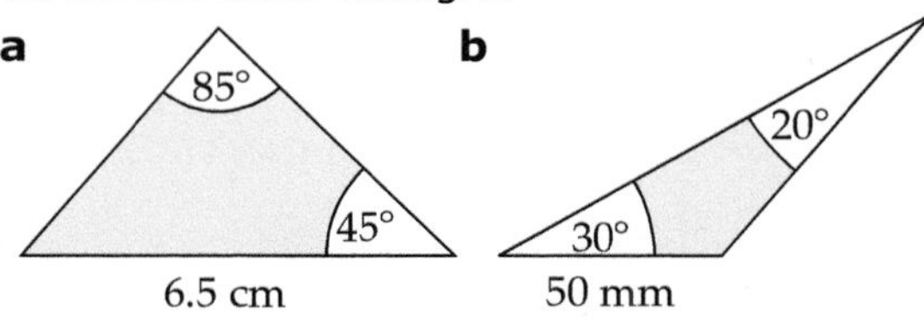

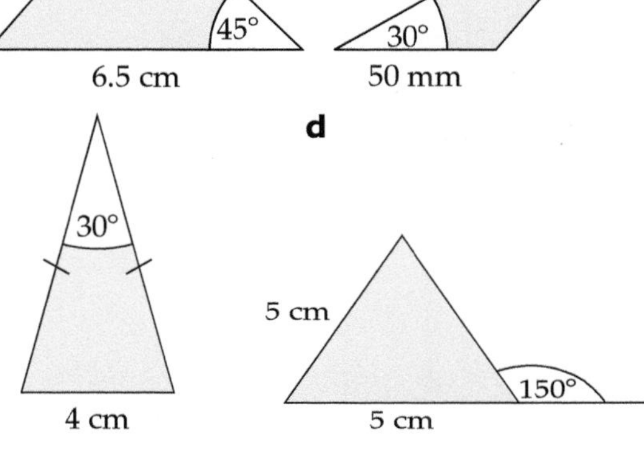

4
- **a** Construct the quadrilateral.
- **b** Measure the four interior angles of the quadrilateral.
  Check that the total is 360°.
- **c** Measure and calculate the perimeter of the quadrilateral.

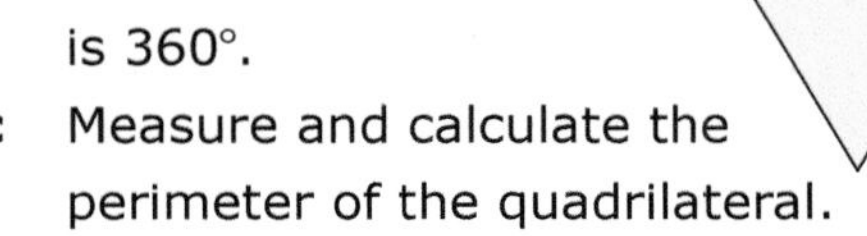

Problem solving

5 **a** Construct and cut out two congruent triangles with these dimensions.

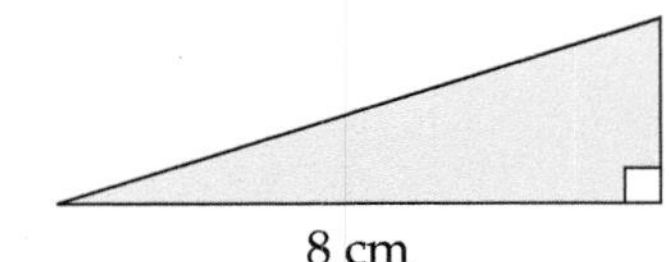

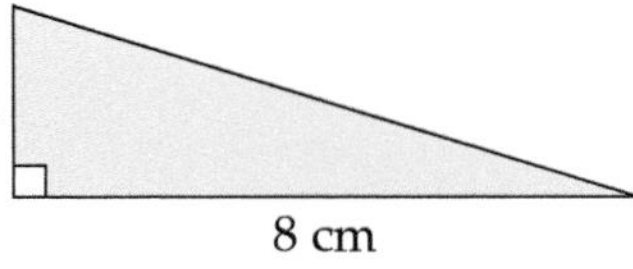

- **b** Fit the triangles together to make a kite.
- **c** Calculate the area of the kite.

6 The spiral of Theodorus is constructed as a sequence of right-angled triangles with the hypotenuse of one triangle being the base of the next.

- **a** Construct your own spiral.
- **b** Measure the distances OA, OB, OC, OD, …
  Do you notice anything special about these lengths?

What would be the area of a square with OB as base?

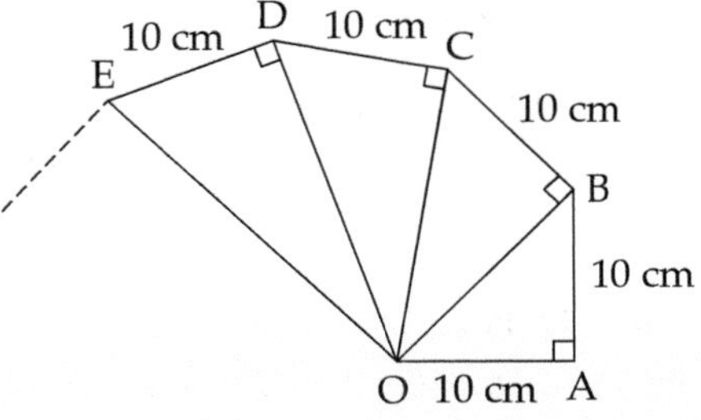

12b Constructing triangles 2

You can **construct** a triangle using a ruler, **compasses** and a protractor.

You always construct **congruent** triangles, when you are given

- either

  the length of all three sides (SSS)

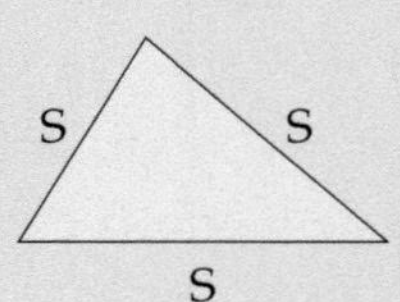

- or

  a right-angle and the length of one side and the **hypotenuse** (RHS)

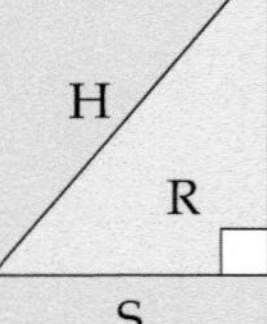

Example

Construct the triangle ABC so that

AB = 6 cm AC = 5 cm BC = 4 cm.

First draw a sketch of the triangle.

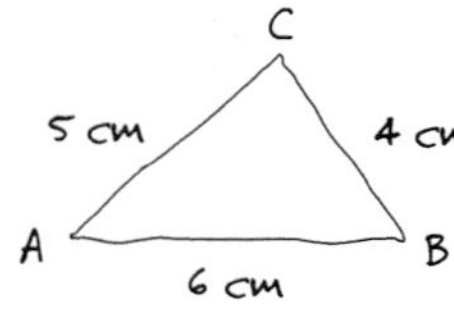

This is SSS.

A ——— B 6 cm

Draw the base line of 6 cm using a ruler.

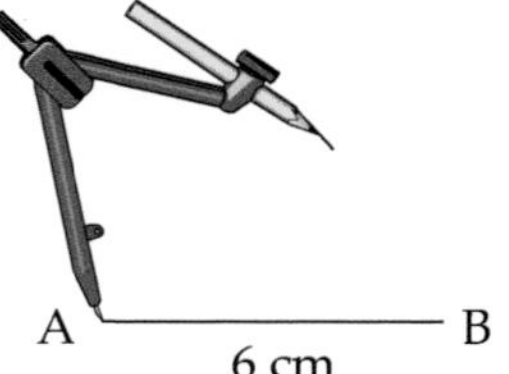

Draw an arc 5 cm from A using compasses.

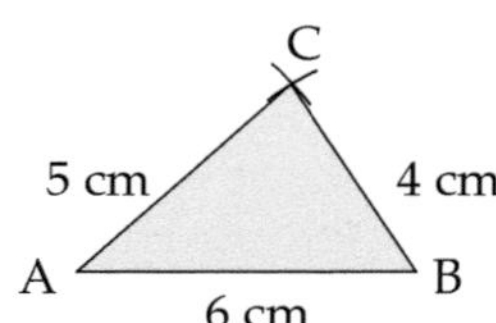

Draw an arc 4 cm from B. Draw AC and BC to complete the triangle.

Example

Construct the triangle DEF so that

DF = 4 cm angle F = 90· DE = 7 cm.

First draw a sketch of the triangle.

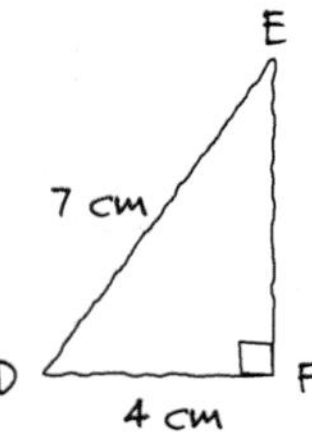

This is RHS.

D ——— F 4 cm

Draw the base line of 4 cm using a ruler and use a protractor to draw an angle of 90° at F.

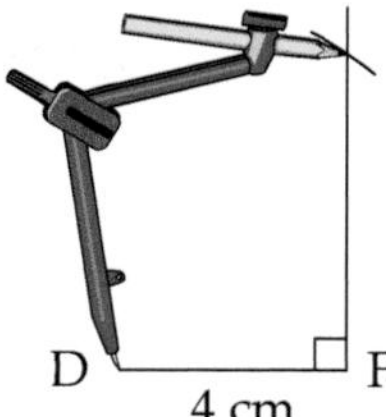

Draw an arc 7 cm from D using compasses.

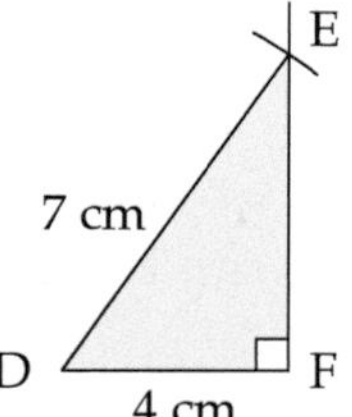

Draw DE to complete the right-angled triangle.

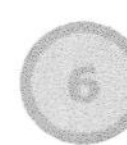

Exercise 12b

1 Construct these triangles, using ruler and compasses.
Measure the angles in each triangle and check that the total is 180°.

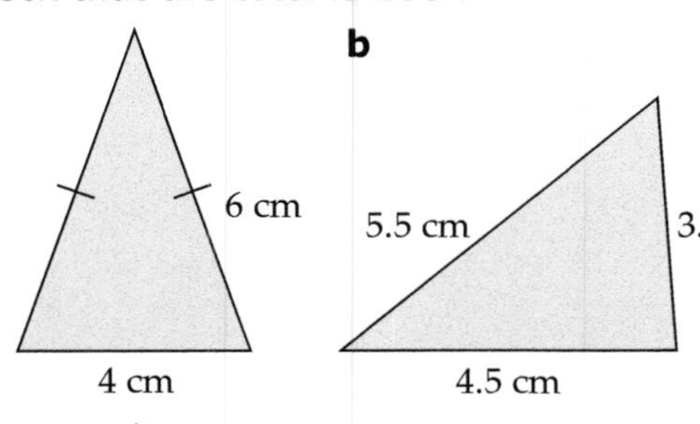

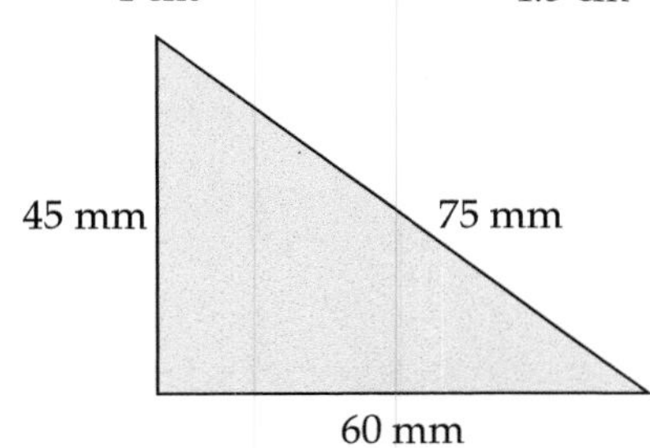

2 Construct these right-angled triangles. Draw a sketch first.

a angle C = 90° AB = 6 cm
BC = 4 cm

b angle R = 90° PR = 3.5 cm
PQ = 6 cm

3 Construct these quadrilaterals.
Measure the length of the diagonals in each quadrilateral.

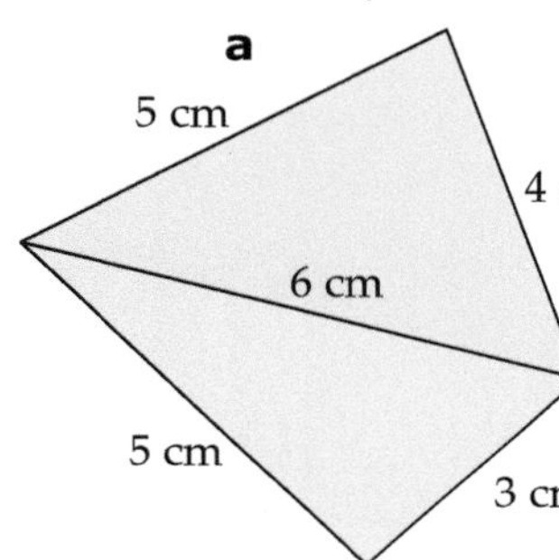

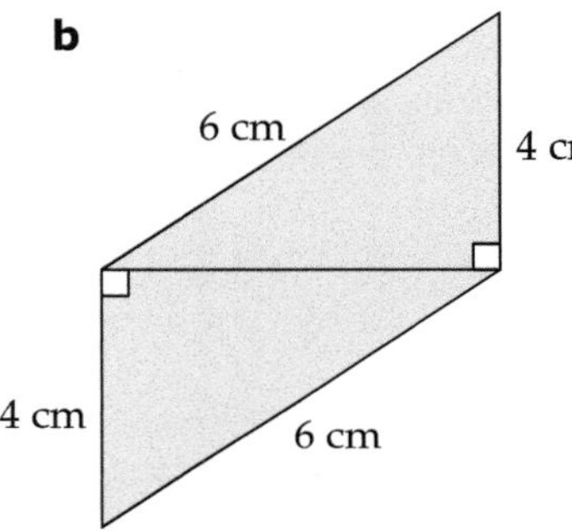

Problem solving

4 A 4 metre ladder is put against a wall. The ladder is 2 metres from the wall at ground level.

a Using a scale of 1 cm to represent 50 cm, construct a scale drawing of the ladder.

b Measure and calculate the distance of the ladder up the wall.

c Measure the angle of the ladder to the ground.

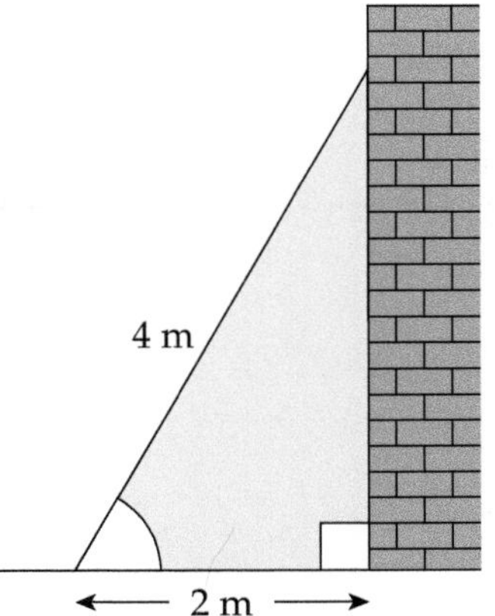

5 Draw a horizontal line measuring 8 cm. Spread your compasses to a distance of 4 cm.
Use the compasses to construct the regular hexagon.
Explain why this method works.

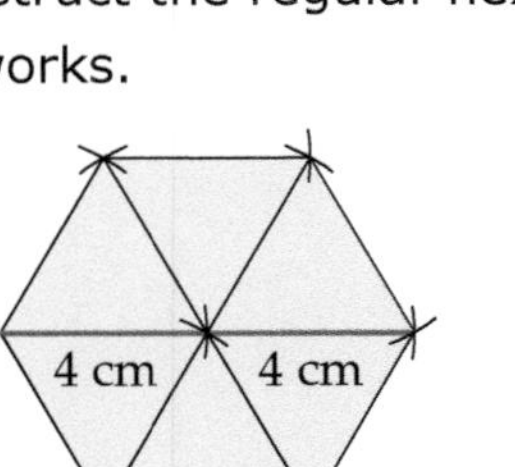

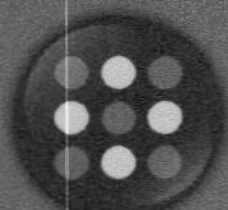

12c Bisectors and perpendiculars

- An angle **bisector** cuts an angle exactly in half.

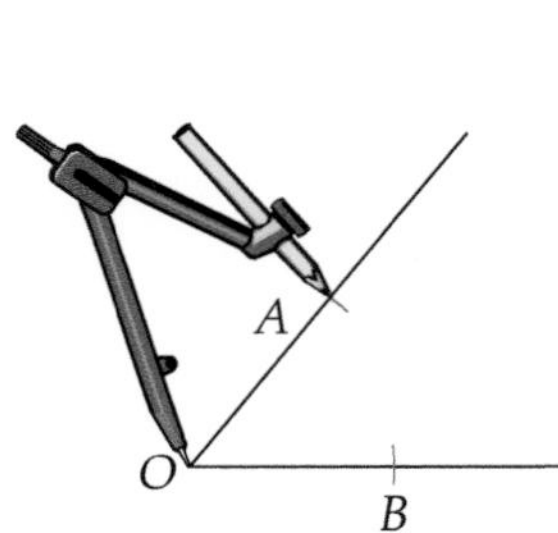

Use compasses to draw an arc on each line.

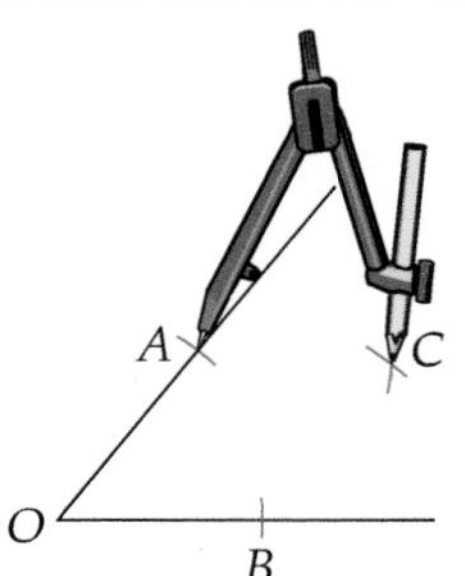

Draw arcs from *A* and *B* that intersect at *C*.

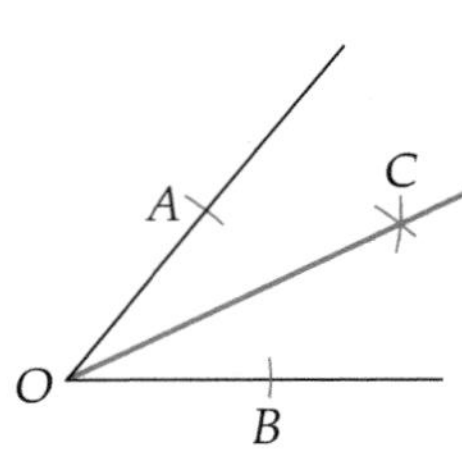

Draw a line from *O* to *C* and beyond.

- You use compasses to construct a **perpendicular** from a point to a line.

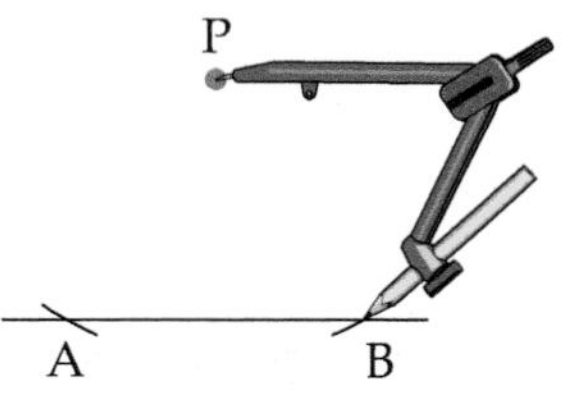

Use compasses to draw arcs from P on the line.

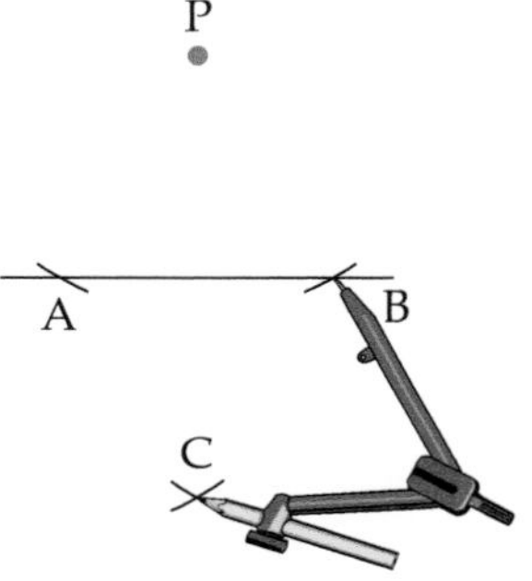

Draw arcs from A and B that intersect at C.

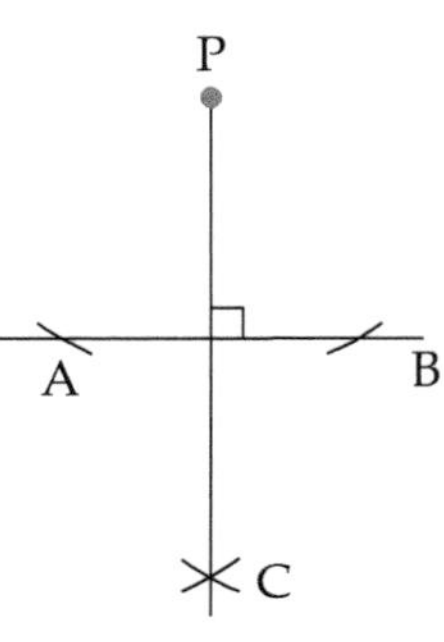

Draw a line from P to C.

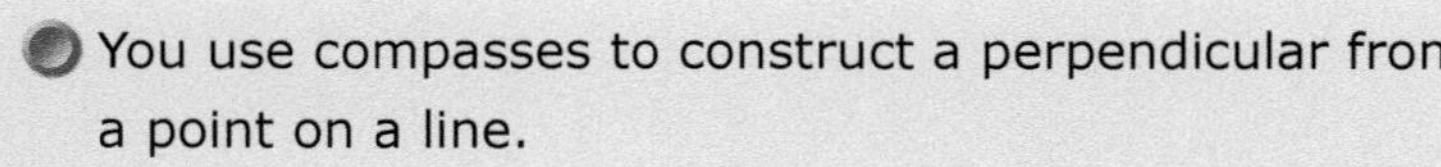

- You use compasses to construct a perpendicular from a point on a line.

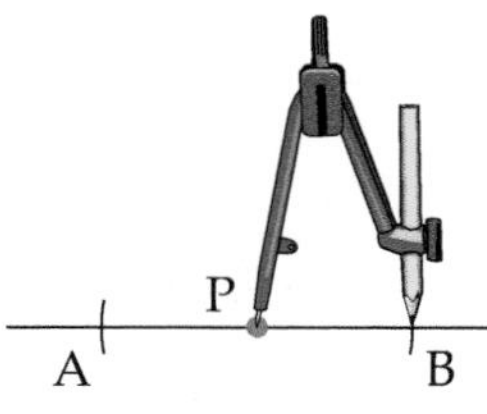

Use compasses to draw arcs from P on the line.

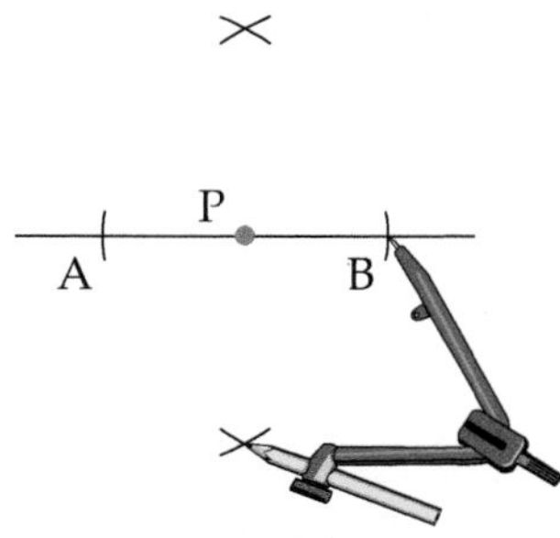

Draw arcs from A and B above and below the line.

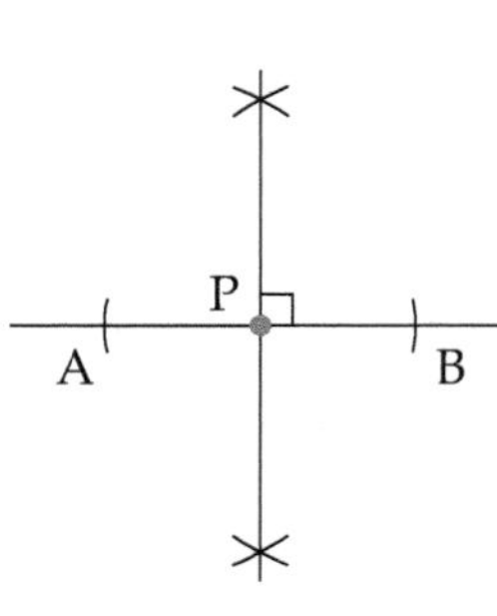

Draw a line between the intersections of the arcs.

Exercise 12c

1 Draw and label these lines.
Using compasses, construct the perpendicular bisector of each line.
Use a ruler and protractor to check your answers.

a AB = 5.8 cm **b** CD = 64 mm
c EF = 7.2 cm **d** 144 mm

2 Draw each angle.
Using compasses, construct the angle bisector of each angle.
Use a protractor to check your answers.

a 124° **b** 78°
c 240° **d** 90°

3 Draw a line AB so that AB = 8 cm.
Mark the point P so that AP = 5 cm and PB = 3 cm.
Construct the perpendicular to AB that passes through the point P.

4 Draw a line AB, with a point P above the line.

P

A ——— B

a Construct the perpendicular to AB that passes through the point P.
b Measure the shortest distance from the point P to the line AB.

Problem solving

5 **a** Using compasses and ruler, construct the two isosceles triangles to form the quadrilateral PQRS.
b State the mathematical name of the quadrilateral.
c Construct the perpendicular line from P to the line SQ.
d Extend the line to the point R and explain why the line PR is a line of symmetry.

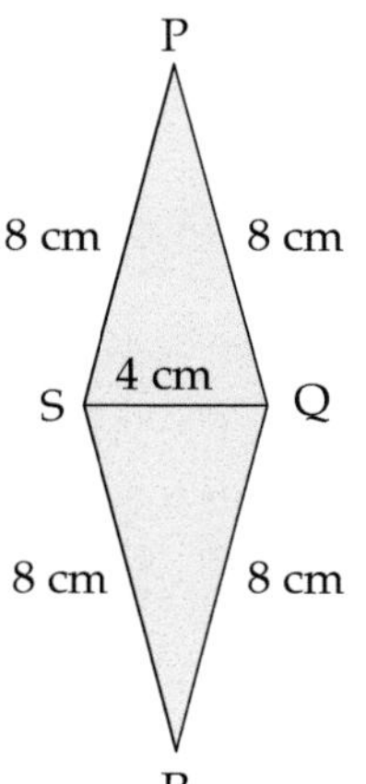

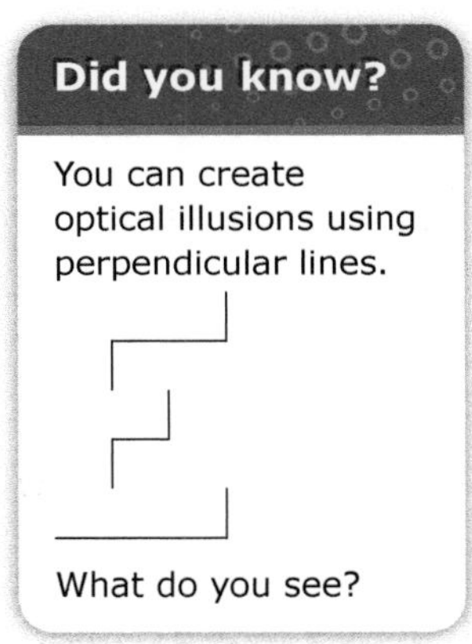

6 In this construction, you are not allowed to measure any lengths.
Draw a horizontal line AB.
Find the midpoint of AB by constructing the perpendicular bisector of the line.
O is the midpoint of AB.
Draw a circle with centre O passing through A, B, C and D.
Using compasses, construct the perpendicular bisectors of AO, OC, OB and OD to find four new midpoints.
Use these midpoints to draw four more circles.

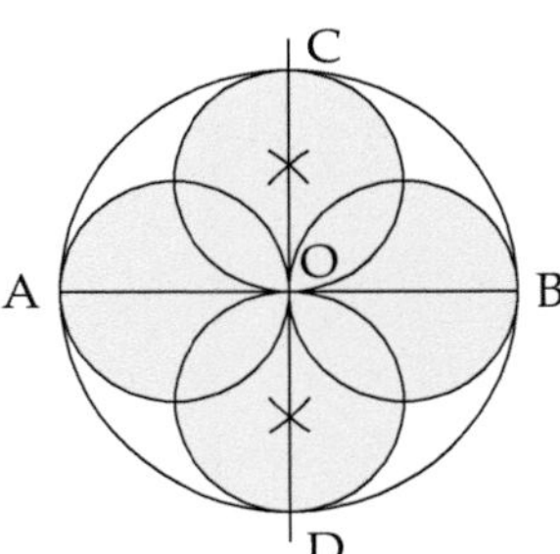

12d Scale drawings

You can use **scale drawings** to **represent** real-life objects.

Length 17 m
Height 5 m

Real-life lengths are reduced or enlarged in proportion using a **scale**. The scale allows you to interpret the scale drawing.

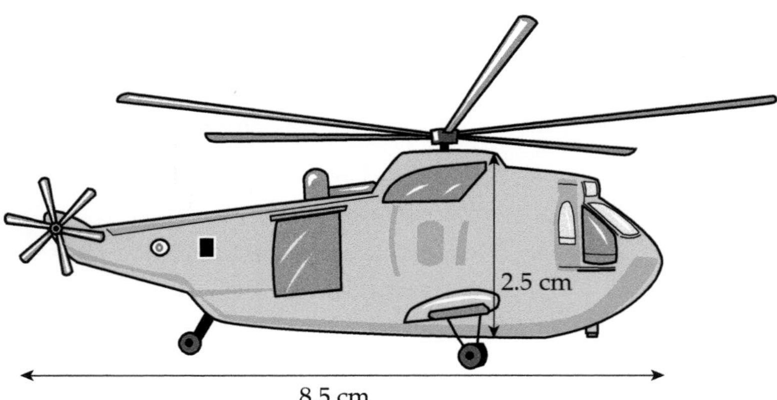

Scale: 1 cm represents 200 cm

The real-life lengths are 200 times larger than in the scale drawing.
8.5 × 200 = 1700 cm = 17 m
2.5 × 200 = 500 cm = 5 m
The real-life lengths are an enlargement scale factor 200 of the scale drawing.

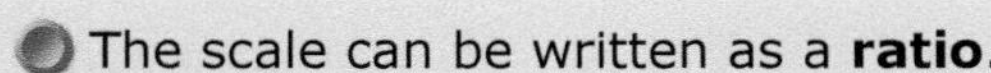

The scale can be written as a **ratio**.

1 : 200 means 1 cm on the scale drawing represents 200 cm, or 2 m, in real life.

The scale for a map is often given as a ratio.

Example

Jamie is using a map with a scale of 1 : 25 000.

a What does 5 cm on the map represent in real life?

b What distance would represent 4 km on the map?

a 1 cm on the map represents 25 000 cm in real life.
5 cm on the map represents 5 × 25 000 cm in real life.
5 × 25 000 cm = 125 000 cm = 1250 m
= 1.25 km

b 4 km = 4000 m
= 400 000 cm
400 000 cm in real life is represented by 400 000 ÷ 25 000
= 16 cm on the map

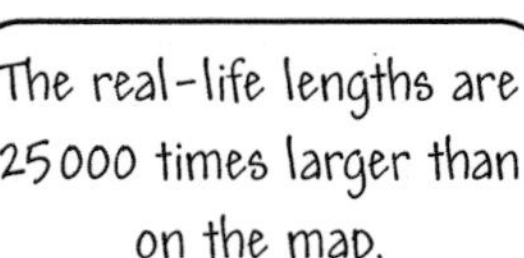

The map's lengths are 25 000 times smaller than in real life.

Exercise 12d

1 This is a scale drawing of a bicycle.

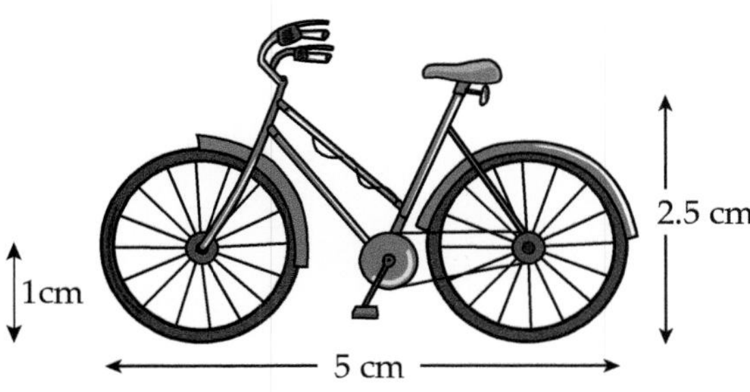

Scale: 1 cm represents 35 cm

Calculate

a the diameter of the wheel

b the length of the bicycle

c the height of the saddle above the ground.

2 The sketch represents a full-size sailing dinghy.
Jenny decides to draw a scale drawing of the dinghy using a scale of 1 : 50.

Calculate the length in the scale drawing of

a the mast

b the length of the boat

c the horizontal length 2.5 m.

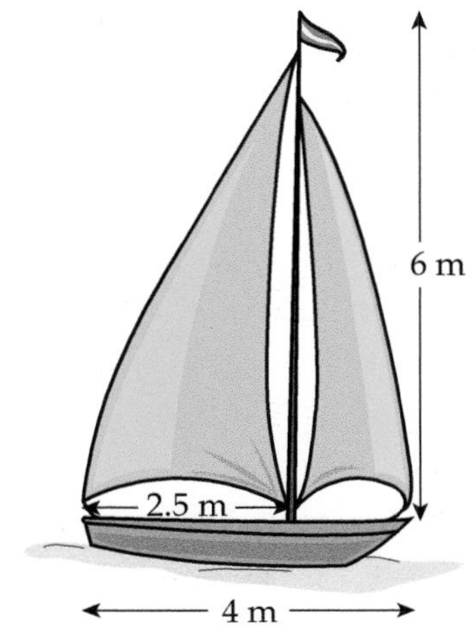

Problem solving

3 A rectangular field measures 40 m by 30 m.
Use a scale drawing to calculate the length of the diagonal of the field.
Remember to state the scale of your drawing.

4 The Kennet and Avon Canal has two right-angled bends at the Avoncliff aqueduct.
Boats find it difficult to pass through this part of the canal and in fact some boats are too long and cannot pass through the bends.

The width of the canal is 5 metres.

a Draw a scale drawing of this part of the canal.
Use a scale of 1 cm to represent 2.5 m.

b What is the longest boat that can pass through the bends?
Start by assuming that the boat has no width and then gradually increase the width of the boat.

Did you know?

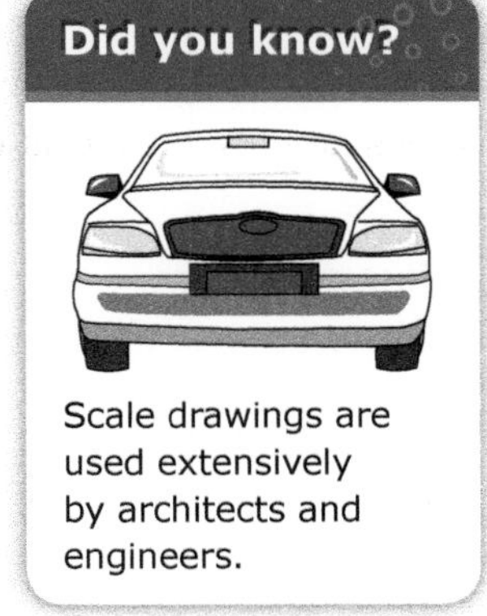

Scale drawings are used extensively by architects and engineers.

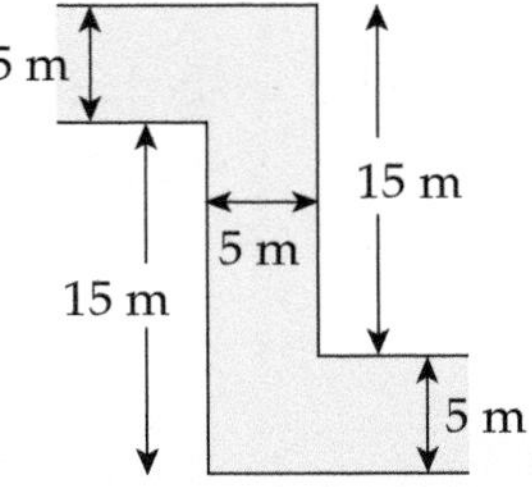

12e Loci

- The **locus** of an object is its **path**.
  - The path of a point that moves according to a rule forms a locus.

▲ The locus of a windmill blade tip is a circle.

- The points on the red circle are the same distance from the centre O.

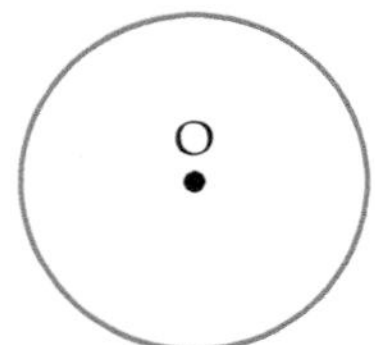

The locus is a circle.

- The points on the red line are **equidistant** from A and B.

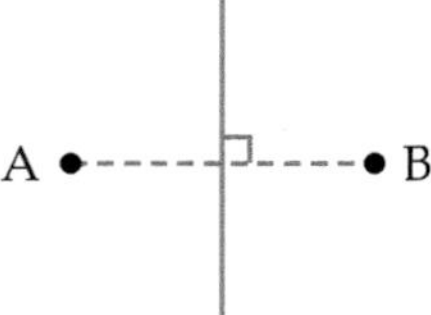

The locus is the **perpendicular bisector** of AB.

- The points on the red line are equidistant from the lines OA and OB.

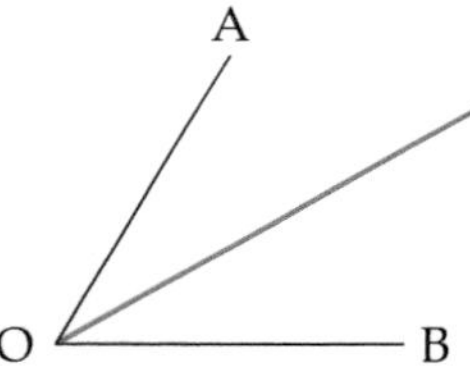

The locus is the angle bisector.

- The points on the red shape are 1 cm from the line AB.

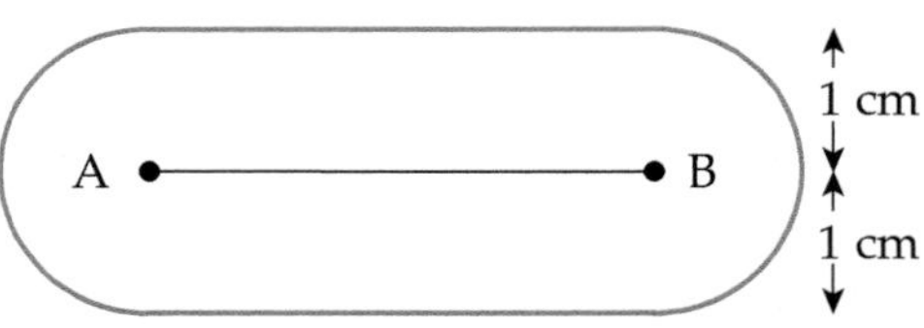

The locus is two lines each parallel to the line AB and two semicircles centred on A and B.

Example

Construct the locus of the point that is equidistant from OA and OB.

B, A, O

The locus is the **angle bisector** of the angle AOB.
Use compasses to construct the angle bisector.

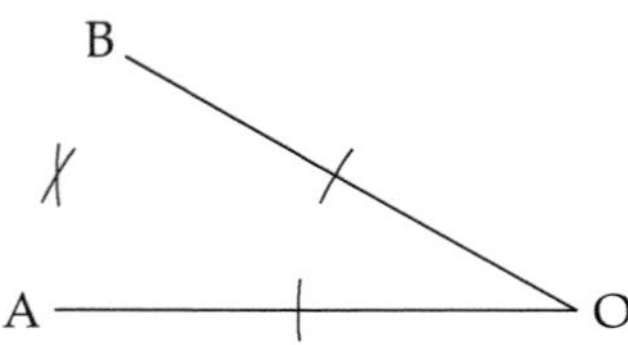

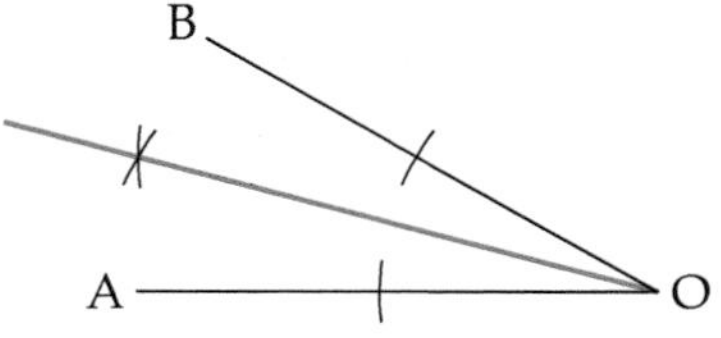

Exercise 12e

1 Draw an angle ROQ of 110°.
Using ruler and compasses, construct the locus of the point that is equidistant from OR and OQ.

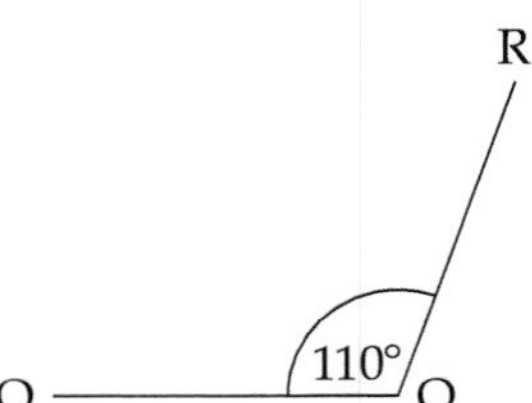

2 Draw the locus of a point that is 35 mm from a fixed point.

3 Two cones A and B are placed 5 metres apart.

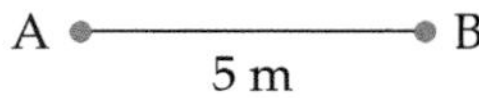

a Draw a scale drawing, using a scale of 1 : 100.

b Using ruler and compasses, construct the locus of the point that is equidistant from the cones.

4 Draw the locus of a point that is 1 cm from a 3 cm long straight line.

Problem solving

5 A straight stream is 2 metres wide.

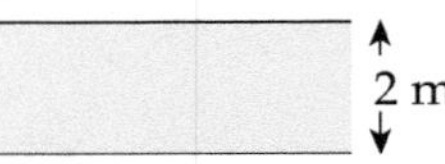

a Draw a scale drawing, using a scale of 1 : 50.

b Draw the locus of the point that is in the middle of the stream.

6 A triangle ABC has an area of 10 cm^2.
The base of the triangle is 5 cm.
Draw the line AB and draw the locus of the point C.

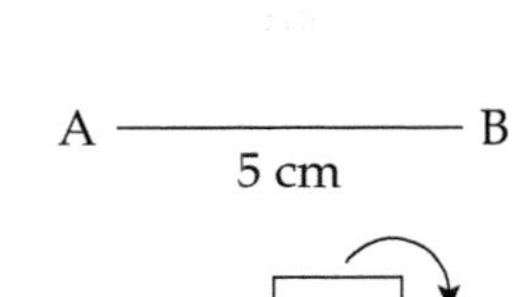

7 Cut out a 2 cm by 2 cm square and place it on a straight line.
The square is rotated clockwise about the point O through an angle of 90°.
The locus of the red cross is the red curve.
The square is now rotated clockwise about the point P, through an angle of 90°.
Draw the locus of the red cross, as the square continues to be rotated about the right-hand vertex on the straight line.

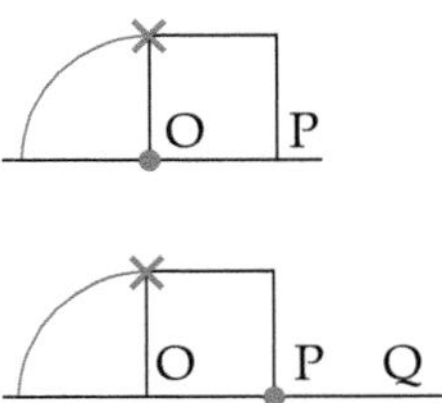

12f Bearings

This indicator board shows the **direction** of places from a hill called Hampsfell in Cumbria.

The numbers are the **bearings** of places from Hampsfell.

Each number is an angle called a **three-figure bearing**.

When you use bearings
- measure from North
- measure in a clockwise direction
- use three figures.

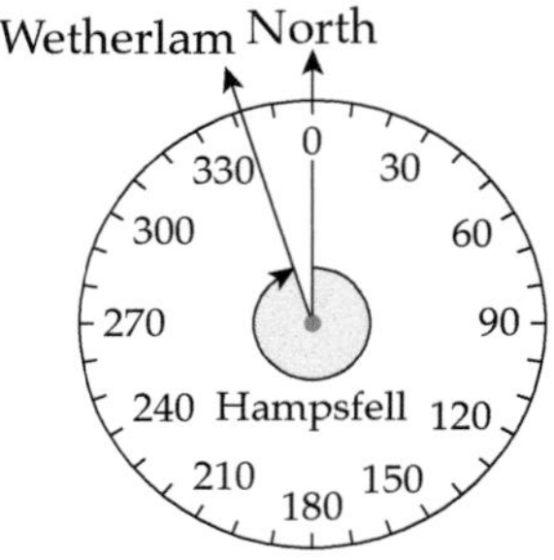

▲ Centre your protractor on Hampsfell.

The three-figure bearing of Wetherlam from Hampsfell is 342°.

Example

Calculate the bearing of

a P from Q **b** Q from P

a Measure the bearing from Q

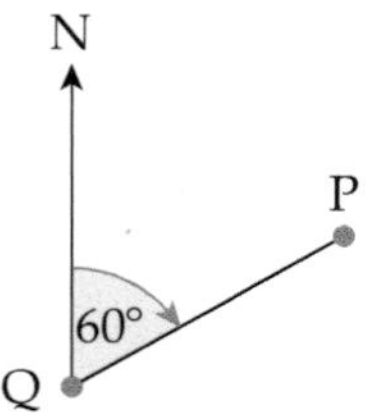

P from Q is 060°

Notice that 60° + 180° = 240°

and 240° − 180° = 60°

You can either add or subtract 180° to find the **reverse bearing**.

b Measure the bearing from P

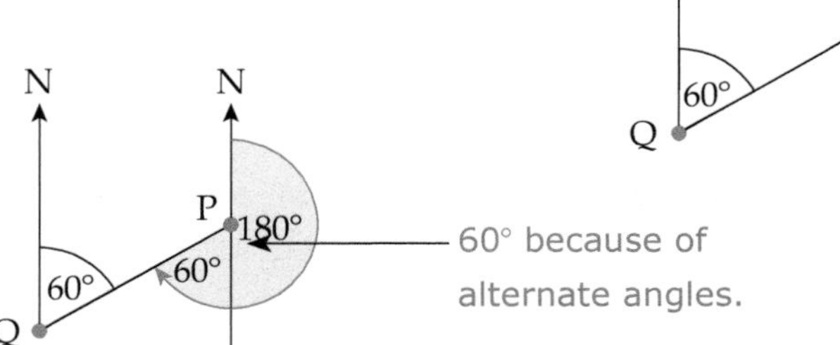

Q from P is 240°

Exercise 12f

1 Measure these three-figure bearings for towns on the Isle of Wight.

- **a** Sandown from Newport
- **b** Freshwater from Newport
- **c** Cowes from Newport
- **d** Ventnor from Newport
- **e** Newport from Ventnor
- **f** Freshwater from Ventnor
- **g** Sandown from Ventnor

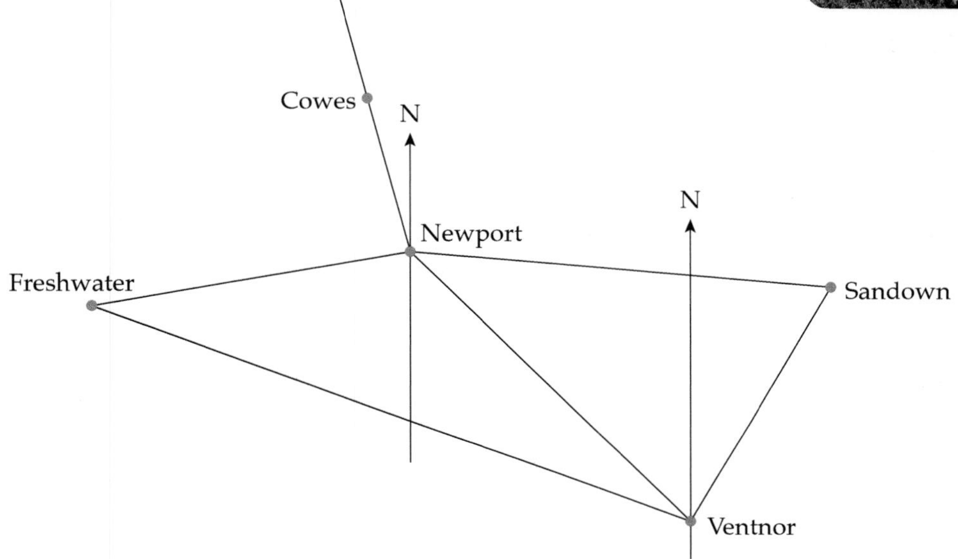

2 Find the bearings of

a B from A **b** D from C **c** F from E **d** H from G **e** J from I

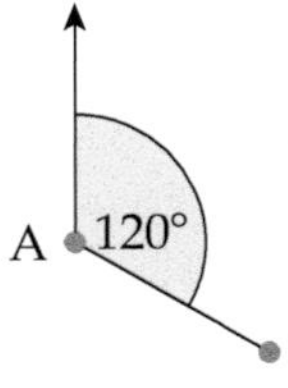

N
C
230°
D

N
F
40°
E

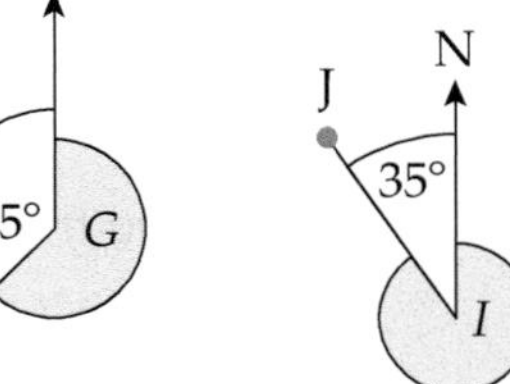

J
N
35°
I

Use the same diagrams to calculate the bearings of

f A from B **g** C from D **h** E from F **i** G from H **j** I from J

Problem solving

3 Andy walks on a bearing of 020°.
He then turns around and returns on a bearing of 200°.
These three-figure bearings use the same digits 0, 0 and 2.
Can you find any other bearing and return bearing that uses the same three digits?

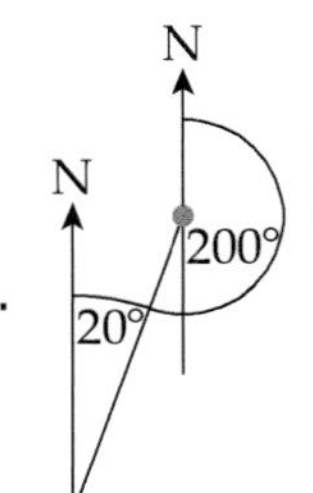

020° + 180° = 200°

4 B is 5 km from A on the bearing 070°.
C is 5 km from B on the bearing 320°.
How far is C from A and what is its bearing?

Use a scale drawing with 1 cm representing 1 km

12 MySummary

Check out

You should now be able to ...

Test it ➡ Questions

You should now be able to ...	Level	Questions
✓ Construct ASA, SAS, SSS and RHS triangles.	6	1, 2
✓ Construct an angle bisector, the perpendicular bisector of a line, the perpendicular from a point on a line and the perpendicular from a point to a line.	7	3
✓ Construct simple loci	6	4, 5
✓ Interpret scale drawings and maps using ratios.	6	6
✓ Use three figure bearings	7	7, 8

Language	Meaning	Example
Perpendicular bisector	A line that cuts a second line at 90°	P, A, B, C
Locus	The path made by the point of an object as it moves	A, B, 1 cm, 1 cm
Congruent	Shapes that are identical: corresponding lengths and angles are the same	ASA, SAS, SSS and RHS triangles are congruent
Construct	To draw accurately using a ruler, protractor and compasses	Bisecting an angle is a construction
Three figure bearing	A direction given as an angle, measured clockwise from north, using three digits	East is 090°

1 Construct these triangles.

a

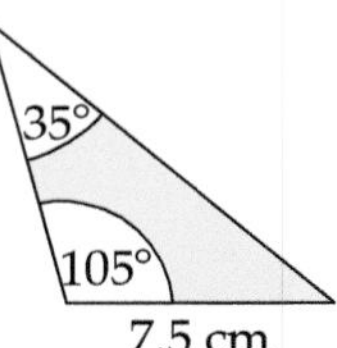

b

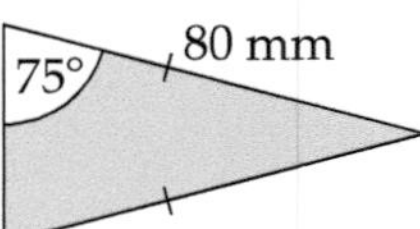

2 Construct these triangles.

a

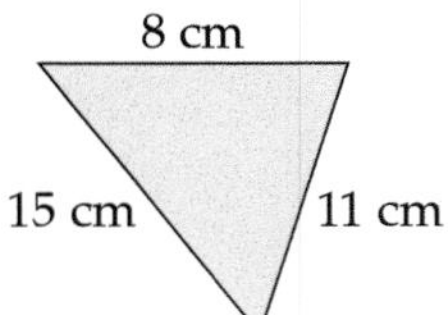

b

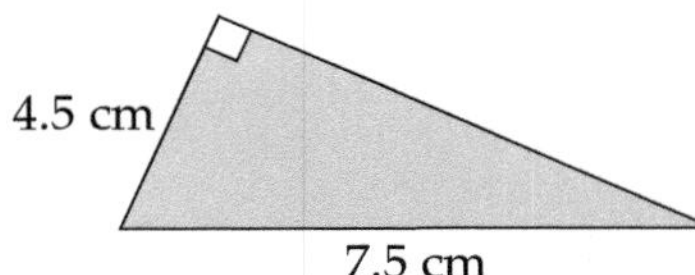

3 Use a ruler and compasses to add the following lines to your earlier constructions.

a On **1b**, the bisector of the angle between the equal sides.

b On **2b**, the perpendicular to the hypotenuse passing through the opposite vertex.

4 Copy this rectangle and construct accurately the locus of a point that is 1 cm from the edge of the rectangle.

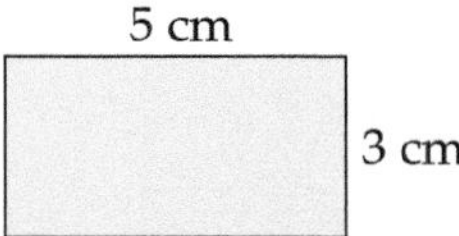

5 Two fences meet at 90° as shown. Copy the diagram and construct the locus of the point which is equidistant from both fences.

6 A circular pond has a radius of 1 m.

a Draw a scale drawing using a scale of 1 : 40

b Draw the locus of the point that is 0.5 m from the edge of the pond.

7 Find the bearings of

a B from A

b A from B

c C from D

d D from C

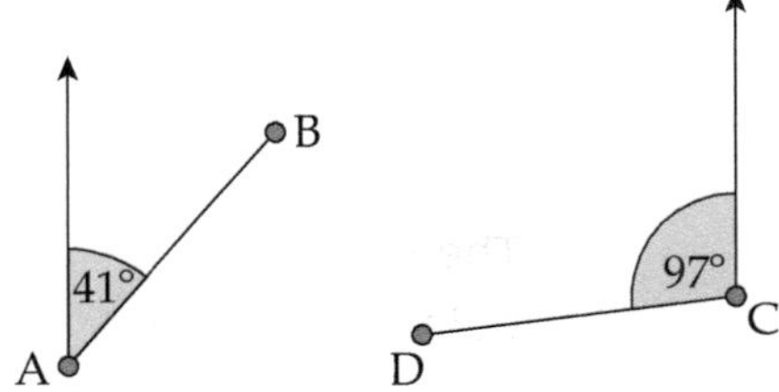

8 Draw the following bearings of B from A and state the bearing of A from B in each case.

a 076° b 195° c 308°

What next?

Score		
0 – 3		Your knowledge of this topic is still developing. To improve look at Formative test: 2C-12; MyMaths: 1086, 1089, 1090, 1103, 1117 and 1147
4 – 6		You are gaining a secure knowledge of this topic. To improve look at InvisiPen: 371, 373, 374 and 375
7 – 8		You have mastered this topic. Well done, you are ready to progress!

12a

1 Construct these triangles.

a

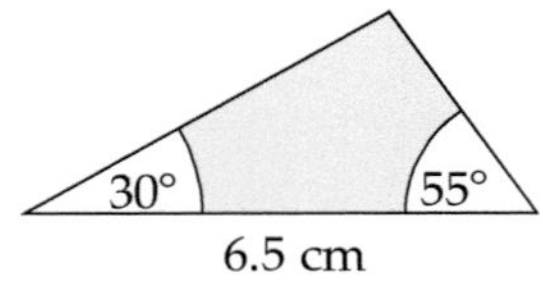

b

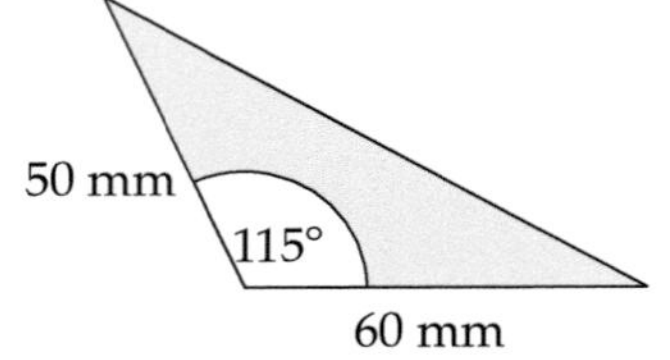

c

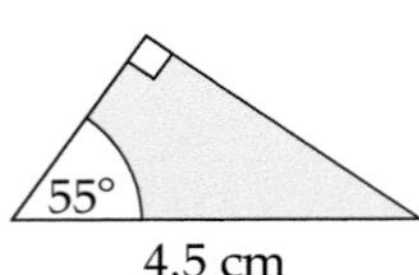

12b

2 Construct these triangles.

a

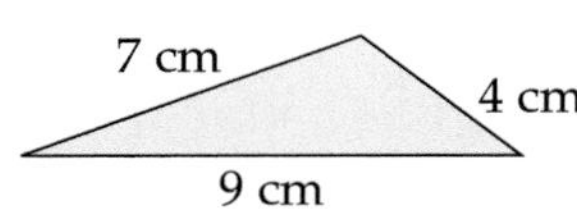

b

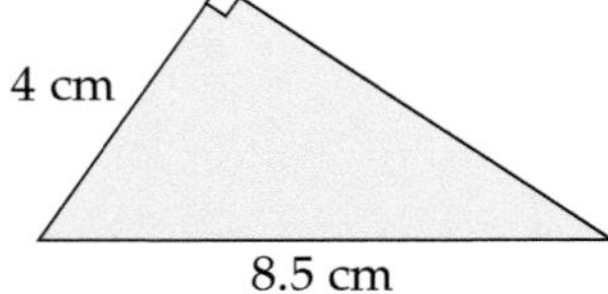

3 Construct these nets, using ruler and compasses.
Each triangle is equilateral.
State the name of the 3-D shape formed by the net.

a

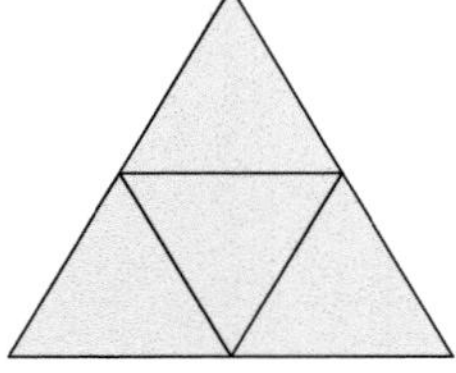

b

12c

4 Make an accurate copy of this diagram of an isosceles triangle.
Construct the perpendicular bisector of the base AB.
Comment on your result.

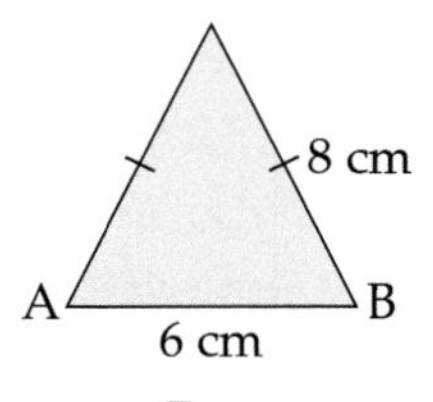

5 Draw a horizontal line and a point P above the line.

a Using compasses, construct the perpendicular to the line passing through P.

b Label your diagram A, B, P and C as shown.

c What is the mathematical name of the quadrilateral APBC?

d Explain why this construction gives a perpendicular line.

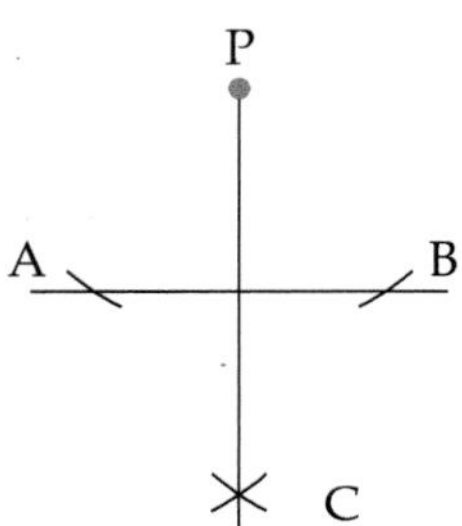

12d

6 The Naze Tower in Essex is 26 metres high and 6 metres wide.

   a Draw a scale drawing of the tower using a scale of 1 : 500.
   Show your calculations for the height and the width of the tower in a scale drawing.

   b Estimate the height of the person in the photograph.

   c Calculate the height of the person in the scale drawing and draw the person on your scale drawing.

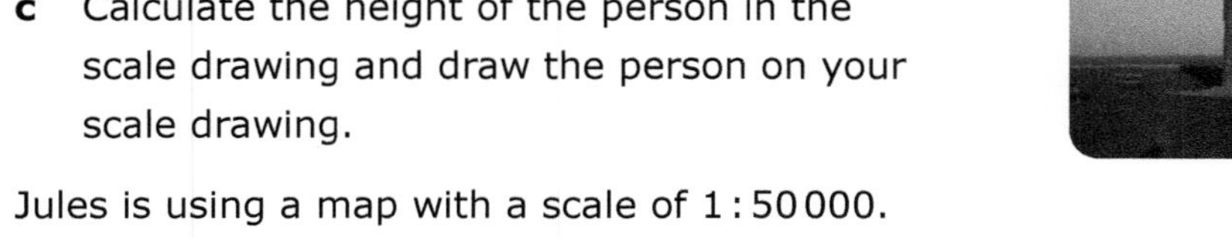

7 Jules is using a map with a scale of 1 : 50 000.
What is the actual distance in kilometres, if the length on the map is

   a 1 cm   b 5 cm   c 1.5 cm   d 3.5 cm   e 4.8 cm?

12e

8 A goat is tethered to a post with a 3 metre length of rope.

   a Using a scale of 1 : 100, draw a scale drawing showing all the grass the goat can reach to eat.

   b The goat is now tethered with the same rope to a wall.
   Draw another scale drawing with the same scale, showing all the grass the goat can now eat.

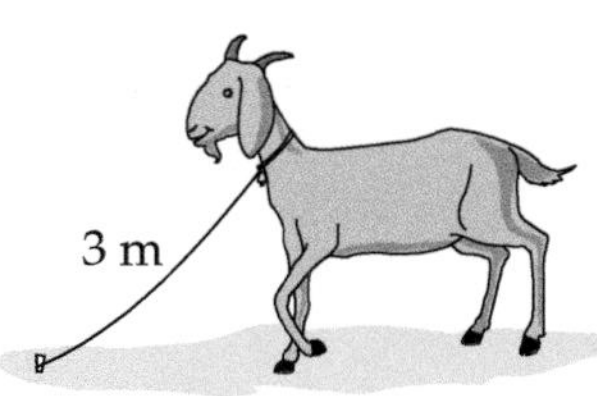

12f

9 The map shows three villages in Derbyshire.
Measure the bearing of

   a Baslow from Bakewell

   b Ashford from Bakewell
   Centre your protractor at Bakewell.

   c Baslow from Ashford
   Centre your protractor at Ashford.

   d Bakewell from Baslow

   e Ashford from Baslow.
   Centre your protractor at Baslow.

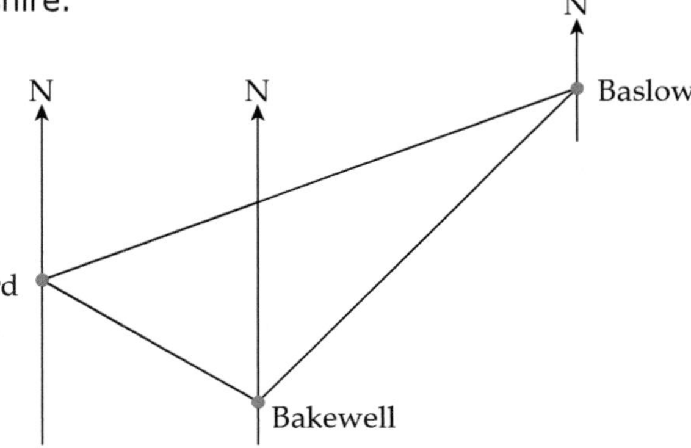

10 Point B is 6 km East of point A.
Point P is on a bearing of 050° from A and 330° from B.
Using a scale drawing, with 2 cm representing 1 km, find the distance of P from A and from B.

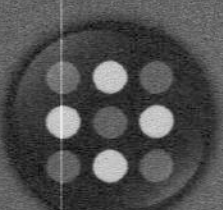

Case study 4: Paper folding

You can explore shapes and angles by simply folding paper.
Origami is an ancient Japanese art using folded paper to create beautiful shapes and figures.

Task 1

Take a square sheet of plain paper and fold it in half diagonally.

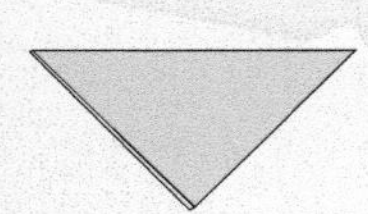

a If you open it out you should have two triangles. What type of triangles are they?

Now fold it in half again.

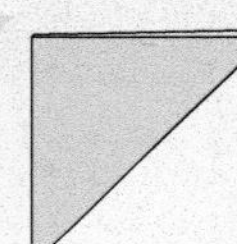

b If you open it out, how many triangles do you have now?

Keep folding it in half – see if you can fold it five times.

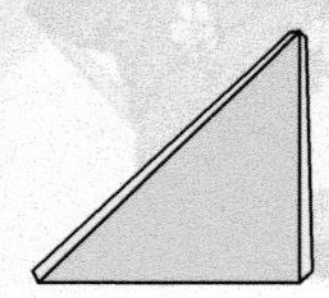

c When you open it out again, how many triangles are there now?

d Look at one of the triangles. Write down its three angles.

e Construct an accurate drawing of the whole triangle pattern.

Check that:

- Your triangles are congruent
- Your angles are accurate

Task 2

Take a square sheet of plain paper. Fold in half vertically, then unfold it again.

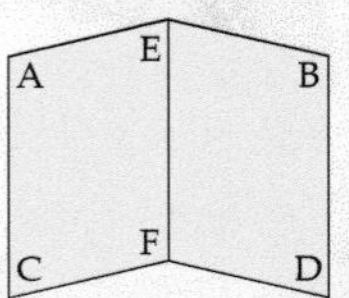

Bring A down to F and make a crease. Open it out again.

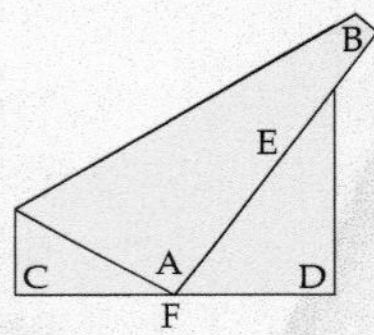

Now do the same with B and F.

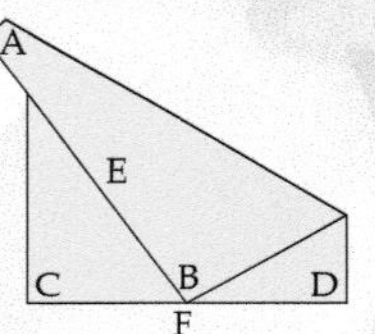

- **Now do the same with C and E, then D and E.**
- **Open out the square and look at the creases.**

a How many triangles are there? What type of triangle are they?

b How many quadrilaterals are there? What type of quadrilateral are they?

c Construct an accurate drawing of the whole pattern.

How many times can you fold a piece of paper in half?

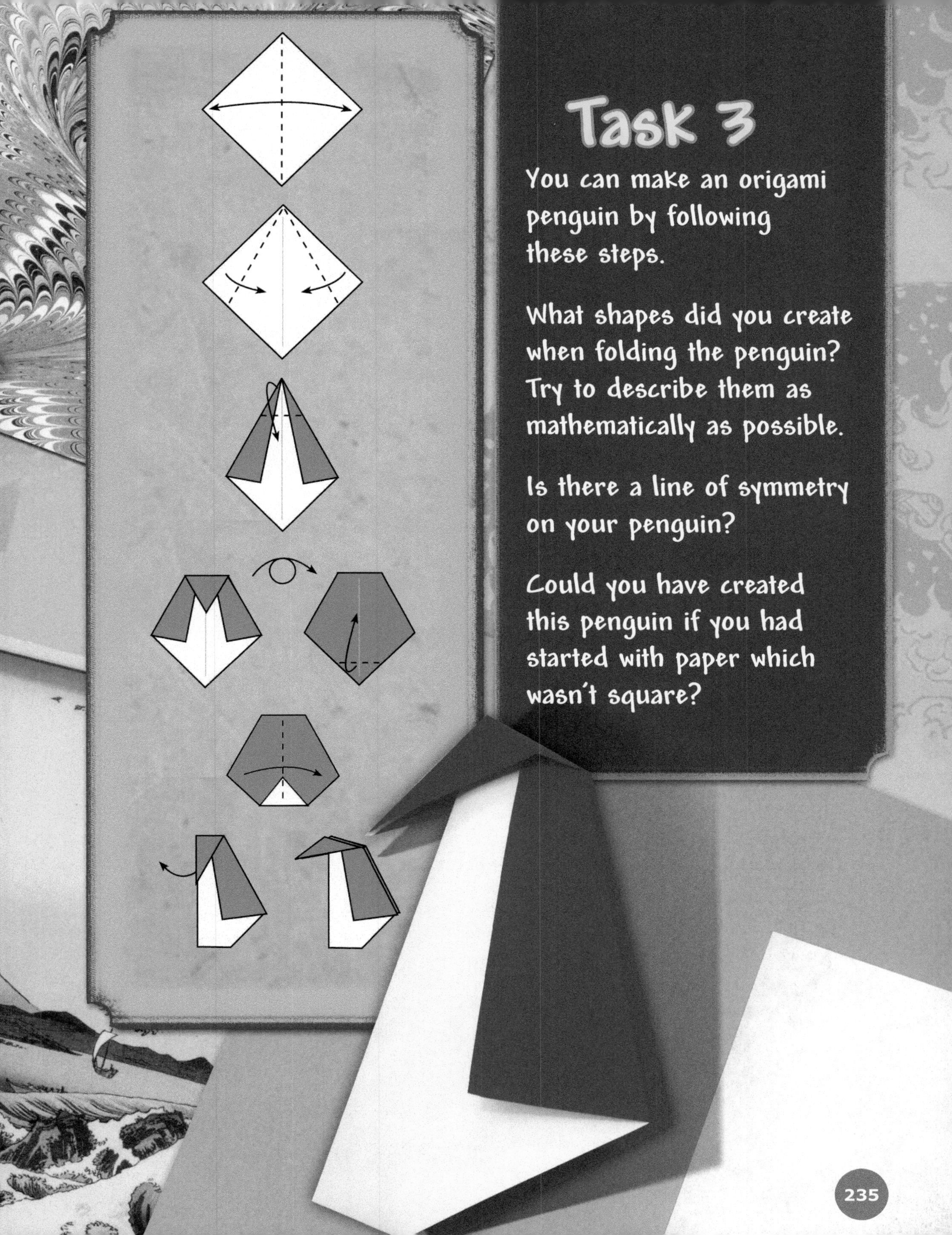

Task 3

You can make an origami penguin by following these steps.

What shapes did you create when folding the penguin? Try to describe them as mathematically as possible.

Is there a line of symmetry on your penguin?

Could you have created this penguin if you had started with paper which wasn't square?

MyAssessment 3

These questions will test you on your knowledge of the topics in chapters 9 to 12. They give you practice in the questions that you may see in your GCSE exams. There are 70 marks in total.

1 Make an accurate copy of this diagram.

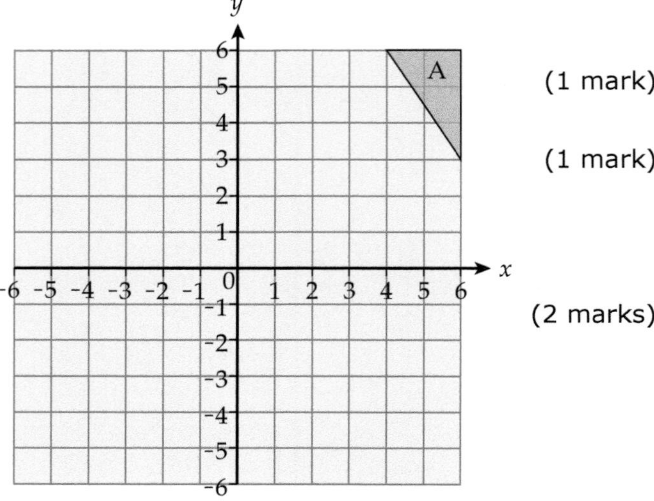

- **a** Reflect the triangle A in the x-axis and label it B. (1 mark)
- **b** Reflect triangle B in the y-axis and label it C. (1 mark)
- **c** Rotate triangle C through 180° about the centre (0, 0). What do you notice about this new position? (2 marks)

2 **a** On a coordinate grid with x and y values from 0 to 10, plot the points A (1, 1), B (5, 1), C (5, 3), D (3, 3), E (3, 5) and F (1, 5) and join successive points AB, BC … FA to make a shape. (4 marks)

- **b** Enlarge the shape by a scale factor of $\frac{1}{2}$ using point (8, 8) as the centre of enlargement. (2 marks)
- **c** Write down the coordinates of the new points A′, B′, C′, D′, E′ and F′. (4 marks)

3 **a** Using only five squares draw a shape that has

- **i** Only four lines of reflection symmetry.
- **ii** Only two lines of reflection symmetry.
- **iii** No lines of reflection symmetry. (3 marks)

- **b** In each case state the shape's order of rotational symmetry. (3 marks)

4 The length of sides of a triangle are $x + 3$, $2x - 1$ and $3x - 4$.

- **a** Write down the simplified expression for the perimeter of the triangle. (2 marks)
- **b** The perimeter of the triangle is 22 cm.
  - **i** Write down an equation for the perimeter. (1 mark)
  - **ii** Solve this equation and hence state the lengths of each side. (3 marks)
  - **iii** What is the mathematical name of this triangle? (1 mark)

5 Solve these equations.

- **a** $3(2p - 1) = 33$ (2 marks)
- **b** $15 - 3y = 3(y - 1)$ (2 marks)
- **c** $\frac{m}{4} + 3 = 7$ (2 marks)
- **d** $\frac{(3x - 2)}{11} = 2$ (2 marks)

6 A rectangle has a length $3n$ and a width $(2n - 3)$.
The area of the rectangle is 80 cm².
Use trial and improvement to find n to two decimal places (5 marks)

7 For these calculations

- **i** Give an estimate of the answer (6 marks)
- **ii** Use your calculator to find the accurate answer to 2d.p. (4 marks)

a $\dfrac{2 \times 3.142 \times \sqrt{2.6^2 + 7.1^2}}{\sqrt{9.8}}$ **b** $\dfrac{\sqrt{5^2 + 2.1} \times (8 - 3.5)}{4 \times 3^2}$

8 A 4 × 4 driver calls in at a petrol station and buys £25 worth of diesel at 139.6 pence per litre.

- **a** How many litres of diesel is bought at this station? (2 marks)
- **b** The next time they buy diesel it costs 140.2 pence per litre. If they fill the 4 × 4 with the same amount of fuel, how much more does it cost? (3 marks)

9 The plan of a local sailing course forms a triangle as shown.
Using a ruler and compasses make an accurate scale drawing of the course.
Use a scale of 1 cm = 100 m.
Leave on all your construction arcs. (4 marks)

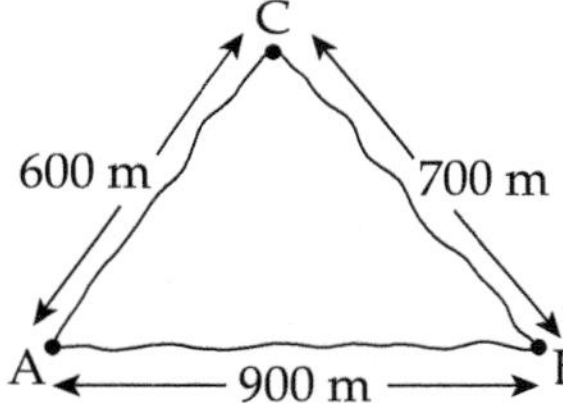

10 A map has a scale 1 : 25 000.

- **a** Two points on the map are 88 mm apart, how far apart are they in real life? (2 marks)
- **b** A road is 5 km long. How long is the road on the map? (2 marks)

11 A cable is to be laid that is equidistant from two fences AB and AC, as shown.
Copy the diagram and then construct the locus of the cable.
Leave on all your construction arcs. (3 marks)

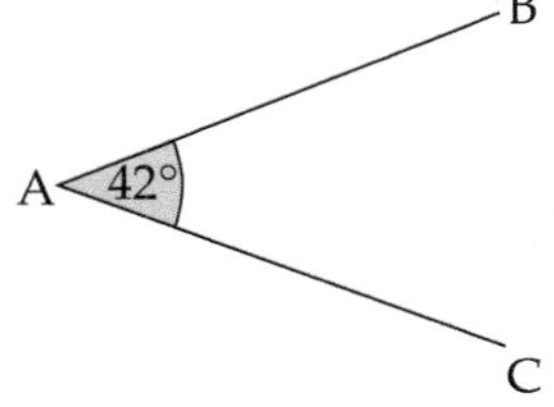

12 The diagram shows a short sailing course.
The race starts at S, goes around the buoy at A and around a second buoy at B before heading back to the start.

- **a** Find the bearing of A from S. (1 mark)
- **b** Find the bearing of S from A. (1 mark)
- **c** Find the bearing of A from B. (2 marks)

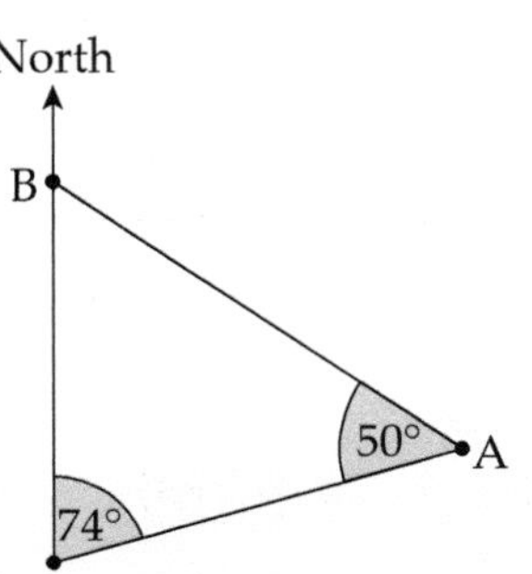

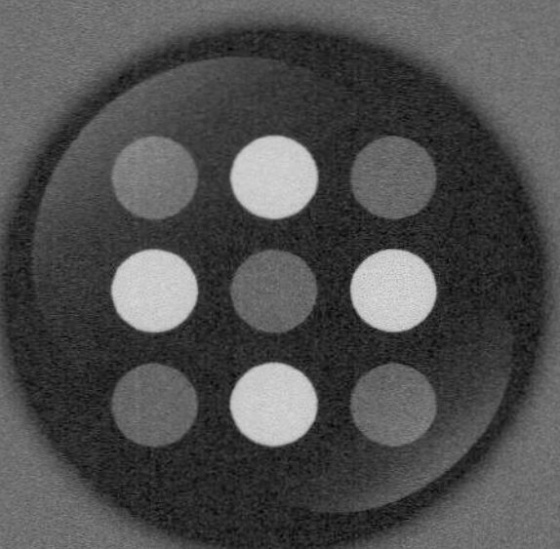

13 Sequences

Introduction

There are lots of different types of sequences, even ones inside you! Every living cell of your body contains genetic information in a molecule called DNA. These DNA molecules contain four different bases (labelled A, T, C and G) which occur many times over. The sequences in which these bases occur determines the physical characteristics of each cell.

What's the point?

Being able to identify and describe a genetic sequence helps doctors fight and treat disease.

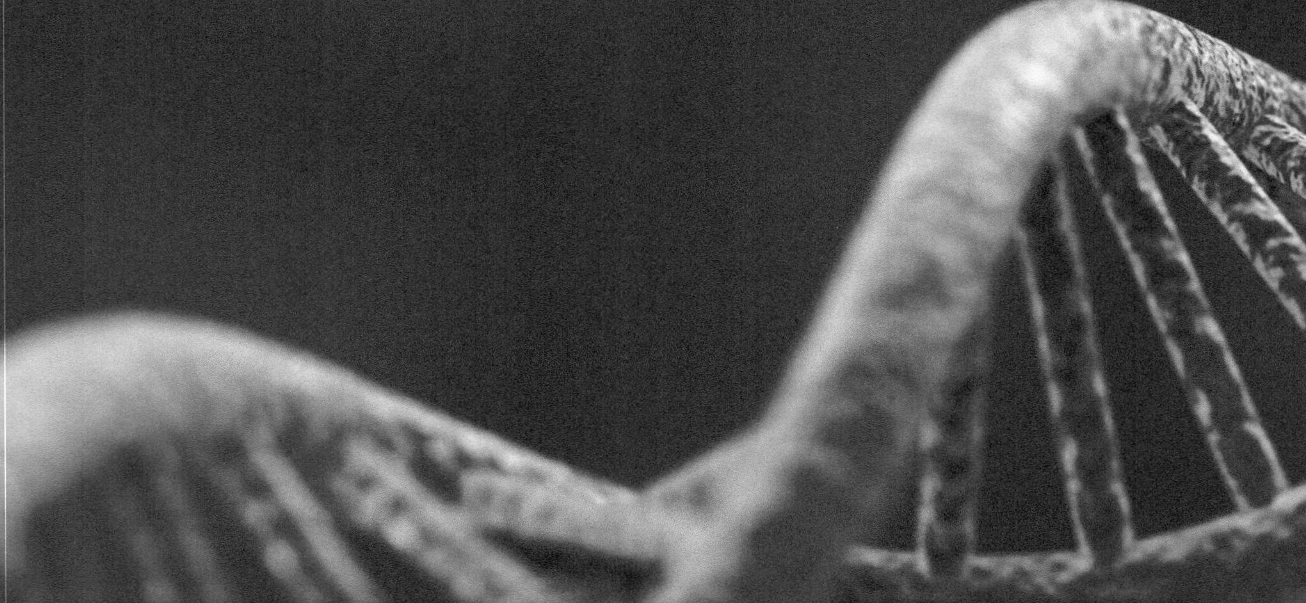

Objectives

By the end of this chapter, you will have learned how to ...

- Describe a linear sequence using a term-to-term rule.
- Describe a linear sequence using a position-to-term rule.
- Recognise and describe geometric sequences.
- Describe a general sequence using a recursive formula.

Check in

1 Continue each of these sequences for two more terms.

a 6, 12, 18, 24, 30, ... b 3, 8, 13, 18, 23, ...

c 90, 81, 72, 63, 54, ... d 720, 360, 180, 90, 45, ...

2 Write the first five terms of the sequences described by each rule.

a The first term is 4. Each term is 5 more than the previous term.

b The first term is 1. Each term is three times the previous term.

c The first term is 10. Each term is half the previous term.

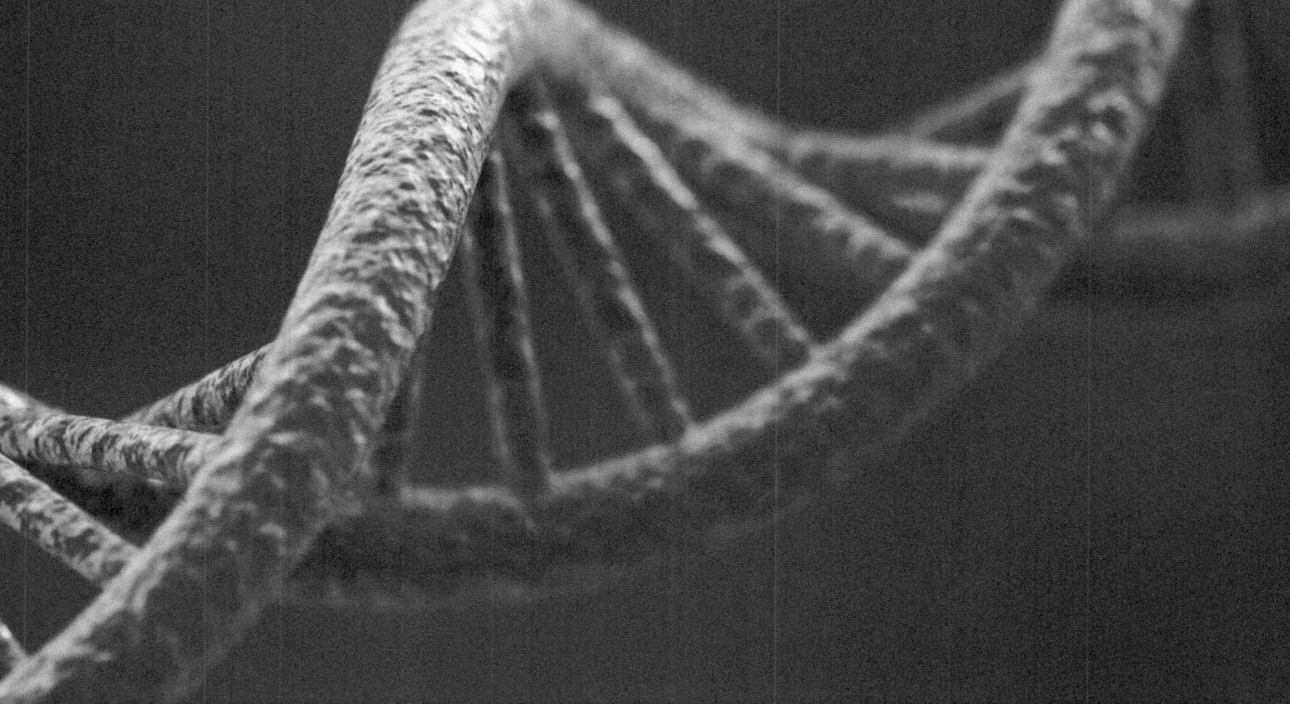

Starter problem

A very bright girl receives £3 a week in pocket money.
She decides to renegotiate her pocket money with her father.
'Dad could I just have 50p pocket money this week?'
'Of course', says her father.
'And next week can I have 20p more?'
'I don't see why not' replies her dad.
'And maybe just 20p more each week from then on?'
'OK – sounds like I'm getting a good deal here – are you sure?'
Investigate.

- A **sequence** is an ordered set of numbers called **terms**.

Sequences often follow rules.

- A sequence can be described by its **term-to-term** rule.

- A sequence is **linear** if it increases or decreases in equal steps.
  - ▶ The increase or decrease is known as the **difference** between terms.

The **term-to-term** rule of the sequence 1, 10, 100, 1000, 10 000 is 'The first term is 1. Each term is 10 times the previous term.'

Example

Write the first five terms of these sequences.

a The first term is 1. Each term is double the previous term.

b The first term is 90. Each term is 9 less than the previous term.

a 1 2 4 8 16

×2 ×2 ×2 ×2

b 90 81 72 63 54

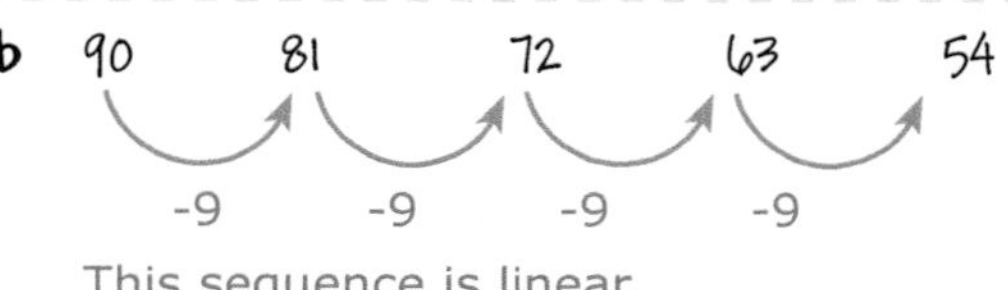

-9 -9 -9 -9

This sequence is linear.

- A sequence can also be described by its **position-to-term** rule.

n is the position number and T(n) is the value of the nth term.

Look at the sequence 1, 4, 7, 10, 13, ...

The position-to-term rule can be expressed as a formula ... ... or in words.

$$T(n) = 3n - 2$$

Multiply the position number by three and subtract two.

Example

Generate the first term and the 100th term of each sequence.

a $T(n) = 4n + 3$

b $T(n) = 105 - 5n$

a $T(1) = 4 \times 1 + 3$
$= 7$
$T(100) = 4 \times 100 + 3$
$= 403$

b $T(1) = 105 - 5 \times 1$
$= 100$
$T(100) = 105 - 5 \times 100$
$= -395$

To substitute into T(n), replace n with the position number of the term that you are looking for.

Exercise 13a

1 Continue each of these sequences for two more terms.

a 1, 6, 11, 16, 21, ...
b 2, 4, 8, 16, 32, ...
c 5, 4.5, 4, 3.5, 3, ...
d 15, 12, 9, 6, 3, ...
e 243, 81, 27, 9, 3, ...
f 1, -2, 4, -8, 16, ...

2 Generate the first five terms of each of these sequences.

First term	Term-to-term rule
1	Add 4 to the previous term
20	Subtract 3 from the previous term
5	Double the previous term

First term	Term-to-term rule
10 000	Divide the previous term by 10
2	Add $\frac{1}{4}$ to the previous term
100	Halve the previous term

3 **i** Write the term-to-term rule for each of these linear sequences.
ii Fill in the missing numbers.

a 4, 8, ☐, 16, 20, ...
b 2, ☐, 8, 11, 14, ...
c 3, ☐, ☐, 24, 31, ...
d ☐, ☐, 19, 16, 13, ...
e 10, ☐, 22, ☐, 34, ...
f 8, ☐, -2, ☐, -12, ...

4 A sequence has term-to-term rule 'add 4'. Write a possible first term for this sequence if all the terms of the sequence are

a even numbers
b multiples of 4
c odd numbers
d not whole numbers.

5 Generate the first five terms of each of these sequences given by their position-to-term rules in words.

a Add 10 to the position number
b Multiply the position number by 5
c Double the position number and add 5
d Multiply the position number by 3 and add 1

6 Generate the first five terms of each of these sequences given by their position-to-term rules.

a $T(n) = n + 3$ **b** $T(n) = n - 1$
c $T(n) = 8n$ **d** $T(n) = 10n + 1$
e $T(n) = 2n + 3$ **f** $T(n) = 50 - n$
g $T(n) = \frac{1}{2}n$ **h** $T(n) = n^2$
i $T(n) = 1 - \frac{1}{n}$ **j** $T(n) = 2^n$

Problem solving

7 Four friends have each written the nth term of a sequence on a card. In what order should the friends stand if they are to arrange themselves in descending order according to the value of

a T(1) **b** T(10) **c** T(100)?

13b Sequences in context

- All linear sequences have position-to-term rules of the form
  $T(n) = an + b$
  where a = the difference between consecutive terms.

To get from the 3 times table to the sequence 4, 7, 10, 13, 16, ... you add 1.

Example

Find the **position-to-term** rule of the sequence 4, 7, 10, 13, 16, ...

a

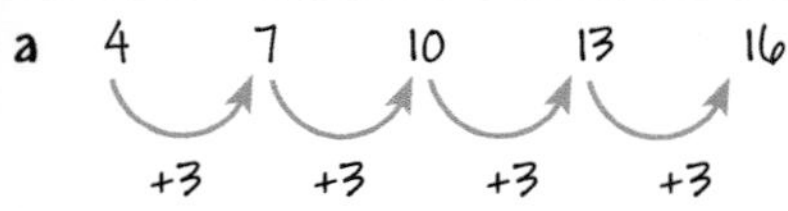

The difference between consecutive terms is 3. The position-to-term rule involves the 3 times table.

Position number, *n*	1	2	3	4	5
3 times table	3 +1	6 +1	9 +1	12 +1	15 +1
***n*th term, T(*n*)**	4	7	10	13	16

Position-to-term rule is in words 'x the position number by 3 and +1'

or as a formula $T(n) = 3n + 1$

Example

Find a rule that relates the number of triangles, n, to the number of straws, m. Explain why the rule works by referring to the diagrams.

1 triangle

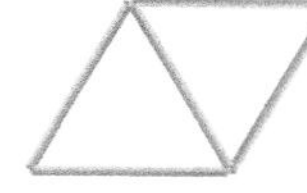
2 triangles

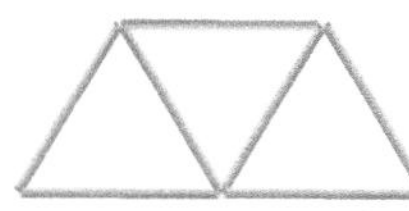
3 triangles

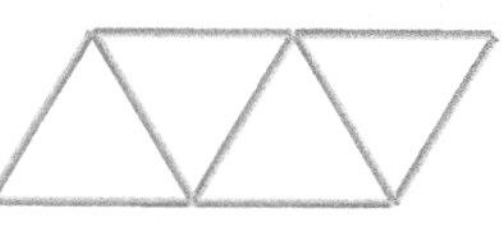
4 triangles

The difference between consecutive terms is 2. So the position-to-term rule involves the 2 times table.

The number of straws forms a sequence 3, 5, 7, 9, ...

Number of triangles, *n*	1	2	3	4
2 times table	2 +1	4 +1	6 +1	8 +1
Number of straws, *m*	3	5	7	9

The rule is in words 'To find the number of straws, m, multiply the number of triangles, n, by 2 and add 1'

in symbols $m = 2n + 1$

The rule works because every new triangle requires 2 straws, plus 1 straw is needed to close the first triangle.

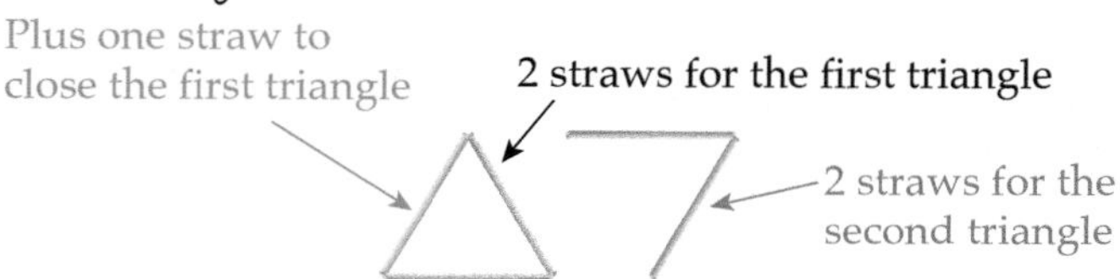

Exercise 13b

1 a Find the difference between consecutive terms in the sequence 5, 7, 9, 11, 13, ...

b Use part **a** to help you copy and complete the table.

Position number	1	2	3	4	5
☐ **times table**					
Term	5	7	9	11	13

c Write the position-to-term rule of this sequence

i in words **ii** in symbols.

2 Match these sequences with one of the *n*th terms on the cards.

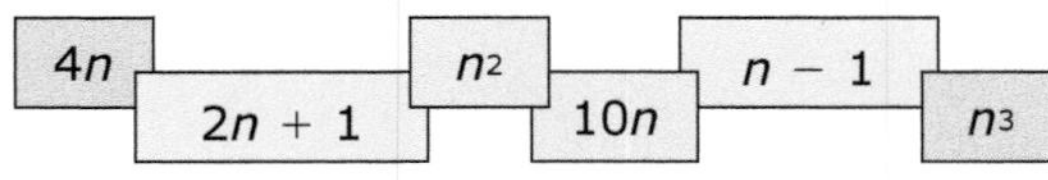

a 10, 20, 30, 40, 50, ...

b 1, 4, 9, 16, 25, ...

c 0, 1, 2, 3, 4, ...

d 4, 8, 12, 16, 20, ...

e 1, 8, 27, 64, 125, ...

f 3, 5, 7, 9, 11, ...

3 Find the *n*th term of each of these sequences.

a 3, 6, 9, 12, 15, ...

b 11, 12, 13, 14, 15, ...

c 7, 9, 11, 13, 15, ...

d 4, 9, 14, 19, 24, ...

4 Find the *n*th term of each of these sequences.

a -5, -2, 1, 4, 7, ...

b $1\frac{1}{2}$, 2, $2\frac{1}{2}$, 3, $3\frac{1}{2}$, ...

c 9, 8, 7, 6, 5, ...

d 3, 1, -1, -3, -5, ...

Problem solving

5 a Find a rule that relates the number of pentagons, *n*, to the number of straws, *m*.

1 pentagon

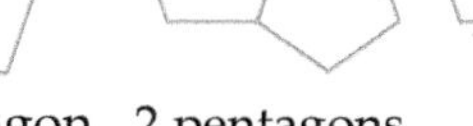
2 pentagons

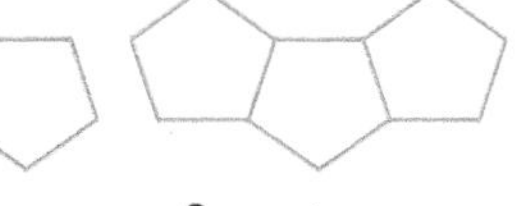
3 pentagons

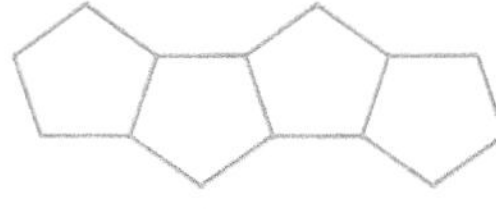
4 pentagons

b Use your formula to find the number of straws in a pattern of 50 pentagons.

c Explain why the rule works by referring to the diagrams.

Hint: construct a table of values.

6 For this pattern of tiles, find a formula that connects the number of red tiles, *r*, to the number of white tiles, *w*. Justify your formula.

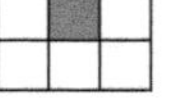 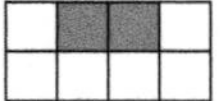 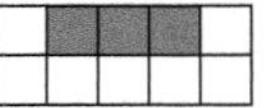 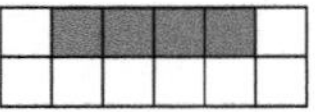

7 The formula that connects the pattern number, *n*, to the number of dots, *d*, is $d = 2(n + 1)$.
Explain why this formula works.

Pattern 1

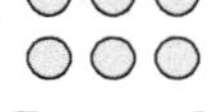
Pattern 2

Pattern 3

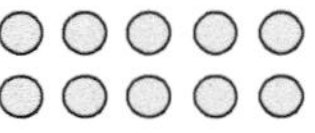
Pattern 4

8 Isobel, a party-planner, needs to seat 54 people at a formal dinner. She has the option of two configurations of tables.
Advise Isobel on the number of tables required for both options.

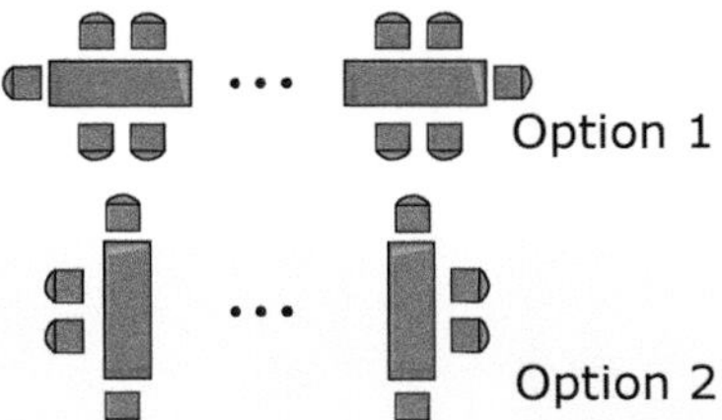

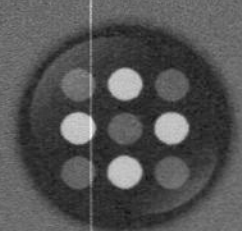

13c Geometric sequences

Jack is exploring sequences involving **indices**.
He starts with 2, and raises it to increasing powers:

$$2^1, 2^2, 2^3, 2^4, 2^5, \dots$$
$$= 2, 4, 8, 16, 32, \dots$$

Jack now tries with 3:

$$3^1, 3^2, 3^3, 3^4, 3^5, \dots$$
$$= 3, 9, 27, 81, 243, \dots$$

In a **geometric sequence**, you multiply each term by a fixed amount to get the next term.

8, 24, 72, 216, 648, ... is a geometric sequence.
$24 = \mathbf{3} \times 8$, $72 = \mathbf{3} \times 24$, $216 = \mathbf{3} \times 72$, etc.

Example

a Generate the first five terms of the sequence following this rule.
Start with 6, and multiply each term by 4 to get the next one.

b Describe a term-to-term rule for this geometric sequence
5, 15, 45, 135, 405, ...

c **i** Write the next two terms of this sequence
200, 100, 50, 25, 12.5, ...

ii Describe a term-to-term rule for the sequence.

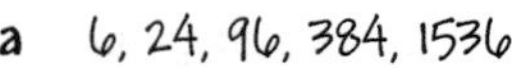

a 6, 24, 96, 384, 1536

b Start at 5 and multiply by 3

c **i** 6.25, 3.125

ii Start at 200 and multiply by 0.5

Example

Geometric sequences occur in real life.
50 birds of prey are introduced to a region of the country.
The population doubles each year for five years, and then increases at a steady rate of 100 birds per year for the next five years.
How many birds are there after 10 years have elapsed?

1st 5 years: 50, 100, 200, 400, 800, 1600
Next 5 years: 1700, 1800, 1900, 2000, 2100
There are 2100 birds after 10 years.

Here's a quicker method.
$(50 \times 2^5) + (100 \times 5)$
$= 1600 + 500$
$= 2100$

Exercise 13c

1 Write the next two terms of each sequence.

a 3, 6, 12, 24, 48, ...

b 4, 12, 36, 108, 324, ...

c 1, 6, 36, 216, 1296, ...

d 1, 10, 100, 1000, 10 000, ...

e 1000, 500, 250, 125, 62.5, ...

f -32, -16, -8, -4, -2, ...

2 Generate the first five terms of the sequence described by each rule.

a Start at 3, multiply by 2

b Start at 4, multiply by 5

c Start at 2, multiply by 8

d Start at -5, multiply by 3

e Start at 8, multiply by -2

f Start at 32, multiply by $2\frac{1}{2}$

3 Describe a term-to-term rule for each of these geometric sequences.

a 2, 10, 50, 250, 1250, ...

b 3, 18, 108, 648, 3888, ...

c 0.5, 1.5, 4.5, 13.5, 40.5, ...

d -4, -16, -64, -256, -1024, ...

e 2, 3, $4\frac{1}{2}$, $6\frac{3}{4}$, $20\frac{1}{4}$, ...

f -2, 10, -50, 250, -1250, 6250, ...

4 Find the 10th term of each of these geometric sequences.

a 5, 10, 20, 40, ...

b 4, 20, 100, 500, ...

c Start at -2 and multiply by 4

d Start at 8 and multiply by -1

e 6, -12, 24, -48, ...

f 20, 10, 5, $2\frac{1}{2}$, ...

Problem solving

5 Cassie is offered a summer holiday job for six weeks.
She is given a choice of payment.
Which option should Cassie choose?
Give your reasons.

Option A
£5 for week 1
£10 for week 2
£20 for week 3
And continuing to double until week 6

Option B
£50 per week
Continuing until week 6

6 Here are two geometric sequences:

Sequence A:	1,	6,	36,	216,	1296, ...
Sequence B:	50,	150,	450,	1350,	4050, ...

After how many terms does sequence A overtake sequence B?

7 Doctor Sequence is exploring some other sequences involving indices!
He starts with the power 2: $1^2, 2^2, 3^2, 4^2, 5^2, \ldots$

a Write this sequence as numbers. What is this sequence commonly known as?

b He now tries the power 3: $1^3, 2^3, 3^3, 4^3, 5^3, \ldots$
Write out this sequence as numbers. What is this sequence commonly known as?
Doctor Sequence is going power-crazy! He writes this sequence.
1, 128, 2187, 16 384, 78 125, ...

c i Write this sequence as powers.

ii Use a calculator to work out the 8th term in this sequence.

13d Recursive sequences

Here is a simple **linear sequence**: 7, 13, 19, 25, 31, ...

T(1) means 'the first term', so T(1) = 7, T(2) = 13, T(3) = 19, ...

> In a linear sequence, there is a constant difference between terms.

Think of the sequence as a flowchart that feeds back on itself:

Term → +6 → Next term

The **term-to-term** rule for this sequence is:

Start from 7 and add 6 to get the next term

You can define this sequence using a **recursive formula**:

$$T(n + 1) = T(n) + 6, \qquad T(1) = 7$$

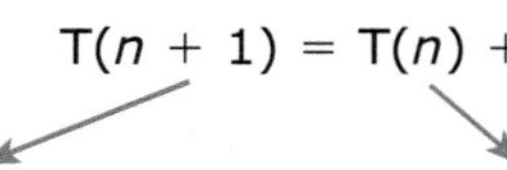

The next or $(n + 1)$th term in the sequence

Any (nth) term in the sequence

This is where you start from

A recursive formula is really just a term-to-term rule! So T(4) = T(3) + 6 just means 25 = 19 + 6.

Example

Write the first five terms of each of these sequences.

a $T(n + 1) = T(n) + 8 \quad T(1) = 3$

b $T(n + 1) = 2T(n) \quad T(1) = 1$

a T(1) = 3 then T(2) = 3 + 8 = 11 T(3) = 11 + 8 = 19, ...

3, 11, 19, 27, 35

b T(1) = 1 then T(2) = 2 × 1 = 2 T(3) = 2 × 2 = 4

T(4) = 2 × 4 = 8, T(5) = 2 × 8 = 16

1, 2, 4, 8, 16

$T(n + 1) = 2T(n)$ is a **geometric sequence**.

In the sequence 1, 2, 4, 8, 16, ... you double each time to get the next term.

> In a geometric sequence, you multiply each term by a fixed amount to get the next term.
> 8, 24, 72, 216, 648, ... is a geometric sequence.

Example

A pond contains frogs and lily pads. Each month for a year,

the number of frogs is given by $T(n + 1) = T(n) + 20$

and the number of lily pads is given by $T(n + 1) = 2T(n) - 3$

At the start of the year there are 8 frogs and 4 lily pads.

Write the sequence of the number of

a frogs for the first 6 months

b lily pads for the first 6 months

a T(2) = 8 + 20 = 28

8, 28, 48, 68, 88, 108

b T(2) = 2 × 4 − 3 = 5

4, 5, 7, 11, 19, 35

Exercise 13d

1 Write the first five terms of each of these sequences.

a $T(n + 1) = T(n) + 1$, $T(1) = 2$

b $T(n + 1) = T(n) + 2$, $T(1) = 0$

c $T(n + 1) = T(n) + 4$, $T(1) = 3$

d $T(n + 1) = T(n) - 2$, $T(1) = -1$

e $T(n + 1) = T(n) - \frac{1}{2}$, $T(1) = 1$

f $T(n + 1) = T(n) - 0.75$, $T(1) = 0.5$

2 Write the first five terms of each of these sequences.

a $T(n + 1) = 2T(n)$, $T(1) = 2$

b $T(n + 1) = 2T(n) + 1$, $T(1) = 0$

c $T(n + 1) = 2T(n) - 1$, $T(1) = 3$

d $T(n + 1) = 3T(n) - 1$, $T(1) = 1$

e $T(n + 1) = -2T(n) + 4$, $T(1) = 1$

f $T(n + 1) = -2T(n) + 3$, $T(1) = 1$

3 Describe each of these sequences using a recursive formula.

a 2, 4, 6, 8, 10, ...

b 3, 7, 11, 15, 19, ...

c -2, 4, 10, 16, 22, ...

d 4, 1, -2, -5, -8, ...

e -5, -9, -13, -17, -21, ...

f $\frac{1}{2}, \frac{5}{4}, 2, 2\frac{3}{4}, 3\frac{1}{2}, \ldots$

4 Describe each of these sequences using a recursive formula.

a 5, 11, ☐, 23, ☐, 35, ...

b ☐, 15, 23, ☐, 39, 47, ...

c 13, 30, ☐, ☐, 81, 98, ...

d 1, 3, 9, 27, 81, 243, ...

e 1, 4, 16, 64, 256, ...

f 5, 10, 20, 40, 80, ...

Careful: the first 3 are linear and have gaps; the last three are geometric.

Problem solving

5 Zachary starts up a savings account with £300. His bank gives him £3 interest each month. At the end of each month he records the amount in pounds sterling in his account:

303, 306, 309, ...

a Write a rule for this sequence using a recursive formula

b Zadie also starts up a bank account with £300. The total amount including interest increases each month according to this formula:

$T(n + 1) = 1.01\ T(n)$

Write out the amounts in Zadie's account for the first five months.

c Who has the most money after a year: Zachary or Zadie?

6 Phoebe is a budding musician. She posts a song on the Internet and very soon it has gone viral! In the first week after its release, the number of hits was only 9, but then the weekly number of hits increased by the recursive formula $T(n + 1) = 2T(n) + 6$. Find the number of hits after

a three weeks **b** 12 weeks

7 Look back at the example on the opposite page. During the year, will the population of lily pads overtake the population of frogs? If so, after how many months?

13 MySummary

Check out

You should now be able to ...

Test it ➡ Questions

You should now be able to ...	Level	Questions
✓ Describe a linear sequence using a term-to-term rule.	5	1
✓ Describe a linear sequence using a position-to-term rule.	6	2 – 4
✓ Recognise and describe geometric sequences.	7	5 – 6
✓ Describe a general sequence using a recursive formula.	7	7 – 8

Language	Meaning	Example
Sequence	An ordered set of terms	2, 4, 6, 8
Term	A number in a sequence	Any of the numbers in the sequence 2, 4, 6, 8
Term-to-term rule	A formula for the next term in a sequence as a function of the current term.	For 2, 4, 6, 8, ... $T(n + 1) = T(n) + 2$
Position-to-term rule	A formula for the term at position n as a function of n	For 2, 4, 6, 8, ... $T(n) = 2n$
General term ***n*th term**	Other names for a position-to-term rule.	
Geometric sequence	A sequence in which the next term is a fixed multiple of the current term.	2, 4, 8, 16, ... $T(n + 1) = 2T(n)$ $T(n) = 2^n$

13 MyReview

1 Find the term-to-term rule and the next two terms for each of these sequences.

a 5, 2.5, 0, -2.5, ...

b 64, 32, 16, 8, ...

c 3, -6, 12, -24, ...

2 Generate the first 5 terms of the sequences given by these position-to-term rules.

a $T(n) = 5n - 1$ **b** $T(n) = \frac{1}{2}n + 1$

c $T(n) = n^2 + 2$ **d** $T(n) = 100 - n^2$

3 Consider this arrangement of tables and chairs.

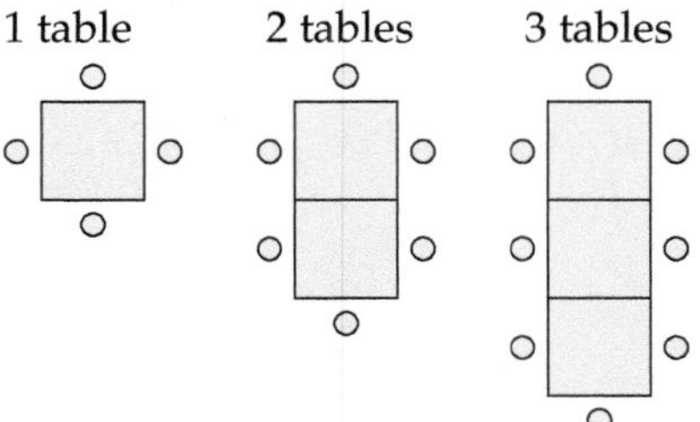

a Copy and complete this table.

Number of tables, *t*	1	2	3	4
...... times table				
Number of chairs, *c*	4			

b Find a rule that relates the number of tables, *t*, to the number of chairs, *c*.

c How many chairs will be needed if there are 10 tables?

d How many tables are there if there are 16 chairs?

4 Find the *n*th term rule for these sequences.

a 19 26, 33, 40, ...

b 10, 21, 32, 43, ...

c 7.5, 8. 8.5, 9, ...

d -5, -10, -15, -20, ...

5 Find the term-to-term rule and the next two terms for each geometric sequence.

a 5, 0.5, 0.05, 0.005, ...

b 0.25, -0.5, 1, -2, ...

c 4, 6, 9, $13\frac{1}{2}$, ...

d 2048, -1024, 512, -256, ...

6 Find the 10th term of the sequence described by each rule.

a Start at 512 and multiply by $\frac{3}{2}$

b Start at 1 000 000 and multiply by -0.1

7 Write out the first 5 terms for each of these sequences.

a $T(n + 1) = 4 - 3T(n)$, $T(1) = 0$

b $T(n + 1) = 2T(n) - 1$, $T(1) = 1$

c $T(n + 1) = 2T(n) - 1$, $T(1) = 2$

d $T(n + 1) = [T(n)]^2 - 1$, $T(1) = 2$

8 Describe each of these sequences using a recursive formula.

a 14, 17, *, 23, *, 29, ...

b *, 62, 47, *, *, 17, 2, ...

c *, -9, 27, –81, *, 729, ...

d 3, *, 6, 9, 13, ...

What next?

Score		
0 – 3		Your knowledge of this topic is still developing. To improve look at Formative test: 2C-13; MyMaths: 1165, 1173, 1920 and 1945
4 – 6		You are gaining a secure knowledge of this topic. To improve look at InvisiPen: 281, 282, 283 and 286
7 – 8		You have mastered this topic. Well done, you are ready to progress!

13 MyPractice

13a

1 Continue each of these sequences for two more terms.

a 3, 6, 9, 12, 15, …
b 2, 5, 8, 11, 14, …
c 1, 10, 100, 1000, 10 000, …
d 50, 44, 38, 32, 26, …
e 1, $1\frac{1}{2}$, 2, $2\frac{1}{2}$, 3, …
f 1024, 512, 256, 128, 64, …
g 2, 1.8, 1.6, 1.4, 1.2, …
h 1, 8, 27, 64, 125, …

2 **i** Write the term-to-term rule for each of these linear sequences.
ii Fill in the missing numbers.

a 4, □, 14, 19, 24, …
b 2, □, □, 14, 18, …
c □, □, -1, -4, -7, …
d 5, □, 19, □, 33, …

3 Generate the first five terms of each of these sequences given by their position-to-term rules.

a $T(n) = n + 10$
b $T(n) = 2n$
c $T(n) = n - 5$
d $T(n) = \frac{n}{3}$
e $T(n) = 2n + 1$
f $T(n) = 10 - n$
g $T(n) = 5n - 2$
h $T(n) = 23 - 3n$

13b

4 Find the *n*th term of each of these sequences.

a 5, 10, 15, 20, 25, …
b 1, 4, 7, 10, 13, …
c -2, 0, 2, 4, 6, …
d 5, 4, 3, 2, 1, …

5 **a** For this pattern of tiles, find a rule that relates the pattern number, *n*, to the number of tiles, *t*.
b Use your formula to find the number of tiles in pattern number 100.
c Explain why your rule works by referring to the diagrams.

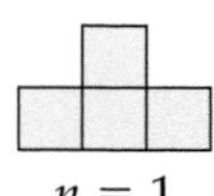
$n = 1$

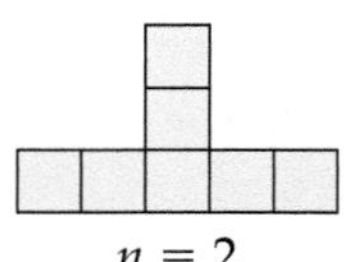
$n = 2$

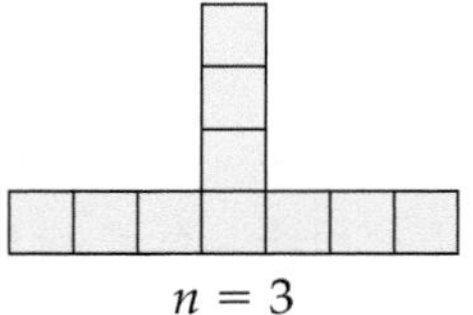
$n = 3$

6 **a** For this pattern of tiles, find a rule that relates the number of red tiles, *r*, to the number of white tiles, *w*.

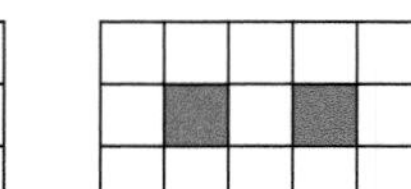

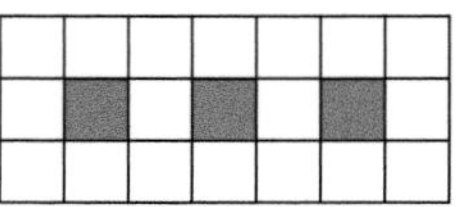

b Use your formula to find the number of tiles in pattern number 100.
c Explain why your rule works by referring to the diagrams.

13c

7 Generate the first five terms of each sequence.

- **a** Start at 3, multiply by 3
- **b** Start at 2, multiply by 4
- **c** Start at 4, multiply by 5
- **d** Start at 16, multiply by $\frac{1}{2}$

8 Find the term-to-term rule and the next two terms for each of these geometric sequences.

- **a** 99, 9.9, 0.99, 0.099, …
- **b** 2, 6, 18, 54, …
- **c** 3, -6, 12, -24, …
- **d** $\frac{5}{16}, -\frac{5}{8}, \frac{5}{4}, -\frac{5}{2}, \ldots$

9 Find the eighth term in each of these sequences.

- **a** Start at 64 and multiply by $-\frac{3}{2}$.
- **b** Start at 1 and multiply by 0.2
- **c** $T(1) = 0.01\ T(n + 1) = 5T(n)$
- **d** $T(1) = 200,\ T(n + 1) = \frac{T(n)}{2}$

13d

10 Write out the first five terms for each of these sequences.

- **a** $T(n + 1) = 17 - 4T(n)$, $T(1) = \frac{1}{4}$
- **b** $T(n + 1) = 3T(n) + 2$, $T(1) = 1$
- **c** $T(n + 1) = 3T(n) + 2$, $T(1) = 0$
- **d** $T(n + 1) = 1 - [T(n)]^2$, $T(1) = 2$

11 Describe each sequence using a recursive formula.

- **a** 4, 7, 10, 13, 16, …
- **b** 3, -1, -5, -9, -13, …
- **c** 2, 8, 32, 128, 512, …
- **d** 3, -9, 27, -81, 243, …

12 Describe each of these recursive sequences using a formula.

- **a** 15, 12, *, 6, *, 0, …
- **b** *, 57, 46, *, 24, 13, …
- **c** *, -16, *, -4, 2, -1, …
- **d** 81, *, 78, 75, *, 66, …

14 3D shapes

Introduction

The food you eat comes in many different forms of packaging. Cartons, boxes, bottles and cans dominate the supermarket shelves. Packaging protects and preserves the things you eat, but it adds to the price of the food and has implications for the environment. Companies design their packaging to cut costs and reduce waste materials.

What's the point?

By understanding surface area and volume, companies can choose the optimum dimensions for packaging to cut costs and help save the environment.

Objectives

By the end of this chapter, you will have learned how to ...

- Name 3D shapes and draw their nets.
- Draw plans and elevations and isometric diagrams.
- Calculate the surface area of a prism.
- Calculate the volume of a prism.

Check in

1. Identify these 3D shapes from the information given and draw a sketch.
   - **a** From above the shape looks like a circle and from the front and side an equilateral triangle.
   - **b** From above the shape looks like a square, from the front a rectangle and from the side an isosceles triangle.
2. For these cuboids calculate
   - **i** their volume
   - **ii** the area of the blue, pink and green faces.

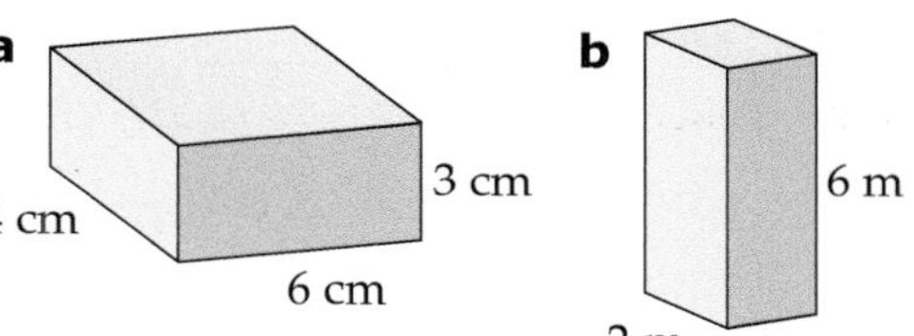

Starter problem

A drinks company needs to design a container to hold exactly 360 mℓ. They are aware of environmental issues and want to minimise the surface area of the container. The current container they use is 12 cm by 6 cm by 5 cm.

Design a container, in the shape of a cuboid, to hold exactly 360 mℓ, which has a smaller surface area than the original container.

Write a report and explain any practical considerations you might need to consider with your design.

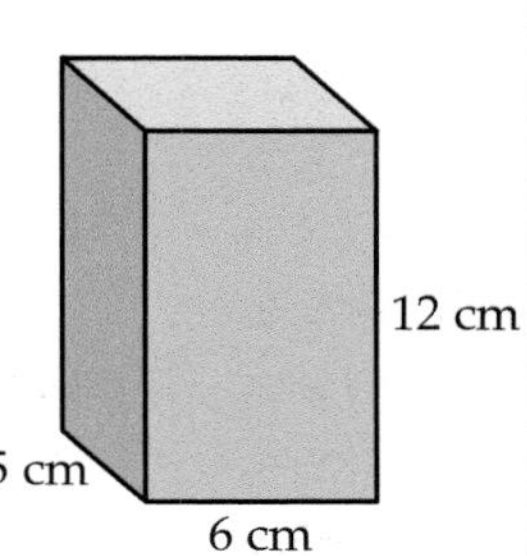

14a 3D shapes

A **solid** is a shape formed in **three dimensions (3D).**

- A **face** is a flat surface of a solid.
- An **edge** is the line where two faces meet.
- A **vertex** is a point at which three or more edges meet.

vertex
edge
face

The plural of vertex is vertices.

You should know the names of these solids.

Cube

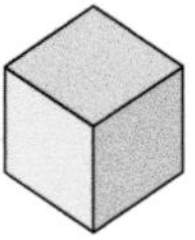

All the faces are square.

Cuboid

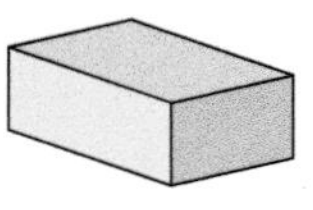

All the faces are rectangles.

Prism

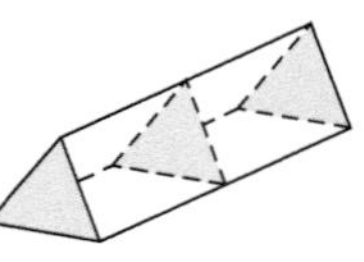

The **cross-section** is the same throughout the length.

Pyramid

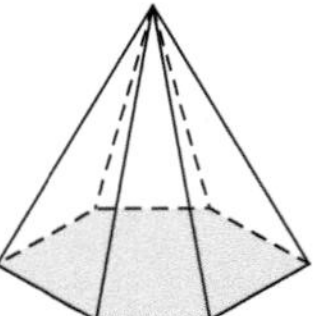

The base tapers to a point.

Example

A square-based pyramid is sliced horizontally.
Describe the cross-sections at different heights.

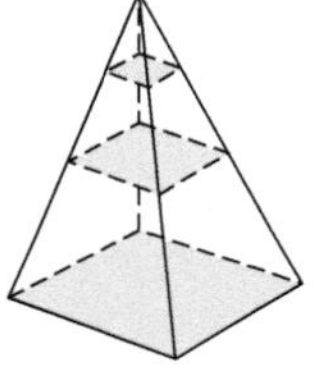

Each cross-section is a square.
The squares decrease in size the nearer the cross-section is to the top vertex.

A **net** is a 2D shape that can be folded to form a solid.

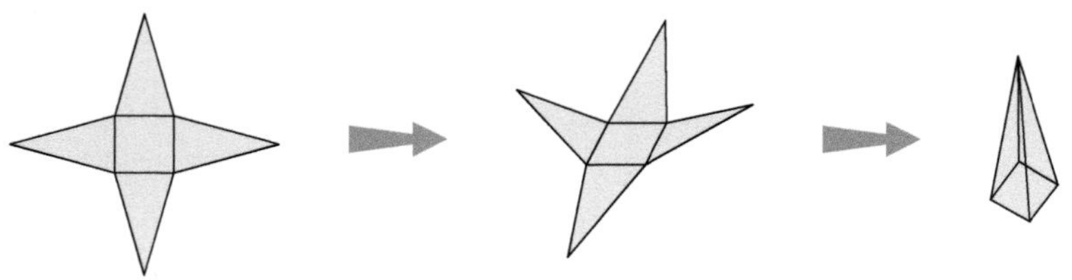

Example

Colour the net of a cube so that the opposite faces have the same colour.
Use the colours yellow, red and green.

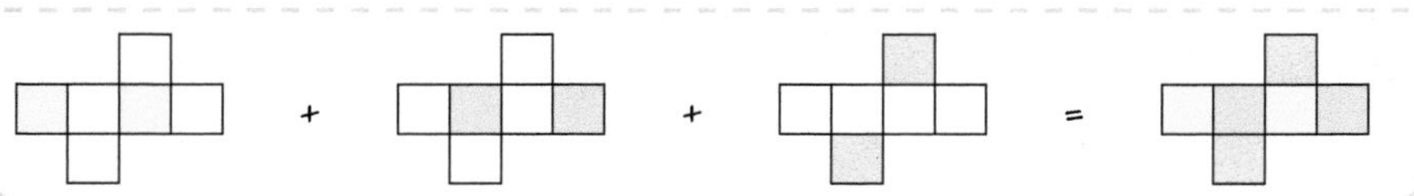

Exercise 14a

1 Each of these nets forms a solid.

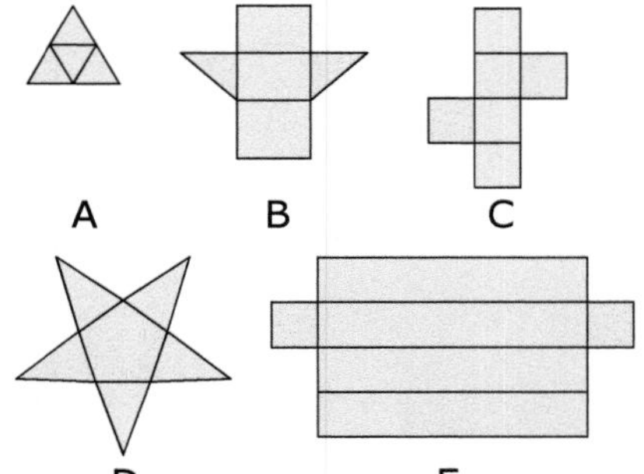

State each solid's

- **a** mathematical name
- **b** number of **i** faces
  - **ii** vertices
  - **iii** edges.

2 A prism is shown.
State the prism's
number of **a** faces
- **b** vertices
- **c** edges.

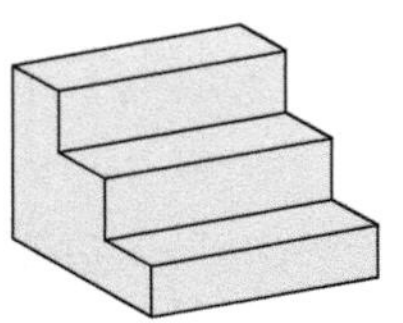

3 A cube has 11 distinct nets.
Try to draw as many of these as you can.

Problem solving

4 **a** Draw a 3D shape with five faces.
- **b** State the number of vertices and edges on your shape.

5 A tetrahedron is made from two blue and two green equilateral triangles.
Find the number of edges where

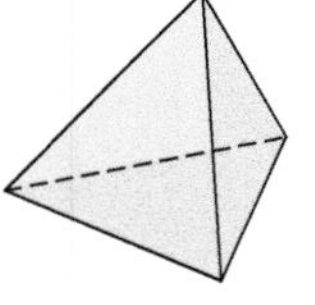

- **a** a blue face meets a blue face
- **b** a blue face meets a green face
- **c** a green face meets a green face.

6 A cuboid can be sliced to give different surfaces.

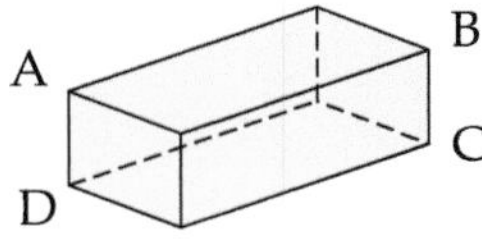

- **a** Describe the shape of the surface if the cuboid is sliced through the points A, B, C and D.
- **b** Is it possible to cut a triangular surface? Draw a diagram to illustrate your answer.

7 An octahedron is made from eight equilateral triangles.
- **a** State the shape's number of **i** faces
  - **ii** vertices
  - **iii** edges.

You can make an octahedron using this net.

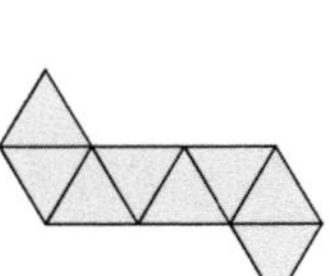

- **b** Copy the net and write the numbers 1 to 8 on the triangles so that the opposite faces of the octahedron add to 9.

Did you know?

Crystals have well-defined 3D structures. Scientists use this fact to investigate how the atoms inside them are arranged.

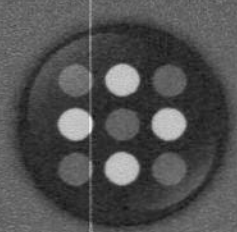

14b Plans and elevations

You can draw diagrams to show a solid viewed from different directions.

- A **front elevation** (F) is the view from the front.
- A **side elevation** (S) is the view from the side.
- A **plan** (P) shows the view from above.

These are the views of the cuboid.

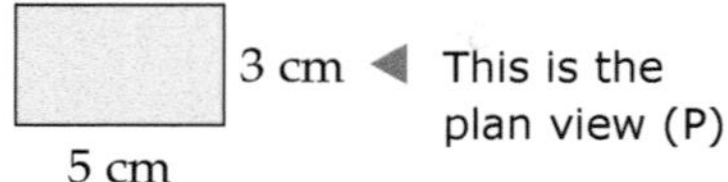

▲ This is the plan view (P).

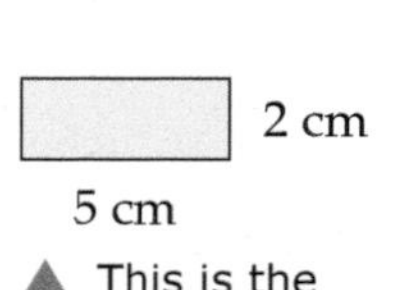

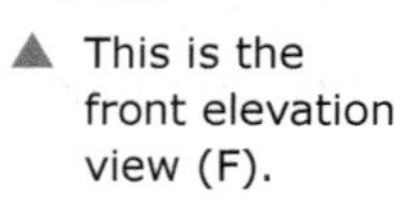

▲ This is the front elevation view (F).

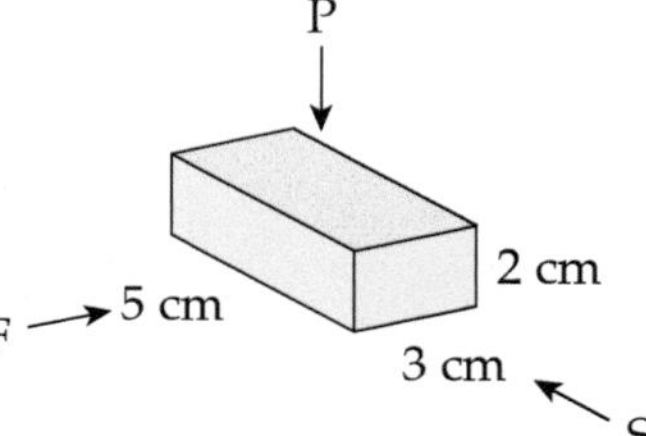

2 cm
3 cm

▲ This is the side elevation view (S).

Example

The diagram shows a square-based pyramid.

Sketch **a** the front elevation (F)
b the side elevation (S)
c the plan view (P).

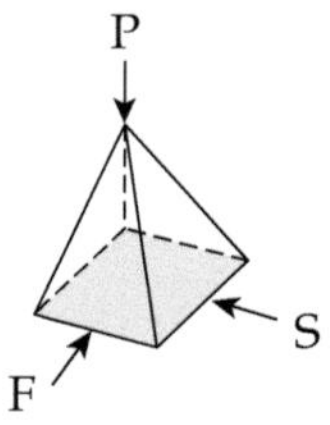

a

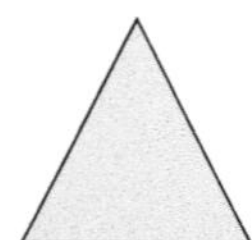

Front elevation

b

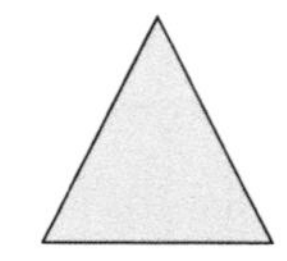

Side elevation

c

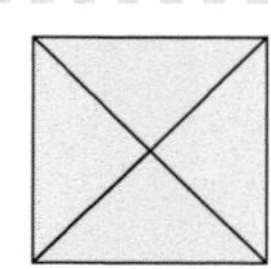

Plan view

Example

The diagram shows the plan view of a solid made from cubes. The number in each square represents the number of cubes in that column.
Draw the solid on **isometric paper**.

1	2
	1

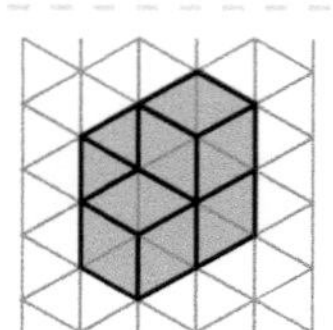

or

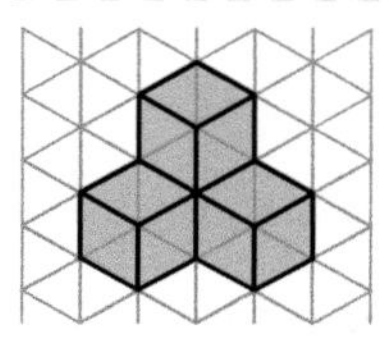

Exercise 14b

1 Sketch the front elevation (F), the side elevation (S) and the plan view (P) of these cuboids.

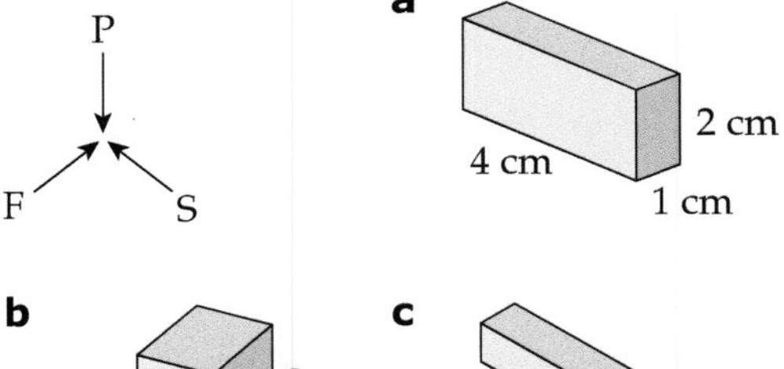

b 3 cm 2 cm 2 cm

c 5 cm 1 cm 1 cm

2 Sketch the front elevation (F), the side elevation (S) and the plan view (P) of these solids.

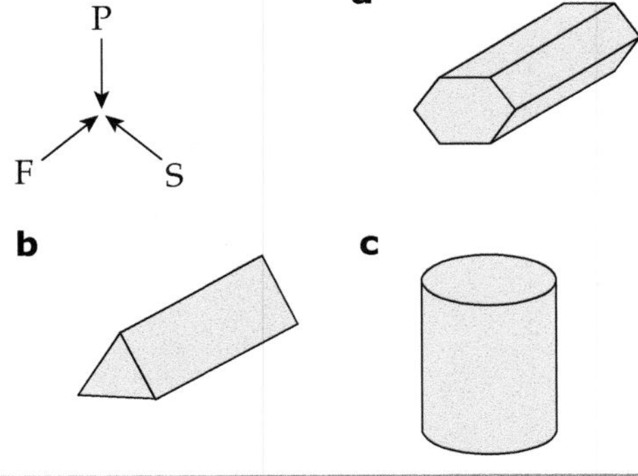

3 The diagram shows the plan view of a solid made from cubes.

The number in each square represents the number of cubes in that column.

a Draw the solid on isometric paper.

b Draw the front and side elevations.

4 A 3D shape is made from cubes. The elevations and the plan view are shown.

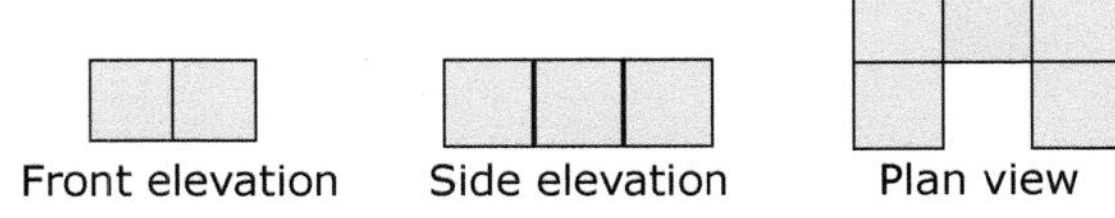

a Draw the solid on isometric paper.

b How many cubes are needed to make the shape?

Problem solving

5 The front and side elevations and the plan views of two solids are shown. The diagrams are jumbled up.

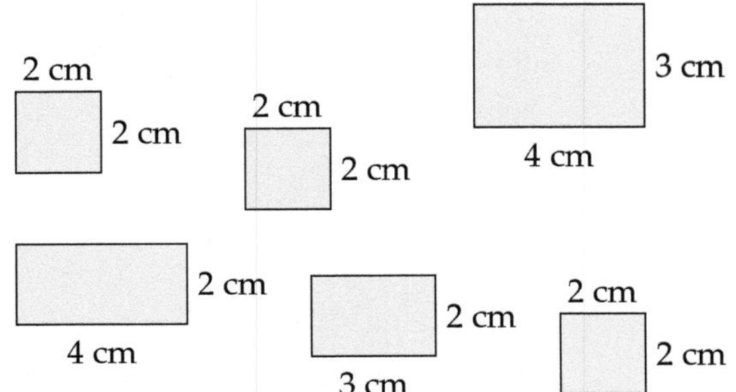

Draw a sketch of each solid, showing the dimensions of the shape and giving the mathematical name in each case.

14c Surface area of a prism

A prism is a solid that has the same **cross-section** throughout its length.

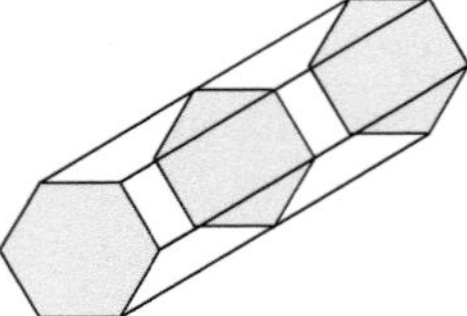

A hexagonal prism.

When you unfold a solid, the 2D shape forms a **net**.

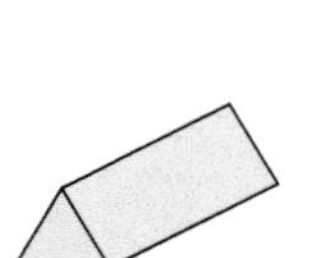

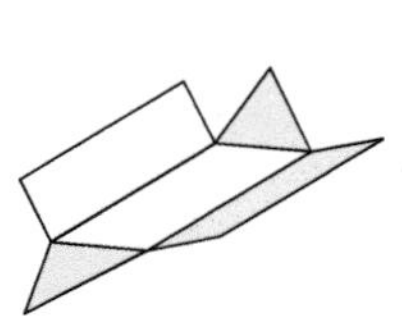

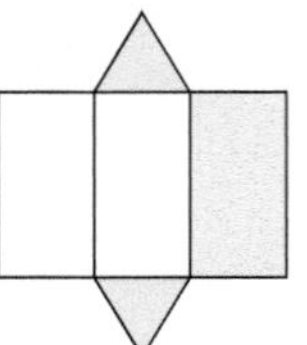

The surface area of a solid and the area of its net are the same thing.

The **surface area** of a solid is the total area of its **faces**.

Example

The surface area of a cube is 13.5 cm². Calculate the length of one side of the cube.

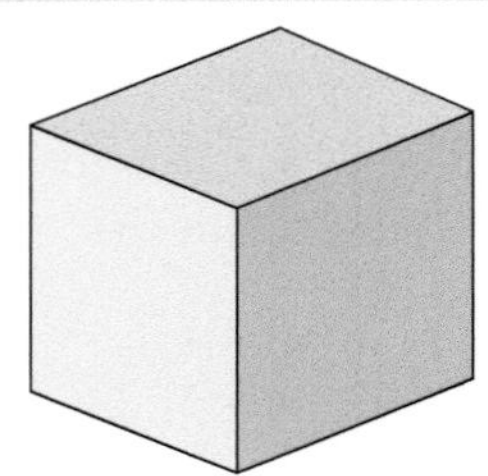

A cube has six square faces.

The area of one face $= 13.5 \div 6 = 2.25\text{ cm}^2$

Length of one side $= \sqrt{2.25} = 1.5\text{ cm}$

Example

a Draw the net of the solid.

b Calculate the surface area of the triangular prism.

3 cm, 4 cm, 5 cm, 6 cm

a

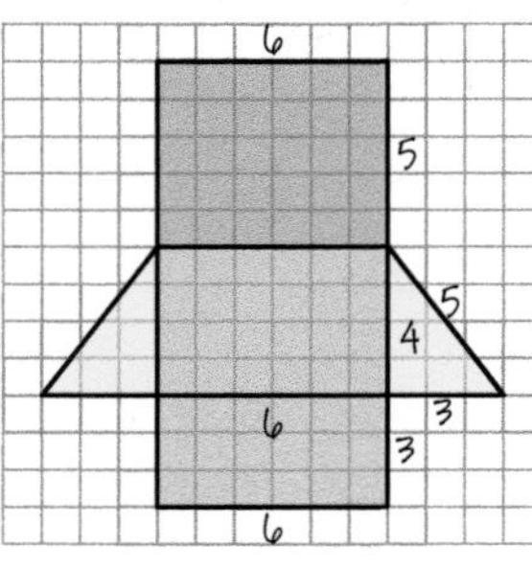

Remember to put the lengths on each edge.

b

Area of the pink rectangle $= 5 \times 6 = 30\text{ cm}^2$

Area of the green rectangle $= 4 \times 6 = 24\text{ cm}^2$

Area of the blue rectangle $= 3 \times 6 = 18\text{ cm}^2$

Area of the yellow triangle $= \frac{1}{2} \times 3 \times 4 = 6\text{ cm}^2$

Area of the other triangle $= \frac{1}{2} \times 3 \times 4 = 6\text{ cm}^2$

Surface area $= 84\text{ cm}^2$

Find the area of each face and then find the total.

Exercise 14c

1 Calculate the surface area of each cuboid.

a

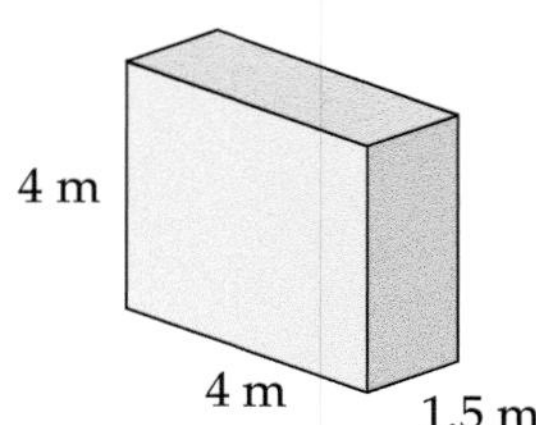

b

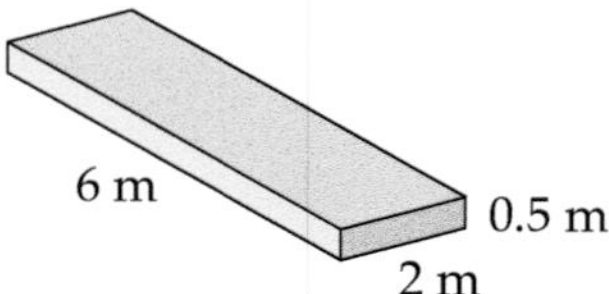

c

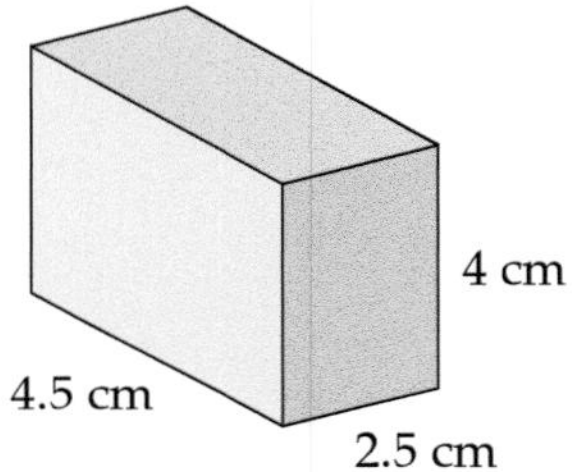

2 Calculate the length of one side of a cube, if the surface area of the cube is

a $1350\,cm^2$ **b** $121.5\,cm^2$ **c** $6\,m^2$

3 **a** Draw a sketch of the net of the prism.

b Calculate the surface area of the triangular prism.

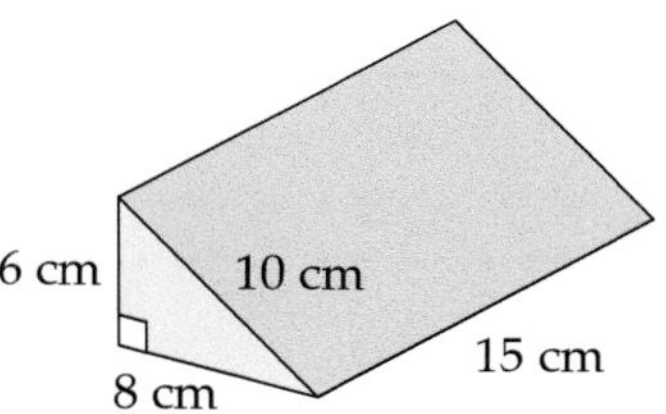

4 **a** Draw a sketch of the net of the prism.

b Calculate the surface area of the prism.

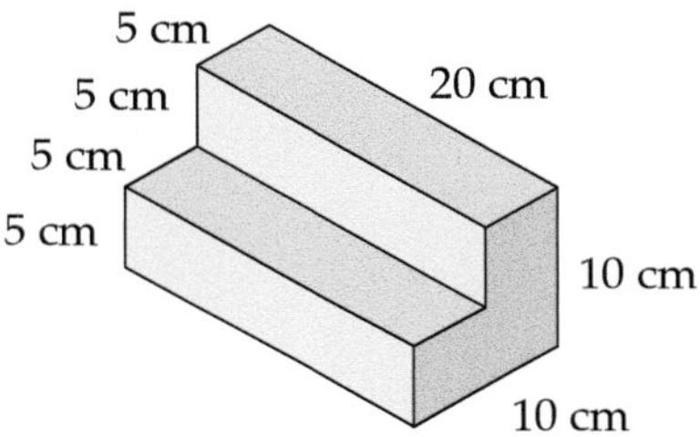

Problem solving

5 A cube has a length of *l*.

Calculate the surface area of the cube in terms of *l*.

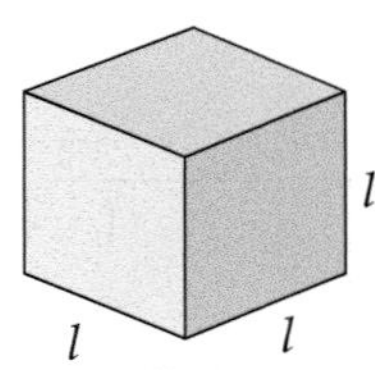

6 The surface area of each cuboid is $78\,cm^2$.

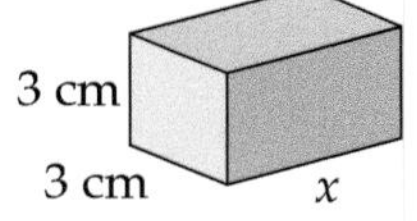

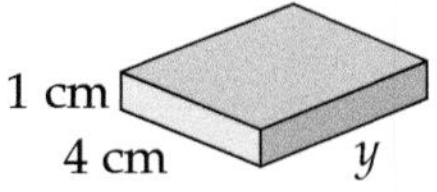

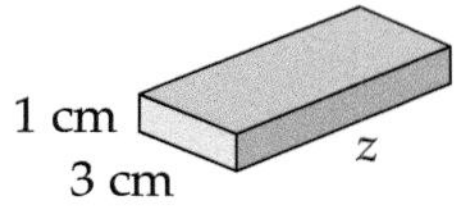

Find the values of *x*, *y* and *z*.

Clues:
x, *y* and *z* form a linear sequence.
x, *y* and *z* are all less than 10.

7 The surface area of a cuboid is $64\,cm^2$.
The length of each side is an integer.
Three cuboids satisfy these conditions. Can you find them?

Hint: one side is less than 3.

14d Volume of a prism

Volume is the amount of space inside a 3D shape.

You measure volume in cubic units.

For example,
a cubic millimetre (mm^3)
a cubic centimetre (cm^3)
a cubic metre (m^3).

Volume of a **cuboid** = length × width × height

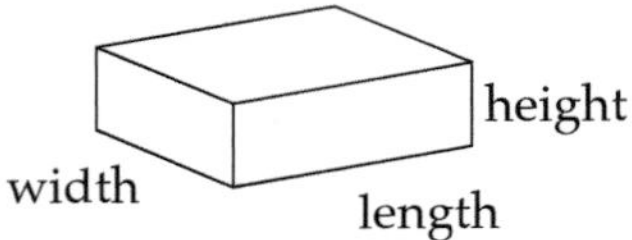

This is the same as Volume = width × height × length
= area of **cross-section** × length

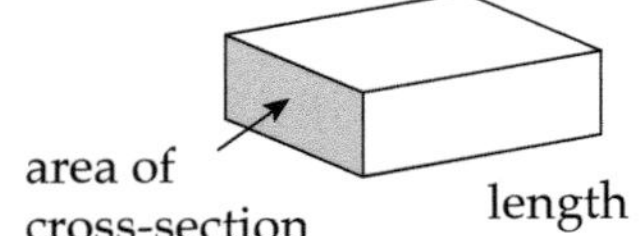

Volume of a **prism** = area of cross-section × length

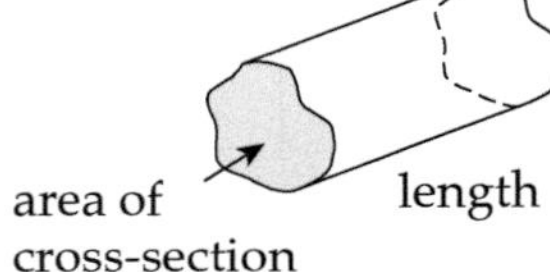

Example

The area of cross-section of a prism is $14\,m^2$.
The length of the prism is 3.5 metres.
Calculate the volume of the prism.

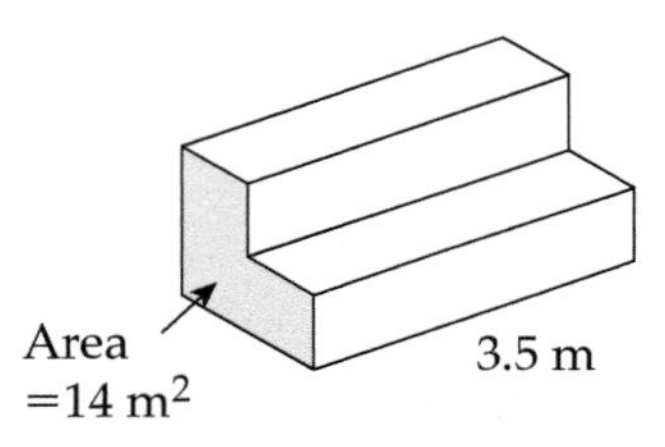

Volume of a prism = area of cross-section × length
$= 14 \times 3.5$
$= 49\,m^3$

The units of volume here are cubic metres.

Example

Calculate **a** the area of the shaded cross-section
b the volume of the prism.

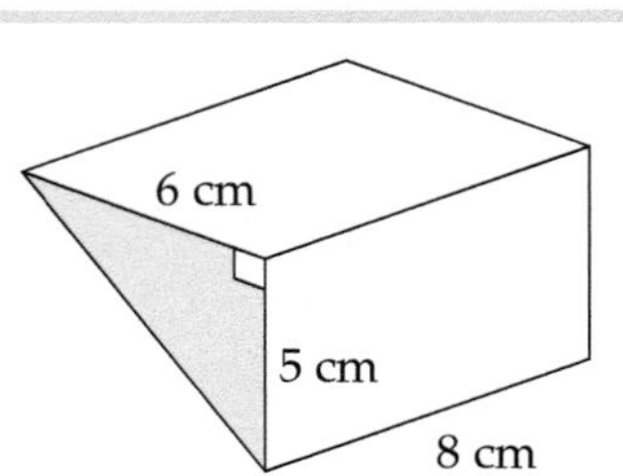

a Area of the red triangle $= \frac{1}{2} \times 6 \times 5$
$= 15\,cm^2$

b Volume of the prism = area of cross-section × length
$= 15 \times 8$
$= 120\,cm^3$

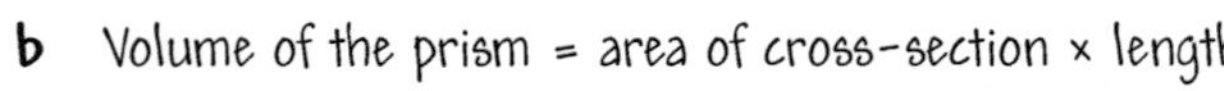

The units of volume here are cubic centimetres.

Exercise 14d

1 A cuboid has dimensions 5 cm by 6.5 cm by 8 cm. Calculate its volume.

2 Two steps are made in the shape of a prism.

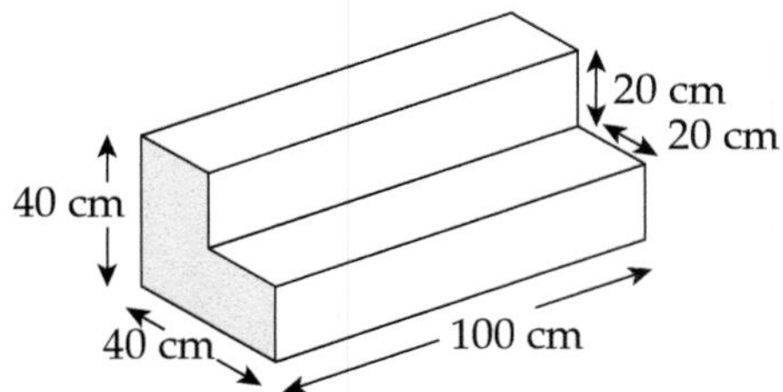

a Calculate the area of the green shape.

b Calculate the volume of the prism.

3 A door wedge is shown.

a State the mathematical name of the shape.

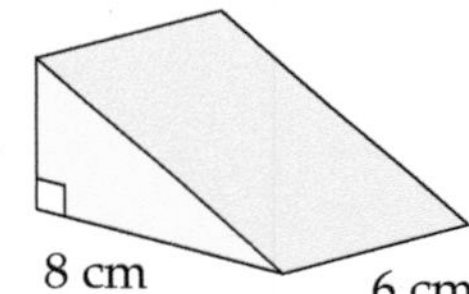

b Calculate

i the area of the triangle

ii the volume of the wedge.

4 A step-up is made in the shape of a prism. The cross-section is an isosceles trapezium.

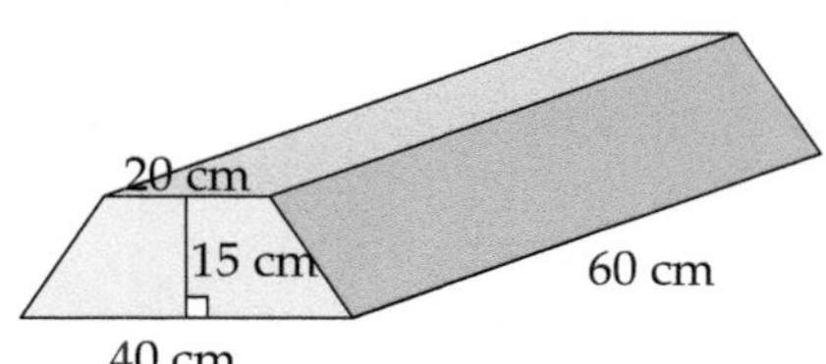

a Calculate the area of the trapezium.

b Calculate the volume of the prism.

5 A cylinder has a length of 15 cm and a radius of 5 cm.

Use $\pi = 3.14$

Calculate

a the area of the circle

b the volume of the cylinder.

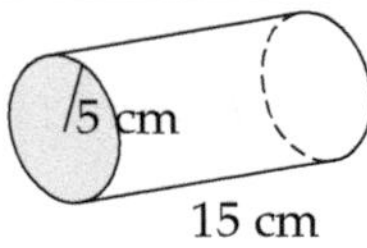

Problem solving

6 A container ship carries 5000 containers.
Each container is a cuboid with dimensions 12.2 m by 2.4 m by 2.6 m.
Calculate the total volume of all the containers.

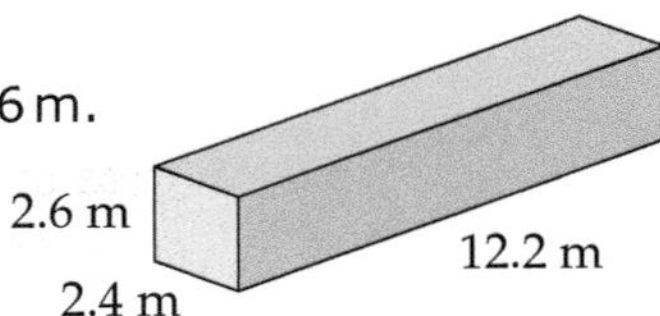

7 The nets of two prisms are shown.
Calculate the volume of each prism.

a

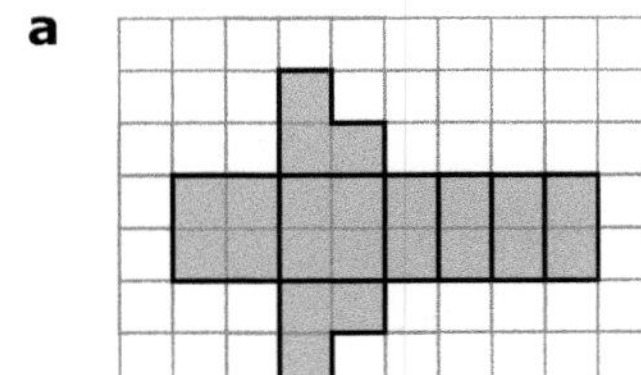

b

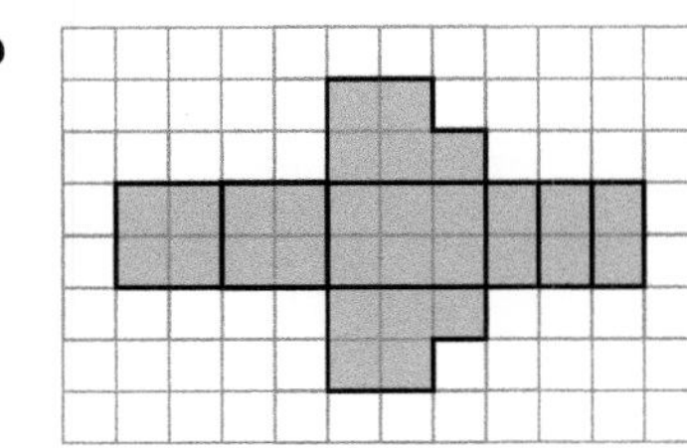

8 A cuboid has faces with areas of 35 cm², 40 cm² and 56 cm².
Find the volume of the cuboid.

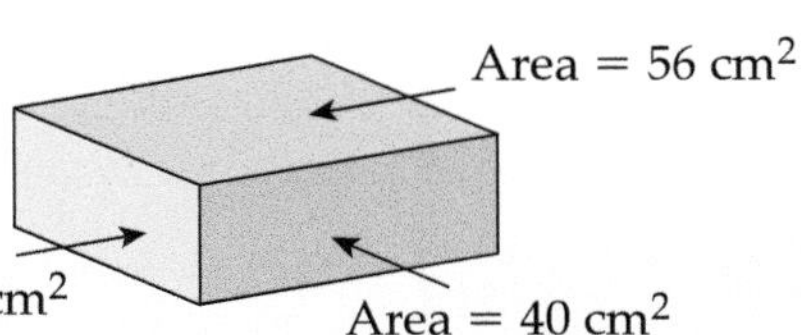

14 MySummary

Check out

You should now be able to ...

You should now be able to ...		Test it ➡ Questions
✓ Name 3D shapes and draw their nets	6	1, 2
✓ Draw plans and elevations and isometric diagrams	6	3, 4
✓ Calculate the surface area of a prism	7	5
✓ Calculate the volume of a prism	7	6, 7

Language	Meaning	Example
Face	A flat surface of a solid shape	vertex, edge, face
Edge	The line where two faces meet	
Vertex	A point where three or more edges meet	
Net	A 2D shape that can be folded to form a 3D shape	
Front elevation	The view of the shape from the front	
Side elevation	The side view of the shape	
Plan view	The bird's eye view of the shape (the view from above).	
Prism	A 3D shape with the same cross-section throughout its length	Cylinder, cuboid

14 MyReview

1

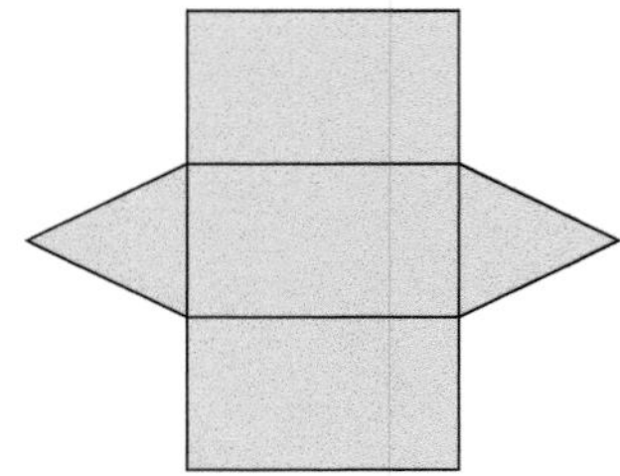

a What is the mathematical name of the solid?

b For this solid state the number of

i faces ii edges

iii vertices.

2 Draw the net of a hexagonal prism. Use different colours to identify opposite faces.

3 a For this solid, sketch

i the front elevation

ii the side elevation

iii the plan view.

b What is the mathematical name of this solid?

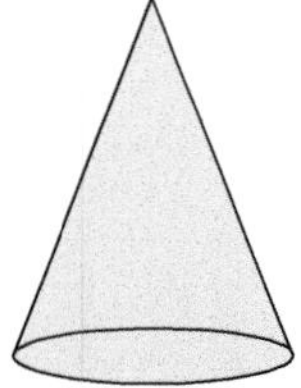

4 A 3D shape is made from cubes. The elevations and the plan view are shown.

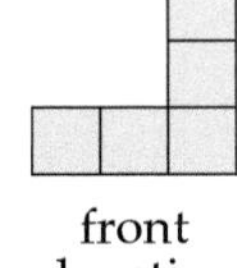

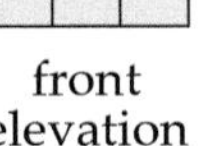

front elevation

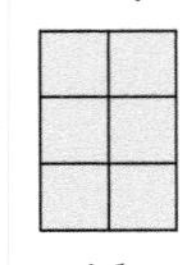

side elevation

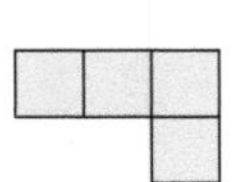

plan view

4 a Draw the shape on isometric paper.

b How many cubes are needed to make the shape?

5 Calculate the surface area of each prism.

a

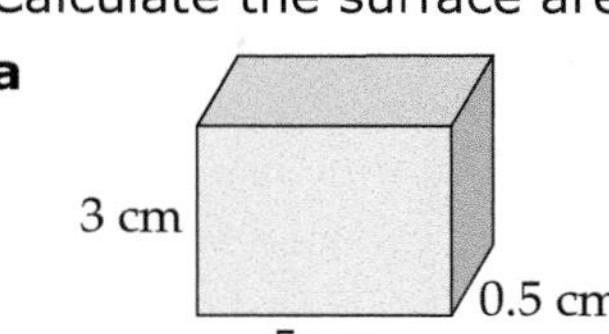

b

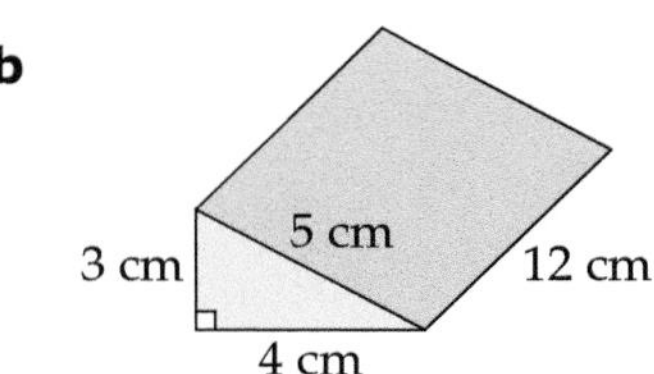

6 Calculate the volume of this cylinder.

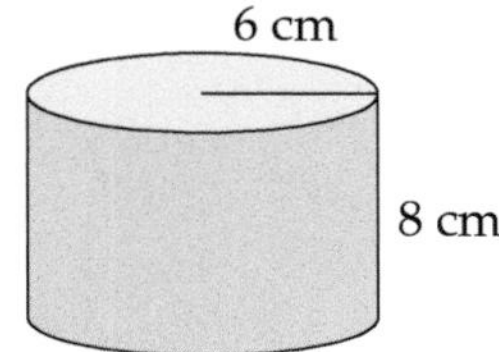

7 Calculate the volume of this prism.

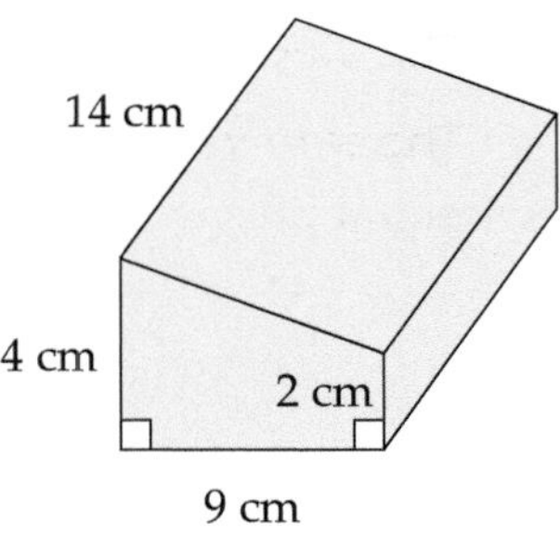

What next?

Score			
	0 – 3		Your knowledge of this topic is still developing. To improve look at Formative test: 2C-14; MyMaths: 1078, 1098, 1106, 1107 and 1139
	4 – 6		You are gaining a secure knowledge of this topic. To improve look at InvisiPen: 321, 324, 325, 326, 327 and 328
	7		You have mastered this topic. Well done, you are ready to progress!

14a

1 On square grid paper, draw the net of a cuboid with dimensions 3 cm by 4 cm by 5 cm.

2 **a** Which shapes are the net of a square-based pyramid?

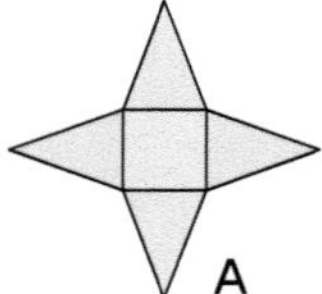

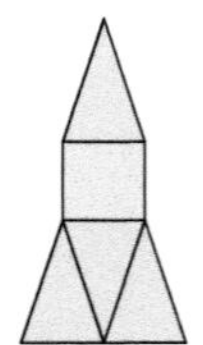

b For a square-based pyramid state the number of

i faces **ii** vertices **iii** edges.

3 On a standard dice the number of dots on opposite faces always adds up to seven. Draw a net for a dice showing the dots.

14b

4 On square grid paper, draw the front elevation (F), the side elevation (S) and the plan view (P) of each solid.

a

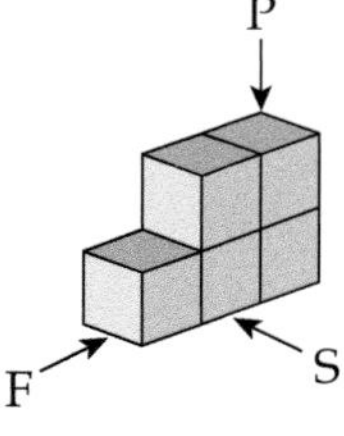

b

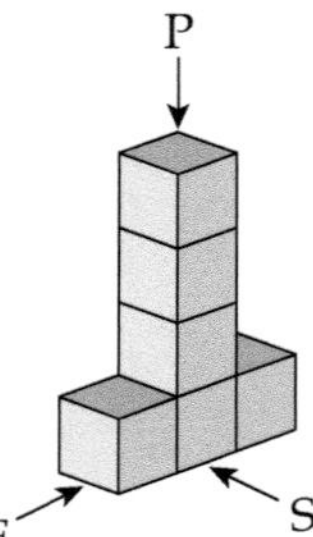

c

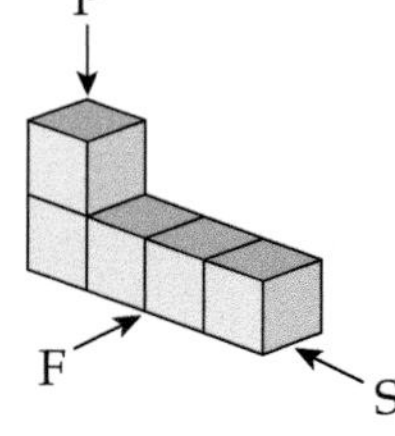

d

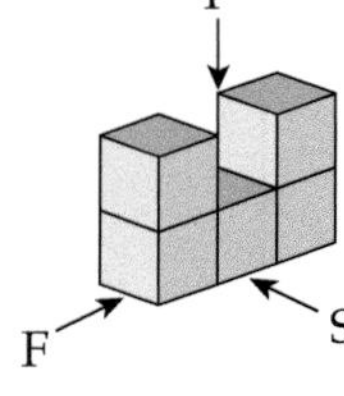

5 A 3D shape is constructed from cubes.
The elevations and plan view are shown.

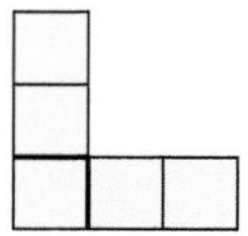

Front elevation

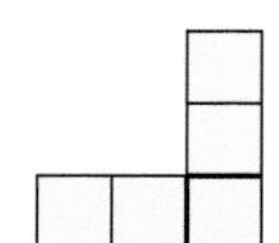

Side elevation

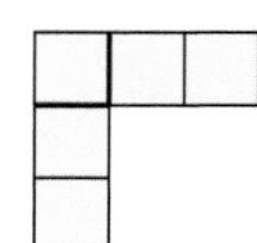

Plan view

a Draw the solid on isometric paper

b How many cubes are needed to make the shape?

14b

6 Calculate the surface areas of these prisms.

a

3 m
4.5 m
2 m

b

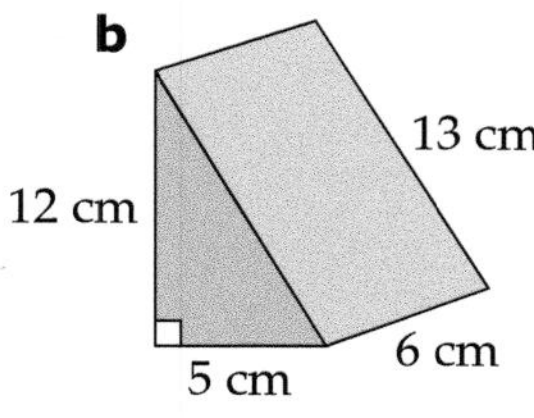

c

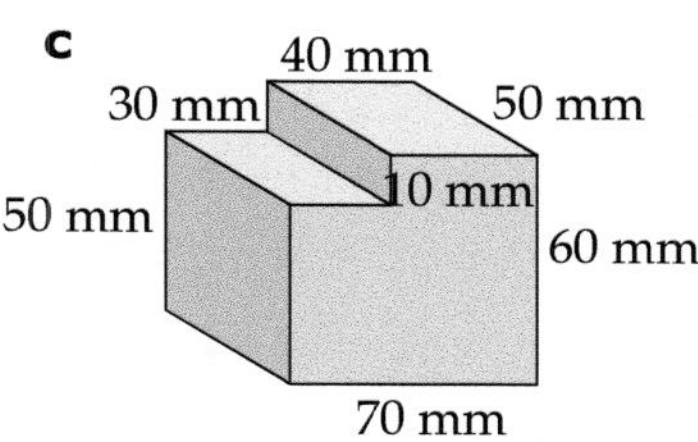

14c

7 **a** Find the nine possible cuboids that can be made using 48 one-centimetre cubes.

b Calculate the surface area of each cuboid.

c Which cuboid has the largest surface area?

d Which cuboid has the smallest surface area?

8 Find the volume of a cube with surface area 150 cm^3.

9 Find the volumes of these prisms.

a

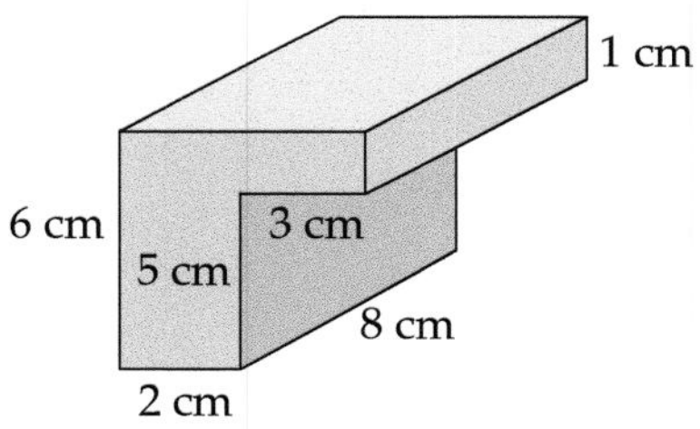

b

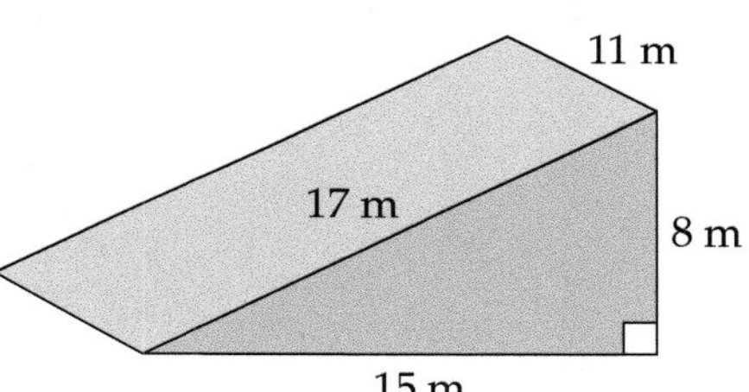

14d

10 A chocolate box has a cross-section of an equilateral triangle.

a State the mathematical name of the solid.

b Draw a sketch of the net, showing the dimensions.

c Calculate

i the surface area

ii the volume of the solid.

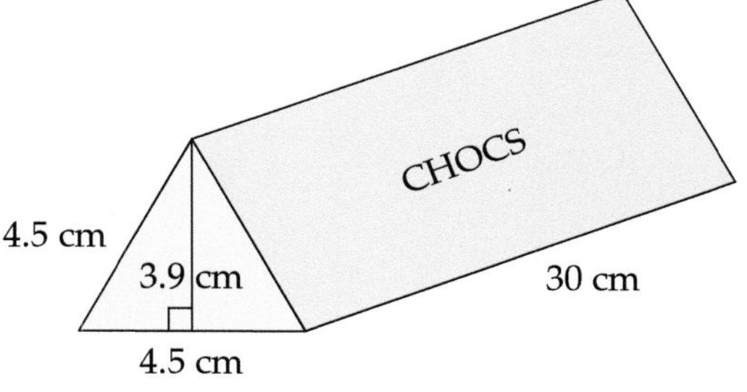

Case study 5: Perspective

For thousands of years, artists have tackled the problem of representing the 3D world in a 2D picture. During the Renaissance, the principles behind perspective were developed and these ideas are still used by artists, architects and graphic designers today.

Task 1

Here are two paintings. The one on the left is from the 14th century, and the one on the right is from the 15th century. Which painting do you think looks most realistic and why?

Task 2

Renaissance artists used the idea that the further away objects are, the smaller they look. This is called foreshortening, and we still use this today.

Look at the two pictures on the right. Picture 1 shows an avenue with seven trees on each side. Picture 2 shows how a computer graphic designer might portray this.

a Describe what is happening to the "trees" as they get further away.
b Draw a similar picture to Picture 2, but with 8 trees on each side.

Compare your picture with a friend's. Whose picture looks most accurate and why?

Task 3

Renaissance artists began to use a single **vanishing point** to add realism. The vanishing point is clearly seen in this photograph.

Check the perspective in the two paintings on the left hand page. Do either of them have a vanishing point?

Task 4

Many Renaissance artists placed the vanishing point near the main subject of their painting. A famous example of this is The Last Supper by Leonardo da Vinci.

The vanishing point is set at the height of the eye-line. In this drawing, the green cuboid appears to be above the viewer and the blue cuboids below.

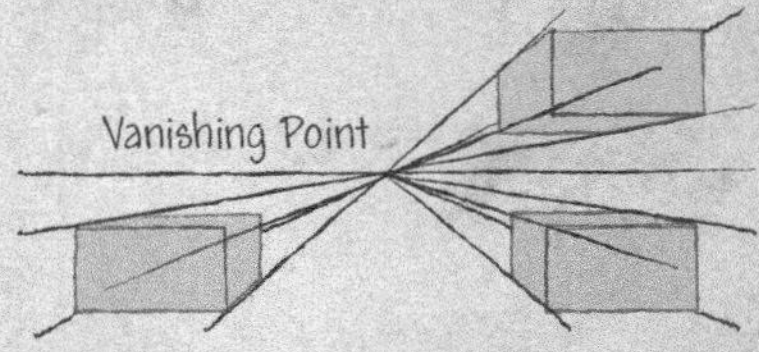

- Make your own drawing of cubes using single point perspective. Describe your findings.
- What do you notice about cubes that are a long way to the left or right of the vanishing point?

Task 5

When an object is edge on, **two point perspective** gives a more realistic impression, using two vanishing points, both on the same horizontal eye line, as in the picture.

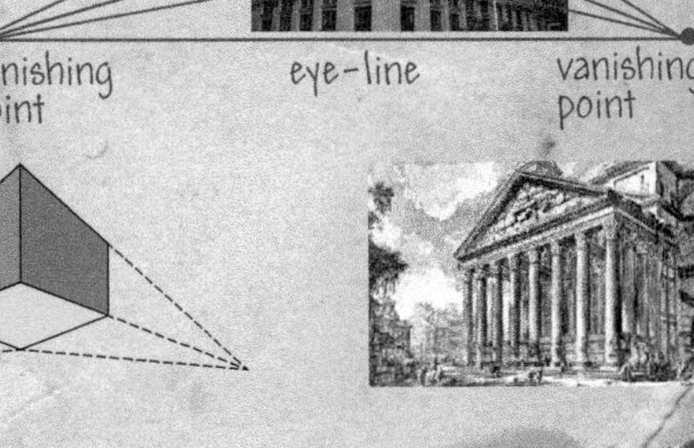

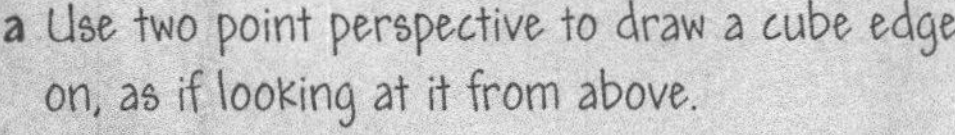

a Use two point perspective to draw a cube edge on, as if looking at it from above.

b Now draw a second cube edge on, this time as if looking at it from below.

Reasearch the meaning of three point perspective.

Try to draw a cube using this perspective.

Hint: Keep your uprights vertical, and place your vanishing points first.

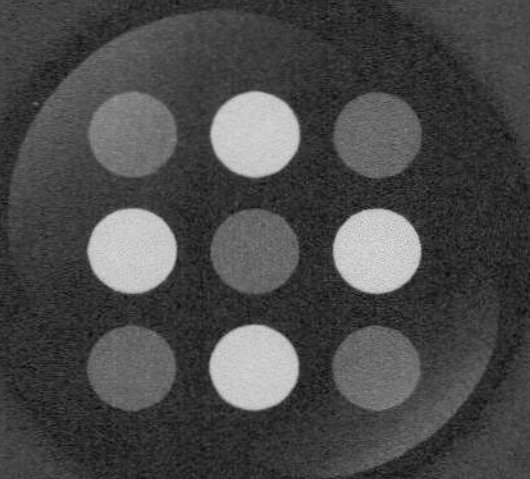

15 Ratio and proportion

Introduction

The idea of creating things which are in proportion is vital to art and architecture. However there is one number, called the 'Golden Proportion', which is supposed to be the most pleasing to the eye.
The Golden Proportion relates to a rectangle whose ratio of length to width is 1.6180339887 : 1. There is evidence that the ancient Greeks and Egyptians used this proportion in the design of many of their buildings, and Renaissance artists used it commonly in their paintings.

What's the point?

The Golden Proportion occurs widely in nature, so it is unsurprising that artists and architects throughout history have chosen to integrate this mathematical dimension into their work.

Objectives

By the end of this chapter, you will have learned how to …

- Simplify and compare ratios.
- Divide a quantity in a given ratio.
- Use the unitary method to solve direct proportion problems.
- Solve ratio and proportion problems.
- Compare proportions.
- Describe quantities in direct proportion using an equation or a graph.

Check in

1 Write each of these ratios in their simplest form.

a 12 : 20 b 42 : 28 c 144 : 108 d 250 cm : 3.5 m

2 Divide 60 cakes in the ratio 2 : 3.

3 4 kg of pears cost 145p. How much do 12 kg of pears cost?

4 An alloy is made from copper and zinc in the ratio 4 : 5.
How much copper needs to be mixed with 60 kg of zinc?

5 In a running club there are 25 beginners, 35 intermediate and 10 advanced runners.

a What proportion of the running club members are intermediate?

b What is the ratio of beginners to advanced runners at the club?

Starter problem

Leonardo da Vinci thought that your head (measured from your forehead to your chin) was exactly one tenth of your height.

Is this true?

Investigate the lengths of different parts of your body to see if any of them are in proportion to each other.

15a Ratio

- You **simplify** a ratio by dividing or multiplying all parts of the ratio by the same number.
  - ▶ A ratio is in its **simplest form** when it contains no units and is written in terms of integers whose HCF is 1.

Example

Write these ratios in their simplest form.

a 12 : 9 : 3 **b** 48 cm : 180 mm **c** 0.4 : 3

a 12 : 9 : 3 → (÷3) → 4 : 3 : 1

Divide all the parts of the ratio by the HCF, 3.

b 48 cm : 180 mm
480 mm : 180 mm
480 : 180 → (÷60) → 8 : 3

Change both quantities to the same units, mm.

c 0.4 : 3 → (×5) → 2 : 15

Multiply all parts of the ratio by 5 to make all numbers whole.

- You can **compare ratios** by expressing them in the **form 1 : *n***.

This means that one of the parts of the ratio has to be 1, and the other part may be a decimal.

Example

Statto is looking at the ratio of goals scored to shots taken by the two strikers who play in the school football team. He finds that the ratio of goals : shots is 7 : 40 for Ree Bok and 4 : 25 for Ade Idas. Which striker is more accurate?

Express both ratios in the form 1 : *n*.

Ree Bok
goals : shots
7 : 40 → (÷7) → 1 : 5.71 (2 dp)

Ade Idas
goals : shots
4 : 25 → (÷4) → 1 : 6.25

Ree Bok scores 1 goal every 5.71 shots.
Ade Idas scores 1 goal every 6.25 shots.
So Ree Bok is the more accurate striker.

Writing both ratios in the form 1:n makes it easier to make comparisons.

Exercise 15a

1 Write each of these ratios in its simplest form.

a	8 : 20	**b**	32 : 28
c	12 : 15 : 24	**d**	45 : 60 : 135
e	80 : 112 : 176	**f**	4 m : 205 cm
g	5 kg : 2800 g	**h**	£3.50 : 80p
i	0.5 : 2	**j**	0.3 : 8
k	1.5 : 5	**l**	1.6 : 2.4
m	4.5 : 6 : 7.5	**n**	0.4 m : 240 cm
o	2.5 kg : 1800 g	**p**	£6.25 : 75p

2 Express each of these ratios in the form 1 : *n*.

a	5 : 10	**b**	3 : 12
c	5 : 25	**d**	8 : 112
e	5 : 9	**f**	3 : 14
g	5 : 17	**h**	8 : 116
i	3 : 8	**j**	7 : 18
k	6 : 11	**l**	3 : 41
m	0.5 : 7	**n**	7 : 0.5
o	0.3 : 1.2	**p**	11.2 : 5.7

Problem solving

3 Here are the shots taken and goals scored for six football players.

Name of striker	Goals scored	Shots taken	Goals : Shots	1 : *n*
Demba Boo	17	43	17 : 43	1 : 2.53
Frank Tores	21	50		
Robin van Winkle	16	35		
Warren Roone	13	34		
Daniel Porridge	19	53		

a Copy and complete the table.

b Use the ratios you have worked out to put the players in order from most to least accurate. Explain your reasoning.

Did you know?

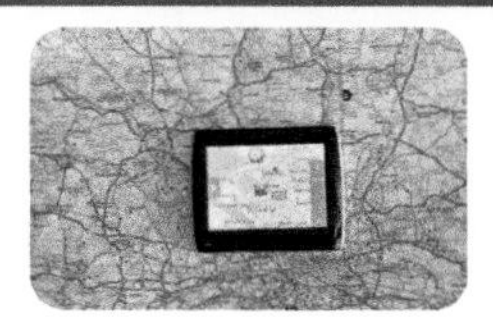

Ordnance Survey is the national mapping agency for the UK. The scale of all of its maps is stated as a ratio. The agency also produces digital maps – just like the ones used in sat-nav systems.

4 The ratios of cotton to other materials in two T-shirts are 3 : 8 and 5 : 14. Write the ratios in the form 1 : *n*. Which T-shirt has the greater proportion of cotton?

5 Brian has made a table using some measurements of distances given in miles and kilometres.

a Copy and complete the table.

b What do you notice about the results? What is the significance of the ratio in the form 1 : *n*?

c Investigate some more quantities in the same way, such as

- pounds : dollars £35 : $68.25
- model bus : real-life bus 62.5 cm : 15 m

d Explain the meaning of the ratio 1 : *n* in each case.

miles	kilometres	miles : km	miles : km
10	16	5 : 8	1 : 1.6
24	38.4		
31.25	50		
50	80		

15b Division in a given ratio

- **Ratios** can be used to divide a quantity into unequal-sized pieces.

- You can divide a quantity in a given ratio by using a **unitary method**.

Example

Naheeda is 7 years old, Marie is 10 years old and Evie is 13 years old.
Their gran gives them £450 to share in the ratio of their ages.
How much money do they each receive?

Dividing the money in the ratio 7 : 10 : 13 requires 30 equal parts.

$$\begin{array}{ccc} & \text{30 parts} & \text{£450} & \\ \div 30 & \downarrow & \downarrow & \div 30 \\ & \text{1 part} & \text{£15} & \end{array}$$

Each part is £15.

Naheeda gets 7 parts.

$$\begin{array}{cccc} & \text{1 part} & \text{£15} & \\ \times 7 & \downarrow & \downarrow & \times 7 \\ & \text{7 parts} & \text{£105} & \end{array}$$

Naheeda receives £105.

Marie gets 10 parts.

$$\begin{array}{cccc} & \text{1 part} & \text{£15} & \\ \times 10 & \downarrow & \downarrow & \times 10 \\ & \text{10 parts} & \text{£150} & \end{array}$$

Marie receives £150.

Evie gets 13 parts.

$$\begin{array}{cccc} & \text{1 part} & \text{£15} & \\ \times 13 & \downarrow & \downarrow & \times 13 \\ & \text{13 parts} & \text{£195} & \end{array}$$

Evie receives £195.

- A quantity can also be divided in a given ratio using the relationship between ratio and **proportion**.

Example

Carole, Sarah and Monty share 5 kilograms of strawberries in the ratio 1 : 2 : 4
How many strawberries do they each receive?

Convert the ratios into proportions and take these fractions of the total.

	Carole	Sarah	Monty
Ratio	1	2	4
Proportion	$\frac{1}{7}$	$\frac{2}{7}$	$\frac{4}{7}$

1 + 2 + 4 = 7 equal parts

Carole receives

$\frac{1}{7}$ of 5 kg = 0.71 kg (2 dp)

Sarah receives

$\frac{2}{7}$ of 5 kg = 1.43 kg (2 dp)

Monty receives

$\frac{4}{7}$ of 5 kg = 2.86 kg (2 dp)

Exercise 15b

1 Divide these quantities in the ratios given.

- **a** 80 cakes in the ratio 2 : 3
- **b** 156 km in the ratio 5 : 7
- **c** £384 in the ratio 4 : 5
- **d** £1.62 in the ratio 1 : 2 : 3
- **e** 96 sweets in the ratio 1 : 1 : 4

2 Divide these quantities in the ratios given. Give your answers to 2 dp as appropriate.

- **a** £13 in the ratio 3 : 5
- **b** 200 m in the ratio 7 : 9
- **c** 4 GB in the ratio 2 : 5
- **d** £40 in the ratio 2 : 3 : 4

Problem solving

3 **a** In a school the ratio of boys to girls is 15 : 16. There are 1085 pupils at the school. How many girls are there at the school?

b A cake mixture contains flour, sugar and margarine in the ratio 4 : 3 : 2. How much sugar is needed to make 630 g of cake mixture?

Did you know?

This symbol was used for the Italian Lira which has now been replaced by the Euro.
₤1936.27: € 1
How often do you see the Lira symbol (₤) used for pounds (£)?

4 Solve these problems.

a A metal alloy is made from tin, iron and nickel in the ratio 3 : 7 : 1. How much iron is needed to mix with 150 kg of tin?

b 3 parts of yellow paint are mixed with 4 parts of red paint to make orange paint. Zahid has 75 ml of yellow paint and 120 ml of red paint.
What is the maximum amount of orange paint he can make?

5 **a** The ratio of KS3 to KS4 pupils in Weregood School is 7 : 5.
Are there more pupils in Year 11 than in Year 7?
Explain and justify your answer.

b Last year Jameela was 110 cm tall. This year she has increased in height by 10%.
What is the ratio of her height last year to her height this year?

6 Great-grandad Vernon died. He has three great-grandchildren, 6-year-old Zoe, 9-year-old Breeze and 15-year-old Jenny. His will gives £1000 to the girls every year, which must be shared in the ratio of their ages.

- **a** Work out the amount each girl receives in the first year.
- **b** Work out the amount each girl receives for the next 10 years.
- **c** Write down what you notice.

Try to use the ratios to explain what is happening.

7 A bag contains red and blue balls that come in two sizes, large and small.
The ratio of red to blue balls is 3:5, the ratio of large red to large blue balls is 1:1, and the ratio of small red to small blue balls is 1:2.
What is the ratio of large to small balls?

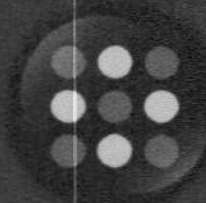

15c Direct proportion

- Two quantities are in **direct proportion** if when one of them increases, the other one increases by the same proportion.

- You can use a **scaling** method to solve problems involving direct proportion.
  - ▶ In this method you multiply or divide both quantities by the same number.

Example

Two litres of orange juice cost £2.60.
What is the cost of 5 litres of orange juice?

Work out the multiplier using division $\frac{5}{2} = 2.5$

×2.5	2 litres	£2.60	×2.5
	5 litres	£6.50	

5 litres of orange juice costs £6.50.

- You can use the **unitary method** to solve problems involving direct proportion.
  - ▶ In this method you always find the value of one unit of a quantity.

Example

a 15 minutes of mobile calls cost 48p.
What is the cost of 23 minutes?

b There are 46 calories in a jaffa cake that weighs 12 g.
How many calories are there in 100 g of jaffa cakes?

a

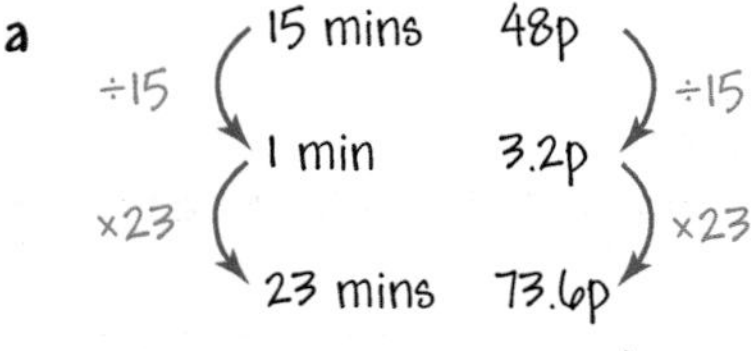

23 voice minutes cost 74p.

b

÷12	46 calories	12 g	÷12
×100	3.8333... calories	1 g	×100
	383.33... calories	100 g	

100 g of jaffa cakes contain 383 cal.

Exercise 15c

1 Use direct proportion to solve each of these problems.

  a 5 kg of pears cost 195p. What is the cost of 15 kg of pears?

  b 40 g of breakfast cereal contain 128 calories. How many calories are there in 100 g of breakfast cereal?

  c A recipe for six people uses 750 ml of stock. What amount of stock is needed for four people?

2 Solve each of these problems, giving your answers to an appropriate degree of accuracy.

  a 5 litres of oil cost £4.79. What is the cost of 18 litres of oil?

  b There are 12 biscuits in a packet. The packet weighs 200 g. What is the weight of 23 biscuits?

  c A car's petrol tank when full holds 48 litres of petrol. On a full tank of petrol Jake can drive 650 km.

    i How far could Jake's car travel on 20 litres of petrol?

    ii How much petrol would he need to travel 130 km?

  d £10 is worth 92.27 Croatian kuna.

    i How much is £325 worth in Croatian kuna?

    ii How much is 1000 Croatian kuna worth in pounds?

  e On average 8 adults weigh 560 kg. On average what would 30 adults weigh?

Problem solving

3 Here are three offers for text messages on a mobile phone. In which of these offers are the numbers in direct proportion? In each case, explain and justify your answers.

A

B

C

4 Use **direct proportion** to copy and complete this conversion table for kilograms and pounds. Write the ratio in its simplest form.

  a Write anything you notice. What do these results tell you about the relationship between pounds and kilograms?

  b How could you quickly change from kilograms to pounds using what you've found out?

Kilograms (kg)	Pounds (lb)	Pounds ÷ Kilograms	Ratio Pounds : Kilograms
1			
	4.4		
5	11		
10			
23			
	110		

  c What about changing from pounds to kilograms? What is the easiest way to convert between the quantities?

15d Ratio and proportion

- You can compare the size of two quantities using a **ratio**.

Example

Dax the cat weighs 6 kg. Tess the dog weighs 7.5 kg.
What is the ratio of Dax's weight to Tess' weight?
What fraction of Tess' weight is Dax?
How many times heavier than Dax is Tess?

Dax's weight : Tess' weight = 6 : 7.5
= 12 : 15
= 4 : 5

Dax's weight is $\frac{4}{5}$ of or 80% of or 0.8 of Tess' weight

Tess' weight is $\frac{5}{4}$ of or 125% of or 1.25 times Dax's weight

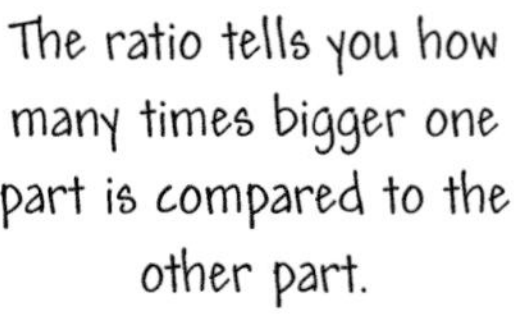

- You can compare two or more parts of the same quantity using ratio or **proportion**.
  - ▶ The ratio compares the size of the parts.
  - ▶ The proportion compares the size of the part with the whole.

Example

In a skiing club there are 20 beginners, 16 intermediate and 8 advanced skiers.

a What proportion of the skiing club members are intermediate skiers?

b What is the ratio of beginners to advanced skiers at the club?

a Total number of skiers = 20 + 16 + 8 = 44

Proportion of intermediates = $\frac{16}{44}$

$= \frac{4}{11}$ (= 36.4% to 1 dp)

b beginners : advanced = 20 : 8

= 5 : 2

The ratio compares how many skiers are in each category.

number of beginners = $\frac{5}{2}$ × number of advanced skiers

number of advanced skiers = $\frac{2}{5}$ × number of beginners

Exercise 15d

1 For each of these diagrams

i Find the ratio of pink : yellow : blue

ii Find the proportion of the shape shaded each colour (as a fraction)

iii Copy and complete these sentences.

pink section = $\frac{\square}{\square}$ × yellow section

pink section = $\frac{\square}{\square}$ of the whole shape

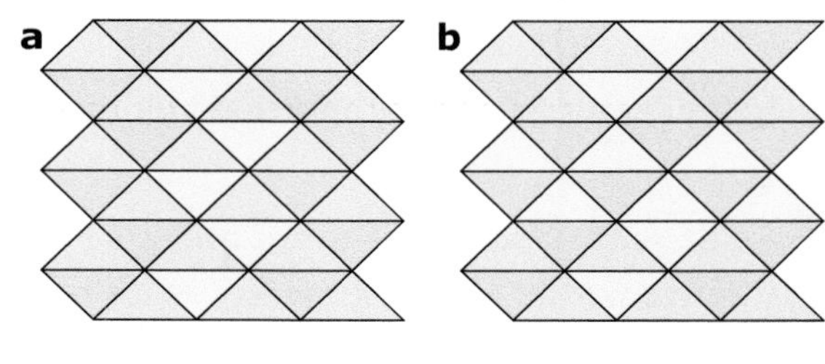

Problem solving

2 In a bag of mixed fruit and nuts there are 75 g of raisins, 30 g of currants and 95 g of nuts.

a Write the ratio of raisins : currants : nuts in the bag.

b How many times more raisins than currants are there?

c What proportion of the bag is nuts?

3 **a** An alloy is made from copper and iron in the ratio 2 : 5.
How much copper needs to be mixed with 45 kg of iron to make the alloy?

b The length and width of a football pitch are in the ratio 8 : 5.
The length of the pitch is 110 m. What is the width of the pitch?

c A cake is made using flour, margarine, ground almonds and sugar in the ratio 4 : 3 : 4 : 5.
How many grams of ground almonds are needed to mix with 180 g of margarine?

d The ratio of protein to carbohydrate in a tin of tomatoes is 12 : 35. If the tin contains 7 g of carbohydrate, how many grams of protein are there in it?

4 **a** $\frac{5}{9}$ of the pupils at a school are girls.
What is the ratio of boys : girls at the school?

b Benni McShot scores $\frac{3}{5}$ of the time he shoots at the goal in a hockey match.
What is Benni's ratio of goals to shots taken?

c Josh is 1.5 m tall. Gary is 20% taller than Josh.
What is the ratio of Josh's height to Gary's height?

d Cinema tickets for an adult and a child cost £9.80. The adult ticket is $1\frac{1}{3}$ times the price of the child's ticket.
How much does each ticket cost?

5 A square and a rectangle have the same area.
The sides of the rectangle are in the ratio 4 : 3.
The perimeter of the rectangle is 294 cm.
What is the length of side of the square? Give your answer to 1 dp.

15e Comparing proportions

- You can compare proportions by converting them to percentages.

Example

Linda is looking at the nutritional information of beef and pork sausages.

a Which type of sausage has the lower proportion of fat?

b How much fat is there in 150 g of beef sausages?
(Give your answer to the nearest gram.)

Pork sausages

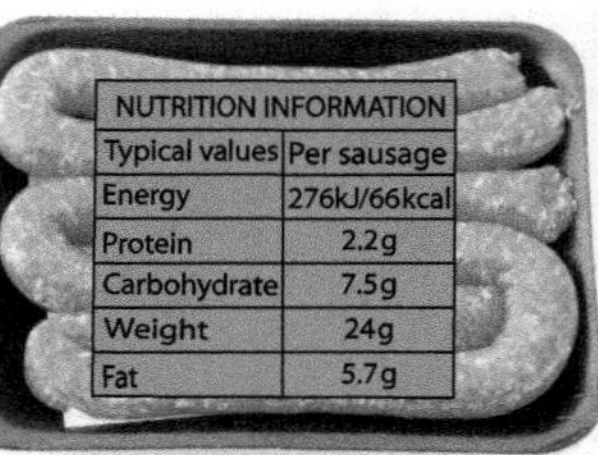

NUTRITION INFORMATION	
Typical values	Per sausage
Energy	276kJ/66kcal
Protein	2.2g
Carbohydrate	7.5g
Weight	24g
Fat	5.7g

Beef sausages

NUTRITION INFORMATION	
Typical values	Per sausage
Energy	450kJ/108kcal
Protein	12.3g
Carbohydrate	4.7g
Weight	55g
Fat	11.1g

Calculate the percentage of fat in each sausage.

a Pork sausage contains
5.7 g of fat in every 24 g
Percentage of fat
= 5.7 ÷ 24
= 0.2375
= 23.75%
= 23.8% (1 dp)

Beef sausage contains
11.1 g of fat in every 55 g
Percentage of fat
= 11.1 ÷ 55
= 0.201 818...
= 20.1818%
= 20.2% (1 dp)

The beef sausage contains a lower proportion of fat.

b Beef sausages are 20.2% fat.
In 150 g of beef sausages there are 20.2% of 150 g of fat
= 0.202 × 150
= 30.3 g
= 30 g (nearest gram)

Write the proportion as a fraction and convert this into a decimal and then a percentage.

- You can express the change in an amount as a percentage of the original amount.

Example

A packet of biscuits increases in weight from 180 g to 210 g. What is the percentage increase in weight?

$$\frac{(210 - 180)}{180} \times 100 = \frac{\overset{1}{\cancel{30}}}{\underset{6}{\cancel{180}}} \times 100$$
$$= 16.7\% \text{ (1 dp)}$$

You can use this formula

$$\text{Percentage change} = \frac{\text{difference}}{\text{original}} \times 100\%$$

to find the percentage change.

Exercise 15e

1 Express each of your answers

- **i** as a fraction in its simplest form
- **ii** as a percentage (to 1dp).

a Four out of every 500 drawing pins produced by a machine are rejected. What proportion of drawing pins are rejected?

b In a survey, 23 out of 40 cats preferred chicken flavour cat food. What proportion of the cats surveyed preferred chicken flavour cat food?

c In class 8X1 there are 35 pupils. 21 of these pupils are boys. What proportion of the class are girls?

2 This table shows the number of grams of fat in different chocolate bars.

a Copy and complete the table.

b Which is the least healthy bar to eat? Explain and justify your answer.

c How many grams of fat would there be in 150g of each chocolate bar? (Give your answers to the nearest gram.)

Chocolate	Weight (grams)	Fat content (grams)	% fat
Kit Kit	21	5.5	
Malties	37	8.5	
Venus bar	65	11.4	
Cream egg	39	6.2	
Twicks	62	14.9	

Problem solving

3 Many food labels give the proportion of energy, protein, carbohydrate, fat, fibre and salt that the product contains.

a Which cereal contains the least amount of fat? Explain your answer.

b Which is the healthiest cereal to eat? Explain your answer.

c How much fat is there in a 40g serving of each cereal?

4 By 1997 about 45% of tropical rain forests had been destroyed around the world. Since then about 175 000 square kilometres have been destroyed every year, which represents about 1.1% of the remainder.

a Estimate the original area of rainforest.

b Estimate the current area.

c Estimate when the rainforests will disappear.

5 Wheat is sold in three different-sized sacks. Work out which size of sack is the best value for money. Explain your answer.

Sack A

Sack B

Sack C

15f Algebra and proportion

- Two quantities A and B are in direct proportion if, as they vary, they remain in the same ratio.
  - ▶ You can write $A \propto B$

The symbol $\propto$ means 'is directly proportional to'.

Example

Here is a recipe for 8 scones.
How much sugar is required to make 12 scones?

Recipe for 8 scones
50 g soft margarine
25 g sugar
200 g self-raising flour

number of scones $\propto$ amount of sugar

Let x be the amount of sugar for 12 scones. $\frac{x}{12} = \frac{25}{8}$ sugar is the numerator in both fractions.

sugar needed for 12 scones, $x = \frac{25 \times 12}{8}$

$= 37.5\text{ g}$

- The graph of two quantities that are in direct proportion is a straight line that passes through the origin.

Example

The table shows the conversion of pounds (£) to New Zealand dollars (NZ$).

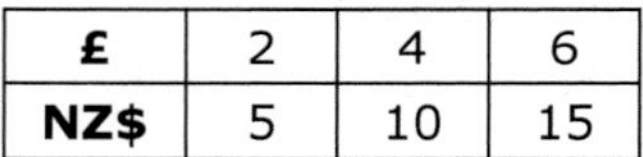

£	2	4	6
NZ$	5	10	15

a Use ratios to find the conversion rate between £ and NZ$.

b Draw a conversion graph and use it to estimate how many NZ$ you get for £5.

a £ : NZ$ = 2 : 5 = 1 : 2.5 The conversion rate is £1 = NZ$ 2.50.

b

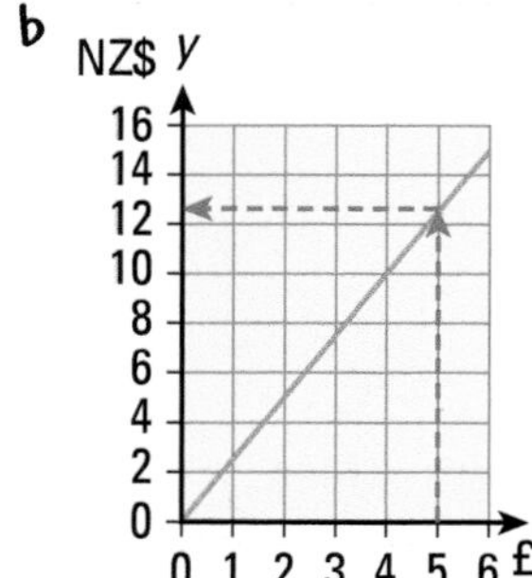

The gradient, $m = 2.5$.
For every 1 unit across you move 2.5 units up.

$c = 0$

The coordinates of the y-intercept are (0, 0).

Using $y = mx + c$, the line is $y = 2.5x$.
This is the conversion rate.

You get NZ$ 12.50 for £5.

Exercise 15f

1 Write whether these quantities are in direct proportion.

a The number of euros purchased for an amount of pounds sterling without a commission fee.

b Temperature in degrees Celsius and temperature in degrees Fahrenheit.

c The amount you earn and the number of years you have worked.

d The circumference and the diameter of a circle.

e The number of hours you spend on your maths homework and the number of marks you receive.

2 For each of these tables, use ratios to work out whether the two quantities are in direct proportion.

a

No. of hours worked	8	12	32
Amount earned in £	72	108	288

b

Length of rectangle, cm	10	15	50
Width of rectangle, cm	8	12	40

Problem solving

3 These are similar triangles.
This means that corresponding sides are in the same ratio.
Work out the height of the large triangle.

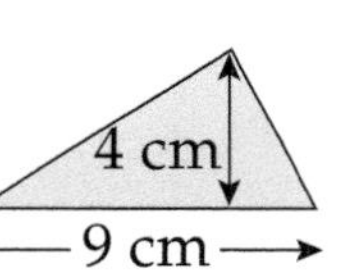

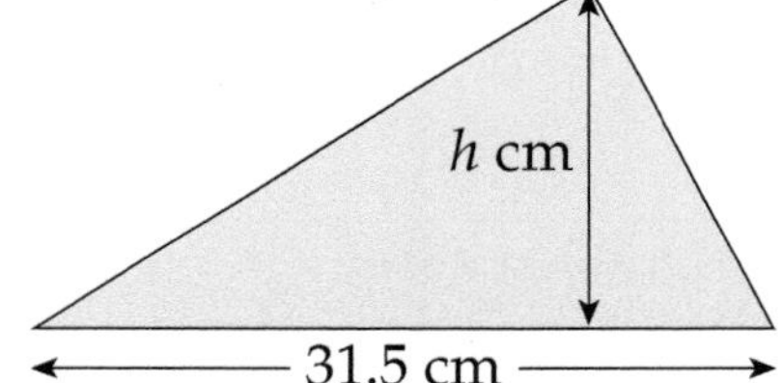

4 The exchange rate for pounds sterling (£) to euros (€) is £1 : € 1.25.

a Copy and complete this table of values.

£	1	4		16
€	1.25		10	

b Draw a conversion graph for £ (x) to € (y) at this exchange rate.

c Use your graph to convert
i £6 to € **ii** €18 to £

d Write the equation of your line.

e Use your equation to help you decide whether you would rather accept a gift of £75 or €100.

5 Two quantities are in **inverse proportion** when one increases at the same rate as the other decreases.
For example, the time a car journey takes is inversely proportional to the average speed of the car.
Suggest some other pairs of quantities that could be inversely proportional.

Check out

You should now be able to ...

Test it ➡ Questions

You should now be able to ...	Level	Questions
✓ Simplify and compare ratios.	6	1 – 2
✓ Divide a quantity in a given ratio.	7	3 – 4
✓ Use the unitary method to solve direct proportion problems.	7	5 – 6
✓ Solve ratio and proportion problems.	7	7 – 8
✓ Compare proportions.	7	9 – 11
✓ Describe quantities in direct proportion using an equation or a graph.	6	12

Language	Meaning	Example
Ratio	A ratio is the relative size of one value to another	1:5
Simplest form	A ratio in which all units and decimals have been removed and the parts have been divided by their HCF	3 : 6 : 27 becomes 1 : 2 : 9
Proportion	A part given as a fraction of the whole	Success is 99% perspiration and 1% inspiration
Direct proportion	Two quantities are in direct proportion if when one quantity increases, the other increases by the same fractional amount	If 10 units of something costs £180, then 15 units will cost £270.
Unitary method	A technique for solving problems in which you first find the value of one unit	5 apples cost £1.20 So 1 apple costs 24 p Hence 3 apples cost 72 p

15 MyReview

1 Write each of these ratios in its simplest form.

a 63 : 18 : 54 b 3.6 kg : 240 g

2 Express each of these ratios in the form 1 : n.

a 12 : 102 b 7 : 1344

3 Divide 500 m in the ratio 3 : 5.

4 Divide £80 in the ratio 2 : 5 : 4, give your answers to 2 dp.

5 14 bananas cost £2.10, what is the cost of 40 bananas?

6 A driver fills up the tank of her car so it has 75 litres of diesel. On a full tank she can drive 900 km.

a How far could her car travel on 65 litres of diesel?

b How much diesel would she need to travel 408 km?

7 A small-animal area at a farm has rabbits and guinea pigs.
$\frac{5}{9}$ of the small animals are rabbits.

a What is the ratio of rabbits to guinea pigs?

There are 15 rabbits.

b How many guinea pigs are there?

8 A meringue is made using egg white and sugar in the ratio
6 : 11. The white from one egg weighs 30 g. How much sugar do you need to make a meringue with 5 egg whites?

9 Davina is 1.6 m, her husband is 15% taller than her.
What is the ratio of Davina's height to her husband's? Write the ratio in its simplest form using whole numbers.

10 Cereal A contains 9 g of sugar per 30 g serving and Cereal B contains 11 g of sugar per 35 g serving. Which cereal is higher in sugar?

11 There are 42 members of a maths society. 18 of these are women, what percentage of the society are men?

12 The distance that Joyce has driven is directly proportional to the journey time. Use ratios to complete the table.

Distance travelled, miles		40		100
Journey time, minutes	30	60	90	

What next?

Score		
0 – 5		Your knowledge of this topic is still developing. To improve look at Formative test: 2C-15; MyMaths: 1036, 1037, 1038 and 1039
6 – 10		You are gaining a secure knowledge of this topic. To improve look at InvisiPen: 153, 191, 193 and 195
11 –12		You have mastered this topic. Well done, you are ready to progress!

15 MyPractice

1 Write each of these ratios in its simplest form.

a	0.4 : 3	**b**	0.6 : 5	**c**	1.2 : 4
d	2.5 : 4	**e**	1.8 : 2.8	**f**	3.2 : 4 : 4.8
g	2 : 3 : 4.5	**h**	1.6 : 2.4 : 6.4	**i**	0.6 m : 360 cm
j	2.2 kg : 1100 g	**k**	£3.75 : 90p	**l**	440 ml : 1.4 litres

2 Express each of these ratios in the form 1 : n.

a	3 : 15	**b**	8 : 12	**c**	10 : 25
d	9 : 12	**e**	15 : 21	**f**	5 : 19
g	6 : 21	**h**	15 : 100	**i**	7 : 12
j	26 : 9100	**k**	3.4 : 68 000	**l**	2.5 cm : 75 m

3 Divide these quantities in the ratios given.

a Divide 140 km in the ratio 2 : 5
b Divide £640 in the ratio 3 : 5
c Divide $728 in the ratio 6 : 7
d Divide 30 cm in the ratio 4 : 3
e Divide 7 MB in the ratio 8 : 7
f Divide €3000 in the ratio 4 : 2 : 1

4 **a** In a school, the ratio of boys to girls is 7 : 9. There are 371 boys at the school. How many girls are there at the school?

b A metal alloy is made from zinc and iron in the ratio 7 : 2. How much iron is needed to make 792 kg of the alloy?

c Gina draws a pie chart to show how the pupils in her school travel home. The pupils travel home by walking, bus or car in the ratio 7 : 3 : 2. How big are the angles she needs to draw for each of the three sectors?

15c

5 **a** 7 litres of petrol cost £7.91. What is the cost of 35 litres of petrol?

b There are 15 cakes in a box. The cakes weigh 420 g. What is the weight of 25 cakes?

c Rene's mobile phone contract means she pays £3.60 for 150 text messages.

i How much would Rene pay for 500 text messages?

ii How many text messages could she have for £2?

6 A wholesaler advertises the following prices for fruit.

Apricots	
3 kg	£22
10 kg	£70
40 kg	£275

Blueberries	
5 kg	£62.50
12 kg	£150
32 kg	£400

Cherries	
4 punnets	£16.50
24 punnets	£99
60 punnets	£247.50

Which of the prices are in direct proportion? Explain your answer.

15d

7 **a** An alloy is made from lead and iron in the ratio 4 : 7.
How much lead needs to be mixed with 8.4 kg of iron?

b The length and width of a netball court are in the ratio 9 : 5. The length of the court is 40.5 m. What is the width of the court?

c The ratio of pop music to rock music CDs in Jermal's collection is 4 : 11. If there are 28 pop music CDs, how many rock music CDs does Jermal have in his collection?

15d

8 **a** $\frac{2}{9}$ of the pupils at a school gym club are boys.
What is the ratio of boys to girls at the gym club?

b Roldova scores $\frac{7}{11}$ of the time he shoots at the goal.
What is Roldova's ratio of goals to missed shots?

c Hannah is 1.75 m tall. Ursula is 20% shorter than Hannah.
What is the ratio of Hannah's height to Ursula's height?

d A bow and set of arrows costs £40.50. The bow is $1\frac{1}{4}$ times the price of the arrows. How much did the bow cost?

15e

9 **a** Copy and complete the table.

b Which is the least healthy food to eat? Explain and justify your answer.

c Which is the most healthy food to eat? Explain and justify your answer.

d How many grams of fat would there be in 250 g of each food? (Give your answers to the nearest gram.)

Type of food	Weight (grams)	Fat content (grams)	%fat
Lamb chops	28	5	
Chocolate bar	26	4.3	
Crisps	35	11.6	
Burger and bun	215	23	
Peas	60	0.4	

15f

10 To convert miles to kilometres, you use the direct proportion relationship

5 miles = 8 kilometres

a Copy and complete this table of values.

Miles	5	7.5		20
Kilometres	8		16	

b Draw a graph to convert miles to kilometres.

c Use your graph to estimate how many kilometres are equivalent to 7 miles.

d Write the equation of your line.

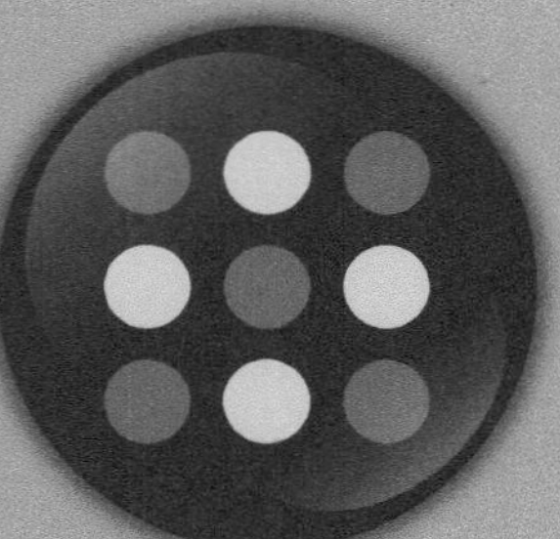

16 Probability

Introduction

In medicine, clinical trials are performed on large groups of people to test the safety and performance of new drugs. Statisticians have to make sure that the tests are fair, to tell if the new drug has worked. They do this by only giving the new drug to half of the people who are in the test. The rest of the people get a fake drug, called a placebo. The statisticians then compare the results of the two groups of people.

What's the point?

Probability is used widely to determine whether or not the findings of a clinical trial are the result of a genuine difference made by the new drug or whether it is just due to chance.

Objectives

By the end of this chapter, you will have learned how to ...

- Systematically list the outcomes for combined events.
- Use a tree diagram to list outcomes and calculate probabilities.
- Identify mutually exclusive events and calculate their probabilities.
- Estimate probabilities using experiments and compare the results to theoretical models.
- Use random numbers to simulate real world data.
- Use Venn diagrams to calculate probabilities.

Check in

1 Simplify

a $\frac{6}{8}$ b $\frac{85}{100}$

c $\frac{18}{27}$ d $\frac{21}{35}$

e $\frac{51}{85}$

2 Evaluate

a $\frac{3}{16} + \frac{4}{16}$ b $\frac{5}{16} + \frac{3}{8}$

c $\frac{3}{7} + \frac{5}{21}$ d $\frac{1}{3} + \frac{1}{5} + \frac{1}{7}$

e $1 - \frac{1}{3} - \frac{2}{5}$

3 A bag contains sweets. There are as many mints as jelly beans. Complete this table.

	Fraction	**Percentage**	**Decimal**
Liquorice		25%	
Chocolate button	$\frac{7}{20}$		
Toffee			0.15
Mint			
Jelly bean			

4 Estimate these probabilities

a obtaining an odd number on the roll of a fair die.

b that you get heads tossing a biased coin if P(tails) = 0.45

c that you get a head and tail when you toss two fair coins.

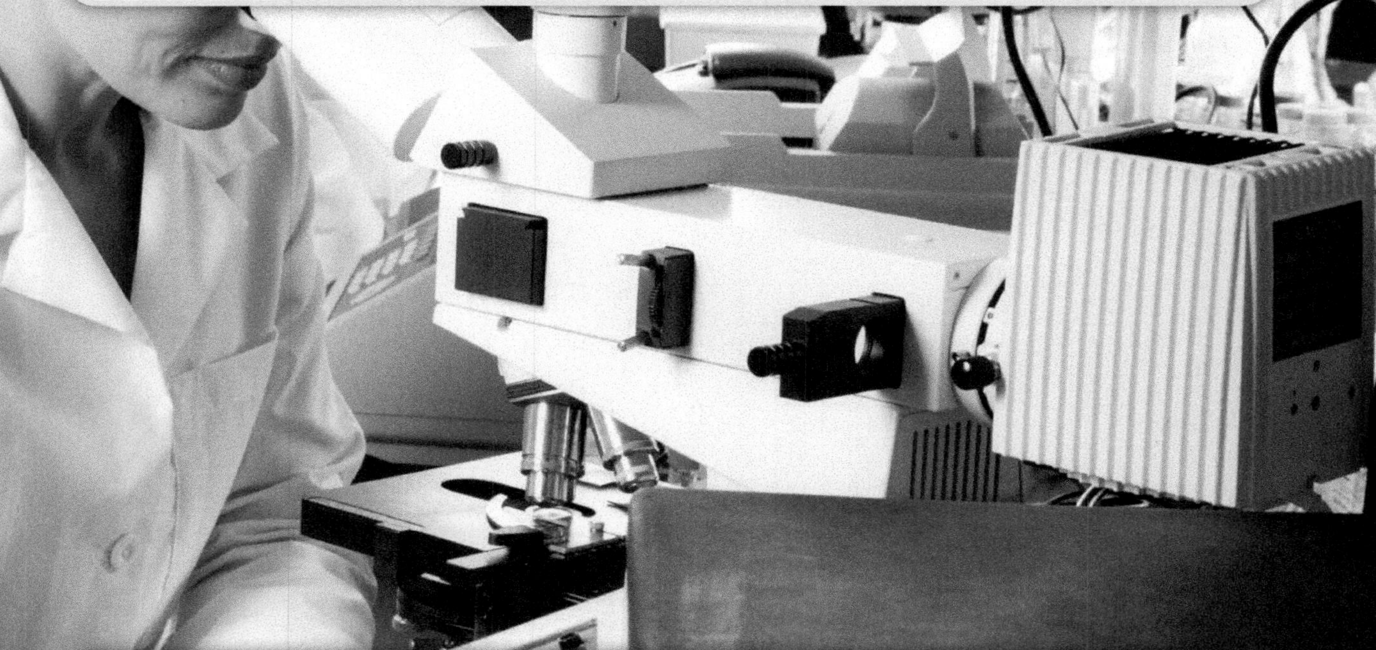

Starter problem

Inside a bag are three cards with the numbers 1, 2 and 3 written on them.
You are allowed to pick one card from the bag and then replace the card in the bag.
What is the probability you pick the same number twice?

16a Two or more events

- A list of all the possible **outcomes** of an event or combination of events is called the **sample space**.

Example

A restaurant offers a set meal.
How many meal combinations could I choose?

Number of combinations $= 2 \times 3$
$= 6$

I could have either the soup or the pate with any one of the three main courses.

- Probability $= \dfrac{\text{favourable outcomes}}{\text{all outcomes}}$

- A table is useful way to show a sample space when two events have **equally likely** outcomes.

Outcomes that occur with the same probability are called equally likely outcomes.

Example

Two fair dice are thrown.

a Show all possible outcomes in a table.

b Calculate the probability of getting a total score of 5.

a

	1	2	3	4	5	6
1	1,1	1,2	1,3	1,4	1,5	1,6
2	2,1	2,2	2,3	2,4	2,5	2,6
3	3,1	3,2	3,3	3,4	3,5	3,6
4	4,1	4,2	4,3	4,4	4,5	4,6
5	5,1	5,2	5,3	5,4	5,5	5,6
6	6,1	6,2	6,3	6,4	6,5	6,6

Each of the 36 outcomes is equally likely.

You write P(A) for the probability that the event A occurs.

b

Sum	1	2	3	4	5	6
1	2	3	4	5	6	7
2	3	4	5	6	7	8
3	4	5	6	7	8	9
4	5	6	7	8	9	10
5	6	7	8	9	10	11
6	7	8	9	10	11	12

The sum of the two scores is shown in each of the 36 cells.
Those with a total of 5 are shaded pink.

$P(\text{Sum} = 5) = \dfrac{4}{36}$

$= \dfrac{1}{9}$

Exercise 16a

1 Two fair coins are tossed.

- **a** Give a systematic listing of all the possible outcomes.
- **b** Give the probabilities of obtaining
  - **i** 0 heads **ii** 1 head
  - **iii** 2 heads.
- **c** How can you check your answers to part **b**?

2 A fair coin is tossed three times.

- **a** List all the possible outcomes.
- **b** In how many of these are
  - **i** exactly 2 heads seen
  - **ii** at least 2 heads seen?
- **c** What is the probability of getting exactly 2 heads when 3 fair coins are tossed?

Problem solving

3 Anneka goes on a weekend break taking 1 skirt, 3 pairs of trousers and 4 tops. How many different combinations can she wear of a top with either a skirt or trousers?

4 Anil is buying an ice-cream. He has to choose between having it in a cone or a tub, whether to have vanilla or strawberry fl vour or both and whether to have a fla e, sprinkles or nothing.
Make a list of all the possible combinations he could choose.

5 Two fair dice are thrown.

- **a** Construct a sample space diagram which shows the higher score showing on the two dice.
- **b** What is the probability that the higher score showing is a 4?

6 The set menu in a restaurant has these options. How many menu combinations are possible for someone

- **a** who has no restrictions on what they will eat
- **b** who does not like cheese
- **c** who is a vegetarian?

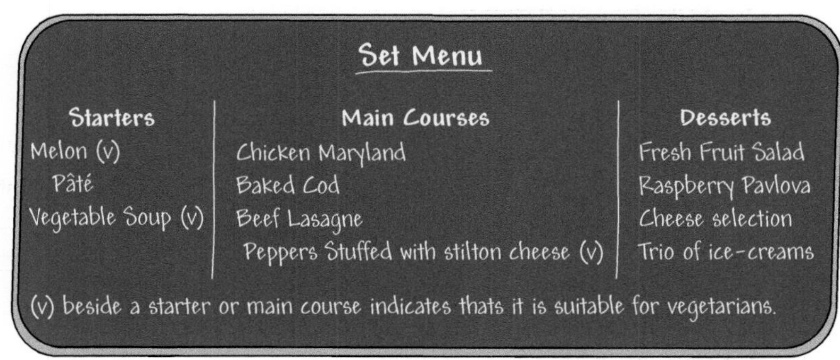

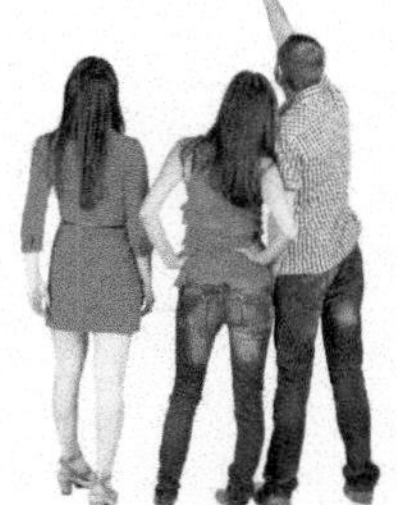

16b Tree diagrams

A **tree diagram** can be used to show a sample space.

This representation is useful when you have two or more events or when the outcomes are not equally likely.

Example

Archie wins a competition and gets to pick one of three identical envelopes which contain £100, £200 or £300. He then must flip coin. If it lands on heads, he doubles his prize money. If it lands on tails, he wins nothing.

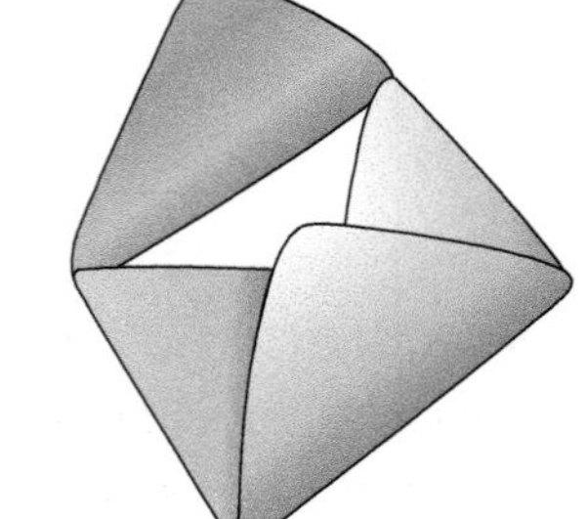

a Show all the possible outcomes in a tree diagram.

b **i** What is the probability that he wins a least £300?

ii What is the probability that he wins nothing?

---

a

Envelope	Double money?
£100	No £0
	Yes £200
£200	No £0
	Yes £400
£300	No £0
	Yes £600

Label each tier of branches. Write the outcomes at the ends of the branches.

b **i** P(wins $\geq$ £300) $= \frac{2}{6} = \frac{1}{3}$

ii P(wins nothing) $= \frac{3}{6} = \frac{1}{2}$

He will go along exactly one of the six routes and each are equally likely, $P = \frac{1}{6}$.

The outcomes at the end of each set of branches are all distinct and can only be reached via one route through the tree. You select either the £100, £200 or £300 envelope and then either double your prize money or end up with nothing.

Exercise 16b

1 A bag contains one red, one blue and one green ball which are identical except for their colours. A ball is taken out, its colour noted and it is put back in the bag. Then a second ball is taken out.

  a Draw a tree diagram to show all the possibilities for the colours of the two balls.

  b **i** What is the probability that red is seen at least once?

  ii What is the probability that green is not seen?

2 Repeat question **1** but this time assume that the first ball is not put back in the bag.

Problem solving

3 The journey Ms Atmar takes to school goes through two sets of traffic lights

  a Draw a tree diagram to show all the possibilities for having to 'stop' or 'go' at the two sets of lights.

  She notices that the first set of lights is on red $\frac{1}{3}$ of the time and the second $\frac{2}{5}$ of the time.

  b If she makes 150 journeys to school in a year, add to the label at the end of each branch the number of journeys that satisfy the conditions for that branch.

  c Using your results from part **b** calculate the probabilities that she stops at

  i neither set of lights

  ii one set of lights

  iii both sets of lights.

> 50 journeys will involve stopping at the first set of lights

4 In the example on the opposite page, if Archie could open the envelope before deciding whether to accept the 'double or nothing' option, what would you advise him to do?

5 **a** A biased coin is twice as likely to show a head as a tail. Calculate **i** P(head) **ii** P(tail)

  b In an experiment the biased coin is tossed three times. Draw a tree diagram to show all the possible outcomes for the experiment.

  c The experiment is repeated 27 times. Add labels to the end of each branch to show the number of times that you expect each outcome to occur.

  d Using your results from part **b** calculate

  i P(0 heads) **ii** P(1 head) **iii** P(2 heads) **iv** P(3 heads)

Did you know?

A famous conundrum in probability is the 'Monty Hall problem'. In one of three envelopes is a prize. You choose one envelope. Monty then opens one of the others and it is empty. Should you now pick the other envelope?

16c Mutually exclusive outcomes

- Two outcomes are **mutually exclusive** if they cannot happen at the same time.

Example

You throw a dice. Which pairs of these events are mutually exclusive?

A: an odd number B: a factor of 6 C: a multiple of 4

A = {1, 3, 5} B = {1, 2, 3, 6} C = {4}

A and C together with B and C are mutually exclusive.

A and B are not mutually exclusive.

A and B both occur if a 1 or a 3 is thrown.

- If a set of mutually exclusive events covers all possible outcomes then their sum of probabilities is 1.

A special case is P(not A) = 1 − P(A)

Example

Emily rolls two fair dice and is interested in whether they show a 5 or 6.

a Illustrate the outcomes using a sample space diagram.

b Calculate the probabilities that

i neither dice shows 5 or 6 **ii** both dice show 5 or 6

iii only one dice shows 5 or 6 **iv** at least one dice shows 5 or 6

a

	1	**2**	**3**	**4**	**5**	**6**
1	1, 1	1, 2	1, 3	1, 4	1, 5	1, 6
2	2, 1	2, 2	2, 3	2, 4	2, 5	2, 6
3	3, 1	3, 2	3, 3	3, 4	3, 5	3, 6
4	4, 1	4, 2	4, 3	4, 4	4, 5	4, 6
5	5, 1	5, 2	5, 3	5, 4	5, 5	5, 6
6	6, 1	6, 2	6, 3	6, 4	6, 5	6, 6

Check: since the four outcomes are mutually exclusive $\frac{1}{9} + \frac{2}{9} + \frac{2}{9} + \frac{4}{9} = 1$, which is the total probability

b **i** P(neither dice shows 5 or 6) blue cells

$= \frac{16}{36} = \frac{4}{9}$

ii P(both dice show 5 or 6) green cells

$= \frac{4}{36} = \frac{1}{9}$

iii P(only one dice shows 5 or 6) purple cells and yellow cells

= P(fir t dice shows a 5 or 6 and second does not)

+ P(second dice shows a 5 or 6 and fir t does not)

$= \frac{8}{36} + \frac{8}{36} = \frac{4}{9}$

iv P(at least one dice shows 5 or 6)

= 1 − P (neither dice shows 5 or 6)

$= 1 - \frac{4}{9} = \frac{5}{9}$

Exercise 16c

1 For each of the following pairs of events say whether or not they are mutually exclusive.

a **i** March 2nd will be the hottest day of next year.

ii it will snow on March 2nd next year.

b The total score when three ordinary dice are thrown will be

i prime **ii** even.

c A rugby player can play international rugby for

i New Zealand **ii** Ireland.

2 A red and a blue dice are thrown together.

a Which pairs of the following events are mutually exclusive?

A the sum of the scores is odd

B the red and the blue dice show the same score

C the total score is less than 5

D the red dice is at least 3 more than the blue dice.

b Give three more pairs of mutually exclusive events.

Define a y new events that you use.

3 A dice is thrown twice, and whether the score is even or odd is recorded each time.

a Draw a sample space diagram to represent this situation.

b Calculate the probability that the **product** of the scores showing is even.

c Using the answer to part **b**, write down the probability that the product of the scores is odd.

4 A fair coin is tossed three times.

a Draw a tree diagram to show all the possible outcomes.

b Use your tree diagram to calculate the probability of getting

i exactly 2 heads. **ii** at least 2 heads.

c The event 'not at least 2 heads' is the same as '0 or 1 head'.

i Use the tree diagram to calculate the probability of getting 0 or 1 head.

ii Show that this equals 1 − P(at least 2 heads).

d P(3 heads) = P(0 heads) and P(2 heads) = P(1 head).

Explain why.

Problem solving

Hint: look back at the list in questions **1** and **2**, lesson **16a**

5 *Without* making a new list, answer the following.

a **i** If I toss a coin 4 times and list all possible outcomes, how many are there?

ii How many of these would have exactly 1 head?

b If the coin was tossed 5 times, how many possible outcomes would there be?

How many of these would have exactly 1 head?

c Can you **generalise** the number of outcomes for *n* tosses of a coin? How many of these outcomes would have exactly one head?

16d Experimental probability

It is not always possible to calculate probabilities using reasoning.

Experiments are sometimes called trials.

- To estimate a probability, repeat an experiment several times and calculate the proportion of successes.

Experimental probability $= \dfrac{\text{number of successes}}{\text{number of trials}}$

Example

Hans is a zoologist who wants to know the relative sizes of the populations of three species of African monkeys, labelled A, B and C.
He records 60 observations.

a Estimate the proportions of each species.

b How could Hans get better estimates?

c Out of another 120 monkeys, Hans counted 62 As, 47 Bs and 11 Cs.
Give the best estimate you can now of the proportions.

---

a Number A = 26 Best estimate $= \dfrac{26}{60} = 43\%$

B = 27 $= \dfrac{27}{60} = 45\%$

C = 7 $= \dfrac{7}{60} = 12\%$

b If Hans took a larger sample, he is more likely to get estimates close to the true proportions.

c Combining the two samples gives the best estimates.

Number A = 26 + 62 = 88 Best estimate $= \dfrac{88}{180} = 49\%$

B = 27 + 47 = 74 $= \dfrac{74}{180} = 41\%$

C = 7 + 11 = 18 $= \dfrac{18}{180} = 10\%$

There are about 50%, 40% and 10% of the three species of monkey.

If Hans recorded another 60 observations, it is almost certain that he would get different results. o it doesn't make sense to give exact values, like 43.3%.

- The larger the sample size, the more accurate the estimated probabilities are likely to be.

You can also use historical data to estimate probabilities.

Computer **simulations** are now widely used to estimate probabilities of complicated sequences of events, where it is too difficult to calculate the theoretical probability by a tree diagram or similar method.

Exercise 16d

1 Keith has a swipe card to enter the building he works in. The system records the time the card is first used each d y. He is supposed to be at work by 8.30 am. Over a month the times recorded were:

8.27	8.24	8.27	8.31	8.30	8.26	8.25	8.29	8.32	8.26	8.28
8.31	8.25	8.27	8.26	8.35	8.26	8.24	8.27	8.27	8.25	8.27

Estimate the probability that Keith is late for work on a randomly chosen day.

Problem solving

2 **a** Make up a tally chart and frequency table for the number of times the vowels (a, e, i, o and u) appear on the page facing this one.

b Give an estimate of the probability of a vowel in English being an 'e'.

3 Choose another page from this book at random.

a Would you expect the proportion of vowels which are 'e' to be the same on that page?

b Repeat question 2 for that page.

c Is the answer the same?

d How could you get a more reliable estimate of the probability of a vowel being an 'e'?

Did you know?

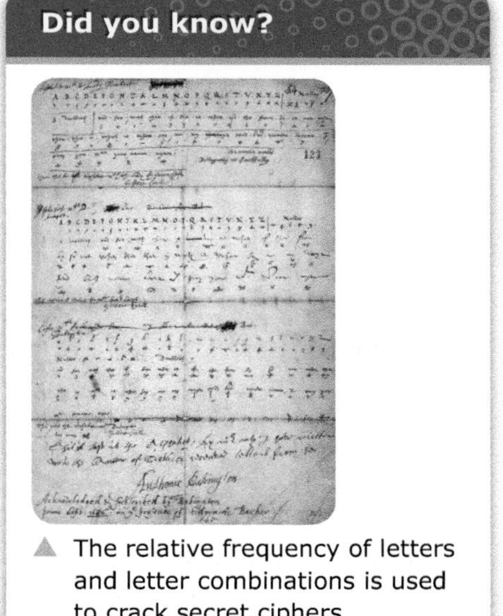

▲ The relative frequency of letters and letter combinations is used to crack secret ciphers.

4 **a** What is the probability that the page number of a page chosen at random from the first chapter of this book will contain the digit 1?

b Could this be used as an estimate of the probability that a page chosen at random from the book will contain the digit 1?

5 How could you estimate the probability of

a being struck by lightning tomorrow

b it raining on your next birthday

c Liverpool winning the next football league title?

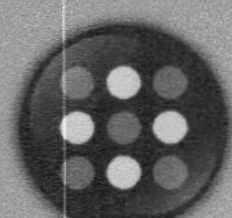

16e Comparing experimental and theoretical probability

Example

A coin is tossed 40 times and shows 18 heads and 22 tails.

a Do these results suggest the coin is biased?

b If it is tossed another 40 times, will it show 18 heads again?

a No. On average a fair coin will show 20 heads in 40 tosses, but anything between about 15 and 25 heads will be seen quite frequently in 40 tosses of a fair coin.

b It is possible to get 18 heads again but not very likely.

In fact there is about a 10% chance of getting 18 heads in 40 tosses of a fair coin.

- The more data used to estimate an **experimental probability**, the more reliable is the result.

Example

Harriet is an archaeologist studying skeletons found at an ancient burial site. It is known that people who lived in that area had head circumferences in three size categories which occurred in the proportions:

A 20% B 50% C 30%

Historians speculate that the area was invaded about this time.

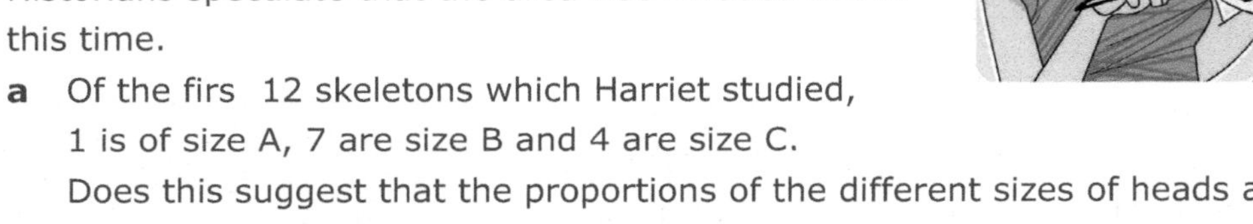

a Of the firs 12 skeletons which Harriet studied, 1 is of size A, 7 are size B and 4 are size C.
Does this suggest that the proportions of the different sizes of heads are different from the known population of the area?

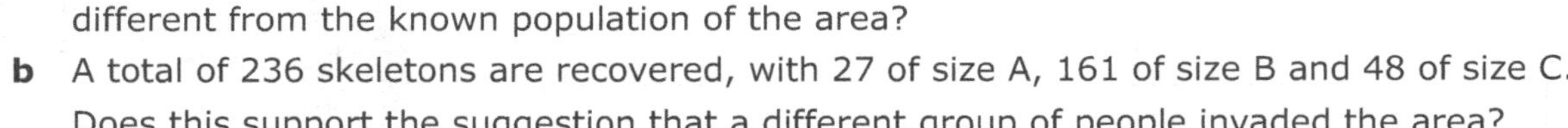

b A total of 236 skeletons are recovered, with 27 of size A, 161 of size B and 48 of size C.
Does this support the suggestion that a different group of people invaded the area?

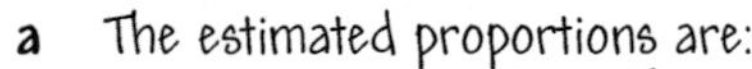

a The estimated proportions are:

A $\frac{1}{12} = 8\%$ B $\frac{7}{12} = 58\%$ C $\frac{4}{12} = 33\%$

It is not possible to say anything strong in support of a differenc , because there are only 12 skeletons.

b The estimated proportions are:

A $\frac{27}{236} = 11\%$ B $\frac{161}{236} = 68\%$ C $\frac{48}{236} = 20\%$

The evidence suggests that the people were not from the local population.

These are based on a small **sample** and so the estimates are not reliable: one skeleton is 8% of the sample.

These are based on a large sample so the estimates should be close to the true proportions: one skeleton is 0.4% of the sample.

Exercise 16e

Problem solving

1 Darrell says that the chance of getting 1 head when you toss 2 fair coins is $\frac{1}{3}$. Ekaterina says he is wrong, and she will prove it to him. She tosses a pair of fair coins 40 times and the table shows the outcomes.

Number of heads	0	1	2
Frequency	8	21	11

a Do you think Darrell is right that the probability of getting 1 head is $\frac{1}{3}$?

b Has Ekaterina proved that Darrell is wrong?

2 Dr McDonald is overseeing a drug trial. He has given one group of patients drug A, another drug B and a third group a placebo. His results are shown in the table.

	Drug A	Drug B	Placebo
Number in trial	96	10	36
Number cured	72	7	17

Write a short report for Dr McDonald saying whether you think the drugs are effective and how a future drug trial might be improved.

A placebo is a 'dummy' medicine.

3 Kenny is testing a set of roulette wheels to see if they are biased. He spins each wheel 60 times and records how often the ball lands in one of three groups of numbers.

	1–12	13–24	25–36
Wheel 1	23	22	15
Wheel 2	17	19	22
Wheel 3	16	17	27
Wheel 4	20	18	22

▲ A European roulette wheel has numbers from 0 to 36 equally spaced around its edge.

a Calculate the theoretical probability of landing in each of the three groups of numbers.

b For each wheel, calculate the experimental probabilities of landing in each of the three groups of numbers.

c Should Kenny recommend that the casino continues to use these wheels?

d For each wheel, do the experimental probabilities add up to 1? If not, why not?

4 If Ekaterina had tossed the pair of coins 4000 times in question **1**, could this have provided a **proof** that Darrell is wrong?
Can you think of any way to provide a proof in a situation like this?

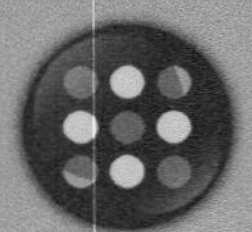

16f Simulating experimental data

Sometimes it is too difficult to calculate probabilities using reasoning. However it may be possible to use a **model** to **simulate** the physical situation.

A model is a set of rules to describe a situation.

A simulation is an implementation of the rules.

Mathematical models are now used widely. Examples include studying the aerodynamics of vehicles, the behaviour of financial mar ets, the growth of cancer cells, climate change,...

- The random number button on a calculator generates numbers between 0 and 1 in such a way that each number is equally likely.

Example

Describe how you could use a calculator to simulate the outcome of rolling a fair dice 10 times.

1 Generate a random number 

2 If the tenths digit is 1, 2,...6 use this as the dice's score, otherwise generate a new random number.

3 Repeat until you have 10 scores.

For example
0.3247668 → 3
0.0982445 → reject

A computer simulation using random numbers is highly unlikely to give the same results twice.

- A simulation should be run several times to see how the values vary.

Example

A simulation of rolling a dice ten times is repeated ten times and the number of occasions when a prime factor of 12 appears is recorded.

2, 4, 3, 6, 4, 7, 3, 4, 4, 5

a Calculate the theoretical probability of getting a prime factor of 12.

b Estimate the same probability using the results of the simulation.

c Do you think a fair dice was being simulated?

a P(prime factor of 12) = P(2 or 3) = $\frac{2}{6} = \frac{1}{3}$

b Each individual simulation gives probabilities $\frac{2}{10} = 0.2$, $\frac{4}{10} = 0.4$, ..., $\frac{5}{10} = 0.5$

A better estimate is to take the mean of the ten simulations.

Best estimate P(prime factor of 12) = $\frac{(0.2 + 0.4 + \cdots + 0.5)}{10} = \frac{4.2}{10} = 0.42$

The range of the estimates is 0.7 − 0.2 = 0.5

The theoretical probability for a fair dice is 0.3 which is close to most of the values obtained. Therefore it is reasonable to think that a fair dice was being simulated.

Exercise 16f

1 For each simulation write out the rules used.

   a Use a calculator to simulate tossing a fair coin ten times.

   b Use a calculator to simulate tossing a biased coin ten times if

      i P(heads) = 0.6

      ii P(heads) = $\frac{1}{3}$

2 **a** Estimate P(heads) using your results from question **1b i**.

   b Repeat part **a** of this question nine more times. Do you get the same estimate for P(heads) each time? If not, why not?

   c What is the best estimate of P(heads) using your simulated data?

Problem solving

3 **a** Using your ten experiments from questions **1a** and **2b** estimate the probability of getting a run of three or more consecutive heads.

   b How do you expect this probability to depend on P(heads)?

4 A coin is tossed 10 times and the number of heads recorded. The result of 30 repeat experiments is shown in the bar chart on the left. A simulation using P(heads) = 0.5 is shown on the right.

Did you know?

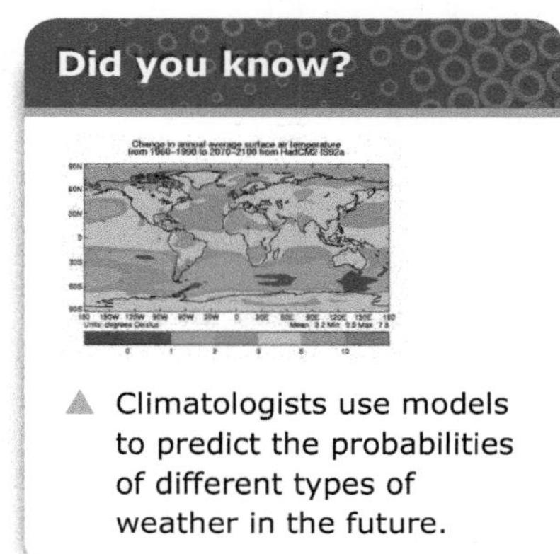

▲ Climatologists use models to predict the probabilities of different types of weather in the future.

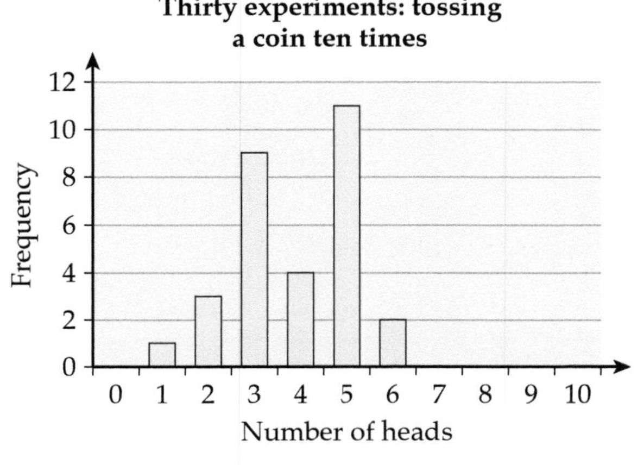

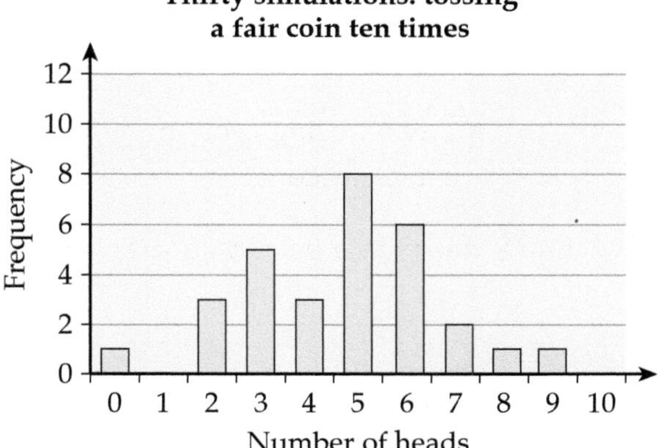

Do you think that the coin used in the experiment is biased?
Explain your reasoning.

5 By using a simulation or otherwise, investigate the effect of changing P(heads) on the number of heads obtained when tossing a coin ten times.
Describe what you find
Using the results from your investigation, estimate P(heads) for the coin used in the experiment in question **4**.

16g Venn diagrams and probability

- The **universal set,** symbol Ω, is the set containing all the elements.

Example

Ω = {2, 3, 6, 7, 11, 15}, P = {prime numbers} and E = {even numbers}

a Write the elements of P ∩ E.

b Write the elements of P ∪ E.

c Which element is in P′ ∩ E′?

---

a P ∩ E = {2}

b P ∪ E = {2, 3, 6, 7, 11}

c 15

Remember ∩ means intersection, ∪ means union and ′ means complement.

- You can use Venn diagrams to work out probabilities.

$$P(A) = \frac{\text{number of elements in set A}}{\text{total number of elements}}$$

P(a) = 1 − P(a′)

Example

Abi sorted the 24 students in her form group into the sets F = {studies French} and G = {studies German}.

She showed her results on a Venn diagram.

a Shade the region F ∩ G′.

b Find P(F ∩ G′)

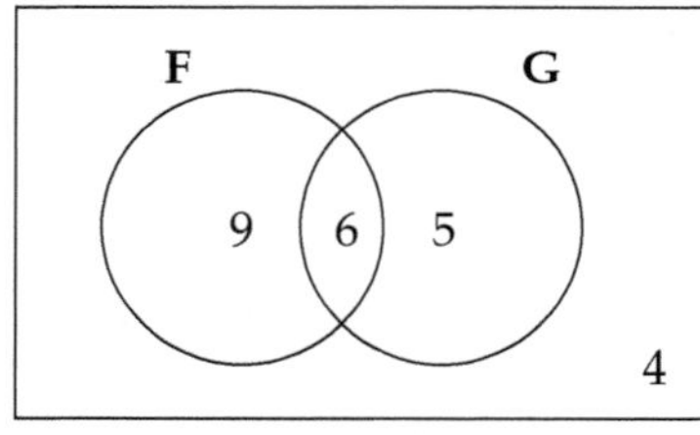

---

a Shade F using vertical lines.

Shade G′ using horizontal lines.

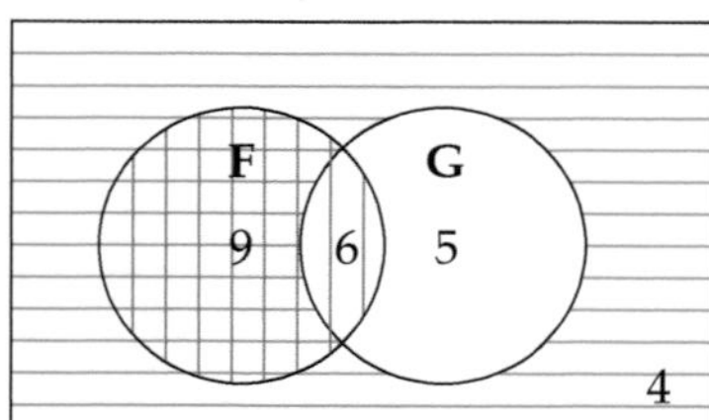

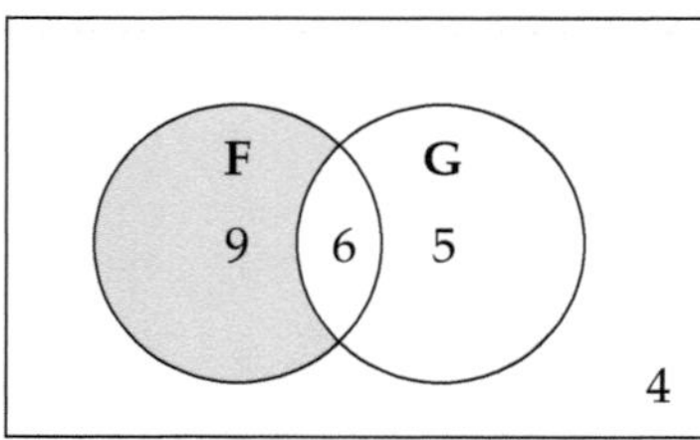

The shading overlaps in the intersection.

b $P(F \cap G') = \frac{9}{24} = \frac{3}{8}$

Exercise 16g

1 For the following sets

a Ω = {whole numbers from 1 to 12},
A = {multiples of 3} and
B = {3, 7, 9, 10, 11}

b Ω = {1,2,3,5,8,13,21,34,55},
A = {numbers less than 20} and
B = {factors of 24}

c Ω = {whole numbers from 1 to 16},
A = {odd numbers} and
B = {prime numbers}

list the elements in

i	A	**ii**	A′	**iii**	B′
iv	A ∩ B	**v**	A ∪ B	**vi**	A ∩ B′.

2 Malik investigates how students in his class keep in touch with their friends after school. He sorts his results into
S = {social media} and T = {texting}.

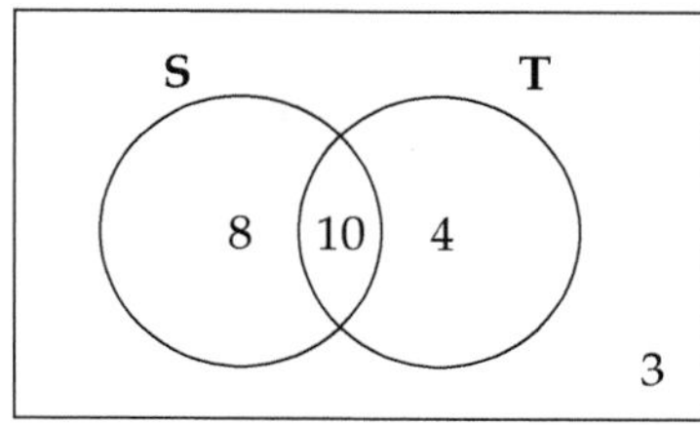

a Find P(S ∩ T).

b Shade the region S ∩ T′.

c Find P(S ∩ T′).

c Shade the region S′ ∩ T′.

e Find P(S′ ∩ T′).

Problem solving

3 Miss Perry is organising a school trip to France.
Her students can sign up to take part in two different activities, a trip to a waterpark or going to the beach.
She shows the results on a Venn diagram.
The trip to the waterpark costs £11 and the trip to the beach costs £7.
Miss Perry collects £393 to pay for the activities.
How many students signed up for both activities?

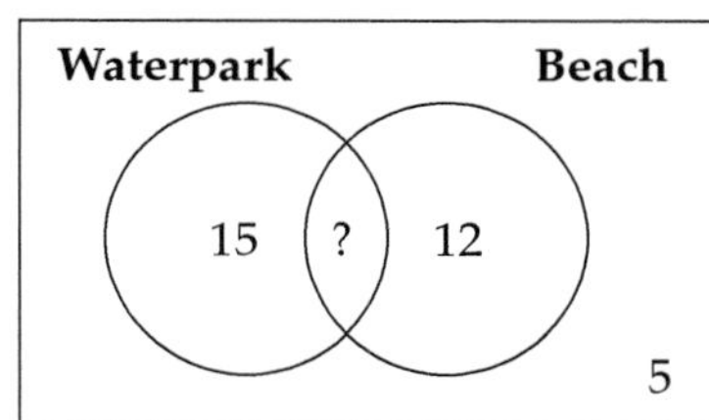

4 Ella has fi e fact cards about a Venn diagram.

Hint: Use the fact that A · B and A′ · B′ are complements.

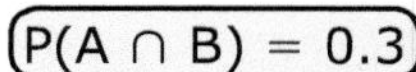

P(A) = 0.5

P(B) = 0.7

P(A ∪ B) = 0.9

There are 2 elements in A′ ∩ B′.

Draw Ella's Venn diagram showing the numbers of elements in each region.

16 MySummary

Check out

You should now be able to ...

Test it ➡ Questions

You should now be able to ...	Grade	Questions
✓ Systematically list the outcomes for combined events.	6	1 – 2
✓ Use tree diagrams to list outcomes and calculate probabilities.	6	3
✓ Identify mutually exclusive events and calculate their probabilities.	6	4
✓ Estimate probabilities using experiments and compare the results to theoretical models.	7	5 – 6
✓ Use random numbers to simulate real world data.	7	7
✓ Use Venn diagrams to calculate probabilities.	7	8

Language	Meaning	Example
Sample space	A list of all the simplest outcomes of an event or combination of events	If you toss 2 coins the outcomes are HH, HT, TH, TT
Independent probability	Two events are said to be independent if and only if the occurrence of one event happening has absolutely no effect on the chances of the other event happening	What you have for tea and who wins the next World Cup
Mutually exclusive outcomes	Outcomes are mutually exclusive if they cannot happen at the same time	Rolling a dice once and getting a 6 and a 2
Relative frequency	The empirical probability of an event, based on the actual frequency relative to the total possible frequencies	If you have 10 hurdles to jump and succeed at jumping 8, your relative frequency is 80%
Experimental probability	$\text{P(event)} = \dfrac{\text{number of times the event occurs}}{\text{number of trials}}$	$\text{P(heads)} = \dfrac{28}{50}$ $= 0.56 = 56\%$
Simulation and Model	Simulation is the imitation of the operation of a real-world process or system over time. The act of simulating something first requires that a model be developed; this model represents the key characteristics of the selected physical or abstract system or process. The model represents the system itself, whereas the simulation represents the operation of the system over time	Computer simulations are a key feature of most of the working world and the gaming industry

1 Jack has a drawer of loose socks. There are lots of black, grey and brown socks. He selects two socks at random. List of all the possible combinations he could choose.

2 Two fair dice are thrown.

a Construct a sample space diagram which shows the difference between the two scores.

b Calculate the probability of getting a difference of 2.

3 The letters from the word CAT are written on individual cards. One card is selected at random then replaced and another card is selected.

a Draw a tree diagram to show all the possibilities outcomes for the two cards.

b What is the probability of drawing the same letter twice?

c What is the probability of drawing the letter C at least once?

4 Two dice are thrown. Are the following pairs of events mutually exclusive?

a *'One of the dice shows a 2.'* and *'The sum of both dice is 9.'*

b *'The product of the two dice is odd.'* and *'The sum of the two dice is even.'*

c *'The difference between the two dice is 1.'* and *'The sum of the two dice is greater than 4.'*

5 A librarian observes that 72 men and 105 women use his library on one particular day.

a Estimate the probability that a visitor to the library is a man.

b The next day there are 250 visitors to the library. Estimate how many will be women.

6 A dice is rolled 20 times and 8 sixes are scored.

a Calculate the experimental probability of scoring a six

b Assuming the dice is fair what is the theoretical probability of scoring a six?

c Does this prove the dice is not fair? Explain your answer.

7 A biased coin has P(heads) = 0.6

a Explain how you could simulate tossing the coin 10 times.

b Explain how you could estimate the probability of getting more than 5 heads in 10 tosses of the coin.

8 **a** Draw a Venn diagram to show the following sets.

Ω = {Whole numbers from 1 to 16}

A = {Factors of 48}

B = {Multiples of 3}

b List the elements in

i A **ii** B **iii** A'

iv $A \cap B$ **v** $A \cup B$ **vi** $A \cap B'$

c Find the probability of each of the sets listed in part **b**.

What next?

Score		
0 – 3		Your knowledge of this topic is still developing. To improve look at Formative test: 2C-16; MyMaths: 1199, 1211, 1262, 1264, 1921, 1922 and 1954
4 – 6		You are gaining a secure knowledge of this topic. To improve look at InvisiPen: 454, 461, 463 and 466
7 – 8		You have mastered this topic. Well done, you are ready to progress!

16a

1 A spinner with 3 equal sections coloured red, green and white is spun twice.

a List all the possible outcomes.

b In how many of these do you get a red and a green?

c In how many of these do you not get a white?

2 Two fair dice are thrown.

a Construct a sample space diagram which shows the product of the scores showing on the two dice.

b What is the probability that the product is at least 20?

3 A lunch menu includes 3 starters, 4 main courses and 2 desserts. How many different menu combinations are there for someone who can eat anything on the menu?

16b

4 A bag contains one black, one white and one purple ball which are identical except for their colours. A ball is taken out, its colour noted and then replaced before a second ball is taken out.

a Draw a tree diagram to show the possibilities of the colours of the two balls.

b **i** What is the probability that the two balls are a black and a white?

ii What is the probability that the two balls are the same colour?

16c

5 A white and a black dice are thrown together and the events A to D are define as

A the sum of the scores is even

B the white and the black dice show different scores

C the total score is less than 3

D the difference between the scores is not more than 1.

Explain why these pairs of events are mutually exclusive or not

i A and B **ii** B and D **iii** B and C

6 The faces of a regular tetrahedron are labelled 1–4 and those of a regular octahedron 1–8. They are both rolled and the number on the bottom face is counted.

a List all possible outcomes.

b Use your list to calculate the probabilities that

i both show prime numbers **ii** only one shows a prime number.

c Without looking at your list, what is the probability that neither shows a prime number?

16d

7 Jorge is making stakes which should be about 1.3 m long.
The lengths of a number of stakes he has made are listed below.
1.27, 1.24, 1.27, 1.31, 1.30, 1.26, 1.25, 1.29, 1.32, 1.26, 1.28
1.31, 1.25, 1.27, 1.26, 1.35, 1.26, 1.24, 1.27, 1.27, 1.25, 1.27

a Estimate the probability that one of his stakes is longer than 1.3 m.

b Explain how a better estimate of this probability could be made.

8 How could you estimate the following probabilities?

a A vowel chosen at random in French is an `a´.

b The National Lottery has a single jackpot winner in the next draw.

c Seeing at least 1 six when 3 dice are thrown together.

16e

9 A trainee in a bank is surprised at how often transactions he sees start with the digit 1. He does a quick tally of 100 transactions.

first digit	1	2	3	4	5	6	7	8	9
frequency	33	19	14	10	6	5	3	4	6

Do you think 1 to 9 are equally likely to occur as the first digit of t ansactions?

16f

10 An otherwise fair dice is biased so that 5 and 6 are both three times as likely to occur as the digits 1–4.

a What are the individual probabilities of obtaining the numbers 1–6?

b Use a calculator to simulate rolling such a dice three times. Write down the rules which you use and your results.

c Repeat your simulation nine more times and use the results to estimate the average sum of the three scores.

d How could you improve the accuracy of your estimate?

16g

11 Rufus is investigating his classmates. He counts the number of students with red hair (R), freckles (F), both or neither. The Venn diagram shows his results.

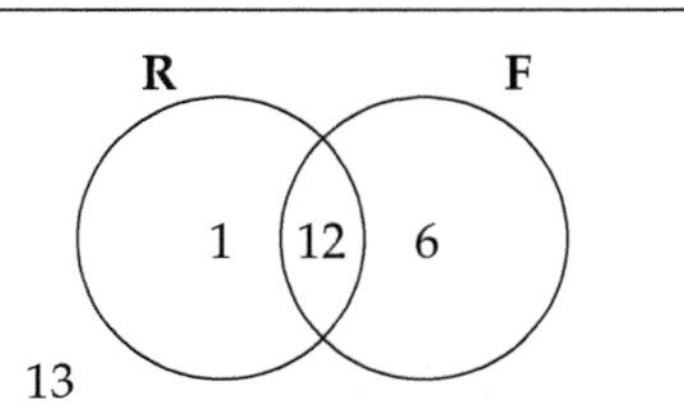

a **i** On a copy of the diagram, shade the region $R \cap F$.

ii Find $P(R \cap F)$.

b **i** On a second copy of the diagram, shade the region $R' \cap F$.

ii Find $P(R' \cap F)$.

Case study 6: Free-range

Free-range eggs are laid by free-range hens. Strict rules must be obeyed for hens to be called 'Free-range.'

Free-range rules

Outside: 1 hen to every 4 m^2

Inside: 7 hens to every 1 m^2

Task 1

The table shows the space allocated to hens in four farms.

a For each farm, work out whether it has free-range hens or not. Show your working.

b For any of the farms that are not free-range, describe what would need to change to make them free-range.

Farm	Number of hens	Outside area, m^2	Inside area, m^2
A	18	60	2
B	250	1000	36
C	120	500	16
D	24	100	4

Task 2

This hen enclosure contains eight hens.
Its total area is 34 m^2, including both outside and inside spaces.
The outside and inside spaces are both rectangular.
Sketch a possible layout for the enclosure, showing that these hens could be free-range. Label your sketch with dimensions.

Task 3

How much would you have to pay for

- **a** 2 dozen free-range
- **b** 2 dozen caged
- **c** 4 dozen free-range
- **d** 4 dozen caged
- **e** 1 free-range
- **f** 1 cagedegg ?

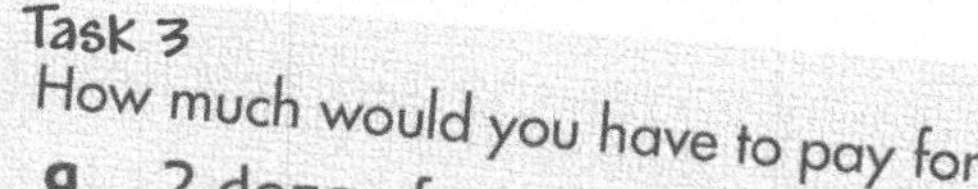

Task 4

Here is a recipe for baked custard. Copy and complete the table.

BAKED CUSTARD (Serves 8)

8 egg yolks
75 g castor sugar
500 ml whipping cream
freshly grated nutmeg

Why do you think that free-range eggs are more expensive than caged eggs? Would you pay more?

Cost of eggs by serving		
	Free-range	Caged
Serves 8	£ 1.28	
Serves 4		£ 0.80
Serves 16		
Serves 12		
Per serving		

MyAssessment 4

These questions will test you on your knowledge of the topics in chapters 13 to 16.
They give you practice in the questions that you may see in your GCSE exams.
There are 75 marks in total.

1 For each of these sequences
   - **i** find the next two terms (3 marks)
   - **ii** find the term-to-term rule. (3 marks)

   a 4, 7, 10, 13, … **b** 19, 14, 9, 4, … **c** -1, 6, 13, 20, …

2 For each of these geometric sequences
   - **i** find the next two terms (3 marks)
   - **ii** find the term-to-term rule. (6 marks)

   a -8, 4, -2, 1, … **b** 0.06, 0.12, 0.24, 0.48, … **c** 125, 50, 20, 8, …

3 The diagram shows the construction of a 3D shape made from six cubes. On grid paper
   - **a** draw a plan view (2 marks)
   - **b** draw a front elevation view (2 marks)
   - **c** draw a side elevation view (from the right hand side). (2 marks)

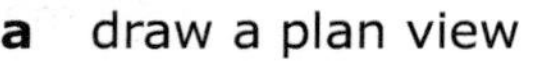

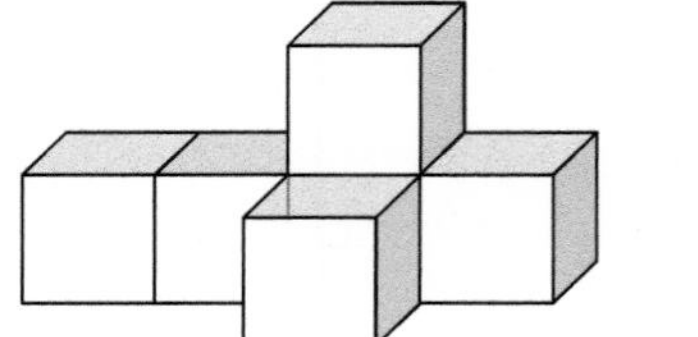

4 For these two prisms calculate the
   - **i** surface area (5 marks)
   - **ii** volume (4 marks)

a

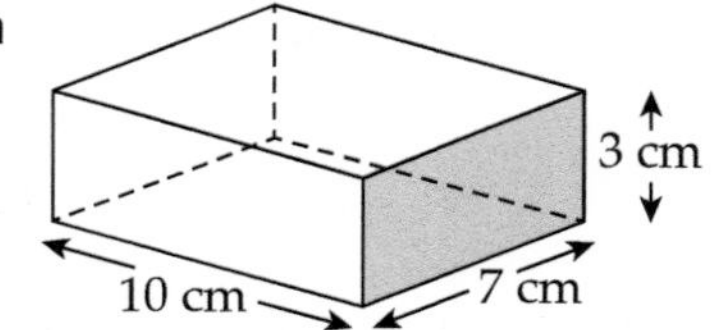

b

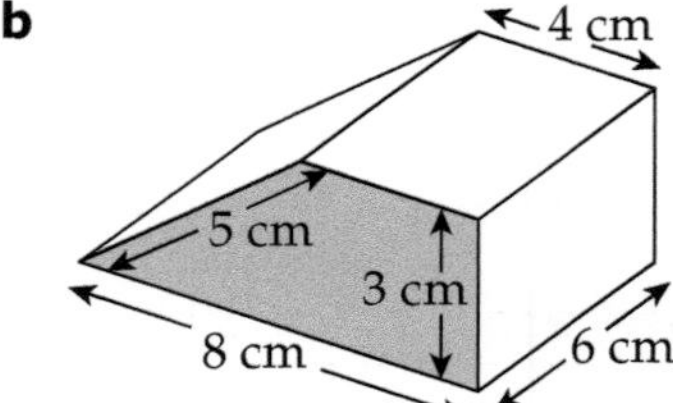

5 Many food items are sold in tins. For the example shown
   - **a** work out the surface area of the tin (3 marks)
   - **b** calculate the volume of the tin. (2 marks)

   Use $\pi = 3.14$

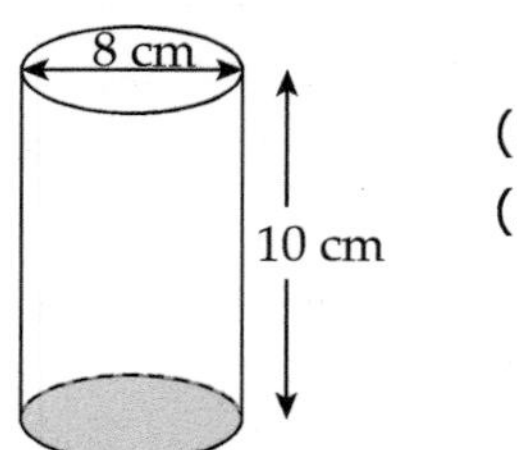

6 Ordinary brass is an alloy of copper and zinc in the ratio 7 : 3 while cartridge brass has a ratio of 13 : 7.

a Which brass has the greater proportion of copper? (3 marks)

b If 10 kg of copper is used to make cartridge brass how much zinc is required? Show your working. (2 marks)

7 Workmen are making a lean concrete mixture of cement, sand and aggregates in the ratio 1 : 3 : 6. They use 2 bags (50 kg) of sand.

a How much cement do they need for the mixture? (2 marks)

b How much concrete do they make altogether (in kilograms)? (3 marks)

c They now mix a new batch of richer concrete in the ratio 6 : 5 : 8. For this they use 2 bags of cement (50 kg).

i How much sand do they use? (2 marks)

ii How much aggregate do they need? (2 marks)

iii How much concrete is made altogether? (2 marks)

8 A photographic image, 8 cm by 6 cm is being enlarged in the ratio of 6 : 5.

a What are the dimensions of the new image? (2 marks)

b What is the scale factor of enlargement? (2 marks)

9 A six-sided dice is thrown and a 2p coin is tossed at the same time.

a What are such events called? (1 mark)

b List all of the possible outcomes in a sample space diagram. (3 marks)

c What is the probability of getting (4, head)? (1 marks)

d Calculate the probability of getting (odd number, tail). (2 marks)

10 Three events are associated with the outcome of rolling an ordinary dice.

A a prime number **B** a multiple of 6 **C** a factor of 8

Which pairs of events are mutually exclusive? (3 marks)

11 An ordinary six-sided dice is rolled 100 times and the scores noted in a frequency table.

Score	1	2	3	4	5	6	Total
Frequency	18	15	12	21	18	16	100

a Determine the experimental probability of obtaining a four. (1 mark)

b How does this compare with the theoretical probability of obtaining a four? (1 mark)

c How could you improve the experimental probabilities? (1 mark)

d How many 'fours' might you expect if you threw the dice 500 times? (1 mark)

12 Consider the sets A and C defined in question **10**.

For the following combined sets **a** $A \cup C$ **b** $A' \cap C'$

i draw a Venn diagram and shade the region containing the set (4 marks)

ii calculate the probability of the set. (2 marks)

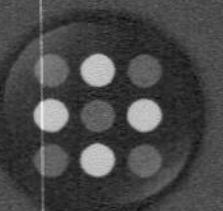

17 Everyday maths

It is getting close to the end of the school year and the time for holidays. Soon you will meet Miss Perry. She is busy getting ready to take Year 8 on a camping trip to France. There is a lot happening and she would like you to help her to solve all the problems she has.

Solving real life problems often requires you to think for yourself and to use several pieces of mathematics at once. If you are going to be successful you will need to practice your basic skills.

- **Fluency** – Do you know how to do arithmetic or algebra?
- **Reasoning** – Can you interpret results and test out your ideas?
- **Problem solving** – Can you cope if a problem involves several steps?

Fluency

If you run a small business you need to be able to do your accounts. Are you making a profit? Is the money you make from sales bigger than all your overheads – wages, rent, materials...?

People often use spreadsheet type programs to help them to do their accounts. However should you trust what they say? It helps if you have a 'feel' for what the right answer should be and if you can quickly do simpler versions of the calculations yourself as checks.

Reasoning

Sometimes finding the answer to a mathematical problem is the easy part. The hardest part can be convincing other people that your solution is the right one.

One way to help persuade other people is by choosing the best graph to show your results.

You also need to be able to back up your results with carefully reasoned explanations.

Problem solving

Controlling a robot is surprisingly complex. It requires breaking down into smaller tasks in order to be manageable.

Each of these smaller tasks might need skills from several different areas of mathematics. To control a robot's movements you will need to use geometry, coordinates and algebra to represent instructions.

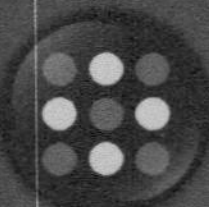

17a Planning the trip to France

Miss Perry is planning a trip for 50 year 8 students.
They will travel from Birmingham to Sarlat in France.

She has to decide whether to travel by coach or train.

Coach	£3560
Ferry berths	£975
Accommodation	£1475
Food	£1450
Insurance	£516
Activities	£1700

Train	£6000
Accommodation	£1550
Food	£1450
Insurance	£500
Activities	£1700

The students would spend 4 days travelling and have 5 days of activities.

The students would spend 3 days travelling and have 6 days of activities.

1 **a** For each possibility work out
  i the total cost of the trips
  ii the costs per student.
  Round the costs to the nearest whole pound (£).

b Which is the most expensive way to travel and by how much?

2 Miss Perry wants to show parents the difference in cost as a percentage of the total cost of the coach trip.
Do the calculation for her giving your answer to the nearest whole percent.

3 By working out the daily cost for each student say which transport method gives the best value for money.
Include only the number of days spent doing activities, and justify your choice.

The group decide to travel by train.
Their journey starts in Birmingham.

These tables show the train times from Birmingham to London, and London to Sarlat (in France)

Depart St Pancras	Arrive Sarlat
04:30	16:50
08:26	18:55
11:05	20:55

Birmingham	23:00	23:00	00:10	05:40	06:40
London	06:50	01:02	07:00	07:00	08:09

When deciding on their schedule they have to take into account these factors.

- When the group arrive in Sarlat they will have to drive for 20 minutes to reach the campsite.
- They have to set-up their tents and this will take about one hour.
- The sun sets at about 8 p.m.
- To be safe, the party will need at least 1 hour to transfer between stations in London.

4 Which trains will the party need to take?

5 What will be their total journey time to the nearest hour?
Remember that French time is one hour ahead of UK time.

From London to Birmingham is about 120 miles.
From London to Sarlat is about 1300 km.

6 What is the total distance between Birmingham and Sarlat stations?
Write your answer in miles or kilometres to the nearest whole unit.

7 Using your answers to questions **5** and **6** to calculate the average speed for the whole journey in kilometres per hour or in miles per hour.

To convert between kilometres (k) and miles (m) use

$$m = \frac{5 \times k}{8}$$

or

$$k = 1.6 \times m$$

8 Miss Perry must pay in advance for the accommodation in Sarlat. She is given a choice: pay £1550 plus an 8% foreign currency handling charge or pay €1840.

If the exchange rate is £1 = €1.18 advise Miss Perry on the best way to pay.

17b Camp Sarlat

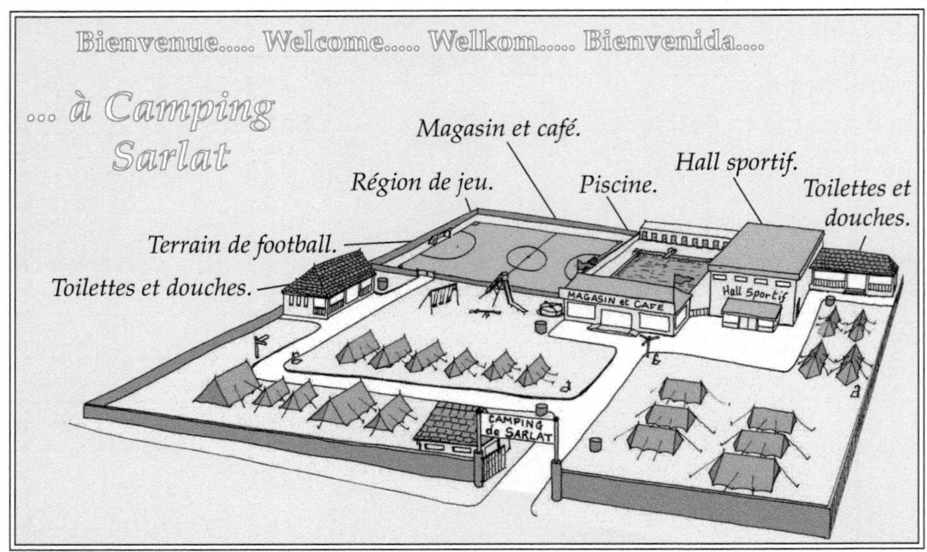

The students are staying in tents. There are three sizes of tent: 2 person, 3 person and 4 person.

1 Working with a partner use the information given to calculate the missing quantity for each tent.

a □ m; Area = 3.3 m²; 2.2 m

b

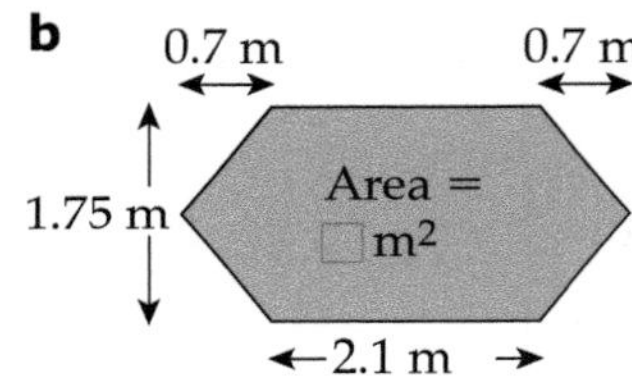

c

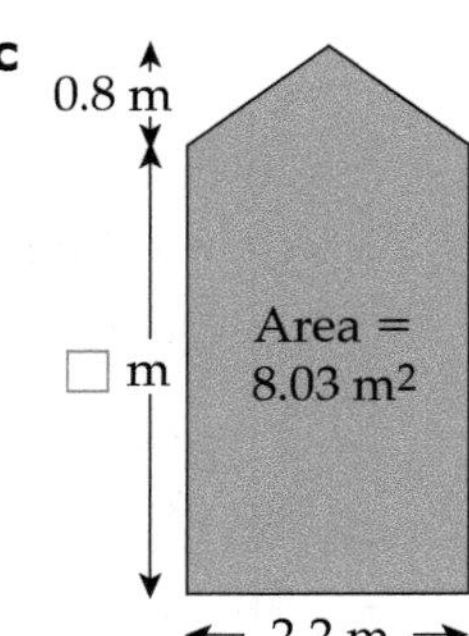

2 The students are shown to their tents. Here are the first five tents – A to E.

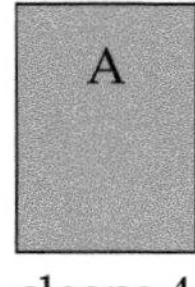

A: sleeps 4 | B: sleeps 2 | C: sleeps 2 | D: sleeps 4 | E: sleeps 3

Again with a partner, use these clues to work out which tents Pete, Cherry, John, Kadeja and Magnus are in.

Boys and girls are in separate tents.

- Fifteen pupils are put in these tents: seven girls and eight boys.
- John's tent is at the end of the row.
- Cherry shares a tent with three other girls.
- The four boys in the tent beside Pete's tent make a lot of noise.
- Kadeja likes her tent.
- Pete, Cherry, John, Kadeja and Magnus are in different tents.

The students are given a map of the camp.

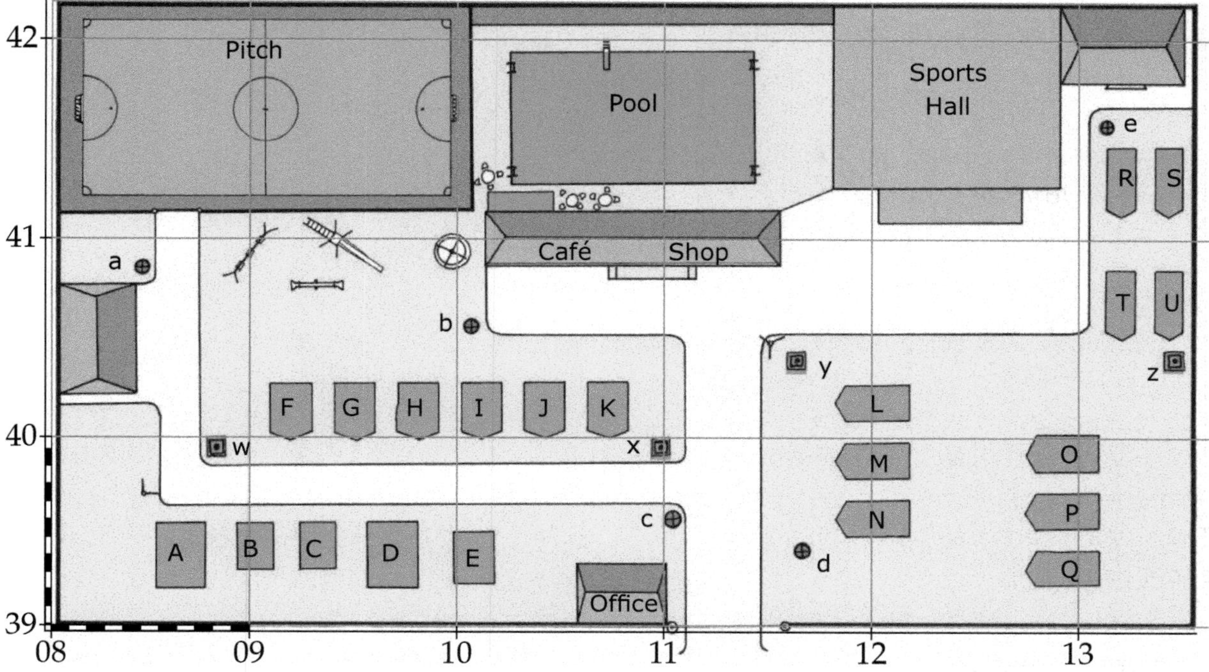

3 **a** Given their six-figure grid references, which tents are these people in?

i Kia is at 104, 402 **ii** Hamad is at 129, 399 **iii** David is at 132, 413

b Where would you be if you were standing at these six-figure grid references?

i 124, 416 **ii** 108, 393 **iii** 113, 410

4 **a** There are five bins around the site, marked ⊕.
Find the bins labeled a – e and give their six-figure grid references.

Bin a is at 084, 408

b There are four water taps around the site marked ▣.
Find the taps labeled w – z and give their six-figure grid references.

5 It is dark and Ronnie walks from 107, 408 to 101, 395.
Which tent does he blunder into?

6 The swimming pool is only half full! It is decided to finish filling it overnight.

$1\,m^3 = 1000$ litres

a The pool is 15 m by 10 m and should be filled to 1.2 m.
What is the volume of the pool?

b The pool can be filled at the rate of 120 litres per minute. How long will it take to finish filling the pool? Give your answers in **i** minutes **ii** hours.

c If the filling operation starts at 10 pm at what time will the pool be ready to use?

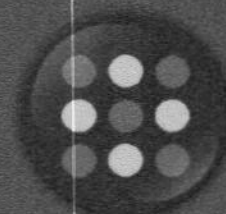

17c The sports day

The next day there is a sports competition.

1 There are 48 students involved in the activities. The pie chart shows the numbers taking part in the morning session.
Measure and calculate how many students are involved in

a football b table tennis
c archery d athletics

Athletics
Table tennis
Football
Archery

2 The numbers involved in the afternoon session are

football	20	table tennis	12
archery	6	athletics	10

Construct and label a pie chart to display this information.

3 Five teams take part in a five-a-side soccer competition.
These are the results.

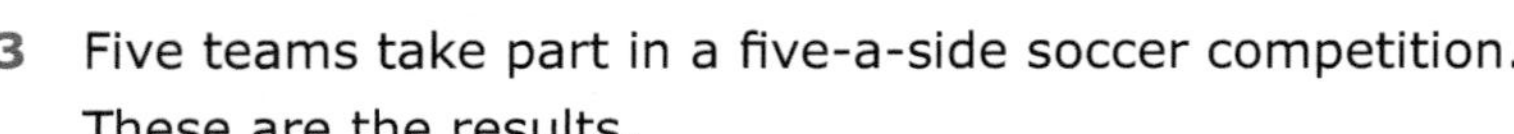

	Games				Goals		Points
	played	won	drawn	lost	for	against	
All Stars	4	0	2	2	6	12	2
Champions	4	2	2	0	7	4	8
Cheetahs	4	1	0	3	10	10	3
High 5	4	1	2	1	7	8	5
Superstars	4	2	2	0	9	5	8

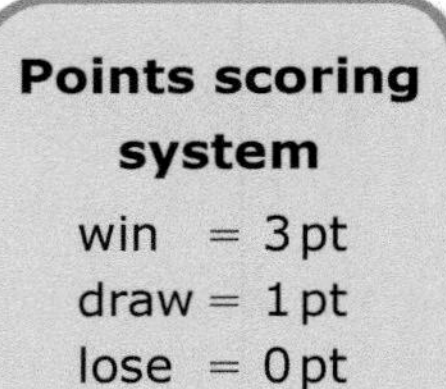

The score boards below show the results of each match.
Using the data in the table above, work out the missing scores from the matches below.

Round 1

High 5	2	v	Superstars	a
Champions	3	v	Cheetahs	1
High 5	b	v	All Stars	2
Cheetahs	0	v	Superstars	2
Champions	2	v	Stars	1

Round 2

High 5	3	v	Cheetahs	2
All Stars	1	v	Superstars	1
High 5	0	v	Champions	c
All Stars	2	v	Cheetahs	d
Champions	2	v	Superstars	2

4 Using the results table and score boards.
a What is the range of goals scored in a match?
b What is the modal average number of goals scored by each team?
c What is the mean average number of goals scored in each match?

5 In the archery competition each student gets to fire four arrows.
Their scores are shown below the targets.

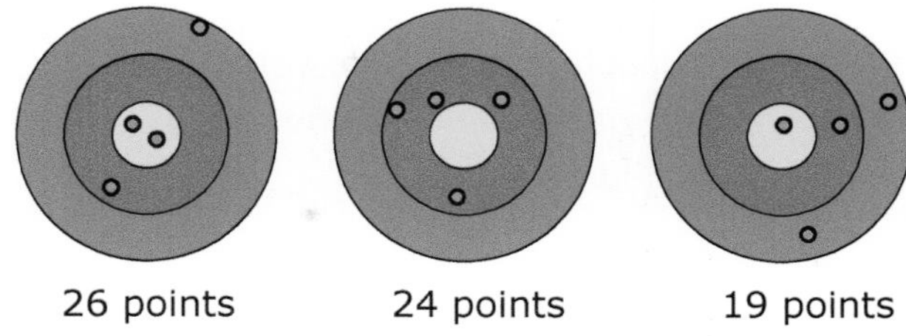

a Using this information, how many points do you get for a hit in the
i red circle **ii** blue circle **iii** gold bull's eye?

b What is the mean average of these scores?

6 A running track has to be marked out for the athletics.
The perimeter must be 400 m. The radius of the semicircles at each end is 40 m.

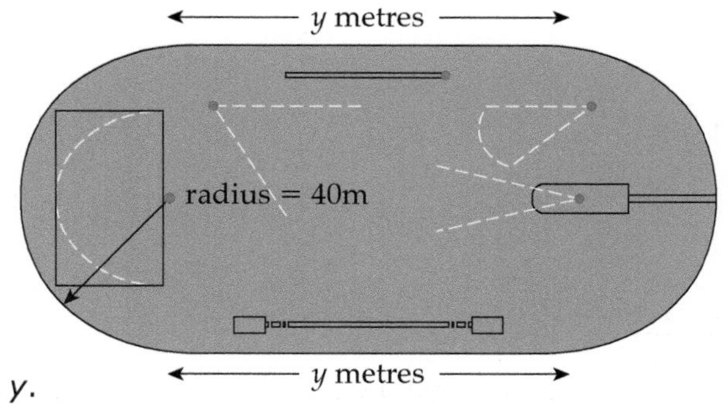

a What is the total distance around the two semicircles?

b Using your answer to part **a**.
Calculate the lengths of the straights, y.
Round your answer to a useful number.

7 Three lanes are marked out.
Each lane is 1 m wide.

The runners run one lap of the track in lanes.
The runner in the inside lane will run 400 m.

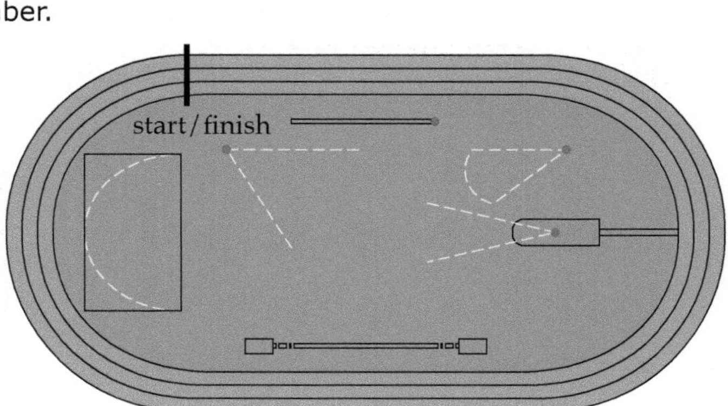

a After one lap, how far has the runner in
i middle lane run **ii** outer lane run?

b How do track markers prevent this when they mark out a real track?

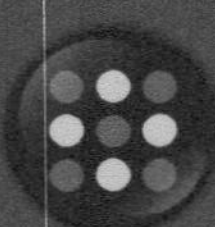

17d The expedition

The group is going on an expedition and must pack their own rucksacks. To be comfortable, the ratio of your body weight to the weight of the rucksack should be 6 : 1.

Bart 36 kg

Gabby 40 kg

Martia 54 kg

Rick 48 kg

Jules 70 kg

Helina 37 kg

1 **a** Calculate the weight of each student's rucksack using the above ratio.
Round your answers to the nearest useful number.

b Steve has 7 kg in his rucksack.
What is his minimum weight?

c Who is closest to the mean weight of the six students?

This is the route the students will take from Camp Sarlat.

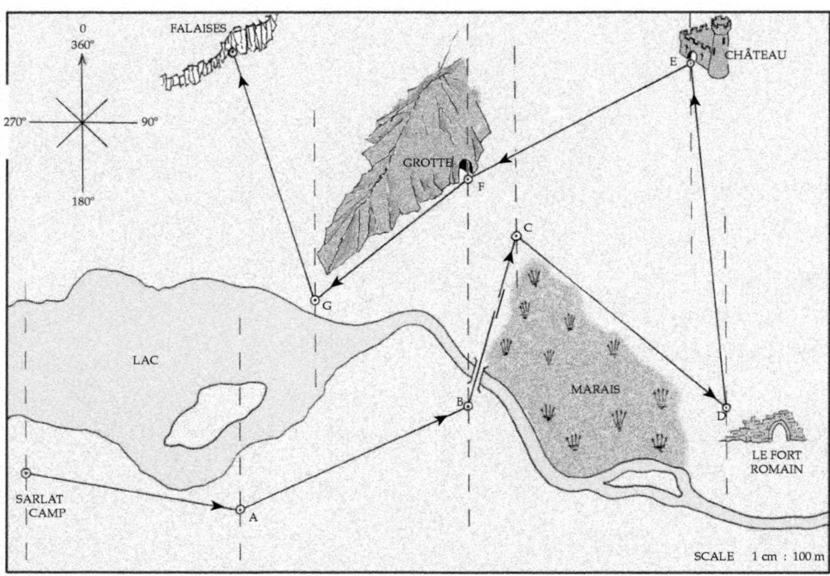

2 Using the scale on the map copy and complete this table of distances and bearings.

Section	3 figure bearing	Distance (m)
A to B	065°	330
B to C		
C to D		
D to E		
E to F		
F to G		

3 **a** In the cave there are drawings that were made in 2150 BC. How many years ago is this?

b The Roman fort was occupied between 74 BC and 48 AD. How many years is this?

At the end of the journey the students learn to mountaineer.

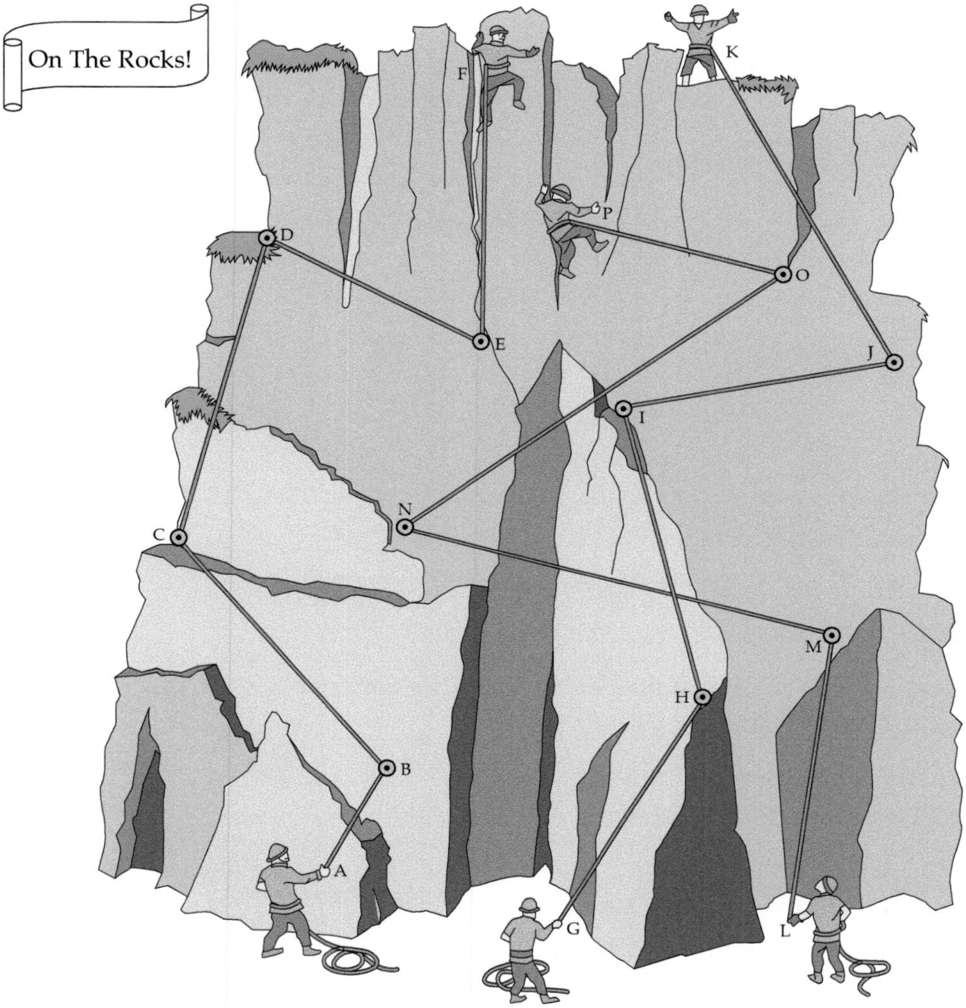

4 Measure accurately and record these

a acute angles

i $\widehat{MNO}$ **ii** $\widehat{DEF}$ **iii** $\widehat{IJK}$

b obtuse angles

i $\widehat{BCD}$ **ii** $\widehat{LMN}$ **iii** $\widehat{GHI}$

c Measure these angles and hence find the reflex angles

i $\widehat{CDE}$ **ii** $\widehat{NOP}$ **iii** $\widehat{ABC}$

5 Using what you know about angles, show that the sections of rope MN and OP are parallel.

6 The scene is drawn to a scale of 1 cm : 1 m (1 : 100).
To the nearest 0.1 m give theses distances in real life.

a MN **b** DE **c** HI **d** CD **e** NO

17e Camp-life

The day started badly for Miss Perry — her tent leaked in the night and she is not pleased. She asks Mr Powell to waterproof the tent for her.

1 The tent is made from a large rectangle and two triangles.

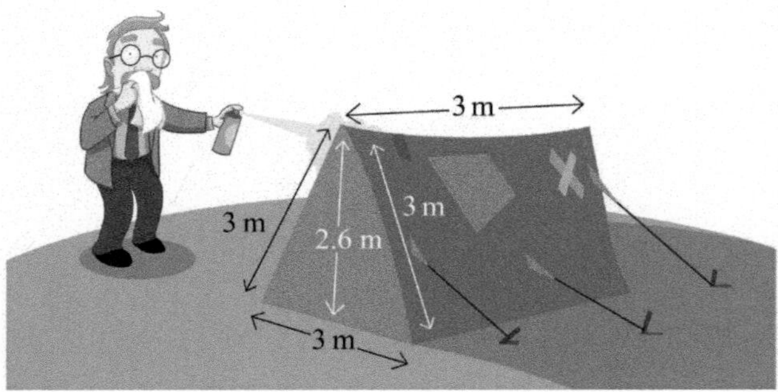

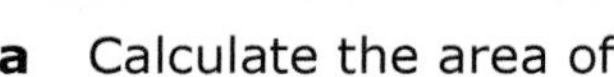

a Calculate the area of **i** the rectangle **ii** a triangle.

b use you answers to part **a** to find the total surface area of the tent.

c How many cans of Seal It! will be needed to spray the whole tent if it takes 250 ml to waterproof every 5 m^2?

Miss Perry refuses to use the showers — they are just too dirty for her! She has a private shower made for her.

2 The students have to carry the water to her shower in containers. Meg and Leroy use different sized containers. They empty their containers in to the shower and fill it exactly.

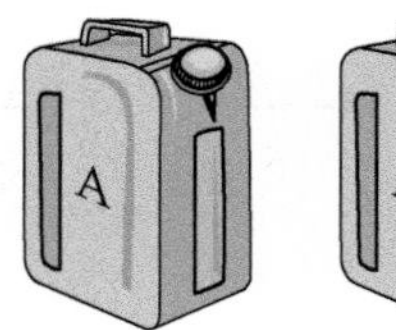

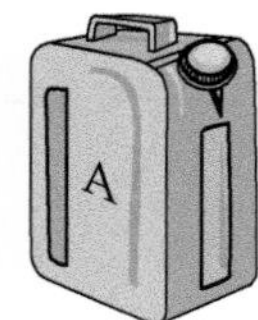

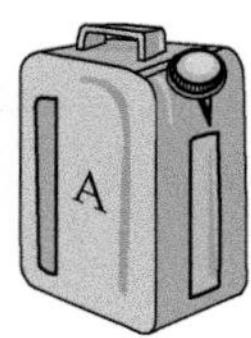

= 50 litres

Leroy empties container A three times and Meg empties container B once. They refill the shower and again fill it exactly.

= 50 litres

This time they use 1 A container and 7 B containers.
Work out how much water each container holds.

While waiting to board the coach to go home, the students gather in the play area.

Sam has placed his sandwich and chocolate bar on the roundabout which is rotating slowly in a clockwise direction.

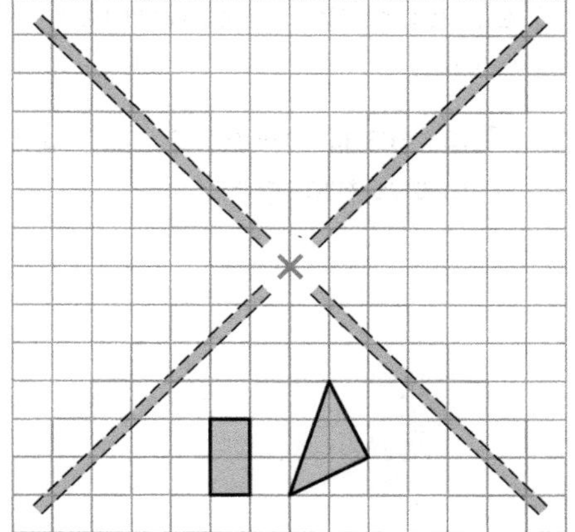

3 On graph paper draw the centre of rotation and the position of the sandwich and chocolate bar.

a Starting from the start positions, rotate the shapes through

i 90° in a clockwise direction and draw the image.

ii 270° in a clockwise direction and draw the image.

b From the start positions the roundabout spins through a total of 1890° before stopping. Draw the final positions of the sandwich and chocolate bar.

4 Claire sits on the see-saw. She weighs 37 kg. Which of the weights shown can be used to balance her?

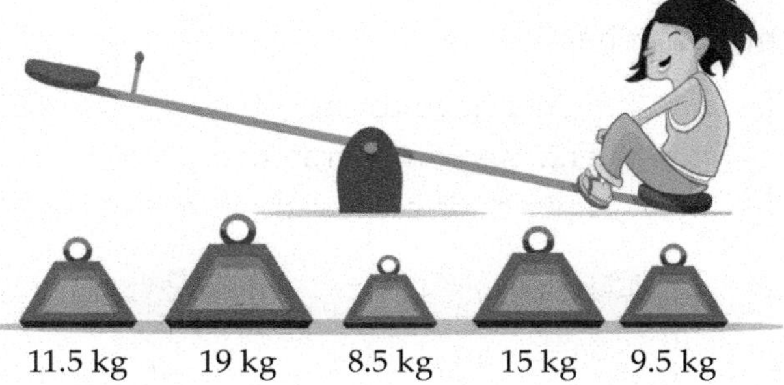

Miss Perry calls to the students from a plane. She explains that her best friend Rupert happened to be flying by and offered her a lift. She decided to hurry home and complete all her unfinished marking.

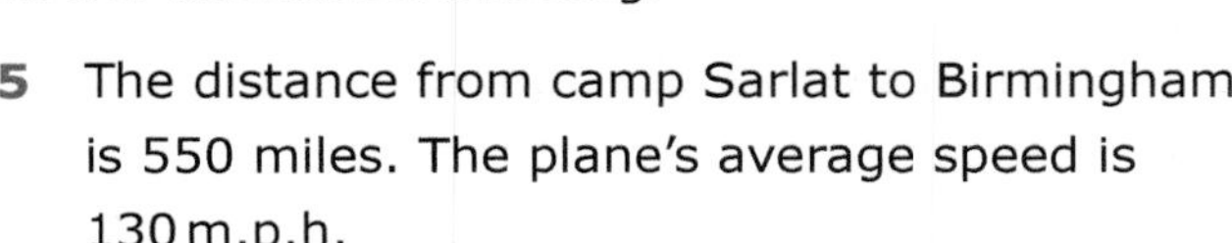

5 The distance from camp Sarlat to Birmingham is 550 miles. The plane's average speed is 130 m.p.h.
There is a 10 m.p.h. wind against the plane all the way back.

How long will it take them to fly home?

Check in 1

1 **a** 1, 2, 3, 4, 5, 6, 10, 12, 15, 20, 30, 60
b 1, 2, 3, 4, 6, 11, 12, 22, 33, 44, 66, 132
c 1, 3, 5, 9, 15, 25, 45, 75, 225

2 **a** HCF = 4 LCM = 24
b HCF = 5 LCM = 60
c HCF = 9 LCM = 54

3 **a** 30 **b** 36 **c** 350

4 2, 3, 5, 7, 11, 13, 17, 19, 23, 29, 31, 37, 41, 43, 47, 53, 59, 61, 67, 71

5 **a** 81 **b** 125 **c** 6
d 4.913 **e** 6.7082...

MyReview 1

1 **a** No **b** Yes **c** No **d** Yes

2 **a** $3^3 \times 11$ **b** $2 \times 5^2 \times 7^2$

3 **a** 9 **b** 1

4 **a** 385 **b** 1764

5 **a** $\frac{31}{18}$ **b** $\frac{9}{20}$

6 **a** 15.8 (1dp) **b** Not possible
c 7.94 **d** -5.43

7 **a** 121 **b** 13
c 512 **d** -4

8 **a** 4^7 **b** 5^7 **c** 12^2
d 4 **e** 72 **f** 2^2

9 **a** 160 **b** 160.1
c 160.10 **d** 160.095

10 **a** 94.5 cm **b** 95.5 cm

11 2.7

Check in 2

1 **a** millimetres, centimetre, metres, kilometres, inch, foot, yard, mile...
b milligram, gram, kilogram, tonne, ounce, pound, stone...
c millilitre, centilitre, litre, fluid ounce, pint, gallon...

2 **a** **i** 74 **ii** 0.39 **iii** 60 **iv** 0.25
b **i** 15 **ii** 54 **iii** 165 **iv** 12.1
c **i** 28 **ii** 0.8 **iii** 300 **iv** 9

3 **a** 26 m, 40 m^2 **b** 21 cm, 30 cm^2
c 75 mm, 312.5 mm^2

MyReview 2

1 **a** l **b** cm **c** km

2 **a** 250 000 cm **b** 0.003 tonnes

3 **a** 9.9 lb **b** 1800 ml

4 **a** 100 ml **b** 250 ml **c** 300 ml
d 460 ml **e** 540 ml

5 117 cm^2

6 24 m

7 24 mm^2

8 160 cm^2

9 8 cm

10 **a** (Isosceles) Trapezium **b** 156 cm^2

11 **a** 153.86 cm^2 **b** 43.96 cm

Check in 3

1 **a** 10 **b** 8 **c** 17 **d** 16
e 10 **f** 12 **g** 25 **h** 4

2 **a** $2x$ **b** $3y$ **c** $3a$
d $2b$ **e** $5p + q$ **f** $8k - 3$
g $5x + y$ **h** $4m - 3n$

3 **a** $\frac{3}{5}$ **b** $\frac{7}{9}$ **c** $\frac{3}{8}$ **d** $\frac{11}{15}$
e $\frac{7}{9}$ **f** $\frac{7}{12}$ **g** $1\frac{3}{20}$ **h** $\frac{23}{24}$

MyReview 3

1 **a** 1 **b** $\frac{1}{9}$ **c** -125 **d** 64

2 **a** 16 **b** -54 **c** $\frac{-1}{12}$ **d** 25

3 **a** 2^3 **b** 3^{-3} **c** x^{11}
d y^{-2} **e** x^5 **f** $8a^{12}$

4 **a** $9 - 2a - 27b$ **b** $8y + 5y^2$
c $11cd + 5d - 2c$ **d** $\frac{q}{2p^2}$

5 **a** $56 - 14a$ **b** $-4b + 14$
c $c^2 + c$ **d** $-2d^2 + 7d$

6 **a** $7r + 10$ **b** $3 - 2s$

7 **a** $4(3x - 1)$ **b** $7(a + 2b)$
c $15p(q + 3)$ **d** $3t(2st - 3)$

8 19

9 $C = 50 + 3.5g$

10 $4t$

11 **a** $x = c + 2b$ **b** $x = y - 19$
c $x = \frac{b}{a}$ **d** $x = y + 3$

12 **a** $\frac{x}{3}$ **b** $\frac{7a}{20}$ **c** $\frac{3 + 2y}{xy}$ **d** $\frac{5p - q}{p^2}$

Check in 4

1 **a** $1\frac{1}{2}$ **b** $\frac{39}{50}$ **c** $\frac{1}{8}$

2 **a** 0.7 **b** 1.35 **c** 0.52 **d** 0.875

3 **a** $\frac{13}{20}$ **b** $\frac{4}{21}$

4 **a** £65 **b** 350 kg

5 **a** $5\frac{5}{7}$ **b** 12

6

Fraction	Decimal	Percentage
$\frac{13}{20}$	0.65	65%
$\frac{1}{8}$	0.125	12.5%

MyReview 4

1 **a** 0.76 **b** 0.6 **c** $0.\dot{2}$ **d** $1.\dot{1}\dot{8}$

2 **a** $\frac{5}{8}$ **b** $\frac{4}{25}$ **c** $\frac{2}{3}$ **d** $3\frac{1}{5}$

3 **a** 0.1, $\frac{1}{9}$, $\frac{2}{15}$, $\frac{1}{7}$ **b** 0.4, $\frac{5}{12}$, $\frac{3}{7}$, $0.\dot{4}$

4 **a** $\frac{10}{21}$ **b** $\frac{23}{30}$
c $\frac{49}{30}$ or $1\frac{19}{30}$ **d** $\frac{29}{54}$
5 **a** $\frac{101}{21}$ **b** $\frac{19}{15}$
6 **a** 16 **b** $3.\dot{3}$ or $3\frac{1}{3}$
7 **a** $\frac{10}{3}$ or $3\frac{1}{3}$ **b** $\frac{3}{20}$
8 **a** 16 **b** $\frac{9}{8}$ or $1\frac{1}{8}$
9 **a** 308 **b** 1205.4
c 827.2 **d** 1.368
10 **a** 73.5 **b** 11.56
11 £7500
12 214
13 30%
14 28%

Check in 5

1 **a** 45°, acute **b** 115°, obtuse
c 295°, reflex
2 **a** $a = 36°$ **b** $b = 18°$ **c** $c = 24°$
3 Interior angles in a square are all 90°.
Interior angles are 80°, 100°, 90° and 90°.
The sum of the interior angles is always 360°.

MyReview 5

1 $a = 86°$ Angles on a straight line add up to 180°
$b = 34°$ Vertically opposite angles are equal
$c = 86°$ Vertically opposite/straight line
$d = 60°$ Vertically opposite/straight line /angles around a point add up to 360°
$e = 187°$ Angles around a point add up to 360°
$f = 82°$ Corresponding angles are equal
$g = 115°$ Alternate angles are equal
$h = 29°$ Angles in a triangle add up to 180°
$i = 99°$ Corresponding angles are equal
2 $a = 134°$ $b = 68°$
3 **a** Parallelogram **b** Isosceles Trapezium
4 **a** 40° **b** 108°
5 Check interior angles are all 120°, allow ±2°
6 **a** 10 cm **b** 125° **c** 55°

Check in 6

1 **a** **i** 11 **ii** -1 **iii** 9
b **i** -3 **ii** 12 **iii** $\frac{1}{2}$
c **i** 4 **ii** 6 **iii** $4\frac{1}{3}$
d **i** 6 **ii** 3 **iii** 3
2 **a**

x	0	2	3
y	1	3	4

b The y-coordinate is equal to the x-coordinate + 1.
c $y = x + 1$

MyReview 6

1 **a**

x	0	1	2	3
y	-5	-1	3	7

b

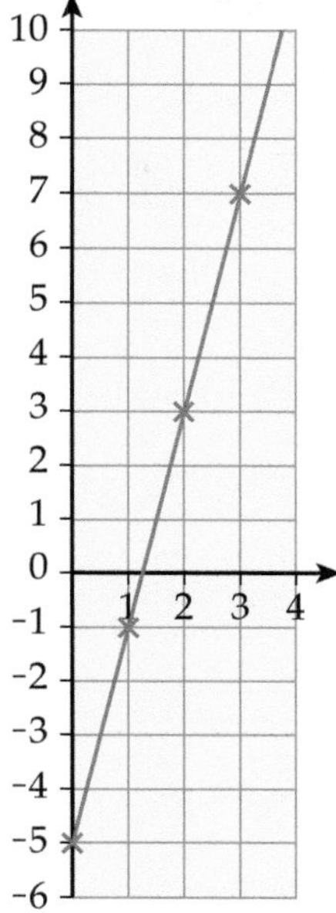

2 No
3 **a** Slope 7, y-axis 3 **b** Slope 1, y-axis -4
c Slope -2, y-axis 8 **d** Slope $\frac{1}{2}$, y-axis 0
e Slope 0, y-axis 5 **f** Slope 5, y-axis 4
4 **a** $y = 4$ **b** $x = -1$
c $y = x + 1$ **d** $y = 1 - 2x$
5 **a**

x	-3	-2	-1	0	1	2	3
x^2	9	4	1	0	1	4	9
-1	-1	-1	-1	-1	-1	-1	-1
y	8	3	0	-1	0	3	8

b

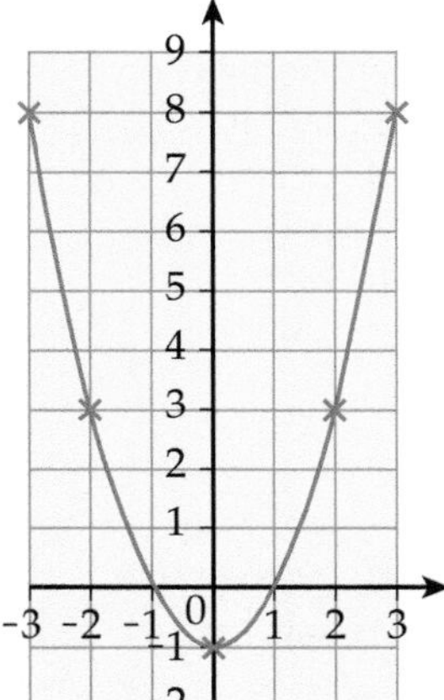

6 **a** (9, 9.5) **b** (-2.5, -4)
7 (11, -1)

8 **a** $y = 11 - x$ **b** $y = 6 - \frac{2}{3}x$
c $y = 3 - 2x$ **d** $y = 26 + 14x$

9
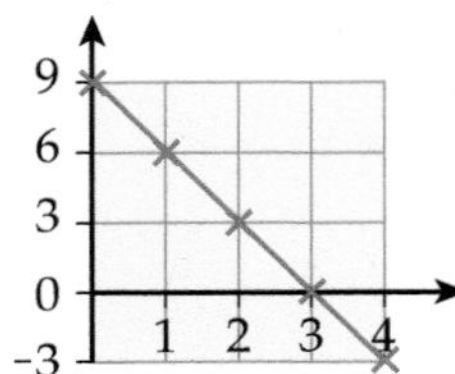

10
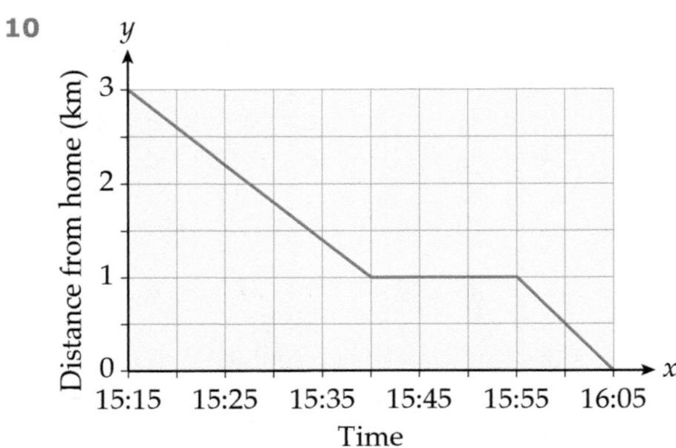

Check in 7

1 **a** 338.32 **b** 204.6
c 365.9 **d** 554.97

2 **a** 60.84 **b** 232.65
c 262.88 **d** 48.705

3 **a** 148.2 **b** 192.1 **c** 380 **d** 170

MyReview 7

1 **a** < **b** >0

2 **a** -7 **b** -4 **c** 5
d -28 **e** -5

3 **a** 6510 **b** 0.0034 **c** 0.24
d 0.062 **e** 3570 **f** 10 400

4 **a** 9.16 **b** 25.6 **c** 11.15 **d** 5.99

5 **a** Sophie, 10.3 kg **b** 1 kg
c Jack, Alex, Emily, Sophie

6 **a** 120.5 **b** 55.92
c 64.2 **d** £24.14

7 Yes

8 **a** 11.465 **b** 192.49
c 18.192 **d** 81.61

9 476.8 g

Check in 8

1 Specific responses which cover all options without any overlap, for example
a At least once a week.
b Less than once a week but at least once a month.
c Sometimes but less than once a month.
d Never

2 None of these people will answer 'never' and those who go to the cinema regularly will be over-represented in the sample she takes.

3 **a** 6 **b** 5.5 **c** 5 **d** 5

MyReview 8

1

Transport	Gender (M/F)	Alone (Y/N)

2

Age	Frequency
≤ 15	0
16 – 19	1
20 – 29	5
30 – 39	6
40 – 49	6
50 – 59	4
≥ 60	2

3 **a**

1	8
2	1 4 6 7 8
3	0 0 2 2 3 8
4	1 2 4 5 7 9
5	0 3 5 9
6	3 8

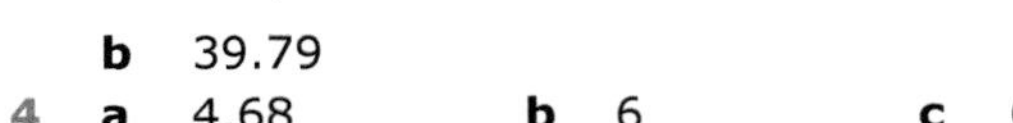

b 39.79

4 **a** 4.68 **b** 6 **c** 6

5 **a**

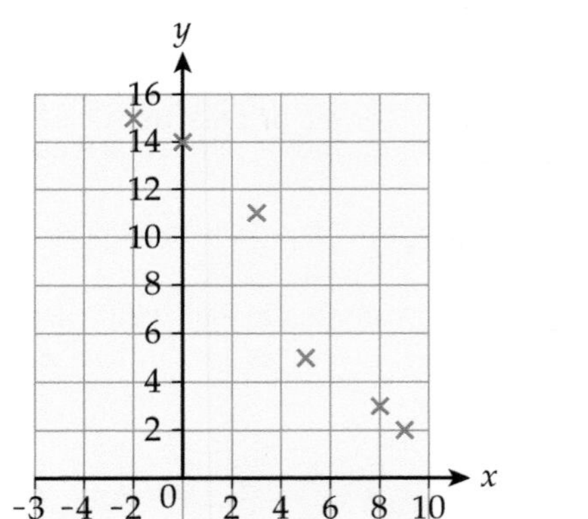

b Negative correlation

6 **a** Girls 0.69, Boys 0.63
b Girls 0.42, Boys 0.59
c Median lower for boys so boys reaction were slightly quicker on average. Range bigger for boys, so girls times were more consistent.

Check in 9

1 **a** 800 mm **b** 200 m **c** 350 cm
d 0.45 km

2 **a** Student drawing
b (0, 2) (4, 2) (2, -2)
c y-axis

MyReview 9

1 **a** Translation of 1 unit left and 3 units down
b Rotation of 90° anti-clockwise about (0,0)
c Reflection in the y-axis, line $x = 0$

2

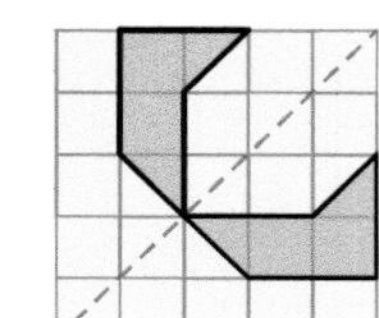

3  **a, b**

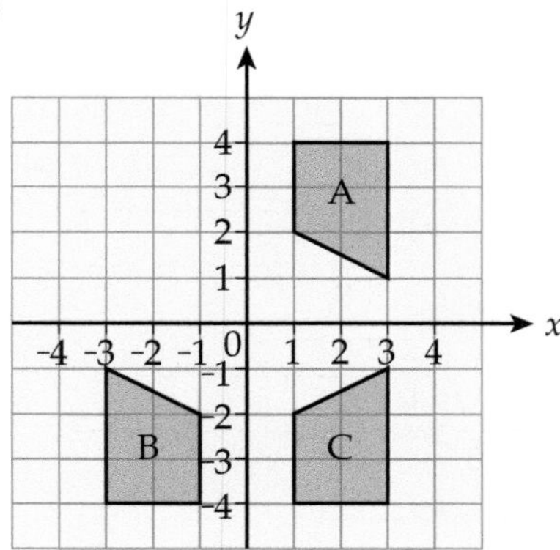

c Reflection in the x-axis, line $y = 0$

4 **a** 10 **b** 2

5 **a** 1 **b** 9

6 scale factor 3, centre of enlargement (2, 9)

7

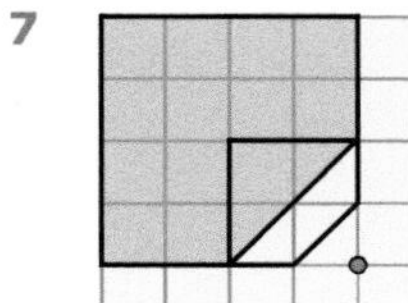

Check in 10

1 **a** $x = 5$ **b** $y = 4$ **c** $p = 4.5$ **d** $k = 3$
e $w = 2$ **f** $z = 5$ **g** $x = 9$ **h** $y = 4$

2 **a** $2a + 10$ **b** $3b - 30$ **c** $x^2 + 2x$
d $ab - 3a$ **e** $3t^2 - 3t$ **f** $6pq + 8p$
g $9k + 2$ **h** $7n + 12$

MyReview 10

1 **a** 0 **b** 4 **c** 5
d 11 **e** 7 **f** -1

2 **a** -2 **b** 4 **c** -6
d 8 **e** -13 **f** -15

3 **a** 53 **b** 10 **c** -12 **d** 40
e 5 **f** 4 **g** -4 **h** 2

4 **a** 6 **b** 15 **c** 3 **d** -7

5 7

6 **a** 1.8 **b** 2.6 **c** 6.9 **d** 1.2

7 3.8

Check in 11

1 **a** 6; 6.1 **b** 16; 15.5
c 217; 217.4 **d** 0; 0.1

2 **a** 12.1 **b** 8.41 **c** 38.16 **d** 3.81

3 **a** 120 **b** 3.8 **c** 0.037 **d** 480

4 **a** 28 **b** 17 **c** 104

MyReview 11

1 **a** 1.12 **b** 41.8 **c** 37 **d** 210

2 **a** 51.72 **b** 750.32
c 42.744 **d** 0.50958

3 **a** 5.9 **b** 68.6 **c** 2.4
d 398.9 **e** 1353.2 **f** 2.3

4 £68.15

5 6.79 m/s

6 Gas = 1224.89 × 4.217 = 5165.36113
Electricity = 1133 × 12.139 = 13753.487
Standing charge gas = 23.276 × 91 = 2118.116
Standing charge electricity = 15.219 × 91
= 1384.929
Total charge = 22421.89313p
Add VAT at 5% gives 23542.98779
So £235.43

7 **a** 7.64 **b** 3 **c** 0.5 **d** 1.07

8 **a** 5 days, 5 hours, 20 minutes
b 1 week, 4 days, 13 hours, 46 minutes, 40 seconds

9 **a** 6.36 kg **b** 1.72 5m

10 **a** 114 $2 \times 3 + 5 = 6 + 5$ not 2×8
b 34 $(-4)^2 = -4 \times -4 = 16$ not -4×4
c 0 $6 - 5 - 1$ not $6 + 5 + 1$
d 160 $(5 \times 8)^2 \div (5 \times 2) = 5 \times 8 \times 4$ not 4^2

Check in 12

1 **a** $a = 40°$ **b** $b = 140°$

2 **a** Student drawing **b** 6 cm

MyReview 12

1 **a** Check ASA: 105°, 7.5 cm, 40°
b Check SAS: 80 mm, 30°, 80 mm
or ASA: 75°, 80 mm, 30°

2 **a** Check SSS: 8 cm, 15 cm, 11 cm
b Check RHS: 90°, 7.5 cm, 4.5 cm

3 **a** The half angle is 15° and the line is the perpendicular bisector of the base.
b The line should cross the hypotenuse at 2.7/4.8 cm.

4

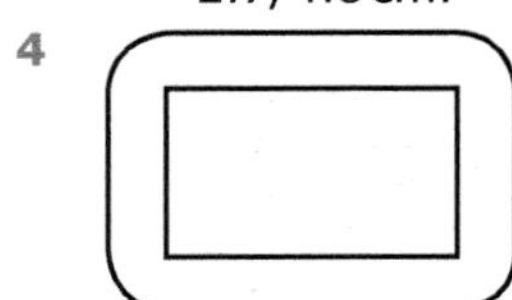

5 The locus is the angle bisector at 45°

6 Radii 2.5 cm and 3.75

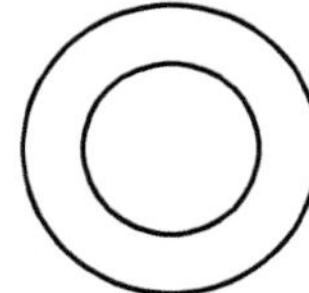

7 **a** 041° **b** 221° **c** 083° **d** 263°

8 **a** 256° **b** 015° **c** 128°

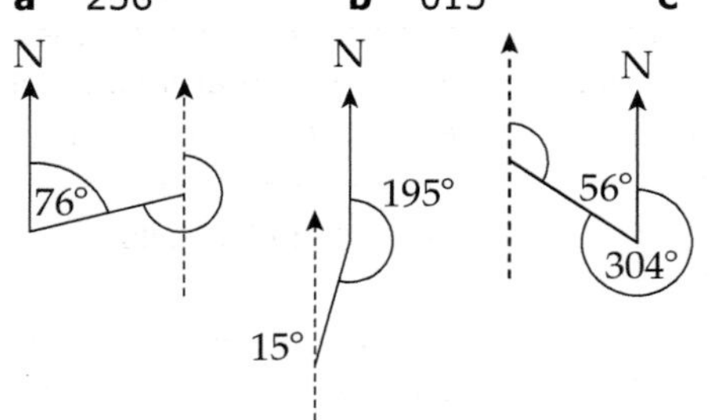

Check in 13

1 **a** 36, 42 **b** 28, 33
c 45, 36 **d** 22.5, 11.25

2 **a** 4, 9, 14, 19, 24, ...
b 1, 3, 9, 27, 81, ...
c 10, 5, 2.5, 1.25, 0.625, ...

MyReview 13

1 **a** Subtract 2.5 from previous term; -5, -7.5
b Halve previous term; 4, 2
c Multiply previous term by -2; 48, -96

2 **a** 4, 9, 14, 19, 24
b 1.5, 2, 2.5, 3, 3.5
c 3, 6, 11, 18, 27
d 99, 96, 91, 84, 75

3 **a**

Number of tables, *t*	1	2	3	4
2 times table	2	4	6	8
Number of chairs, *c*	4	6	8	10

b $c = 2t + 2$ **c** 22 **d** 7

4 **a** $7n + 12$ **b** $11n - 1$
c $\frac{1}{2}n + 7$ **d** $-5n$

5 **a** Divide previous term by 10;0.0005, 0.00005
b Multiply previous term by -2: 4, -8
c Multiply by $\frac{3}{2}$: $20\frac{1}{4}$, $30\frac{3}{8}$
d Divide by -2: 128, -64

6 **a** 19683 **b** -0.001

7 **a** 0, 4, -8, 28, -80 **b** 1, 1, 1, 1, 1
c 2, 3, 5, 9, 17 **d** 2, 3, 8, 63, 3968

8 **a** $T(n + 1) = T(n) + 3$ $T(1) = 14$
b $T(n + 1) = T(n) - 15$ $T(1) = 77$
c $T(n + 1) = -3T(n)$ $T(1) = 3$
d $T(n + 1) = T(n) + n$ $T(1) = 3$

Check in 14

1 **a** Cone, check drawings
b Triangular prism, check drawings

2 **a** **i** 72 cm^3
ii blue 12 cm^2, pink 24 cm^2, green 18 cm^2
b **i** 24 cm^2
ii blue 12 m^2, pink 4 m^2, green 12 m^2

MyReview 14

1 **a** Triangular prism
b **i** 5 **ii** 9 **iii** 6

2 One possible net is

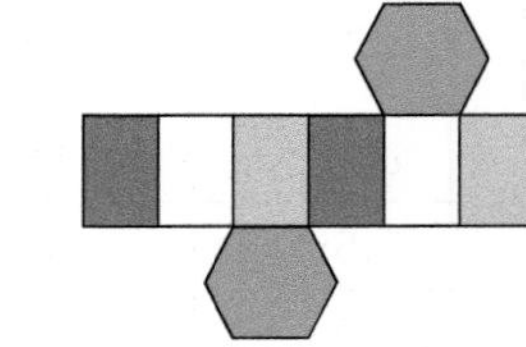

3 **a** **i** **ii** **iii**

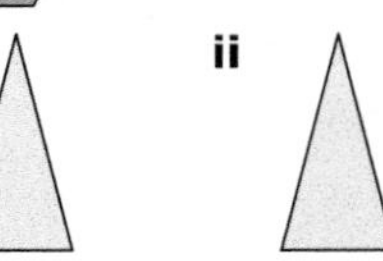

b Circular pyramid or Cone

4 **a**

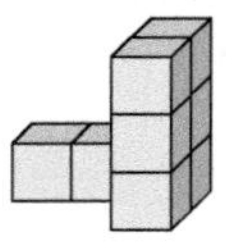

b 8

5 **a** 38 cm^2 **b** 156 cm^2

6 904.3 cm^3

7 378 cm^3

Check in 15

1 **a** 3 : 5 **b** 3 : 2
c 4 : 3 **d** 5 : 7

2 24 : 36

3 435p

4 48 kg

5 **a** $\frac{1}{2} = 50\%$ **b** 5 : 2

MyReview 15

1 **a** 7 : 2 : 6 **b** 15 : 1
2 **a** 1 : 8.5 **b** 1 : 192
3 187.5 m, 312.5
4 £14.55, £36.36, £29.09
5 £6
6 **a** 780 km **b** 34 litres
7 **a** 5 : 4 **b** 12
8 275 g
9 20 : 23
10 B
11 57.1%
12

Distance travelled, miles	20	40	60	100
Journey time, minutes	30	60	90	150

Check in 16

1 **a** $\frac{3}{4}$ **b** $\frac{17}{20}$ **c** $\frac{2}{3}$
d $\frac{3}{5}$ **e** $\frac{3}{5}$
2 **a** $\frac{7}{16}$ **b** $\frac{11}{16}$ **c** $\frac{2}{3}$
d $\frac{71}{105}$ **e** $\frac{4}{15}$
3

	Fraction	**Percentage**	**Decimal**
Liquorice	$\frac{1}{4}$	25%	0.25
Chocolate button	$\frac{7}{20}$	35%	0.35
Toffee	$\frac{3}{20}$	15%	0.15
Mint	$\frac{1}{8}$	12.5%	0.125
Jelly bean	$\frac{1}{8}$	12.5%	0.125

4 **a** $\frac{1}{2}$ **b** 0.55 **c** $\frac{1}{2}$

MyReview 16

1 (Black, Black), (Black, Grey), (Black Brown) (Grey, Grey), (Grey, Brown) (brown, Brown)
2 **a**

	1	2	3	4	5	6
1	0	1	2	3	4	5
2	1	0	1	2	3	4
3	2	1	0	1	2	3
4	3	2	1	0	1	2
5	4	3	2	1	0	1
6	5	4	3	2	1	0

b $\frac{2}{9}$

3 **a**

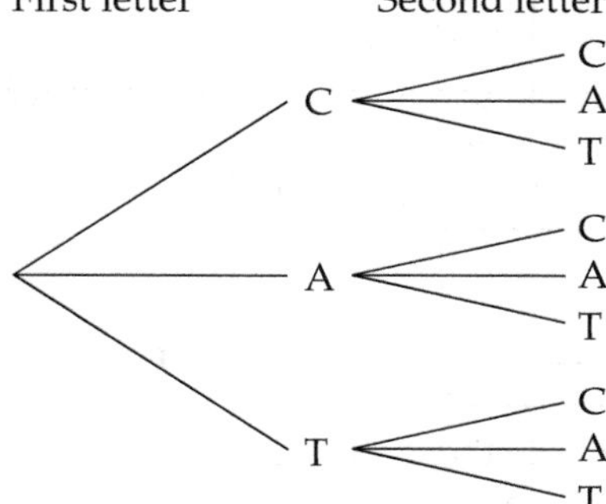

b $\frac{1}{3}$ **c** $\frac{5}{9}$
4 **a** Yes **b** No **c** No
5 **a** 0.41 **b** 148 women
6 **a** 0.4 **b** $\frac{1}{6}$ or 0.167
c No, although we did not get the expected results this does not prove it is unfair: the result of each throw is random and you won't necessarily get a six exactly $\frac{1}{6}$ of the time.
7 **a** Generate a random number, R#.
If R# $\leq$ 0.6 heads otherwise tails.
Repeat 10 times.
b For the sample in **a**, count a success if number of heads > 5.
Generate many samples and estimate P $\approx$ number of success $\div$ number of samples.
8 **a**

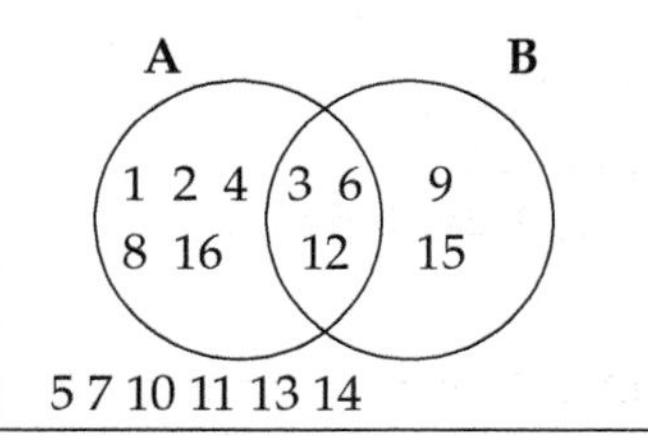

b **i** A = {1, 2, 3, 4, 6, 8, 12, 16}
ii B = {3, 6, 9, 12, 15}
iii A′ = {5, 7, 9, 10, 11, 13, 14, 15}
iv A ∩ B = {3, 6, 12}
v A ∪ B = {1, 2, 3, 6, 8, 9, 12, 15, 16}
vi A ∩ B′ = {1, 2, 4, 8, 16}
c **i** $P(A) = \frac{8}{16} = \frac{1}{2}$ **ii** $P(B) = \frac{5}{16}$
iii $P(A') = \frac{8}{16} = \frac{1}{2}$ **iv** $P(A \cap B) = \frac{3}{16}$
v $P(A \cup B) = \frac{9}{16}$ **vi** $P(A \cap B') = \frac{5}{16}$

2D shape 258
3D shape 254, 255, 354
volume of 260

A
addition
of fractions 8, 70
of indices 12
inverse of 54
mental calculations 128
written calculations 208
alternate angles 88
angle bisector 222, 226
angle(s)
alternate 88
corresponding 88, 94
exterior 96
exterior, of polygon 92
exterior, of triangle 90
interior 96
interior, of polygon 92
interior, of triangle 90
parallel lines and 88
of rotation 164
vertically opposite 88
annulus 34
appproximate solutions to equations 188
approximation 128, 130, 132
arc 32, 36
area
of circle 34
metric units for 24
of parallelogram 30
of rectangle 28
of trapezium 30
of triangle 28
arrowhead 90
symmetrical properties 168
averages 146, 148

B
back bearing 228
bar chart 144
base 28, 254
bearings 228
BIDMAS 42, 206, 212
bisectors 222
brackets 206, 207
expansion of 48, 56, 60
factoring 50

C
calculator skills 202, 204
cancelling 46, 72
capacity
imperials units for 26
metric units for 24
centre of enlargement 170, 172
centre of rotation 164, 166
checking answers 202
chord 34
circle
area of 34
circumference of 32
circumference 36
of circle 32
class intervals 142
collection of terms 46
common denominator 58, 70, 80
comparing ratios 270
compasses 220, 222
compensation 128, 132
complement (′) 300, 301
congruent shapes 94, 96, 164, 230
congruent triangles 218, 220
construct 218, 220, 230
conversion (converting)
between fractions, decimals and percentages 78
between units 204
coordinates 108
correlation 152, 156
corresponding angles 88, 94
corresponding sides 94
cross-multiplying 186
cross-section 254
of cuboid 260
of prism 258
cube 254
volume of 47
cube root 10, 18
by trial-and-improvement 16
cuboid 254
dimension of 256
surface area 49
volume of 47, 260
curved graph 106

D
data collection 140
data handling cycle 138, 156
data logging 140
decagon 92
decimal places, rounding of 14
decimal(s) 68
conversion of fraction into 68
fractions and percentages, converting between 78
recurring 68, 80
terminating 68, 80
decomposition 6
denominator 80
diameter 32, 36
difference between terms 240
dimensions of cuboid 256
direct proportion 274, 275, 282
direction 228
directly proportional to (∝) 280
distance, imperials units for 26
distance-time graph 112, 116
distributions, comparing 154
divisibility tests 4
division 186
expressions involving 46
using factors 200
of fractions 72
in given ratio 272
of index form numbers 12
of indices 44
inverse of 54
long 212
mental calculations 130
of negative integers 124
using partitioning 200
of powers of 10 126
written calculations 200, 210
doubling in sequence 244

E
edge 254, 262
elevation 256
enlargement 170, 172, 174
equally likely outcomes 288
equation 182, 184, 192
with fractions 186
real life 190
of straight line 104
equidistant points 226
equilateral triangle 90
equivalent calculation 200, 212
equivalent fraction 58, 70, 80
equivalent reflections 166
equivalent whole-number calculation 198
estimates 14
evaluation of formula 54
expansion (expanding) of brackets 48, 56, 60, 192
experimental probability 294, 296, 302
explicit equation 110, 116
expression(s) 46, 48, 172, 192
factorising 50, 60
simplification of 56, 60
writing 56
exterior angle 96
of polygon 92
of triangle 90

F
face 254, 258, 262
factor tree 6, 18
factorising expressions 50, 60
factor(s) 4, 18, 50
division using 200
multiplication using 198
form 1: *n* 270
formula 52, 190
rearranging 54
subject of 54

fraction key 202
fraction(s) 14
addition of 8, 70
algebraic 58, 60
brackets in 206
cancelling of 72
conversion into decimal 68
decimals and percentages, converting between 78
division of 72
equations with 186
equivalent 58, 70, 80
improper 80
multiplication of 72
of a number 72
subtraction of 6, 70
frequency table 142, 148
front elevation 256, 262
function, graph of 102

G
general term of sequence 240, 248
geometric sequence 244, 246, 248
gradient 104, 112, 116
graph
curved 106
distance-time 112, 116
of implicit functions 110
of linear functions 102
real life 112
scatter 152
sketch 112
statistical 144, 150
straight line 104
time series 114, 115
grouped frequency tables 142, 146

H
heptagon 92
hexagon 92
hexagonal prism 258
hexagonal pyramid 254
highest common factor (HCF) 8, 18, 50
hypotenuse 220
hypothesis 138, 140, 156

I
image 164, 170, 172, 174
imperial measurement 26, 36
implicit equation 110, 116
improper fraction 80
independent probability 302
index (indices) 12, 18
in algebra 42
division 44
multiplication 44
power of number
in sequences 244
simplification of 48
index form 12
index laws 44
index notation 12, 60, 126, 132
indices *see* index
instrument, measuring 26
intercept 104, 116
interior angle(s) 96
of polygon 92
of quadrilateral 90
of triangle 90
intersection
of two lines 88
of two sets (∩) 300
inverse operation 54, 186, 210, 212
percentage change and 76
inverse proportion 281
isometric paper 256
isosceles trapezium 90
symmetrical properties 168
isosceles triangle 90

K
kite 90, 91
symmetrical properties 168

L
length
imperials units for 26
metric units for 24
like terms 46, 56, 60
line of symmetry 168
linear equations 182, 184, 192
linear function 102, 116
linear sequence 240, 246
locus (loci) 226, 239
long division 200, 212
long multiplication 212
lowest common multiple (LCM) 8, 18, 58, 70

M
mass
imperials units for 26
metric units for 24
mean 148, 154
median 146, 154
median class 146
mental calculations
addition 128
division 130
multiplication 130
subtraction 128
metric measurement 24, 36
metric units 24, 26
midpoint 108, 116
mixed number 80
modal class 146
mode 146
model 298, 302
moderate correlation 152
multiples 4, 18
multiplication 186
expressions involving 46
using factors 198
of fractions 72
of index form numbers 12
of indices 44
long 212
mental calculations 130
of negative numbers 48, 124
using partitioning 198
of powers of 10 126
written calculations 198, 210
mutually exclusive outcomes 292, 302

N
negative correlation 152
negative integers 124, 132
negative number
cube root of 10
multiplication 48
net 258, 262
no correlation 152
nonagon 92
*n*th term 242, 246, 248
numerator 80

O
object 164, 170, 172, 174
octagon 92
operation 206
operator 206
order of magnitude 202, 212
order of operations 206
order of rotation symmetry 168
outcome 288

P
parabola 106, 116
parallel lines 96
angles and 88
parallelogram 90
area of 30
symmetrical properties 168
partitioning 128, 132
division using 200
multiplication using 198
path 226
pentagon 92
percentage change 74, 76
percentage decrease 74
percentage increase 74
percentages 80
conversion of proportions to 278
fractions and decimals, converting between 78
perimeter 36
period 114
perpendicular bisector 222, 226, 230
perpendicular height 28
perpendicular lines 88, 96
perpendicular to line 222
pi 32
pie chart 144, 150
plan 256
plan vew 262
polygon 96
properties of 92
population 140, 156
position-to-term rule 240, 242, 248
positive correlation, strong 152

positive number, cube root of 10
power key 202
power *see* index
powers of 10 12, 126
prime factor decomposition 6, 18
prime factors 4, 6
  cube roots and 10
  square roots and 10
primes (prime number) 4, 5, 18
prism 254, 262
  surface area of 258
  volume of 260
probability
  experimental 294, 296, 302
  independent 302
  theoretical 296
problem solving approach138
proportion 272, 276, 282
  algebra and 280
  comparing 278
  conversion to percentages 278
  direct 274, 275, 280, 282
protractor 218, 220
pyramid 254

Q
quadratic function 106
quadrilateral 92, 96
  interior angles of 90
  properties of 90
questionnaire 141

R
radius 32, 36
range 146, 154
ratio 224, 270, 276, 282
  division in given 272
real life equations 190
real life graphs 112
rearrangement (rearranging)
  of formula 54
  of implicit equations 110
reciprocal 42, 60
record sheet 140
rectangle 90
  area of 28
  symmetrical properties 168
recurring decimal 68, 80
recursive formula 246
recursive sequences 246
reflection 166, 174
reflection symmetry 168
regular octagon 92
regular pentagon 92
regular polygon 92
regular shape 96, 169
relative frequency 295, 302
remainder 204
representation 224
reverse bearing 228
rhombus 90
  symmetrical properties 168
right-angled triangle 90, 220
rotation 164, 166, 174
rotation symmetry 168
rounding down 14
rounding up 14
rule 218, 220

S
sample 140, 156, 296
sample space 288, 302
scale 26, 224
scale drawings 224, 225
scale factor 170, 172, 174
scalene triangle 90
scaling 274
scatter diagram 156
scatter graph 152
sector 34
segment 34
semicircle 35
sequence 240, 242, 248
  geometric 244, 246, 248
  recursive 246
sexagesimal numbers 205
short division 68, 200
side elevation 256, 262
sign change key 202
similar shapes 170, 172
simplest form of ratio 270, 282
simplification
  of expression 46, 48, 56, 60/
  of ratio 270
simulation 294, 298, 302
  of experimental data 298
sketch graph 112
slope of line 104
solution of (solving) equation
  172, 184
speed 112
square 90
  symmetrical properties 168
square-based pyramid 254
square root 10, 18
  calculator key 202
  by trial-and-improvement 16
statistical investigation,
  planning 138
stem-and-leaf diagram 144, 150
straight line, equation of 104
subject 110
  of formula 52
substitution 42
  of formula 52
subtraction
  of fractions 8, 70
  of indices 12
  mental calculations 128
  written calculations 208
surface area
  of cuboid 49
  of prism 258
  of solid 258
symmetry 168

T
term 240, 248
term-to-term rule 240, 246, 248
terminating decimal 68, 80
tessellation 93, 166
three-dimensional shape 254,
  255, 354
  volume of 260
three-figure bearing 228, 230
time series 114, 115, 156
transformation 164, 170
  combinations of 166
translation 164, 166, 174
trapezium 90
  area of 30
  symmetrical properties 168
tree diagrams 290
trend 114
trial-and-improvement method 16,
  188, 192
trials 294
triangle 92
  area of 28
  congruent 218, 220
  construct of 218, 220
  corresponding angles in 94
  corresponding sides in 94
  equilateral 90
  isosceles 90
  properties of 90
  right-angled 90, 220
  scalene 90
triangular prism 254
two-dimensional shape 258
two point perspective 267

U
union (∪) 300
unitary method 76, 282
  direct proportion 274
  division in given ratio
    using 272
  percentage change and 76
universal set (Ω) 300

V
vanishing point 267
variable 42, 52, 54, 102, 140
  evaluation of 54
Venn diagram , 300
vertex 254, 262
vertically opposite angles 88
volume
  of cube or cuboid 47, 260
  of prism 260

W
whole number 14
written calculations
  addition 208
  division 210
  multiplication 210
  subtraction 208